ROME OF THE PILGRIMS
AND MARTYRS

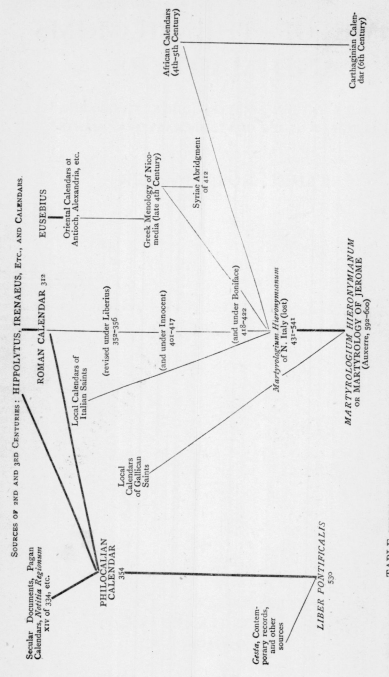

SOURCES OF 2ND AND 3RD CENTURIES: HIPPOLYTUS, IRENAEUS, ETC., AND CALENDARS.

EUSEBIUS

ROMAN CALENDAR 312

Secular Documents, Pagan Calendars, *Notitia Regionum* xiv of 334, etc.

Oriental Calendars of Antioch, Alexandria, etc.

African Calendars (4th–5th Century)

Carthaginian Calendar (6th Century)

Greek Menology of Nicomedia (late 4th Century)

Syriac Abridgment of 412

(revised under Liberius) 352–356

(and under Innocent) 401–417

(and under Boniface) 418–422

Local Calendars of Italian Saints

Martyrologium Hieronymianum of N. Italy (lost) 431–541

MARTYROLOGIUM HIERONYMIANUM or MARTYROLOGY OF JEROME (Auxerre, 592–600)

Local Calendars of Gallican Saints

PHILOCALIAN CALENDAR 354

LIBER PONTIFICALIS 530

Gesta, Contemporary records, and other sources

TABLE SHOWING THE RELATIONS OF THE *LIBER PONTIFICALIS*, MARTYROLOGIES, ETC.

Frontispiece

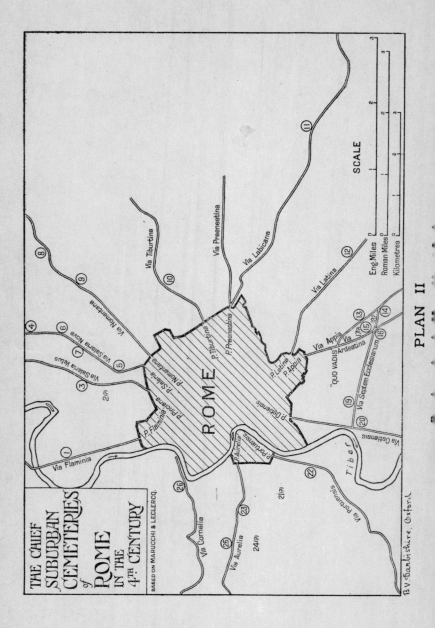

THE CHIEF
SUBURBAN
CEMETERIES
of
ROME
IN THE
4TH CENTURY

BASED ON MARUCCHI & LECLERCQ.

SCALE

Eng. Miles
Roman Miles
Kilometres

PLAN II

B.V. Darbishire. Oxford.

ROME

Via Flaminia

Via Salaria Vetus

Via Salaria Nova

Via Nomentana

Via Tiburtina

Via Praenestina

Via Labicana

Via Latina

Via Appia

Via Ardeatina

"QUO VADIS"

Via Septem Ecclesiarum

Via Ostiensis

Via Portuensis

Via Aurelia

Via Cornelia

Tiber

P. Flaminia

P. Pinciana

P. Salaria

P. Nomentana

P. Tiburtina

P. Praenestina

P. Latina

P. Appia

P. Ostiensis

P. Portuensis

P. Aurelia

PLAN II

THE CHIEF SUBURBAN CEMETERIES OF ROME IN THE FOURTH CENTURY

FLAMINIA	.	.	1. *Valentini.*
SALARIA VETUS	.	.	2. Ad Septem Columbas [in Clivum Cucumeris].
,, ,,	.	.	3. Basillae ad S. Hermetem [S. Pamphilii].
,, NOVA	.	.	4. Priscillae ad S. Silvestrum.
,, ,,	.	.	5. *Maximi ad S. Felicitatem.*
,, ,,	.	.	6. Jordanorum ad S. Alexandrum.
,, ,,	.	.	7. Thrasonis ad S. Saturninum.
NOMENTANA	.	.	8. *Ostrianum* [*Coem. Majus* or *Ad Nymphas Petri*].
,,	.	.	9. *S. Agnetis et Emerentianae et Nicomedis.*
TIBURTINA	.	.	10. *Cyriaci ad S. Laurentium* [*et S. Hippolytum*].
LABICANA	.	.	11. Ad duas Lauros ad SS. Petrum et Marcellinum [S. Castuli].
LATINA	.	.	12. Aproniani ad Sanctam Eugeniam [S. Gordiani].
APPIA	.	.	13. Praetextati ad S. Januarium.
,,	.	.	14. Catacumbas ad S. Sebastianum.
,,	.	.	15. Calixti ad S. Xystum.
ARDEATINA	.	.	16. Domitillae Nerei et Achillei ad S. Petronillam.
,,	.	.	17. Balbinae ad SS. Marcum et Marcellianum.
,,	.	.	18. Basilei ad S. Marcum.
OSTIENSIS	.	.	19. Commodillae ad SS. Felicem et Adauctum.
,,	.	.	20. *Pauli in praeda Lucinae* [*Theclae et Timothei*].
PORTUENSIS	.	.	21. Ad insalatos ad S. Felicem.
,,	.	.	22. Pontiani ad Ursum Pileatum.
AURELIA	.	.	23. *S. Pancratii* [*Processi et Martiniani*].
,,	.	.	24. *S. Lucinae ad S. Agatham ad Girulum.*
,,	.	.	25. Calepodii ad S. Calixtum.
CORNELIA	.	.	26. *S. Petri.*

All the cemeteries are mentioned in the *Index Coemiteriorum* of the fourth century (see p. 98) except those in italics, some of which are the oldest of all.   Owing to the undefined area of the cemeteries, the incompleteness of the excavations and disputed identifications, the position of the cemeteries can only be indicated approximately.

It was over some of these shrines that the earliest basilicas were built. See p. 15.

ROME OF THE PILGRIMS AND MARTYRS

A STUDY IN THE MARTYROLOGIES, ITINERARIES SYLLOGÆ, & OTHER CONTEMPORARY DOCUMENTS

BY

ETHEL ROSS BARKER

AUTHOR OF "BURIED HERCULANEUM"

WITH FOUR MAPS

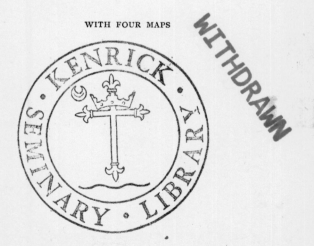

METHUEN & CO. LTD.
36 ESSEX STREET W.C.
LONDON

First Published in 1913

C'est la vérité qui est notre voie et notre vie . . .
notre piété n'est point dans l'illusion et dans le
mensonge.

TILLEMONT, *Mémoires* . . . I. xiv.

PREFACE

IN approaching the study of the stones of Christian Rome with the object of collecting some material for elucidating the still obscure story of the first three centuries of Christianity, the student is constantly confronted with certain early Christian documents—the *Liber Pontificalis* or History of the Popes, the *Itineraries* or Pilgrims' guide books, the *Acta Martyrum* or Acts of the Martyrs, the *Martyrologies*, and the *Syllogæ*, or Collections of Inscriptions.

Many questions at once arise. What is the date and authorship of these documents? What the general character of their contents? In what sense are they of historical value? What is their precise relation to the monuments? What light does the collated evidence of monument and document throw on the history of the period? What texts are available, and what have scholars already contributed to the subject? The answer to some of these questions is to be found in certain great monographs, too long and sometimes too technical for any but the specialist, and inaccessible from their rarity or costliness: a few points have been treated in foreign periodicals difficult to collect. Very little has been written in English: all the texts are in Latin, there are practically no translations, and there is no adequate account in a single book of the total results of research.

This book is an attempt to supply the need of a connected history of all these documents; to show their relation one to the other; and to collate the topographical information on the martyrs' shrines which is contained in them all, and forms a link between them. There is further, in the introductory chapters, a description, derived from contemporary sources, of the pilgrimages to Rome in the early ages; and in the last chapters, an indication of the method of applying the documentary evidence to the identification of the monuments as revealed by the excavations, which are now in progress day by day in the catacombs.

While some of these documents are mainly topographical, others are only incidentally so. These latter have been described in all their aspects, so that each document may be judged as a whole. Each section of the book, therefore, is complete in itself within the prescribed period.

There are many chapters here which do but present the results of the recent researches of scholars in their respective branches—of Duchesne and De Rossi; of Delehaye, Harnack, and Leclercq; of Marucchi, Wilpert, and many others; and there is scarcely a line which does not owe something to these great specialists who have, one and all, dealt with questions of historical fact in a spirit of scientific criticism.

It is hoped the book may interest the general reader, for whose benefit a large number of translations from the originals have been made. These are as literal as possible, and shortcomings in matter and form are, sometimes at least, faithful reflections of the Latin. In quoting the Latin itself, the curious spellings, so characteristic of the documents, have generally been preserved. The student too may perhaps find some help in it; especially in the bibliography, appendices, and footnotes, which form an introduction to more specialized study in these or kindred subjects.

Documents so different in character have each required a different method of treatment. In some the human interest prevails: others seem but to furnish a theme for topographical and literary disquisition. Yet even the latter are in touch with life. As we study the *Index Oleorum*, can we not see the figure of Abbot John trudging patiently down the suburban roads, tying his little labels of Saints to his bottles of holy oil? So too, in the confusion of the Sylloge of Centula we can watch the monastic scribe laboriously and unsuccessfully piecing together two imperfect originals; and in the wearisome lists of the Itineraries we can hear the feet of the pilgrims passing to and fro to the shrines.

In a book of this kind, involving minute research over a large field, mistakes in detail are almost inevitable. Corrections of these, and suggestions in respect of the matter dealt with, will be most gratefully received from those who are interested in the subject.

It remains to express my most grateful thanks to the many who have assisted me with advice and encouragement: especially to Commend. O. Marucchi, Professor of Christian Archæology in the University of Rome, who has interpreted for me some difficult passages in the Syllogæ; and to the Rev. J. Arbuthnot Nairn, D.Litt., Headmaster of Merchant Taylors' School; and to Mrs. Stuart-Moore, who have given me much helpful criticism and advice, and by whom the proof-sheets have been read; and to Miss M. Nicholson who has revised some of the proof-sheets.

E. R. B.

All Saints, 1912

CONTENTS

INTRODUCTION

CHAP.   PAGE

I. TOPOGRAPHY AND MONUMENTS 1

II. THE PILGRIMAGES AND THE SHRINES . . . 16

III. THE PILGRIMAGES: THE BELIEFS OF THE PILGRIMS . 35

PART I

THE DOCUMENTS

IV. THE *LIBER PONTIFICALIS*: SOURCES AND DATE . 48

V. THE *LIBER PONTIFICALIS*: FORM OF THE LIVES, PAPAL CHRONOLOGY, THE MARTYRED POPES, DISCIPLINARY DECREES 63

VI. THE *LIBER PONTIFICALIS*: THE INVENTORIES OF ECCLESIASTICAL PROPERTY 84

VII. THE ITINERARIES 93

VIII. THE ITINERARIES (*continued*) 112

IX. ACTS OF THE MARTYRS: CRITICISM, ANCIENT AND MODERN 127

X. ACTS OF THE MARTYRS: THE *ACTA PROCONSULARIA* . 134

XI. ACTS OF THE MARTYRS: CLASSIFICATION OF THE TEXTS: THREE CLASSES OF AUTHENTIC DOCUMENTS . 146

XII. ACTS OF THE MARTYRS: CLASSIFICATION OF TEXTS: THREE CLASSES OF AUTHENTIC DOCUMENTS (*contd.*) 161

XIII. ACTS OF THE MARTYRS: DOCUMENTS OF THE FOURTH CLASS 178

xi

CHAP.   PAGE

XIV. ACTS OF THE MARTYRS: THE WORK OF TRADITION
     AND OF THE HAGIOGRAPHERS 185

XV. ACTS OF THE MARTYRS: THE ROMAN *GESTA* .   . 199

XVI. THE MARTYROLOGY OF JEROME: PLACE AND DATE
     OF COMPILATION 205

XVII. THE MARTYROLOGY OF JEROME: THE ANCIENT
      SOURCES 218

XVIII. THE *SYLLOGAE*: THEIR SOURCES AND LITERARY
       STYLE   230

XIX. THE *SYLLOGAE*: ANALYSES   240

XX. THE NEW SYLLOGE OF CAMBRIDGE: THE *SUMITE*
    CONTROVERSY   254

XXI. THE *SYLLOGAE*: SOME EXAMPLES OF INSCRIPTIONS . 278

XXII. DOCUMENT AND MONUMENT   297

PART II

APPENDICES

I. BIBLIOGRAPHY

A. General Bibliography

    1. (*a*) DICTIONARIES AND (*b*) HISTORY   .   . 320
    2. PATRISTIC—(*a*) Texts, (*b*) Translations .   . 322
    3. ARCHAEOLOGY—(*a*) General, (*b*) Catacombs . 323

B. The Documents

    1. *LIBER PONTIFICALIS*—(*a*) Text and History, (*b*)
       Philocalian Calendar, (*c*) Papal Chronology . 325
    2. THE ITINERARIES—(*a*) General Topography and
       Plans, (*b*) General Texts, (*c*) Monographs . 327
    3. ACTS OF THE MARTYRS—(*a*) General History,
       (*b*) Texts, (*c*) Translations   .   .   . 330
    4. THE MARTYROLOGY OF JEROME AND OTHERS 333
    5. THE *SYLLOGAE*—(*a*) General History, (*b*) Sylloge
       of Verdun, (*c*) Sylloge of Cambridge, (*d*) Dis-
       cussions on (*b*) and (*c*)   335

CONTENTS

PAGE

II. LIST OF POPES, WITH DATES, PLACES OF BURIAL, ETC. 336

III. (*A*) *DEPOSITIO EPISCOPORUM* AND (*B*) *DEPOSI-TIO MARTYRUM* OF THE PHILOCALIAN CALENDAR, WITH (*C*) LIST OF MARTYRS IN IT ARRANGED ALPHABETICALLY 337

IV. *INDEX COEMITERIORUM XVI.* AND THE TRUE NUMBER OF THE CEMETERIES 340

V. LIST OF PASSIONS IN THE PASSIONARY OF GREGORY (Sixth Century) 341

VI. LIST OF SEVENTY-SEVEN MARTYRS OF THE FIRST THREE CENTURIES IN ADO'S MARTYROLOGY (Ninth Century) 343

VII. LIST OF MARTYRS WHOSE PASSIONS ARE REFERRED TO IN THE CHAPTERS ON THE ACTS OF THE MARTYRS 346

INDEX 351

TABLES AND PLANS

TABLE SHOWING RELATIONS OF *LIBER PONTIFICALIS*, MARTYROLOGIES, ETC. . . . . . *Frontispiece*

PAGE

TABLE OF SHRINES ON THE VIA APPIA (COLLATED FROM THE ITINERARIES) 298

FACING PAGE

I. PLAN OF ROME IN THE FIRST SEVEN CENTURIES OF OUR ERA I

II. PLAN OF THE SUBURBAN CEMETERIES OF ROME . 92–93

III. PLAN TO ILLUSTRATE THE ITINERARY OF EINSIEDELN . 119

IV. PLAN OF THE AREAS OF S. CALLIXTUS, VIA APPIA . 297

ROME OF THE PILGRIMS AND MARTYRS

INTRODUCTION

CHAPTER I

TOPOGRAPHY AND MONUMENTS

General topography—The fourteen regions of Augustus—Persistence of paganism—Secular buildings under Christianity—The preservation and adaptation of pagan monuments—Splendour of Rome in the sixth century—Destruction of the monuments—Ecclesiastical Rome : buildings prior to the Peace of the Church—The triumph of Christianity : the parish churches (*tituli*)—The churches for the stations—The basilicas and other churches—Churches without Rome.

> Exaudi regina tui pulcherrima mundi
> Inter sidereos Roma recepta polos,
> Exaudi genetrix hominum genetrixque deorum,
> Non procul a caelo per tua templa sumus.[1]

Quam speciosa potest esse Hierusalem coelestis, si sic fulget Roma terrestris![2]

General Topography—Hills, Bridges, Monuments.— Before entering on a detailed study of the early Christian monuments of Rome, and of the documents which interpret them, it is well to form a general idea of the form of the city, of the civil and ecclesiastical divisions, and of the change

---

[1] Claudius Rutilius Namatianus, *De Reditu suo*, i. 47 : "*Hear me, O Rome, thou loveliest queen of the world which thou hast made thine; thou who hast been welcomed among the constellations of heaven ! Hear me, O mother of men, O mother of the gods; by thy temples we are not far from the heavens where they dwell.*"

[2] *Vita Fulgentii*, c. 13, in Migne's *Patrologia Latina* ("*P.L.*"), 65, col. 130 : "*If earthly Rome glows before us in such splendour, what must be the beauty of the heavenly Jerusalem !*"

in the character of her monuments at the transition from paganism to Christianity.[1]

The public buildings, the palaces, the mansions of the rich were usually situated on one or other of the seven hills —on the Palatine and Capitoline in the very heart of Rome, and on those curving round them in a semicircle on the east, from north to south: the Quirinal, Viminal, Esquiline and Coelian.[2]

In the depressions between the hills, so much deeper in those days than now, lay, for the most part, the great chain of forums, the markets, the circuses, the Colosseum, and the long lines of the arches of the aqueducts. The Tiber, flowing S-shaped from north to south, bounds the city on the west, though two great districts, the Vatican and the Trastevere (*Transtiberim*) with the Janiculum, lay to the west of it, and are connected with the rest of the city by seven bridges.

The whole city, excluding the Vatican, but including the Janiculum, was encircled by the immense towered wall, raised by Aurelian (270–276), and repaired by Honorius in 403. It was pierced at intervals by seventeen gates, through which the pilgrim passed out along the great highways; and on these roads all round Rome, at a radius of from two to three miles, are the catacombs, some thirty in number.

These main roads, to which we shall constantly refer, are, proceeding in a clockwise direction from the north: the Viae Flaminia, Salaria Vetus and Nova, Nomentana, Tiburtina, Praenestina, Labicana, Latina, Appia, Ardeatina, Ostiensis, Portuensis, Aurelia, Cornelia.

Within the Aurelian Wall is the inner girdle of the Servian Wall, pierced also by gates about ten in number.

The Fourteen Regions of Augustus.—The city was divided in the time of Augustus into fourteen regions, each controlled by forty-eight overseers (*vicomagistri*) and two

---

[1] For this chapter I am greatly indebted to Grisar, *History of Rome and the Popes* (see Bibliography—ITINERARIES), to which the reader should refer for details.   Many points alluded to in these introductory pages are treated at length in the following chapters.

[2] The names of the "seven" hills are variously given, even in the ancient records.

curators of public monuments (*curatores*).   Each region was subdivided into districts (*vici*) from 7 to (in a single case) 78 in number, making a total of 424. These *vici* contained, in various proportions, mansions (*domus*), tenement houses (*insulae*), barracks, baths (*balnea*), mills (*pistrina*), warehouses (*horrea*).

We cannot linger here to enumerate the monuments of every description — fountains, drains and aqueducts; basilicas, temples and theatres ; forums, porticoes and statues of the gods—in a word, all the " marvels of Rome," to which nearly every writer of the time alludes, and which he sometimes describes with a wealth of detail.

At this point the question arises : How did the transition from paganism to Christianity affect the monuments ?

Persistence of Paganism.—All evidence, literary and monumental, shows that paganism died hard ; that long after the Edict of Milan (313) Isis, Cybele, Mithra, together with the ancient gods of Rome, were worshipped side by side with Christ, not only by the village folk (*pagani*), but by emperor and patrician.   Rome was not, even externally, wholly Christianized before the days of Theodosius (379–395), the friend of Ambrose, the last great emperor who united under his rule East and West.   Even in 382 the praetorian prefect Flavianus Nichomachus celebrated in public the mysteries of Cybele, submitted to the *taurobolium*—the bloody baptism of Mithra—and through a solemn three months purified the city from the pollution of Christianity.   As late as the days of Leo the Great (440–461) we find that pope rebuking his flock because, when they have mounted the great flight of steps to S. Peter's

> before entering the basilica they turn round and bend themselves to the rising sun, and with bowed heads incline their bodies in honour of the splendid orb.   We greatly grieve at this, done partly through the vice of ignorance, partly in a spirit of paganism.[1]

The Sacramentary of Leo,[2] compiled about the sixth century from more ancient documents, still preserves a prayer against " vain superstitions and diabolical figments "

---

[1] *Sermo* 27, in *P.L.* 54, 218.

[2] Feltoe, *Sacramentarium Leonianum*, or in *P.L.* 55, coll. 83 and 377.

and for the abolition "of every rite of pestilential antiquity (*pestiferae vetustatis*), and the renouncing of all abominations."

The fifth century poem of Rutilius, quoted at the head of this chapter, celebrates the glories of the ancient gods alone. In a sermon, too, of Augustine [1] we read :

> Look how many Christians are half heathen : they have joined us with their bodies, but never with their heart and soul.

Secular Buildings under Christianity.—Yet paganism died out at length. What, then, was the fate of the ancient buildings ?

In the purely secular buildings all Roman citizens, whether Christian or pagan, took pride and delight. Christians still flocked to circus and theatre : even gladiatorial games continued to the time of the Emperor Honorius (395–408), and Pope Leo reproaches his flock [2] for preferring these diversions to attendance in church on the feast of Peter and Paul, the anniversary too, of the day when Genseric the Hun ceased plundering Rome :

> Devils are served with more zeal than the holy apostles, and senseless spectacles attract bigger crowds than the burial-places of the martyrs. Was it the circus sports which saved you from falling by the sword, or was it not rather the intercession of the saints who brought salvation to the city, who snatched it away from captivity, who defended it from slaughter ? Was it through the circus sports or the care of the saints, by whose prayers sentence of divine wrath is averted, that we, who merited destruction, are preserved for pardon ?

The Emperor Theodosius [3] (379–395) expresses the general feeling when he says :

> It is not seemly that aught should be destroyed from which the time-honoured pleasures of the Roman people have been derived.

Yet the troubled times through which Rome was passing,

---

[1] *Sermo* 62, in *P.L.* 38, 423.   Cf. *infra*, p. 27.

[2] *Sermo* 84, in *P.L.* 54, 433.

[3] For references to the imperial edicts quoted in this chapter see the fine edition of Mommsen and Meyer, *Theodosiani Libri xvi . . .*, *lib. xv: De Operibus Publicis*, i. p. 801, 3 vols. : Berlin, 1905.

and, above all, the transference of the seat of government to Constantinople must have rendered many of the public buildings useless.

The Preservation and Adaptation of Pagan Monuments.—Many of these secular buildings were converted at that period into places of Christian worship. For example, the ancient Senate House (*Curia Senatus*) in the Forum was converted into the Church of S. Hadrian by Pope Honorius (625–640), and the imperial library in the Forum, at the foot of the Palatine, into S. Maria Antiqua about the sixth century. The secular basilica of the Sessorian Palace became under Constantine the Church of the Holy Cross (*S. Croce in Gerusalemme*). The circular covered market (*Macellum Magnum*)[1] on the Coelian Hill was converted by Pope Simplicius (468–483) into the round church now called S. Stefano Rotondo. The church of S. Andrew Catabarbara on the Esquiline, which has now disappeared, was built in the time of Simplicius in the hall of the mansion of Junius Bassus (consul in 317). S. Balbina on the Aventine, existing in the sixth century, was probably once part of the house of Cillo, the favourite of Septimius Severus, and the Baths of Novatus, or Timothy, near the present church of S. Pudentiana, were converted by Pius I. (158–167) into a parish church, known as the *Titulus Romanus*.

Some of the temples, too, which were perhaps for secular rather than religious purposes, were converted into churches. Thus the so-called Temple of the Holy City (*Templum Sacrae Urbis*) with the rotunda of Romulus[2] attached, which stands in the Forum, was probably used as a registry for the survey and assessment rolls, or perhaps as a library.[3] On to it was affixed the marble slab on which was engraved the plan of the city made by Septimius Severus.[4] This building was converted into a church dedicated to SS. Cosmas and Damian by Felix IV. in 526. Again, the Temple of

---

[1] The best example of a *Macellum* is to be seen in the Forum of Pompeii.

[2] Infant son of the Emperor Maxentius.

[3] Huelsen, *Forum Romanum*, Rome, 1906 (trans. in English and French).

[4] *Infra*, p. 94.

Saturn in the Forum was the storehouse of state treasure, and was used as such by the Christians.

In the pagan temples, dedicated to strictly religious purposes, worship might cease owing to change of faith, persecution, or worldly wisdom. The buildings were, however, preserved as national monuments and museums. Further, many a statue was brought from some inner shrine into the light of day, and, its divinity forgotten but its beauty worshipped, adorned the public baths or the forums.

As an example of many similar edicts we may quote that of Honorius (395–408):

> As strongly as we forbid idol worship, so strongly do we desire to preserve public monuments as ornaments to the city.

Again the same Emperor, in 408, decrees:

> In towns and suburbs, temples are to be treated as state property, but their altars must be everywhere overthrown.

Of the statues, Theodosius remarks in one of his decrees:

> These images are to be prized for their value as works of art . . . not to be feared on account of their divinity.

And the Christian poet Prudentius (*b.* 348) puts into the Emperor's mouth the words:[1]

> Cleanse the marble statues which have been defiled by your hateful lustrations, and leave them in their simple beauty. They are the works of great masters, and it is my will that they adorn your city, and be no longer disfigured by an evil use of them.

Splendour of Rome in the Sixth Century.—Neither the sack of Rome in 410 by Alaric the Goth, who respected nothing save the shrines of Peter and Paul, nor the systematic plundering in 455 by the Vandal Genseric,[2] who

---

[1] *Contra Symmachum*, i. 500, in *P.L.* 60.

[2] He carried off even the copper cooking pots of the imperial palace of the Palatine.

bore off down the Tiber shiploads of the finest statues, and vast treasures of gold and precious stones from pagan and Christian monuments, to beautify his African capital, permanently impaired the beauty of the eternal city.

Procopius, the Greek historian, writes in the sixth century:[1]

> I know of no people who so love their city as the Romans, and they are zealous to beautify and preserve her. Though she suffered from the barbarians she preserved her buildings and her adornments.

About the same period Cassiodorus, the minister of Theodoric and, later, the monk of Vivarium, writes:[2]

> The ancients reckoned seven wonders of the world, . . . but who would any longer think much of these when in one single city he sees so much for amazement?

Innumerable passages in very different writers of about the same date bear witness to the enduring splendour of Rome.

Destruction of the Monuments.—It is in the main to the later political disasters of the city, the perpetual warfare of the Middle Ages, and the hand of Time that we owe the loss of many of the monuments of Rome.

Yet the Romans themselves are responsible for the deliberate destruction of certain of their monuments when materials were required for new buildings. This is not, however, a peculiar characteristic of the early Christian, but a habit of the Romans as a people, in the fifth as in the twentieth century. This fact accounts for the vast number of antique columns and of sculptures, as well as of less recognizable fragments, incorporated into the Christian basilicas.

The edicts and codes of the Emperors Valentinian (364–379), Theodosius (379–395), Majorian (457–461) and Justinian (527–565) illustrate these facts.

Valentinian enacts:

> Whoever wishes to erect any new building in the city

---

[1] *De Bello Gothico*, iv. 22.
[2] *Variarum libri duodecim*, 7; No. 15 in *P.L.* 69, col. 719.

must procure his own materials; he is not at liberty to use everything which happens to come handy, to dig up the foundations of famous monuments, to cut anew stones taken from public structures, to deface public buildings by appropriating thence blocks or slabs of marble.

Honorius permitted buildings which were quite in ruins to be put up to sale. Majorian, moved by the fact that private dwellings were erected with the stones of public buildings, forbids any one to lay sacrilegious hands on temples or monuments.

Ecclesiastical Rome—Buildings prior to the Peace of the Church.—To the splendour of the surviving pagan monuments the citizens of Rome added the beauty of the Christian basilicas.

Even before the Peace of the Church, many a private house,[1] whose natural construction of inner court (*atrium*) and outer portico lent itself so admirably to purposes of Christian worship, had been consecrated permanently. Thus the house of the patrician lady Cecilia, that of Pope Clement, that of Pudens (the host of S. Peter),[2] all became churches which are standing to-day. The larger houses had private halls (*basilicae*) attached: some of these too, as we have seen,[3] were converted into Christian basilicas, whose architecture seems to be derived mainly from the public secular basilica, and partly from the plan of a private house.[4]

Further, a few oratories at least, of a humble character, had been raised already over the graves of the martyrs of the catacombs.

Of Anacletus, the third pope, we read in the *Liber Pontificalis*:[5]

[1] The plan of Roman houses can be seen admirably at Pompeii.

[2] This tradition has strong historical evidence in its support : see Barnes, *S. Peter in Rome*, London, 1906, with bibliography, on the whole question of Peter's sojourn and martyrdom in Rome.

[3] *Supra*, p. 5.

[4] This point is much disputed : the similarity to a secular basilica is obvious, though the weight of modern scholarship seems to incline to the *house* as the chief model of the Christian basilica.

[5] *Liber Pontificalis*, ed. Duchesne. For an account of this document see *infra*, Chaps. IV.–VI. For further details on the erection of the churches see Chap. VI.

Anacletus constructed the memorial chapel (*memoria*) of blessed Peter, inasmuch as he had been ordained priest by blessed Peter.[1]

A confirmation of this fact is found in the words of the Roman priest Gaius,[2] writing early in the third century:

I can show you the trophies (*tropaea*) of the apostles if you go on the Vatican or on the Ostian Way:[3] there will you meet the trophies of those who founded the Church.

Eusebius, speaking of the transition from paganism to official Christianity under Constantine, says:[4]

We saw temples again rising from their foundations . . . receiving a splendour far greater than the old ones which had been destroyed.

Optatus,[5] Bishop of Milevis in Numidia (*circ.* 365–378), referring to the very beginning of the fourth century, says there were more than forty Christian basilicas in Rome at that period.

The Triumph of Christianity—Parish Churches (*tituli*). —From the reign of Constantine, the money formerly expended on baths, amphitheatres and palaces was diverted to the erection, at incredible speed, of great basilicas over the tombs of the martyrs, and of rotundas on the model of the pagan *mausolea* and *nymphea* to serve as tombs and baptisteries; while the palace on the Lateran which belonged to the Princess Fausta became in 313 the headquarters of the Bishops of Rome.

We have only to turn over the pages of the *Liber Pontificalis* to find a minute account of the number of the buildings, and of their amazing splendour.

This growing Church required organization[6]: in the early days as a persecuted sect; in the third century when, it

---

[1] See Barnes, *op. cit.*, for the Petrine question.
[2] Eusebius, *Historia Ecclesiastica*, ii. 25.
[3] The burial-place of S. Paul.
[4] *Hist. Eccles.* x. 2.
[5] *De Schismate Donatistarum*, ii. 34, in *P.L.* 11, col. 954.
[6] See Kehr, *Regesta Pontificum*, 2 vols.: Berlin, 1906.

appears, the catacombs (hitherto respected as private property) were recognized by the government as the property of
a burial confraternity, of which the Bishop of Rome was
the responsible representative; in the fourth century, with
the sudden increase in her material resources, and the
simultaneous thronging into the fold of thousands of half-
Christianized pagans.

There is no reason to doubt the statement of the *Liber
Pontificalis* that Peter appointed seven deacons in Rome,
and that succeeding popes, Fabianus (240–254) and others,
maintained that institution.

Of more practical importance, as a guide to historical
investigation, is the division of the city into parish churches
(*tituli*),[1] each with a priest attached. Anacletus, the third
pope, according to the *Liber Pontificalis*, appointed twenty-
five such priests. The fifth pope, Evaristus, made a similar
appointment, and finally we read that Marcellus in 308

> established twenty-five *tituli* in the city of Rome as
> dioceses for baptism and reception of penitents among
> the multitude who were converted from paganism, and
> for the (care of the) burial-places of the martyrs.[2]

No doubt the persecutions of Domitian (81–96) and
Diocletian (284–305) necessitated the reorganization of the
parishes and accounts for the attribution to several popes of
similar decrees concerning the *tituli*.

The comparative antiquity of, at least, most of the *tituli*,
which no doubt were formed gradually, is proved by the fact
that the names of some of them occur in fourth-century
inscriptions.[3] We have, further, a complete list of the twenty-
five together with a few more, with the names of the priests
attached, appended as signatures to the decrees of the

---

[1] Barnes, *S. Peter in Rome*, points out that *titulus* as used here means a
consecrated stone altar, and quotes the old Latin version of Genesis xxviii. 18,
recording the dream of Jacob at Bethel : "And Jacob arising in the morning
took the stone which had lain under his head, and set it up for a title (*erexit in
titulum*), pouring oil upon the top of it." The word, however, might well be
derived from the ordinary classical meaning of *titulus*, a boundary stone (also,
the inscription on a boundary stone). For *tituli* see *infra*, Chap. V. p. 76.

[2] *i.e.* for the administrations of the cemeteries.

[3] De Rossi, *Inscriptiones Christianae*, i. No. 262 (cf. 377).

Roman Council of 499,[1] and again a list almost exactly similar appended to the decrees of the Council held under Gregory the Great in 595,[2] where the number given is twenty-four, *S. Anastasia*, though it was certainly a titular church, being omitted.

The names of these *tituli* occur so frequently in the documents which we are about to study that a complete list, parallel with that of the secular divisions of the city into fourteen regions, may be useful. It will be seen that the *tituli* are usually clustered together in districts remote from the heart of the city: another proof, perhaps, of antiquity. Further, scarcely a single *titulus* has been founded on the site of a famous secular monument.

It will be noted that in this ancient list of churches, as well as in a similar list of the cemeteries which were attached to them,[3] the names used are those of the founders. It is only in the following centuries, when the bodies of the martyrs were brought from the catacombs, and laid in the ancient titular churches, that the latter were called after the saint who lay beneath the altar. Even then, in early documents, the name appears without the prefix *sanctus*. Between the sixth and the eighth century the names of the *tituli* are frequently changed, and by this we can detect, as by a sort of pulse chart, the fluctuating popularity of various saints and the results on the hagiographical traditions.[4]

Except in the case of the *titulus Cyriaci*, of which no traces have been discovered as yet, churches called by one or other of the ancient names stand to-day[5] on the ancient sites; and to-day, as in ancient times, the Cardinal priests of the Roman Church take their titles from the "titular" churches to which they are appointed.[6]

---

[1] Thiel, *Epistolae Romanorum pontificum*, pp. 651-3.

[2] *Gregorii I. Registrum epistolarum*, v. 57, ed. Ewald and Hartmann, t. i. pp. 562-7.

[3] For *Index Coemiteriorum* see *infra*, pp. 97-102 and 340. For the *Notitia regionum urbis XIV.*, see p. 95. Cf. Plans I. and II.

[4] *Infra*, Chap. XIV. with bibliography.

[5] Cf. Baedeker, *Guide to Italy, Rome*: this book with its admirable plans and concise historical notices is of real assistance in identifying the ancient sites.

[6] *E.g.*, Cardinal Bourne holds the title of S. Pudentiana. (See No. 10 in the list.)

LIST OF THE REGIONS AND *TITULI* [1]

REGIONS.	*TITULI.*
I. Porta Capena [2]. . .	1. Titulus Crescentianae (or Sixti [II.]?). 595. (San Sisto.)
II. Caelimontium [3] . .	2. Byzanti or Pammachii. 401–417. (SS. Joannis et Pauli.)
	3. (Aemilianae? or) Quattuor Coronatorum. Fourth century.
III. Isis and Serapis [4] . .	4. Clementis. 366–384.
	5. Marcellini et Petri. 595.
	6. Apostolorum (or Eudoxiae, or ad Vincula Petri). 431.
	7. Equitii or Silvestri. 499. [(San Silvestro e Martino ai Monti.)
IV. Templum Pacis [5] . .	No titulus.
V. Regio Esquiliae . .	8. Praxedis. 491.
	9. Eusebii. Fourth century.
	10. Pudentis or Pudentianae. 384.
VI. Alta Semita [6] . . .	11. Vestinae (S. Vitalis). 401–417.
	12. Gai or Susannae. Fourth century.
	13. Cyriaci. 499.
VII. Via Lata [7]	14. Marcelli. 308.
VIII. Forum Romanum. .	No titulus.
IX. Circus Flaminius [8] .	15. Lucinae, or Laurentii in Lucina. [9] S. 366.
	16. Damasi, or Laurentii in Damaso. 366–384.
	17. Marci (San Marco). S. 336.
X. Palatium	No titulus.
XI. Circus Maximus [10] .	18. Anastasiae. S. 366–384.

---

[1] For more detailed information, see Duchesne, *Mélanges d'archéologie et d'histoire*, t. vii. p. 217 (1887); *Liber Pontificalis*; Grisar, *op. cit.* S appended to the name of a church denotes a stational church (see *infra*, p. 14, n. 1). Later names of *tituli* are in brackets. The modern Italian name is only added where the Latin name is not sufficient for identification. The date indicates the period when the church is first mentioned.

[2] *Porta Capena* is in the Servian Wall, south-east of Rome on the Via Appia.

[3] North of Region I., with the Lateran palace on the east.

[4] Contains the Flavian Amphitheatre (Colosseum).

[5] Includes the *Sacra Via*, running from the Colosseum through the Arch of Titus to the Forum.

[6] The name of a path going straight up the Quirinal (modern *Via del Quiri-nale* and *Via Venti Settembre*).

[7] The *Via Lata* forms the lower part of the Via Flaminia, and leads up to the Pincian Hill.

[8] Includes the low lands of the Campus Martius with the Circus Flaminius.

[9] *i.e.* S. Laurence in (the parish of) Lucina.

[10] In the low land south-west of the Palatine Hill (Region X.).

Regions.		Tituli.	
XII. Piscina Publica [1]		{ 19. Fasciolae.[2] (SS. Nerei et Achillei.)	377
		{ 20. Balbinae. 595.	
XIII. Aventinus		{ 21. Sabinae. 422-432.	
		{ 22. Priscae (? Tigridae). 499.	
XIV. Transtiberim		{ 23. Julii et Callisti (S. Maria in Trastevere). S. 341-352.	
		{ 24. Caeciliae. Fourth century.	
		{ 25. Chrysogoni. S. 499.	

There were, further, many churches which were not *tituli*, or, if *tituli*, fulfilled some other function as well.

The Churches for the Stations.—For example, another list of churches comes from the seventh century Itinerary [3] *De locis sanctis martyrum* (Concerning the holy places of the martyrs). After a description of the route to the various catacombs comes the following list :—

NOW THESE ARE THE CHURCHES WITHIN ROME

1. The Constantinian Basilica (the Lateran Basilica).
2. S. Maria Maggiore.[4] 352-366.
3. S. Anastasia. T.[5]
4. S. Maria Antiqua (in the Forum).
5. S. Maria Rotunda (the Pantheon).
6. S. Maria in Trastevere.[6] T.
7. SS. James and Philip (Santi Apostoli).[7]
8. SS. John and Paul. T.
9. SS. Cosmas and Damian. 526-530.
10. S. Laurence (*i.e.* in Lucina). T.
11. S. Peter in Chains. T.
12. S. Hadrian (in the Forum).
13. S. Chrysogonus. T.
14. S. George (San Giorgio in Velabro).
15. S. Clemente. T.
16. S. Agatha.[8] 459-472.
17. S. Stephen (San Stefano Rotondo). 468-483.
18. S. Mark. T.

---

[1] A great pond on the low lands near the Baths of Caracalla.

[2] *Infra*, p. 187.

[3] *Infra*, p. 115. Dates and words in brackets are not found in the original.

[4] Known in earlier times as the Liberian Basilica, founded by that pope (352-366); repaired and dedicated to S. Mary by Sixtus III. (432-440).

[5] T indicates a *titular* church.

[6] Formerly called the *Basilica Julii*, founded by that pope (341-352).

[7] Also known as the *Basilica Julia*.

[8] Now S. Agatha dei Goti, in the Suburra : founded originally by Ricimer for the Arian Goths of Theodoric.

19. S. Marcellinus.   T.
20. S. Michael Archangel (that near S. Peter's).
21. S. Boniface (S. Alessio on the Aventine).
22. Bas (*i.e.* basilica) : (here is a blank space).
23. Bas   ,,   ,,   ,,
24. Bas   ,,   ,,   ,,
25. Bas   ,,   ,,   ,,
26. Bas   ,,   ,,   ,,

In all these churches Stations [1] are held at appointed seasons.

Of these twenty-six churches for the stations, of which
the names of twenty-one are given, nine have appeared
already in the list of titular churches, though under different
names sometimes.

The Basilicas and other Churches.—Some of the blank
spaces should, no doubt, be filled in with the names of stational
churches *without* Rome, such as (1) S. Peter's on the Vatican
and perhaps (2) S. Paul's.   In the time of Gregory the Great
(3) S. Valentine on the Via Flaminia and (4) S. Sabina on
the Aventine were stations.   The omission of the great
Sessorian (5) Basilica of Constantine (Region V.), where
Helena placed the relic of the true Cross, is inexplicable ; it was
certainly a stational church in the seventh century.   These
five, then, if our conjectures are correct, should fill the five
blank spaces.   The other great basilicas—the Constantian
Basilica (Lateran), the Liberian (S. Maria Maggiore) and
the Julian (Santi Apostoli)—all appear in this list of stational
churches.   If we add the names of S. Andrew Catabarbara [2]
on the Esquiline, and quite near, S. Bibbiana, both founded
by Simplicius (468–483), and the *Basilica Theodorae*, now
unknown, but existing in 418, our list of important
Roman churches existing in the sixth century is fairly
complete.

Churches without Rome.—Further, without the walls,

---

[1] A *station* was the reunion of the faithful at some appointed spot for public
prayer, recitation of psalms, etc.   These stations probably originated before even
the second century, and usually took the form of vigils.   The liturgy here recited
is the origin of the evening and night recitation of Vespers, Matins and Lauds
—the most primitive part of the Roman office.   These vigils were usually
terminated by a stational Mass.   The stations in Rome for many of the Masses
are still indicated in the Roman Missal, and are observed on certain occasions.
[2] *Supra*, p. 5.

over the shrines of the martyrs were innumerable basilicas and oratories, some of them existing even before the Peace of the Church. A long list could be made from the *Liber Pontificalis* of those in existence in 530, the date of the compilation of that volume, and as they are frequently referred to in the Itineraries, etc., a list of the more important, arranged topographically with the name of the original founder, may be of use.

LIST OF SUBURBAN ROMAN CHURCHES [1]

VIA FLAMINIA.—Basilica of S. Valentine, founded by Julius I. (341–352).

VIA SALARIA.—S. Felicitas, founded by Boniface I. (418–423)'; and, just within the walls, S. Saturninus, founded by Felix IV. (526–530); and the Basilica of Silvester, founded by that pope (314–337).

VIA NOMENTANA.—S. Agnes, founded by Constantine.

VIA TIBURTINA.—S. Laurence, founded by Constantine (*Basilica ad Corpus*), and a second larger basilica, above it, by Sixtus III. (432–440). S. Agapitus, founded by Felix III. (483–592), and S. Stephen by Simplicius (468–483).

VIA LABICANA.—SS. Marcellinus and Peter near the Emperor Constantine's villa *Ad duas lauros*.

VIA LATINA.—S. Stephen, founded by Leo I. (440–461).

VIA APPIA.—*Basilica Apostolorum ad Catacumbas* (S. Sebastian), founded by Damasus (366–384). S. Cornelius, founded by Leo I.: the oratory of S. Sixtus (II.), and that of S. Soteris, all in the Catacomb of S. Callixtus.

VIA ARDEATINA.—Basilica of S. Mark, built by that pope (337–341); SS. Nereus et Achilleus, restored by Pope John I. (523–526); Basilica of Damasus, erected by Damasus.

VIA OSTIENSIS.—S. Paul's, founded by Constantine; SS. Felix and Adauctus, restored by John I. (523–526).

VIA PORTUENSIS.—Basilica of Julius, built by Pope Julius (341–352) to the martyr Felix.

VIA AURELIA.—S. Pancras, built by Pope Symmachus (498–514), and also a church to S. Agatha.

VIA CORNELIA.—S. Peter's, founded by Constantine.

---

[1] For details see *infra*, Bibliography—CATACOMBS, and the *Liber Pontificalis*, under the names of the respective popes. Cf. Plan II.

CHAPTER II

THE PILGRIMAGES AND THE SHRINES

The CATACOMBS — Most ancient monuments—Adornments by popes—Destroyed by the barbarians—The Lombard invasion and translation of bodies.—The PILGRIMS at S. Peter's and at the Catacombs—Descriptions of pilgrimages in Jerome, Prudentius, Chrysostom, Augustine—Emperors and patricians at S. Peter's—The sermon of Leo—English kings in Rome—The popes and the Eastern Church—Arrangements for the pilgrims — Excesses of the pilgrims described by Paulinus and Augustine.—RELICS, their character and uses—Some historic relics.

Τῶν δὲ δούλων τοῦ Χριστοῦ καὶ τὰ σήματα λαμπρὰ τὴν βασιλικωτάτην καταλαβόντα πόλιν, καὶ αἱ ἡμέραι καταφανεῖς ἑορτὴν τῇ οἰκουμένῃ ποιοῦσαι . . . καὶ οἱ τάφοι τῶν δούλων τοῦ σταυρωθέντος λαμπρότεροι τῶν βασιλικῶν εἰσιν αὐλῶν.
Chrysostom, *Hom. in 2 Cor.* (No. xxvi.).[1]

The Ancient Tombs of the Catacombs.—The most ancient Christian monuments must be sought in the many-storeyed catacombs[2] which, lying along the great highways which radiate from Rome, encircle the city within a radius of three miles from the Aurelian Wall. Here, from the first century to the fourth, among a thousand undistinguished dead, were laid the bodies of the martyrs in graves, cubicles or crypts. These shrines were usually of considerable size, and bore inscriptions; the crypts were adorned with frescoes, hung with lamps, and formed into little chapels where once a year at least, on the anniversary of the death (*natalis*), the feast of the saint was kept. Sometimes, even in the earliest days, tiny oratories were raised above the crypt.

Adornment by the Popes.—With the Peace of the Church, succeeding popes vied with each other in adorning

---

[1] Migne, *Patrologia Graeca* ("*P.G.*"), 61, 582. For translation see *infra*, p. 21.

[2] For a description see *infra*, Bibliography—CATACOMBS.

the martyrs' shrines, in raising memorial chapels and basilicas, and in repairing the damages suffered, especially by the northern catacombs, in the invasions of Rome, notably in that of Witigis in 535.   Several popes provided that Masses should be said more or less frequently on days other than the anniversaries.[1]

The Lombard Invasion and the Translation of Bodies.— Then came the Lombards in 756; and the shrines were again invaded and desecrated.   Paul I. (757–768), who first translated within the walls certain of the bodies of the martyrs, writing in 761 to the Abbot of S. Stephen and S. Sylvester, after graphically describing the ruin wrought by the barbarians, continues : [2]

> The faithful have ceased by indolence and by negligence to render at the cemeteries the cult which is due : animals have penetrated into these : they have been transformed into cattle-sheds and sheep-folds : they have been defiled by every kind of corruption.   I have witnessed this indifference for such holy places, and deplored it profoundly, and I have thought good, with the help of God, to withdraw from these ruined places the bodies of the martyrs, the confessors and the virgins of Christ ; and, amid hymns and spiritual songs, I have transported them to the city of Rome, and have placed them in the church which I have recently constructed in honour of S. Stephen and S. Sylvester on the site of the house in which I was born. . . .

Succeeding popes tried in vain to maintain worship in the ancient shrines; Pope Pascal (817–824) finally transferred the last of the bodies to churches within the city.   For eight centuries the catacombs were deserted, and fell into ruin. In the sixteenth century they were again discovered, and plundered, rather than excavated.[3]   Finally in modern times

---

[1] *Liber Pontificalis*, ed. Duchesne, under *Vigilius* (537–555), *John III.* (561–574), *Sergius I.* (687–701), *Gregory III.* (731–741).   The question of the development of the cult of the Martyrs is of the highest importance.   For a detailed treatment see E. Lucius, *Die Anfänge des Heiligenkults in der Christlichen Kirche*, Tübingen, 1904 ; H. Delehaye, *Les Origines du culte des Martyrs*, Brussels, 1912.   Cf. *infra*, Chaps. XIV., XV.

[2] Mansi, *Concilia*, xii. 646.   Cf. De Rossi, *Roma Sotterranea*, i. 220.

[3] An exception must be made in favour of Bosio (1576–1629) who inaugurated the scientific method of research.

2

the great De Rossi, and later scholars who are proud to call themselves his pupils, have undertaken the systematic excavation of the earliest monuments of Western Christianity.

The Pilgrims at S. Peter's.—During the seven centuries prior to the Lombard invasions the catacombs were a centre of devotion.[1]   Pilgrims from every land: some from the remote East, some faring to or from the holy places in Jerusalem; swarthy Africans, Spaniards, and the fair-haired children of the North from German forests, from the lowlands of the Rhine, from the far shores of Britain and Ireland, all flocked to Rome.   They availed themselves of the admirable roads which bound together the Empire from the Euphrates to the Pillars of Hercules, and from Ethiopia to farthest Britain.   They trod in the steps of ambassadors, scholars and tourists; merchants, actors and doctors; quacks, magicians, destitute aliens and the rest who sought fame, fortune or food in Rome.   They came to perform a penance imposed, to seek answers to their prayers, remission of their sins, healing in their sickness, and relics to take home.

Among all the martyrs, Peter has ever maintained the first place in the affections of the pilgrims; and his shrine surpassed all the others in the splendour of the gifts received.[2]

Next in favour was the shrine of S. Paul.   The golden vessels of these two churches were respected by Alaric the Goth when he sacked Rome.   Those of S. Peter's were guarded "by a consecrated virgin now advanced in years" in a house far distant from the basilica.   The contemporary Spanish historian, Orosius,[3] vividly describes the incident. When a Gothic chieftain burst into the house, the custodian said to him:

'These are the sacred vessels of Peter the apostle. Touch them if you dare.   You will see what will

---

[1] Guiraud, "Rome ville Sainte au Vième siècle," in *Revue d'histoire et de littérature*, 1898.

[2] These are recorded in the *Liber Pontificalis* under the lives of successive popes.

[3] Orosius, *Hist.* vii. 39, in *P.L.* 31, 1163.   This work was translated into Anglo-Saxon by Bede.

happen.' . . . But the barbarian, moved to religious
awe, and touched by the fear of God and the fidelity
of the virgin, reported the matter to Alaric, who ordered
all the vessels, as they were, to be carried to the basilica of
the Apostle. [A great procession is formed]. . . . Raised
high over their heads the gold and silver vessels are
borne along publicly : the holy procession is defended
by drawn swords : barbarian and Roman raise hymns
aloud to God. The trumpet of salvation rings far and
wide amid the slaughter in the city . . . the chosen
vessels (*Vas*) of Christ rush together from all sides to
the vessels of S. Peter, and many pagans mingle with
the Christians.

The Pilgrims in the Catacombs.—From these two
churches most of the pilgrims passed on to the catacombs.
They usually started from the North, from the Via Flaminia,
and passed round Rome in a clockwise direction from shrine
to shrine till they had completed the circuit.

And in addition to the pilgrim, the hundreds who were
drawn to Rome primarily for some business, ecclesiastical
or secular, would not fail to pay a visit to the shrine of
S. Peter at least.

Who were the pilgrims who made this journey ?
What was the point of view of the simpler pilgrims,
of the priests and bishops who directed them, of the
learned doctors of the Church ? Were there any abuses,
obvious even to those who devotedly believed in pilgrimages ? Were there any voices raised against the whole
practice ?

We find answers to all these questions in stories of
individual pilgrims preserved in national records, in friendly
letters, in acrimonious pamphlets, in sermons, in treatises,—
all contemporary with the pilgrimages, and of indubitable
authenticity. Incidentally some vivid pictures of the pilgrims
themselves are presented. The material is abundant, the
difficulty only in the choice. We will content ourselves with
the quotation of a few representative passages, and confine ourselves mainly to writers of the fourth and fifth
century.

Then, with these documents in our hands as commentaries, we will walk in the footsteps of the pilgrims along the tracks that connect the shrines,[1] pass down the broad stairs to this tomb, ascend again to another, descend once more to a third: we will read the *graffiti*[2] scrawled on the passage walls and in the crypts; look at the frescoes, inscriptions, and phials containing the martyrs' blood, on which the pilgrims gazed fifteen hundred years ago. Then we will make a longer halt at some shrine converted into a liturgical chapel, adorned with marble and fine stuffs, where the frescoes are blurred by the smoke of the candles, and where great lamps, fed with oil of balsam, burn perpetually before the shrine. It was here the weary pilgrims would rest awhile on the stone bench that runs round the walls, while over the altar tomb the priest said the Mass of the saint in the words still used on their festivals to-day ; or some great preacher, Jerome, Augustine, Leo the Great, delivered in the basilicas above the tombs, sermons which we can still read after fifteen hundred years.

Descriptions of the Pilgrimages :—By Jerome.— S. Jerome (346–420), in a passage recalling his boyhood, describes the catacombs :[3]

> When I was a boy in Rome being instructed in liberal studies, on Sundays, with others of my own age, I used to wander about the sepulchres of the apostles and martyrs ; and I often went into crypts dug out of the depths of the earth, which have along the walls, on each side as you enter, bodies of the dead ; and everything is so dark that those words of the prophet are almost fulfilled :—' They descend alive into hell ' (Ps. liv. 16). Now and then (*raro*) a light from above modifies the horror of the darkness, but it seems rather a hole pierced to let down the light than a window. . . .

---

[1] Schneider is attempting to discover some of these ancient tracks, of the highest importance for determining the sites : see *Nuovo Bullettino di archeologia cristiana*, 1910, p. 17.

[2] De Rossi points out that the discovery of *graffiti* and broad stairways in the course of excavations always indicates the proximity of a consecrated shrine visited by pilgrims.

[3] *Commentarium in Ezechielum*, xii. 50, in *P.L.* 25, 375. (The greater part of S. Jerome has been translated by Wace and Schaff ; see Bibliography—PATRISTIC.)

In another passage he describes the pilgrims at the shrines : [1]

> Where save at Rome do they crowd with such zeal and frequency to the churches and sepulchres of the martyrs? Where, as here, does *Amen* re-echo like heavenly thunder, and the temples, emptied of their idols, shiver? Not that Rome has a faith different from that of all the Churches of Christ, but because devotion in her is greater, and simplicity in belief.

By Prudentius.—Prudentius [2] (b. 348) describes the pilgrims to the tomb of Hippolytus :

> In the morning they rush to greet him : all the youth worship : they come, they go, till the setting of the sun. They press kisses on the shining metal of the inscription : they pour out spices : they bedew his tomb with tears. And when . . . his feast day returns, what throngs are forced thither by their earnest zeal . . . : the wide fields can scarce contain the joy of the people. . . .

In the words of the Fathers and in the pages of history we read of the reverence paid by emperors and kings to the shrine of Peter. The Fathers generally draw therefrom the moral of the pre-eminence of the spiritual over the material, and inculcate the virtue of humility.

By Chrysostom.—Chrysostom [3] (347–407) in one of his most eloquent sermons says :

> Of the servants of Christ the very tombs are glorious, seeing they have taken possession of the most royal city : and their days are well known, making festivals for the world. . . . The tombs of the servants of the Crucified are more splendid than the palaces of kings . . . he that wears the purple goes to embrace these tombs and, laying aside his pride, stands praying to the saints to be his advocates before God . . . the son of Constantine the Great thought he should be honouring his father with great honour if he buried him in the Porch (*atrium*) of the Fisherman . . . the place that

---

[1] *Comm. in Epist. Galat.* ii., in *P.L.* 26, 355.

[2] *Peristephanon*, xi. 189, in *P.L.* 60, 550.

[3] *Hom.* 26 *in* 2 *Cor.* xii. 10, in *P.G.* 61, 582 (trans.: Pusey, *Library of the Fathers*).

doorkeepers fill in the halls of the kings is filled by kings in the basilica of the apostle.[1]

By Augustine.—Similar in tenor are the words of Augustine:[2]

> . . . Behold what is noble and pre-eminent in this world—the emperor comes to Rome: whither does he hasten? To the temple of the emperor or to the memorial of the Fisherman?

Emperors and Patricians at S. Peter's: the Sermon of Leo.—In February 450 the western emperor Valentinian III., with his wife Eudoxia, the daughter of the great Theodosius, and his mother Galla Placidia, paid one of his rare visits to Rome, and on the 22nd ("the anniversary of the Chair of Peter" as we read in the Philocalian Calendar of the fourth century[3]), after attending the vigil, and offering rich gifts, they all entered the Basilica of S. Peter in full state, and Leo the Great (440–461) preached the sermon:[4]

> . . . See! the government of the first and greatest city of the world has been bestowed by Christ on a poor man of no account like Peter. The sceptres of kings have bowed down before the wood of the Cross: the purple of the Court has submitted to the blood of Christ and of the holy martyrs. The emperor, decked with his glittering diadem and accompanied by a host of warriors, comes to seek the Fisherman's intercession, and desires to be adorned with his merits rather than be decked with jewels. The noble and exalted prostrate themselves before the burial-place of a man of the lowest estate.

Conviction, loyalty, or the fashion soon induced patrician

---

[1] An allusion to the tombs of Valentinian (364–379) and Honorius (395–423) at the entrance of S. Peter's in Chrysostom's day: at a later date Otho II. was buried there and some of the Anglo-Saxon kings who died when pilgrims to Rome: see *infra*, p. 23.

[2] *Comm. in Psalm*, cxl., in *P.L.* 37, 1830. (For translation see Schaff, *op. cit.* in Bibliography.)

[3] *Infra*, Appendix III. *B.*, *Dep. Mart.*

[4] Morin, *Anecdota Maredsolana*, i. 409, 1893, from a new codex. Cf. Leo, *epist.* 55, in *P.L.* 54, 858. (Selections from Leo have been translated in Wace and Schaff, *op. cit.*)

and plebeian to follow the emperor's example. Prudentius [1]
describes the scene:

> . . . They come to the holy sanctuaries of the
> followers of the Nazarene . . . the descendants of the
> Anii, the noble children of the Probi . . . the high-born
> Anicius . . . the Olybrii lay low the fasces of the
> Bruti before the threshold of the martyrs. . . . After
> this turn your eyes on the people: what part of them
> does not despise the altar . . . of Jupiter? Every man
> of them who . . . treads the stony ways . . . to the
> heights of the Vatican where lie the ashes of the beloved
> father (Peter).

The sovereigns of the newly-converted Teutonic peoples
were among the most devout of pilgrims.

When Charlemagne and his suite went to spend their
Easter in Rome in 774, they performed the last thirty miles
on foot, and Charlemagne ascended the steps of S. Peter's
on his knees, kissing each step as he went up. The pope
received him, they embraced, prayed in the church, and then
" descended together to the body of blessed Peter."

English Kings at S. Peter's.—Many of our Anglo-
Saxon kings [2] from time to time ceased to fight for their
precarious crowns in order to make a visit to Rome.
Cadwalla, after many a bloody deed, went to Rome and was
baptized by Pope Sergius

> On the holy Saturday before Easter in the year of
> our Lord 689, and being still in his white garments, he
> fell sick and departed this life on the 20th of April, and
> was associated with the blessed in heaven.

He was named Peter, and was buried in S. Peter's, and
honoured with a long epitaph.[3] His successor, Ina, gave up
his kingdom, having reigned thirty-seven years:

> and went away to Rome to visit the blessed apostles
> . . . being desirous to spend some time of his pilgrimage

---

[1] *Contra Symmachum*, i. 550, in *P.L.* 60, 164.

[2] See Bede, *Historia Ecclesiastica*, in *P.L.* 95 (also edited with translation
by Giles, *Patres ecclesiae anglicanae*, London, 1843: also translated by A. M.
Sellar); *Anglo-Saxon Chronicle* (in Bohn's Library together with Bede's
Ecclesiastical History).

[3] *Infra*, p. 231.

on earth in the neighbourhood of the holy place, that he might be the more easily received by the saints in heaven. The same thing was done by many of the English nation, noble and ignoble, laity and clergy, men and women.[1]

Another king imitated the example of Ina:[2]

Coinred, who had for some time nobly governed the kingdom of the Mercians, did a much more noble act by quitting the sceptre of his kingdom and going to Rome (709), where, being shorn when Constantine was pope, and made a monk at the threshold of the apostles, he continued to his last hour in prayers, fasting and almsgiving. . . . With him went the son of Sighere, king of the East Saxons, whose name was Offa, a youth of most lovely age and beauty, and most earnestly desired by all the nation to be their king. He with like devotion quitted his wife, lands, kindred and country for Christ and for the gospel. . . . He also, when they came to the holy places at Rome, receiving the tonsure, and adopting a monastic life, attained the long-wished-for vision of the blessed apostles in heaven.

Ethelwulf in 855

went to Rome in great state and remained there twelve months . . . [later] Alfred, his third son, he sent to Rome; and when Pope Leo heard that Ethelwulf was dead he consecrated Alfred king, and held him as his spiritual son at confirmation, even as his father Ethelwulf had requested on sending him thither.

Alfred's sister, Queen Ethelswitha, died on her way to Rome, and her body lies in Pavia.

It would be tedious to multiply names. A single remark of the *Chronicle* shows the frequency of these journeys from England to Rome:

In that year (899) no journey to Rome was undertaken except that King Alfred sent two couriers with tithes.

Truly might Leo I.[3] exclaim:

(Peter and Paul) have raised Rome to such glory

---

[1] Bede, *op. cit.* v. 7.   [2] *Ibid.* v. 19.

[3] *Sermo* 82 in *P.L.* 54, 422 (trans. in Wace and Schaff, *op. cit.*): the translation above is not entirely by Wace and Schaff.

that she has become a holy nation, an elect people, a royal and priestly city, and the head of the world, thanks to the blessed seat of Peter. . . . And what a multitudinous offspring these two glorious plants of the divine seed have produced, her thousands of blessed martyrs bear witness; who, in emulation of the triumph of the apostles, have girt our city with a people robed in purple, whose glory shines far and wide: and they have crowned her, as with a diadem, studded with the splendour of innumerable precious stones.

The Pope and the Eastern Church.—In the letter of Theodoret,[1] Bishop of Cyrrhus in Syria, to this same Leo we have the view of a learned Oriental:

. . . Your city is great among all because she is the head of the world, and sees great multitudes pressing within her walls; . . . but her chief glory is the faith to which the divine Paul bore witness. . . . Your city possesses the bodies of Peter and Paul, the fathers of us all, our masters in the faith, whose tombs illumine the hearts of the faithful. These blessed two, inspired by God, have arisen in the East, and spread on all sides their rays: but it is in the West they have found their setting, it is from the West that they illumine the world. It is they who have given to your seat an incomparable glory: they are the most precious of your possessions.

Arrangements for the Pilgrims.—Arrangements were made for the comfort of this throng of pilgrims. They brought with them introductions, and were received on the way in the Bishops' houses, in monasteries and in guest-houses. Pope Symmachus (498–514) had established three hospices in Rome, at S. Peter's, S. Paul's and S. Laurence's; and Belisarius, the general of Justinian, built and magnificently endowed a hospice in the Via Lata. In the time of Charlemagne there was a special guest-house for the Franks, the *Schola Francorum*; and other little national colonies were formed,—Saxons, Frisians, Lombards—in the precincts of S. Peter's. Here also were two great fountains

---

[1] *Ep.* lii. in *P.L.* 54, 847 (trans. in Wace and Schaff, *op. cit.* vol. iii. p. 293, Ep. cxiii.).

for the pilgrims to wash in,[1] stalls at which to buy food and "objects of piety," and a place under the arcades of the Atrium where, from the earliest days, the poor were fed on the feast day of S. Peter.

Ansa, wife of the Lombard king Desiderius, built a hospice about 740 on Mount Garganus, on the Adriatic: Paul the Deacon put up an inscription on it:

> Go on thy way safely, pilgrim from the western shores, who seekest the temple of blessed Peter and the rock of Garganus and the blessed cavern. Safe under his protection thou shalt not fear the robber's dagger, nor cold nor storm in the dark night: the queen has provided you with spacious shelter and with refreshment.

Excesses of the Pilgrims described by Paulinus and Augustine.—The pilgrims at times took only too good advantage of the opportunities afforded them. Their devotions paid, they indulged freely in revels and feasting, a characteristic also of an ordinary funeral repast[2] in those days. Many passages from the Fathers have illuminated for us this phase of the complex aspects of the pilgrimages.

When Eustochium, that pious daughter of the pious Paula, sent a present to Jerome on the Feast of S. Peter, he replied to her with some serious advice conveyed in a light tone, and remarked:[3]

> We must be careful to celebrate the Feast (of S. Peter) not so much by abundance of food as by exaltation of spirit: for it is absurd to try to honour by such excess a martyr whom we know to have pleased God by his fasting.

No doubt the description of the scenes at the tomb of S. Felix of Nola which we owe to Paulinus of Nola[4] would apply to the Roman pilgrims:

> In throngs they spend the whole night in vigils and

---

[1] We have the inscription for the fountain (*cantharus*) in the Atrium of S. Paul's. See *infra*, p. 286.

[2] See Augustine, *Confessions*, vi. 2; Paulinus of Nola, *Ep.* xiii. in *P.L.* 61, 207.

[3] *Ep.* 31 *ad Eustochium*, in *P.L.* 22, 445 (trans. Wace and Schaff).

[4] *Carmen*, xxvii. 555, in *P.L.* 61. For Paulinus' life, cf. *infra*, p. 36.

rejoicing. . . . Would that this rejoicing manifested
itself in sober (*sanus*) prayers, and that they did not
fill high the wine cups on the threshold of the saints, . . .
The simple credulously hold that the saints rejoice in
the fumes of the wine poured forth on their sepulchres
. . . the altar tomb (*mensa*) of Peter receives what the
doctrine of Peter abhors.

Another description of these excesses, their origin, and
the effort of the Church to combat them is found in a letter
which S. Augustine wrote in 395, when still only a priest,
to Alypius, Bishop of Thagaste,[1] stating how he dealt
with the question. After describing how he rebuked his
congregation he continues :

> Lest, however, any slight should seem to be put by
> us on those who before our time tolerated . . . such
> manifold excesses of an undisciplined multitude, I
> explained to them the circumstances out of which this
> custom seems to have necessarily risen in the Church,—
> namely, that, in the Peace . . . crowds of heathen
> who wished to assume the Christian religion were kept
> back, because, having been accustomed to celebrate
> the feasts connected with their worship of idols in
> revelling and drunkenness, they could not easily refrain
> from pleasures so hurtful and habitual. Therefore it
> seemed good to our ancestors, making for a time a
> concession to their infirmity, to permit them to celebrate,
> instead of the festivals which they renounced, other feasts
> in honour of the holy martyrs ; which were observed not
> as before with a profane design but with similar self-
> indulgence. . . . The example of daily excess in the
> use of wine in the church of the blessed Apostle Peter
> was brought forward in defence of the practice. I said
> in the first place that I had heard that these excesses
> were often forbidden, but because the place was at a
> distance from the bishop's control, and because in such
> a city the multitude of carnally-minded people was
> great, the foreigners especially, of whom there is a
> constant influx . . . the suppression of so great an evil
> had not been possible.

S. Augustine again, in a well-known passage in his

[1] *Ep.* 29 *ad Alypium*, in *P.L.* 33, 114 (trans. Wace and Schaff).

Confessions,[1] describes how in Milan his mother was bringing the usual offerings for the anniversaries of the saints. The same custom prevailed in Rome. She was wont to bring with her—

> A basket full of pottage, bread and wine to be tasted by herself, and then given away . . . when called upon to attend the memorials of the dead ; . . . and when she learnt that that illustrious preacher and godly prelate (Ambrose) had forbidden these things to be done even by those who did them in all sobriety, lest any occasion of excess should be given to the intemperate, and, further, because these memorials were too like the superstitious *Parentalia* (funeral feasts) of the Gentiles, she willingly submitted, and in place of her basket full of fruits of the earth she learned to bring to the memorials of the martyrs a bosom full of purer offerings, so that she might give what she could to the poor, and that thus the Communion of the Lord's Body, in imitation of whose Passion the martyrs were sacrificed and crowned, might be celebrated at the anniversaries in this way.

The Character and Uses of Relics (for Dedications of Churches, etc.).—As we study the story of individual pilgrims we shall note that the majority of them brought back relics.[2] What were these relics? What view did the pilgrims take of them?

Very often it is a bishop who requires relics of the martyr to whom his church is dedicated, in order to place them in the altar, even as in quite primitive days the altar stone [3] (*titulus*) was itself a martyr's tomb. The gift of relics made by the popes to kings and great people is a commonplace of papal correspondence. We shall note, too, how often deacons were sent with petitions for these treasures, and further, often brought back from the archives documents of historical importance incorporated by a Bede [4] or a

---

[1] Bk. vi. 2, in *P.L.* 32, 719 (trans. by Bigg, " Library of Devotion " : London, 1905).

[2] A. de Waal, "Andenken an die Romfahrt im Mittelalter," in *Römische Quartalschrift*, 1900, p. 54, with further bibliography.

[3] *Supra*, p. 10.   [4] *Infra*, p. 37.

Gregory of Tours [1] into their histories.   These relics could heal sicknesses, save from shipwreck, and, on one occasion at least, were miraculously preserved amid the flames.   In some few cases the relics were, or professed to be, actual portions of the body of the saint, or else a splinter of the true Cross enclosed in a cross, or a minute fragment of the chain which had bound Peter or Paul, or of the gridiron of Laurence and such like.

In the vast majority of cases, however, the relics were nothing but objects which had been in proximity to the holy tombs,—a cloth which had been placed on the tomb of S. Peter or S. Paul ; a key or a golden model of a key which had unlocked the door of their confession ; a lamp or a little vessel [2] containing oil that had burnt before the shrines of the martyrs ; facsimiles of the nails of the true Cross ; medals with portraits of the apostles.   Some of the familiar portraits of Peter and Paul made with gold leaf inserted in crystal (*vetri*) no doubt served this, as well as other purposes. A tiny medal somewhat of this character, with a metal ring attached for hanging round the neck, has actually been found in the catacomb of Priscilla.[3]   There was in the precincts of S. Peter's then as to-day, a depot of "objects of piety" to supply the needs of pilgrims.   Such relics are very similar to the objects brought home by the Catholic pilgrim now,—a blessed medal, a rosary laid on the tomb of a saint, some grains of earth from the catacombs enclosed in a crucifix,—and were probably regarded in much the same light then as now.

The passages illustrating these statements are numerous : reference to a few only will be sufficient for our purpose. Among the bishops who sought for relics we read that Amantius, Bishop of Como,[4] visited Rome in 440, and returned with relics of SS. Peter and Paul and placed them in

---

[1] *Infra*, p. 31.

[2] There are some beautiful examples of such vessels in the Treasury of Monza : see *infra*, pp. 102 and following.   For illustrations see Garucci, *Storia dell' arte cristiana*, vol. vi. pl. 433–435 : Prato, 1880.

[3] De Rossi, in *Bull. di archeol. crist.* 1864, p. 81 ; 1891, p. 127 ; Garucci, *op. cit.* tav. 174, 176.

[4] Ughelli, *Italia Sacra*, v. 258 : Venice, 1720.

his Cathedral Church dedicated to these apostles. Germanus, Bishop of Auxerre,[1] brought into Britain in 429 "relics of all the apostles and of several martyrs," and worked many miracles with them.

The letter of Gregory the Great to Palladius, Bishop of Saintes[2] (*Santones*) in Gaul is worth quoting :

> Leuparic your presbyter, the bearer of these presents, when he came to us, informed us that your Fraternity has built a church in honour of the blessed apostles Peter and Paul and also of the martyrs Laurence and Pancras; and placed there thirteen altars, of which we learn that four have remained as yet undedicated, because of your desire to deposit there relics of the above-named saints. And, seeing that we have reverently supplied you with relics of the saints Peter and Paul and also of the martyrs Laurence and Pancras, we exhort you to receive them with reverence, and deposit them with the help of the Lord ; providing before all things that supplies for the maintenance of those who serve there be not wanting.

For the same purpose Avitus, Bishop of Vienne in Southern France, sends his deacon Julian to Pope Symmachus (498–511) to beg for a fresh supply of relics.[3]

Some Historic Relics.—Among the innumerable presents of this kind offered to kings and bishops we read how Pope Pelagius I. (555–560)[4] sent relics to King Childebert by the monks of the monastery of the island of Lérins, off Provence, and to Sapaudius, Bishop of Arles, through a sub-deacon called Homobonus. Pelagius II.[5] in 580 sent Aunarius, bishop of Auxerre, relics "with blessing attached" (*cum cohaerente sibi sanctificatione*).

A few drops of the holy oil which had burnt before the martyrs' shrines, collected into little bottles, was a sufficiently magnificent present for the great Pope Gregory to make to

---

[1] Bede, *Ecclesiastical History*, i. 18.

[2] *Gregorii Magni Epistolae*, vi. 49, in *P.L.* 77, 834 (trans. Wace and Schaff, *op. cit.*).

[3] *Aviti Vitensis Epistolae*, xxvii., in *P.L.* 59, 243.

[4] Jaffé, *Regesta Pontificum Romanorum*, No. 942. For Lérins, see *infra*, p. 250, and note 1.

[5] *Ibid.*, No. 1048.

the Lombard queen Theodelinda for the cathedral which she had founded at Monza.   They have been preserved as the greatest of treasures to the present day, and form the subject of countless learned treatises.[1]

A similar relic, some *Oleum S. Crucis*, or oil burnt before the shrine of the Holy Cross, was presented to Pope Gregory the Great by the ex-consul Leontius.[2]

A most instructive passage is found in the pages of Gregory of Tours.   Agiulphus,[3] the deacon of Gregory, visited all the sanctuaries of Rome, and brought back some relics for the church of Tours.   He recounted to Gregory all he had seen there, and all that he had heard concerning the passions and shrines of the martyrs.   This has been embodied in the *De Gloria Martyrum*[4] of Gregory, in which the following passage occurs :

> S. Peter is buried in a church called from ancient times the Vatican. . . . His sepulchre, which is placed under the altar, is very rarely entered.   However, if any one desires to pray, the gates by which the place is fenced are opened, and he goes in above the sepulchre ; and then having opened a little window (*i.e.* the *fenestrella confessionis*) puts his head within, and makes request concerning his needs.   Nor is the result delayed, if only the petition be a just one.   For if he desires to carry away with him some blessed memorial, he throws within a little handkerchief that has been carefully weighed, and then, watching and fasting, he prays most fervently that the apostle may give an effective answer to his devotion.   Wonderful to say, if the faith of the man prevails, the handkerchief, when it is raised from the tomb, is so filled with divine virtue that it weighs much more than it did before ; and then he who has raised it knows that he has obtained the favour which he sought.   Many also make golden keys to unlock the gates of the blessed sepulchre ; then they take away those which were used before as a sacred treasure, and

---

[1] For a full account of the treasure see *infra*, p. 102.

[2] *Gregorii Magni Epistolae*, lib. viii., No. 35 in *P.L.* 77, 938.   (Wace and Schaff, *op. cit.*)

[3] Duchesne, "Le *Liber Pontificalis* en Gaule" in *Mélanges d'archéologie et d'histoire*, 1882, 277 ; Gregory of Tours, *Historia Francorum*, x. 1.

[4] *De Gloria Martyrum*, i. 28, in *P.L.* 71, col. 728.

by these keys the infirmities of the afflicted are cured. For true faith can do all things.

As a further illustration of the practices here mentioned, we find certain bishops petitioning Pope Hormisdas in 520 to lay some cloths (*brandea*) actually *upon* the tomb of the Apostles Peter and Paul :[1] they ask, further, for a portion of the chains of the apostles, and a fragment of the gridiron of Laurence. Their requests are granted.

Again, one of the keys described above was sent by Gregory the Great to Theoctista,[2] sister of the Emperor Mauricianus and governess of the royal children. In the letter which accompanies it the pope says :

> I beg you to take especial care to instruct in good morals the little lords you are bringing up. . . . Further, I send you, as a blessing from S. Peter the Apostle, a key from his most sacred body : with respect to which key the miracle has been wrought which I now relate.

Then follows the story of the sacrilegious Lombard who was trying to steal what he believed to be a golden key, and cut his own throat by mistake.

A similar key was sent by him to Anastasius, patriarch of Antioch,[3] with the words :

> I have sent you the keys of blessed Peter the Apostle who loves you : these, laid upon the sick, are splendid with many miracles.

These keys sometimes contained in addition actual relics of S. Peter's chains,[4] as did those sent to King Childebert[5] "which, hung round the neck, will protect you from evil." Many of the pilgrims so wore their relics, on twisted chains (*tortulae*).[6]

When the Empress Constantina made a bold request to Gregory the Great for the head of S. Paul, the pope replies :[7]

> I am distressed that I neither can nor dare do what

[1] Borgia, *Vaticana Confessio*, p. clxi : Rome, 1776.
[2] Greg. *Ep.* lvii., No. 26 in *P.L.* 77. [3] *Ibid.* i. 6.
[4] *Ibid.* i. 30.   [5] *Ibid.* vi. 6.   [6] *Supra*, p. 29.
[7] *Ibid.* iv. 300.

you enjoin. For the bodies of the apostles Peter and Paul glitter with so great miracles and terrors in their churches, that one cannot even go to pray there without great fear. . . . Moreover, let my most tranquil lady know that it is not the custom of the Romans, when they give relics of saints, to presume to touch any part of the body : but only a cloth (*brandeum*) is put into a box (*pyxis*), and placed near the most sacred bodies of the saints : and when it is taken up, it is deposited with due reverence in the church that is to be dedicated, and such powerful effects are thus produced there as might have been if the bodies themselves had been brought to that special place. . . . But since so religious a desire of my most serene lady ought not to be wholly unsatisfied, I will make haste to transmit to you some portion of the chains which S. Peter the apostle himself bore on his neck and hands, from which many miracles are displayed among the people : if, at least, I should succeed in removing it by filing. . . . A priest attends with a file, and in case of some seekers a portion comes off so quickly from these chains that there is no delay ; but in the case of other seekers, the file is drawn a long time over the chains, and yet nothing can be got from them.

Of the miraculous powers ascribed to such relics we have further examples. The deacon Agiulphus, who was bringing back manuscripts to Gregory of Tours, was nearly shipwrecked on his journey home,[1] but in the end all on board reached their journey's end—

For there were on board relics of the apostles, of S. Paul, of SS. Laurence and Pancras, of S. Chrysanthus and the maiden Darias, of S. John and the other Paul his brother. . . .

This same Gregory of Tours[2] tells of a certain John who went on a pilgrimage to the Holy Land, and was healed of leprosy. Coming back " he fell among thieves in the lofty solitudes of the Alps." They beat him, left him half dead, and threw on to the fire the little casket (*capsa*) in which

---

[1] Gregory of Tours, *De Gloria Martyrum*, i. 83.
[2] *Ibid.* i. 19.

were relics.   The relics remained intact, and John recovered
and went back to Gaul.

Gregory himself was given a cloth in which the Holy
Cross had been wrapped up.   He tore the stuff into small
fragments, and apportioned them to various religious houses,
whereby were wrought miracles of healing.[1]

Beside the human interest in these stories, these relics
have often thrown light on historical questions, as in the case
of the celebrated treasure of Monza.

---

[1] Gregory of Tours, *De Gloria Martyrum*, i. 6.   For further examples of
pilgrims see *supra*, pp. 23, 24.   Cf. p. 37.

CHAPTER III

THE PILGRIMAGES: THE BELIEFS OF THE PILGRIMS

Some individual pilgrims: early martyrs, pilgrims from Gaul, Paulinus of Nola, English pilgrims—Pilgrimage privileges attached to local churches—The beliefs of the pilgrims as shown in the *graffiti*—Spirit of materialism—Burial *ad Sanctos*: views of Augustine—Jerome on pilgrimages—The inscription of Achilles at Spoleto—The controversial pamphlets of Jerome and Vigilantius.

Unde duo ista praeclara divini seminis germina in quantam subolem pullularint, beatorum millia martyrum protestantur : quae, apostolicorum aemula triumphorum, urbem nostram purpuratis et longe lateque rutilantibus populis ambierunt, et quasi ex multarum honore gemmarum conserto uno diademate coronaverunt.—Leo, *Sermo*.[1]

Individual Pilgrims: Early Martyrs.—We may linger yet a little over the personalities of the pilgrims; who are sometimes interesting in themselves, and whose records throw light on the beliefs of that day. The writers of the *Acta Sanctorum*[2] love to relate how several of the early martyrs perished while in prayer at the tombs of their forerunners. Zoe, one of the converts of the martyr S. Sebastian,[3] was arrested as she was praying at the shrine of S. Peter on his feast day. Her fellow-convert Tranquillianus cried : " Are women to win their crowns before us ? Why then should we live ? ": and, descending to the tomb of S. Paul on the octave of his feast, he too was martyred. These *Acta* are almost all compilations of the fifth and sixth century, but occasionally they have preserved the tradition aright, and at least give us the traditions as known to the pilgrims.

[1] *Supra*, p. 25.   [2] *Infra*, p. 128.
[3] *Acta Sanctorum* (" *A.SS.*"), Jan. 20.

We come again to genuine historical pilgrims with Fulgentius of Africa,[1] the historian of the Vandal invasion, who came to Rome in 500 and

> reverently went all round to all the holy places of the martyrs.

Pilgrims from Gaul.—Among the earliest of the foreign pilgrims were those from Gaul, which had given many martyrs to the Church. Hilary, Bishop of Arles in 429, was wont to visit the sanctuary of the apostles and martyrs,[2] and, as a true pilgrim, made the whole journey on foot. Apollinaris Sidonius (430–483), Bishop of Clermont - Ferrand,[3] who has described his journey, was in Rome in 456 and again in 467.

Gregory of Tours[4] tells a characteristic story of Aravatius (or Servatius), Bishop of Tongres in the middle of the fifth century. Fearing the possible horrors of a Hunnish invasion of Gaul, the bishop made a pilgrimage to Rome to fast and to pray for the intercession of the apostle to avert the scourge. S. Peter replies that God has sanctioned the invasion, but that Servatius shall be spared the sight by swift death. One wonders if the bishop went home comforted.

Paulinus of Nola.—An ardent pilgrim and devout believer in relics was Paulinus,[5] once a wealthy patrician of Bordeaux, then Senator and Consul of Rome. In 394 he gave up wealth and position to live a life of monastic poverty with his wife at Nola in Southern Italy, where he built a great church to S. Felix; and of this district he became bishop in 409. He was in constant correspondence with Augustine and Jerome. He was wont to make an annual pilgrimage to Rome on 29th June, "the anniversary of the blessed apostles" (*beatorum apostolorum natalis*).

In 399 he writes to his friend Severus,[6] saying he has been ten days in Rome, and spent all the mornings in prayer at the sanctuaries of the apostles and martyrs, and the afternoons in visits. Again, in 340 he writes to

---

[1] *P.L.* 65, 130.   [2] *A.SS.* May 5.   [3] *A.SS.* August 23.
[4] *Historia Francorum*, ii. 5, in *P.L.* 71.
[5] *Infra*, pp. 41, 44.   [6] *Ep.* 17, in *P.L.* 61, 235.

Delphinius,[1] Bishop of Bordeaux, that he has made his wonted pilgrimage to Rome on the anniversary of the blessed apostles, and been kindly received by Pope Anastasius.

Chrysostom expresses regret in one of his sermons that he cannot visit the shrine of S. Paul:[2]

> If I were free from ecclesiastical cares, and my body were in sound health, I would eagerly make a pilgrimage merely to see the chains that had held Paul captive.

The English Pilgrims.—The national chronicles of the various peoples would yield much further interesting information on pilgrims.[3]   Let us confine ourselves, however, to the pages of *The Anglo-Saxon Chronicle* and to Bede's *Ecclesiastical History*, to see what adventurous and pious Englishmen made the somewhat perilous journey to Rome during the sixth and seventh centuries.[4]   In the preface to his history, Bede writes that Nothelm (who was afterwards Archbishop of Canterbury)

> with the permission of Pope Gregory sought the archives of the holy Roman church . . . and brought documents home to be inserted by me in my history.

We have seen already how Germanus, Bishop of Auxerre, brought into Britain "relics of all the apostles and of several martyrs" (429). Mellitus, Bishop of London, sat in the Roman Synod of 605. A certain Wighard,[5] on his way to Rome in 665 for consecration as bishop, died there. Pope Vitalian writes to King Oswy to inform him of the fact, and to tell him that Wighard lies in the Church of the Apostles. With the letter the pope also sends presents,

> relics of the blessed apostles Peter and Paul and of the holy martyrs Laurence, John and Paul, Gregory and Pancras.

---

[1] *Ep.* 20 ; cf. *Epp.* 43, 45.   [2] *Hom.* 8 *in Ephes.*, in *P.G.* 62, col. 57.

[3] There is an admirable monograph on famous pilgrims from Gaul by Zettlinger, "Die Frankischen Rompilger bis zur zeit Gregors des Grossen" in the *Römische Quartalschrift*, Supplementheft xi. p. 1.

[4] See *supra*, p. 23.   There is a special rite for blessing the robes, and the pilgrim's staff and scrip in the Sarum Missal, with prayers for the safety of the traveller.

[5] Bede, *Hist. Eccles.* iii. 29.

To the Queen Elfleda he sends

> a cross with a golden key in it, made out of the most holy chains of the apostles Peter and Paul.

Wilfred,[1] the great Archbishop of York, journeyed to Rome in 678 and on two other occasions, accompanied once by " Biscop called Benedict," Abbot of Wearmouth, Bede's own monastery.

Willibrord,[2] monk of Ripon, the English missionary of Friesland, " made haste " to go to Rome in 692—

> hoping to receive from the pope some relics of the blessed apostles and martyrs of Christ: to the end that when he destroyed the idols, and erected churches in the nation to which he preached, he might have the relics of the saints to hand to put into them: and having deposited them there, might accordingly dedicate these places to the honour of each of the saints whose relics they were.

Willibrord's foresight was crowned with success, and he returned to Rome four years later to be made archbishop of his new converts.

Bishop Acca, a pupil of Wilfred of York—

> made it his business to procure relics of the blessed apostles and martyrs of Christ from all parts, and place them in altars. . . .

He accompanied Wilfred to Rome on one occasion (709). It would be tedious to prolong the list, but the names of Oftfor, future Bishop of Worcester and disciple of Archbishop Theodore; of Archbishop Wulfred (812); and of Wigbert, Bishop of Sherbourne (812), are worth recording.

Pilgrimage Privileges in Local Churches.—For the benefit of the pious who could not make the pilgrimage to Rome, churches were built in honour of S. Peter, often on the actual plan of S. Peter's in Rome. If we search the charters of foundations granted by the kings, and the papal

---

[1] *A.SS.* April 24, and Bede, *op. cit.*

[2] For Alcuin's life of Willibrord see Jaffé in *Bibliotheca rerum Germanicarum,* vi. 39 : Berlin, 1866.

charters of privileges,[1] we find such is the case for many of our English churches. For example, the Cathedral of Peter-borough[2] was founded and dedicated to S. Peter as a monastic church during the years 650–656. In the charter of 656 of King Wulferus, nephew of the famous Penda of Mercia, we read:

> . . . I will also that here we all seek S. Peter, we who are not able to go to Rome.

And in the charter of privileges granted by Pope Agatho (678–682):

> (This church) where, as we possess blessed Peter in the body, so you possess him ever present in the spirit: where by you, and all your kingdom he is sought out, as if at Rome, and venerated by the pious prayers of the faithful.

There follows a long passage conferring on this local S. Peter's, privileges equivalent to those to be obtained in Rome. The Abbey church of S. Peter's, Westminster, was conse-crated, according to the legend, by S. Peter himself, and to it, as to the Cathedrals of Exeter, Gloucester, Ely, and the Abbey of Ripon, special privileges were attached.[3]

In the Chronicle of Eadmer the Monk [4] (eleventh century) we read, of the Cathedral of Canterbury:

> That church was the work of Roman workmen, as Bede bears witness in his history, and was in some part an imitation of that church of blessed Peter, the prince of the apostles, in which his holy relics are venerated by pilgrims from all the world.

Beliefs of Pilgrims as shown in the *Graffiti*.—Some of our documents, monumental and literary, enable us to pene-trate a little deeper into the spirit of the pilgrims. On the inscriptions of the catacombs we must not linger here. Of special interest, however, are the scrawlings (*graffiti*) on the wall of passage and cell made by these ancient tourists in

---

[1] Dugdale, *Monasticon* (Eng. trans. by Colly): London, 1846.
[2] *Ibid.* i. 344 (note *h*) and 379.   [3] *Ibid., op. cit.* for charters.
[4] *P.L.* 159. Cf. Bede, *op. cit.* i. 33: "Augustine . . . recovered a church which, he was informed, had been built by the ancient Roman Christians."

the neighbourhood of the shrines of martyrs.[1]   Many a time
have these *graffiti*, unearthed after fifteen hundred years,
directed the unerring instinct of De Rossi to the shrine itself.
In the majority of cases the pilgrim left his own name on the
wall, coupled with a prayer to the local saint for his intercession.   In the crypt of S. Cecilia in S. Callixtus there is
something like an official list of a body of priests who visited
her shrine.   The pilgrim sometimes added his nationality or
profession, and the odd variety of names proves from what
far distant lands these travellers fared.

A few of these *graffiti* taken at random in S. Callixtus
will serve as examples:

> JERUSALEM CIVITAS ET ORNAMENTUM MARTYRUM.
> (The heavenly) Jerusalem, city and glory of the martyrs.
> PETITE SPIRITA SANCTA[2] UT VERECUNDIUS CUM SUIS
> BENE NAVIGET.
> Pray, Holy Spirits (of the dead) that Verecundius
> may make a safe voyage with his friends.
> SANTE SUSTE IN MENTE HABEAS IN HORATIONES
> AURELIU REPENTINU.
> Holy Sixtus (II., pope) remember in thy prayers
> Aurelius Repentinus.
> MARCIANUM SUCCESSUM SEVERUM SPIRITA SANCTA
> IN MENTE HAVETE ET OMNES FRATRES NOSTROS.
> Holy spirits, remember Marcianus Successus Severus
> and all our brothers.

In S. Priscilla, near the tomb of the martyr Crescentianus
we find:

> SALVA ME DOMNE CRESCENTIONE.
> Save me, Lord Crescentianus.

In SS. Peter and Marcellinus:

> MARCELLINE
> PETRE PETITE
> PRO GALL . . .
> CHRISTIANO.
> O Marcellinus and Peter, pray for Gallus a Christian.

[1] Many of the *graffiti* are addressed by friends and kinsmen to their own
dead—not martyrs, and, touching and beautiful as they are, do not concern
us here.

[2] *Spiritum* (neuter) is late Latin for *spiritus*.

Materialism : Burial *Ad Sanctos*.—All through the story of the pilgrimages we discern here, too, that everlasting tendency of human frailty to materialism in things spiritual. Among the early Christians it manifested itself in various ways,—in an eager desire to be buried near the martyrs—in a devotion to the relics rather than the spirit of the martyrs —in a desire to secure worldly welfare rather than spiritual gifts from these all-powerful intercessors.

As we walk down the passages of the catacombs how many frescoes over a martyr's tomb do we not find ruthlessly pierced that one or more shelf-like graves (*loculi*) may be provided for the dead who wish to lie " beside the martyrs." Again and again in the inscriptions on their tombs we read the words AD MARTYRES, AD SANCTOS—(Buried) Near the martyrs, Near the Saints.

The more scrupulous spirits did not commit this violence. The noble epitaph of Damasus [1] set up by the graves of the martyred popes in S. Callixtus terminates with the words :

> I confess that I, Damasus, would fain have laid my limbs here, but I fear to disturb the holy ashes of the saints.

Again, in the epitaph of the deacon Sabinus who was buried in all humility at the entrance of the basilica of S. Laurence, " a doorkeeper of the holy place," we read :

> It profits nothing that he digs a grave close by the tombs of the pious. It is a life of virtue which brings him near the merits of the saints. Let us cleave to them not in body but in spirit, which shall itself be the salvation of our bodies.

Views of Augustine.—Paulinus of Nola thought that such pious desires were not altogether foolish, and buried his infant son near the tomb of the martyr Justus in Alcala, and commended himself and his wife to the prayers of the saint. He writes, however, to ask Augustine's opinion, and the latter replies by his treatise *On Care to be given to the Dead* (*De Cura pro Mortuis gerenda*),[2] written about 421. He says that the very good do not require such help, and the very bad are

---

[1] *Infra*, pp. 291, 292.   [2] *P.L.* 40, 591 (trans. Schaff, *op. cit.*).

beyond it: and that the bodily proximity to the saint's tomb is *only* beneficial because visitors to the tomb were reminded to offer prayers to the saint on behalf of the dead man buried near, and that these prayers alone can profit him.   He adds that the Church, as the common mother of us all, makes a general commemoration of her dead for the especial benefit of those who have no kinsman to pray for them.

There is much more of great interest on the same subject; and the treatise is still the basis of arguments in favour of the beliefs and practices we are describing.

Augustine combats another aspect of materialism in an eloquent sermon preached on the feast of SS. Peter and Paul,[1] immediately after the sack of Rome by Alaric in 410, and endeavours to persuade his flock to seek spiritual rather than material benefits from the saints:

> See, Beloved, what things are laid upon the servants of God in this world, on account of the future glory which shall be revealed to us. . . . Men say "the body of Peter lies in Rome—the body of Paul, the body of Laurence: the bodies of the other holy martyrs lie in Rome: and Rome is in misery, Rome is laid waste, afflicted, crushed, consumed by fire.   Great is her desolation by death through famine, through pestilence and through the sword.   Where are the memorials of the martyrs? . . . Lo, when we sacrificed to our gods Rome stood, Rome flourished, . . . now that these sacrifices are forbidden, see what Rome suffers." . . . You are not called to inherit the earth, but to win heaven. . . . Lay up for yourself treasures in heaven, . . . the sanctuaries of the apostles which ought to prepare you for heaven, are they only to serve to protect your theatres? . . . was S. Peter martyred and buried in Rome in order that the stones may not fall from your theatres?

Jerome on Pilgrimages.—Both in the friendly correspondence and in the acrimonious controversial pamphlets of a group of famous men, we gain further light on the question of pilgrimages and veneration of martyrs.

Paulinus, Bishop of Nola, an ardent pilgrim, had

[1] *Sermo* 296, in *P.L.* 38, 1352.

evidently intended to prolong his travels as far as Jerusalem, and writes to consult Jerome, who was living in Bethlehem and keeping a hospice for pilgrims. Jerome writes about 395 to dissuade Paulinus from his purpose,[1] on the ground that it is contrary to his vocation as a monk (*monachus*) to visit such a busy and crowded city as Jerusalem :

> What is praiseworthy is not to have seen Jerusalem but to have lived a good life while there, . . . the city we are to praise and seek is not that which has slain the prophets, and shed the blood of Christ, but that which is made glad by the streams of the river, and which is set upon a mountain, and so cannot be hid. . . . Access to the courts of heaven is as easy from Britain as from Jerusalem, for the kingdom of God is within you. . . . When I take into consideration your vows and the earnestness with which you have renounced the world, I hold that as long as you live in the country, one place is as good as another. . . . Seek Christ in solitude. . . . My advice does not concern bishops, priests, or the clergy, for these have a different duty. . . . I am speaking only to a monk. . . . Had the scenes of the Passion and of the Resurrection been enacted elsewhere than in a populous city with a court and garrison, with prostitutes, play-actors and buffoons . . . then the city would be a desirable abode for those who have embraced the monastic life . . . the true temple of Christ is the believer's soul.

That Jerome did not disapprove of pilgrimages, however, is clear from many other portions of his writings : for example, in the letter of condolence to Eustochium on the death of her mother Paula, he mentions in the course of his eulogy the holy places she has visited.[2]

Inscription of Achilles at Spoleto.—The same spiritual point of view is put before the pilgrim in an inscription[3] set up by Achilles, Bishop of Spoleto, about 430, in the

---

[1] *Ep.* 58, in *P.L.* 22, 579 (trans. Wace and Schaff, *op. cit.*).

[2] *Ad Eustochium, Ep.* 108. Cf. *ad Marcellum, Ep.* 46, in which Jerome urges many reasons in favour of pilgrimages.

[3] De Rossi, *Inscriptiones Christianae urbis Romae* ("*I.C.*"), ii. p. 113. Cf. *Bull. Arch. Crist.*, 1871.

church dedicated by him to S. Peter, which contained relics of the chains of the apostles. Spoleto was for this reason itself a place of pilgrimage, and lay on the road of the traveller from Milan, down the Via Flaminia to Rome. The inscription reads :

> Achilles, the devoted bishop of Christ our Lord, raised this lofty temple in honour of holy Peter. Let no one think that this court has no share in his venerated name because it is not the home of his body. Great Rome preserves his venerated sepulchre, where for the name of Christ he suffered and died. But monuments cannot confine his merits (*meritum*), nor the stones which contain his body hold his spirit. For a victor over this world, having overcome death, his triumphant spirit journeyed to the stars to the highest God. Since he rested in Christ while life lasted, so, when he died, the martyr, body and spirit, returned to Christ, Who offers to all believers (the merits of) His saints, through whom He brings aid to his suppliant servants.[1]

Controversial Pamphlets of Jerome and Vigilantius.— There were not lacking those, however, who raised their voices against the veneration paid to the martyrs. The Emperor Julian (360–363), the satirist of Christianity in general, mocks at those

> who adore at unclean sepulchres for the purpose of deriving from them magic powers.[2]

Cyril of Alexandria,[3] in a well-known pamphlet, defends the " honour and veneration paid to the holy martyrs."

The next opponent of the veneration paid to the saints, and also of all forms of asceticism, was Vigilantius, a Spanish priest and at one time a friend of Paulinus of Nola and Jerome. His pamphlet on the subject, written about 403, is

---

[1] Cumque sit in Christo vita durante repostus
　　Ad Christum totus martyr ubique venit,
　　Ille suos sanctos cunctis credentibus offert
　　　Per quos supplicibus praestat opem famulis.

[2] Neumann, *Juliani Imperatoris librorum contra Christianos quae supersunt*, Leipsic, 1880.

[3] *Contra Julianum*, x., in *P.G.* 76, 1018.

now lost: his views were supported by his bishop, and also spread in Gaul.

To stem the tide of this fifth-century Protestantism, Desiderius, priest of Aquitaine, and Riparius, a priest of Aquileia, wrote to consult Jerome at Bethlehem. Jerome replies at once to the letter of Riparius:[1]

> You tell me that Vigilantius . . . has again opened his fetid lips, and is pouring forth a torrent of filthy venom upon the relics of the holy martyrs: and that he calls us who cherish them ashmongers and idolaters. . . . We refuse to worship or adore, I say not only the relics of martyrs, but even the sun and moon,[2] the angels and archangels. . . . For we may not serve the creature rather than the Creator. . . . Still we honour the relics of the martyrs that we may adore Him whose martyrs they are. . . . And do we, every time we enter the basilicas of the apostles and prophets and martyrs, pay homage to the shrines of idols? Are the tapers which burn before their tombs only the tokens of idolatry? . . . if the relics of martyrs are not worthy of honour, how comes it that we read: " Precious in the sight of the Lord is the death of His saints." . . . You tell me, further, that Vigilantius execrates vigils, . . . the vigilant one will not hearken to the Saviour's words: " What, could ye not watch with me one hour?"

Some time later the actual pamphlet of Vigilantius was sent to Jerome, and in 406 the latter wrote an answer in his *Contra Vigilantium*.[3] We have no means of knowing if Jerome is representing his opponent fairly in the following quotations:

> "What need is there," you (Vigilantius) say, "for you to pay such honour, not to say adoration, to the thing, whatever it may be, which you carry about in a

---

[1] Ep. cix., *ad Riparium*, in *P.L.* 22, 906 (trans. Wace and Schaff).

[2] For this curious remark, compare Pope Leo's prohibition against bowing before the rising sun, *supra*, p. 3.

[3] *P.L.* 23, 339 (trans. Wace and Schaff). Of this pamphlet Dean Fremantle, in his life of Jerome (in *Dict. of Christ. Biog.*, ed. Wace and Piercy) remarks: " This is the treatise in which Jerome felt most sure he was in the right, and the only one in which he was wholly in the wrong." Who shall judge between Jerome and the Dean?

little vessel and worship?" . . . "Why do you kiss and adore a bit of powder wrapped up in a cloth?" . . . "Under the cloak of religion, we see what is almost a heathen ceremony introduced into the churches: innumerable tapers are lighted, while the sun is still shining, and a bit of paltry powder wrapped up in a costly cloth is kissed and worshipped. Great honour do men of this sort pay to the blessed martyrs who, they think, are to be made glorious by trumpery tapers, when the Lamb who is in the midst of the throne, with all the brightness of His majesty gives them light."

To this Jerome replies :

Madman, who in the world ever adored the martyrs. . . . And have you the audacity to speak of the "mysterious something or other which you carry about in a little vessel and worship." I want you to know what it is you call "something or other." Tell me more clearly . . . what you mean by the phrase "a bit of powder wrapped up in a costly cloth in a tiny vessel." It is nothing less than the relics of the martyrs which he (Vigilantius) is vexed to see covered with a costly veil, and not bound up with rags or hair cloth . . . [here follow examples of honours paid by the emperors to the relics]. Are the bishops not only sacrilegious but silly into the bargain, because they carry that most worthless thing, dust and ashes, wrapped in silk in a golden vessel? Are the people of all the churches fools, because they go to meet the sacred relics? . . .

He then goes on to argue that the saints "who follow the Lamb whithersoever He goes" are all about us, and not necessarily confined "in a place of refreshment or under the altar of God, that they cannot leave their tombs." He continues :

You say in your pamphlet, that as long as we are alive we can pray for one another, but once we die, the prayer of no person for another can be heard. . . . If apostles and martyrs, while still in the body, can pray for others . . . how much more must they do so when once they have won their crowns, have overcome and triumphed? . . . Shall Vigilantius the live dog be better than Paul the dead lion? You bring before me an apocryphal book called Esdras, read by you and those of your

feather, and in this book it is written that after death
no ones dares pray for others.   I have never read the
book : for what need is there to take up what the
Church does not receive? . . . As to the question of
tapers . . . once upon a time even the apostles pleaded
that the ointment was wasted : but they were rebuked
by the voice of the Lord.   Christ did not need the
ointment, nor do the martyrs need the light of tapers :
yet that woman poured out her ointment in honour of
Christ, and her heart's devotion was accepted. . . .
Does the Bishop of Rome do wrong when he offers
sacrifices to the Lord over the venerable bodies of the
dead men Peter and Paul . . . and judges their tombs
worthy to be Christ's altars?   And not only the one
bishop, but the bishops of the whole world?

Having thus gained some idea of the belief touching the
saints, their relics and their shrines, which was held by
those who compiled the documents concerning them, we
can examine these documents in some detail for further
light on the history of martyrs.

PART I.—THE DOCUMENTS

CHAPTER IV

THE *LIBER PONTIFICALIS*: SOURCES AND DATE

THE SOURCES:—Papal records of the second century: Hegesippus and Irenaeus—Records of the third century: Eusebius and Hippolytus—The Philocalian (Liberian) Calendar of 354—Patristic literature of the fourth century —The Roman Catalogue of the fifth century—The Laurentian fragment of 520. THE DATE:—Prefatory letters of Damasus and Jerome proved apocryphal—The language of the *Liber Pontificalis*—Summary of contents—View of Duchesne: the latest date-limit is seventh century: earliest limit sixth century: book belongs to early sixth century, the Gothic period, and the precise date is 530, fixed by Felician and Cononian abridgments—View of Mommsen: date early seventh century.

Isti sunt viri per quos tibi Evangelium Christi, Roma, resplenduit. . . . Isti sunt qui te ad hanc gloriam provexerunt ut gens sancta, populus electus, civitas sacerdotalis et regia per sacram beati Petri sedem caput orbis effecta, latius praesideres religione divina quam dominatione terrena.[1]

Leo Magnus, *Sermo* lxxxii. *in Natali apostolorum Petri et Pauli.*

AMONG the documents which throw light on the monuments of Rome, the first place must be given to the *Liber Pontificalis* or Acts of the Popes. It is fitting, too, to begin our detailed studies with the leaders of the Church— her directors in things temporal and spiritual, and often, too, the first to show their flock the path to martyrdom. In this book are recorded, among other things, the death of each pope, and his place of burial, the buildings he erected over the martyrs' shrines, the donations he received, his

---

[1] *P.L.* 54, 422: "*These are the men through whom the Gospel of Christ shone upon you, O Rome. . . . These are the men who have raised you to such glory that you have become a holy race, a chosen people, a royal priestly city through the holy seat of blessed Peter, and you rule the capital of the world with wider sway through divine religion than by earthly domination.*"

liturgical and disciplinary decrees. Here, then, we have a sort of guide to the monuments which once existed, nearly all of which have now been identified.

Papal Records of the Second Century :—Hegesippus, Irenaeus.—It seems probable that the Christian Church from the earliest days remembered, by oral tradition or written record, those who ruled over her: hence the claim of any given city to be an apostolic foundation is not necessarily fictitious. It was the purpose of investigating the question of apostolic succession which, in the time of Pope Anicetus (about 167–175), brought Hegesippus, a Syrian, to Rome, where he drew up a list of popes from Peter to his own day.[1] Irenaeus,[2] writing on the same question in the time of Eleutherius (? 182–189), extends the list to that pope, and in his letter to Pope Victor[3] (?189–199) part of the same list is repeated backwards; elsewhere in his works certain details of their lives are given.[4] Linus is identified with the "Linus mentioned by S. Paul in his epistle to Timothy";[5] Clement "had talked with the apostles," and had written an epistle to the Corinthians;[6] Telesphorus was martyred.

The order of the popes in this tradition of Irenaeus, followed later by the historian Eusebius, is—Peter, Linus, Anacletus, Clement, Evaristus, Alexander, Sixtus (I.), Telesphorus (martyr), Hyginus, Pius, Anicetus, Soter, Eleutherius, Victor.

An anonymous writer[7] of the time of Zephyrinus (199–217) states that Victor (189–199) was the thirteenth pope after Peter; which agrees with the list given above.

A passage in Tertullian[8] and recent studies[9] on ancient

---

[1] Quoted in Eusebius, *Historia Ecclesiastica* ("*H.E.*"), iv. 22, *P.G.* 20. See *infra*, Bibliography—LIBER PONTIFICALIS: Papal Chronology, and Appendices II. and III.   The dates of the early popes can be given only approximately.

[2] Irenaeus, *Contra Haereses*, ii. 31, *P.G.* 7; also quoted in Eusebius, *H.E.* v. 6.

[3] Eusebius, *H.E.* v. 24.

[4] Irenaeus, *Contra Haer.* i. 25 and 27, iii. 3 and 4.   [5] 2 Timothy iv. 21.

[6] See Lightfoot, *Apostolic Fathers*, pt. i. vols. i. and ii.

[7] Quoted in Eusebius, *H.E.* v. 28.

[8] *De Praescriptionibus*, 30, in *P.L.* 2.

[9] Harnack, *die Zeit des Ignatius*, p. 74, Leipsic, 1874 : cf. *infra*, Bibliography —LIBER PONTIFICALIS : Papal Chronology.

4

papal catalogues, show that from the time of Victor the
names were accompanied by dates.

**Papal Records in the Third Century :—Eusebius and
Hippolytus.**—The papal list is carried down to Marcellinus
(296–308) by Eusebius in his *Chronicle* and in his *Ecclesiastical History*, but there are slight variations in the length of
rule attributed to some of the popes in these two lists.[1]

In the early part of the third century we come to the
interesting personality of Hippolytus, the learned Roman
priest, whose statue, discovered in 1551 near his place of
burial on the Via Tiburtina, stands now in the Christian
Museum of the Lateran.   Hippolytus is seated in a chair : on
its arms and back are engraved the names of his works, including that of the famous *Chronicle*, or universal history of the
world, which contained, among purely secular records, a list of
the popes down to 235, carried on by an anonymous and contemporary writer to 254.   The original document, in Greek,
has been lost, but it appears in the *Liber Generationis*[2]
(which Mommsen[3] and Krusch[4] have shown to be a Latin
translation from the Greek chronicle) ; this, enlarged and
brought up to date is embodied in the famous *Philocalian
Calendar*, which is the foundation of the *Liber Pontificalis*.

Philocalian (Liberian) Calendar of 354. — This
Calendar[5] is named *Liberian*, since it was compiled in 354
under Pope Liberius.   It is called *Philocalian*, after its
author Philocalus ; who, as secretary of Pope Damasus (366–
384), also carved, in the beautiful characters which bear
his name, the epitaphs of the martyrs in the catacombs.
The Calendar forms part of a composite work signed by
the compiler, *Furius Dionysius Filocalus titulavit*, and
dedicated to a certain Valentine, unknown, but probably
a private patron who appreciated beautiful writing.   The

---

[1] S. Jerome, in his Latin version of the *Chronicle* of Eusebius (*P.L.* 27),
replaces the original figures by those found in the *Ecclesiastical History*.

[2] Contained in a mutilated manuscript at Cheltenham, in the library of Sir
Thomas Phillipps.

[3] Mommsen, *Ueber den Chronographen vom Jahre 354*.

[4] Krusch, *Neues Archiv*, t. vii. (1882) p. 457.

[5] Duchesne, *Liber Pontificalis*, i. p. vi ; cf. *infra*, Bibliography—PHILOCALIAN
CALENDAR, and Appendix III.

whole forms a manual of universal history, combined with the kind of information found in directories and almanacs.

1. The *Liber Generationis*.—The compilation contains, as we have seen, the chronicle of Hippolytus (the *Liber Generationis*), a history which very properly begins at Adam, and passing through the divisions of the world to the sons of Noah, gives the story of the Jewish kings, priests and prophets and of certain of the Macedonian and Persian monarchs.

2. Annals of the City of Rome.—Another item in Philocalus' work is the history of the city of Rome, with a list of consuls and prefects, kings and emperors, down to the period of the author; closed by a citation of that most useful topographical account of the fourteen regions into which the Emperor Augustus had divided the city, the *Notitia regionum xiv urbis Romae*,[1] remarkable because no single Christian building is mentioned in it.

3. Pagan Calendar.—There is, further, a surprisingly pagan calendar which contains the names of gods, the anniversaries of victories, and notes the days for games and feasts. For December 25 we read the Mithraic entry: "The birthday of the Invincible" (*Natalis Invicti*).

4. *Depositio Episcoporum* and *Depositio Martyrum*.—In the Christian portion of the work is a paschal table and, most important for our purpose, the Christian Calendar proper, consisting of a list of the anniversaries of the burial days of the popes (*depositio episcoporum*) and one of the martyrs (*depositio martyrum*), with the names of the catacombs where they were buried. Those popes who were at once bishops *and* martyrs,[2] namely, Callixtus (217–222), Pontianus (230–235), Fabianus (236–251), and Sixtus II. (257–259), appear in the second list only, among the martyrs.

The first list is as follows :—

> The burial day of the bishops.
> Dec. 27. Dionysius in Callixtus.
> Dec. 30. Felix in Callixtus.
> Dec. 31. Silvester in Priscilla.

[1] *Infra*, pp. 95, 96.

[2] There is great uncertainty as to which of the other popes were actually martyrs. See *infra*, pp. 66–73, and Duchesne, *op. cit.* i. p. lxxxix. See *infra*, Appendix III. for text.

Jan. 10. Miltiades in Callixtus.
Jan. 15. Marcellinus in Priscilla.
Mar. 5. Lucius in Callixtus.
Apr. 22. Gaius in Callixtus.
Aug. 2. Stephen in Callixtus.
Sept. 26. Eusebius in Callixtus.
Dec. 8. Eutychianus in Callixtus.
Oct. 7. Marcus in Balbina.
Apr. 12. Julius on the Via Aurelia at the third milestone in Callixtus.[1]

The *Depositio Episcoporum* begins at the same date as the list of the prefects of Rome.

Both the list of bishops and that of the martyrs is derived from the Roman Calendar of 312,[2] compiled at the Peace of the Church.

The *Depositio Martyrum* [3] contains over fifty names of martyrs, all of whom suffered in Rome, except the three African martyrs, Cyprian, Bishop of Carthage, and Perpetua and Felicitas. A few extracts will show the form of the document :—

Dec. 25. Christ born in Bethlehem of Judaea.[4]
Jan. 20. (pope) Fabianus (buried) in Callixtus and Sebastian in the Catacombs.[5]
Jan. 21. Agnes in (Via) Nomentana.
Feb. 22. The feast (*natale*) of the Chair of Peter.

. . .

June 29. Peter in the Catacombs,[6] and Paul on the Via Ostiensis in the consulship of Tuscus and Bassus (258).

. . .

[1] *i.e.* in the Cemetery of Calepodius, where Pope Callixtus was buried : not in the "Cemetery of Callixtus" on the Via Appia. For the catacombs and martyrs mentioned see Index.

[2] *Infra*, Chap. XVII., *Martyrology of Jerome.*

[3] For a complete list see *infra*, Appendix III., *B* and *C*.

[4] This is the first definite reference to the *feast* of Christmas, though Clement of Alexandria (about 190), Hippolytus (about 120) and other writers had discussed the date, which varied between March and December and other months. The feast was introduced at Antioch about 375 (S. John Chrysostom, *Sermon for Christmas Day*, in *P.G.* 49, 351). The feast of the Epiphany was more ancient.

[5] The catacombs now known as S. Sebastian, on the Via Appia.

[6] *i.e.* of S. Sebastian. See *supra*, p. 8, note 2 : cf. p. 305.

Aug. 6. (pope) Sixtus (II.) in Callixtus, and in Praetextatus, Agapitus and Felicissimus.

Aug. 11. Laurence in (Via) Tiburtina.

Oct. 14. (pope) Callixtus on the Via Aurelia at the third milestone.

There are no fixed church festivals, other than feasts of martyrs, mentioned in this Calendar except Christmas Day. This list is important, not only for topographical reasons, but as indicating what martyrs were venerated in Rome in the fourth century.

5. **The Papal Biographies.** — There follows in our document a chronological list of the popes from Peter to Liberius, with the length of their reign in years, months and days, and the date, indicated by the consuls. Occasionally a few other facts are added. The earlier portion of the list is derived from Hippolytus. It contains a few errors in the order of the popes, and where it differs from the Irenaean list [1] the latter is certainly correct. We cannot be sure that these errors were in the original document of Hippolytus, and "Cletus-Anacletus" of the Calendar looks like a copyist's blunder. The point of divergence from the Irenaean tradition [2] are indicated below by italics:—

Peter Linus *Clement Cletus Anacletus* Aristus (for Evaristus). . . . *Anicetus Pius* Soter. . . .

The form into which these notices of the popes are cast is invariable; the dates, derived from those of the contemporary consuls and emperors, are not always correct. The notice of any one of the popes will serve as an example of the style:

Alexander (reigned) VII years II months I day. He reigned in the times of Trajan from the consulship of Palma and Tullius to that of Helianus and Veter (109-116).

---

[1] This list is followed in the Canon of the Mass: *Communicantes et memoriam venerantes beatorum Apostolorum et Martyrum tuorum Petri et Pauli . . . Lini, Cleti, Clementis, Xysti, Cornelii. . . .*

[2] *Supra*, p. 49.

Patristic Literature of the Fourth Century. —
There are very slight variations in those papal lists of
the fourth and fifth centuries, which we find mainly in the
patristic literature defending apostolic continuity against
heretics. The African bishops Optatus[1] and Augustine,[2]
the unknown author of the *Poem against Marcion*,[3] Jerome
in his Latin translation of the Greek *Chronicle* of Eusebius,[4]
and Epiphanius,[5] have all given lists copied later by the
historians of the fifth century.

Roman Catalogue of the Fifth Century. —There is
also a well-known Roman Catalogue of the fifth century[6]
depending partly on S. Jerome and partly on the Liberian
Catalogue, and in some respects more correct than the latter,
i.e. it gives Anacletus and omits his double, Cletus; and
places Clement after Anacletus, and Anicetus after Pius, in
accordance with the most ancient tradition preserved in
Irenaeus. All subsequent catalogues are derived from this,
and such catalogues were widely known in the East as well
as the West.[7]

The Laurentian Fragment. —Of the various other
papal chronicles, the most important is perhaps the mutilated *Laurentian Fragment*,[8] written about 520, in the
time of Pope Hormisdas, and discovered in a sixth-century
manuscript at Verona. It is independent of the *Liber
Pontificalis*, and contains contemporary lives of the popes
Anastasius and Symmachus; it is schismatical, and supports
the anti-pope Laurence, the opponent of Symmachus, and is
perhaps a fragment of a lost *Liber Pontificalis*. The rivalry
between Symmachus (498–514) and the anti-pope called

---

[1] Optatus, *De Schismate Donatistarum*, ii. 3, in *P.L.* 11.

[2] Augustine, *Epistola Generoso*, No. 53 in *Corpus scriptorum ecclesiasticorum
Latinorum*, t. xxxiv. 1.

[3] Fabricius, *Poetarum veterum ecclesiasticorum opera*, 258, Bâle, 1564. The
work is probably of the late fourth century, see Duchesne, *Liber Pontificalis*,
i. p. xi.

[4] *P.L.* 27.

[5] *Adv. Haereses*, xxvii. 6, in *P.G.* 41, col. 571.

[6] Duchesne, *op. cit.* i. p. xii.

[7] Cureton, *Ancient Syriac documents*, pp. 41, 63, London, 1864.

[8] Duchesne, *op. cit.* i. p. xxx; De Rossi, *Roma Sotterranea*, i. 122;
Mommsen, *Liber Pontificalis*, p. viii.

forth a mass of poetry and literature, a good deal of which was pure forgery.[1]

The *Liber Pontificalis* : **The name of the work.**—Such are some of the contributions to early papal history. They are all more or less absorbed into a work which, in spite of obvious defects, remains a noble monument of Christian history,—the Acts of the Popes.   There are many manuscripts of this document which bear no title at all;[2] later appear various headings,—*Acta Beatorum pontificum*, *Gesta pontificalia* (in the *Martyrology* attributed to Bede),[3] and, finally, the name it usually bears, the *Liber Pontificalis*.

Prefatory Letters of Damasus and Jerome apocryphal.—The compiler put his book under the patronage of Pope Damasus (366–384) and his learned friend S. Jerome in two letters placed at the beginning.   Jerome writes :

> Jerome to the blessed Pope Damasus.
> Our humility implores the glory of thy sanctity . . . that thou wouldst deign to narrate to us in order the deeds (*gesta*) that have been done in thy seat, the deeds from the reign of the blessed Peter the apostle up to your[4] own times : that our humility may know who of the bishops of the seat mentioned above deserved to be crowned with martyrdom, or who on the other hand is known to have transgressed the Canons of the Apostles.   Pray for us most blessed pope (*papa*).

To which Damasus replies :

> Damasus bishop to Jerome priest.
> . . . Whatever deed (*gestum*) has been done which we could find by the zeal of our office (*sedis*), we have sent rejoicing to thy affection.   Pray for us that we may have a holy resurrection, brother and priest.   Farewell in Christ our Lord God. . . .

It might have seemed suitable that this friend of Jerome, this great pope who had set the church in order, repaired the catacombs, sought out the history of the martyrs and set up epitaphs in their honour, should occupy himself with the history of his predecessors who lay in the sacred

---

[1] See *infra*, p. 81.   [2] Mommsen, *op. cit.* p. xii.
[3] Bede, *Martyrologium, viii. idus Aug.*, in *P.L.* 94, col. 999.
[4] The *thy* . . . *your* is in the original.

precincts of the Vatican, or in the great papal crypt of S. Callixtus, or in that most ancient cemetery of Priscilla. But the authenticity of these letters was disproved, as early as the seventeenth century, by Schelestratus.[1] The poverty and inaccuracy of the fourth-century records in this volume, and the discrepancies between the *Liber Pontificalis* and Jerome's *Chronicle*, are alone sufficient to disprove the authorship of Damasus.

The contents of the *Liber Pontificalis* may give us some clue to the disputed question of the date. The weight of evidence seems to be in favour of Duchesne's view, which is accepted by most scholars.[2]

The Date and the Language of the *Liber Pontificalis*. —We may note, first, that the language of the *Liber Pontificalis* is the popular decadent Latin similar to that of the *Gesta Martyrum*[3] of the fifth and sixth centuries, and of the Christian inscriptions of the same date, though the style of the book compares favourably with the *Gesta*. One orthographical peculiarity of the *Liber Pontificalis*, namely, the spelling *Maburti* for *Mavorti* (the consul of 527), appears in two dated Roman inscriptions of the year of that consul.[4]

Date and the Summary of Contents. —The *Liber Pontificalis* contains lives of the popes from Peter to Pius II. (1458–1464). For present purposes we shall seldom need to carry our investigations beyond Silverius (536–537).

The nucleus of the book is, as we have seen, the brief records of the popes down to Liberius (352), contained in the Philocalian Calendar, which is itself based on earlier sources.

For the period following, down to Gelasius (492), there is no indication of dates, except for Felix III. (483); and the accounts are unreliable, and obviously not by a contemporary hand.

For the eight popes that follow, from Anastasius (496) to Agapetus (535), we have a contemporary record of which

---

[1] Schelestratus, *Antiquitates Ecclesiae*, i. 369, Rome, 1692 ; cf. Mommsen, *op. cit.*

[2] But cf. *infra*, pp. 61–2.   [3] See *infra*, Chaps. XIII., XIV., XV.

[4] De Rossi, *Inscriptiones Christianae*, i. pp. 460, 463.

the minute exactitude can be checked by numerous contemporary documents. The story is vivid, full of detail and passionately partisan.

A contemporary, or rather two contemporaries, record the life of Silverius (536–537), who lived in the stormy days when Belisarius, the great general of Justinian, was winning back Italy from Theodatus, the Gothic king (534–536), who succeeded Theodoric (493 – 534). The account is again vivid and partisan. There was the same rivalry between Goth and Byzantine in the ecclesiastical as in the political world ; the writer of the first part of the life is Byzantine in sympathy, and pours contempt on Silverius as a creature of Theodatus :

> Silverius . . . was raised up by the tyrant Theodatus, without deliberation of the Assembly, which Theodatus corrupted by money : and he threatened with the sword any of the clergy who would not consent to the ordination. . . . But after two months, by the divine will, Theodatus the tyrant perished and Witigis was made king (536–540).

Witigis then goes to Ravenna, and carries off by violence the daughter of Queen Amalasuenta. Justinian, under whose protection she was, " sent Vilisarius (Belisarius) with an army to liberate all Italy from the captivity of the Goths."

Belisarius takes Naples and sacks it (536), enters Rome in December, and undergoes there a terrible siege by Witigis :

> In those days the city was besieged so that none might come out or enter in. Then all possessions both private and of the state and of the church were consumed by fire : but the men perished by the sword : some fell by the sword, some by famine, some by disease. And the churches and the bodies of the holy martyrs were exterminated by the Goths. . . .

After a year the Goths raise the siege (538) and fly to Ravenna, and a universal famine ensues. All these facts are accurate and can be checked by Procopius and other writers. It may be noted, however, though the *Liber Pontificalis* does not relate it, that Silverius had been deposed in March 537, that is, so soon as Belisarius arrived in Rome, and Vigilius (537–555), the Byzantine candidate had been enthroned as pope.

It is at this point that a fresh hand is visible. Immediately after the account of the famine following the siege of Rome in 538, we read:

> At the same time Belisarius went to Naples (536), set it in order, and afterwards came to Rome in (536). He was kindly received by Silverius.

This is immediately followed by the story that the Empress Theodora, the wife of Justinian, sent an order to Silverius to reinstate the patriarch Anthemas, whom he had deposed for heresy. The "blessed" Silverius refused: Belisarius was sent to Rome to depose him: false witnesses were brought forward (it is evident that the analogy of the trial of our Lord is in the writer's mind), and Silverius was deposed, made a monk, and died in exile in the Pontian Isles, in West Italy, where miracles of healing were worked at his tomb.

Thus we see that Silverius, who enters on his career as the creature of the Gothic king, supported by fraud and violence, ends his days as the "blessed" Silverius and almost a martyr. It is clear, too, that we have a double account of the capture of Naples and the siege of Rome, and that, in fact, a different writer, with different politics from his predecessor, has taken up the work in the middle of the life of Silverius.

View of Duchesne : the Latest Date limit, Seventh Century.—These facts, taken in combination with others, will be of some assistance in determining the date of the original *Liber Pontificalis*. The latest possible limit of date that can be fixed is the seventh century, as the Naples manuscript [1] (ending at Conon, d. 687) is of that date. Bede also frequently borrows from it.[2]

Earliest limit of Date, Sixth Century.—The inaccuracy of the facts from Liberius (352–366) to Anastasius (496) shows that the book was compiled later than the fifth century.

---

[1] Duchesne, *op. cit.* i. p. clxxvi.

[2] *Monumenta Germaniae Historica: Auctorum Antiquorum t.* xiii. pp. 223, 334, ed. Mommsen, Berlin, 1898 ; Quentin, *Martyrologes du moyen age*, 1908.

To what portion, then, of the sixth century or early seventh century does the *Liber Pontificalis* belong? To the days of the Gothic kings,—Theodoric (493–526), Theodatus (534–536), Witigis (Vitigis) (536–540), Totila (541–552),— or to the brief years of the triumph of Justinian from 552 onwards?

It belongs to early Sixth Century, the Gothic Period.— Now, of the great ecclesiastical changes which took place under the Byzantine restoration, there are no traces in the *Liber Pontificalis*,[1] and a writer under Justinian would certainly have betrayed, by anachronisms in the history of earlier popes, the circumstances of his own day. This, then, would indicate the Gothic period as the date of the book. Further, though the language in which it is written could perhaps belong to either period, certain details of expression could belong only to the days of the Gothic domination, as, for example, the mention of the *single* Latin consul and the omission of the Greek representative.[2] For this second reason, then, the book seems to belong to the Gothic period and to be therefore earlier than 552.

A third fact points to this conclusion. In the list of œcumenical, or universal, councils given in the *Liber Pontificalis* under Hilary (461–468), three only are mentioned,— Nicæa, Ephesus, Chalcedon,—and the second council, that of Constantinople (381), is omitted. This council, however, was not recognized as œcumenical until Vigilius (537–555), who speaks of it with enthusiasm.[3] The *Liber Pontificalis* therefore appears to be earlier than 540, that is, to belong to the early portion of the sixth century, a date already indicated by Schelestratus[4] in the seventeenth century.

Precise Date, 530, fixed by Felician and Cononian Abridgments.—De Rossi[5] and Duchesne have even determined the actual year when the first compiler began his work. There exists a condensed account of the Lives of the

---

[1] Duchesne, *op. cit.* i. p. xxxvii.

[2] After the division of the empire one consul represented the West and the other the East.

[3] Jaffé, *Regesta Pontificum Romanorum*, i., Nos. 910, 925. See also Labbé, *Concilia*, vii. p. 1139, where, in a document of 483, this council is omitted.

[4] Schelestratus, *Ant. Eccles.* i. 354.   [5] *Roma Sotterranea*, i. 122.

Popes, proved by Mommsen and Duchesne to be derived from the *Liber Pontificalis*. It is known as the Felician Abridgment,[1] since it stops at the death of Pope Felix in 530. The document was compiled in France, certainly not earlier than the end of the sixth century. Duchesne[2] shows, fairly conclusively, that it was known in Gaul by 590, and used by Gregory of Tours (538–594) in his *Historia Francorum* and *De Gloria Martyrum*.

From the fact that the Felician Abridgment stops abruptly at Felix, Duchesne has concluded that the original *Liber Pontificalis* stopped at this date, namely, 530 : that the compiler then took up the work under Boniface (530–532) and carried it on as far as Silverius (536–537) : in the middle of this life occurs, as we have seen, the curious change of hand, where a second compiler took up the work. The compiler, then, of 530 would have been a contemporary of the preceding popes also, as far back at least as Anastasius (496) ; and the accuracy of these lives, from Anastasius onwards, has already been noted, and is now accounted for.

There is yet another abstract from the *Liber Pontificalis* known as the Cononian Abridgment,[3] since the papal list is carried down to Conon (686–687). It was compiled in a Burgundian monastery in 741. This must have been made from one of the earliest copies brought over the Alps. This document is used in a French chronicle, compiled by various authors about the year 800 at Autun, which exists in a manuscript at Leyden.[4]

A comparison of the *Liber Pontificalis* with the Felician and Cononian Abridgments will reveal the interesting fact that the compilers of these two documents had before them, as far as the year 530, an earlier version of the *Liber Pontificalis* than the edition, retouched and revised, which we

[1] Duchesne, *op. cit.* i. pp. xli, 48 ; Lipsius, *Chronologie der Römischen Bischöfe*, 1869.

[2] Duchesne, " Le *Liber Pontificalis* en Gaule," in *Mélanges d' Archéologie et d' Histoire*, 1882, p. 277.

[3] Duchesne, *op. cit.* i. pp. liv, 48 ; Mommsen, *op. cit.* p. xv.

[4] Waitz in *Neues Archiv*, t. v. (1880) p. 475. See *infra*, Bibliography—LIBER PONTIFICALIS.

possess. The Cononian Abridgment, for the years 530 to 687 (where it ends), follows the *Liber Pontificalis* as we have it, which seems a confirmation of the fact that the original book ended in 530.

View of Mommsen : Date early Seventh Century.— Such is Duchesne's account in his great work on the *Liber Pontificalis*. De Rossi, as we have seen, is in agreement with him, and so, too, is Lipsius,[1] on the main points, though the last writer places the first edition of the book some half-century earlier than Duchesne.

Mommsen, however, while paying a tribute to the work of Duchesne, and agreeing with him on many points, ascribes the *Liber Pontificalis* to the first decade of the seventh century and the Felician Abridgment to the eighth.[2]

The reasons, which are somewhat technical, do not seem entirely convincing, and leave some difficulties unsolved. It is possible, of course, that the writer of the lives of Anastasius and his successors, whom Duchesne believes to be a contemporary, may, as Mommsen says, have been only using contemporary documents; but if this is so, the abrupt termination of the Felician Abridgment is unexplained. Mommsen, again, denies Duchesne's assertion that Gregory of Tours is using the *Liber Pontificalis*, and points out that neither Pope Gregory I. (d. 604), nor Isidore of Spain (d. 636), nor the compiler of the *Chronica Francica* of 642, known as Fredegaire,[3] seem aware of the existence of the *Liber Pontificalis*, and that it is Bede who first mentions it.

The style, too, Mommsen thinks, is rather of the decadent seventh century than of the early part of the sixth, when Theodoric the Goth was ruling and his minister Cassiodorus was writing.

Duchesne has maintained his original views in a series

---

[1] See *infra*, Bibliography—LIBER PONTIFICALIS : Papal Chronology.

[2] Mommsen, *op. cit.* Prolegomena. Waitz places the *Liber Pontificalis* at the end of the seventh century, and the Felician Abridgment at the end of the sixth century. For his contributions to the subject see Bibliography.

[3] *Mon. Germ. Hist. : Script. Rer. Meroving.* vol. ii. ed. Krusch, Hanover, 1888.

of articles,[1] and the question has been discussed with an urbanity on both sides which does not always distinguish such literary contests.

The date, however, of the *Liber Pontificalis* is definitely fixed by universal consent between 530 and 710, and the weight of evidence seems to indicate precisely the year 530.

A study of the manuscripts from the seventh to the fifteenth century shows how frequently the work was revised and brought up to date, and bears witness to its popularity. It exercised great influence, was an indispensable volume in every episcopal and conventual library, and a model for all similar compositions. Many writers, including our own Bede, are indebted to it, and the *Martyrology of Jerome*[2] is related to it.

It was first printed in Mayence by Busaeus in 1602, under the title of *Anastasii*[3] *bibliothecarii Vitae seu Gesta Romanorum Pontificum*.

---

[1] Duchesne, "La date et les recensions du *Liber Pontificalis*," in *Revue de questions historiques*, vol. xxvi. p. 493 (1879); "Le premier *Liber Pontificalis*," *ibid*. vol. xxix. p. 246 (1881); "La nouvelle édition du *Liber Pontificalis*," in *Mélanges d'Archéologie et d'Histoire*, vol. xviii. p. 381 (1898).

[2] See *infra*, Chap. XVII.

[3] See Bibliography. Anastasius was for a long time the reputed author of the work. There were no less than three editions between 1718 and 1724 by Bianchini, Muratori and Vignoli respectively, all based on the same inferior manuscript.

CHAPTER V

THE *LIBER PONTIFICALIS*: FORM OF THE LIVES, PAPAL CHRONOLOGY, THE MARTYRED POPES, DISCIPLINARY DECREES

FORM OF THE LIVES—Examples: Linus, Telesphorus—The contemporary lives of Anastasius, etc—Statements in the *Liber Pontificalis* on PAPAL CHRONOLOGY.—THE MARTYRED POPES: (1) In the Philocalian Calendar (2) In the fifth-century liturgies (3) In the *Liber Pontificalis*: sources of Error—A comparison of the *Liber Pontificalis* with the *Gesta Martyrum*: for 1. Urban, 2. Cornelius, 3. Gaius, 4. Marcellus, 5. Sixtus II., 6. Pontianus, 7. Lucius, 8. Marcellinus—Date and place of burial.—DISCIPLINARY DECREES: Sources of the statements in the *Liber Pontificalis* (1) Authentic: examples of Decrees (2) Forgeries: *Constitutum Silvestri* and the *Constitution of the Synod of Bishops* —Forgeries in the Lives of Silvester, Julius, Liberius, Felix, Sixtus III., etc.

Statuit ei Dominus testamentum pacis, et principem fecit eum : ut sit illi Sacerdotii dignitas in aeternum.

Missale: Commune unius martyris pontificis (*Ecclesiasticus* 45).[1]

Form of the Lives.—The statements in the lives of the earlier popes in the *Liber Pontificalis* are arranged under the same invariable headings as are found in the original source—the Philocalian Calendar. Some of these statements, however, are somewhat enlarged in the later work : the parentage and country of the pope are given, and almost invariably are added the disciplinary decrees enacted, buildings erected, the number of priests, deacons and bishops ordained, and the date and place of burial.

As typical lives may be quoted those of Linus, the successor of Peter, and, according to Irenaeus, the Linus of the epistle to Timothy ;[2] and that of Telesphorus, the eighth pope from Peter.

---

[1] " *The Lord established with him a covenant of peace, and made him a prince, that he should hold the honour of the priesthood for ever.*"

[2] *Supra*, p. 49.

63

Linus, an Italian by nation, of the region Tuscia : his father was Herculanus. He sat (in the episcopal chair) 11 years 3 months 12 days. He lived in the time of Nero, from the consulship of Saturninus and Scipio (50 A.D.) to that of Capito and Rufus (67). He is crowned with martyrdom. In accordance with the precept of blessed Peter, he decreed that a woman should enter the church with veiled head. He made 2 ordinations,—15 bishops and 18 priests (*presbyteros*). He was buried beside the body of blessed Peter in the Vatican on December 23rd.

Telesphorus, by nation a Greek, and an anchorite, ruled 11 years 3 months 21 days : he lived in the times of Antoninus and Marcus. He decreed[1] that the seven weeks before Easter should be kept as a fast. He was crowned with martyrdom. He decreed that Masses at night should be celebrated on the anniversary (*natalis*) of our Lord Jesus Christ : for usually no one may celebrate Mass before the third hour is past, at which hour our Lord ascended the cross. And before the sacrifice, the angelic hymn was to be sung, that is *Glory to God in the highest* and the rest, but only on the night of the anniversary of the Lord. He was crowned with martyrdom.[2] He was buried beside the body of blessed Peter in the Vatican on January 2nd. He made 4 ordinations in the month of December, 12 priests, 8 deacons and 13 bishops in different places. The bishopric was vacant 7 days.

Contemporary Lives of Anastasius, etc.—For the lives of a few only of the earlier popes are any additional facts given. Truly with the Peace of the Church under Pope Silvester (314–337), we find inserted in the lives long inventories of church property;[3] but it is not till the time of Anastasius (496–498) and his successors that the hand of a contemporary draws a vivid picture of the great figures that come upon the scene. He describes the conflict between Theodoric the Goth and Justinian : how Belisarius and Witigis wasted the fair face of Italy : how successive popes —Anastasius, Hormisdas (514–523), John (523–526)—strove to heal the schism with the Eastern Church caused by the

---

[1] *Infra*, pp. 77–79.
[2] Note that this is recorded twice.   [3] *Infra*, p. 84.

papal excommunication of the heretic patriarch Acacius; and how the rulers of the East and West threw themselves into the struggle. Then comes a description of the long dissensions [1] between the "blessed" Symmachus (498–514) and the antipope Laurence; and of the judgment of Theodoric, who, after summoning the antagonists to his court at Ravenna, decided in favour of Symmachus, "who loved the clergy and the poor, and was good, prudent, kindly and gracious." We note that this excellent, if unorthodox, monarch is freely called a heretic by the writer of the life of Pope John; and so great is the mental preoccupation with the burning theological questions of the day, that Pope Agapitus, sent on a political mission by Theodatus, the successor of Theodoric, to Justinian, discourses at length to that emperor on the dual nature of Christ. Then comes the curious double record of the life of Silverius, with whose death, six years after the date of the compilation of the original *Liber Pontificalis*, we may close our investigations.

Statements in the *Liber Pontificalis*: (1) Papal Chronology; (2) Martyred Popes; (3) Disciplinary Decrees.— Concerning ourselves especially with those lives of the earlier popes which may throw some light on the history of the martyrs, their shrines, and their cult, let us consider how far the statements of the *Liber Pontificalis* are reliable as regards (1) the papal chronology, which is important for determining other dates; as regards (2) the martyred popes, and the places of their burial; for these statements, collated with those found in the Martyrologies, Itineraries, Acts of the Martyrs and Syllogae, and all applied to the elucidation of the monuments, form an integral part of our present study; as regards (3) the disciplinary decrees, which sometimes concern the cult of the martyrs, and the means taken for collecting documents concerning them. These decrees must be considered as a whole, in order to determine their sources and authenticity; as regards (4) the records of buildings raised by the popes as a memorial to the martyrs.

The statements in the *Liber Pontificalis*, relating to this early period, require severe scrutiny. For this we must

---

[1] For the literature called forth by this struggle see *infra*, p. 87.

5

refer the reader to Duchesne's critical notes. We shall here merely indicate the line of criticism that may be taken, or point out occasionally the particular source, whether authentic or apocryphal, of these statements. Even inaccurate statements have historical value, as indicating the condition of things at the time of the writer.

Papal Chronology.—The first question that arises is that of the chronology of the popes. We have already noted the double tradition,—the Irenaean and the Liberian,[1] —and that, in most cases, the *Liber Pontificalis* follows the second, and less correct, source. On the other hand, for the duration of the rule of each pope, where the two sources differ, the *Liber Pontificalis* has followed the fifth-century Catalogue[2] in preference to the Liberian.[3] The length of the duration of the vacancies is usually incorrect. It is only with Pontianus (230–235) that dates of accession can be determined with certainty: they are doubtful for the preceding popes.

For the facts as to the parentage of the popes, the sources are too uncertain to inspire any confidence. The same is true as regards their country of origin up to Felix III. (483–492), after which period the statements can be checked. According to the ascriptions of the *Liber Pontificalis*, of the 56 popes who ruled up to 530, 26 were Roman, 11 Italian, 9 Greek, and 3 African, among whom was Gelasius: Damasus was a Spaniard and Anicetus a Syrian. The statements can sometimes be traced to local tradition or the *Acts of the Martyrs*.[4]

The Martyred Popes (1) in the Philocalian Calendar.— A question of considerable interest arises in connexion with the martyrdoms of the popes as recorded in the *Liber Pontificalis*. The sources of the information may usually be traced either to genuine historical fact, or to an obvious confusion of such facts, or to a definite tradition.

---

[1] *Supra*, pp. 49–54.　　　　　　　[2] *Supra*, p. 54.

[3] See Duchesne, *op. cit.* i. p. lxxx, for a comparative table of dates. For a full discussion of the whole subject see *infra*, Bibliography—LIBER PONTIFICALIS : Papal Chronology.

[4] On the question of the *ordinations* see Harnack, " Ueber die Ordinationen im Papstbuch," in *Sitzungsberichte der Königlichen Preussischen Akademie der Wissenschaften*, 1897, p. 761 : Berlin.

Combining the biographical notices of the popes with the *Depositio Martyrum*, both found in the Philocalian Calendar, we find that the first martyrdom [1] recorded is that of Callixtus (217–222), followed by those of Fabianus (236–251), of Cornelius (251–253), which is recorded in the words " he fell asleep with glory " (*cum gloria dormitionem accepit*), and of Sixtus II. (257–259). All these martyrdoms are thoroughly authenticated from contemporary, or reliable, historical evidence ; and, except in the case of Callixtus, who was buried elsewhere, by the existence of tomb and epitaph in the catacomb of S. Callixtus on the Via Appia.

If we add to the list Telesphorus (142–154), on the contemporary authority of Irenaeus,[2] and, Pontianus (230–235), who, like Cornelius, died from the results of the hardships of exile, the roll of martyr popes is perhaps complete.

(2) In the Fifth-Century Liturgies.—Tradition has, however, increased the number. In the liturgies of the fifth century, the period of the formal crystallization of the Canon of the Mass (which, in essentials, is far older), nearly all the popes up to the Peace of the Church find a place as martyrs.

Here, in these liturgical Martyrologies, as in the case of the late *Acts of the Martyrs* (*Gesta Martyrum*) of the same period, may be noted that remarkable rise of apocryphal literature in the fifth century, which Gelasius, Hormisdas and other popes endeavoured to control.[3]

(3) In the *Liber Pontificalis* : Sources of Error.—In the *Liber Pontificalis*, as we have it,[4] the crown of martyrdom is ascribed to twenty-two of the thirty-two popes who preceded Silvester. Many of the sources of these erroneous or doubtful statements can be traced.

For example, Pope Clement is called a martyr by Rufinus[5] (345–410), by Pope Zosimus[6] (417–418) and

---

[1] For the martyrdoms of these popes see *infra*, Index, and *infra*, p. 200.

[2] *Contra Haereses*, iii. 3, in *P.G.* 7, 851.　　　　[3] *Infra*, p. 192.

[4] In this second edition which we possess (*supra*, p. 60), four additional names are found, namely, Anicetus, Eutychianus, Gaius, Marcellus, which do not appear in the abridgments derived from the first edition. For a complete list see *infra*, Appendix II.

[5] Jerome, *Apologia adversus libros Rufini*, ii. 17, in *P.L.* 23, 439.

[6] *P.L.* 20, 650.

by Gregory of Tours[1] (d. 594). The story of his passion,[2] a fourth-century document at the earliest, probably arose out of the confusion between the pope and a martyr called Clement, venerated in the Chersonesus.[3]

Again, Pope Alexander is probably confused with the authentic martyr Alexander, who is buried on the Via Nomentana;[4] and Sixtus I. with Sixtus II., who was, in fact, martyred.

Thus a confusion of persons is probably responsible for some of the false ascriptions of martyrdom.

It is fairly certain, too, that neither Victor (189–199) nor Anteros (235–236) were martyrs, as their deaths are recorded in the *Philosophumena*[5] of the early third century without any mention of martyrdom.

A Comparison of the *Liber Pontificalis* with the *Gesta Martyrum*.—These traditions of the martyred popes were embodied in various *Gesta Martyrum* (or *Passiones Martyrum*), of which some are lost ; ten, however, still exist.[6] Their dates of compilation range from the fourth to the sixth century, and the records hover between the fourth class of such documents, which contain some grains of truth, and the purely apocryphal. There are no *Gesta* for two authentic martyrs —Telesphorus and Fabianus—and the spurious *Passion of Cornelius* does not invalidate the fact of his martyrdom.

A comparison of these *Gesta* with the very few details of the martyrdoms given in the *Liber Pontificalis*, will show the obvious dependence of the latter on the *Gesta* in two cases : for that of Urban, who is only a Confessor, according to the *Liber Pontificalis*, and for Cornelius, who is counted a martyr, having died of the hardships of exile. In a few other lives there are slight resemblances between the *Liber Pontificalis* and the *Gesta*, but for Sixtus II. there are marked differences existing between the authentic record in the *Liber Pontificalis* and the *Gesta* as we have them. For three lives, Pontianus,

---

[1] *De Gloria Martyrum*, c. 35, 36, in *P.L.* 71.
[2] Funk, *Opera Patrum Apostolicorum*, iii. 29.
[3] De Rossi, *Bull. arch. crist.*, 1864, p. 5 ; 1868, p. 18.
[4] Marucchi, *Le Catacombe Romane*, p. 379.
[5] *Philosophumena*, ix. 12, *P.G.* 16 (3), 3381.
[6] See *infra*, Chap. XV.

brother Gavinius and the daughter, called Susanna, of the priest Gavinius, was crowned with martyrdom.]

4. Marcellus (308–309).—The story of Marcellus in the *Liber Pontificalis* is hopelessly confused : it depends on the *Passion of Marcellus* : [1]

> When Marcellus was setting the church in order, he was seized by Maxentius, who tempted him to deny that he was a bishop,[2] and to humiliate himself by sacrificing to demons. Marcellus contemptuously mocked at the words and precepts of Maxentius, and he was condemned to the service of the public transports [3] (*in catabulum*). He served in the stables many days, and ceased not to serve God by prayer and fasting. But in the ninth month by night all his clergy came and rescued him from the stables. And a certain matron Lucina, a widow, who had lived with her husband Mark fifteen years, took up (? the body of) the blessed man : and she dedicated her house under the name of the Parish church (*titulus*) of blessed Marcellus,[4] where day and night with hymns and prayers they confessed our Lord Jesus Christ. Hearing this, Maxentius sent and again seized blessed Marcellus, and ordered that boards should be laid down in the church, and that the animals for the public transports should be brought there, and that blessed Marcellus should look after them. During his service in the stables he died, clothed only in a garment of goats' hair (*nudus amicto cilicio*). The blessed Lucina took his body, and buried him in the cemetery of S. Priscilla on the Via Salaria on January 16th.

5. Sixtus II. (257–259).—For an example of the occasional differences between the *Gesta* as we have them, and the *Liber Pontificalis*, the accurate record of Sixtus II., as given in the latter, may be quoted, and compared with the un-

---

[1] *A.SS.*, Jan. 16.

[2] Marcellus, though a bishop in the sight of the Church, had probably not been recognized by the civil power, owing to the confiscation of property during the Diocletian persecution. This perhaps accounts for the omission of his name in the *Depositio Episcoporum* of the Philocalian Calendar.

[3] This involved the care of the animals. In the *Passion* also it is said that the church in the house of Lucina was converted into these stables.

[4] The modern church of S. Marcellus in Via Lata.

authentic *Passion of Laurence*,[1] of the sixth century, where
the story of Sixtus is found :

> Sixtus was crowned with martyrdom. He lived in
> the time of Valerian and Decius when there was a great
> persecution. At the same time he was seized by Valer-
> ian and brought that he might sacrifice to demons.
> He despised the precepts of Valerian.[2] He was be-
> headed on August 6th, and with him six deacons besides,
> Felicissimus and Agapitus, Januarius, Magnus, Vincentius,
> and Stephen. And priests ruled over the church from
> the consulships of Maximus and of Gravio (Glabrio) for
> the second time (255) to Tuscus and Bassus (258). . . .
> And after the passion of blessed Sixtus, on the third
> day, blessed Laurence his archdeacon suffered on August
> 10th, and the sub-deacon Claudius and Severus the
> priest and Crescentius the reader (*lector*) and Romanus
> the doorkeeper (*ostiarius*) . . . Sixtus was buried in the
> cemetery of Callixtus on the Via Appia : the six deacons
> named above were buried in the cemetery of Praetextatus
> on the Via Appia : the above named blessed Laurence
> in the cemetery of Cyriaca in the property called
> Veranus, in a crypt with many other martyrs. . . .

**6. Pontianus (230–235), 7. Lucius (253–254) and 8. Marcel-
linus (296–308).**—The passages quoted below from the
Liber Pontificalis depend on some *Gesta* now lost:

> Pontianus . . . was crowned with martyrdom. . . . At
> the same time Pontianus the bishop and Hippolytus the
> priest were exiled by Alexander to Bucina (?),[3] in Sardinia,
> in the consulship of Severus and Quintianus (235). In
> this same island he was torn and tortured with cudgels,
> and he died October 30th. . . . And blessed Fabianus,
> with the clergy, brought him back by sea, and buried him
> in the cemetery of S. Callixtus on the Via Appia.

> Lucius . . . was crowned with martyrdom . . . he
> was exiled : afterwards by the will of God he returned
> safe to the church . . . he was beheaded by Valerian [4]
> on March 4th . . . he was buried in the cemetery of
> S. Callixtus on the Via Appia.

---

[1] *A.SS.*, Aug. 6.
[2] Note the similarity of phrase in the life of Marcellus.
[3] Another reading is *in insula nociva* (in an unhealthy island).
[4] An anachronism: Valerian's persecution began in 257 ; Lucius was dead in 254.

. . . At this time (reign of Diocletian) there was a great persecution, so that within thirty days, seventeen thousand Christians of both sexes throughout all the provinces were crowned with martyrdom. Wherefore Marcellinus was brought to the sacrifice to offer incense: which he did. And a few days after, being penitent, he was beheaded and crowned with martyrdom for the faith of Christ, together with Claudius and Cyrenus and Antonius. And after this their holy bodies lay exposed in an open space, for an example to the Christians, for twenty-four days by order of Diocletian. And then Marcellus the priest, with the priests and deacons took up their bodies by night, and singing hymns they buried them on the Via Salaria, in the cemetery of Priscilla, in the chamber (*cubiculum*) which lies open (*patet*) to the present day, as Marcellus himself had ordered after his repentance, when he was being led to execution ; the chamber is in a crypt near (*juxta*) the body of S. Crescentius.[1]

Date and Place of Burial.—The anniversaries of the burial days of the popes, given in the *Liber Pontificalis*, agree with those of the Philocalian Calendar (*depositio episcoporum*), of the earlier portion of the *Martyrology of Jerome*, and with those given in the earliest liturgical tradition.

The place of burial indicated is also, with few exceptions, exact.[2] Such topographical facts are usually correct even in the most apocryphal documents, such as some of the *Gesta* ; for the obvious reason that the shrines were in existence, well known, and frequently objects of pilgrimage.

Many of the papal tombs have been identified by actual excavation, and will be described in due course.

Disciplinary Decrees.—There are few popes to whom is not attributed in the *Liber Pontificalis* some disciplinary decree, often vaguely described in the formula :

He made a constitution (*constituit, fecit constitutum*) about the church, which is to-day laid up in the archives of the church.

---

[1] For the famous forgeries, *Gesta Liberii* and *Gesta de Sixti Purgatione*, which have supplied details for the lives of certain popes who suffered persecution, but not death, see *infra*, p. 82.

[2] See *infra*, p. 220, and Appendix II.

In other places the compiler briefly notes the decrees, merely stating the fact they were enacted, rather than giving a full exposition of contents. These statements are isolated one from another, so that it is impossible to deduce a complete body of law or custom on any of the points of which the decrees treat,—liturgical uses, baptism, penance, fasting, the discipline and organization of the various orders of clergy, the treatment of heretics, etc.

Such decrees were usually promulgated at the councils held annually by the popes on the anniversary of their ordination (*natale ordinationis*).

Sources of the Statements in the *Liber Pontificalis*: (1) Authentic Sources.—The value of this record of decrees passed lies mainly in the information which it gives as to the discipline of the Church at the date of compilation of the *Liber Pontificalis* in the sixth century.

To determine the accuracy of the statements, it is necessary to discover the sources of information. Whenever these sources can be traced, they prove to be sometimes genuine, sometimes apocryphal. More often, however, it is impossible to check the statement, as there remains no complete codified collection (*ordo*, *consuetudo*) of laws made specifically for the Church in *Rome* to which we can refer. But no doubt these local Roman edicts closely resembled those letters of instructions (decretals) issued by the popes to the other churches throughout the world, from the time of Clement the fourth pope onwards. These decretals possess almost the authority of the laws or canons made in the Œcumenical Councils, and are binding on the universal Church.[1]

Dionysius' Collection of Canons of the Councils and of the Apostles.—These authentic Canons, together with the so-called *Canons of the Apostles*,[2] had already been

---

[1] See C. J. Hefele, *A History of the Christian Councils to 787*, 5 volumes (English translation by W. Clark, Edinburgh, 1871–1896). See *infra*, Bibliography—GENERAL HISTORY.

[2] The latter collection is a compilation of the fourth or fifth century, declared apocryphal by Gelasius (492–496) in his decree *De Recipiendis* (see *infra*, p. 182) and by Hormisdas (514–523). Dionysius himself felt dubious of its authenticity. See Hardouin, *Concilia*, i. col. 1.

collected into a final edition, and translated into Latin by Dionysius, a Scythian monk settled in Rome, about 500 under Symmachus (498–514). This was soon followed by his edition of the Papal Decretals from Siricius (384–399) to Anastasius (496–498). These two works were held in high esteem, commended by Cassiodorus,[1] the founder of the monastery of Vivarium in Calabria, and accepted as an official version (*liber canonum*) by the popes.

There would certainly be a copy of these in the archives of the Roman Church; but curiously enough the writer of the *Liber Pontificalis* has made little use of the great collection, and of the twenty decretals he quotes, from Siricius (384–399) to Hilary (461–468), two only are found in Dionysius' collection,—concerning the reconciliation of heretics under Siricius, and concerning the Sabbath fast under Innocent (401–417).

In other cases where the sources of an edict have been traced, we often find it ascribed, in the *Liber Pontificalis*, to some pope other than the one who is quoted as author in the original document: and the edict is usually *ante*dated in the *Liber Pontificalis*. Sometimes, on the other hand, a pope is said to issue a rule when he is only confirming an ancient custom.

But, though frequently misdated, most of the edicts found in the *Liber Pontificalis* were really enacted, and were certainly in force in the sixth century, and many of them earlier.[2]

Examples of Decrees : (1) Duties of the Clergy.—A few examples of the decrees will indicate their general character and historical value.

Several of them concern the discipline of the clergy, especially as regards their duties in collecting the records of the martyrs, and the care of the cemeteries.

We read that Clement (90–112 (?))

Made seven regions and apportioned them to faithful

---

[1] Cassiodorus, *De institutione divinarum litterarum*, c. 23, in *P.L.* 70, col. 1137. For text of Decretals and Canons see *P.L.* 67.

[2] Some of the statements, however, are derived from less respectable sources. See *infra*, p. 80.

notaries of the Church who were diligently and curiously
to seek out, each in his own region, the deeds (*gesta*)
of the martyrs.[1]

Again Anteros (235–236)

Sought out diligently the *Gesta Martyrum* by means
of notaries and laid them up in the Church.

And Fabianus (236–251)

Allotted the regions to deacons, and made seven
subdeacons who should superintend the seven notaries,
and faithfully collect the *Gesta Martyrum*.

As regards these statements, it is probable that deacons
did exist from the very earliest times in Rome, as in
Jerusalem.   The seven regions were organized by Fabianus
in all probability : it is doubtful if these existed as early as
Clement.   The true function of the notaries is clearly defined
in the *Liber Pontificalis* under " Julius " (337–352), namely,
to afford legal assistance to the bishops in their judicial
functions and to preserve documents relating to the
donations to the church.[2]   Though it is an established fact
that individual *notarii* from the earliest times collected the
Acta and *Gesta* of the martyrs,[3] the *notarii* were not created
for this purpose specifically ; nor is there any other evidence
in support of the existence of an established order of
notaries at all, as early as Clement.   The purpose of these
statements, an example of antedating, is to lend authority
to the *Gesta* at a moment when the Church was much
occupied in discriminating between authentic and apocryphal
documents.[4]

With regard to the care of the martyrs' tombs we read :

Dionysius (259–269) allotted churches to the priests,
and arranged the cemeteries and parishes in dioceses.

And—

Marcellus (308–309) made parishes in the city of
Rome, as dioceses for the baptism and imposition of

---

[1] See *infra*, p. 134 *et seq.*   [2] *Infra*, Chap. VI. ; *L.P.* under " Julius."
[3] *Infra*, p. 136.   [4] *Infra*, p. 192.

penance on the many converts from paganism, and for the administration of the tombs of the martyrs.

Since the former pope ruled after the persecution of Valerian (253–266), and the latter after that of Diocletian (284–305), it seems probable that they did in fact carry out a scheme of reorganization which the necessities of the times rendered imperative.

As an example of postdating we note that Zephyrinus (199–217) is only re-enforcing a primitive custom when he commands the presence of all the clergy and faithful laity at the ordinations "whether of a clerk, a levite (*i.e.* deacon), or a priest."

There is no confirmation elsewhere of the decree of Lucius (253–254) that two priests and three deacons should everywhere accompany the bishop as witnesses to his life (*propter testimonium ecclesiasticum*). The difficulties of finding witnesses in the accusations brought against Pope Symmachus (498–514) may have appeared to the writer of the *Liber Pontificalis* an excellent reason for suggesting such a practice. Gregory the Great in the council of 595 replaced the laymen in attendance on the popes by clergy or monks; but the avowed purpose was that the example of the bishop might minister to the edification of his attendants. This ordinance may have suggested to the writer of the *Liber Pontificalis*, or to a later reviser, the decree ascribed to Lucius.

There is a reference to the most ancient hierarchy of the clergy in the decree of Gaius (283–296) that none should be a bishop unless he had already passed through the lower degrees of the priesthood—doorkeeper (*ostiarius*), reader, exorcist, acolyte (*sequens*), subdeacon, deacon and priest. This decree is repeated under Silvester with the addition of the office of "keeper of the martyrs."

(2) **On Fasting.**—There are several decrees on the subject of fasting. Telesphorus [1] (142–154) ordained a fast of seven weeks before Easter. Now it is true that fasts of varying duration had been kept from the earliest times, and Telesphorus had in fact made decrees on the question, as

---

[1] *Supra*, p. 64.

we see from Irenaeus' letter to Pope Victor;[1] but a fast of seven weeks' duration is posterior to the time of Pope Gregory I. This fact is adduced by Mommsen as a reason for attributing the *Liber Pontificalis* to this later period, while Duchesne holds that the writer is trying to introduce a salutary reform by making a false historical statement.[2]

A decree of Eleutherius (182–189) on the subject is evidently directed against the Manichaean heresies on the subject of evil, and the consequent practice of abstinences:

> He again established that no reasonable human food which God had created should be refused by Christians, especially those baptized (*i.e.* no longer mere catechumens).

A similar purpose inspires the decree of Miltiades (311–314) that none of the faithful should fast on Sunday or Thursday, because on those days the pagans keep a sacred fast; this is directed against the Manichaeans as well as the pagans.

The number of decrees in the *Liber Pontificalis* and elsewhere, directly or indirectly concerning heretics, penitent and impenitent, and the powerful effect exercised by these heretics, as we shall see presently, on Christian literature,[3] show yet again how heresies and schisms—the double divergence in dogma and discipline—came near to strangling the infant Church, like another Herakles, in the very cradle.

(3) Liturgical Decrees.—Among liturgical decrees are several concerning the Canon of the Mass,[4] which, however, throw little light on that obscure period of its history in the third and fourth centuries,—the period of transition from the Greek liturgy of the second century, quoted by Justin Martyr (about 165) and by other writers, to the crystallized Latin

---

[1] Eusebius, *Hist. Eccles.* v. 24, in *P.G.* 20, col. 502.

[2] Mommsen might well have drawn attention to the edict under Lucius (*supra*, p. 77) concerning the clerical attendants on the pope. Was the writer giving his own interpretation of a custom in force already in his own day, or only a counsel of perfection *before* Gregory had introduced the change?

[3] See *infra*, pp. 192–195.

[4] Cabrol, *Dict. Arch. Chrét.*, art. "Canon"; *Catholic Encyclopedia*, art. "Mass, Liturgy." The best book on the subject is Adrian Fortescue, *The Mass*: London, 1912.

rite[1] of the sixth century. To the existence of this Latin rite the letter of Pope Vigilius to Profuturus in 538 bears witness,[2] as does also the Sacramentary of Leo (sixth century, and almost contemporary with the compilation of the *Liber Pontificalis*) and that of Gelasius (early eighth century).[3] This rite is, in all essentials, the Canon of the Mass as it exists to-day.[4]

The *Liber Pontificalis* attributes various small modifications to Alexander (121–132), Telesphorus (142–154), and Leo I. (440–461); but none to Damasus (366–384), who probably had some share in forming the Canon; nor to Gelasius (492–496), to whom a constant tradition ascribes a strong influence on it, and who gave his name to one of the earliest Sacramentaries; nor to Vigilius (537–555), who legislated concerning the Preface of the Mass,[5] as we see in the letter referred to above.

We may examine the decree attributed to Telesphorus as an example of such edicts, and of the antedating of them. It is stated that he introduced the use of the *Gloria in Excelsis*, and caused Masses to be celebrated on Christmas Eve: the number is not specified. Now the feast of Christmas (*Natalis Domini*) was probably not observed in Rome till the fourth century.[6] There is no Mass for Christmas Eve even in the Sacramentary of Leo (sixth century), but *three* Christmas Masses[7] were said in the time of Gregory.[8]

A vague decree that Masses are to be said above (*supra*)

---

[1] The change of language does not necessarily imply a total change of rite, and there are passages in Justin, as in fourth and fifth century Fathers, which still appear in the Canon of the Mass in use to-day. The ultimate origin of the Mass is probably the liturgy of the Jewish Passover.

[2] *P.L.* 69, col. 18.

[3] Muratori, *Liturgia Romana Vetus*, t. i. pp. 318 *et seq.*, and p. 696.

[4] Gregory the Great (590–604) made some additions, and in the eighth century the Roman Canon was fused with the Gallican rite, and the *order* of the prayers rather lamentably confused.

[5] *i.e.* the passage *Vere dignum et justum est, aequum et salutare* . . . (Truly it is fitting and right, just and salutary . . .).

[6] See *supra*, p. 52, note 4. The *Gloria* was sung at an early period in Christmas and Pontifical Masses, but not generally in the ordinary Mass till the sixth century.

[7] See *Roman Missal* for text.

[8] *Gregorii Homilia*, i. 8, in *P.L.* 76, 1103 : "Because by the goodness of God we are about to-day (Christmas day) to celebrate thrice the office of the Mass, we cannot speak at length on the passage of the Gospel that has been read."

the *Memoriae,* or shrines of the martyrs, is attributed to Felix (269–274). Feasts of the martyrs were certainly kept in the East from the second century.[1]   S. Augustine[2] describes the Mass celebrated on the anniversary of the martyrdom of S. Cyprian at his tomb. The custom of saying Mass over the body of a martyr was firmly established in Rome by the fourth century.[3]   But if, as seems likely, the funeral feast (*agape*) was closely associated with the Eucharist, the practice goes even farther back to the very earliest times, and is an inheritance from paganism.

Among edicts concerning other ceremonies, Alexander (121–132) ordered that houses should be blessed by sprinkling them with water mixed with salt, as is, in fact, done at the present day among Catholics ; and Eutychianus (275–283) that of the fruits of the earth only beans and grapes should be blessed on the altar. This refers to the blessing of the firstfruits on the altar during the Canon of the Mass.[4]   Ascension Day was the occasion chosen from the fourth century at latest.

There are many edicts concerning vestments : among these a decree of Stephen (254–257) forbidding priests and deacons (*sacerdotes et levitas*) to wear their consecrated garments elsewhere than in church.

Sources of the Statements in the *Liber Pontificalis* : (2) Forgeries.—In addition to the authentic sources of the

---

[1] In the *Martyrdom of S. Polycarp* (see *infra*, p. 162, and Eusebius, *Hist. Eccl.* iv. 15) we read : We gathered up his bones, more precious than jewels, and more glorious than tried gold, and deposited them in a fitting place.   There also, as far as we can, the Lord will grant us to gather together, and celebrate the anniversary (*natalis*) of his martyrdom in joy and gladness, both in commemoration of those who have finished their contest, and to exercise and prepare others for the future.

[2] *Sermo*, 310, c. 11, in *P.L.* 39, col. 1413.

[3] Prudentius, *Peristephanon*, xi. 171, in *P.L.* 60, 549.

[4] For the text of these prayers see *Roman Missal,* and compare the *Gelasian Sacramentary* in Muratori, *op. cit.*   The prayer for the blessing of the firstfruits (*fruges novae*) in the latter runs : Bless, O Lord, these firstfruits, whether of grapes or beans, which Thou hast deigned to bring to maturity by the dew from heaven, and the inundation of the rains, and by serene and tranquil weather ; that we should receive them with thanksgiving, in the name of our Lord Jesus Christ, through whom all these things, O Lord, are good.

Liber Pontificalis, there is also a group of forged documents, from which are derived certain of the decrees, as well as other details in the lives.

Forgeries :—*Constitutum Silvestri* **and** *Constitution of the Synod of the Bishops.*—Most of the edicts quoted above bear true witness, as we have seen, to the customs of the time of the writer. But the entire lives of Silvester (314–337) and of his immediate successors depend partly on a famous group of forgeries of the year 501, whose purpose is to glorify Symmachus at the expense of his rival, the anti-pope Laurence.[1] The best known of these is the *Constitutum Silvestri*,[2] which claims to be a collection of the Canons promulgated by that pope, at a council held in the Baths of Trajan in Rome, in the presence of the recently baptized Constantine.[3] In certain of the clauses of these false edicts those heretics are condemned who were offering opposition to Symmachus.

A second *Constitutum Silvestri*[4] purports to be drawn up also by Silvester in the Baths of Trajan in the presence of Constantine some years later, as a confirmation of the Council of Nicæa (in 325). Duchesne calls it the Constitution of the *Synod of the Two hundred and Seventy-five Bishops*, to distinguish it from its predecessor.

Forgeries and the Life of Silvester.—The disciplinary edicts given by the *Liber Pontificalis* in the life of Silvester depend on these documents, and especially on the second,[5] but the importance of the variations from the originals shows how little respect the writer of the *Liber Pontificalis* felt for his documents. He actually divides the various pseudo-edicts of the Synod of the Bishops among *six* popes: Evaristus (112–121), Victor (189–199), Zephyrinus (199–217), Silvester (314–336), Siricius (384–399) and Boniface (418–423),—a remarkable series of antedated edicts!

[1] See *supra*, p. 54, Maassen, *Geschichte der Quellen und der Literatur des Canonischen Rechts im Abendlande*, i.

[2] *P.L.* 8.

[3] As a matter of history, Constantine was baptized on his deathbed at Nicomedia.

[4] Hardouin, *Concilia*, i., col. 285, and *P.L.* 8.

[5] For parallel passages see Duchesne, *op. cit.* i. p. cxxxviii.

6

Derived from the *Constitutum Silvestri* is that decree of Silvester found in the *Liber Pontificalis* which, as Duchesne says,[1] was never proclaimed, nor applied, nor found in any authentic text :

> No layman shall bring a charge against a member of the clergy . . . no one of the clergy, for any cause whatsoever, shall go into Court, nor plead his cause before the public judge, but only before the Church.

A portion of this edict is repeated under Julius (337–352), and bears witness to the jealousy between civil and ecclesiastical courts.

The following edict of Silvester (314–337), though derived from the same apocryphal source, is on many points in agreement with authentic documents.   It enacts, as in the edict of Gaius,[2] that the future bishop must pass through the lower steps of the hierarchy, and further that

> He must be approved in every respect, and have good witness to his character from those outside his house, be the husband of one wife, married with the blessing of the priest.

Forged *Gesta* also a Source of the Lives of Julius, Liberius, Felix, Sixtus III.—Belonging to this group of forgeries, and of the same date, is the *Gesta Liberii*, whose purpose is again the glorification of Symmachus, by showing that he is the antitype of the Liberius (352–366) who was persecuted by the Arian emperors.   History is not so well assured as to the conduct of Liberius under persecution.[3]

The *Gesta Liberii* have supplied certain facts, too, in the lives of Julius, Liberius himself, and Felix II.; but the compiler has used the legend with great freedom, combined it with other sources, and produced a document hostile in spirit to Liberius, and hence opposed to the *Gesta Liberii*.

In another document of this group, the *Gesta de Sixti*

---

[1] Duchesne, *op. cit.* pp. 189, 190, notes 20, 23.

[2] *Supra*, p. 77.

[3] For a discussion of the much-disputed question as to the orthodoxy of Liberius, see F. Savio, *Nuovi Studi sulla questione di Papa Liberio*, Rome, 1909.

purgatione,[1] is related the story of the vindication of Sixtus III. (432–440) from false charges before the Emperor Valentinian. Under these names of Sixtus and Valentinian, the writer describes a pretended triumphant refutation before Theodoric, of the accusations brought against Symmachus (499–514). As a matter of history, neither Sixtus nor Symmachus were given an opportunity of justifying themselves. This fantastic story has been used with modifications in the life of Sixtus III. in the *Liber Pontificalis*.

There are some curious incidents, derived from similar sources, recorded in the lives of other popes. Two may be quoted here as examples.

The legend of the finding of "the Cross of our Lord Jesus Christ" in the time of pope Eusebius (309–311), and that of the baptism, and simultaneous healing of leprosy of the Emperor Constantine by Silvester, are derived from the *Acta Silvestri* and *De Inventione Crucis* respectively, both apocryphal works, condemned in the Gelasian decree *De Recipiendis*.[2]

In another passage we read that Pope Eleutherius received a letter from Lucius, King of Britain, asking to be made a Christian. Bede repeats this statement in his *Ecclesiastical History*.[3] The origin of the legend is probably the existence of a famous British Christian corps of soldiers in the Roman armies in Gaul, in the fifth century, or perhaps the frequent immigrations from Britain to Gaul, or, perhaps, the presence in Rome, in the fourth century, of the celebrated British monk Pelagius, and others of the same country.[4]

---

[1] Baronius, in *Annales Ecclesiastici*, anno 443, t. vii. p. 462, ed. 1741, gives the *Gesta*, which he characterizes as *corrupta, depravata, mendosissima*.

[2] See *infra*, p. 182. [3] Bede, *Hist. Eccles.* i. 4.

[4] Duchesne, *op. cit.* i. chap. ii. ; Mommsen, "De Historia Brittonum," in *Neues Archiv*, 1894, p. 291 ; Bede, *op. cit.* i. x. ; Williams, *Christianity in Early Britain*, Oxford, 1912.

CHAPTER VI

THE *LIBER PONTIFICALIS*: THE INVENTORIES OF ECCLESIASTICAL PROPERTY

Ecclesiastical buildings in Rome and their endowments—Gifts under Silvester, Liberius, Damasus, Sixtus III. and others—Royal gifts—Restorations after the ravages of the barbarians—Criticism of the records and their sources—Number of Churches in the sixth century—Inventories of treasures—The landed properties of the Church—The inventory of S. Peter's—Sources of the records: charters of Foundation—The *Charta Cornutiana*.

Domine Deus in simplicitate cordis mei laetus obtuli universa: et populum tuum, qui repertus est, vidi cum ingenti gaudio: Deus Israel, custodi hanc voluntatem.
Missale, In Anniv. Dedic. Eccles. (1 *Paralip. xxix.*).[1]

Ecclesiastical Buildings in Rome and their Endowments.—From the earliest times we have brief notices of buildings erected by the popes:—the *Memoria* over the tomb of Peter, erected by Anacletus (78–90);[2] structures in the catacombs, and other buildings by Zephyrinus (199–217), Callixtus (217–222), and Fabianus (236–251). But it is only with the Peace of the Church in 312 that begin those fuller notices of the foundation, adornment and endowment of the famous Roman basilicas, which form the most reliable and not the least interesting portion of the *Liber Pontificalis*.

These churches were raised in nearly every case over some ancient shrine of a martyr, and sometimes replaced or incorporated a chapel already existing.

Gifts under Silvester. — At the "suggestion" of Silvester, Constantine founded no less than nine churches.

---

[1] "*O Lord, in the uprightness of my heart I have willingly offered all these things: and now I have seen with joy Thy people who are present here. . . . O God of Israel, prepare their heart unto Thee.*" (Authorized Version, 1 Chron. xxix.)

[2] A. S. Barnes, *S. Peter in Rome*; cf. Dufourcq, *Étude sur les Gesta Martyrum romains*, 101.

These include the Constantinian basilica, known as the Lateran, S. Peter's, S. Paul's, the basilica[1] built in the Sessorian Palace, "where Constantine enclosed in gold and gems the wood of the Holy Cross of our Lord Jesus Christ," and basilicas by the tombs of S. Agnes, on the Via Nomentana, and of S. Laurence, on the Via Tiburtina.

Liberius.—Liberius (352–366) began the Liberian basilica,[2] which retains, at the present day, more of its ancient beauty than almost any church in Rome.

Damasus.—Damasus (366–384) was a great builder:

> He made two basilicas: one to blessed Laurence near the theatre,[3] and another on the Via Ardeatina, where he himself rests:[4] and the Catacombs where lay the bodies of the holy apostles Peter and Paul,[5] (in which place is the platonia, where were laid their holy bodies) he adorned with verses.[6] And he sought and found many bodies of the saints, of whom he told in verses.[7]

Then follows an inventory of this basilica to S. Laurence which was called after himself, *Titulus Damasi.*

Sixtus III. and Others.—Sixtus III. (432–440) embellished the Liberian basilica, and we still read in mosaic, over the triumphal arch: "Sixtus the Bishop for the people of God." He also erected a second great basilica to S. Laurence, made a monastery for the service of the catacomb, where S. Peter and S. Paul and, later, S. Sebastian had lain; and erected in the papal crypt of S. Callixtus, a marble tablet inscribed with the names of the bishops who lay there.[8]

---

[1] Now S. Croce in Gerusalemme.

[2] Now S. Maria Maggiore, or Our Lady of the Snows.

[3] San Lorenzo in Damaso, near the Theatre of Pompey.

[4] Not yet discovered. For a summary and bibliography of the whole question see E. Barker, "S. Callixtus," in *Journal of Roman Studies*, vol. i. pt. i., London, 1911.

[5] Where is now the Church of S. Sebastian, Via Appia. See A. S. Barnes, *op. cit.* chap. v.

[6] De Rossi, *Inscriptiones Christianae*, ii. pp. 32, 89, 105.

[7] *Epigrammata Damasi*, ed. Ihm, in the series *Anthologia Latina*. For these and other inscriptions see *infra*, Chaps. XVIII.–XXI., especially Chap. XXI.

[8] For the inscriptions he put up in the Liberian basilica and in S. Callixtus see *infra*, pp. 282, 292.

Hilary (461–468) gave an immense treasure of church plate, Gelasius (492–496), "the lover of the poor," and Symmachus (498–514) raised basilicas and oratories, John I. (523–526) beautified the catacombs, Felix IV. (526–530) converted into the Church of SS. Cosmas and Damian[1] the pagan temple to the little Roman prince, Romulus (309), on the Via Sacra in the Forum. Indeed, nearly every pope in his day, contributed something to the splendour of the churches, and especially to the shrine of S. Peter, to which the greater part of the offerings flowed.

Royal Gifts.—Emperors and kings, too, were munificent in their donations. Under pope Hormisdas (514–523), vessels of gold and silver, precious fabrics, and books of the gospels bound in gold, and set in gems came from the Eastern emperor, Justinus, for the shrine of S. Peter; two silver candlesticks from Theodoric; "a golden crown (*regnus*) with precious stones from Clovis, the Christian king of the Franks;" and, a few years later, under John II. (533–535), equally splendid gifts from Justinian.

Restorations after the Ravages of the Barbarians.—The successive ravages of the barbarians necessitated frequent restorations. Celestinus (422–432) made gifts to the Julian basilica,[2] and to S. Peter's and to S. Paul's, after the sack of Rome by Alaric (Aug. 410); though the Gothic king seems to have shown respect to the sacred vessels of S. Peter's and extended protection to fugitives to S. Peter's and S. Paul's.[3]

The Emperor Valentinian, at the request of Pope Sixtus III. (432–440), gave a silver ciborium to the Lateran basilica, to replace that carried away by the barbarians under Alaric; and in the life of Leo (440–461) we read that, after the Vandal invasion, he replaced the sacred vessels in all the parish churches, besides executing other improvements.

A Criticism of the Records and their Sources.—It is noticeable that in the *Liber Pontificalis* there is no mention, under Siricius (384–399), of three churches at least which

---

[1] For the inscription see *infra*, p. 287.   [2] S. Maria in Trastevere.
[3] *Supra*, p. 18; cf. Orosius, *Historiarum liber vii.*, c. 39, in *P.L.* 31, col. 1163.

were connected with his name—S. Pudentiana, S. Clement and the Church of the Apostles (also called S. Peter *ad vincula*) on the Esquiline. This fact raises the questions: How far are these records in the *Liber Pontificalis* adequate or accurate, and what are their sources?

The Number of the Churches in the Sixth Century. —Taking the middle of the sixth century as the limit of our investigation, the *Liber Pontificalis* mentions twenty parish churches (*tituli*)[1] as built up to that period in Rome. That there were in reality twenty-five at least is clear, for their names and those of their parish priests are appended to the account of the Roman Council of 499.[2]

In the list, too, of suburban churches, many are missing which appear in the seventh-century Itineraries[3] and certainly date from the fifth century or earlier.

As a walk round the city would have enabled the writer to complete his lists, one may conjecture that he is using, somewhat mechanically, written documents which are either incomplete or abridged by himself.

The Inventories of their Treasures.—It is noticeable that he is not writing as an historian or connoisseur : the structure and architectural features of the church, the sculptures and mosaics are passed over in silence, or only mentioned to indicate the marbles that covered the pillars, or the weight of gold used to gild the apse, or the jewels in t es of a statue. For it is with the objects of value ta iter is preoccupied, and in the lives from Silves 7) to Sixtus III. (432–440), for which period the most detailed, we find, for the nineteen church uring that period, accounts of the gifts made to ch at foundation, set out in minutest detail, and a rding to the same plan : namely, there is, first, ue of liturgical vessels, containing always the sar vhich vary only in number and value, with a note terial

---

[1] On *tituli* see *supra*, pp. 9 *et seq.* ; cf. H. Grisar, *History* *: Popes in the Middle Ages*, i. p. 188, London, 1911 (the translation delta).

[2] *Monumenta Germaniae Historica, Auctorum Antiquo* *.* 410, ed. Mommsen, Berlin, 1894.

[3] *Infra*, Chaps. VII., VIII.

of which they were made, and the weight. A second catalogue contains a list of lamps and candelabra, described with the same detail.

The Landed Properties of the Church.—These catalogues are followed by a list of landed properties for the endowment of the churches, and especially to provide for the expenses of the lighting (*in servitio luminum*).[1] These properties (*massae, fundi, agri, possessiones*) are generally situated near the church: for instance, S. Agnes had property in the Via Nomentana and the Via Salaria; S. Laurence in the Via Tiburtina.

Other Roman churches were supported by lands in S. Italy, Sicily, Africa, Numidia. The churches of S. Peter and S. Paul depended on revenues from the eastern provinces. The revenues of these lands are given in *solidi*[2] and sometimes in kind. For through the ports of these far-off lands flowed the treasures of the East—oil from Cyprus, myrrh from Arabia, nard and pepper from India, cinnamon, saffron and cloves from the Moluccas, and balm from the banks of the Jordan. Some of these were offered to the service of the dead, and for the lights of the Sanctuary. Gregory the Great[3] sends aloes and incense, storax and balm, "as offerings to the bodies of the holy martyrs." In 408, part of the ransom paid by Rome to Alaric was three thousand pounds (σταθμοί) of pepper,[4] and in the eighth century Lullus, the future bishop of Mayence, sends to Eadburga, abbess of Thanet, a handsome present of storax and cinnamon.[5]

The Inventory of the Church of S. Peter's.—It is worth while to examine one of these inventories. We may choose, as the most complete and most famous, that recording the donation of Constantine to the ancient little

---

[1] I am indebted to my friend, Rev. O. Apthorp, for the fact, that from similar charters of the thirteenth century in England, we learn that the lights in many English churches, too, were paid for out of landed properties devoted to the purpose.

[2] A *solidus* was worth about £6.

[3] *Gregorii Epistolae*, ix. 52, in *P.L.* 77, col. 989.

[4] Zosimus, *Historia*, v. 41.

[5] Jaffé, *Monumenta Moguntina*, in *Bibl. rer. Germ.*, t. iii. p. 214.

shrine of S. Peter, already   inc   of Pope
Anacletus, at the end o   is Constantine converted into the   ur   r's, only
destroyed when the prese   in the
fifteenth century. The ac   ur   with the
emperor's other donations,   of

  At the same time   ne   made a
basilica to blessed Pe   st   temple
of Apollo. The tomb   it   of Saint
Peter he thus covered   to   shut in
on every side with (on   it was
fixed :[2] at the head 5   he   : at the
right side 5 feet: at th   fe   5 feet :
above 5 feet; thus he   th   blessed
Peter the apostle, and   ve   adorned
it above (*i.e.* on the alt   it   columns
and other columns car   ne   brought
from Greece.

  And he made an ap   *ba*   ng with
plates of gold; and a   od   l Peter,
above the bronze whic   it,   cross of
purest gold, weighing   ds   to the
measurement of the p   n   : CON-
STANTINE AUGUSTUS   E   A SUR-
ROUND THIS ROYAL   [rine of
S. Peter] WITH A COUR   SPLEN-
DOUR,[3]—written in lett   o   s itself.
He made also candela   ed   feet in
height, 4 in number, wr   ve   statues
of the apostles, weighin   po
  4 golden chalices, wi   f   acinth [4]
each of which has 4   an   ghs 12
pounds.

---

[1] For certain difficulties in the read   lat   cisms and
explanation of the text, see the admir   sti   . Barnes,
S. Peter in Rome and his Tomb o   E   oo, with
bibliography, and Duchesne, *op. cit.*   donations
of Constantine, obviously taken from   nt   *emporum*
Ratione.
[2] *i.e.* the whole was built up with
[3] The original is CONSTANTINUS   r   TA HANC
DOMUM REGALEM SIMILI FULGORE   LA   c).
[4] The prase is a kind of green jasp   is

2 silver *metretae*[1] (vessels for holding the wine) weighing 200 pounds.

20 silver chalices weighing each 10 pounds.

2 golden *amae* (vessels for holding the oblations of wine) weighing each 10 pounds.

5 silver amae, each weighing 20 pounds.

A golden *patena* (plate) with a tower (*turris*)[2] of purest gold, with a dove adorned with jewels of prase and of jacinth, with 215 pearls, weighing 30 pounds.

5 silver *patenae* each weighing 15 pounds.

A golden crown before the body which is to serve as a stand for candles (*farus cantharus*), with 50 dolphins, which weighs 35 pounds.

32 silver *fara*[3] in the nave of the basilica with dolphins; weighing each 10 pounds.

In the right aisle of the basilica 30 silver stands for candles, weighing each 8 pounds.

The altar itself of silver gilt is adorned on all sides with jewels of prase and jacinths and pearls (*albis*), the number of jewels 400, weighing 350 pounds.

An incense-burner of purest gold adorned with jewels on all sides, to the number of 60, weighing 15 pounds.

Further, the gift which Constantine Augustus offered to blessed Peter throughout the diocese of the East:[4]—

In the city of Antioch :
  the house of Datianus producing 240 solidi.

.   .   .   .   .   .

  a bath in Cerateas producing 42 solidi (mills, gardens, etc.).

In the suburbs of Antioch :
  the property of Sybille given to Augustus, producing 322 solidi, 150 decades of leaves of papyrus, 200 pounds of spices, 200 pounds of oil of nard, 35 pounds of balsam.

In the suburbs of Alexandria :
  (various properties).

Throughout Egypt in the suburbs of Armenia :

.   .   .   .   .   .

---

[1] Really a *measure* of about 40 litres.

[2] Used for containing the consecrated Host.

[3] *Farus, i,* is feminine, but *fara* is the plural given in *L.P.* Similarly *Cantara* (sic) is plural of *Cantharus* or *Canthara* (m. or f.).

[4] One of the twelve dioceses into which Diocletian divided the empire. Selections only are quoted from this portion of the document.

The property Passinopolimse producing 800 solidi, 400 decades of leaves of papyrus, 50 medimni of pepper, 100 pounds of saffron, 150 pounds of storax, 200 pounds of spiced cassia, 300 pounds of oil of nard, 100 pounds of balsam, 100 measures of linen, 150 pounds of cloves, 100 pounds of oil of Cyprus.

. . . . .

. . . . . .

In the province of the Euphrates in the suburb of Cyprus :
[varied produce].

. . . . .

Such is the form of these inventories. They are sometimes greatly condensed. In the donation to the basilica of S. Paul we read merely :

All the holy vessels, whether of gold or silver or bronze Constantine gave, as in the basilica of blessed Peter the apostle, so in the basilica of blessed Paul the apostle. And he also placed a golden cross over the tomb (*locus*) of blessed Paul the apostle, weighing 150 pounds.

Then follows the list of landed properties.

A further examination of some other of the inventories will show they are not quite complete. After Sixtus III., the details concerning the landed property are omitted. Frequently the fact is just stated,—that a basilica has been built, or a cemetery adorned or church plate supplemented.

The Sources of the Records : Charters of Foundation. — The character of these records, the choice of facts, the minuteness of detail, and the uniformity of the manner of expression, indicate as sources of the information, the original charters of foundation or donation, church inventories, account books and such-like; the phraseology used in some cases indicates documents of considerable antiquity.[1]

Some of these original records were no doubt found in those archives of the Roman Church to which the writer of the *Liber Pontificalis* frequently refers.

[1] Duchesne, *op. cit.* i. pp. cl, cxlix.

We have seen that under Julius (337–352) the notaries are entrusted with the care of documents concerning wills, donations, debts, etc., preserved in the ecclesiastical chests;[1] some of these documents may have provided material for the inventories of the *Liber Pontificalis*. Duchesne, however, conjectures that the bulk of the inventories may have come from the offices of the Treasurer of the holy See (*Vestiarius sanctae Sedis*).[2] The first we hear of this treasury is in the life of Pope Severinus, under whose predecessor it had been sacked (in 638) by the Roman army for the sake of "the money heaped up by Honorius" (625–638). We have no means of knowing how long it had been established; but some such institution must have been necessary from the moment that the Church held property.

The *Charta Cornutiana.*—We do not possess the originals of any of the inventories used by the writer of the *Liber Pontificalis*; but Duchesne quotes at length[3] an example of just such a charter of foundation as must have been the source of those records. It is known as the *Charta Cornutiana*: the manuscript, which is of the twelfth century, is in the Vatican. The charter is dated 471, and by it Flavius Valila Theodorius gives a house on the Esquiline to a little country church near Tivoli. The document opens with the further donation of a dozen farms, for the repair of fabric, and service of the lights; and of land for the houses and gardens of the clergy. Then follows a list of liturgical vessels and other furniture, "for the adornment of the same church and the celebration of the above mentioned holy mystery." Finally, there is a long list of beautiful stuffs and linens of lovely design and colour, and of certain codices —the four gospels, psalter, etc. These last two items are usually omitted in the inventories of the *Liber Pontificalis*, which in all other respects closely resemble the form of the *Charta Cornutiana*.

---

[1] *Supra*, p. 76.   [2] Duchesne, *op. cit.* i. p. cliii.
[3] Duchesne, *op. cit.* i. p. cxlvi.

CHAPTER VII

THE ITINERARIES

The Itineraries and their authors.—Plan of Rome of Septimius Severus (A.D. 193–211).—*Notitia urbis regionum XIV.* (334) and *Curiosum urbis* (357).—*Laterculus Polemii Silvii* (449).—Topography of Zaccarias of Mitylene (540). —*Index Coemiteriorum* (fourth century) appended to *Notitia* : date and the number of the cemeteries (16?).—The Papyri of Monza (sixth century): the tradition of the treasure : the pilgrimage of Abbot John : text of the labels *(pittacia)* and the list of labels *(index oleorum)* : Sepulcri's theory as to the origin of the papyri : history of the treasure : topographical value of the papyri and the position of *Sedes* of S. Peter.

Accipe hunc baculum sustentationis itineris ac laboris peregrinationis tuae : ut devincere valeas omnes catervas inimici, et pervenire securus ad limina sanctorum, quo pergere cupis : et peracto obedientiae cursu, ad nos iterum revertaris cum gaudio. Per Christum. . . .
Missale ad usum ecclesiae Sarum : servitium peregrinorum.[1]

The Itineraries and their Authors.—It was to guide the pilgrims on their way, that the Roman Itineraries [2] were compiled, between the fifth and the eighth centuries. The information afforded by them is adequate to its purpose, if not very copious. We find, as a rule, a list of shrines given, the cemetery in which they are found, and the most striking oratory, etc., which stands in that cemetery above ground. It is the rarest thing to find any biographical note. We are told, further, on what road, and, sometimes, on which side of the road, the cemeteries lie ; the precise nature of their monuments,—crypt, or basilica, or oratory;—whether above or below ground ; method of access ; even, sometimes, the number of

---

[1] The blessing of the pilgrim's staff: *Take this staff to support you on the journey and in the toil of your pilgrimage: that you may be able to overcome all the bands of enemies, and reach in safety the thresholds of the saints whither you desire to journey: and having performed the command laid upon you, may return to us again with joy, through Jesus Christ. . . .*

[2] *Infra*, Bibliography—ITINERARIES.

93

steps the pilgrim ascended or descended; and the relative positions of the shrines among themselves. The Itineraries all follow a definite topographical order, moving round Rome either clockwise—starting from the Via Flaminia and passing by the Via Salaria and Via Nomentana, to end at the Vatican on the Via Cornelia—or counter-clockwise, from the Via Aurelia by the Via Portuensis, Via Ostiensis, Via Appia, etc. The distance of the shrines, measured in miles from the Aurelian Wall, is sometimes stated.

De Rossi has called the Itineraries "the topographical key of the suburban tombs of the martyrs and the popes."

The precision and the phraseology of these documents make it evident that they were written on the spot, and hitherto it has been accepted that the pilgrims themselves were the authors of the Itineraries. Schneider [1] has, however, recently suggested that they were written by residents in Rome, most probably by some lower order of clerk; and that an educated or wealthy pilgrim may have purchased a copy, or even made his own copy, and taken it back to his native land. The suggestion in itself appears likely to be true, and if none of the reasons adduced by Schneider, taken alone, afford absolute proof, yet taken together they afford a pretty strong argument in favour of his theory.

Under the general name of Itineraries we will discuss, not only the Christian Itineraries proper, but also some important secular works of topography kindred to them, which throw light on the Christian monuments: also some Christian topographical documents, such as the *Papyri of Monza*, of a different form from the Itineraries.

Plan of Rome of Septimius Severus.—Various official documents enable us to form a vivid and minute picture of imperial pagan Rome; but the most precious of all, the plan of Rome as it was at the beginning of the third century, has been lost since the Middle Ages, save for a few fragments preserved in the garden of the Capitoline Museum. The

---

[1] G. Schneider, "Gli autori e il criterio di compilazione degli antichi itinerari delle Catacombe Romane," in *Nuovo Bullettino di archeologia cristiana*, 1909. For technical terms of architecture, etc., used, *ibid.* 1911, p. 153, and cf. 1910, p. 17.

original plan[1] was engraved on marble by orders of Septimius Severus (193–211) and affixed to the exterior wall of
the Temple of Romulus[2] in the Forum.

Notitia urbis regionum XIV.—Our next document is a sort
of municipal guide to the city.   The *Notitia urbis regionum
XIV.* (Register of the fourteen regions of the city)[3] was compiled under Constantine in 334 from earlier documents in
the urban archives.   It describes the boundaries of the
regions, and the streets and monuments in them.   There are
appended two supplemental lists, *i.e.* one of the monuments,
classified under "obelisks," "theatres," "bridges," "aqueducts," etc., the other a brief epitome (*breviarium*) of the
first list.   No Christian building is mentioned.   The *Notitia*
was incorporated into the Philocalian Calendar of 354; and
into the *Notitia Dignitatum utriusque imperii*[4] (Register of
the officials of both empires, *i.e.* Eastern and Western),
compiled in the time of Honorius (395–408) at the final
division of the Empire.

Curiosum Urbis.—The *Curiosum Urbis Romae regionum
XIV. cum breviariis suis* is practically the same as the
Notitia and was compiled about 357.   In this document also
there is no mention of Christian buildings; and had we no
other evidence on the topography of Rome than these two
early and authentic records, we might conclude, not unreason-
ably, that there were no Christian monuments—and hence,
perhaps, no Christians—at the beginning of the fifth century,
when the *Notitia Dignitatum* was compiled.

The description of a single region will show the general
character of the rest.

REGION XI.   THE GREAT CIRCUS (*Circus Maximus*).   It contains the Temple of the Sun and Moon
and the Temple of Mercury, the sanctuary of the
Mother of the Gods and of Jove: (temple of) Ceres,
12 gates, the Porta Trigemina, (the statue of) Apollo
looking skyward, of Hercules with an olive, the district

---

[1] Richter, *Topographie von Rom.*   See *infra*, Bibliography—ITINERARIES.
[2] *Supra*, p. 5.   [3] For a complete list see *supra*, p. 12.
[4] *Infra*, p. 199.   O. Seeck, *Notitia Dignitatum*, Berlin, 1876.   The *Notitia
Regionum* has not been printed in this edition.

Velabrum, the Arch of Constantine : (the region contains) 21 quarters (*vici*), 21 little temples (of the Lares) (*aediculae*), 48 superintendents (*vicomagistri*), 2 overseers of monuments (*curatores*), 2500 (IID.) tenement houses (*insulae*), 89 mansions (*domus*), 48 warehouses for food (*horrea*), 44 public baths (*balnea*), 90 fountains with basins (*laci*), 20 public mills (*pistrina*). It contains 11,500 feet (XID.).

The supplemental list of the monuments takes the following form :—

1. 28 LIBRARIES.
2. 6 OBELISKS.—In the Circus Maximus 2, the lesser measuring 87 feet, the greater 122 feet. In the Vatican 1, 75 feet in height, etc. . . .
3. 8 BRIDGES.—Aelian, Aemilian, Aurelian, Molvian, Sublician, Fabrician, of Cestius, of Probus.
4. 7 HILLS.—Coelian, Aventine, Tarpeian, Palatine, Esquiline, Vatican, Janiculum.
5. 8 OPEN SPACES (*Campi*) [list].
6. 11 FORUMS [list].
7. 10 BASILICAS (pagan) [list].
8. 11 PUBLIC BATHS (*Thermae*) [list].
9. 19 AQUEDUCTS [list].
10. 29 ROADS [list of those within, and leading out of, the city].

The remaining information is still further condensed in the *Breviarium*, which reads :

2 Capitols, 2 Circuses, 2 Amphitheatres, etc. . . . 37 gates, 423 districts (*vici*) . . . 46,602 tenement houses (*insulae*) . . . 856 public baths (balnea) . . . 254 public mills (*pistrina*), 46 *lupinariae*. . . .

Laterculus Polemii Silvii.—The *Laterculus Polemii Silvii* (Register of Polemius Silvius) is a register of *imperial* Rome. It was compiled in 449 by Polemius Silvius, and consists of a list of the emperors and the Roman provinces and dioceses, and, under the heading, " What there is at Rome " (*Quae sint Romae*), a brief note of the hills, bridges and buildings. The writer ignores the pagan temples : of the Christian buildings he merely remarks that there are " some sacred buildings together with innumerable holy tombs of the martyrs." Perhaps the " sacred buildings " include pagan temples.

Topography of Zaccarias of Mitylene.—A small contribution to Christian topography, is found in the *Ecclesiastical History*[1] of Zaccarias the Rhetorician, who was afterwards Bishop of Mitylene in Lesbos. It was written in 540 under Justinian, and incorporated in it is a somewhat inaccurate description of Rome, under the title of "A Short History of the Beauties of the City of Rome." This is based on some earlier document (probably the *Notitia* or *Curiosum*), since many statues and other treasures are enumerated, which had disappeared long before 540, during the Gothic invasions. The only reference to Christian monuments is in the following extract:

> . . . There are in Rome the (? two) Churches of the Blessed Apostles and 24 (? other) Catholic Churches, 2 great (secular) basilicas, 324 great spacious roads, 2 capitols, 80 great golden statues of the gods . . . and there are 5000 places of burial, where they gather together and bury (the dead). . . .[2]

It is unknown from what early document Zaccarias derives his information on this point. The number of twenty-six churches almost corresponds with that given in the itinerary *De Locis Sanctis*.[3]

***Index Coemiteriorum* (Fourth Century).**—The first document of real importance for the Christian monuments was discovered by De Rossi, in a beautiful fifteenth-century manuscript in the Vatican. Of the various documents copied by this fifteenth-century scribe, one was an eleventh-century manuscript of the *Notitia Regionum*, exactly corresponding with the text of that document as found in the *Notitia Dignitatum* (date about 400), with the highly

---

[1] The Syriac Codex in the Vatican is corrupt, and the translation of Cardinal Mai (*Scriptorum veterum nova Collectio*, x. p. xii, and p. 361 : Rome, 1838) somewhat obscure. There is an epitome of this Codex in a manuscript in the British Museum : see Ign. Guidi, "Il testo Syriaco della descrizione di Roma nella storia attribuita a Zaccaria" in *Bull. della Commissione archeologica Communale di Roma*, 1884, p. 218.

[2] According to De Rossi's emendations of Mai's text : followed also by Guidi. See *Roma Sotteranea*, i. p. 130. The "five thousand places of burial" might include pagan as well as Christian tombs.

[3] This number almost corresponds to that of the twenty-five parish churches of Rome (*tituli*) (see *supra*, pp. 12, 13).

7

important addition of a list of sixteen cemeteries in Rome (*Cimiteria totius Romam* (sic) . . . *Cimiteria XVI.*).

The following is the text of the Vatican Codex *re-arranged* in topographical order:[1]

INDEX XVI COEMITERIORUM OF THE VATICAN CODEX
ARRANGED IN TOPOGRAPHICAL ORDER

Via Flaminia. . . .   *Cemetery of S. Valentine.*

Via Salaria Vetus . .
1. Coemiterium ad Sanctam Columbam ad caput S. Joannis in Clivum Cucumeris.
   [C. Coem. ad septem palumbas, etc.]
   [L. Coem. ad septem columbas, etc.]
2. Coemiterium Basillae ad S. Hermen Via Salaria. P.
   [C. L. Coem. Basille ad S. Hermetem. Via Salaria Vetere.]

Via Salaria Nova. . .
3. C. L. Coem. Priscillae ad S. Silvestrum Via Salaria. P.
   Cemetery of Maximus at S. Felicitas.
4. C. L. Coem. Jordanorum ad S. Alexandrum Via Salaria. P.
5. C. L. Coem. Thrasonis ad S. Saturninum Via Salaria. P.

Via Nomentana . . .
Cemetery of S. Agnes. P.
or *Emerentianae*, or "*Ostrianum*" or "*Coem. Majus*" or "*Ad Nymphas Petri.*"

Tiburtina . . . . .   *Cemetery of S. Laurence, of Hippolytus.* P.

Via Labicana . . . .
6. Coem. ad duas lauros ad SS. Petrum et Marcellinum Via Labicana. P.[2]
   [C. Coem. inter duas lauros ad S. Marcellianum[3] Via Labicana.]
   [L. Coem. inter duas lauros ad S. Marcellinum et Petrum.]

---

[1] The order of the cemeteries in the *manuscript* is : Priscilla, Jordani, Praetextatus, Domitilla, Catacumbas (S. Sebastian), Callixtus, ad duas Lauros, Balbina, ad Sanctam Columbam, Felix, Pontianus, Basilla, Basileus, Commodilla, Calepodius, Thraso. The letter *P* indicates that the cemetery is mentioned in the *Depositio Martyrum* or *Depositio Episcoporum* of the Philocalian Calendar (*infra*, Appendix III.).

There are other manuscripts of this Index, *e.g.* those of the *Biblioteca Chigiana* and of the *Biblioteca Laurenziana*. The letters *C, L* indicate the readings of the *Chigiana* and *Laurenziana* respectively (see *infra*, Appendix IV.). The names of the *chief* cemeteries omitted are added in italics. For the Index of cemeteries in the *Mirabilia Urbis Romae* see *infra*, p. 124.

[2] Under a different name in the Philocalian Calendar (see *infra*, Appendix III.).

[3] A mistake for *Marcellinum*.

[Via Latina]	Not in Vatican codex.
[Making a seventeenth cemetery]	[C. L. Coem. Aproniani ad sanctam Eugeniam [1] Via Latina.]

Via Appia . . . . .
  7. C. L. Coem. Praetextati ad S. Januarium Via Appia. P.
  8. C. L. Coem. Catacumbas ad S. Sebastianum Via Appia. P.
  9. C. L. Coem. Calisti ad S. Xystum Via Appia. P.

Via Ardeatina. . . .
  10. C. L. Coem. Domitillae, Nerei et Achillei ad S. Petronillam Via Ardeatina.
  11. L. Coem. Balbinae ad SS. Marcum et Marcellianum Via Ardeatina. P.
  [C. Coem. Balbinae ad SS. Marcum et Marcellinum [2] Via Ardeatina.]
  12. C. L. Coem. Basilei ad S. Marcum [3] Via Ardeatina.

Via Ostiensis . . . .
  13. C. L. Coem. Commodilla ad S. Felicem et Adauctum Via Ostiensi.
  Cemetery of Paul, and of Thecla and Timothy.

Via Portuensis . . .
  14. C. Coem. ad insalatos ad S. Felicem Via Portuensi. [L. Coem. ad(o)mphalatos, etc.]
  15. C. L. Coem. Pontiani ad Ursum pileatum, Abdon et Sennen Via Portuensi. P.

Via Aurelia . . . .
  Cemetery of S. Pancras.
  16. C. L. Coem. Calepodii ad S. Calixtum Via Aurelia. P.[4]
  Cemetery of Lucina at S. Agatha ad Girulum.

Via Cornelia . . . .   *Cemetery of S. Peter on the Vatican.*

The information contained in this Index is in agreement with the best authenticated information from other sources.

The Date.—Since this document was appended [5] to the *Notitia Regionum* and the *Notitia Dignitatum*, it is clear that it is an official, secular list. That it is of the same

---

[1] See *infra*, p. 193.

[2] A mistake for *Marcellianum* (see *supra*, *Via Labicana*, No. 6).

[3] Marcus is the pope (337–341) who built a basilica in the cemetery of Balbina, in the cemetery now called S. Callixtus : the foundations have been identified. The other Marcus and Marcellianus, fellow-martyrs of the Diocletian persecution, were *first* buried in the same catacombs, and then transferred to a basilica on the Via Ardeatina.   The whole question of these burial-places is controversial (see *S. Callixtus* . . . in *Journal of Roman Studies*, vol. i. pt. i. p. 107 : London, 1911).

[4] Under a different name in the Philocalian Calendar.

[5] *Supra*, p. 97.

date as the documents to which it is appended is also clear. Among other reasons we remark that, while in the *Notitia* there is no mention of the later monuments erected between 379 and 383 by Gratian, so in the Index there is no mention of the basilica for his own tomb made by Damasus (366–384) on the Via Ardeatina.

The Number of the Cemeteries in the Index and in the Philocalian Calendar.—If, again, we compare the list of cemeteries in the Index with those in the *Depositio Martyrum* and *Depositio Episcoporum* of the Philocalian Calendar, we shall find a close resemblance; especially when we consider that the Index is a secular list of cemeteries, while the Calendar is only concerned with martyrs' anniversaries for liturgical purposes. The Index, as we have seen, contains sixteen cemeteries, the Calendar fourteen. No less than eleven are common to both documents, and, with two exceptions,[1] bear identical names (Nos. 2, 3, 4, 5, 7, 8, 9, 11, 15).

Three cemeteries omitted in the Index appear in the Calendar, *i.e.* (1) S. Agnes on the Via Nomentana; (2) SS. Paul, Timothy and Cyriacus, on the Via Ostiensis; and (3) S. Laurence on the Via Tiburtina. On the other hand, the Calendar omits five given in the Index (Nos. 1, 10, 12, 13, 14). If to those given in the Index (in one or other of the manuscripts), namely, seventeen, we add the three in the Calendar which are omitted in the Index, and also two more omitted in both documents (S. Peter's, and S. Valentine on the Via Flaminia), we have a list of twenty-two, which includes all the chief cemeteries.[2]

De Rossi and other scholars account for the omission of some half-dozen important cemeteries from the Index by a mutilation of the manuscript.

Rampolla, who had more material to work on than De Rossi, believes the manuscript to be complete.

If, then, the manuscripts are complete, why are at least

---

[1] The two exceptions are the (1) *Coem. ad duas lauros ad SS. Petrum et Marcellinum Via Labicana* (No. 6), referred to in the Calendar in *V. id Sep. Gorgoni in Via Labicana*, and (2) *Coem. Calepodii ad S. Calixtum Via Aurelia* (No. 16), referred to in the Calendar in *Prid. id. Oct. Calisti in Via Aurelia*.

[2] For a full discussion see *infra*, Appendix IV.

half a dozen important centres of cemeteries omitted ?[1]   It is a fact, though it may be unconnected with the omissions in the Index, that at nearly all these places omitted, building operations were being carried on, as we learn from the *Liber Pontificalis*: that is (1) on the Via Flaminia, in the cemetery sometimes called S. Valentine, where that martyr lay, Pope Julius (337–352) was actually engaged, at the time of the compilation of the Index, in raising the basilica to S. Valentine ; (2) on the Via Nomentana Constantine was raising a basilica over the tomb of S. Agnes, and also (3) on the Via Tiburtina over the tomb of S. Laurence.   Also at the shrines of (4) S. Peter, Via Cornelia, and of (5) S. Paul on the Via Ostiensis, Constantine was building great basilicas. Both these shrines are omitted in the Indexes, though the cemetery of Felix and Adauctus on the Via Ostiensis, near S. Paul's, is mentioned.

The building operations probably rendered these particular catacombs inaccessible. What havoc and ruin was wrought in them can easily be imagined, and several passages in the *Liber Pontificalis* and elsewhere bear witness to it. We read how Damasus (366–384)[2] found the remains of the martyrs—scattered, lost, submerged in water —and buried them.   Perhaps, then, these five cemeteries were omitted as not being in actual use?   They all appear in the Philocalian Calendar, except S. Valentine's and S. Peter's.

Possibly, too, some of those omitted were still private property, and others small or unimportant, and therefore not entered on the Index. The precise history of each of these cemeteries, to be elucidated by excavations not yet undertaken, remains an interesting and important question to investigate.

---

[1] Neither in the fourth century nor in the present day can the "number" of cemeteries be very precisely defined.   In the days of the Itineraries, various portions of what we now consider one cemetery were *each* called "a cemetery." For example, the cemetery now known as S. Callixtus contained, according to the Index, S. Callixtus (proper) near the shrine of Sixtus II., and the cemetery of S. Basileus at the shrine of Pope Mark.   The famous cemeteries are usually agglomerations of various burial centres.

[2] *Infra*, p. 279; *Damasi epig.* 4, ed. Ihm ; *Gesta Liberii*, in *P.L.* viii., 1392 ; *Vita Damasi*, in *L.P.*

It is probable that all the cemeteries were private property till the third century, and some of them later. They are still called, in these fourth-century documents, by the ancient names—those of their owners [1]—or, sometimes, are indicated by the name of the locality. Thus we have the cemeteries of Priscilla (3), Apronianus (17), Praetextatus (7), Domitilla (10), Commodilla (13), the Jordani (4) and Thraso (5), or else the "Cemetery at the sign of the Seven Doves" (*ad septem Columbas*) (1), "At the Bear in the Cap" (*ad Ursum Pileatum*) (15), "Between the two Laurels" (*inter duas Lauros*) (6). To these indications is often added the name of the principal shrine in the cemetery—as the Cemetery belonging to Praetextatus at the shrine of S. Januarius (7). In later days the cemeteries were known by the names of the martyrs themselves—as the cemetery of S. Sebastian (i.e. *ad Catacumbas*) (8).

The Papyri of Monza.—We pass on from these purely secular documents to the study of the famous relics preserved in the Cathedral of Monza, a town about eight miles from Milan. The cathedral is associated with the Lombard kings, whose iron crown is preserved there; and especially with Queen Theodelinda, who founded it in 590, and to whom Pope Gregory the Great (590–604) wrote several letters,[2] accompanied, it seems, by relics which still form the nucleus of the cathedral treasure. The chief of these consists of forty-four vessels, about eight centimetres in height: twenty-eight are of glass, and sixteen of pewter. They once contained oil from the lamps burning before the shrines of the martyrs in Rome, and remains of it can still be detected in some of them.

---

[1] Cf. the names of the *tituli*, *supra*, p. 12.

[2] See *Monumenta Germaniae Historica Epistolarum tomus*, ii. 431, for a charming letter of Gregory, congratulating Theodelinda on the birth of her son, and the fact that he will be a Catholic : he tells her he himself has gout, and sends her several presents—a cross containing a small relic of the wood of the true Cross, a copy "of the holy Gospel," and rings set with jacinths and pearls for the lady's daughters. From "Pauli Historia Langobardorum," in *Mon. Germ. Hist. Script. Rer. Langob.*, p. 117, we learn that Gregory wrote four books on the lives of the Saints, and sent them to Theodelinda; and further, of all the good the Queen did for the Catholic Church (p. 118) and of a letter of thanks (p. 119) from Gregory. Some of the letters are translated in Wace and Schaff, *Post-Nicene Fathers*, 1900. Cf. *supra*, p. 30.

All have a string round them for fastening a label. Many of these labels have been lost: a few were found detached by Marini,[1] and some, though damaged, are still attached to the bottles. In all, nine labels (*pittacia ampullarum*) are still in existence.

Further, a list (*notula, index oleorum*)[2] has been made on a diptych of the names inscribed on the labels. The text of this Index is very close to that of the labels, with a few additions and corrections; it contains some names which, obviously, were once found on labels now lost.

Both the labels and the Index are in Lombard characters, and most scholars believe the two are contemporary.[3]

The Tradition of the Treasure—Gregory and Theodelinda.—According to the tradition, a certain Abbot John, in the time of Pope Gregory, collected, according to a common practice of the time, small measures of the holy oils burning before the shrines of the martyrs, as a present from that pope to Theodelinda, Queen of the Lombards. The fact that there was an authentic correspondence and interchange of gifts between Gregory and Theodelinda, and that she founded the Cathedral of Monza (in 590) appears to support the tradition.

The Pilgrimage of Abbot John.—John may have been an inhabitant of Rome, or he may have been sent from Lombardy by the Queen. It is just possible he bought his oils at what would now be called a "depôt for objects of piety." It seems more likely, however, that, as a pious pilgrim, he performed himself the somewhat arduous journey from shrine to shrine: and that he would do it according to the route traced out for us in various Itineraries. At whatever road he *began*, or whether he went round Rome clockwise, or counter clockwise, the *order* of his visits can be indicated by the route:

Viae Cornelia, Salaria Vetus, Salaria Nova, Nomentana, Tiburtina, Appia, Ardeatina, Ostiensis, Aurelia.

---

[1] Gaetano Marini, *I papiri diplomatici raccolti ed illustrati*, p. 208 : Rome, 1805.

[2] For text of the Index and of some of the labels see *infra*, pp. 105–8.

[3] But see *infra*, p. 108.

This list can be read forwards (for clockwise direction) or backwards (for counter clockwise direction).

Text of Index and Labels.—As he walked from road to road, John would fill each bottle with various oils, and tie on a label containing the names of the saints. We might expect, then, that a group of names on a label would indicate that these saints lay all together on the same road. Excavations have enabled us to identify all the shrines mentioned in the Index and the labels (except the *Sedes ubi prius sedit Petrus* of Label VII.), and this conjecture is proved true for Labels I., II., III., IV., V., VIII., IX.,[1] *i.e.* all the shrines mentioned on each single label, are in the same road. If, however, there were a great number of saints on one road, naturally more labels than one were necessary. For example, the seventeen saints of the Via Appia are divided between Labels IV. and VIII. The sixteen saints of the Via Salaria Nova are divided between Labels II., part of VI., and VII. The remaining part of VI., and the Label V. contain saints of the Via Salaria Vetus. It may be noted that the Salaria Vetus and Salaria Nova were adjacent roads.

From this it is clear (1) that any given label does not *necessarily* contain *all* the names of shrines on any given road; (2) the names on any single label do not *always necessarily* belong to shrines on the same road.

The following text of the Index, with the spelling as given by Sepulcri, and with the additions of the road, and of the number of the corresponding label, will show the relation of Index and labels. It will be seen that some labels are missing; but there could never have been *many* more than twelve. The few lacunae in the existing labels can easily be supplied from the Index.[2]

It may be noted that no shrines are mentioned in the Index, nor found on the labels, for the Viae Portuensis, Latina,

---

[1] *Infra*, pp. 105–8.

[2] The arabic numerals indicate the correct *topographical* order of the labels. For the actual text, with its curious misspellings, and for photographs of the diptych and *pittacia*, see Sepulcri, *I papiri della Basilica di Monza* . . . (*op. cit.* in Bibliography—ITINERARIES : PAPYRI OF MONZA).

Labicana, Flaminia.[1] Perhaps bottles and labels were lost before the list was made.

INDEX OLEORUM

Roads		Labels (*pittacia*)
1. Via Cornelia .	Sci Petri Apostholi	Label lost
11. Via Ostiensis .	Sci Pauli Apostholi	Label lost
12. Via Aurelia . .	Sci Pancrati Sci Arthemi Sce Sofiae cum tres filias suas (*sic*) Sce Paulinae Sce Lucinae Sci Processi Sci Martiniani	Label I.
5. Via Salaria Nova	Sci Grisanti Sce Dariae Sci Mauri Sci Jason et alii Sci multa milia Sci Saturnini Sce . . . pinionis	Label II.
7. Via Tiburtina .	Sci Systi Sci Laurenti Sci Yppoliti	Label lost
Within Rome on the Coelian Hill	Scorum Johannis et Pauli	Label III.
6. Via Nomentana	Sce Agnetis et aliarum multarum martyrum Sci Y . . . ion	Label lost
9. Via Appia . .	Sce Sotheris Sce Sapientiae Sce Spei Sce Fides Sce Caritas Sce Ceciliae Sci Tarsicii Sci Cornilii et multa milia Scorum	Label IV.

[1] The cemetery on this road is also omitted in the *Index Coemiteriorum.* See *supra,* p. 98.

INDEX OLEORUM—continued

Roads		Labels (*pittacia*)
2. Via Salaria Vetus	Sci Johannis Sci Liberalis [Sce Lucine] Scs Blastro et multorum Scorum . . . alii Sci id est CCLXII. in unum locum et alii CXXII. . . . XLV. quos omnes Justinus prb collega Sci Laurenti martyris sepelivit	Label V.
3. Via Salaria Nova	Sce Felicitatis cum septem filios suos (*sic*) Sci Bonifati	Label VI.
Via Salaria Vetus	Sci Hermitis Sci Proti Sci Jacynti Sci Maximiliani Scs Crispus Scs Herculanus Scs Bauso Sca Basilla	
Not certainly known . . .	Oleo de Side (*sic*) ubi prius sedit Scs Petrus	Label VII.
4. Via Salaria Nova	Sci Vitalis Sci Alexandri Scs Martialis Scs Marcellus Sci Silvestri Sci Felicis Sci Filippi et aliorum multorum sanctorum	
8. Via Appia . .	Sci Sevastiani Sci Eutycii Sci Quirini Sci Valeriani Sci Tiburtii Sci Maximi Sci Orbani Sci Januarii	Label VIII.

INDEX OLEORUM—continued

Roads		Labels (*pittacia*)
10. Via Ardeatina	Sce Petronillae Sci Petri Apostoli Sci Nerei Sci Damasi Sci Marcelliani Sci Acillei Sci Marci	Label IX.
	Quae olea sca temporibus Domni Gregorii Papae adduxit Johannis indignus et peccator Domnae Theodolindae Reginae de Roma.[1]	

TEXT OF SOME OF THE LABELS

Arranged Topographically

Via Nomentana

Lost

Via Salaria Nova

4.
| Sedes ubi prius sedit Petrus et oleo[2]
[Scs Vitalis scs Al]³exander scs Martialis scs Marcellus
[. . .]⁴ sci Silvestri sci Felici sci Filippi et aliorum
multorum Scorum. | VII. |

5.
| Sci Grisantis [scsque Darias scs Maurus][5]
Sci Jason et ali[i sancti multa milia]
Sci Saturnini [et scs aupinio (?)] | II. |

[1] " The holy oils which in the time of our Lord Pope Gregory, the unworthy sinner John brought from Rome to the Lady Queen Theodelinda."

[2] Position not determined : the other shrines are on the road indicated. Note the order of this label, VII. (No. 4), and the following, II. (5) is *interchangeable*, since both contain names of shrines on the *Via Salaria Nova* and no others—except for the doubtful *Sedes Petri*.

[3] Words in brackets are supplied from the Index.

[4] Illegible name omitted in the Index.

[5] Words in brackets in this label were legible in the time of Marini. See *supra*, p. 103, note 1.

VIA SALARIA NOVA AND VETUS

3.	$\overline{Sca}$ Felici[tas cum septem filios suos] Scs Bonifatius Scs Hermis Scs Protus Scs [Jacynthus Scs M]aximilianus Scs Crispus Scs Herculanus [Scs Bauso $\overline{Sca}$ Ba]silla	VI.

VIA SALARIA VETUS

2.	$\overline{Scs}$ Systus $\overline{Scs}$ Liberalis Scs . . . Scs Blastro et multa milia s[corum] et alii CXXII. et alii $\overline{Sci}$ XL.	V.

A glance at the indications of the order of the roads in the text quoted above, will show that the *Index oleorum* is not written in topographical order. The writer probably took each bottle as it came to hand, and copied the label; so that the *groups* in the Index are correct if the labels are so. It is obvious the topographical order of the *labels* should be—V., VI., VII., II. (or II., VII.), IV., IX., I., —or the reverse way.[1] In conclusion, then, the merely topographical value of the *Index oleorum* taken *by itself* is little; the labels, however, arranged in proper order, give some valuable indications of the position of shrines in many cases.

Sepulcri's Theory as to the Origin of the *Papyri*.— The tradition of the origin of the papyri of Monza is accepted by most scholars. It is in harmony with the known historic facts concerning the relations of Gregory and Theodelinda, and with all other evidence concerning the customs of pilgrims and collectors of relics.[2] Sepulcri,[3] however, notes that there is no evidence beyond the tradition, that it was Gregory who sent these treasures to Theodelinda; and he thinks that this donation was ascribed to the pope through the tendency to concentrate round one famous name deeds performed in reality by many different

---

[1] *Supra*, p. 103.

[2] See *supra*, pp. 16–47. Schneider in his article on the authors of the Itineraries (*op. cit.* p. 94, note) accepts this tradition, as is evident from an incidental reference to the *papyri* on p. 90. So also does Bonavenia (see *infra*, p. 111, note 2).

[3] *Op. cit.* p. 104.

individuals. It is so that Diocletian has become responsible for many persecutions of which he was innocent, and Anulinus, for every cruel sentence executed on the martyrs during several centuries. Sepulcri asserts that the *pittacia* are inscribed by different hands, and is inclined to date them at the end of the seventh century; basing his reasons on a minute study of the handwriting and of the extremely bad Latin. He notes certain mistakes in the topography which do not appear in the Itineraries contemporary with Pope Gregory, and *do* appear in the *Itinerarium Einsiedlense*[1] of the eighth century. He regards the Index as of slightly later date than the labels. Moreover, he states that the *Sce Sapientiae*, *Spei, Fides* (sic), *Charitas* (sic) of the Papyri, do not appear in the Martyrologies till the ninth century.

Taking this last statement first, however, we note, that in the catacomb of S. Callixtus, not far from the crypt of S. Cecilia, in exactly the place which the label indicates, has been found a fragmentary inscription of the fourth century, on a great marble slab, with the names PISTIS (= FIDES) SPES:[2] a fact which entirely invalidates this particular argument of Sepulcri. None of the other reasons he adduces in disproof of the ancient tradition appears quite convincing. The topographical errors are very slight, and mankind is liable to such errors in any century. The bad Latin, which is, moreover, characteristic of many sixth-century documents, amounts to little more than extraordinary Lombard misspellings of a string of proper names. Perhaps John was a Lombard. If, too, the Abbot was writing his labels *en route*, this would perhaps account for peculiarities in the calligraphy. One clings rather fondly to this old and picturesque tradition, till the severe light of higher criticism has really shown there is nothing in it.

History of the Treasure.—The history of the treasure is not without interest. The *Ampullae* and the *Index* were originally kept, with other relics, in a wooden coffer. In a general catalogue of the cathedral treasure made in 1042, there is a brief note of them: the number of the vessels is given as forty-two, and before this entry is an imperfect tran-

---

[1] *Infra*, p. 119.   [2] Marucchi, *Le Catacombe Romane*, p. 170.

scription of the *Index oleorum*. This inventory was made on the occasion of the transference of the *ampullae* to a marble urn, placed behind the high altar. The *ampullae* were exposed to the veneration of the public in the thirteenth century, and put back again. In 1576 they were again exposed, and finally placed under the altar in the side chapel of S. Maria, and a fresh inventory was made. In 1606 they were enclosed in crystal cases, and placed in two tabernacles by the pillars of the high altar.

The vicissitudes of the *Index* are not so well known. It was discovered in the local library Settaliano by Mabillon in 1685; and there studied also by Muratori,[1] Frisi, Gori, Ruinart, Marini, and others. It finally reached the library of the Conte di Firmiano, and was restored to the basilica in 1782. In 1881 *Ampullae* and *Index* were placed together in the Cathedral Treasury.

The Topographical Value of Labels in Test Case of the *Sedes* of S. Peter.—A test case for the topographical value of the labels may be examined, which will also give an example of the method of using the documents.

The only shrine about whose position there is any doubt is the *Sedes ubi prius sedit Petrus*, quoted on Label VII.[2] Of other shrines on that label, *Vitalis* and *Alexander* and *Martialis* are in the Cemetery of the Jordani, and *Marcellus*, etc., in Priscilla; both cemeteries being on the Via Salaria Nova. Hence, the *Sedes* would belong either to the nearest group on its own label, *i.e.* Cemetery of the Jordani on the Via Salaria Nova; *or* to the label which had last been filled up, but was too small to contain all the names. If the labels are taken in the natural topographical order, VII., II., VI., V., the label in question (VII.) would come next to the lost label of the Via Nomentana, so that the *Sedes* might have properly belonged to that group. If, however, the labels were taken in an equally natural order, *i.e.* II., VII., VI., V., then the Sedes *might* possibly belong to the group *Grisantis*, *Darias*, etc., in Label II.; *i.e.* shrines in the Cemetery of Thraso on the Via Salaria Nova.

[1] *Anecdota Latina*, ii. 191 : Milan, 1697.
[2] For list of labels see *supra*, p. 107.

It makes no difference to this question whether the pilgrim was moving clockwise or counter-clockwise.

If then we grant, as seems reasonable, that the pilgrim was making his journey in a natural manner, and if we expect that he is employing his usual methods of label-writing in the case of the *Sedes*, we have, as we have seen, three alternative places where the *Sedes* might be: *i.e.* either (1) on the Via Nomentana; or else on the Via Salaria Nova in one of its two cemeteries—*i.e.* either in the (2) Cemetery of Thraso or (3) the Cemetery of the Jordani.

There has been much discussion as to the precise place "where Peter first sat."[1] An old and strong tradition points to the neighbourhood of S. Agnes in the Via Nomentana, and Bonavenia thinks the label supports the tradition. Marucchi believes that the words *sedes ubi Petrus* . . . have been displaced, and should come on Label VII., after *Martialis*, and belong to the Marcellus-Silvester group of Priscilla. This seems a somewhat arbitrary supposition, and, if correct, would deprive the labels of the sole topographical value they possess—that of correct grouping.

Much other evidence has been brought to bear on the question of the locality of the *Sedes*, but the testimony of the Papyrus of Monza does not contribute anything final to the solution.[2]

---

[1] *i.e.* the place where he exercised his episcopal functions in the official chair —*Sedes* or *Cathedra*. See Philocalian Calendar, *Depositio Martyrum*, where February 22nd is marked as the feast day (cf. *supra*, p. 52).

[2] For a full discussion of the whole question see Bonavenia, *La Silloge di Verdun*, 1903, and a series of articles (mainly by Marucchi) in the *Nuovo Bullettino di archeologia cristiana* from 1900 onwards; and in the *Römische Quartalschrift*, 1907. The discovery, in 1900, of the ancient Baptistery of S. Priscilla affords, perhaps, stronger support to Marucchi's opinion than the Papyrus of Monza (see Marucchi, *Le Catacombe Romane*, and *Nuovo Bullettino* and *Römische Quartalschrift* quoted above).

CHAPTER VIII

THE ITINERARIES (*continued*)

De Locis Sanctorum Martyrum of the Würzburg Codex (sixth or seventh century)—Two Salzburg-Vienna Codices : (1) *Notitia Ecclesiarum urbis Romae* (or *Itinerarium Salisburgense*) (seventh century, depending on document of fourth) ; (2) *Epitome de Libro de Locis Sanctis Martyrum* (sixth or seventh century)—*Notitia Portarum viarum ecclesiarum circa urbem Romam* (*Itinerarium Malmesburiense*) (649–683)—*Itinerarium Einsiedlense* (eighth century)—*Ordo Romanus* of Benedict and *Mirabilia urbis Romae* (twelfth century)—The Itineraries and the identification of the monuments.

It is a great penance that a layman lay aside his weapons, and travel far barefoot, and nowhere pass a second night, and fast and watch much and pray fervently by day and by night, and willingly undergo fatigue, and be so squalid that iron come not on hair or on nail.

Edgar, King of England, Ancient Laws (ed. Thorpe).

THE documents to be described in this chapter are strictly Itineraries.

De Locis Sanctorum Martyrum of the Würzburg Codex.—The *De Locis Sanctorum Martyrum quae sunt foris civitatis Romae* was found by Eckhart in a Codex of the ninth or tenth century, appended to a manuscript of the *Martyrology of Bede* at Würzburg ; and published by him in 1729 in his *Commentarii de rebus Franciae Orientalis* (i. pp. 831–833). It is almost the same as the *De Locis Sanctis Martyrum* of the Salzburg Codex, and is the basis of that document.

Two Salzburg-Vienna Codices : (1) Notitia Ecclesiarum urbis Romae (Itinerarium Salisburgense) ; (2) De Locis Sanctis Martyrum.—At Salzburg in 1777 was found and printed a manuscript of the works of Alcuin, at the end of which were two topographies of Rome.[1] The first, a manuscript of

---

[1] The manuscripts of the two topographies are now in Vienna. De Rossi saw them there, and detected the various interpolations, especially numerous in ye second document (*De locis sanctis*) : see *Roma Sotterranea*, i. 136.

the tenth century, was named *Notitia Ecclesiarum Urbis Romae* (Notice of the Churches of the City of Rome), somewhat incorrectly, since it deals almost entirely with the cemeteries outside the wall; it is usually called now the *Itinerarium Salisburgense*. The second of the documents, of the ninth or tenth century, preserved in the Salzburg manuscript, is known as *De Locis sanctis martyrum quae sunt fores civitatem Romae* (Of the holy places of the martyrs without the city of Rome), a title not entirely correct either, since many shrines mentioned in it are within the city. The title in the manuscript is *De Libro de locis . . . (From the book* concerning the holy places . . .) and indicates that the document is an epitome of some other volume. It is indeed based on, and almost exactly similar to the Würzburg manuscript discovered by Eckhart,[1] with additional notes from other sources. The particular topographical arrangement, described below, indicates, too, an epitome, rather than an original document. Some German pilgrim must have carried home with him the original versions of these manuscripts.

The dates of the documents can be determined pretty exactly.

1. Notitia Ecclesiarum (Itin. Salisburgense).—The *Notitia Ecclesiarum (Itinerarium Salisburgense)* is earlier than 649, since it ignores the translation of the bodies of Primus and Felicianus from their shrines on the Via Nomentana to the Church of S. Stephen, on the Coelian Hill, by Theodore (642–649).[2] It is earlier also than 642, since there is no mention of Anastasia, who was martyred in Persia in 627, and whose body was brought to Rome by Theodore in 642. Neither are the repairs of the catacomb of S. Valentine on the Via Flaminia, by Theodore, mentioned. It is, however, later than Honorius (625–638), since that pope is referred to three times, as embellishing the cemeteries of S. Valentine on the Via Flaminia, S. Agnes on the Via Nomentana and S. Pancras on the Via Aurelia.

---

[1] *Supra*, p. 112. Marini confused together the manuscripts from Würzburg, Salzburg and Einsiedeln (see *infra*, p. 119).

[2] For this and the following statements see Duchesne, *Liber Pontificalis*, under the name of each pope.

8

A peculiar feature of this Itinerary is, that from the notices of the papal tombs can be constructed a complete list (with two omissions) of the popes from Silvester (314–335) to Celestinus (422–432). Why does the papal list suddenly cease here? Dufourcq[1] conjectures that the original Itinerary was written under Sixtus III. (432–440), the successor of Celestinus; and that it, in turn, depends on the early Roman Calendar of 312,[2] contemporary with the reorganization of the Church under Silvester, which is also the source of the *Depositio Episcoporum* and *Depositio Martyrum* in the *Philocalian Calendar*.

At the latest, then, this document is of the early seventh century: whilst parts of it may very possibly be of the fifth, and depend on documents of the beginning of the fourth. If this is the case, we know from it the precise name, place of burial and date of anniversary of the martyrs something like ten years after the last persecution, a fact which makes this Itinerary of the highest importance. Dufourcq remarks that the Itineraries of the seventh century differ little in information from this document, and prove the continuity of the tradition.

This *Itinerarium Salisburgense* is a true Itinerary of the highest value, from which we can exactly follow the pilgrim in the route he took. After visiting the shrine of SS. John and Paul, on the Coelian Hill, within the city, he starts on his circular tour outside the city from the Via Flaminia, in the north, proceeding clockwise. The points of the compass are clearly indicated, as well as the positions of the shrines, on the right or left hand side of the road. The nature of each shrine is also recorded—whether above (*sursum*) or below (*deorsum*) ground; whether a sepulchral chamber (*cubiculum*), which may be above or below ground, or a church (*ecclesia*), which is always above ground, or an underground chamber (*antrum, spelunca, sub terra*).[3]

[1] See Dufourcq, *Études sur les* Gesta Martyrum *romains*, p. 21, for a full discussion of this important point.

[2] *Infra*, p. 224.

[3] Cf. Schneider, "I termini dell' architettura cimiteriale . . . negli Itinerari dei pellegrini," in *Nuovo Bull.* 1911, p. 153. Cf. *ibid.* 1909, p. 79; 1910, p. 17. For certain difficulties as to the route see De Rossi, *R.S.* i. 138, 147.

The Itinerary begins:

Firstly in the city of Rome rest the bodies of the blessed martyrs John and Paul, in a great and very beautiful basilica. Then you enter (and go) through the city towards the North, till you come to the Porta Flaminia, where lies the martyr Saint Valentine, on the Via Flaminia, in a great basilica which Honorius repaired; and other martyrs in a northern direction (*plaga*) underground. Then you go towards the East, until you come to the church of John the martyr, on the Via Salaria, where rest Diogenes, the martyr, and in another cubicle Boniface, the martyr, and Fistus (*Sixtus*) under the earth. . . . Afterwards on the same road you come to Saint Pampulus (*Pamphilius*), martyr, to whom you descend under the earth by 24 steps. Then you come to Saint Felicitas on another road which is also called Salaria: there she rests in a church above ground, and Boniface pope and martyr in another place, and her son down below under the earth . . . afterwards ascending on this same road you come to the church of S. Silvester. . . .

So the pilgrim continues by the Viae Nomentana, Tiburtina, Appia, Ardeatina, Ostiensis, Aurelia, to end at the Via Vaticana and the " Basilica of Blessed Peter." [1]

2. *De Locis Sanctis Martyrum.*—The *De Locis Sanctis Martyrum* of the Salzburg Codex is perhaps a trifle later than the *Notitia Ecclesiarum (Itin. Salis.).* In this document are mentioned, as already on the Via Ostiensis, the relics of S. Anastasia. The Itinerary, then, is later than 642. It seems possible, however, that it was written not long after this date, for it speaks of the " magnificent adornments " (*mirifice ornata*) of the Catacomb of S. Valentine, on the Via Flaminia, which was, in fact, restored by Theodore ; and of " the marvellous beauty " of the Basilica of S. Agnes, on the Via Nomentana, which was restored by Honorius (625–638); also the Basilica of S. Laurence on the Via Tiburtina is described as "*new* and wonderfully beautiful"; S. Laurence was rebuilt by Pelagius II. (579–

---

[1] There follows an account of a pilgrimage to Milan.

590). So this Itinerary appears to be of the seventh century.[1]

In this the pilgrim starts at S. Peter's and journeys counter-clockwise. The Itinerary opens with the following passage :—

> First in the western part of the city by (*juxta*) the Via Cornelia at the first milestone (without the city) Peter rests in the body, and all the pontifical order except a few, rest in the same place in their own tombs. . . . Near this same road Saint Rufina and Saint Secunda . . . and many other saints lie.
>
> Thence, not far off on the left hand, near the Via Aurelia, S. Processus, S. Marcianus, S. Pancras, S. Paulinus, S. Arthemius, S. Felix, S. Callixtus, S. Calopus (?) with many others lie buried.
>
> Near the Via Portuensis, which is also in the western part of the city, S. Abdon, S. Sennen . . . and the place of sleep of S. Beatrix.
>
> But in the southern part of the city by the Via Ostiensis, Paul the Apostle lies, and Timothy bishop and martyr, of whom the Book of Silvester speaks, sleeps there. . . .

The Itinerary then continues by the Viae Ardeatina, Appia, Latina, Labicana, Tiburtina, Nomentana, Salaria. Then follow the words: "These are the churches within the city of Rome," with a list of twenty-six churches (of which five places are left blank), where liturgical stations were held.[2]

It will be seen that this Itinerary is less precise than the *Notitia Ecclesiarum*. Is it correct topographically? Examining the opening sentences we note:

(1) That the graves of Rufina and Secunda are, in fact, ten to thirteen miles distant from the city.

(2) The very next sentence runs: *Not far off on the left hand, near the Via Aurelia, S. Processus, etc.*

Now the saints mentioned in this group lie on *both* sides

---

[1] De Rossi and Dufourcq think it may even be contemporary with Pelagius, and that the Itinerary as we have it, is only a second edition of a late sixth-century document.

[2] *Supra*, p. 13.

of the Via Aurelia, at distances from one to three miles from the Aurelian Wall. The rest of the Itinerary will furnish similar examples. The explanation of the apparent inaccuracy is that the directions are given with respect to the *roads* and not to the shrines. Thus, "Not far off on the left hand" refers to the *Via Aurelia* (and not to the shrines); that road being near the Via Cornelia and on the left of a pilgrim walking out of the city down the *Via Cornelia*. Though such indications are not as precise as one might wish, there is yet not that topographical confusion in the Itinerary which appears to exist at the first glance, and the document offers a striking example of the need of careful interpretation.

Notitia Portarum Viarum . . . (Itin. Malmesburiense).— It is to an English historian that we owe the preservation of one of the most reliable of the Itineraries. The *Notitia Portarum Viarum Ecclesiarum circa urbem Roman*[1] (Notice of the gates, roads and churches round the city of Rome) has been inserted by William of Malmesbury in his *Gesta Regum Anglorum* (Deeds of the English Kings), of the twelfth century, in his account of the Crusade under Pope Urban II.: hence the document is often known as the *Itinerarium Malmesburiense*. The date of this Itinerary can be determined pretty exactly. We find that Primus and Felicianus have already been removed from their resting-place in the catacombs on the Via Nomentana to the church of S. Stephen on the Coelian Hill. This translation took place under Pope Theodore (642–649): the Itinerary is therefore later than that pope. On the other hand, the majority of the martyrs are still in the catacombs, whence their bodies were removed to various churches in Rome by Paul I. (757–767). The Itinerary is therefore earlier than Pope Paul. Since, however, there is no mention of Simplex, Faustinus and Beatrix, who were translated from the cemetery of Generosa on the Via Portuensis to S. Bibiana in 683 by Pope Leo II. (662–684), De Rossi thinks the Itinerary is probably earlier than 683. At all events, the

---

[1] Best edition, Duff Hardy, *Willelmi Malmesburiensis Gesta regum anglorum*, London, 1840.

document is of the seventh or early eighth century, and was very likely compiled between 649 and 683. It is curious to find the only version of this complete and reliable Itinerary in the works of the twelfth-century English monastic historian.

In this Itinerary the pilgrim is supposed to start in succession from each of the fourteen gates of Rome that open in the Aurelian Wall, whence the great roads, lined with cemeteries, stretch out over Italy. He starts at the Porta Cornelia (or Porta S. Petri) and passes on, in a clockwise direction to the Porta Flaminia, Porta Porticiana (*i.e.* Pincian Gate) . . . Nomentana, Tiburtina . . . and round to the Porta Aurelia.

A brief extract will suffice to show the character of the document :—

THE FOURTH GATE

The fourth gate on the Via Salaria which used to be called the Gate of S. Silvester. There, near the road, rest S. Hermes and S. Vasella (*Basilla*) and Protus and Jacinthus, Maxilianus (*Maximillianus*) Herculanus, Crispus ; and in another place rest the holy martyrs Pamphilius, Quirinus (descending) seventy steps below the earth. Then comes the basilica of S. Felicitas where she rests, and Silanus her son, and not far off the martyr Boniface. In the same place, in another church, are Chrysanthus and Darias and Saturninus and Maurus and Jason and their mother Hilaria and innumerable other saints. And in another basilica S. Alexander, Vitalis, Martialis, sons of S. Felicitas : and seven holy virgins, Saturnina, Hilarina, Dominanda, Rogantina, Serantina, Paulina, Donata. Then the basilica of S. Silvester, where he lies covered with a marble tomb : and the martyrs Celestinus, Philip and Felix : and there three hundred and sixty-five martyrs rest in one sepulchre : and near by, Paul and Crescentianus, Prisca, Semetrius (?), Praxed and Potentiana rest.

Bede tells a story which illustrates the manner in which, on one occasion, at least, an Itinerary of the Far East became known in the remotest parts of England.

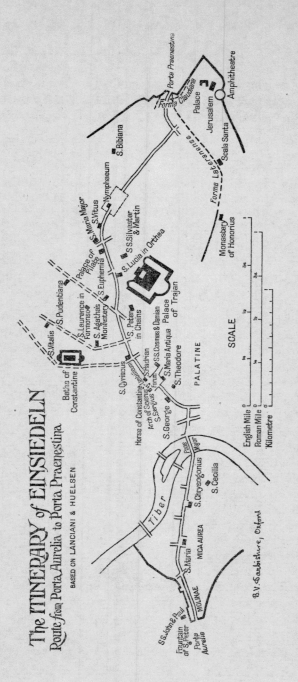

The ITINERARY of EINSIEDELN
Route from Porta Aurelia to Porta Praenestina

BASED ON LANCIANI & HUELSEN

SS.John & Paul
Fountain of S. Peter
Porta Aurelia
MOLINAE
S. Maria MICA AUREA
S. Chrysogonus
S. Cecilia
Tiber
Pons Major
PALATINE
S. Theodore
S. Maria Antiqua Palace of Trajan
SS. Cosmas & Damian
S. George
S. Peter in Chains
Arch of Severus S. Sergius Forum S. Hadrian
Horse of Constantine Umilicus
S. Cyriacus
S. Agatha's Monastery S. Euphemia
S. Vitalis S. Pudentiana
S. Laurence in Palace of Palace of Fuon Formosus Filate
Baths of Constantine
S. Lucia in Orthea
SS. Silvester & Martin
S. Maria Major SS. Vitus
Nymphaeum
S. Bibiana
Porta Praenestina
Forma Claudiana
Palace Jerusalem
Amphitheatre
Scala Santa
Forma Laterenensis
Monastery of Honorius

SCALE
English Mile
Roman Mile
Kilometre

B. V. Darbishire, Oxford

PLAN III

Based on plans by Lanciani and Huelsen

In his *Ecclesiastical History* [1] he has inserted a portion of an Itinerary of Jerusalem. He copied it, he says, from the work of a learned Irish abbot, Adamnan, "a good and wise man, and remarkably learned in Holy Scripture." He then tells how Adamnan obtained his information:

> Arculf, a French bishop, had gone to Jerusalem for the sake of the holy places. . . . Returning home by sea, a violent storm drove him upon the western coast of Britain (703). After many accidents he came to the aforesaid servant of Christ, Adamnan, . . . who committed to writing all that Arculf said he had seen remarkable in the holy places. . . . Adamnan presented this book to Alfrid (King of Northumbria), and through his bounty it came to be read by lesser persons. . . . I believe it will be acceptable to our readers if we collect some particulars from the same, and insert them in our history.

Itinerarium Einsiedlense.—Slightly different in character on account of its original method of sight-seeing, and from its inclusion of a number of secular monuments among the Christian buildings, is the *Itinerarium Einsiedlense* preserved in a manuscript of the ninth or tenth century in the library of the Monastery of Einsiedeln, in Switzerland. It was first published by Mabillon in 1685,[2] but all other versions have been superseded by that of De Rossi, and the new edition by Lanciani.[3]

Appended to it is a collection (*Sylloge*) of inscriptions copied from the monuments, which affords some assistance in determining the date. The latest of the inscriptions quoted in this Sylloge are of the time of Pelagius II. (578–590) and Honorius (625–640). Also in the Sylloge the epitaphs of Protus (No. 72), and Jacinthus (No. 73) (on the Via Salaria Vetus); of Nereus and Achilleus (No. 74) (on the Via Ardeatina); and of Felix and Adauctus (No. 76) (on the Via Ostiensis) are quoted as still in position in the catacombs.

These facts would indicate the seventh or the early part of the eighth century, prior to the translation of the bodies.

---

[1] *Eccles. Hist.* v. 15.   [2] *Vetera Analecta*, iv. 350.
[3] *L'Itinerario di Einsiedeln* . . . (*op. cit.* Bibliography—ITINERARIES).

But though the general topography of Rome, as described in this Itinerary, indicates a date prior to the alterations undertaken by Pope Leo IV. (847–855), yet several features of the city are noted which point to a period not earlier than the days of Charlemagne. The document would therefore appear to be of the later part of the eighth century. Comparing it with some of the earlier Itineraries, we note the city does not seem to have changed greatly.

It is one of the most precise and vivid of all the Itineraries. It takes the pilgrim a series of eleven walks in Rome in every direction : for example, Route 3 is from the Porta Nomentana (near the Baths of Diocletian) on the north-east, to the Forum in the west central district of Rome ; Route 4, from the Porta Flaminia in the extreme north-west to the Via Lateranensis, passing by the basilica of that name in the extreme south-east ; Route 9, from the Porta S. Petri, near S. Peter's, on the right bank of the Tiber, at the end of the Via Cornelia, right down to the south, and the tomb of S. Paul on the Via Ostiensis. On each excursion are indicated, in two parallel columns, the monuments passed on the right hand and on the left. Where the pilgrim passes under an arch (Arch of Severus), or arch of an aqueduct (the *Forma Virginis*—the pure or virgin water), or through a forum (*Forum Romanum*), or over a bridge (the *Pons Major*), the name of the monument is written between the two columns. Sometimes portions of different routes are the same.

Let us follow in detail the sixth route. By means of the text below and the plan (III), together with the detailed knowledge we have of the monuments mentioned, many of which, either in their original form or rebuilt, still stand, we can realize Rome as that eighth-century German pilgrim saw it, as easily as the modern traveller finds his way about with his Baedeker.

ITINERARIUM EINSIEDLENSE.

Route 6. From the PORTA AURELIA as far as the PORTA PRAENESTINA

On the left	*On the right*
The Fountain of S. Peter(?), where is his prison.	The Windmills (*Molinae*). *Mica Aurea.*
SS. John and Paul.	S. Maria, S. Chrysogonus, S. Cecilia.

OVER THE *Pons Major*

S. George and S. Sergius. The Palatine. S. Theodore.

UNDER THE ARCH (? OF SEVERUS)

The Capitol. The Umbilicum. S. Maria Antiqua.

THE HORSE OF CONSTANTINE

S. Hadrian. SS. Cosmas and Damian.

THE ROMAN FORUM

S. Cyriacus and the Baths of Constantine. The Palace of Trajan. There is (the Church of S. Peter) in Chains (*ad vincula*).

THE SUBURRA

The Monastery of S. Agatha.
S. Laurence *in Formonso*.
S. Vitalis (or Vitus).
S. Pudentiana and S. Euphemia.
The Palace of Pilate (?). S. Maria Maggiore. S. Vitus. A Fountain (*nymphaeum*).
S. Bibiana.
Claudian Aqueduct.

S. Lucia in Orpheus (? *Orthea*).
SS. Silvester and Martin.
The Palace near Jerusalem.
Jerusalem.
The Amphitheatre (sc. *Castrense*).
The Lateran Aqueduct.
The Monastery of Honorius.
The Porta Praenestina.

ON THE VIA PRAENESTINA WITHOUT THE WALL

Claudian Aqueduct. S. Helena. SS. Marcellus and Peter.

The pilgrim starts, as we see, from the Porta Aurelia (now S. Pancras) in the Aurelian Wall at a point a mile west of the Tiber. He goes in an easterly direction, down the steep Janiculum, past the windmills (*Molinae*), follows the road called *Mica Aurea* to cross the Tiber at the Pons Major (Aemilian Bridge). In the Trastevere district, through which he has just passed, he has seen on his right three famous churches, still standing: S. Maria (in Trastevere), S. Chrysogonus and S. Cecilia. On his left are the heights where now stands S. Pietro in Montorio, built there in 1472 owing to a false legend which identified this spot as the place of S. Peter's martyrdom. Neither "the prison" nor the "fountain" can be identified. There appears, from other authorities, to have been a church of the fellow-martyrs, John and Paul, on the hill, but it cannot be identified with certainty.

Crossing the bridge, and passing through the Argiletum, he sees, on the heights to the right, the mansions of the

Palatine Hill, with the little circular church of S. Theodore at its foot, and, on the left of the road, what is now San Giorgio in Velabro, with the Capitol rising high beyond. Passing under an arch, which we cannot certainly identify, he finds himself in the Forum, by the "Umbilicum," the marble-faced brick column that was "the sacred heart of Rome"; just on his road is the equestrian statue of Constantine. He only notes, on his left, the Church of S. Hadrian, which was converted into a place of Christian worship by Pope Honorius (625–638), having formerly been the Curia or Senate House. On the right, some way off, is S. Maria Antiqua, whose structure can still plainly be seen, and which is still adorned by wonderful Byzantine frescoes of the time of Justinian. Before its conversion into a church it had formed part of the library of the Imperial Palace. Quite near, on the right, is the Church of SS. Cosmas and Damian, converted into a church by Pope Felix (526–529) from the Temple of the Holy City, with its round church attached, built to the memory of Romulus, the infant son of the Emperor Maxentius.

On his leaving the Forum, the portion of the route as far as S. Lucia, in the district called Orpheus (?), is identical with Route 1 (from the Porta S. Petri to S. Lucia *in Orpheo*), and the same monuments are mentioned in both. Leaving, on the left, the Church of S. Cyriacus and the Baths of Constantine, near the Quirinal; and on the right, the Palace of Trajan (just north-east of the Colosseum), and the church dedicated by the Empress Eudoxia to the Chains of Peter (S. Pietro in Vincoli), standing high up on the Viminal, he passes through the Suburra to enter on a district thick with famous churches all existing to-day: S. Agatha *in Suburra*, S. Laurence (*in Formonso* or *in Panisperna*), S. Vitalis, S. Vitus, S. Bibiana and S. Pudentiana,—around which cluster traditions of Peter and Pudens and Priscilla,—S. Euphemia (in the Vico Patricio) and S. Maria Maggiore, still one of the most beautiful churches in Rome. Does the unexplained *Palace of Pilate* refer to some building standing where is now the *Scala Santa*, the flight of twenty-eight marble steps said to have been taken from the Palace of Pilate in Jerusalem, by the Empress Helena, who brought it to Rome in 326 and placed it near her former palace, recently given to the popes?[1] It would stand quite near the Monastery of S. Honorius, but on the pilgrim's right, rather than left, as stated. The Church of S. Praxed (San Prassede), with the ancient mosaics, is omitted from the Itinerary. The next church, S. Martin, on the right, was built by Pope Symmachus, and the oratory near was called perhaps after Silvester.[2] Thence the pilgrim passes under the Arch of Gallienus down the Via Labicana Antica to the "Palace near Jerusalem,"—the famous Sessorian palace whose secular basilica was converted under Constantine into a church (Jerusalem), now known as the Church of S. Croce in Gerusalemme. Near by is the Amphitheatre called Castrense, and then some more churches. Far away on the right is the Monastery, dedicated to S. Andrew, and founded by Honorius (625-640), on the spot where now stands the great Lateran hospital. As the pilgrim at length ends his journey, he passes out by the Porta Praenestina, with the beautiful arches of the Aqua Claudia (called also Marcia, Tepula, Julia) and the Aqua Lateranense (Celimontana) stretching out on his left and right.

Ordo Romanus **of Benedict and** *Mirabilia urbis Romae.*— The *Ordo Romanus* [3] of Benedict the Canon, of the twelfth century, giving an accurate account of the processions made by the pilgrims through Rome, describes a city of too late a date to be of very great assistance for the study of an earlier Rome. Since, however, for part of the way it follows one of the routes of the Einsiedeln Itinerary, it sometimes elucidates the latter. The *Mirabilia urbis Romae* of a date a trifle earlier, gives us some interesting details among many doubtful statements. It contains a list of monuments classified under: "the walls of the city," "the names of the gates," "the arches," etc.

Under "hills" and "baths" are the following entries:—

Of the Hills.—These are the hills within the city:

---

[1] Pilgrims still ascend these steps (now covered with wood) on their knees.
[2] The origin of these two (?) churches has not been determined with certainty.
[3] See Lanciani, *L'Itinerario di Einsiedeln* . . .

Janiculum.   Aventine which is also called the Quirinal.
The Coelian Hill.   The Capitol.   The Palatine.   The
Esquiline.   The Viminal.

Of the Baths.—The Baths of Antoninus.   The Baths
of Domitian. Of Maximius. Of Licinius. Of Diocletian.
Of Tiberius. Of Novatian. Of Olympias. Of Agrippina.
Of Alexander.

There are two brief notices of Christian monuments :

These are the places which are found mentioned in
the Passions of the Saints : Without the Appian Gate
where the Blessed Sixtus (II.) was beheaded, and where
the Lord appeared to Peter who said to Him : Lord,
whither goest Thou ? (*Domine, quo vadis ?*) . . .

The Aqua Salvia near S. Anastasius where the
blessed Paul was beheaded.   The garden of Lucina [1]
where is the Church of S. Paul and where he rests. . . .

There follows a list of cemeteries : [2]

INDEX COEMITERIORUM IN THE MIRABILIA URBIS ROMAE

Via Flaminia omitted.

Via Salaria Vetus . .	1. Coem. ad clivum cucumeris. I.
	2. Coem S. Hermetis et Domitillae.[3] I.
	[Coem. S. Marcelli Via Salaria Vetere, in *Ordo Benedicti Canonici*].
Via Salaria Nova . .	3. Coem. Priscillae ad pontem Salarium. I.
	4. Coem. Felicitatis.
	5. Coem. Thrasonis ad S. Saturninum. I.
Via Nomentana . . .	6. Coem. S. Agnetis.
	7. Coem. Fontis S. Petri.
Via Tiburtina. . . .	8. Coem. in agro Verano ad S. Laurentium.
Via Labicana. . . .	9. Coem. inter duas lauros ad S. Helenam. I.
Via Latina.	10. Coem. Gordiani foris portam Latinam.

---

[1] *i.e.* the private crypt of Lucina on the Via Ostiensis.

[2] I have added the names of the roads, and arranged the whole in the same topographical order as the Index of the Vatican Codex (*supra*, p. 98), that the two may be compared : they are in the main identical.   Of the nineteen cemeteries given in the *Mirabilia*, thirteen are in the Vatican Index, and are indicated by the letter I.   There are some mistakes in the remaining six, from mutilation of the names or confusion between two different cemeteries.   The MS. of the Index of the *Mirabilia* is in topographical order (except for two mistakes) and begins at the *Coem. Calepodii* of the Via Aurelia, proceeding in a counter-clockwise direction.

[3] "Domitillae" is a mistake.   It should, I think, be transposed with the "Jordanorum" of No. 14.

Via Appia	{	11. Coem. Calixti juxta Catacumbas. I.
		12. Coem. Praetextati inter portam Appiam. I.
Via Ardeatina . . .	{	13. Coem. Balbinae Via Ardeatina. I.
		14. Coem. Jordanorum [1] Nerei et Achillei Via Ardeatina. I.
Via Ostiensis . . .	{	15. Coem. S. Cyriaci Via Ostiense.
		[Coem. Innocentium ad S. Paulum, from *Ordo Benedicti Canonici*.]
Via Portuensis . . .	{	16. Coem. Ursi ad Portuensem (viam). I.
		17. Coem. S. Felicis Via Portuensi. I.
Via Aurelia	{	18. Coem. Calepodii ad S. Pancratium. I.
		19. Coem. S. Agathae ad Girulum.
		[Coem. Julii Via Aurelia, in *Ordo Benedicti Canonici*.]

There are further notices of Christian buildings scattered about the document.   For example :

In the Palace of Licinius is the temple of Honor and of Diana.   Where is now S. Maria Maggiore was the temple of Cybele.   Where now stands S. Peter *ad Vincula* (S. Peter in chains) was the temple of Venus.

The Itineraries and the Identification of the Monuments.—The passages quoted above have been taken at random from various parts of the Itineraries merely to show the general character of these documents.

To derive any topographical information of value from them, it is necessary to focus the attention on a definite area, combine the information obtainable from *all* the Itineraries with regard to it, and then study the actual monuments mentioned in them.

In this collation of document and monument, it is necessary to remember that the Itineraries are not always in accord, nor complete, nor quite accurate.   With regard to the monuments, there are in the catacombs, both crypts below, and also oratories above ground, that have either not been certainly identified, or perhaps wrongly identified. Moreover, no single one of the catacombs has been entirely excavated, and a vast number of monuments have perished. Yet the fact remains that the co-ordinated study of the Itineraries and monuments has enabled us to establish with certainty the place of burial—and hence the *existence*—of a

[1] " Jordanorum " is a mistake.

large number of martyrs and confessors of the first three centuries. In cases where shrines, such as S. Soteris, and S. Zeno, have not been identified, we sometimes know where to look for them, thanks to the united testimony of the various Itineraries. It was, indeed, in this way that the site of shrines, buried deep and without sign of existence, beneath field and garden, was first determined; and actual excavation has, again and again, justified the accuracy of the Itineraries, and the correct interpretations of De Rossi and his disciples.[1]

[1] To compare adequately the information derived from the Itineraries with the actual monuments as they have been revealed, and are daily being revealed, by excavation, would require volumes. As an example of method, a brief study has been made of the shrines on the Via Appia and the Via Ardeatina, *infra*, Chap. XXII.

CHAPTER IX

ACTS OF THE MARTYRS: CRITICISM, ANCIENT AND MODERN

The task of criticism.—Criticism in the sixteenth century (Baronius, Tille-mont).—The *Acta Sanctorum* and the *Analecta Bollandiana* of the Bollandists.—The *Acta Sincera* of Ruinart.—The Theory of Interpolation.—Authentic docu-ments and modern critics.—Modern methods of criticism.—Monuments and documents throwing light on the *Acta.*

Contenta nitore suo veritatis, pura simplicitas, eo pulchrior quo incultior recte sentientibus esse solet.[1]—Baronius, *Annales Eccles.* t. iii. p. 262 (1738).

Task of Criticism.—For the lives of the Roman martyrs of the first three centuries,[2] we have a mass of documents known as *Acta, Vitae, Passiones, Gesta,* which have been compiled in the course of many centuries, and differ widely in historical value.

The task of the critic is to discover the date, circumstances of composition, and sources of the documents; to classify them according to their degree of authenticity; and, in the case of the less trustworthy compositions, to sift the few grains of historical truth from the mass of legend and rhetoric in which they are embedded.

Criticism in the Sixteenth Century.—These problems of criticism are not peculiar to the twentieth century. While the Golden Legend (*Legenda aurea*) of the Dominican poet,

---

[1] " *Pure simplicity is content with the splendour of the truth which is hers, and the less she is adorned the more beautiful she appears to those who feel aright.*"

[2] All criticisms on the authenticity of the *Acta Sanctorum* refer to the lives of saints of *these centuries only.* For texts of *Passions,* etc., see Bibliography—ACTS OF MARTYRS, and APPENDIX VII. Nearly every Passion referred to is found in the *Acta Sanctorum* (*A.SS.*) of the Bollandists under the date mentioned: many are found in Ruinart, *Acta Sincera* (*A.S.*) and translations into French, and critical notes in Leclercq, *Les Martyrs* . . .

Jacobus de Voragine (1230–1298), reveals the absolute confidence reposed in these records in the Middle Ages, the critical spirit was already awake in the sixteenth century. Cardinal Baronius (1538–1607), friend of S. Philip Neri, and author of the *Ecclesiastical Annals* (1508–1607), regards the *Acta* with suspicion,[1] but though some of the documents were, as Baronius says, vitiated " by the craft of Satan, the foolishness of the faithful (*colentium*), and the depravity (*nugacitas*) of heretics," he uses them as material for his history.

Tillemont, too, in his *Mémoires pour servir à l'histoire ecclésiastique* has applied sound criticism to many of the Passions. His conclusions, if at times sceptical, appear only too just.[2] He writes:

> The death of the saints is the greatest and most certain fact in their history, while their earlier life is almost always obscure.

Again, he concludes his criticism of the *Acts of S. Caesarius* [Nov. 4] with the words:

> I think that the safest course is to leave him among the number of those whose sanctity we know, while we are ignorant of all the rest.

The fifteenth and sixteenth centuries saw various editions of the Lives of the Saints. Mombritius published in Milan, in 1475, his *Sanctuarium, sive vitae Sanctorum, collectae ex codicibus manuscriptis*[3] (Collected Lives of the Saints), Lipomann, in 1551, at Rome, his *Historia de Vitis Sanctorum* (History of the Lives of the Saints); and the Carthusian Surius, in 1562, at Lübeck, his work, *De probatis sanctorum historiis* (The Authentic Histories of the Saints). In spite of the attempts at criticism of the age, these writers are more preoccupied with the elegancies of their own style than the historical contents of the documents.

The *Acta Sanctorum* of the Bollandists (1643 . . .).—

---

[1] *Annales Ecclesiastici*, t. iii. p. 262.

[2] Tillemont, *Mémoires pour servir à l'histoire ecclésiastique*, i. 6, ii. 573.

[3] This has been re-edited in 1910 by the Benedictine Fathers. See Bibliography—ACTS OF MARTYRS.

It was the Jesuit, Hubert Rosweyde (1569–1629) of Antwerp, who first conceived the necessity for a collation of the texts, with a view to restoring the original readings; but it was left to another Jesuit, Bollandus of Antwerp (1596–1665), and his fellow-workers and successors, to carry out the idea in the sixty-four great volumes already published of the *Acta Sanctorum*. The work has been carried on in Belgium, in the face of many difficulties, from 1643 to the present day, and is still incomplete. The ideal of the Bollandists has not, perhaps, always been realized, owing to inadequacy of material, imperfection of method, and diversity of authors. It is unfortunate that the biographies are arranged according to the calendar, instead of in chronological order, grouped according to the respective localities of the saints.

The modern Bollandists are collecting material for future volumes in the *Analecta Bollandiana*, published quarterly since 1882 in Brussels, and in their study of the manuscripts are laying a sure foundation for some final edition of the Lives of the Saints. They have already published catalogues of the manuscripts in the libraries of Belgium, and of Paris and Chartres, examined their age, origin, form and contents, and have given us many new or revised texts of the Lives.

The value of their work has been justly estimated by Salomon Reinach:[1]

> The Bollandists, modest men of learning, are quietly accomplishing an immense labour . . . there reigns in the *Analecta* a spirit of tolerance, urbanity and liberal criticism calculated to astonish those who, for lack of information, place in the same category all the writers of the Society of Jesus.

The criticism of the earlier Bollandists seemed very advanced in their own day. In the first volume for April, Papebroch, the fellow-worker of Bollandus, cast doubt on the tradition that Elijah founded the Carmelite order;[2] whereupon the first fourteen volumes of the *Acta* were censured

---

[1] *Revue Archéologique*, 1895, p. 228; cf. Duchesne, in *Bulletin Critique*, April 1890.

[2] *Acta Sanctorum*, April 8 (*De Alberto patr. Hieros*).

by the Office of the Inquisition at Toledo in 1695, though only one of the volumes, the *Propylaeum Maii*, was put on the Index of forbidden books,[1] where it remained till 1900. Papebroch died broken-hearted, protesting to the last that he was a faithful son of the Church.

The *Acta Sincera* of Ruinart (1689).—In the period following, Ruinart, a Benedictine, attempted to sift from the volumes of the *Acta Sanctorum* those records relating to the first three centuries which he believed to be authentic. The result is the volume, *Acta Sincera*, containing about a hundred and twenty documents of various character. Even this modest number has been greatly reduced by modern criticism.

The Theory of Interpolation.—It is in the *Acta Sanctorum* of the Bollandists that we first find, vaguely indicated in various passages, the theory that the later legends reproduce some original authentic document which can be distinguished by the critic from the mass of fiction that has overlaid it. This is known as the Theory of Interpolation.[2] It is implicitly accepted by Ruinart.

A more sceptical estimate of the *Acta* is that of Cardinal Valerius, the friend of S. Carlo Borromeo, who was of opinion that the majority are mere rhetorical monastic exercises on a given martyr.

The Theory of Interpolation has found able exponents in modern times. Edmond Le Blant, in his learned study, *Les Actes des Martyrs: Supplément aux* Acta Sincera *de Ruinart,* has applied the theory in a detailed examination of a vast number of apocryphal legends, in which he hopes to discover traces of the original documents. The same principle inspires the critical methods of De Rossi, Allard, Heuser, Aubé and Neumann.

Authentic Documents and Modern Critics.—The number of documents now unanimously recognized as in various degrees authentic, at least in their main outlines, by Preuschen, Krüger, Leclercq, Delehaye, Van den Gheyn, and Harnack, is about forty. The Benedictine Dom Leclercq

---

[1] *Index librorum prohibitorum*, p. 301, Turin, 1891.
[2] See *infra*, p. 197.

has published a French translation of these *Acta*, with critical notes, in the first three volumes of his invaluable work *Les Martyrs,—Recueil de pièces authentiques*; he relegates to the appendix documents containing only a slight substratum of truth.

Delehaye, one of the Bollandists, shows a more sceptical spirit than Ruinart or Leclercq, and in his illuminating volume, *Les Légendes hagiographiques*, he reduces the hundred odd documents of the *Acta Sincera* of Ruinart to thirteen, and classes among "historical romances" several of Leclercq's "authentic" records.   Perhaps the divergence between these two modern critics is rather of words than ideas: an "authentic" document of inferior value contains only a small proportion of truth, while the historical romance may be based on the essential facts of the story.

It is a good omen in the cause of truth when we find a long roll of ecclesiastics and monks, from Baronius and Rosweyde in the past, to Leclercq and Delehaye in our own day, applying sound principles of historical criticism to these legends, with the purpose of restoring, in a few cases at least, the austere beauty of the original documents.   We may perhaps apply to all these writers, in some degree, the tribute paid to the greatest of ecclesiastical historians, Mgr. Duchesne, on his reception among the "Immortals" of the French Academy: "He combined a sceptical mind with a religious spirit."   We have here a definition of the ideal critic of hagiographical documents.

Modern Methods of Criticism.——We have indicated the nature of the problem of criticism, and the spirit in which past ages have dealt with it.   What material have we in the twentieth century towards a final solution?

The task is one of peculiar difficulty.   There are few good texts, no fixed principles of criticism, and seldom any history of the documents; while, with a few exceptions, the best records are compilations of the fifth and sixth centuries, that is to say, composed from two to five hundred years subsequent to the events.

We need not dwell here on the methods of criticism—philological and historical—universally employed in establishing the character of all texts, but confine ourselves to the methods peculiar to an investigation of hagiographical records. In dealing with these we need to study not only the external facts, but, as Tillemont pointed out in his preface to the *Mémoires*, to penetrate deeply into the spirit which inspires the genuine records of the martyrs, and so to learn to recognize the true from the false by a certain unerring instinct. There is something quite distinctive in the spirit which dominates those Passions known to be authentic, and these can be used as a touchstone for testing less trustworthy records.

The investigation of the causes of successive deformations of the originals is a natural continuation of this task.[1]

Again, no text can be finally established till all the manuscripts from remote libraries and monasteries are in our hands. We are sometimes put on the track of such documents by references in later writers. For example, Ado, Archbishop of Vienne (860–874), states that in compiling his Martyrology he used "a venerable and ancient" Calendar of Ravenna sent by the pope to some bishop of Aquileia.[2] Again, Pope Gregory I., in a famous letter of 598, states that he has in his possession "a single volume" concerning the deeds of the martyrs "which contains very little."[3] The Ravenna Calendar has not been found; but a search for the book referred to by Gregory resulted in the discovery of a Passionary of the Roman martyrs.[4] Research on these lines may bring to light other ancient documents.

This brings us to the question—What are the original sources of our Lives, and how far have the sources been faithfully embodied in later compilations?[5]

Documents and Monuments throwing Light on the Lives.—Again, the contents of the Lives can be checked by information derived from contemporary literature,—both from pagan writers, especially when they are dealing with

---

[1] See *infra*, Chap. XIV.

[2] See *infra*, p. 299, and cf. Dufourcq, *Étude sur les* Gesta Martyrum *romains*, p. 31.

[3] *Infra*, p. 201.

[4] See *infra*, Appendix V., p. 341, and cf. Dufourcq, *op. cit.* p. 78.

[5] See *infra*, Chaps. X.–XV.

methods of criminal procedure, local customs, or social conditions,[1] and also from patristic literature [2] and early liturgies. We find some curious similarities between the last class of literature and the Lives. Many documents—Calendars, Martyrologies and Itineraries—dating from the fourth to the eighth centuries, deal solely with the history of the martyrs, but tell us little more than the name of the saint, place of his shrine, and anniversary of his death.

The actual monuments in Rome—tombs, crypts, sculptures, frescoes, epitaphs—throw further light upon the question. Stones cannot lie, but how strangely has their story been interpreted!

In collating our various sources of information—Lives, Calendars, monuments—we are faced with the delicate task of determining their mutual relations and interdependence. Do the Lives depend on the Calendars, or *vice versa*? How many stories did the popular imagination weave, inspired by the frescoes of some venerated shrine? What pious romances in our *Acta* were based on the simple entry of a name and date in the Martyrology? How many names have crept into the Calendar of saints and martyrs from passages imperfectly understood in the Lives? [3]

Such are, roughly speaking, the main lines of investigation with which we shall deal, beginning with the question of the original sources of the documents.

[1] *Infra*, p. 197.
[2] Harnack, *Geschichte der altchristlichen Literatur bis Eusebius*, erster Theil, Bd. ii. p. 808 . . . ; cf. Bibliography—PATRISTIC.
[3] See *infra*, Chap. XIV.

CHAPTER X

THE ACTS OF THE MARTYRS: THE *ACTA PROCONSULARIA*

Acta Proconsularia and the *Notarii.*—The *Acta Publica.*—Christian copies of the *Acta Publica.*—Destruction of documents under Diocletian.—The formula of the *Acta Proconsularia* (identification of accused, charge, etc.). — The preparation for martyrdom.

Tamquam aurum in fornace probavit illos, et quasi holocausti hostiam accepit illos.
Commune plurimorum Martyrum (*Liber Sapientiae*).[1]

Acta Proconsularia* and the *Notarii.—Among the main sources for all subsequent Lives of the Martyrs, are the *Acta Proconsularia*, that is to say, the official records of the trials of the martyrs before the proconsuls in the provinces, or the praetors in Rome.

Shorthand notes (*notae*) were taken of the proceedings by clerks (*notarii, exceptores*), and then copied out to form part of the public acts (*acta publica*) of the judicial archives (*archivium proconsulis*). In several works of art we see the *notarii*[2] taking down their notes. Asterius, Bishop of Amasia, in Pontus (fourth century), in a sermon[3] in honour of S. Euphemia, martyred [Sept. 16] under Diocletian, describes one of a series of paintings on canvas which adorned her shrine:

> The judge is seated on a raised bench, looking at the maiden with an angry countenance. Around are the guards and many soldiers and clerks (*notarii*), holding their tablets and their styles. One of these, raising his

---

[1] " *He tried them as gold in the furnace, and received them as a burnt sacrifice.*"
[2] Cf. Le Blant, *Supplément aux* Acta Sincera *de Ruinart*, pp. 62, 65 ; *Les Persécuteurs et les martyrs*, p. 1, etc.
[3] *P.G.* t. 40, col. 335. See Ruinart, *Acta Sincera* ("*A.S.*").

hand from his wax-covered tablet, is looking fixedly at the maiden, as if to ask her to speak more distinctly, so that not having any difficulty in hearing, he may avoid all error in the transcription of her answers.

There are many references to these *notarii* in pagan and Christian literature.

In the Acts of Maximus [1] [May 14] we read:

> While Magnilianus the clerk was taking down the answers of the Christians, the Proconsul Gabinius said to him: "Have you taken down the names of all?" Magnilianus answered: "If your worship commands I will read my text." The Proconsul said: "Read it." Then Magnilianus said: "The names I have taken down are as follows: Maximus, Dadas, Quintilian."

In various Acts the conversions of *notarii* are recorded,— of Neon [2] and Eustratius, [3] and of Cassian [Dec. 3], the African clerk who, converted in court by the constancy of the prisoner, the soldier Marcellus [Oct. 30], flung down his tablets and perished, pierced in a hundred places by his own stylus. The story of S. Genesius of Arles [Aug. 25] is worth quoting:

> S. Genesius . . . studied with great application, and exercised with great success that useful art by which he was able at a single stroke to take down words on paper, and by the speed of his hand equal the rapidity of the discourse of an orator, and to render, word for word, with abridged notes, the pleadings of counsel, the depositions of witnesses, and the answers of the accused. . . . Now it happened one day, while he was performing his duties as clerk of the court before the judge at Arles, there was read out an impious and sacrilegious edict which the Emperors had published throughout all the Provinces. The ears of the pious clerk were wounded, and his hand refused to imprint them on the wax. He did more, he rose, he flung down his registers at the feet of the judge, and renounced for ever such an evil employment.

He then, "in accordance with the precept of the Gospel,"

---

[1] *Acta Sanctorum* of the Bollandists ("*A.SS.*"), May 14.
[2] *Acta S. Speusippi, A.SS.*, Jan. 17.
[3] Surius, *De probatis sanctorum historiis*, Dec. 12.

seeks to hide himself, fleeing from town to town. Then the story continues:

> Yet, as he thought that he had need to be fortified in the faith by baptism, for he had not yet been regenerated by water and the Holy Spirit, he sent his demand to the bishop by some faithful persons: but whether the bishop was meanwhile arrested himself, or that he, distrusting the youth of Genesius, would not risk conferring the sacrament, and put it off: the bishop only told him that his blood shed for Jesus Christ would take the place of the baptism he had so ardently desired to receive. And I think myself that it was not without a special dispensation of Providence that the bishop made difficulties. It was without doubt that heaven wished alone to consecrate him, and that Jesus Christ had prepared him a double baptism, that of water and blood which flowed from the side of the divine Saviour. . . .

He was finally captured and executed on the banks of the Rhone.

The *Acta Publica*.—The great collection of *Acta Publica*, stored, as we have seen, in the *Archivium Proconsulis*, were frequently consulted; both by the judge, on taking up his annual functions, for information with regard to cases passed on to him;[1] and also by historians, as they themselves bear witness.[2] The Byzantine writer, Lydus,[3] who died in 565, states that he was able to use the *Acta Publica* as far back as the reign of Valens, that is, for a period of two centuries.

Copies by Christians of *Acta Publica*.—The Christians regarded these records with positive veneration, and sometimes sought permission from the officials to make copies of them.[4] Sometimes, no doubt, they took down their own notes in court,[5] and from both these sources copies would

---

[1] Le Blant, *op. cit.* p. 68.

[2] Apuleius, *Floridorum libri quattuor*, i. 9.

[3] Lydus, *De Magistratibus Populorum Romanorum*, l. iii. c. 20.

[4] *Passio S. Pontii*, in Baluze, *Miscellanea*, t. i. p. 33.

[5] We read in the *Liber Pontificalis*, i. pp. 123, 147, 148, that there existed, from the time of Clement, official Christian *notarii* for this purpose. Duchesne (*ad loc.*) and Delehaye (in *Les Légendes hagiographiques*) point out the improbability of this statement. (See *supra*, p. 76.)

be multiplied. S. Cyprian,[1] in the third century, in a letter to his priests and deacons, writes :

Finally, note the days on which they (the martyrs) depart this life, that we may celebrate the memories of them among the memorials of the martyrs . . . and that there may be celebrated here by us oblations and sacrifices in commemoration of them.

In the *Acts of S. Felix* [Jan. 14] we read :

We carried away with us the remains of his blood, together with the *Gesta* (i.e. *Acta*), that we might enjoy his aid in this present life, and, in the future, under his patronage, attain life everlasting with the help of our Lord Jesus Christ who crowned his martyr with peace.

The Christians no doubt at times ran some risks in obtaining and circulating copies, and the government did not favour such proceedings. Sometimes its wrath fell upon the clerks. In the *Acts of S. Victor, the Moor* (Mar. 8) we read :

Then Anolinus (*sic*) the magistrate ordered all the clerks (*exceptores*) who were in the palace to be seized, that no one might conceal any documents or papers, if he possessed them. Then they all swore by the gods and by the safety of the Emperor, that no one concealed any document; and when they had all brought their papers, Anolinus had them burnt before him by the executioner; an action which greatly pleased the Emperor.

We may remark of this Anolinus (or Anulinus) that he is the typical bloodthirsty persecutor of the Christian imagination. He figures in the *Acta* at an impossible number of places, and during a period exceeding the span of human life. The concentration in one person of many persecutors satisfied the double mental need for historical simplification and for a spectacle of deep-dyed iniquity.

On other occasions the documents were seized in the hands of the Christians;[2] sometimes, as in the trial of

---

[1] *Cypriani epistolae*, xii. 2, ed. Hartel, t. iii. 502, in Series *Corpus Scriptorum Latinorum*.

[2] Prudentius, *Peristephanon*, i. 75–78 (*P.L.* 60, col. 767).

S. Vincent of Saragossa [Jan. 22], it was forbidden to report the proceedings. Though we are here using very doubtful authorities, it is probable that they depict a true condition of affairs.

Destruction of Documents under Diocletian.—How many such documents there were in the hands of the Christians it is impossible to say, and also what varying degrees of accuracy they may have possessed.

Modern historians lay stress on the universal destruction of documents under Diocletian, but again, we know little of the truth of the matter. Eusebius [1] relates that together with other property, Diocletian ordered the destruction of the Christian writings. In the authentic *Acts of S. Saturninus* [Feb. 11], who, with his forty-seven companions, was arrested, "while celebrating the mystery of the Eucharist," at Carthage in 304, we find they were martyred on the double charge of holding illegal meetings, and of refusing to give up the holy books to idolaters. Some of the books, given up by more timid Christians, were publicly burnt in the Forum.

Such incidents are frequently recorded, and, even when found in apocryphal Acts, indicate clearly the nature of the Diocletian persecution. In this same year, 304, the deacon Euplus [Aug. 12] was beheaded in Catana with a copy of the gospels hung round his neck ; and the three maidens, Agape, Irene and Chione [April 3], of Thessalonica, fled to the mountains with the sacred documents, and endured untold hardships till their arrest in the following year.

The Church, when the persecutions were over, dealt severely with those who had given up the sacred books (*traditores*). In S. Augustine [2] we read a detailed account of the trial, in 320, of a certain Silvanus, bishop of Cirta. He was accused by the deacon Nundinarius of this offence, committed when the bishop was only a subdeacon and serving under a certain bishop Paul, now dead. In the course of the evidence is read the official report (*Acta*) [3] of certain

---

[1] Eusebius, *Historia Ecclesiastica*, viii. 2 (*P.G.* 20, col. 744).
[2] Augustine, *Contra Cresconium*, iii. 29, 70 (*P.L.* 43, coll. 512 and 539).
[3] Text in Gebhardt, *Acta martyrum selecta* ; and elsewhere.

domiciliary visits made by the flamen Felix to seize church treasure in accordance with the Emperor's edict. These *Acta* are different, of course, from the official *Acta Proconsularia*. The passage may be quoted as throwing light on the method of procedure and, incidentally, on the functions of the different orders of the Church hierarchy; the incidents, moreover, are not without a touch of humour.

. . . When the officials came to the house where the Christians were accustomed to assemble, Felix, perpetual flamen and curator of the colony of Cirta, said to the bishop Paul: "Bring out the writings of the Christian law and anything else you have here, that you may obey the edict." Paul said: "The readers (*lectores*) have the writings, but what we have here we will give you." Felix said to the bishop: "Produce the readers or send for them." Paul said: "You know them all." Felix said: "We do not know them." Paul said: "They know them at the office of public records (*officium publicum*), that is the clerks (*exceptores*) Edusius and Junius know them." Felix said: "The question of the readers, on which the officials (*officium publicum*) will enlighten us, can wait: give us what you have yourself."

Here follows a list of names of church officials present,—with the exception of the readers, who were perhaps in hiding,—namely, the bishop Paul, four priests (*presbyteri*), three deacons, four subdeacons, among whom is the Silvanus in question, six sextons (*fossores*) "and other sextons."

Then Victor, the secretary of Felix, takes an inventory, not without interest, of church plate and clothing for the poor; and Felix appeals in turn to the subdeacons and sextons to bring out treasures, and reminds them that their words are taken down. Then, in the words of the *Acta*:

Afterwards in the library were found empty cupboards. There Silvanus brought out a vase (*capitulata*) and a silver lamp which he declared he had discovered behind a coffer; and they said to him: "If you had not found them, you would have been a dead man." Felix said: "Search diligently that nothing remains." Silvanus said: "Nothing remains, we have brought out everything."

There is a further search in the dining-room (*triclinium*), with little result, and then :

> Felix said: "Bring out the writings you have, that you may obey the imperial edict." Catulinus (the subdeacon) produced a very large document. Felix asked the subdeacons: "Why have you only given me one: bring out the writings that you have." The subdeacons answered: "We have no more, because we are subdeacons; but the readers have the documents." Felix said: "Point the readers out to us." Two of the subdeacons said: "We do not know where they are." Felix said: "If you don't know where they are, tell me their names." The subdeacons answered: "We are not traitors (*proditores*); here we are, have us killed." Felix said: "Take them into custody."

The *Acta* then continue to describe six more visits, producing some thirty documents.

Again, we find the testimony of the *Acta* invoked at the Council of Arles in 314[1] in a clause directed against *traditores*; and by Cyprian[2] and Eusebius[3] to prove public apostasies.

The Formula of the *Acta Proconsularia*.—The use of the *Acta Proconsularia* with which we are mainly concerned, is their embodiment, with various degrees of accuracy, in the Christian records of the martyrs. None of the original *Acta Proconsularia* have come down to us, but from a comparison of other pagan records of criminal procedure[4] with the authentic Christian documents which embody the *Acta*, we can restore the formula of the original *Acta*,[5] and use it as a test in criticizing documents of doubtful authenticity.

The official account of a trial opened with the name of the consuls (to date the year), the day of the month, the names of the judge, and of city and building where the trial took place,

---

[1] *Concil. Arel. anno* 304, c. xiii., in Labbé, *Concilia.*

[2] *Cypriani epistolae*, 67, 86, ed. Hartel.

[3] Eusebius, *Hist. Eccles.* v. 18, in *P.G.* 20, col. 479.

[4] Rambaud, *Le Droit criminel romain dans les Actes des martyrs*, Lyons, 1885 ; Walter, *Histoire du droit criminel chez les Romains*, 1863.

[5] For fuller details consult Le Blant, *op. cit.*

and the name of the accused. This formula occurs again and again.

As a typical example we may quote the authentic *Acts of Cyprian*:[1]

> When the Emperor Valerian was consul for the fourth time, and Gallienus for the third, on August 30th, in his private audience chamber, Paternus, proconsul of Carthage, said to Cyprian the bishop.

Then follows a more or less lengthy identification of the accused,[2] in the course of which he is asked his name, parents, country, profession, and social status. This is followed by the actual prosecution, in which the form of interrogation varied. For the persecution of the Christians assumed very different aspects at different epochs,[3] and in different parts of the empire at the same epoch. At least half the period between the first persecution of Nero in 64 and the Peace of the Church in 312 was passed in tranquillity: for the persecutions were intermittent. They were sometimes the result of a caprice on the part of the Emperor—as under Nero and Domitian: sometimes dictated by an outburst of Jewish or pagan prejudice: sometimes inspired by a settled imperial policy. The persecution was directed now against the Christians as a corporate body—in which case the bishops and clergy alone suffered, and property was confiscated, as under Valerian in 258: now against converts and their instructors, as under Septimius Severus in 202–203. Under Decius, in the persecution of 250, individuals—men, women and children—were systematically sought out and accused, often on anonymous information, in the hope of restoring the worship of the ancient gods, and totally suppressing Christianity. Under Diocletian in 303 the policy appears to have been one of the total extermination of a sect of invincible obstinacy.

[1] See *infra*, p. 147.

[2] Eusebius, *Hist. Eccles.* v. 1; Baluze, *Misc.* t. i. p. 22; *Passio S. Pioni* and *Passio S. Symphoriani* (Ruinart, *A.S.*).

[3] See Bibliography—ACTS OF MARTYRS: General History; Cabrol, *Dict. arch. chrét.: Accusations contre les chrétiens*, p. 266; Mommsen, "Der Religionsfrevel nach römischen Recht," in *Historische Zeitschrift*, 1890.

It was in these last two cruel persecutions that the greater number of the victims fell.

The processes against them were carried out sometimes in accordance with already existing laws,—as, for example, those against illegal associations or against treason—which applied to pagan and Christian alike. Sometimes the prosecution was in accordance with a definite edict or rescript. There were no witnesses, and in nearly every case recantation would have secured the acquittal of the accused; for the purpose of the judge, even in the application of torture, was to secure such a recantation, as is clearly seen in the authentic *Acta*.

Again, the interpretation and execution of the law would vary with different judges, the peculiar conditions of the locality, and the particular circumstances of each case.

The Christians were accused now of crimes and infamous practices; and we find, in the case of the martyrs of Lyons,[1] that many apostate Christians were executed on these charges alone, and were " sadly tormented by their own consciences." They were sometimes charged with holding illegal meetings, as we have seen, or with magical practices, and a refusal to give up their sacred writings. Frequently the mere profession of the name of Christian was its own condemnation. A passage in the *Passion of S. Saturninus* [Feb. 11] throws light on the last two accusations. Felix, one of the accused, has just confessed to being a Christian. " I do not care what you call yourself," said the judge, " but tell me if you have been present at illegal meetings or refused to give up the sacred writings." Most frequently the charges brought against them resolved themselves into that of treason,—a refusal to perform their military service or to pay the formal worship due to the divinity of the Emperor. In the case of noble Romans,—Pomponia Graecina, Flavia Domitilla, Clement the Consul, Acilius Glabrio,—it is difficult to distinguish the political from the religious offence. Finally, the penalties might involve banishment, death, confiscation of property, private or collective, and refusal of permission of burial, though this last is somewhat rare.

[1] Eusebius, *Hist. Eccles.* v. 1, 2.

This complexity of cause and character in the persecutions is brought out in *Acta* which for other reasons are accepted as authentic, and is in itself a reason for regarding certain *Acta* as authentic, at least in parts. In the actual trial scenes these *Acta* usually show us, on the one hand, the judge as the impassive Roman official, conscientiously discharging his duty in a rapid capable manner in accordance with the lines laid down by law or edict; and on the other the Christians, serene and confident, answering briefly in the words they had been instructed to utter.[1]

The Preparation for Martyrdom.—For the martyrs came to their trial "prepared and exercised," as Eusebius says. At the first threat of persecution the pastors gathered their flock around them to instruct the candidates for martyrdom, and themselves often set a practical example. For the persecutions were frequently directed against ecclesiastics alone, and they form a large proportion of the martyrs.

So Cyprian writes:

> Since fresh persecution is near . . . let us be ready and armed for the combat . . . let us fortify ourselves by the Body and Blood of Jesus Christ, and, satisfied with this divine food, let us find in the Eucharist our safeguard against the enemy.

And his disciples, condemned to the mines of Numidia, answer him when he is already in banishment after his first trial:[2]

> Like a good and true teacher you have first pronounced in the *Acta Proconsularia* what we your disciples, following you, ought to say before the judge; and as with a trumpet call, you have roused to battle the soldiers of God equipped with heavenly arms.

We read, on the other hand, in Eusebius, how the faithful of the churches of Lyons and Vienne, owing to the suddenness with which the persecution came upon them, went to their trial "unprepared and untrained."

[1] Le Blant, "La Préparation au martyre," in *Mémoires de l'Acad. des Inscriptions*, t. xxviii. 2ⁱᵉ partie; Rufinus, *Historia Monachorum*, c. xix., in *P.L.* 21, col. 441.
[2] See *infra*, p. 148; *Cypriani epistolae*, ed. Hartel, 54, 72 (2), 78.

Again, in the times of the Diocletian persecution, the priest, Epictetus, gave the following instructions to Astion:[1]—

> If, dearest son, the judge shall ask us to-morrow what is your race, your name, of what province are you and whence do you come,—let us answer him nothing at all, neither tell our name, race, or country of origin: but let us only say this, that we are Christians, and this is our name, this our race, this our country ... and again, if after this confession he orders us to be put to the torture, let us say nothing else as we lie in torment except "Lord Jesus, may Thy will be done in us."

Astion and his companions carried out in full their instructions. After enduring many tortures they were finally beaten

> until they breathed forth their spirit. And those blessed athletes of Christ said nought save "Lord God, may Thy will be done in us."

S. Chrysostom,[2] again, in a sermon on S. Lucianus, a priest of Antioch [Jan. 7, 312?], after relating how to each of the questions of the judge the Saint replied, "I am a Christian," continues:

> For he knew in such conflicts there was no need of eloquence but of faith, not of fluency of speech, but of a spirit fired with the love of God ... for he who says "I am a Christian" has told all,—his country, his estate and profession.

In fact, when we turn to the *Acta* we find the same dialogue between judge and accused repeated perpetually "What is your name?" "I am a Christian," or, "First I will say the most beautiful name of Christian." "What is your condition?" "The coming of Christ has set me free." "What is your country?" "Our true father is Christ, and our mother the faith by which we believe in Him." "Have you a wife, children or parents?" "No," replied Irenaeus of Sirmium, who had a wife and children. "Who then were those weeping round you at the last audience?" "God has said," replied Irenaeus, "'He who prefers his father, his mother

---

[1] *Vitae SS. Epicteti et Astionis*, xii., xvii., in Rosweyde, *Vitae Patrum*, 216, 218, Antwerp, 1628 (also in *P.L.* 73, col. 593).

[2] *Homilia in S. Lucianum*, 83 (*P.G.* 50, col. 524).

his wife, his brother or his children to Me, is not worthy of Me.'" The last quotation is from *Acta* of dubious authenticity; but the answer is in harmony with primitive sentiment. Of the martyr Carpus [April 13], undergoing torture, we read:

> He continued to repeat "I am a Christian," till the moment when, fainting from excess of suffering, he lost his voice.

Again, to the question: "Where have you hidden your sacred books?" we find a fixed form of reply: "They are written in my heart."

Though some of the examples quoted occur in apocryphal Acts, in which later compilers frequently assisted their failing imaginations by borrowing, for their own narratives, some happy or edifying phrase on the lips of an early martyr, yet the fact seems established by Le Blant that the martyrs did indeed receive definite instructions as to their words when on trial.

On the lips of the martyrs in their agony we hear the same cries, in this case surely inspired by the same need, rather than any form of instruction. "Lord, help Thy servants,"—"Lord Jesus Christ, help me by Thy passion,"—"O give victory to my heart and body to endure torments." They are summed up in the single petition of Perpetua at her baptism, for grace to endure suffering;[1] and a fitting commentary is found in the words of Phileas of Alexandria [Feb. 4] at his martyrdom: "Now that I begin to suffer pain, I begin to be a disciple of our Lord Jesus Christ."

Later compilers love to imagine miraculous deliverances in answer to these prayers; but in the authentic records the martyrs usually endure to the end, and "by patience they consummate their martyrdoms," to quote the words of Tertullian.

We have thus reconstituted approximately the form of the official *Acta Proconsularia*, and established a standard of criticism for documents based upon them. These we will now examine, and attempt to classify, according to their fidelity to the *Acta* and other sources.

[1] *Passio S. Perpetuae*, in *Texts and Studies*, vol. i., 1891 (see *infra*, p. 165).

10

CHAPTER XI

ACTS OF THE MARTYRS: CLASSIFICATION OF THE TEXTS: THREE CLASSES OF AUTHENTIC DOCUMENTS

Authentic texts as touchstones of criticism.—Number and classification of authentic texts—CLASS I. Documents depending on the *Acta Proconsularia*—Examples: (1) *Acts of Cyprian*—(2) *Of the Scillitan Martyrs*—(3) *Of Justin Martyr*—(4) *Of Fructuosus.*

Μετὰ ταῦτα δὴ λοιπὸν εἰς πᾶν εἶδος διῃρεῖτο τὰ μαρτύρια τῆς ἐξόδου αὐτῶν. ἐκ διαφόρων γὰρ χρωμάτων, καὶ πάντοιων ἀνθῶν, ἕνα πλέξαντες στέφανον προσήνεγκαν τῷ πατρί. ἐχρῆν δ᾽οὖν τοὺς γενναίους ἀθλητὰς ποικίλον ὑπομεινάντας ἀγῶνα, καὶ μεγάλως νικήσαντας ἀπολαβεῖν τὸν μέγαν τῆς ἀφθαρσίας στέφανον.[1]

Eusebius, *Hist. Eccles.* v. 1.

Authentic Texts as Touchstones of Criticism.—Since, as we have seen, none of the original *Acta Proconsularia* have survived, the word *Acta*, used by hagiographers, indicates a document which is, or professes to be, derived from these originals. Genuine documents of this description stand in the first class as regards authenticity.

Strictly speaking, we are concerned with the Acts of the Roman martyrs only. Since, however, these documents are of doubtful authenticity, and cannot be analysed without some touchstone whereby to test them, we must extend the limits of our inquiry, and briefly indicate those Acts of the Eastern, Gallican and African churches which may provide us with types of every kind of authentic document. These will serve as models of the style of genuine *Acta*, supply examples of Roman procedure in trials of Christians, and show the mutual attitude of judge and accused; they will

---

[1] "*After this, by death through every kind of martyrdom, they wove a single crown of divers colours, and all kinds of flowers, and offered it to the Father. For these valiant athletes had to undergo a manifold contest, and win a great victory before they could carry off the great crown of immortality.*"

146

also afford authentic information on the circumstances of
the imprisonment and death of the martyrs. Further, these
facts can frequently be checked by information derived from
other sources, and the authenticity of the *Acta* themselves
proved from contemporary evidence. The text of these
documents, too, will illustrate, better than pages of criticism,
the spirit in which the martyrs met their death. It is, after
all, this spiritual atmosphere pervading certain *Acta*, which
is, as it were, the hallmark of authenticity.

The Number and Classification of Authentic Texts.—
There exist in all, as at present discovered, about forty
documents of high historical value, and twelve of these are
of first-hand authority. They cover the whole period of the
persecutions; many recount martyrdoms of the second
century—of the Scillitan martyrs, Ignatius, Polycarp, the
martyrs of Vienne and Lyons, Carpus, Apollonius, Thecla.
The Decian persecution of 250 has given us the Acts of
Procopius, Pionius and Acacius. The systematic persecution
of the Christians as a body, accompanied by confiscation of
property under Valerian, in 258 and 259, produced many others
—of Pope Sixtus II. in Rome,[1] of Jacobus and Marianus, and
of Montanus and Lucius, both in Africa, and of Fructuosus in
Spain; and the other persecutions have found worthy historians.

Even the authentic documents may be divided into
three classes: I. Those records depending directly on the
original *Acta Proconsularia*. II. Documents depending
mainly on the accounts of eye-witnesses. III. Records
depending on documents of Classes I. and II.

**Class I.:—Documents depending on the *Acta Procon-
sularia*: (1) *Acta S. Cypriani*, 258.**—In the *Acta Proconsularia
S. Cypriani*[2] [Sept. 14, 258] we have a record which is

---

[1] The fact of his martyrdom is certain, but there exist no authentic *Acta*
(see *supra*, p. 71).

[2] *Cypriani epistolae*, ed. Hartel, p. cx, in Series *Corpus Scriptorum Latinorum Ecclesiasticorum*, t. iii. ; for a translation see Pusey, *Library of the Fathers*,
vol. iii. ; cf. Monceaux, "Examen critique des documents rélatifs au martyre de
Saint Cyprien," in *Revue Archéologique*, Série 3, t. xxxviii., 1901, pp. 249–271 ;
Studia Biblica, iii. 217, iv. 189. Where no other reference is given, the text of
the *Acta* mentioned in the following pages is found in the *Acta Sanctorum* (*A.SS.*)
of the Bollandists under the date mentioned.

unique. It is a compilation of three distinct documents:
(i) A copy of the official *Acta Proconsularia* of the first trial
in 257, after which the bishop was banished; (ii) a copy of
the *Acta* of the second trial in 258, when he was executed;
(iii) a brief account of his death, added by the compiler,
together with a few words to connect the various parts. In
some of the manuscripts the third part is omitted, in others
the break between Parts I. and II. is evident. In spite
of the length and the familiarity of the document it is quoted
in full below, as affording the most perfect type of a Roman
trial:

When the emperor Valerian was consul for the
fourth time, and Gallienus for the third, on August 30th,
in the private audience chamber, Paternus the proconsul
said to Cyprian the bishop: "The most sacred emperors
Valerian and Gallienus have deigned to give me letters
in which they have commanded those who do not
follow the Roman religion to observe that ceremonial
henceforth. For this reason I have sought you out;
what do you answer me?" Cyprian the bishop
answered: "I am a Christian and a bishop; I know
no other gods but the one and true God who made
heaven and earth, the sea and all that is in them.
This God we Christians serve: to Him we pray day
and night, for ourselves and for all men, and for the
safety of the emperors themselves." Paternus the proconsul said: "Do you persist in this intention?" Cyprian
the bishop answered: "A good intention, which acknow-
ledges God, cannot change." Paternus the proconsul
said: "You will, then, according to the edict of Valerian
and Gallienus depart an exile to the city of Curubis."
Cyprian the bishop answered: "I depart." Paternus
the proconsul said: "The emperors have deigned to
write to me not only about the bishops, but about the
priests: I wish therefore to know from you who are the
priests who live in this town." Cyprian the bishop
answered: "By your laws you have wisely forbidden
any to be informers (*esse delatores*): so I am not able to
reveal their names, and betray them. But they can be
found in their towns." Paternus the proconsul said:
"I will to-day seek them out in this place." Cyprian
said: "Our discipline forbids that any should volun-
tarily give himself up, and this is contrary to your

calculations; but you will find them if you look for them." Paternus the proconsul said: "I will find them," and added: "The emperors have also forbidden any assemblies to be held in any place, and also access to the cemeteries. If any then has not observed this salutary precept, he incurs the penalty of death." Cyprian the bishop answered: "Do what is ordered you." Then Paternus the proconsul ordered the blessed Cyprian to be exiled. When he had already been some time in his place of exile (A.D. 258) Galerius Maximus the proconsul succeeded to Aspasius Paternus the proconsul. The former ordered the holy Cyprian, the bishop, to be recalled from exile and brought before him. When Cyprian, the holy martyr chosen by God, had returned from the city of Curubis (where he had been in exile according to the decree of the then proconsul Aspasius Paternus), he remained in his own gardens according to the imperial decree, hoping daily that they would come for him, as had been revealed to him (in a dream). And while he was staying there, suddenly on September 13th, in the consulship of Tuscus and Bassus (258), two officers of the proconsul came to him, one the chief gaoler of the proconsul Galerius Maximus who had succeeded Aspasius Paternus, and the other marshal of the guard of the same office. They put him in a carriage, and placed him between them, and took him to Sexti, whither Galerius Maximus the proconsul had retired to recover his health. This same Galerius Maximus the proconsul ordered the trial of Cyprian to be deferred to another day, and the blessed Cyprian was taken to the house of the chief gaoler of this same Galerius Maximus the proconsul, and remained as a guest with him in the quarter called Saturn, between the Street of Venus and the Street of Health. Thither all the brethren came together. And when holy Cyprian learnt this, he ordered that the young girls should be protected, since all remained together in that quarter before the gate of the officer's house. The next day, September 14th, in the morning, a great crowd came together to Sexti according to the command of Galerius Maximus the proconsul, who ordered Cyprian on that same day to be brought before him in the court called Sanciolum. When he was brought, Galerius Maximus the proconsul said to Cyprian the bishop:

"You are Thascius Cyprianus?" Cyprian the bishop answered: "I am." Galerius Maximus the proconsul said: "You have made yourself the pope (*papa*) of these sacrilegious men?" Cyprian the bishop answered: "Yes." Galerius Maximus the proconsul said: "The most sacred emperors have ordered you to sacrifice." Cyprian the bishop answered: "I will not sacrifice." Galerius Maximus said: "Reflect." Cyprian the bishop answered: "Do what is commanded you: there is no place for reflexion in so just a matter." Galerius Maximus, having discussed the matter with his council, gave sentence most reluctantly (*vix et aegre*) as follows: "You have lived long in sacrilege; you have gathered round you many accomplices in unlawful association; you have made yourself an enemy to the Roman gods and their holy religion; and our most pious and sacred princes, Valerian and Gallienus, the August,[1] and Valerian, also most noble Caesar,[1] have not been able to recall you to the practice of their rites. Therefore, since you are found to be the author and ringleader of shameful crimes, you yourself shall be made an example to those whom you have associated with you in your crime: your blood shall be the confirmation of the laws." At these words he read the decree from a tablet: "Thascius Cyprianus shall be put to death by the sword." Cyprian the bishop said: "Thanks be to God."

When this sentence was passed, the crowd of the brethren said: "Let us be beheaded with him." For this reason a tumult of the brethren arose, and a great crowd followed him. So Cyprian was led forth into the plain of Sexti, and there he took off his cloak, and knelt down, and prostrated himself in prayer to God. And when he had taken off his dalmatic[2] and given it to his deacons, he stood up in his linen undergarment, and waited for the executioner. When the executioner came, Cyprian ordered his friends to give him twenty-five pieces of gold. Sheets and napkins were laid down before Cyprian by the brethren. After this, blessed Cyprian bandaged his eyes with his own hand (*manu sua oculos texit*). When he could not himself fasten the sleeves of his garments, Julian the priest, and Julian the

[1] *Augustus* and *Caesar* were titles bestowed on the emperors.
[2] An ordinary secular tunic, afterwards an exclusively ecclesiastical vestment.

subdeacon fastened them for him. So blessed Cyprian suffered ; and his body was laid in a place near by, to satisfy the curiosity of the pagans. Thence by night it was carried away with candles and torches, with prayers and with great triumph, to the gravel yard of Macrobius Candidianus the procurator, which is on the road to Mappala, near the reservoirs. A few days after Galerius Maximus the proconsul died.

These *Acta Cypriani*, as well as others describing this persecution, show clearly that the edicts of Valerian were directed against the clergy only, and that the multitude of the faithful could freely approach their bishop, bury him in triumph, and carry away napkins, soaked in his blood, as relics. The document shows also the precise charges brought, the method of investigation, the judge's desire that his prisoner should recant, and the general consideration with which the bishop was treated.

At the end of the year 257 a copy of the *Acta* of that year was in the hands of the confessors condemned to the mines in Numidia, as we see from the letter they wrote to Cyprian quoted above.[1]

The authenticity of these *Acta* is further attested by letters of Cyprian himself,[2] and of Pontius, his friend and deacon, who wrote the *Passion of S. Cyprian*,[3] based partly on the *Acta*. S. Augustine,[4] in a sermon in honour of S. Cyprian, refers to the " Passion of the blessed Cyprian which has just been read," and describes the deeds of the martyr in words closely resembling the *Acta* as we have them.

(2) Acts of the Scillitan Martyrs, 180.—There is no other record whose authenticity, based on internal and external evidence, is so well attested as that of the *Acta Cypriani*, though a certain number of documents closely reproducing the originals may be classed with them. Of these the best known are the *Acts of the Scillitan Martyrs*[5] [Carthage, July 17, 180]:

On July 17th under the consulship of Praesens for

---

[1] *Supra*, p. 143.   [2] *Epistolae*, 76, 80, 81.   [3] *Infra*, p. 163.
[4] *Sermo* 14, in *P.L.* 46, col. 864 ; and *Sermones* 309-313, in *P.L.* 38, col. 1410.
[5] *Texts and Studies*, i. p. 104, 1891. The Latin version appears to be the original form of the *Acta*.

the second time, and of Claudian—Speratus, Nartzalus and Cittinus, Donata, Secunda and Vestia appeared in the private audience chamber at Carthage. The proconsul Saturninus said: "You can obtain grace from our master the emperor if you return to a reasonable frame of mind." Speratus answered: "We have never done any evil nor lent ourselves to any iniquity: we have never said any evil, but have returned thanks for ills suffered because we obey our emperor."

The proconsul Saturninus said.—"We also, we are religious, and our religion is simple. We swear by the happiness of our master the emperor, and we pray for his safety. You should do the same."

Speratus.—"If you truly wish to lend me an attentive ear, I will explain to you the mystery of the true simplicity."

Saturninus.—"I will not lend my ear to your impertinences against my religion. Swear rather by the happiness of our master the emperor."

Speratus.—"I do not acknowledge the kingdom of this present age, but I only serve with greater fidelity my God Whom no man has seen, and Whom mortal eyes cannot see. I have not committed theft. If I labour at any trade, I pay the taxes, because I know our Lord the King of Kings and of all peoples."

The proconsul Saturninus addressing himself to the other accused persons.—"Give up this vain belief."

Speratus.—"There is no dangerous belief except that which permits homicide and false witness."

The proconsul Saturninus.—"Cease to be the accomplices of this folly."

Cittinus.—"We have, and we fear only one God, our God who is in heaven."

Donata.—"We render to Caesar the honour due to Caesar, but we fear God only."

Vestia.—"I am a Christian."

Secunda.—"I am a Christian and wish to remain so."

Saturninus to Speratus.—"Do you remain a Christian?"

Speratus.—"I am a Christian."

All the accused associated themselves with him.

Saturninus.—"Do you wish for a delay to reflect?"

Speratus.—"In so just a cause there is no need to reflect."

Saturninus.—"What do you keep in your archives?"

THREE CLASSES OF AUTHENTIC DOCUMENTS 153

Speratus.—"The books of the Gospels, and the Epistles of Paul, a holy man."

Saturninus.—"Take thirty days' delay, and reflect."

Speratus said again.—"I am a Christian."

All the accused associated themselves with him.

Saturninus the proconsul read the decree on the tablet:

"Speratus, Nartzalus, Cittinus, Donata, Vestia, Secunda and others have declared that they live in the manner of the Christians; and to the proposal made them to return to the manner of living of the Romans, have persisted in their obstinacy: we condemn them to die by the sword."

Speratus.—"Let us thank God."

Nartzalus.—"This very day as martyrs we shall be in heaven. Thanks be to God."

The proconsul Saturninus ordered the herald to read the arrest:

"I order that:—

"Speratus, Nartzalus, Cittinus, Veturius, Felix, Aquilinus, Laetantius, Januaria, Generosa, Vestia, Donata and Secunda be put to death."

They all said.—"Thanks be to God."

Thus all at the same time were crowned with martyrdom, and they reign with the Father and the Son and the Holy Spirit. Amen.

The similarity between these *Acta* and those of Cyprian is apparent. The doxology appended indicates that they were read liturgically.

(3) Acts of Justin Martyr, 163.—The Greek *Acts of Justin* the philosopher [April 13, 163?],[1] one of the earliest authentic accounts of a martyr in Rome, may be quoted:

Justin and those who lived with him, were brought before the prefect of Rome, Rusticius. As soon as they were before the tribunal Rusticius said to Justin: "Submit to the gods and obey the emperors." Justin answered: "No one can be blamed or condemned for having followed the laws of our Lord Jesus Christ." *Rusticius.*—"What science do you study?" *Justin.*— "I have successively studied all the sciences: but in the end I abide in the doctrine of the Christians, though

[1] *Studi e Testi*, vol. viii. p. 25, 1902.

it is displeasing to those led away by error." *Rusticius.*
—"Unlucky man, is that the science you love?"—"Yes,
I follow the Christians because they possess the true
doctrine." "What is this doctrine?" "This is the
doctrine the Christians follow religiously: to believe
in one God, Creator of all things visible and invisible.
To confess Jesus Christ, the Son of God, foretold of
old by the prophets, the future judge of the human
race, Messenger of salvation, Master of all those who
are willing to learn of Him. I, a weak man, am too
feeble to be able to speak worthily of His infinite
divinity: it is the work of the prophets. Throughout
the centuries, by inspiration from on high, they have
announced the coming into the world of Him Whom
I call the Son of God." The prefect asked in what
place the Christians assembled. "Wherever they can,"
answered Justin. "Do you think," he continued, "that
we all assemble in the same place? Not at all. The
God of the Christians is not shut up anywhere; invisible, He fills heaven and earth; in all places the
faithful adore Him, and praise Him." "Come, tell me,"
said Rusticius, "the place where your meetings take
place and where you assemble your disciples."

"I have lived up to this day near the house of a
certain Martin, beside the Baths of Timothy.[1] This
is the second time that I have come to Rome, and I
know no other dwelling save that. To all those who
wished to come and find me, I have imparted the true
doctrine."

—"You are then a Christian?"

"Yes, I am a Christian."

The prefect said to Chariton.—"Are you a Christian,
you too?"

—"By the help of God I am."

The prefect said to Charita.—"Are you also of the
faith of Christ?"

She answered.—"By the grace of God I also am a
Christian."

Rusticius said to Euelpistus.—"And you, what are
you?"

Euelpistus.—"I am a slave of Caesar, but being a Christian

---

[1] Close to the house of Cornelius Pudens (who was connected, on very good
evidence, with the sojourn of S. Peter in Rome), which is now the site of the
Church of S. Pudentiana (see *supra*, p. 8).

I have received liberty from Christ; by His benefits, by His grace I have the same hopes as these others."

Rusticius to Hierax.—" Are you a Christian?"

Hierax.—" Certainly I am a Christian : I love and adore the same God as these."

Rusticius.—" Is it Justin who has made you a Christian?"

Hierax.—" I have always been a Christian and I shall be always."

Paeonius got up and said.—" I also, I am a Christian."

The prefect.—" Who has instructed you?"

Paeonius.—" I learnt the good doctrine from my parents."

Euelpistus said.—" For myself, I listen with great pleasure to Justin, but I learnt the Christian religion from my parents."

The prefect said.—" Where are your parents?"

Euelpistus.—" In Cappadocia."

The prefect to Hierax.—" And you, of what country are your parents?"

Hierax.—" Our true father is Christ, and our mother the faith by which we believe in Him : my parents according to the flesh are dead. For the rest, I was brought hither from Iconium in Phrygia."

The prefect said to Liberianus.—" What do you call yourself? Are you too a Christian and impious towards the gods?"

Liberianus.—" I am a Christian, and I love and adore the true God."

The prefect returned to the case of Justin.—" Listen, you who are called eloquent, and who think you possess the true doctrine : if I have you beaten and then beheaded, do you think you will then mount to heaven?"

Justin said.—" I hope to receive the reward destined for those who keep the commandments of Christ, if I suffer the punishments you promise me. I know that those who have lived thus will keep the divine favour till the end of the world."

Rusticius.—" You think, then, that you will mount to heaven to receive a reward there?"

Justin.—" I do not think it, I know it. I am so assured of it, that I have no doubt about it of any kind."

The prefect.—" Enough: come, and all together sacrifice to the gods."

Justin.—"No one in his senses will abandon piety for error."

The prefect—"If you do not obey orders you will be tortured without mercy."

Justin.—"It is our most earnest desire to suffer in the cause of our Lord Jesus Christ, and be saved : so that we may present ourselves, assured and tranquil, before the terrible tribunal of this same our God and Saviour whither, according to the divine ordinance, the whole world will pass all together. What thou wilt, do quickly : we are Christians, and do not sacrifice to idols."

Then the prefect passed sentence :

"That those who have not consented to sacrifice to the gods, and obey the orders of the emperor, shall be beaten and led away to suffer the penalty of death in accordance with the laws."

In consequence the holy martyrs, glorifying God, were led to the ordinary place of execution, and after being beaten they were beheaded, thus consummating their martyrdom in the confession of Christ.

Some of the faithful took up their bodies secretly, and put them in a suitable place, sustained by the grace of our Lord Jesus Christ, to Whom be glory for ever and ever. Amen.

The peculiar interest of these *Acta* lies in the ancient confession of faith by Justin, in the topographical allusion to one of the earliest places of worship in Rome, and in the answer of Euelpistus, showing that as early as 163 there was a second generation of Christians in Cappadocia.

Other Examples of Class I.—The *Passion of SS. Maxima, Donatella and Secunda* [1] [Africa, July 30, 304 (?)] may be included in this class. Like the Acts of Justin, it closes with the doxology. In this document every detail of the judicial proceedings is correct and according to ancient custom—the early hour of the trial, the formula of interrogation, the various ranks of the officials.

Closely related to this in type are the *Passion of S. Typasius* [2] [Ticabis, N. Africa, Jan. 11, under Diocletian]

---

[1] *Analecta Bollandiana*, 1889, p. 5; 1897, p. 64.   *Texts and Studies*, vol. i. p. 106, 1891.   *Bulletin critique*, ii. p. 229, 1882.

[2] *Anal. Boll.*, 1890, p. 116.

and the *Acts of Maximilian*, the conscript of Numidia [March 12, 295]; those of *Marcellus*, a centurion [Tangiers, Oct. 30, 298], of *Maximus* [Ephesus (?), May 14 (or April 30), 250], and of *Cassian* (Tangiers, Oct. 30, 258).

(4) Passion of Fructuosus, 259.—The *Passion of S. Fructuosus*, Bishop of Tarragona [Jan. 21, 259], quoted below, combines a version of the *Acta* with details that only an eye-witness could have supplied. S. Augustine in a sermon,[1] and Prudentius in a poem,[2] quote from a passion closely resembling, and probably identical with, the document before us. It is written in the style of the third century, and the indications of dates and days of the week are correct and evidently noted by a contemporary. This characteristic noting of days and dates appears also in the *Passion of S. Pionius*.[3]

In the reign of Valerian and Gallienus, in the consul-ship of Aemilius and Bassus, on January 16th, a Sunday, Fructuosus the bishop, Augurius and Eulogius, deacons, were arrested. Fructuosus had just gone to bed when the soldiers arrived. They were called Aurelius, Testucius, Aelius, Pollentius, Donatius and Maximus. The bishop, hearing the sound of their steps, jumped out of bed, and came to the threshold of the door. The soldiers said to him : "Come, the governor has sum-moned you with your deacons." Fructuosus answered : "Let us go. Will you let me put on my shoes ?" "As you like." They took them to prison. Fructuosus exulted at the thought of the crown which was offered him : he prayed without ceasing. All the community came to see him, they brought him food, and com-mended themselves to his remembrance. On one of the days which followed his imprisonment, he baptized a catechumen called Rogatianus. The accused remained six days in prison. The sixth day, January 21st, a Friday, they appeared in court.

The governor Aemilianus said.—" Bring in Fructuosus the bishop, Augurius and Eulogius the deacons." An official answered : " They are present."

Aemilianus said to Fructuosus.—"You know the orders of the emperors ? "

[1] *Sermo* 213, c. 2, 3, in *P.L.* 38, col. 1248.
[2] *Peristephanon*, vi., in *P.L.* 60, col. 767.
[3] *Infra*, p. 169.

Fructuosus.—" No, but I am a Christian."

Aemilianus.—" They have ordered you to adore the gods."

Fructuosus.—" I adore one God only, Who has made heaven and earth, the sea and all things."

Aemilianus.—" Do you know that there are gods ? "

Fructuosus.—" I know nothing of it."

Aemilianus.—" You will learn it."

Fructuosus raised his eyes to heaven and prayed in silence.

Aemilianus.—" Who then will be obeyed, feared and honoured, if one refuses worship to the gods, and adoration to the emperors ? "

Aemilianus said to Augurius the deacon.—" Do not listen to what Fructuosus says."

Fructuosus answered.—" I adore God the almighty."

Aemilianus to Eulogius the deacon.—" Do you adore Fructuosus ? "

Eulogius.—" I do not adore Fructuosus, but I adore the God Whom Fructuosus adores."

Aemilianus to Fructuosus.—" You are a bishop ? "

Fructuosus.—" I am."

Aemilianus.—" You *have* been." He ordered all three to be burnt alive.

During the passage to the amphitheatre the people showered pity upon Fructuosus, for all, Christians and pagans, loved him. He was the perfect type of a bishop, such as the Holy Spirit had portrayed it by the hand of that vessel of election, the doctor of the Gentiles. The brethren who thought of the glory which awaited him, were more inclined to joy than sadness. Several among them presented to those who were to die a cup of spiced wine. " The hour for breaking fast has not yet sounded," said Fructuosus. It was ten o'clock. The martyrs had solemnly celebrated in prison the day of the station [1] the preceding Wednesday, and they advanced, joyous and calm, to finish the station of that day, Friday, with the martyrs and the prophets, in the paradise which God has prepared for those whom He loves. At the moment when they reached the amphitheatre a man rapidly approached the bishop. It was his reader, Augustalis, who, with tears in his eyes, asked permission to unfasten his shoes. " Go away, my child,

[1] See *supra*, p. 14, note 1.

I will take off my shoes myself," said the martyr, tranquil, joyous and assured of obtaining the promise of the Lord. When this was done, one of our people, Felix, took the right hand of the bishop, praying him to have remembrance of him. The old man then said : " I must think of the Catholic Church spread from the East to the West." As the moment approached when the martyr was going to meet glory, rather than suffering, in the presence of his brethren, under the attentive gaze of the soldiers, who could hear these words dictated by the Holy Spirit, Fructuosus said : " You will not be deprived of your shepherd : the goodness and promise of God will not fail you, either now, or in the future. What you see is but the misery of an hour."

Having comforted the brethren, the martyrs advanced towards the place which was to be their salvation, grave and radiant at the moment of obtaining the fruit which the Scriptures promise. Like the three Hebrew children,[1] they brought to mind the Trinity. In the midst of the flames the Father did not abandon them, the Son aided them and the Holy Spirit stood in the midst of the furnace. When the cords which bound their wrists were burnt, free in their movements they knelt down in the ordinary attitude of prayer, assured of their resurrection, and recalling by hands outstretched the triumph of Christ : they did not cease to pray till the moment when they gave up their spirit. Then divine miracles manifested themselves : the sky opened and two of our brethren, Babylas and Mydonius, belonging to the house of the prefect, and even the daughter of this officer, saw Fructuosus and his deacons, with brows crowned, entering into heaven while their dead bodies were still fastened to the stake. They called Aemilianus : " Come, see your condemned prisoners ; see how according to their hope you have opened heaven to them." Aemilianus ran up, but he was unworthy to enjoy this sight.

The community was sorrowful, like a flock of sheep deprived of their shepherd : uneasiness oppressed all, not that they pitied Fructuosus, on the contrary, they envied him.

At nightfall the faithful hastened to the amphitheatre :

---

[1] A favourite subject for frescoes in the Roman catacombs from the third century.

they carried with them wine to extinguish the bones half carbonized in the fire. Then each took for himself some portions of the ashes as relics. Another miracle exalted the faith of the brethren and served as a lesson to the youngest. It was needful that Fructuosus should bear witness in his death both to the resurrection of the body, and to the truth of that which he had promised in our Lord and Saviour when he taught in this world by the mercy of God. It happened, then, that after his martyrdom he appeared to the brethren, and warned them to restore, without delay, whatever portion of his ashes, each one, by devotion, had carried away; so that they might be gathered together into the same place. He also appeared to Aemilianus: he was accompanied by his deacons, and all wore the robe of glory. He rebuked the judge roundly, showing him the uselessness of what he had done, for these whom he saw in glory were those whom he thought to be buried in the earth.

O holy martyrs, proved by fire as precious gold, covered with the breastplate of faith and the helmet of salvation, as the price of the victory over the devil whose head you have crushed, you have received a diadem and an imperishable crown!

O holy martyrs, you have merited a dwelling in heaven, standing on the right hand of Christ, blessing the Father Almighty and His Son our Lord Jesus Christ. God has received His martyrs in peace for their faithful confession. Glory and honour to Him for ever. Amen.

CHAPTER XII

ACTS OF THE MARTYRS: CLASSIFICATION OF TEXTS: THREE CLASSES OF AUTHENTIC DOCUMENTS (*continued*)

CLASS II. Documents depending on eye-witnesses : Passions of Ignatius, Polycarp, Procopius, Cyprian, Perpetua, of Jacobus and Marianus—CLASS III. Documents depending on records of Class I. or Class II. : Passions of Pionius, of Montanus and Lucius—Characteristics of genuine documents.

Justorum animae in manu Dei sunt, et non tanget illos tormentum malitiae. Visi sunt oculis insipientium mori : illi autem sunt in pace.[1]
In Vigilia Omnium Sanctorum (*Liber Sapientiae*, 3).

Class II. : Documents depending on Eye-Witnesses. —Other sources of information are the writings of the martyrs themselves, or records by eye-witnesses. These documents we may place in a second class. In them we miss the impersonal note of the *Acta*, but we have sometimes a vivid and touching record of the incidents. They are usually known as *Passions* : their value varies greatly, according to the opportunities and abilities of the writers. The best of them very nearly approach the original *Acta* in historical value, and include nine documents of established authenticity. Five of these are preserved for us by Eusebius, who clearly indicates the original sources.[2]

(1) Passion of Ignatius, 107.—For Ignatius,[3] Bishop of Antioch [Rome, Feb. 1, 107], he quotes first the saint's

---

[1] " *The souls of the righteous are in the hand of God, and there shall no torment touch them. In the eyes of the foolish they seem to die : but they are in peace.*"

[2] There are some other authentic accounts of martyrdoms which are not *Passions* to be found in the Ecclesiastical History of Eusebius, and in other writers.

[3] Eusebius, *Historia Ecclesiastica*, iii. c. 36 ; Lightfoot, *Apostolic Fathers*, pt. ii. vols. i. and ii.

authentic Letter to the Romans, written at Smyrna on his
way to martyrdom at Rome, a first-hand authority; next a
passage from Irenaeus, a second-hand authority; thirdly,
he mentions tradition (λόγος δ' ἔχει).

(2) Passion of Polycarp, 156 ?—An encyclical letter
written by the Church of Smyrna to that of Philomelium,
records the martyrdom of Polycarp,[1] Bishop of Smyrna
[April 25, 156?].

(3) Martyrs of Vienne and Lyons, 177.—For the martyrs
of Vienne and Lyons [2] [June 2, 177] we have the letter written
from those churches to their brethren in Asia and Phrygia.

(4) Martyrs of Alexandria, 250.—For the martyrs
who suffered at Alexandria (in 250) the letter written by
their bishop, Dionysius, to Fabius, Bishop of Antioch.[3]

(5) The Passion of Procopius, 250.—The *Passion of
Procopius*,[4] the reader [Caesarea in Palestine, July 8, and Nov.
22, 250], first recorded in a book of Eusebius, the *Martyrs of
Palestine*, is preserved in a Latin Passionary. Eusebius was
himself an eye-witness of that persecution, and a shortened
form of the passion is found in his Ecclesiastical History:

> Procopius was the first of the martyrs of Palestine.
> He was a man of celestial grace. From his infancy
> to his martyrdom he had sought, all his life, chastity and
> all the virtues. His body was so emaciated that one
> might have thought it without life: but his spirit was so
> valiant beneath the action of the divine words, that one
> might have thought that it alone sustained the life of
> the body. He lived on bread and water, and moreover
> only ate every two or three days, and sometimes only
> once a week. His contemplation was prolonged night
> and day. All his study was that of the holy books:
> beyond this he knew little. Born in Jerusalem, he had
> settled at Scythopolis, where he fulfilled the office of
> reader, exorcist and official translator of the Scriptures.
> This he did by reciting to the people, in the common

---

[1] *Hist. Eccles.* iv. c. 15; Lightfoot, *op. cit.* vol. iii.; *Studia Biblica*, i. 175,
ii. 105.

[2] *Hist. Eccles.* v. c. 1, 2.   [3] *Hist. Eccles.* vi. c. 41.

[4] Eusebius, "Paralipomena," in *Die Griech. Christ. Schriftstellen*, vol. 2,
II. p. 907, Leipsic, 1908; also in *Hist. Eccles.*, Appendix to bk. viii.;
Anal. Boll., 1897, 113 (see *infra*, p. 195).

tongue, the passage of the holy books read in the liturgy in Greek. Transferred with his colleagues from Scythopolis to Caesarea, he was taken at the gate of the city, and conducted straight before the governor Flavianus, who commanded him to sacrifice to the gods. "There are not many gods but one only, Creator of all things," said Procopius. The governor, touched, was contented with the answer, and sought something else : he commanded Procopius to offer incense to the emperor. "Listen," said Procopius, "to these lines of Homer : ' It is not good to have so many masters; let there be one master, one king.' "

At these words the judge fancied he saw some intention to insult the emperor, and pronounced sentence of death. So Procopius attained to glory. It was July 7, the day of the Nones, as the Latins say, of the first year of the persecution. He was the first martyr of Caesarea. Jesus Christ reigns. To Him be honour and glory for ever. Amen.

(6) Passio Cypriani, 258.—In the *Passion of Cyprian* [1] we have recorded some incidents in the life, trial, and martyrdom of the Bishop of Carthage by his deacon, Pontius, his friend and companion in exile. The writer is therefore an eyewitness, who has also access, as he tells us, to the *Acta S. Cypriani*. And yet this document, accepted as contemporary with the events, is little but a panegyric of Cyprian ; it is inadequate as concerns his life, and, though five times the length of the *Acta*, omits much, notably the incidents of the passion, and contains little more than the original document, with which, in certain details, it is discrepant. It is instructive to compare these two accounts as an illustration of the difference between a primary and secondary document. A few extracts are given below from the small portion which deals with the trial and death.

. . . Banishment followed on these excellent and pious actions, for impiety always makes this return, paying back good with evil. And what this priest of God replied to the interrogations of the proconsul, there are the Acts which relate it. He is shut out from the city, he

[1] See *supra*, p. 147. For a translation see Roberts and Donaldson, *Ante-Nicene Fathers*, vol. viii.

who did good for the salvation of the city, he who had laboured that the eyes of the living should not suffer the horror of the infernal dwelling. . . .

. . . .

At last that other day dawned, that destined, that promised, that divine day which, if the tyrant himself had wished to put off, he would not have been able : a day joyful at the knowledge of the future martyr, and radiant with the clear light of the sun, when all clouds were scattered through the whole circle of the earth. He left the house of the chief officer, himself an officer of Christ and God, and he was encompassed on all sides by an army of a mixed multitude. . . . But when he had come to the praetorium, as the proconsul had not yet come forth, a private place was allotted him.

. . . .

So the judge read the sentence from the tablet . . . a spiritual sentence not rashly to be spoken, a sentence worthy of such a bishop and such a witness, a glorious sentence in which he is called the ringleader of the sect ; and enemy of the gods ; and told that he was to be made an example to his people, and that the law would begin to be confirmed by his blood. . . .

. . . .

And when he left the doors of the praetorium, a band of soldiers accompanied him ; and, lest anything should be lacking in his passion, centurions and tribunes stood on each side of him . . . but now his eyes being bound by his own hands he tried to hasten the executioner whose duty it was to wield the sword, and who could hardly grip it with trembling fingers in his failing right hand, until, at the right hour for the glorification, power was given from above to strengthen his hand for carrying out the death of this so rare spirit.

. . . .

His passion being thus accomplished, brought about that Cyprian, who had been an example of all good, was also the first in Africa to dye his priestly crown with martyrdom . . . for from the time at which the list of bishops in Carthage is recorded, no one at all, even of the good men and priests, is said to have suffered death.

. . . .

Greatly, oh greatly do I exult at his glory, yet grieve more that I stayed behind,

(7) Passion of S. Perpetua, 202 or 203.—The fierce persecution of the later years of Septimius Severus (193–211) produced many martyrs. Among the most celebrated is S. Perpetua.

The author of the *Passion of S. Perpetua*[1] [Carthage, March 6, 202 or 203] states that Perpetua and her companion, Saturus, wrote the account of their own visions, and that he himself, an eye-witness, added the story of the martyrdom. This statement has been accepted as true, and Dr. Armitage Robinson distinguishes the differences of style in the three portions. He further conjectures that Tertullian himself may have been the compiler of the work, and he believes the Latin version to be the original of the Greek translation— and not *vice-versa*. S. Augustine quotes freely from these Acts in his sermon for S. Perpetua's day.[2]

The story is familiar to all. Perpetua had many relatives living, and was of distinguished birth and education. She was twenty-two, married, with an infant at the breast. Her five companions were also young; two were slaves and catechumens, of whom one was Felicitas, who was waiting for the birth of her child. The father of Perpetua ill-treated his daughter on account of her faith. She seized the opportunity of his absence from home to receive baptism, in consequence of which she was imprisoned. The martyrs received some alleviations in their captivity from the ministrations of two " dear deacons " who looked after them, and Perpetua was permitted to have her child with her.

Perpetua then has the first of her celebrated visions:

> I saw a brazen ladder of marvellous length, for it reached to heaven, and very narrow, for one could only mount singly. On the steps of the ladder were fastened iron instruments of all sorts,—swords, lances, hooks, knives,—arranged so that if one mounted carelessly and without looking above his head, he would have been torn to pieces, and his flesh would have remained spiked

[1] J. Armitage Robinson, in *Texts and Studies*, vol. i. 61, 1891 ; Pio Franchi de' Cavalieri, in *Römische Quartalschrift*, 1896, Suppl. 5 ; *Anal. Boll.* 1892.

[2] *Sermo* 280, 281, 282, in *P.L.* 38, col. 1280.

on all these instruments of iron. At the foot of the ladder was crouched a dragon of marvellous greatness, who lay in ambush for all those who were mounting the ladder, and terrified them to prevent their mounting. Saturus (the catechist) mounted first. He had just given himself up for our sake, because he was absent when we were arrested. He reached the summit of the ladder, and turned to me and said: "Perpetua, I am waiting for you: but take care the dragon does not bite you." I answered: "In the name of Jesus Christ he will do me no harm." As if he were afraid of me, the dragon gently raised his head, but when once I had reached the first rung I crushed him. I mounted then and discovered an immense garden, in the midst of which there was seated a man of tall stature, with white hair, clothed like a shepherd: he was seated and busy in milking his flock. Around were many thousands in white robes. The shepherd raised his head, looked at me, and said: "You have come well, my child, you have come without hindrance." He called me and gave me a piece of curdled milk. I joined my hands to receive it, and I ate, while all those present answered, *Amen*.

The subject of the martyr having overcome the dragon, mounting to heaven by a ladder, is represented in a fresco in the catacombs of S. Callixtus.[1] The subject of our Lord represented as a Shepherd milking His flock, and other conceptions, almost identical, are also found in the catacombs with a Eucharistic significance. In the earliest days of the Church, the Eucharist was received in the hands, folded crosswise, and those present said *Amen*.

The visions here recorded throw light on Christian iconography, and further show that the minds of these martyrs were saturated with passages from the Apocalypse, and from that popular allegory, the *Shepherd of Hermas*.[2] This reproduction of current literature, and also of passages from early liturgies,[3] is a fairly common feature of the *Acta*.

[1] Wilpert, *Le pitture delle catacombe romane*, p. 445, pl. 553, 1910 (Italian translation from the German original).

[2] Lightfoot, *op. cit.*, "Miscellaneous Texts," 1891.

[3] Cabrol, *Dict. Arch. Chrét.: Actes des Martyrs*, p. 418.

After Perpetua has resisted the prayers of her father to recant, the prisoners are tried. The dialogue closely resembles that in other authentic Acts. They are condemned to the beasts, and sent back to prison to await death, while the child of Perpetua is taken from her. They pass the time in prayer. Perpetua prays for her brother Dinocrates:

> During that night I had a vision: I saw Dinocrates coming forth from a place of darkness, and many others were there, burning with heat and with thirst. Dinocrates had on a soiled dress: his face was sad, pale, disfigured by the wound which he had when he died. Dinocrates had been my brother in the flesh, dead at seven years old of a cancer in the face in circumstances which caused horror to every one. Between him and me I saw a great space which neither the one nor the other could pass. In the place where Dinocrates was, I saw a basin full of water, whose edge was too tall for a child to reach. Dinocrates stood on tiptoe as if to drink, and I was grieved to see this basin full of water, and the edge too high for him to reach.

She awoke from her dream and continued to pray night and day for him. Then she had another vision:

> The place which I had seen full of darkness, was full of light, and Dinocrates was cleansed in body, well clothed, cared for, refreshed. The wound in his face was healed, and the edge of the basin had become lower, and reached half way up him: the child drank freely. On the edge of the basin was a golden vessel filled with water: Dinocrates drank of this water but it diminished not. When he had drunk enough he went away, and began to play like the child that he was. Then I awoke, and understood that my brother had quitted the place of suffering.

This vision shows the belief of the Church in the efficacy of prayers for the dead. S. Augustine, in *The Origin of the Soul*, discusses the vision at length and states that Dinocrates was suffering for sins committed after baptism.[1]

---

[1] *De Origine Animae*, i. 10, and iii. 9. It seems very unlikely in the circumstances that the child *was* baptized.

On the eve of martydom Perpetua has yet another vision: she sees herself, as a male athlete, anointed with oil, wrestling and overcoming an immense Egyptian in the arena,—a symbol of the devil.

Felicitas, whose one grief was that her martyrdom was to be delayed, three days before the games, in answer to the prayers of her comrades, gave birth to a daughter, who was adopted by a Christian woman. One would like to know the story of this child of Felicitas.

The story of their death, related with such simplicity, is too familiar to need quotation.

(8) Passion of Jacobus and Marianus, 259.—Of the same type is the less well-known *Passion of SS. Jacobus and Marianus*[1] [April 12, 259] respectively deacon and reader in the Church of Cirta, who perished in the same persecution as the bishops Sixtus II. in Rome, Cyprian in Carthage, and Fructuosus at Tarragona.

The author relates that he was united to these martyrs "by a particular affection and a close friendship." A few extracts must suffice. After Jacobus and Marianus had been seized, tried and tortured they were sent back to prison, thanking God for the joy of their recent victory. Marianus in a dream sees a judge on his platform, and a throng of confessors condemned to death. Among them is Cyprian, martyred that very year: a loud voice calls on Marianus, and Cyprian helps him on to the platform among the confessors. Then the scene changes, and amid the gardens of Paradise (described with exquisite feeling), Cyprian offers Marianus a cup of water from a heavenly source. Jacobus, too, has a vision of a divine figure who offered him two purple girdles, one for himself and one for his friend, and bade them quickly follow him. He awakes, trembling with joy. Their fellow-confessors, also, have visions. Their death is recorded as follows:—

They led the confessors to the place of triumph: it was an enclosed valley traversed by a river whose banks rose in a gentle slope like the seats of a natural amphi-

[1] *Studi e Testi*, i. 47, 1900; Dufourcq, *Études sur les* Gesta Martyrum *romains*, iii. 135.

theatre. The blood of the martyrs flowed in a little stream to the river, and this scene had a mysterious symbolism for the saints, who, baptized in their own blood, went to receive in the waters as it were new purification. . . . The executioner having a number to strike, placed his victims in long rows so that the blows flew wildly from one head to another. . . . According to custom they bound the eyes of the condemned before execution : but no darkness could limit the free range of vision of their hearts, in which was shed an ineffable and dazzling light. . . . When all were killed the mother of Marianus, joyous as the mother of the Maccabees, and assured now that the passion of her son was fulfilled, congratulated, not so much him as herself, for having brought forth this child. She embraced the body, fruit and glory of her own body, and lovingly kissed the severed neck. Oh blessed Mary, blessed mother of such a son, happy to bear so beautiful a name. . . .

We may add to this class the *Passion of Carpus, Papylus, and Agathonice* [1] [Pergamos, April 13, 160–180 (?)], considered by Harnack to be a contemporary document of the second century ; that of *Apollonius* [2] the senator [Rome, April 8, 183 (?)], and that of *Crispina* [3] [Tebessa in Africa, Dec. 5, 304].

Class III. : Documents depending on those of the first two Classes.—Texts of the third class depend on the documents of the first and second classes, and include the remaining twenty-four Passions which Leclercq recognizes as authentic. Some of these have suffered severely from interpolations, and Delehaye [4] very justly relegates nearly half of them to the inferior class of historical romances.

(1) Passion of S. Pionius, 250.—Among the better authenticated documents is the *Passion of S. Pionius*, the priest [Smyrna, March 12, 250], which appears to be nearly

[1] Text in Aubé, *Revue Archéologique*, December 1881, p. 348 ; cf. *L'Église et L'État dans la seconde moitié du troisième siècle*, Appendix I. p. 499. Duchesne, *Bull. Crit.*, May 1882, p. 469.

[2] Text in *Anal. Boll.*, 1895, p. 284. See Leclercq, *Les Martyrs*, i. p. 112, for bibliography ; F. C. Conybeare, *The Acts of Apollonius* (for translation).

[3] *Studi e Testi*, vol. ix. p. 23, 1902.

[4] Delehaye, *Les Légendes hagiographiques*, p. 136.

contemporary with the events, and is full of vivid local colour. Eusebius [1] gives a summary of the incident; and of the sub-ject-matter of the long speeches Pionius made in the forum on his way to judgment, and in prison : a portion of the Passion which would otherwise seem the most open to suspicion. The historical fact that the persecution of the Christians was frequently caused by the enmity of the Jews is brought out in these Acts. The scene in the forum may be quoted :

> When they arrived in the forum, an immense crowd poured into it, occupying all the empty spaces, and covering to the roof the pagan temples and houses. There was an incredible number of women there, because it was the Sabbath, and so the Jews of the town were free. The immense throng of all ages wanted to see : those who were too short got up on stools and on boxes, showing great ingenuity in remedy-ing their natural defects.

Pionius then makes a lengthy speech, addressed especially to the Jews, and quoting from the Jewish law. Even the writer of the Passion remarks, "He said many other things, for his speech was of great length, and there was no end to it."

The trial follows much the usual course. Pionius and his companions return to prison, and pass their time "in evil-smelling cellars," in chanting hymns, and in silent meditation. They are visited by the faithful, by pagans anxious to convert Pionius, by those "weeping hot tears" who had succumbed and sacrificed to idols, and by those also who had been pressed by the Jews to return to the synagogue. Pionius makes them another "long discourse," full of com-passion, and weeping himself. Among his fellow-prisoners is a woman, Macedonia, a Montanist; and at the stake Pionius suffers with Metrodorus, a Marcionite priest. The statement of the unwelcome fact that Pionius suffered with two heretics seems a guarantee of authenticity ! Their death is recorded as follows :

> They put up the stakes to which Pionius and Metro-dorus (the Marcionite priest) were fastened. . . . Pionius

[1] Eusebius, *Hist. Eccles.* iv. c. 15, in *P.G.* 20, col. 363.

kept his eyes and spirit fixed on the sky. They brought wood and fuel: the fire flamed up with a joyful crackling. Pionius had closed his eyes, and prayed in silence that he might rest in blessedness. Soon after, his face lighted up with a great joy: he said *Amen*, and gave up his spirit like a soft breath: commending it to Him from Whom he awaited his reward, and Who has Himself promised to do justice to spirits unjustly condemned, and saying: " Lord, receive my spirit."

The precision of the days and dates further confirms our impression that we are here dealing with an authentic document:

This passed in the proconsulship of Julius in Asia, Proculus and Quintilianus being magistrates: under the third consulship of the emperor Decius, and the second of Gratian: according to the Romans, the fourth day before the ides of March (March 12): according to the Asiatics, the twelfth day of the sixth month: finally, according to our method of reckoning, a Saturday at 10 o'clock, in the reign of our Lord Jesus Christ, to Whom be honour and glory for ever and ever. Amen.

(2) **Passion of Montanus and Lucius, 259.**—The writer of the *Passion of Montanus and Lucius* [1] [Carthage, Feb. 24, 259] states that the saints themselves wrote the greater part. The document is obviously modelled on the *Passion of S. Perpetua*, but the accent of truth can be detected in spite of the imitation, the verbosity and the accumulation of marvels which disfigure it. It was probably compiled some years after the event by a writer whose style occasionally recalls that of S. Cyprian.

The earlier part of the recital is in the first person, and records the hardships of the life in prison and the series of visions that encouraged the confessors—that of the matron, Quartellosa, who partakes of a cup of milk,[2] an ancient

---

[1] Pio Franchi de' Cavalieri, in *Römische Quartalschrift*, 1875, Suppl. 8 ; *Anal. Boll.*, 1899, p. 67 ; *Studi e Testi*, 1900, vol. iii. p. 7, and 1909, fasc. 3, p. 1.

[2] Cf. The vision of Perpetua, *supra*, p. 166.

symbol of the Eucharist, being especially interesting. The passage following illustrates a common Christian practice:

> The next day, as we were waiting for the hour when the administrator of the prison should bring us, not food, for we had had none for two days, but something to make us feel our privation, suddenly, as drink comes to him who thirsts, and food to him who hungers, and martyrdom to him who longs for it, even so the Lord granted us refreshment (*refrigerium*) by means of the priest, dearest Lucian, who forcing his way through the strictest barricade, sent us two cups by means of Herennienus, subdeacon, and Januarius, the catechumen, who brought to all that Food which diminishes not. This help sustained the sick and weak . . . and all rendered to God thanks for His glorious deeds.

A very human incident occurs in prison. Montanus had had with a certain Julian, a sharp discussion about a woman who, excluded from Communion, had yet partaken. When the dispute was ended " there was a certain coldness between the confessors." The following night Montanus has a vision. They are all together, a great company of martyrs, with Cyprian and Lucius, clothed in white, and with flesh whiter than their white raiment, in an immense plain bathed in light. Montanus perceives some stains on his own breast. On waking he told the story to Julian and added: " Whence came these stains? It is because I am not reconciled with Julian. . . . So I conclude, dearest brothers, that we should strive with all our strength to preserve peace and concord and oneness of mind among us."

The story of the trial and tortures is told by the friend of the confessors, and their deaths are recorded in the following words :—

> The executioner was ready, his long sword already suspended above the neck of the condemned, when they saw Montanus lift his hands to heaven, and heard him pray God with a loud voice . . . that Flavian, separated from his companions, might follow in three days. And as if to give a pledge that his prayer was granted, he tore in two pieces the bandage that bound his eyes, and bade them keep the other half for Flavian.

.   .   .   .

Now that he was sure to die, Flavian walked full of joy, and talked freely to those about him. . . . As he talked, his spirit dwelt already in the Kingdom where, in a few moments, he would reign with God ; . . . after he had encouraged each one there, and given the kiss . . . he mounted on to a little height and said . . . "Dearly beloved brothers, you have peace among you if you remain in peace with the church : preserve oneness of spirit in love . . . our Lord Jesus Christ Himself said shortly before His Passion, 'I leave you the commandment to love one another.'"

Other Documents of the Third Class.—Very similar in character, and belonging to this class, are the *Acts of Acacius*, Bishop of Antioch in Pisidia [March 31, 250], of the priest, *Saturninus*, and his companions [Carthage, Feb. 11, 304], of *Agape, Irene, and Chione* [1] [Thessalonica, April 3, 304], of *Felix*,[2] Bishop of Tibiuca in North Africa [Aug. 30, 303], of *Phileas and Philoromus* [Alexandria, Feb. 4, 306],[3] and perhaps the *Passion of S. Thecla* [Iconium, about 47], rejected by Baronius, but now generally accepted as a composition of the second century.[4]

We have now examined three classes of documents, of which those in the first two classes possess a high degree of truth, and those in the third retain at least the main outlines of the story.

Characteristics of Genuine Documents.—To distinguish sharply between authentic documents and those of inferior value is not possible, even after applying the critical tests indicated above, as the various classes do, in fact, overlap. Yet certain of the records are pervaded by a peculiar spiritual atmosphere : they are stamped genuine as with a hall-mark. It may be possible to define in words something of this spirit and its manner of expression.

[1] *Studi e Testi*, 1902, vol. ix. p. 1.

[2] *Anal. Boll.*, 1897, p. 27 ; 1903, p. 460.

[3] Le Blant in *Anal. Boll.*, 1897, and in *Nuovo Bullettino di archeologia cristiana*, 1906, p. 27.

[4] For bibliography see Leclercq, *op. cit.* p. 141 ; Cabrol, *Dict.: Actes des Martyrs*, p. 374 ; F. C. Conybeare, *op. cit.* for translation. Text in Gebhardt, *Acta martyrum selecta*.

(1) Simplicity of Style.—The heroic story is told in simple language as if it were an ordinary event : whether the martyr is at his trial, or in prison, or suffering torture or death, there is a perfect measure in word and deed. " So Jesus Christ crowned them with peace,"—thus concludes the story of the death of many a martyr. Again, of the seven sons of Symphorosa [1] [July 17] we read :

> They gathered up the remains, and placed them in tombs : their names are written in the book of life.

And of Crispina : [2]

> " I bless God who has thus deigned to deliver me from your hands. Thanks be to God ! " And signing her brow with the sign of the cross and stretching out her neck, she was beheaded for the name of our Lord Jesus Christ to Whom is honour for ever and ever. Amen.

These are a few out of many examples.

(2) Homeliness of Certain Incidents.—Many a homely incident, a human touch, bring these martyrs very near to us : Cyprian, who cannot fasten the sleeve of his garment ; Fructuosus, who jumps out of bed at the knocking of the soldiers at his door, and asks if he may stop and put on his shoes ; Montanus and Lucius, who await death with so perfect a courage, yet quarrel over the orthodoxy or morals of one of the women, their fellow-prisoner, and then make peace again with such exquisite charity ; Perpetua in prison who, when her infant is restored to her there, " suffered no more ; all my pains and anxieties passed away and the prison became for me a house of pleasure." How natural, too, is her ex-clamation—" When we were put in prison I was terrified, because I had never endured such darkness." And again, after being worn out by the persecution and pleading of her father, she writes, on his departure : " He did not come back for several days, and I thanked God : his absence was such a relief."

(3) Inspiration of Certain Phrases.—Yet, here and

---

[1] Leclercq, *op. cit.* i. 209. This Passion is certainly based on an authentic document.

[2] *Supra*, p. 169.

there, in the simple narrative, some inspired utterance flashes forth almost unconsciously from the white heat of spiritual experience.   Thus, at the end of the account of the horrors inflicted on the martyrs at Lyons, we read :

> So they wove one crown of divers colours and all kinds of flowers, and offered it to the Father.

After Polycarp had been martyred

> They gathered up his charred bones, more precious than precious stones and purest gold.

Phileas cries :

> I have never suffered ; and now that I begin, I begin to be a disciple of our Lord Jesus Christ.

There is the mother " who died seven times over at the death of each of her sons ; " and Blandina, one of the martyrs of Lyons, is described as

> A noble mother that had fired her sons to fight valiantly, and sent them on first as victors to the great King.

(4) The Individuality of the Martyrs.—These repeated stories of martyrdoms might well become monotonous, yet, from the very force of their truth, these *Acta* unconsciously preserve the sharp outlines of individuality and variety of psychology, so that the persons of the drama live before us. There is the Bishop Polycarp, eighty-six years old, whose one thought is for his flock, and who, on the way to martyrdom, prays

> For all those whom he had known in his long life, great and small, illustrious and obscure, and for the whole Catholic Church throughout the world. . . .

Ignatius, in his desire for martyrdom, implores his fellow-Christians not to prevent his condemnation :

> Let me offer myself a sacrifice while the altar is ready. . . . I am the wheat of God, and am ground by the teeth of wild beasts that I may be found pure bread.

Bishop Pothinus of Lyons[1] is ninety and

> so weak in body that he could scarcely draw breath, and yet the ardour of his soul and eager desire for martyrdom roused his remaining strength.

Contrast with these Perpetua, as revealed in her auto-biography, who can be humorous in an African prison. Truly she writes of herself:

> I have always been gay, I shall be more gay in another world.

She goes singing to her death on that " day of victory, day of glory, promised and divine day," and her last thought is for another. After being tossed in the arena she gets up, and seeing her companion, Felicitas, lying on the ground, she goes to her, gives her a hand to lift her up, and kisses her.

How different again is Flavian.[2] In prison, awaiting his death, he sees in a vision the martyred Cyprian, in whose footsteps he is longing to follow. How natural is the question he asks Cyprian—" Does the death-blow hurt?" and Cyprian replies:

> The body suffers nothing when the spirit is with God.

The same note of triumphant ecstasy is struck by Symphorosa, who cries:

> Whence comes this joy that I can be sacrificed with my sons to God?

And by the martyr " who did not feel her tortures because the Lord suffered in her place." Even so Carpus, as they lit the fire at the stake, cries out:

> Blessed be Thou, Lord Jesus Christ, Son of God, who has deigned to make me, a sinner, companion of Thy heritage.

From these triumphant saints we turn to Blandina, a slave woman, " delicate, infirm, despised." Her mistress had grave fears for her constancy: we can almost hear her discussing the question with the anxious bishop! After

---

[1] Eusebius, *Hist. Eccles.* v. c. 1.
[2] *Passion of Montanus and Lucius*, Leclercq, *op. cit.* ii. 143.

watching the tortures, the heroisms and the apostasies of her fellow-citizens, Blandina herself died fearless, "talking with God." For there were apostates as well as martyrs, and the fears of the Church were better justified in some cases than in that of Blandina.

And how subtly drawn again are the different characters, and the precise circumstances of the apostacy! There were those who rushed to deny their faith, and those who succumbed only at the sight of the wild beasts, or to the prayers of their kinsfolk, or after enduring torture. Some, like the woman Biblias,[1] after a first apostasy returned and won their crown.

But amid all this diversity, the vast majority of the martyrs are alike in their burning enthusiasm, unflinching courage and joyous serenity; and it is this perhaps that is their most striking characteristic. "Assured and tranquil," "grave and radiant"—the words occur again and again in the *Acta*. Amid the horrors of prison, and tortures, worse than death, they pray and sing and meditate. And what visions of peace are theirs! They dream of shining plains and flowing rivers, and themselves, a white-robed throng, refreshed at celestial waters, and sharing in the heavenly banquets; or of the Good Shepherd receiving the faithful in the gardens of Paradise, fresh with fountains, where strange birds flutter among the leaves of the trees. These are the pictures we see above their shrines on the walls of the catacombs.

[1] Eusebius, *Hist. Eccles.* v. 1.

CHAPTER XIII

ACTS OF THE MARTYRS: DOCUMENTS OF THE FOURTH CLASS

History of the documents up to the fourth century.—The hagiographical collections of Eusebius.—Pilgrimages and monasticism.—Records of the Roman martyrs in the fourth century (Damasus, Augustine).—The Church on the authenticity of the *Gesta*.—Poverty of authentic records in the sixth century (Gregory the Great).—Martyrologies of the seventh and eighth centuries.

O Vetustatis silentis obsoleta oblivio.[1]
Prudentius, *Peristephanon*, i. 73.

Documents of the Fourth Class.—Of the vast number of hagiographical records dealing with the first three centuries we have found only forty which may be called authentic. As regards the rest, for our present purpose we may neglect altogether those documents which are forgeries or pure inventions. There remain, however, a large number of records which certainly contain some grains of truth. Pending further criticism of the individual Passions, we may place them, a strangely mixed company, in a fourth class and attempt to delineate some of their common characteristics, whether of form or contents, to show the conditions under which they were composed, and thence account for the process of successive deformations. The best of the Passions of Roman martyrs belong to this class.

History of the Documents up to the Fourth Century.—There are few details of the history of these documents. Copies of the Christian versions of the *Acta* were no doubt multiplied, and encyclical letters carried the name of many a martyr beyond the bounds of his own locality. These *Acta* were read liturgically in most of the churches from the middle of the second century. A general council of the African

[1] *P.L.* 60: "*Alas, for the dim oblivion of the silent ages!*"

178

churches at Hippo in 393[1] authorizes this custom on the anniversaries of the martyrs, when, as we learn from Cyprian, Masses were offered, and feasts celebrated at their shrines.[2]

No doubt, already even in those early days, the compilers filled in from their imagination the bare outlines of the historic fact. Then came the destruction of the records under Diocletian. Wherever these Acts and Passions were used liturgically it was a practical local necessity, as well as a pious duty, to replace the original documents as far as might be : from oral tradition, from such scant documents as remained, and from pure imagination.

Hagiographical Collections of Eusebius.—There is, however, no record of any hagiographical *collection* prior to the great works of Eusebius. The most important of these was his *Collection of Ancient Martyrdoms* (Συναγωγὴ τῶν μαρτύρων ἀρχαίων)—a complete account of the subject, now lost, but known in Alexandria, though not in Rome, as late as the sixth century.[3] A few of these Passions survive in liturgical documents. This work established, on a sure historical basis, the *Martyrology of Asia Minor*, which we have in an abridged Syriac translation in a manuscript of A.D. 412 ; and this latter document is one of the sources of the so-called *Martyrology of S. Jerome.*[4]

Many records of the martyrs are found in the familiar *Ecclesiastical History.* In this the writer often refers us to his earlier work. Finally, in the *Martyrs of Palestine* (Περὶ τῶν ἐν Παλαιστίνῃ μαρτυρησάντων), Eusebius describes the persecution at Caesarea from 303 to 310, of which he was an eye-witness.

These records of Eastern martyrs need not detain us.

Pilgrimages and Monasticism.—With the sudden triumph of the Church in 312, following so closely on the horrors of the Diocletian persecution (303–304), there swept over Rome a passionate wave of enthusiasm for the martyrs ;

---

[1] Hardouin, *Concilia*, i. 886.
[2] See *supra*, p. 137. Cf. Tertullian (about 160–240), *De Corona*, c. 3, in *P.L.* i, col. 79 : " We offer Masses for the dead on their anniversaries as a commemoration rite."
[3] See *infra*, p. 183.   [4] See *infra*, Chap. XVI.

and precisely at this date was compiled the Roman Calendar [1] (containing brief notices of the date of their deaths and the locality of the shrines), and in 354 the Philocalian Calendar,[2] containing a list of forty-seven Roman martyrs and three African.

The great Constantinian basilicas and oratories were being built in honour of the martyrs; Pope Damasus (366–384) restored and decorated their shrines in the catacombs, and his famous secretary, Philocalus, author of the Calendar, carved in beautiful characters the epitaphs [3] composed by his master.

During the centuries that followed, the faithful flocked to the catacombs,[4] and pilgrims came from east and west to worship at the shrines of the martyrs.

Eastern monasticism, too, was taking root in the West. There arose, at that moment, a double need: of an oral tradition to satisfy the pilgrims, and of written documents for liturgical and private use in the monasteries. To supply these needs the Roman *Gesta* [5] appeared.

On what historical truth were they based?

Records of the Roman Martyrs in the Fourth Century: Damasus, Augustine.—Already in the early fourth century the fame of the martyrs who sowed the seed of the Church had paled before the more recent and familiar glories of the heroes of the Diocletian persecution. The names of Telesphorus, the martyr pope,[6] and of Justin, the philosopher,[7] both of the second century, nowhere appear; and the forty-seven Roman martyrs of the Philocalian Calendar all belong to the third century.

If we turn to the epitaphs of Damasus, we derive little definite information from them, save the fact of the existence of the martyr, and the place of his shrine. The verses are filled up with generalities and platitudes, and the poet himself seems conscious of his ignorance. "Anti-

---

[1] *Infra*, p. 224. [2] *Supra*, p. 50.

[3] *Epigrammata Damasi*, ed. Ihm; cf. *infra*, p. 291.

[4] Chaps. II., III. on Pilgrimages.

[5] The word *Gesta* (deeds) was applied, from the fifth century onward, to the lives of the martyrs, as well as the older words *Acta* (for a document presumably based on the *Acta Proconsularia*), *Passiones*, *Vitae*.

[6] *Supra*, p. 67. [7] *Supra*, p. 153.

quity could not retain the names or the number of the Saints" (*Sanctorum . . . nomina nec numerum potuit retinere vetustas*),[1] he inscribes on the shrine of an unknown martyr. Yet Damasus as a child knew some of the actual actors in the drama: "An executioner told this to me, Damasus, when I was a child."

Prudentius,[2] in his *Crown of Martyrs* (409), sadly echoes him:

> We saw innumerable ashes of the saints in Rome . . . You ask the names and inscriptions carved on their graves? It is difficult for me to answer . . . many sepulchres give the name of the martyr and some epitaph, but there are also mute marbles closing silent tombs . . . Christ alone has their names complete.

The same poet, after singing of the deeds of his own Spanish saints, mentions only Hippolytus, Pope Sixtus II. and Laurence out of all the Roman martyrs. And the incidents he records are legendary. It is indeed just these saints, with the addition of Agnes, Sebastian and Agatha, whom alone of the Roman martyrs we find mentioned in S. Augustine and S. Ambrose.[3] On the rare occasion when the *Acta* exist, S. Augustine quotes them freely and accurately, as we have seen in the cases of Cyprian, Perpetua, Fructuosus.[4] It is obvious, then, that authentic records were lacking. Even in favoured Africa there seems a dearth of such documents, for S. Augustine in one of his sermons[5] says:

> While we can hardly find any *Gesta* of the other martyrs which we can read on their festivals, the Passion of this saint (Stephen) is in a canonical book.

The Church on the Authenticity of the *Gesta*.—In the general organization of affairs in the fifth and sixth centuries,

---

[1] *Epig.* No. 42.

[2] *Peristephanon*, xi.: S. Hippolytus, in *P.L.* 60, col. 530.

[3] For a complete list of references see Dufourcq, *Études sur les* Gesta Martyrum *romains*, p. 28.

[4] *Supra*, Chap. XI.　　　　　[5] *Serm.* 315 in *P.L.* 38, col. 1426.

the Church paid especial heed to fixing the canonical and authentic books.[1]

In the Roman Synod of 494, held under Pope Gelasius (492–496),[2] nearly all the *Gesta* of the martyrs are excluded, in the decretal *De Recipiendis*, from the number of authentic works:

> . . . The *Gesta* of the holy martyrs . . . in accordance with ancient custom, by a special precaution are not read in the Roman Church : because the names of those who wrote them are entirely unknown ; and they are considered to be written by the infidels or the ignorant, and contain what is superfluous or inadequate to the truth : as, for example, the Passion of a certain Ciricus and Julitta[3] [June 16], and of George, and other Passions of this kind, which are said to have been composed by heretics. Wherefore, lest the slightest occasion of mockery should arise, they are not used in the Roman Church . . . the Acts of blessed Silvester, chief (*praesul*) of the apostolic seat (may be read), also the writing about the Finding of the Cross of our Lord, and the Finding of the head of John the Baptist. For they are new records, and some Catholics read them : but when these come into the hands of Catholics let them follow the precept of the blessed Apostle Paul : " Prove all things, hold fast that which is good."

This document points to the existence in the fifth century of many *Gesta* of doubtful authenticity.

A desire to establish the authenticity of the *Gesta* is apparent in the mind of the compiler of the *Liber Pontificalis*. Pope Clement (?90–112), he tells us,[4] allotted the seven regions of the city of Rome to faithful notaries of the Church, who should eagerly seek out, each in his own district, the *Gesta* of the martyrs : further, Anteros (235–236) continues this organization, and Fabian (236–251) appoints seven sub-deacons to overlook the notaries. Again, the compiler

---

[1] *Liber Pontif.*, ed. Duchesne, i. page c.

[2] Thiel, *Epistolae Romanorum Pontificum*, i. 458 : Leipsic, 1872 ; or in *P.L.* 59, col. 168. It is not absolutely certain that Gelasius is the original author of the decretal he is promulgating, which has been ascribed to Damasus (366–384). On the *Decretum Gelasianum* see *Texte und Untersuchungen* (3[te] Reihe, 8[te] Band), vol. 38, 1912. Cf. *infra*, p. 192.

[3] *Anal. Boll.*, 1882, p. 192.

[4] See *supra*, p. 75.

of the Constitution of Silvester[1] (*Constitutum Silvestri*), a forgery of the year 501, states that at the Council held by this pope sat fourteen notaries of the Church, who narrated in order the *Gesta* of the martyrs. Duchesne treats these statements with the scepticism which they deserve.

Poverty of Authentic Records in the Sixth Century : The Passionary of Gregory : the Martyrology of S. Jerome.—Another document bears witness to the paucity of authentic records in the sixth century. This is the famous letter of Pope Gregory,[2] written in 598 in answer to a letter from Eulogius, Bishop of Alexandria, asking for a copy of the *Collection of Ancient Martyrdoms* (Συναγωγή) of Eusebius. Gregory writes that he is not even aware of the existence of the volume for which Eulogius asks him, and possesses nothing except the other books of Eusebius ; a Roman Calendar with no details beyond the date and place of the martyrdoms (identified as the famous *Martyrology of S. Jerome*[3]) ; and "a single volume which contains very little"[4] (*The Roman Passionary of Gregory*).

Martyrologies of the Seventh and Eighth Centuries. —Suddenly, however, in the seventh and eighth centuries appear the many famous Martyrologies : that called by the name of the Venerable Bede (672-735) at Yarrow ; that of Rabanus Maurus in Germany (about 845) ; that of Florus of Lyons (848) ; that of Ado, Archbishop of Vienne (860-874) ; and that of Usuard (875).[5]

By this time, too, we find, from a letter dated 794 of Pope Hadrian to Charlemagne,[6] that Passions may be read "even in church" when the anniversaries are celebrated : further, in an eighth-century manuscript[7] there is a note that Passions are to be read at Office in the Church of S. Peter.

It is then mainly between the fourth century, when there are practically no documents, and the ninth, with its detailed

---

[1] *Liber Pontif.* i. page c. ; cf. *supra*, p. 81.

[2] Jaffé, *Regesta pontificum Romanorum*, i. 180 ; Leipsic, 1885.

[3] *Infra*, p. 215.   [4] See *infra*, p. 201.

[5] Texts of martyrologies are in *P.L.* 94, col. 799 ; 110, col. 1121 ; 119, col. 95 ; 123, cols. 201 and 599. See *infra*, p. 228.

[6] *P.L.* 98, col. 1284.

[7] *MS. Parisin.* 3836. See Cabrol, *Dict. : Acta Martyrum*, p. 387.

Martyrologies, that the lives of the martyrs are compiled. How, during those ages, has the double influence of oral tradition and of written document affected the original historical facts?   What are the characteristics of the *Gesta*? Can we by study of them define their date more closely? What residuum of truth do they contain?

CHAPTER XIV

ACTS OF THE MARTYRS: THE WORK OF TRADITION AND OF THE HAGIOGRAPHERS

The work of tradition: The imagination of the people; the suggestion of the monuments; tradition and epigraphy.—The work of the hagiographers: Anachronisms and mistranslations; expansions of the original documents; plagiarisms; variety of the tradition and conventionality of the *Gesta*; polemical character of the *Gesta* (preoccupations with questions of authenticity; heretics and the deformation of the *Gesta*; asceticism and oriental influence).—Example of the successive deformations of the *Passion of S. Procopius*.—The residuum of truth in the *Gesta*: Le Blant and the Theory of Interpolation.

Multitudo martyrum quorum nec numerum nec nomina colligere potuimus. Dominus enim eos in libro vitae conscripsit.[1]

Gregory of Tours, *Hist. Franc.* i. 27.

The Work of Tradition on the *Gesta*.—The hagiographical traditions,[2] while preserving a vast body of truth, have yet been contaminated by those errors inherent in the nature of all traditions, as well as by some peculiar to themselves; and the very preservation, modification, and deformation of these traditions depend on the living cult of the Martyrs as it has survived through all the ages, sometimes as a reasonable veneration of the heroes of Christianity, but often debased by materialism, ignorance, and superstition.

The Imagination of the People.—It was around the shrines, venerated by the faithful, and visited by pilgrims, that for five hundred years tradition wove the legends embodied in the *Gesta*; and the dependence of the *Gesta* on these traditions rather than on authentic documentary

[1] " *A multitude of martyrs . . . whose names and number we cannot collect; but God has written them in the book of life.*"

[2] Delhaye, *Les Légendes hagiographiques*, to whose work I am indebted for this chapter; cf. works quoted above, p. 17, note 1.

185

sources is shown by the fact that in them are preserved the names of many authentic martyrs who are yet
unknown to the Philocalian Calendar (an obvious source,
it might seem) or even to the Martyrology of Jerome. In
the somewhat rare cases where the topographical statements
are identical in *Gesta* and Calendar [1] it is because they both
depend on local tradition. However ruthlessly these *Gesta*
may be criticized, even the least reliable have often preserved accurately the name, and place and date of burial
of a martyr otherwise forgotten. Of these martyrs who
lay in the catacombs,— a servant of the household of
Caesar, some Greek pilgrim worshipping at the shrine of
S. Peter, a lad surprised on the road bearing the Eucharist,
—what was known, save that when the call came they were
ready, and laid down their lives, and were buried with
rejoicing? At their shrines, year after year, on their
anniversaries,—their "birthdays" (*natales*),—Mass was celebrated. And if there were no other details of these
otherwise obscure lives to satisfy the fervour of the simple,
and the desire for edification on the part of their instructors,
what wonder that the lively Latin imagination should have
supplied them; should have coloured the story with the least
remote memories of the great Diocletian persecution; confused names, places, and dates; brought into the account the
politics, the theology, the controversies of a later day;
and heightened the strange and the miraculous element to
the further glory of the local shrines, and to strike awe into
the foreign pilgrim?

Suggestions of the Monuments.—The human mind is
ever prone to materialize the spiritual, and no doubt, pilgrim
and guide alike were more interested in a legend about this
stone or that relic, than in the spiritual combats of the
martyrs; and thus the monuments, frequently misinterpreted,
gave rise to many deformations of the truth. In Prudentius'
Hymn to S. Hippolytus [2] the poet seeks for his facts in
the frescoes depicting the martyr's death by being torn

[1] For a complete analysis see Dufourcq, *Études sur les* Gesta Martyrum *romains*, Paris, 1900.

[2] *Peristephanon*, xi. in *P.L.* 60, col. 767.

asunder by wild horses. The whole story resembles too closely the legend of the Greek hero Hippolytus to escape suspicion.[1]

We have seen[2] how the bishop Asterius, consults the paintings at S. Euphemia's shrine to supply him with details of her martyrdom. Again we read, in the *Passion of S. Eleutherius* [April 13],[3] that the saint preached to the beasts, and that they all raised their right foot to praise God. Is it a picture of Orpheus, adorning the martyr's shrine that the writer is unconsciously describing?

Often a legend of fellow-martyrs or of brothers develops around the shrines of saints whose only connexion is that they are buried near each other.

The confusion of the monuments resulting from the sack of Rome, and the subsequent restorations must have contributed further to deformations of the legends.

Delehaye gives a curious example of a name creating a legend.[4] The parish (*titulus*) where stands the Church of SS. Nereus and Achilleus was known as that of *Fasciola*. History is uncertain as to the origin of the name, but legend knows no doubts, and relates that when the blessed Peter left prison his leg had been injured by the heavy chain, "and the bandage (*fasciola*) fell off before the Septisolium in the Via Nova." We may remark, in passing, that the topographical exactitude of the details does not prove the truth or antiquity of the legend.[5]

Tradition and Epigraphy.—A misunderstanding of the epitaph of Damasus[6] to Felix and Adauctus [Aug. 30] has given rise to the story of two brothers, both called Felix, which we find in Ado's Martyrology; to the romance known as *Vita Sancti Felicis presbyteri* [Jan. 14], in the *Acta*

---

[1] Cf. *Studi e Testi*, 1908, t. xix. p. 123, for other classical reminiscences.

[2] *Supra*, p. 134.   [3] *Studi e Testi*, 1901, vi. p. 137.

[4] Delehaye, *op. cit.* p. 53.   [5] *Infra*, p. 198.

[6] "Oh how truly and rightly named Felix, happy, you who with faith untouched, and despising the prince of this world have confessed Christ, and sought the heavenly kingdom. Know ye also, brothers, the truly precious faith by which Adauctus too hastened a victor to heaven. The priest, Verus, at the command of his rector, Damasus, restored the tomb, adorning the thresholds of the saints" (*Epigrammata Damasi*, No. 7, ed. Ihm).

Sanctorum ;[1] and to endless further confusion of the historical facts. It seems probable, too, that the *Passion of SS. Digna and Merita* [September 22] owes its existence to another epitaph misinterpreted, in which the words *digna et merita* (worthy and deserving) are used as epithets.[2] Another epitaph of Damasus,[3] misunderstood, gave rise to the legend that Eastern pilgrims came to steal the bodies of Peter and Paul.

Such is the fashion in which tradition worked upon the original historical facts. A critical study of these Roman *Gesta*, created around definite shrines, would throw further light on the inquiry.[4]

The Work of the Hagiographers: Anachronisms: Mistranslations.—When we turn to the *Gesta* in which these traditions are embodied, internal evidence confirms the belief that they were written between the fourth and the ninth centuries. The philological peculiarities[5]—of orthography, vocabulary, syntax, and structure of sentence —show that they belong to that period when classical Latin was developing, gradually and unbeautifully, into the modern languages of Europe.

Further, there are mistakes of fact which no writer contemporary with the events could have made,—in the chronology, in the identity of places and persons concerned, in the titles of officials. The incidents and attendant circumstances recorded are those of a period subsequent to the persecutions : for example, the *Gesta* of the martyrs of the first and second centuries are highly coloured with the fresher recollections of the Diocletian persecution.

Sometimes a trivial blunder betrays the fact that our document is a Greek translation from a Latin original, as in the *Passion of S. Leo and Paregorius* [June 30],[6] where we

---

[1] See *Anal. Boll.*, 1897, p. 19.   [2] *Anal. Boll.*, 1897, p. 30.

[3] *Ep. Dam.* 26 : "Here (*i.e.* Catacombs of S. Sebastian) . . . lay S. Peter and S. Paul. . . . The East sent us disciples, a fact which we gladly acknowledge . . . but it was Rome who merited to guard (the bodies of) her citizens (*i.e.* Peter and Paul, who had lived and died in Rome)."

[4] Dufourcq, *op. cit.*

[5] Dufourcq, *op. cit.* p. 45, with bibliography; F. G. Mohl, *Introduction à la chronologie du Latin vulgaire*, Paris, 1899.

[6] Ruinart, *Acta Sincera*, with reference to Greek version.

find δεύτερος (=the second) as a rendering, without sense, of the Latin *secundus* (=favourable *or* second) (*Imperatoribus . . . quos secundos servatores et deos . . . nos vocamus*).

These mistakes have sometimes a far-reaching consequence on the tradition. For example, in the *Passion of S. Marciana* [Jan. 9] we read that when the saint was exposed to a lion in the arena, the beast, having smelt her (*odoratus*) refused to touch her. A copyist wrote " adoratus " for " odoratus," and hence the mediaeval legend of the lion in adoration.[1]

The *Acts of the Scillitan Martyrs* opens with the familiar formula :

> *Praesente bis et Candiano consulibus* . . .
> When Candianus was consul, and Praesens for the second time . . .

The transcriber took *praesente* for a present participle, and boldly altered the rest of the text to make sense. Later transcribers, however, were not contented with his rendering, and still further " emended " the readings, till the chronology of these authentic Acts was in confusion.[2]

The Expansions of the Original Documents.—These confusions of fact, and anachronisms are due to sheer mistakes. More deliberate offences on the part of the compilers have further deformed the records. In late documents we note the tendency to expand the original, and in the rare cases in which we possess the latter, a close comparison of the double or triple record is most instructive. Of the original *Acts of the Scillitan Martyrs* referred to above, we have several later versions, each more inaccurate and lengthy than the last.

We have already quoted the early version of these *Acts*.[3] The following extract from a somewhat later version will illustrate the tendency to expansion :—

> In those days, brought into the private audience chamber of Carthage *by the officials*, Speratus, Nartzalus

---

[1] *Breviarium Gothicum*, July 12 in *P.L.* 86, col. 1149.

[2] Delehaye, *op. cit.* p. 89; Monceau, *Histoire littéraire de l'Afrique chrétienne*, i. p. 62, Paris, 1901.

[3] *Supra*, p. 151.

. . . (etc.) were addressed *all together* by the proconsul Saturninus, who said : " You can win pardon from our lord the emperor if you return to a reasonable frame of mind and *observe the ceremonies of the gods.*"

Holy Speratus said : " *We are not conscious* of ever doing evil, *neither by deed nor consent* have we lent ourselves to iniquity. We are never found to have spoken ill of any, but evilly treated *and harassed* we have ever given thanks to God, *nay, we have ever prayed for those whose enmity we have unjustly endured.* Wherefore we look to our emperor, by whom this rule of living is permitted to us."

This difference in style is clearly seen by a comparison of the familiar and authentic record of the martyrdom of Ignatius [1] with the Greek text of the *Acta* of the fourth century.[2] In spite of the existence of five versions, discordant in some details, of this fourth-century document, these Acts contain a considerable amount of truth. Some extracts will show the general style. There is, first, the dialogue between Ignatius and the Emperor Trajan at Antioch :

When he was before the emperor this prince said to him : " Who are you, evil spirit, who dare to violate my orders, and to inspire others with contempt of them ? " Ignatius replied : " None but you, prince, ever called Theophorus (it was thus Ignatius was named) by this insulting name. Far from that, it is the evil spirits which tremble and fly at the voice of the servants of the true God. I know that I am hateful to them, which is what you intended to say. Christ is my King, and I destroy their snares." " And what is this Theophorus ? " said the emperor.

" It is whoever carries Jesus Christ in his heart."

" Do you think, then, that we have not also in our hearts the gods who fight for us ? "

" Gods ? You deceive yourself, they are only demons. There is only one God Who has made heaven and earth and all they contain : and there is only one Jesus Christ, the only Son of God, of Whose love I am assured."

" Whom do you say ? What, this Jesus whom Pilate fastened to a cross ? "

[1] *Supra*, p. 161.   [2] Lightfoot, *Apostolic Fathers*, ii. 2, p. 363.

" Say, rather, that this Jesus Himself fastened to the cross sin and its author, and that He gave, since then, to all those who bear Him in their breast, the power to lay low hell and its might."

" You bear, then, Jesus Christ within you ? "

" Yes, assuredly," answered Ignatius ; "because it is written : I will dwell in them and will accompany all their steps."

After the sentence and the thanksgiving of Ignatius, and details of the long voyage to Rome the Acts conclude :

All Rome had rushed to the amphitheatre, and drank with avidity the blood of the martyr who, having been given to two lions, was in an instant devoured by these cruel animals. They left of his body only the largest bones, which were gathered up with respect by the faithful, carried to Antioch, and placed in the church as an inestimable treasure. . . .

Such variations from the original tradition arise out of blunders or simple verbosity. But there are other and more potent causes of deformation.

Plagiarisms.—Frequently the writer is indulging in pure romance, for the sake of imparting pleasure or edification : he borrows incidents wholesale from the lives of other saints to fill out his own meagre story, and even pagan myths find a place in his pages. That the results were incoherent mattered little, and if at the end he can scarcely distinguish fact from fiction, it is pretty certain his audience will accept the whole as fact.

Variety of the Tradition and Conventionality of *Gesta.* —The *Gesta* were compiled at a period when the traditions were living and infinitely varied in the forms in which they were embodied. The compiler was forced to use those which were available; out of these he always seems to choose the most commonplace version. He simplified complicated historical facts; he obliterated delicate psychological distinctions of character; he omitted those homely details which carry conviction of authenticity ; he developed the simple utterances of the martyrs into interminable harangues; he fastened on the miraculous element and exaggerated it; and finally produced those dreary documents in which the martyrs have no distinctive personality; all share in the same remarkable antecedents; utter the same interminable platitudes, by which they convert innumerable multitudes; undergo impossible tortures prolonged by improbable miracles; and frequently perish by the simple expedient of having their heads cut off. How far are we here from the spirit of the genuine records! And it is, unfortunately, this type of document that proved popular. Hence it is always the conventional version of a Passion which is reproduced in numerous manuscripts, while the more characteristic records, in the rare cases when they exist, are found in a few manuscripts only.[1]

Polemical Character of the *Gesta.*—Sometimes the *Gesta* are polemical or didactic in character.[2] The writers are preoccupied with just those questions, doctrinal and disciplinary, that are discussed in papal decretals and other documents whose dates we know, and which so accurately reflect the spirit of some definite epoch, and indicate the phases of some controversy.

(1) Preoccupations with Questions of Authenticity.—For instance, the energy displayed by the Church of the fifth and sixth centuries in establishing a list of canonical and authentic writings[3] is reflected in the anxiety with which the compilers of the *Gesta* seek to gain confidence for their work. Again and again they insist on the authenticity of the *Gesta*, on the edification to be derived from reading them, especially as a defence against the activities of the heretics. The writer states that his work was dictated by the martyr himself, or based on one of his letters, or on original *Acta*, or on newly discovered documents. The official Church, however, more sceptical, as often, than her children, regarded these compilations with distrust, and the Gelasian edict[4] was no doubt bitterly resented by many an unknown writer.

(2) Heretics and the Deformation of the *Gesta.*—There is frequent reference to heretics in the *Gesta*, many of which

---

[1] See Catalogue of Manuscripts, published in the *Analecta Bollandiana*.
[2] Dufourcq, *op. cit.* p. 323.   [3] *Supra*, p. 181.   [4] *Supra*, p. 182.

are permeated by the fierce controversial atmosphere of the
period.   Some are written with the avowed purpose of com-
bating heresies by spreading abroad the knowledge of the
martyrs.   The compiler of the *Acts of Nereus and Achilleus*
passionately deplores the zeal of heretics, and the lukewarm
spirit of Catholics.   Sometimes it is the heretics themselves
who compile the *Gesta*, and modify the tradition for their
own purposes—as witness again the Gelasian decretal.[1]   We
have some definite facts on this point in the works of the
learned Rufinus,[2] between whom and S. Jerome there existed
such bitter enmity.   Writing in 397 he says:

> Whenever the heretics have found, in any of the
> renowned writers of old days, a discussion of things
> pertaining to the glory of God . . . they have not
> scrupled to infuse into these writings the poisonous
> taint of their own false doctrines.

After giving examples of interpolations made in the
writings of Clement of Rome, Clement of Alexandria,
Origen, and others, Rufinus continues:

> The whole collection of letters of the martyr Cyprian,
> is usually found in a single manuscript.   Into this
> collection certain heretics, who hold a blasphemous
> doctrine about the Holy Spirit, inserted a treatise of
> Tertullian . . . and from the copies thus made they
> wrote out a number of others; these they distributed
> through Constantinople at a very low price.

The Catholics were not behindhand in furnishing orthodox
versions of the legends by the same methods.
In the ancient Armenian version of the *Acts of Eugenia*[3]

---

[1] *Supra*, p. 182.
[2] Epilogue to Rufinus' *Translation of Pamphilius' Apology for Origen*,
Wace and Schaff, "Ante-Nicene Fathers," vol. iii. p. 421.   We find there a
further account of an ingenious falsification of a word in a manuscript bearing
on a controversial question.
[3] *P.L.* 21, col. 1105; F. C. Conybeare, in *Monuments of Early Christianity*,
London, 1894, for translation and criticisms.   The nucleus of the story is of the
third century, about 225; the Armenian text about 250; the Latin version about
400 (by Rufinus of Aquileia (?)).   Discoveries in the catacombs have established the
truth of parts of the Acts.   Cf. Dufourcq, *op. cit.* p. 222.

13

[Dec. 25] we read that this saint chose as her model, Thecla, the convert of S. Paul. The fact, however, that Thecla, a woman, had administered the rite of baptism was unacceptable to Christians of a later day; and in the fourth-century Latin Acts of Eugenia the name of Thecla does not appear.

The compilers sometimes frankly reveal their methods. Thus a certain Hilarion, in editing the *Acts of Athanagines*, a martyr of Nicomedia, who was perhaps an Arian, states that he has "made orthodox all that was said."

Again, the various versions of the *Acts of Peter* and the *Acts of Paul*[1] which replaced the primitive traditions, are due to the Manichaean controversy. This controversy also explains that preoccupation with the question of the voluntary nature of martyrdom which appears in the *Passions of Processus and Martinianus*,[2] the gaolers of S. Peter, of Andrew,[3] and of *Thomas*,[4] and elsewhere. The Catholic *Passion of S. Cyriacus* [Aug. 8] appears to be a romance actually based, in a spirit of rivalry, on the story of Manes, the founder of Manichaeism. A clause in the Gelasian decretals, defining the orthodox belief concerning the Apostle Paul, is implicitly directed against the Manichaeans. Thus the Acts mentioned above, and others coloured by this controversy, may be dated as of the fourth and fifth centuries.

(3) Asceticism in the *Gesta*.—To this epoch belongs that enthusiasm for the ascetic life which was filling the West with monasteries. It is expressed in the *Gesta* by an exaltation of the virtue of virginity, at the expense of historical truth and the true teaching of the Church. As examples similar to many others may be noted the *Passion of Nereus and Achilleus* [May 12], which contains a long attack on marriage,[5] and those of *S. Cecilia*,[6] *SS. Chrysanthus and Darias* [Oct. 25], and *SS. Julian and Basilissa* [Jan. 9].

---

[1] Lipsius, *Acta apostolorum apocrypha*, vol. i., 3 vols. Leipsic, 1891.

[2] *A.SS.*, July 2.   [3] Lipsius, *op. cit.* vol. ii.

[4] Lipsius, *op. cit.* vol. iii.

[5] Tillemont criticizes this Passion as "une très méchante pièce, digne des Manichéens, ennemis du mariage" (*Mémoires*, ii. p. 127).

[6] Mombritius, *Sanctuarium*, i. p. 332 (ed. 1910).

Here, too, the zeal of the compilers was perhaps spurred into rivalry by the ascetic virtues of the heretics.

(4) Oriental Influence on the *Gesta*.—We may note, in theology, politics, art, the potent influence of the East upon Rome. Here, again, the *Gesta* reflect the spirit of the age. Many a record of oriental martyrs is found among the Roman *Gesta*; and their shrines are seen in the catacombs; S. Anastasia and SS. Cosmas and Damian[1] take their place beside Laurence and Sebastian and Agnes; and a large number of *Gesta* of Roman martyrs are full of incidents which connect them with the East.

Such are but a few of the influences which have moulded the *Gesta*.

Example of the Deformation of a Document : *Passion of S. Procopius.*—Delehaye has pointed out that we have a unique example of the process of the deformation of the original sources, in the various *Passions of S. Procopius*;[2] because for this saint, by a rare good fortune, there exists not only the contemporary Passion, but also a series of records, proving independently his existence and very early cult.

S. Procopius [July 8 and Nov. 23] was martyred at Caesarea in Palestine, under Diocletian; and the original account of Eusebius, an eye-witness, in the *Martyrs of Palestine*, has been preserved for us in a Latin Passionary. It is a simple, dignified, and very human document.

In a Greek manuscript in Paris, and in a Latin Passionary at Monte Cassino, the main outlines of the story are embodied in a version known as the *First Legend of S. Procopius*. It is seven times the length of the original; full of inaccuracies, of rhetoric, and of incidents, miraculous and otherwise, invented and borrowed from other sources.

Based on this and considerably longer, is a *Second Legend* —a fantastic confusion of incidents from half-a-dozen different Passions, with scarcely a fact correct. It was well known in the eighth century.

---

[1] *Supra*, pp. 12, 13.
[2] See *supra*, p. 162 ; Delehaye, *op. cit.* p. 142.

Differing little from this is the *Third Legend*, of which the Greek version is published in the *Acta Sanctorum* of the Bollandists.[1] The account is extremely lengthy, and the whole truth contained in it can be summed up in two lines : Procopius of Jerusalem was martyred by the sword, under Diocletian, by the judge, Flavianus.

We may add that the writer of the first legend was in possession of the original document of Eusebius, as is evident from many similarities. If only we had the sources of the later Passions of other martyrs, we might find an equally small residuum of truth in these; while, on the other hand, if we had not, in this rare example, ample evidence to prove the existence and cult of S. Procopius, the spurious character of the Passion in the *Acta Sanctorum* might justly lead us to doubt if he existed at all.

The confusion, first, between the Procopius, reader and exorcist of Eusebius' record, and the Procopius who has become a pagan convert and soldier in the second legend; and, secondly, between the Caesarea in Palestine and that in Cappadocia, has caused endless confusion in the Oriental calendars: the least of which is a double entry for S. Procopius—July 8 for the soldier, and November 22 for the reader and exorcist.[1]

The Residuum of Truth in the *Gesta*.—We have thus indicated in a general manner the work of tradition and of the hagiographer on the historical facts relating to the martyrs. All authorities, from the Jesuit Delehaye, who is perhaps the severest critic, to Leclercq, Harnack, and Bardenhewer, who are somewhat more lenient in their judgments, agree that there is some residuum of truth in these *Gesta* of the fourth class; even if, as in the case of S. Procopius, it is only the fact of the existence of a saint, of his shrine, and of his cult. We may further note that the legendary character of the *Gesta* of any saint does not necessarily invalidate his existence; and that, in fact, the saints whose existence is best authenticated, and at whose shrines the faithful assembled, have suffered most from the extravagances of tradition.

---

[1] *Synaxarium ecclesiae Constantinopolitanae*, pp. 245, 805, in *Acta SS.*, November, propylaeum (ed. Delehaye, 1902).

There now remains the laborious and delicate task of determining what is the residuum of historical fact in the *Gesta*.

By bringing all our critical apparatus—philological, historical, psychological—to bear on each of the *Gesta*, we can frequently approximate to a true result.

Le Blant and the Theory of Interpolation.—Certain critics of these legends have, as we have said, accepted implicitly or explicitly, the Theory of Interpolation,[1] which supplies a general principle of criticism applicable to all *Gesta*. Le Blant, in a work of great learning, has, in fact, applied it to over two hundred of the Acts which are excluded even from Ruinart's *Acta Sincera*. He attempts to show that traces of original documents may be discerned even in the most fictitious records. He perceives these traces in passages which correctly reproduce the formulae of the pagan *Acta Proconsularia*; or in the official names of that complicated hierarchy which assisted at the arrest, trial, and execution of prisoners; or in the names of the buildings (theatre, circus, tribunal, secretarium, etc.) where the trials took place. He catches a glimpse of early manuscripts, in the use of words, phrases, and technical terms belonging to the first three centuries; in the precision of certain indications of day, date, month, and year; and in the knowledge shown of the ancient costume, and of curious incidents, social customs, and details of legal procedure of the period. He lays peculiar stress on the exactitude of topographical detail, especially in the Roman Acts.

Most modern authorities on the subject, as we have seen, adopt this theory, though they vary in the method of application.

But, though we were to accept Le Blant's conclusions, the grains of gold in these legends are few and hard to distinguish. Even granting, for the moment, the dependence of these *Gesta* on earlier documents, this fact is of little use to us if we remain in ignorance of the character of these authorities: they might well be more ancient than the *Gesta* without possessing a high degree of authenticity.

[1] *Supra*, p. 130.

But can we accept all these characteristics which Le Blant indicates, as equally valid proofs of dependence on an original source? If we consider the anxiety of the writers of the *Gesta* to gain credit for their work as depending on reliable sources,[1] and their shameless plagiarism,[2] it seems natural to suspect that in some cases at least the archaisms are the result of deliberate copying of *any* older document that came to hand. Again, topographical exactitude[3] indicates nothing except that the writer of the Roman *Gesta* in the fifth or sixth century is perfectly well acquainted with, say, the shrine of Nereus and Achilleus, or of Felicitas and her seven sons. We have already seen what errors arise from traditions woven around shrines.[4]

These remarks are only intended to indicate that Le Blant's application of the Theory of Interpolation is open to criticism. That it sometimes has resulted in the discovery of truth is equally certain. Fitly to appraise the justice of his results would demand an exhaustive study of each of the two hundred and twenty *Gesta* of which he treats, and the experimental application of his theory to others, especially in cases where we possess some independent material wherewith our conclusions may be checked.

[1] *Supra*, p. 192.
[2] *Supra*, p. 191 ; Delehaye, *op. cit.* chap. iii.
[3] *Supra*, p. 186.
[4] *Supra*, pp. 185 *seqq.*

CHAPTER XV

ACTS OF THE MARTYRS: THE ROMAN *GESTA*

Dates of the Roman *Gesta* : Internal evidence—External evidence : references to *Gesta* in Gregory of Tours.—Connexion of the *Gesta* with the *Liber Pontificalis*, with the *Passionary of Gregory the Great*, and with the *Martyrology of Ado*.—An examination of individual *Gesta*.

Bonum agonem subituri estis in quo agonothetes Deus vivus est : Xystarches Spiritus Sanctus : Corona aeternitatis brabium angelicae substantiae, politia in caelis, gloria in saecula saeculorum.[1]—Tertullian, *Ad Martyres*.

Dates of the Roman *Gesta* : Internal Evidence.—If we now turn our attention to certain of the Roman *Gesta*, we can in some cases bring forward fresh evidence for ascribing them to the fifth and sixth centuries. If a certain general similarity, philological and psychological, characterizes, as we have seen, the later Passions in general, a yet closer relationship of form and of spirit binds together many of our Roman *Gesta*,—as Dufourcq has demonstrated in his " *Gesta Martyrum* romains,"—and indicates that they were compiled at more or less the same period. On purely philological grounds, this period cannot be earlier than the fifth century ; since the technical terms employed, especially those of officials, belong to the age subsequent to the division of the Empire in 395.[2] The word *Gesta* itself, as applied to the deeds of the martyrs, appears first in the fifth century.

External Evidence : References to *Gesta* in Gregory of Tours.—On the other hand, we have, as we have seen,

[1] " *You are about to pass through a noble struggle, in which the master of the games is the living God: in which the trainer is the Holy Spirit: in which the prize is an eternal crown of angelic substance, citizenship in heaven, and glory for ever and ever.*"

[2] For an analysis of these terms, and a comparison with the *Notitia Dignitatum* (ed. Seeck, Berlin, 1876), of the time of Honorius, see Dufourcq, *op. cit.* p. 279.

references in the fifth- and in the sixth-century writings to *Gesta* already in existence.[1]   Gregory of Tours (d. 594), too, in his book *Concerning the Glory of the Martyrs*[2] (*De gloria martyrum*), mentions three *Gesta* of Roman martyrs,—the *Gesta of Pope Clement*[3] [Nov. 23] (the *fact* of whose martyrdom is dubious), of *Chrysanthus and Darias* [Oct. 25], and of *S. Pancras*[4] [May 4].   With regard to the other Roman martyrs he says :

There are many martyrs of the city of Rome whose Passions and history have not come down to us entire.

Connexion of the *Gesta* with the *Liber Pontificalis*. —There are ten *Gesta Martyrum* existing which record the passions of the popes prior to the Peace of the Church, namely, the *Passions of Clement, Alexander,*[5] *Callixtus,*[6] Urban (in the *Passion of S. Cecilia*),[7] *Cornelius,*[8] *Stephen,*[9] *Sixtus* II.,[10] Gaius (in the *Passion of S. Susanna*),[11] *Marcellus,*[12] and *Eusebius.*[13]   The *Liber Pontificalis*[14] of the sixth century borrows[15] from these *Gesta* for the lives of Urban and Cornelius, and possibly depends on them for the few incidents recorded of Gaius and Marcellus, while the record there of Sixtus II. is independent of the *Gesta*.   It makes no use of the other *Gesta* quoted above.

For certain popes, however, namely, Pontianus, Lucius, and Marcellinus, the *Liber Pontificalis* depends on *Gesta* now lost; as perhaps also for the mere fact of martyrdom recorded for the other popes.

[1] See *supra*, pp. 76, 182.

[2] *De gloria martyrum*, c. 35, 38, 39, 40 ; in *P.L.* 71, col. 737.

[3] Mombritius, *Sanctuarium*, i. p. 341, ed. 1910 ; *P.G.* 2, col. 617 ; F. Funk, *Opera patrum apostolicorum*, ii. p. 29.   This spurious passion was not adopted in the Roman liturgies before the ninth century.   The Clement venerated in the Chersonesus is not identical with the pope.   See *supra*, p. 67.

[4] *Anal. Boll.*, 1891, p. 53.

[5] Confused with the authentic martyr of the Via Nomentana.   See *A.SS.*, May 3.

[6] *A.SS.*, October 14.

[7] Mombritius, *op. cit.* i. p. 332, ed. 1910 ; Surius, *De probatis sanctorum historiis*, November 22.

[8] Schelestratus, *Antiquitates ecclesiae*, i. p. 188.   [9] *A.SS.*, August 2.

[10] *A.SS.*, August 6.   [11] *A.SS.*, August 11.   [12] *A.SS.*, January 16.

[13] *A.SS.*, September 26.   [14] *Supra*, Chaps. IV.–VI.   [15] See *supra*, p. 68.

The *Gesta* and the Passionary of Gregory the Great.—
The most important indication, however, of the existence of
Roman *Gesta* is found in the letter, dated 598, about the
Martyrologies, of Gregory the Great to Eulogius, Bishop of
Alexandria, referred to above.[1] In it he mentions "a single
volume containing very little."

Dufourcq[2] proves, fairly conclusively, that he has discovered this volume in a tenth-century manuscript, known as
the *Codex Vindobonensis*, in the Imperial Library in Vienna.
Among other documents in the Codex, is a copy of a
Passionary of Roman origin which Dufourcq attributes to the
latter part of the sixth century at latest, which he calls the
Passionary of Gregory. It contains[3] the *Gesta* of twenty-seven
Roman martyrs, five Umbrian, and four of other places,
arranged liturgically, in fairly correct order, except in the case
of the nine saints foreign to Rome, who are all out of place,
and probably interpolated later at the expense of some other
martyrs. Internal evidence shows that the *Passionary* is an
incomplete and modified version of some earlier volume, as
yet undiscovered, which Dufourcq calls the Book of Martyrs
(*Liber Martyrum*).

Thus, from internal and external evidence, it is clear that
there were already some *Gesta* of Roman martyrs in existence
in the fifth and sixth centuries.

The *Gesta* and the *Martyrology of Ado*.—In the ninth-
century *Martyrology of Ado*[4] are one hundred and seventy-
eight Roman martyrs or groups of martyrs : to one hundred
and twenty-nine of these are attached brief Lives, from four to
thirty lines in length, and for seventy-seven of these Lives Ado
quotes various " Passions" and " Gesta" as his authorities.
We may note that about twelve of the seventy-seven saints
mentioned are in the Philocalian Calendar, and another twelve
in the *Passionary of Gregory*, but that only some four names
are common to the three lists,—Pope Callixtus, Agapitus,
Alexander, and Cyriacus. We can conclude, then, that a
large number of *Gesta* were in existence before the ninth

---

[1] *Supra*, p. 183.
[2] Dufourcq, *op. cit.* p. 77.   [3] For a complete list see Appendix V.
[4] *P.L.* 123, col. 139. For full list see Appendix VI.

century, and that some of them, as we have shown, existed in the fifth and sixth.

An Examination of Individual *Gesta*.—A critical examination of individual *Gesta* will enable us to fix a more definite date for certain of them, and will incidentally afford us illustrations of the action of tradition.

For example, the *Gesta of S. Cecilia* are earlier than the first compilation of the *Liber Pontificalis* (514–523), since the latter uses these *Gesta*. On the other hand, they are later than Tertullian (d. 240), whose Apology is quoted; later than the publication in 416 of the *De Trinitate* of S. Augustine; and later than the history of the Vandal persecution (*de persecutione Vandalica*),[1] published in 486 by Victor, Bishop of Vita, an eye-witness : both works being quoted or copied in the *Gesta*. The date, then, of their compilation is between 486 and 523.

By somewhat similar methods we may definitely ascribe to the fourth century, with developments in the fifth and sixth, the *Acta Petri*;[2] to the fifth century the *Gesta of the Greek Martyrs*,[3] and of *S. Sebastian* [Jan. 20]; to the early sixth century those of *S. Pancras* [May 4], *S. Laurence* [Aug. 10],[4] and *S. Eusebius* [Sept. 26]. The *Gesta of John and Paul* [June 25] were probably written between 498 and 514, while the *Gesta of Processus and Martianus* [July 2], and of *Nereus and Achilleus* [May 12], are of the sixth century.[5]

A further investigation on similar lines will no doubt enable us to fix the dates of other individual *Gesta* with greater certainty, and perhaps within narrower limits.

To criticize in detail the *Gesta* which concern the early Roman martyrs would require volumes dealing largely with minute details of monumental, as well as of literary, evidence. Dufourcq, in his original and enlightening work, has briefly discussed some seventy of them. As an example of the *method* of criticism we may take the *Gesta of S. Callixtus*, the pope (217–222).

---

[1] *P.L.* 58.
[2] Lipsius, *Acta Apostolorum apocrypha*, 3 vols., Leipsic, 1891–1903.
[3] De Rossi, *Roma Sotterranea*, iii. p. 201.
[4] Surius, iv. p. 581.   [5] For further details see Dufourcq, *op. cit.*

The story of the martyrdom of Callixtus, condensed from the *Gesta of Callixtus* [Oct. 14], is as follows:—

> In the time of Macrinus and Alexander, the consul Palmatius accuses the Christians of burning a part of the Capitol, and partly burning various other places. The soldiers whom he sends to seize Callixtus in the Trastevere are blinded: a vestal virgin, Juliana, is seized by the devil on a day of solemn sacrifice. Palmatius is baptized by Callixtus in the quarter called Ravenna, as well as his wife and forty-two persons of his house. Palmatius, arrested by the tribune Torquatus, confesses Christ before Alexander, and is handed over to the Senator Simplicius. He heals Blanda, wife of Felix; and converts Simplicius and his family, who are baptized by the priest Calepodius and the bishop Callixtus. Calepodius is beheaded on the first of May: his body, thrown into the Tiber, is taken out and buried in the cemetery which bears his name, on the tenth of May. Callixtus hides in the house of Pontianus in the quarter called Ravenna: he converts the soldier Privatus, but is discovered and thrown into a well. The priest Asterius buried him in the cemetery of Calepodius, on the Via Aurelia, on the eve of the fifteenth of October.

With regard to these *Gesta* Dufourcq points out, with full references to the original authorities, that the Church of S. Callixtus, still in existence, is mentioned in documents as early as 352; that the district Ravenna is, in fact, in the Trastevere, and so called because a portion of the fleet from Ravenna was quartered there. Further, the year, day, and place of burial are attested in the Philocalian Calendar (354), the Martyrology of Jerome, and the Itineraries. The cemetery of Calepodius and the ruins of the cemetery where Callixtus is stated to have been buried have been discovered on the Via Aurelia.[1] The manner of the death of Callixtus indicates rather the vengeance wreaked in a popular rising than the execution of a legal sentence, and the charge against the Christians seems inspired by the same feeling: these facts

[1] Marucchi, *Le Catacombe Romane*, p. 62.

are in harmony with history, for Callixtus perished in the reign of Alexander Severus, who was favourable to the Christians. The general conclusion is, therefore, that these late *Gesta Callixti* have preserved for us the historic facts.

CHAPTER XVI

THE MARTYROLOGY OF JEROME: PLACE AND DATE OF COMPILATION

The Calendars in general.—The Martyrology of Jerome: The Codex of Berne, the Codex of Epternach, and others—The original compilation of the Martyrology at Auxerre, in Burgundy, in the sixth century, between 592 and 600 —Quotation from the Calendar of Auxerre—Gallicisms in the terms used— The contents of the document: The prefatory letters (Chromatius and Heliodorus to Jerome), etc.—Extract from the Martyrology.—References by Cassiodorus and Gregory the Great to the Martyrology.—A North Italian version, between 431 and 541.

O Lector, vive, lege, et pro me ora . . . Tuorum, Domine, quorum nomina scripsi sanctorum, eorum quaeso suffragiis miserum leva Laurentium : tuque idem, Lector, ora.

Laurentius presbyter (*circ.* 705) in *Martyrologium Hieronymianum.*[1]

The Calendars in General.—Every Church from the earliest times possessed its diptychs and calendars. "You have, O Christian, your tables of feasts" (*fastos*), says Tertullian. These primitive records formed the basis of the first Martyrologies, which were compiled about the time of the Peace of the Church,—the *Roman Martyrology* of 312,[2] the *Greek Menology* of the fourth century,[3] the *African Calendar*[4] of about the same date. These early calendars were then combined in various ways to form a general Martyrology (*Martyrologium Universale*), including saints

---

[1] Laurence, the priest and scholar and the friend of the English bishop, Willibrord, wrote this prayer at the beginning of the manuscript of the *Martyrology of Jerome*, which he was transcribing: "*O Reader, live, read, and pray for me . . . Do Thou, O Lord, by the suffrages of Thy saints whose names I have inscribed here, lift up, I pray Thee, miserable Laurence: and do thou also, Reader, pray for him.*" See supra, p. 38.

[2] *Infra*, p. 224.   [3] *Infra*, p. 218.

[4] *Infra*, p. 219.   For the relations of the documents see frontispiece.

of all lands; and were brought up to date by the addition of the names of later saints. The Martyrology was then adapted for local use by the addition of local saints, local church dedications, translations of relics, and lists of bishops. During the troubled centuries for Italy that followed, the copies of these Martyrologies disappeared. It is in the libraries of France, Germany, and the British Isles that we now find manuscripts of them, dating roughly from the sixth century onward; together with the popular abbreviated versions (*Breviaria*), which are often more correct, being based on better manuscripts, now lost, than the unabbreviated versions of the Martyrologies which we possess.

Those who used the Martyrologies, and especially the monks, found they required something more than a mere entry of the name of the saint, and place and date of burial. Hence, to provide edifying reading, passages from the *Gesta Martyrum*[1] were often inserted into the old Martyrology and so formed the *historical* Martyrologies of Bede, Ado, and other ninth-century compilers.

Martyrology of Jerome: The Codex of Berne, of Epternach, and others.—The whole process is illustrated in the great central Martyrology of the western world, the Martyrology of Jerome, which gathers up the substance of the most remote Calendars, and is the source of all later Martyrologies. We will examine it in detail, starting with the *latest* form, when the document has been adapted for local use, and tracing it back to the earliest sources, when we shall find it is related as "brother" or "cousin" to some of the ancient documents we have already described.

The Martyrology which bears the name of Jerome (*Martyrologium Hieronymianum*) is, then, as we have seen, a compilation from various sources, with later additions. In this it resembles the *Liber Pontificalis* and the *Itineraries*.

Forty of the manuscripts in which this Martyrology is preserved have been described by De Rossi, and more fully

[1] See *infra*, p. 229.

by Duchesne in his great work.[1]   The two most important
texts are (1) the Codex of Berne (*Codex Bernensis*), discovered
by De Rossi, and considered by him to be the most important manuscript of all, owing to the fullness of its topographical details—a point which would especially appeal
to De Rossi.   It has been published separately in a convenient little volume by the Bollandists.[1]   The second
highly important manuscript is (2) the Codex of Epternach
(*Codex Epternacensis*).   This document is slightly abbreviated,
even to the actual words, from some other earlier text.
We owe this great manuscript, which Duchesne considers
the best, to the English bishop, Willibrord, the missionary of
the Frisians,[2] and to Laurence, his friend and scribe, whose
petition is inscribed at the head of this chapter.   It is from
this Codex that quotations are usually made in these pages.
These two manuscripts, together with two others, have been
published jointly by De Rossi and Duchesne in four parallel
columns : no one has as yet attempted a final version of the
Martyrology.

The other manuscripts depend on these two, and vary
greatly in general character, in accuracy, and in the omissions
and additions found in them.   We can account for this by
the fact that the original compilation, with its primitive roll
of Eastern, Roman, and African martyrs,[3] had to be adapted
now for monastic use, now for liturgical use, in various
districts and local churches ; each of which made additions
of their own local saints.   To quote only two examples, the
Codex of Corvie (*Codex Corbeiensis*), in France (Somme),
contains a number of local French saints otherwise unknown.
Again, when the Martyrology had passed through the hands
of Bede [4] it appeared enriched with the names of the English
saints of Canterbury and Northumbria,—Augustine, Paulinus,
King Oswald, Cuthbert, and others.

**The Original Compilation of the Martyrology ; Gallic
in Origin.**—But beneath all these variations we can discern

---

[1] See Bibliography—MARTYROLOGY OF JEROME.
[2] See *supra*, p. 38.
[3] For a full account of these original sources see *infra*, pp. 218-228.
[4] Bibliography—MARTYROLOGY OF JEROME.

one early original common text of the compilation. To discover this, to describe its character, date, and birthplace, let us turn for some indication to the Calendar itself, and study the lists added by the local churches.

We are struck first by the large proportion of Gallic saints: there is scarcely a day on which one name at least does not appear. Further, while the rest of the Calendar is in considerable confusion, the notices of the Gallic saints are accurate and sometimes detailed.

Of the Sixth Century.—*It is clear, then, that Gaul is the birthplace of that compilation of the Calendar preserved in the manuscripts we now possess.* Further, while for the saints of other lands the commemorations cease after the fifth century, the notices of Gallican saints include those of the sixth century. *The approximate date, then, of this Gallic version is the sixth century.*

But place and date can be defined more precisely.

Of Auxerre in Burgundy.—These Gallic saints all belong to Southern Gaul, and are, moreover, very unequally distributed among the different cities. To take a few cases only: for Auxerre (*Autussiodorum*) we find thirty names in the Martyrology, for Autun (*Augustodunum*) twenty-five, for Lyons twenty-six.[1] Then, with a sudden drop, eight for Vienne, the home of so many martyrs,[2] seven for Tours, and only two or three apiece (rarely five or six) for forty other places.

It is clear, then, that the Martyrology was compiled for the use of Auxerre, or Autun, or Lyons. Among these three, Auxerre, as we see, has a pre-eminence which is all the more remarkable because the local saints of that town are less important than those of Lyons or Autun. Further, for Auxerre we have the list of the burial days (*Depositio*) of her seventeen bishops complete (with one exception), and to one bishop, Germanus (418–448),[3] no less than three festivals are assigned. For this church, too, the topography is exact

---

[1] For text of this portion of the Calendar see De Rossi and Duchesne, *Martyrologium Hieronymianum*, in *A.SS.*, Nov., p. xli. For information on the Gallic bishops and saints see Duchesne, *Fastes Episcopaux de l'ancienne Gaule*, 2 vols., Paris, 1900, and Gams, *Series Episcoporum Ecclesiae Catholicae*, 1 vol., Ratisbon, 1873.

[2] *Supra*, p. 162.   [3] *Supra*, p. 30; cf. p. 210.

and there is frequent mention of festivals, of translations of relics, and anniversaries of dedications of churches, all totally unimportant save locally.

For Lyons, on the other hand, we note that only fourteen bishops are mentioned and twelve are omitted.

For Autun, though the episcopal records are too mutilated to enable us to check the Martyrology by them, the festivals of that church are obviously recorded less completely than for Auxerre.

Auxerre, then, is the birthplace of the Gallican version of the Martyrology.

Between 592 and 600.—If we further examine the commemorations for Auxerre and Autun we shall be able to define the date more exactly. It was De Rossi[1] who first remarked that in the notices for the bishops of Auxerre, for all, with one exception, the date of burial (*Depositio*) is noted in the usual way according to the model of the *Depositio Episcoporum* of the Philocalian Calendar and kindred documents. For Bishop Aunarius (or Aunacharius) (*c.* 561–605),[2] however, the anniversary of his consecration as bishop is mentioned, and there is no notice of his death; from which we conclude that the Martyrology was compiled *in his lifetime*. Again, turning to the notices of the bishops of the neighbouring town of Autun, we note precisely the same fact concerning Bishop Syagrius,[3] who was consecrated bishop about 561 and died in 600. Thus the evidence seems sufficient for affirming that the *Martyrology of Jerome was compiled at Auxerre in the sixth century in the lifetime of Aunarius, Bishop of Auxerre, and of Syagrius, Bishop of Autun*, i.e. *between 560 and 600.*

A third series of commemorations of Gallican bishops confirms this fact. We read for January 21 the entry:

XII. kal. feb. . . . Arvernius depoŝ [beati][4] aviti eᵽi.

Jan. 21. . . . In the district of the Arverni (*i.e.* Avergne) the burial of blessed Avitus, bishop.

---

[1] *Roma Sotterranea*, ii. p. xvi.   [2] *Gams, op. cit.* p. 50.
[3] *Ibid.* p. 499; cf. Duchesne, *Fastes*, ii. p. 427.
[4] In *Codex Bernensis*.

14

This Avitus was the teacher and friend of Gregory of Tours, to whom the latter so often refers in his works, and from whom we learn that Avitus was alive in 591.[1] From the Martyrology we learn that Avitus did not die *before* January 21, 592.

Therefore, the Martyrology is not earlier than 592 nor, as we have seen, later than 600.

Quotation from the Calendar of Auxerre.—A brief quotation from that part of the Calendar concerning the saints of Auxerre (*Kalendarium Autissiodorense*) which has proved so important for determining the date and birthplace of the Martyrology is not without interest:[2]

April 15.—In Auxerre in Gaul, the dedication of the baptistery, which is near the basilica of S. Germanus, bishop and confessor, where are laid the relics of S. John the evangelist. On the same day the dedication of the altar of S. Julianus, martyr, who came from the district of Brest [*Brivate*].

May 1.—In the city of Auxerre the burial of S. Amator, bishop.

May 6.—At Auxerre the burial of Valerian, bishop.

May 26.—At Auxerre the Passion of Priscus.

June 30.—At Auxerre the burial of S. Germanus, bishop and confessor, and the anniversary of Aunarius, bishop.

Sept. 22.—At Auxerre, Germanus, bishop: in Gaul, in the city of Auxerre, the arrival and reception of the body of S. Germanus, bishop and confessor, from Italy.

Oct. 1.—In Gaul, in the city of Auxerre, the burial of S. Germanus, bishop and confessor.

Gallicisms in the Terms used for the Festivals.—

---

[1] Gregorius Turonensis, *Hist. Franc.* x. 6, in *P.L.* 71.

[2] See also *Martyrologium insignis ecclesiae Autissiodorensis* (of tenth century), in *P.L.* 138, col. 1209.

Further, as Duchesne points out,[1] the very names of the feast days are Gallican, and certain feasts are either absent from the Roman Calendar or found there under another name. For example, the entry of the Martyrology of Jerome

KL. JAN. [LAETANIAS INDICENDAS][2] CIRCŪCISIO DNI [NRI IHU XRI SECD CARNĔ].

Jan. 1.—Litanies to be sung. The Circumcision of our Lord Jesus Christ according to the flesh.

is known in the Roman Calendars as the *OCTAVUM DOMINI*, that is the Octave of Christmas Day.

The following entry is unknown to the Roman Calendars, at least on the day indicated :—

XV kl. feb depoŝ sčae mariae[3] et cařh petri in roma.[4]
Jan. 18.—The burial of S. Mary [the Virgin] and the Chair of Peter in Rome.

The following entries are altogether unknown in the early Roman Calendar :—

VIII k aᵽ hieroŝ dñs crucifixus est.
VI k aᵽ resurř dñi ñi ihū hieroŝ.
V noñ m[ai] in hierosolima inventio scae crucis [dñi nři ihū xři ab helena regina in monte golgotha post passionĕ dñi anno ducentissimo XXXIII regnante constantino imperatore].
IV k seᵽ passio sčï iōh babtiŝ.
VI k jañ adsumpto sčï iōh evanǧ apud ephesū et ordinatio episcopatus sčï Jacobi ff dñi qui ab apostolis primus ex Judaeis hierosolimis est aepiscopus ordinatus et in medio paschae martyrio coronatus hierosol cuius paŝ VIII k aᵽ.

March 25.—At Jerusalem the Lord was crucified.
March 27.—Resurrection of the Lord Jesus at Jerusalem.

[1] The brief assertions made here are proved by many references to other calendars given in Duchesne, *op. cit.* p. xl.
[2] The passages in brackets are from the *Codex Bernensis* in all the quotations which follow.
[3] Unknown also in the African Calendars.
[4] This feast of S. Peter was kept in Rome on February 22, as we see from the Philocalian Calendar (fourth century).

May 3.—At Jerusalem the Finding of the holy Cross [of our Lord Jesus Christ by Helena the queen on Mount Golgotha in the two hundred and thirty-third year after the Passion of the Lord in the reign of Constantine the emperor].

Aug. 29.—The Passion of S. John the Baptist.

Dec. 27.—The Assumption of S. John the Evangelist at Ephesus, and the ordination as bishop of S. James the brother of our Lord who, first of the apostles, was ordained bishop by the Jews at Jerusalem, and in the middle of Easter was crowned with martyrdom at Jerusalem, whose Passion is March 25.

The Notices of Monthly Litanies a Gallicism.— Another Gallicism in this Calendar is the rubric at the beginning of each month : *LAETANIAS INDICENDAS, i.e.* that litanies were to be sung. From the earliest times at Rome and elsewhere litanies were universally recited on certain days of the year, as we learn from many liturgical documents and edicts bearing on them. But the recitations of *monthly* litanies is characteristic of Auxerre, as we see from the decree [1] of Bishop Aunacharius (Aunarius) (*c.* 561–605), " that every month on the first of the month a litany is to be celebrated " at one of the twelve (stational) urban basilicas (which he enumerates), and " on other days of the months as above."

Having thus determined the date and place of origin of the earliest compilation that we possess, let us turn to the document itself, and examine it in its entirety.

The Contents of the Document :—(1) The Prefatory Letters of Chromatius and Heliodorus to Jerome, with Reply of Jerome.—According to a common custom of the time, one of the earliest compilers commended his work to the public by two prefatory letters which claimed to be the correspondence with Jerome of two bishops of North Italy,—of Chromatius of Aquileia, the friend of Ambrose, and of Heliodorus of Altinum. Chromatius and Heliodorus

---

[1] *De Gestis episcoporum Autissiodorensium, pars prima, cap. xix.*, in *P.L.* 138, col. 234. For texts of some tenth-century litanies (based on earlier documents) see *P.L.* 138, col. 885. There are to be found in these *Gesta* some interesting details on the history of the diocese of Auxerre.

write that in a council of bishops held at Milan, at the
summons of "the august and most religious" Emperor
Theodosius,

> We all unanimously determined to write to your
> Charity (*ad tuam Caritatem*) to ask you to examine
> in the archives the most famous Ferial of Eusebius,
> priest of Caesarea in Palestine, and to send us notes of
> the feast days of the martyrs; that the Office of the
> martyrs may be performed better and more perfectly
> through your holy industry.

The reply of Jerome is as follows:

> Jerome, priest, to Chromatius and Heliodorus, bishops.
> It is well established that our Lord receives daily (in
> the liturgy) the triumphs of His martyrs whose passions
> we have found, written by saint Eusebius of Caesarea.
> For when the Emperor Constantius entered Caesarea,
> and bade the bishop ask for some favour for the church
> at Caesarea, Eusebius is said to have answered . . .
> that he was possessed by an earnest desire, that what-
> ever action in the Roman state had been taken with
> regard to the saints of God throughout the whole
> Roman world, as one judge succeeded another, should
> be sought and examined by a careful scrutiny of all the
> public monuments; and that, by the royal command,
> notices taken from the archives should be sent to
> Eusebius himself, concerning the names of the martyrs,
> under what judge they suffered, in what province or
> state, on what day, and by what manner of death they
> won the palm of perseverance.[1]

After describing how Eusebius' petition was granted, and
how he compiled his history of the martyrs from the
documents so provided, Jerome continues:

> And since, offering the sacrifice daily to God, you
> desire to remember the names of those who on that day
> on which the sacrifice is offered stood up as victors over
> the devil, and glorious and shouting for joy with the
> triumph of their martyrdom reached the presence of
> Christ their King—for this reason we have arranged the
> feast days month by month, and day by day as you
> deigned to command me, saying that there would be an

---

[1] Cf. *supra*, p. 179.

everlasting commemoration of our humble self when the feast day of the names of the saints is celebrated on all the days through the spaces of the years.

He then explains that, since for each day of the year there are, from all lands, at least five hundred martyrs, he has abbreviated the Calendar for fear of wearying his readers. Further, that he has arranged all together at the beginning, out of the due order of the months, the feast days of the apostles.

(2) **Prefatory Notices of the Apostles.**—Thus the compiler prefaced the work, and though the letters appear to be apocryphal, we shall see that the facts contained in them are true.

The Calendar opens, as stated in the letter, with a brief biographical notice of each of the apostles, including Judas, Paul and Matthias. There follows a notice of ten feast days dedicated to them, from which a few quotations may be made:[1]

June 29.—The anniversary of the apostles Peter and Paul in Rome.

Nov. 30.—The anniversary of Andrew the apostle in the city of Patras in the province Achaia.

Dec. 27.—The anniversaries of the apostles S. James the brother of our Lord and of John the evangelist.

June 24.—The anniversary of the falling asleep (*dormitio*) of John, the apostle and evangelist, in Ephesus.

. . . .

(3) **Some Extracts from the Martyrology.**—Then begins the Calendar proper at December 25. For each day of the year there are a large number of saints: their country is usually indicated, and for some, more minute topographical details are given. A brief extract will show the general character of the document. Preference has been given to those days which contain some details on Roman martyrs:

Dec. 25.—In Bethlehem the birth of our Saviour the Lord Jesus Christ according to the flesh. At Rome,

[1] *Codex Bernensis.*

Jovinus Pastor Victoriana Agellius Euticetus Simphroniana Saturninus Timedus Ignatius Cyriacus Gagus
Januaria Dativus.   And in the cemetery of Apronianus
on the Via Latina at Rome, the passion of S. Eugenia
Virgin.[1] Sirmius and Anastasia.   At Milan, Felicitas,
and in Pergamos, Saturninus.   At Constantinople, S.
Anastasius, virgin.

Jan. 16.—At Rome on the Via Salaria in the cemetery
of Priscilla the burial (*depositio*) of S. Marcellus, pope
and confessor; and on the Via Appia in the cemetery
of Callixtus, the passion of S. Martha.   Audeinus,
martyr.   On the Via Corniva (? Cornelia) in the cemetery,
nine soldiers, and another thirteen whose names are preserved written in the book of life.   In Africa, Saturninus,
Faustinus, Fravianus and six others.   At Arles the
burial of S. Honoratus, bishop.

June 11.—At Rome on the Via Salaria the anniversary
of Saint Basilla.   Also on the Via Nomentana, at the
seventh milestone from the city, the anniversary of S.
Crispolius, Restitutus and elsewhere the translation
of the body of Fortunatus, bishop and martyr.   In
Aquileia, Emeritus Aritus Victorianus Victor, and
elsewhere the anniversary of Nabor and Felix.

**References to the Martyrology by Cassiodorus and
Gregory the Great.**—Some earlier version of this work
was known to Cassiodorus (469–562), the minister of
Theodoric, and the founder of the Monastery of Vivarium.
He writes to his monks in about 541 urging them to read
constantly [2]

> The Passions of the martyrs, which you will certainly
> find among other things in the letter of S. Jerome
> to Chromatius and Heliodorus—those martyrs who
> flourished all over the world ; that their holy invitations
> pricking you on, may lead you to the heavenly
> kingdoms.

This work is again referred to in a famous letter of

---

[1] *Supra*, p. 193.
[2] *De institutione divinarum litterarum*, c. 32, in *P.L.* 70, col. 1147.

Gregory the Great,[1] which is important also for the references it contains to other works. Eulogius, Bishop of Alexandria, had written to him, asking for the well-known volume of Eusebius, *A Collection of Ancient Martyrdoms.* Gregory writes, in answer, in 598, that he knows nothing of this work, and then continues :

> Except what we read in the books of this same Eusebius (*i.e.* in the *Ecclesiastical History*) concerning the deeds (*gesta*) of the martyrs, I know of nothing, either in our own archives, nor in the libraries of the city of Rome (except a few things collected in a single volume, *i.e. Passionary of Gregory*). But we have collected into a single volume (*i.e. Martyrology of Jerome*) the names of nearly all the martyrs with a separate passion for each day, and on all these days we celebrate the Mass in honour of them. But what each one suffered is not related in the same volume, but only the name, the place and the date of the passion is given. . . .

The last part of this letter describes a document so closely resembling the Martyrology of Jerome that there can be little doubt as to the correctness of Duchesne's identification. Gregory seems to have in his mind, too, the contents of the prefatory letters.

This Version was an Earlier Compilation than the Gallican, and made in North Italy between 431 and 541.— Is it possible to discover traces in our Gallican edition of that earlier compilation know to Cassiodorus?

Setting aside the Gallican additions, of which we have given an account, and also the fundamental portions derived from very ancient Roman, Eastern and African Calendars, which we will discuss in detail presently, what remains? We may note in passing a few Spanish saints from Cordova, Tarragona (Fructuosus,[2] Augurius and Eulogius), Valentia.

---

[1] *Gregorii Magni Epistolae,* viii. 29, in *P.L.* 77, col. 930, or in Jaffé, *Regesta pontificum Romanorum,* No. 1517. Many older scholars, as well as Duchesne and nearly all modern scholars, have so identified the work referred to by Cassiodorus and Gregory (see *supra,* p. 201). It is to Dufourcq, *Études sur les* Gesta Martyrum *romains,* that we owe the identification of the *Passionary of Gregory* referred to in this letter (see *supra,* p. 201, and Appendix V.).

[2] January 21 (*XII. kal. Feb.*). For authentic Acts see *supra,* p. 157.

Also a few from Dalmatia, Pannonia (S. Quirinus), Rhaetia and the neighbouring districts. Except in local calendars, S. Alban is the only English saint whose name appears in the Martyrology. We note, however, a very large number of saints from various cities of Italy and Sicily —from Milan, Aquileia, Ravenna, Verona, Placentia, Perugia, Spoleto ; and in the south from Capua, Naples, Nola, Puteoli, Baiae, Beneventum, Catana, Syracuse. The entries are correct, and the topography detailed. The feast days too, of their bishops, as late as the fourth century, appear—Ambrose (d. 397), Paulinus of Nola (d. 431) and others. It is for *Northern* Italy that we have the greatest number of names —for Milan, Aquileia, Ravenna—and it is precisely for North Italy, too, that feasts of translations of relics, dedications, etc., of purely local interest, are inserted.

All these facts point to an earlier *North Italian version of the Martyrology*. This version it is to which Cassiodorus refers, and which must have been compiled between 431, as it records the death of Paulinus of Nola, and 541, the date of Cassiodorus' letter. Cassiodorus, as we have seen, knew the version when it was already prefaced with the correspondence of Chromatius and Heliodorus with Jerome. Yet again we find that these apocryphal letters preserve something of historical truth, when they make the request for a version of the Martyrology emanate from two northern bishops (Aquileia and Altinum) sitting in council at Milan.

CHAPTER XVII

THE MARTYROLOGY OF JEROME: THE ANCIENT SOURCES

The ultimate sources of the Martyrology and their combination: (1) Greek Menology of the fourth century, and Syriac abridgment of 412, (2) African Calendar of the fourth or fifth century and Carthaginian Calendar of the sixth, (3) The Roman portion of the Martyrology: Quotation of papal entries—Similarity with the Philocalian Calendar.—Four papal ordinations indicate four periods of compilation of Martyrology.—The original Roman Calendar of 312 and subsequent revisions—Other double papal entries—An analysis of the entries for the Roman martyrs.—Views of Krusch on the date and place of compilation of the Martyrology; Luxeuil, seventh century.—Later Martyrologies.

Nos insensati vitam illorum aestimabamus insaniam, et finem illorum sine honore : ecce quomodo computati sunt inter filios Dei, et inter sanctos sors illorum est.—*Commune Martyrum* (*Liber Sapientiae*, iii.).[1]

The Ultimate Sources of the Martyrology and their Combination.—We have described in the last chapter the local additions to the Martyrology, and have thereby been enabled to trace something of its history.

We now come down to the fundamental portion; which consists of the feasts of martyrs of (1) the East, (2) of Africa, (3) of Rome. We shall find that the sources of these entries can be traced back to very early national Calendars. There are, moreover, a few saints common to two, or even to all three of the Calendars, as SS. Peter and Paul, the martyred Pope Sixtus II., Cyprian of Carthage, Perpetua of Africa.

(1) Greek Menology of the Fourth Century and the Syriac Abridgment of it in 412.—Let us consider first the sources of the Oriental portion of the Martyrology, which is accurate, and abounds in topographical detail.

[1] " *We fools accounted their lives madness, and their end without honour : now are they numbered among the sons of God, and their lot is among the saints.*"

There is in existence a *Syriac Martyrology* of the year 412.[1] Comparing this document with the Martyrology of Jerome we find the two so similar that it is clear they are derived from a common source. The Martyrology of Jerome is, however, a good deal fuller in detail. *The original source of both these documents is some Greek Menology* (Martyrology) *of Asia Minor, compiled probably at Nicomedia in the fourth century*, and itself depending on earlier Calendars (of Antioch, Alexandria, etc.) and the works of Eusebius. Duchesne thinks the Syriac abridgment of 412 was probably made from the Martyrology of Jerome, though others believe it may have been derived *direct* from the Greek Menology.

The arrangement of this Syriac version is interesting. The saints in it are divided into two classes : (1) the martyrs of the Eastern Roman Empire, (2) the martyrs of the Far East —of Babylon and Persia—all arranged, not in the order of the Calendar, but according to their position in the hierarchy.

Here again we note the correctness of the facts recorded in the prefatory letters which make the works of Eusebius one of the sources of our Martyrology.

(2) The African Calendar of the Fourth or Fifth Century and a Carthaginian Calendar of the Sixth Century. —The African Calendars have the peculiarity of referring to their saints, at times, not by their names, but by the name of the town or district to which they belong : *SS. Scillitanorum, SS. Maxilitanorum, SS. Turburbitanorum* (the Scillitan martyrs . . .). The roll of African saints appears in the Martyrology of Jerome with, as a rule, the single topographical indication " In Africa."

This portion of our Calendar may be compared with a well-known *Martyrology of Carthage* of the sixth century.[2]

---

[1] The most ancient manuscript is preserved in the British Museum. It has been published, with an English translation, where it can easily be studied, by W. Wright, *Journal of Sacred Literature*, t. viii. (new series), 1866, pp. 45, 423, and re-edited by Graffin, *A.SS.*, November. Fuller details of the Eastern Calendar are found in Duchesne, in *Mélanges d'archéologie*, 1885, quoted in Bibliography—MARTYROLOGY OF JEROME.

[2] Mabillon, *Vetera Analecta*, iii. 398 ; Ruinart, *Acta Sincera*, at the end ; and Duchesne, *A.SS.*, Nov., p. lxxi.

The two documents (of which the Martyrology of Jerome is the fuller) are closely alike, and depend on those numerous and accurate early Calendars for which Africa was famous.[1] The immediate source of this Carthaginian Martyrology was a Calendar compiled before the Vandal invasion, since the names of none of those martyrs who perished at that period are found in it. It is therefore of the fourth or fifth century.[2]

(3) **The Roman Portion of the Martyrology.**—We now come to the study in the Martyrology of Jerome of the Roman martyrs with whom we are especially concerned. We note first the accuracy of the topographical details given, —the information as to basilicas and stational churches, the precision with which the locality of shrines on the suburban roads are noted. These topographical notices should be compared with those given in the *Liber Pontificalis*, the Itineraries, and the *Gesta Martyrum*. To illustrate this part of the Calendar, we will extract those portions referring to the bishops of Rome. Such an extract will illustrate all the general characteristics referred to above; it possesses, moreover, a peculiar historic interest, and will furnish facts for determining some important dates. For this series of entries, too, there exists ample collateral evidence, documentary and monumental. We will further note certain errors that have crept in, which will be of assistance in forming a critical estimate of the document:

THE PAPAL ENTRIES IN THE MARTYROLOGY.[3]

January

(3rd) III *non jan.*—Rom(æ) Antheri pap(a)e.
(10th) IIII *id jan.*—Rom in Cimiter(io) Via Appia

---

[1] *Supra*, p. 178.

[2] Achelis, *Die Martyrologien, ihre Geschichte und ihr Wert*, 1900 (see Bibl.), believes the document to be of Catholic origin, not, as some hold, a Donatist compilation.

[3] The text following is taken almost entirely from the *Codex Bernensis*. There is a further discussion of some of the details on pp. 223–226. I have added in brackets the letters which complete the contracted forms, and sometimes the *correct* form of a name, for the assistance of the reader.

       Caelesti (Callixti) (depositio) Melchiades[1] (sic)
       epi (scopi).

(16th) XVII *kl. febs.*—Rom̃ Via Salaria in cimiterio
       Prescelle (Priscillae) depos̃(itio) Sc̃i Marcelli
       papae et conf̃(essoriss).[2]

(20th) XIII *kal feb.*—Rom(a)e Via Appia in Cim̃(iterio
       Callisti) Fabiani[3] epi.

March

(4th) IIII *non mar.*—Rome in Cimiterio Calesti Via
       Appia depos̃ Julii epi(scopi).[4]

(12th) IIII *id mart.*—Rome depositio Sc̃i Innocenti epi.[5]

(14th) *prid id mar.*—Rome Leonis epi et martyris . . .[6]
       Innocenti[7] epi.

April

(11th) III *id aprael.*—Rome Leonis papę.

(12th) *pridi id apl.* — Rome in Cimit Calepodi Via
       Aurelia tertio miliario depos̃ Juli epi.

(22nd) X *kl mai.*—Roma(e) in cimit Calesti Via Appia
       Sc̃i Gagi (Gaii) papę.

May

(17th) XVI *kl jun.*—Rome Via Salaria Vetere . . .
       depositio Liberi epi.[8]

(25th) VIII *kl jun.*—Via Nomentana miliario VIII
       natal(is) Urbani epi.[9]

[1] Correct. See *VI. non. Jul.* (July 2), which is the day of the *ordination*, not of burial. Translation: "*At Rome on the Via Appia in the cemetery of Callixtus the burial day of Melchiades, bishop.*" The other passages can be readily translated from this example.

[2] There is the second (and incorrect) entry for Marcellus ; cf. *Non. Oct.* (Oct. 7). The *name* here should be *Marcellinus*, who is omitted altogether.

[3] Among martyrs (*Dep. Mart.*) in Phil. Cal.

[4] The name *Julii* is a mistake for *Lucii* (see Phil. Cal.) ; the correct entry for Julius is on *prid. id. Apr.* (April 12), as in Phil. Cal.

[5] Correct. See *XII. kal. Jan.* (Dec. 21) for day of ordination. The entry for *prid. id. Mart.* (March 14) is a mistake (?).

[6] The single example of the subsequent addition of a pope later than Boniface (418–422). The entry for the following day is that of his translation.

[7] A mistake (?). This is the third entry for Innocent. See note 5 above.

[8] For day of burial see *VIII. kal. Oct.* (Sep. 24). This is day of ordination.

[9] Topographically incorrect : not in Phil. Cal.

July

(2nd) VI *non jul.*—Romae. In cimiteř Damasi . . .
Via Appia in cimiterio Calesti natal(is) Eutici
et depoš Melc(h)iadis (Miltiadis) pape.[1]

August

(2nd) IIII *non ags.*— Romae in cimiť Calesti Via
Appia sči Stefani eṗi et mař.

(6th) VIII *id ags.*—Rome in cimiť Calesti Via Appia
nat(a)l(is) Sixti [2] eṗi.

(9th) V *id ags.*—Rome in cimiterio Calesti Via Appia
depositio Dionisi [3] eṗi.

(13th) *Id a(u)gustas.*—In Via Appia Calesti Scorum
Pontiani eṗi.[2] . . .

September

(4th) *prid no sep.*—Rome in cimiť Maximi Via Salaria
Bonifaci eṗi.

(14th) XVIII *kl oct.*—Romae Via Appia in cimiterio
Calesti Cornili eṗi et Dionisi eṗi.[4]

(24th) VIII *k oč(t).*— Roṁ depoš Liberi eṗi.[5]

(26th) VI *kl oct.*—Rome Via Appia in cimiťr Calesti
depoš sči Eusebii eṗi.

October

(7th) *nonas oct.*—Rome Via Appia depositio Marcelli
eṗi et Marci eṗi.

(14th) *prid id oct.*—Rome Via Aurelia in cimiterio
Calepodi Calesti eṗi.[6]

---

[1] A mistake : this is the day of his ordination. See *IIII. id. Jan.* (Jan. 10)
footnote.

[2] In *Dep. Mart.* of Phil. Cal.

[3] Day of translation : for day of burial see *VII. kal. Jan.* (Dec. 26). Cf.
XVIII. kal. Oct. (Sep. 14).

[4] Cornelius is not in the Phil. Cal. This is the third entry for Dionysius. Is
it a mistake? For burial see *VII. kal. Jan.* (Dec. 26) and translation *V. id.
Aug.* (Aug. 9).

[5] Not in *Codex Bern.* but in *Codex Eptern* Cf. *XVI. kal. Jun.* (May 17).

[6] In *Depos. Mart.* of Phil. Cal.

December

(8th) VI *id dec.* Roṁ depoŝ Euticiani ep̄i.[1]
(10th) IIII *id dec.* — Roṁ . . . Pontiani[2] . . . Roṁ
 Damasi ep̄i.[1]
(11th) III *id dec.* Roṁ depos Damasi.[1]
(20th) XIII *k jañ.*—Roṁ depoŝ Zephirini ep̄i.[3]
(21th) XII *kl jan.*—Rome dep̄ Sc̄i Innocenti ep̄i.[4]
(26th) VII *kl janu(a)r.*—Roṁ dep̄s Sc̄i Dionisi.[5]
(29th) IIII *kl januar.*—Roṁ . . . Bonefatii ep̄i de
 ordinatione.
(30th) III *kl januar.*—Roṁ Felicis ep̄i.
(31st) *pr kl jan* Roṁ . . . depoŝ Sc̄i Silvestri ep̄i.

Similarity with the Philocalian Calendar.—We note
at once a close resemblance between these entries in the
Martyrology, and the papal list compiled from the *Depositio
Episcoporum* and *Depositio Martyrum* of the Philocalian
Calendar.[6] The formula of entry—name, date, place of
burial—is the same. Both documents really begin with
Pope Lucius (253–254), any earlier bishops who are given
in either, being martyrs, namely, Callixtus (217–222),
Pontianus (230–235), Fabianus (236–250) and Cornelius
(251–253).[7]

[1] Not in *Codex Bernensis*.
[2] Not in *Codex Bernensis*. This entry is the date of the translation of his
relics from abroad, where he died a martyr : he is in *Depos. Mart.* of the Phil.
Cal.
[3] Not in Phil. Cal.
[4] This entry is a mistake : it is the day of the *ordination* of Innocent. For
day of burial see *IV. ides Mart.* (March 12). Cf. *Prid. id. Mart.* (March 14).
[5] Cf. *XVIII. kl. Oct.* (Sep. 14) ; also *V. id. Aug.* (Aug. 9) for
translation.
[6] *Infra*, Appendix III.
[7] The last pope is omitted from the *Depositio Martyrum* of the Philocalian
Calendar, probably by a copyist's error. It is curious, however, that we find in
the Martyrology the names of the earlier popes, Zephyrinus (199–217) and
Anteros (235–236), who were not martyrs. The third name, Urban, for May 25
(*VIII. kal. Jun*) is probably not the *pope* (227–233) at all, but that Bishop
Urban who played a part in the martyrdom of S. Cecilia (p. 69). Further, while
Marcellus (304–309) is omitted from the Philocalian Calendar, perhaps because
he was not recognized by the Government (p. 71), he appears correctly in the
Martyrology on October 7 (*non. Oct.*), while *Marcellinus* (296–304) is wrongly
entered as *Marcellus* in the Martyrology on January 16 (*XVII. kal. Feb.*).

Both the Calendars, too, in reality end at Julius (337–352). It is true that the Martyrology carries the list down to Boniface (418–422), but there is a complete cessation of all topographical details for the popes between Julius and Boniface (*i.e.* for Liberius, Felix II., Damasus, Siricius, Anastasius, Innocent I., Zosimus) till we come to Boniface himself. The name of Leo the Great (440–461) on March 14 (*prid. id. Mart.*) is the only pope later than Boniface who appears in the Martyrology. He is, of course, added by a later hand.

We thus see the close resemblance between the Philocalian Calendar and the Martyrology. It is true that the latter, being designed for ecclesiastical and liturgical use, contains more details than the Philocalian Calendar, which was an almanac of secular information.

Four Papal Ordinations as Indication of Date.—There is, moreover, an entry peculiar to the Martyrology, namely, the feast of the ordination (*de ordinatione*) of four popes: (1) For Miltiades (or Melchiades). For this pope there are *two* entries of deposition: January 10 (*IIII. id. Jan.*), which is correct, and July 2 (*VI. non. Jul.*), which is a mistake, and is in reality the day of his *ordination*, as we know from other sources. (2) For Liberius (352–366) the day of his death is marked September 24 (*VIII. kal. Oct.*), which is correct, and May 17 (*XVI. kal. Jun*), which is a mistake, and is really the day of ordination. (3) For Innocent (401–417) March 12 (*IV. idus Mart.*) is correctly given as the day of burial; December 21 (*XII. kal. Jan.*) is the day of his ordination. (4) For Boniface (418–422) alone are both entries correct, namely, December 29 (*IIII. kal. Jan.*) as the day of ordination (*de ordinatione*) and September 4 (*prid. non. Sep.*) as day of deposition.

The Original Roman Calendar of 312 and Subsequent Revisions.—Since the days of consecration of the bishops were observed only *in their lifetime*, and, as soon as they were dead, the commemoration of their day of burial was substituted, it follows that the original Roman Calendar was completed under Miltiades, about 312, and subsequently revised three times,—under Liberius, Innocent and Boniface.[1]   Boniface, as we have seen, is the last of the popes mentioned in the Calendar, with the exception of Leo the Great (440–461) March 14,—an addition by a later hand.

We remark, further, that though no dedications of churches in Rome are noted as a rule, there are no less than four such entries for churches dedicated under Sixtus III. (432–440), namely, the Baptistery of the Lateran, on June 29 (*III. kal. Jul.*), S. Peter-in-Chains on August 1 (*kal. Aug.*), S. Maria Maggiore on August 5 (*non. Aug.*), and the churches of SS. Sixtus (II.), Hippolytus, and Laurence on November 2 (*IV. non. Nov.*).   These notices seem to be added to the Martyrology by a contemporary, and to be the latest revision which we can trace.

It is on this Calendar of 312, too, as we have already shown, that the Philocalian Calendar depends: this fact accounts for the close similarity between the Philocalian Calendar and the Martyrology,—two documents independent of each other,—and further accounts for the fact that the paschal table of the Philocalian Calendar begins at the arbitrary date of 312.

Hence the ultimate source of the Roman portion of the Martyrology of Jerome is the so-called *Calendar of Miltiades* of about the year 312, which was completed only some dozen years later than the last persecution, and composed at the first moment the Church enjoyed peace.   The martyrs' graves, sealed and inscribed, were as yet untouched by barbarian invasions.   We can, then, with very few exceptions, rely on the Martyrology as topographically correct, especially when we note the agreement between this document and the Itineraries compiled on the spot with the actual tombs before the writers' eyes.   The anniversaries, too, are usually reliable.   In the actual names themselves there are occasional blunders, which are not surprising when we consider how difficult is accuracy in this respect,

[1] It is so that the date of the compilation of the sixth-century Gallican version was determined by the entries of the days of ordination of Aunacharius and Syagrius.   See *supra*, p. 209.

15

and through how many copyists' hands this ancient Martyrology has passed.[1]

Other Double Papal Entries.—In addition to the four double papal entries noted above, we remark the same double entries for several other popes.   In some cases it is obviously a mistake,—sometimes merely a mistake of one day, resulting, possibly, from a copyist's error (it is so easy to write *IIII* for *III*, or *XVII* for *XVIII*, or copy a line twice over !); or possibly from a confusion of the day of death, and day of burial.   Sometimes, also, it can be explained, as Dufourcq has pointed out, by the fact that the second date is the day of translation of relics.

A list of these nine double (or sometimes treble) entries may be useful for reference.[2]

	DEPOSITIO.	
Pontianus .	*id. aug.* (Aug. 13th).	*IV id. dec.* (Dec. 10th) (translation).
Dionysius .	*VII kal. jan.* (Dec. 26th).	*V id. aug.* (Aug. 9th) (translation).
Marcellus .	*non. oct.* (Oct. 7th).	*XVII kal. feb.* (Jan. 16th). Name should be Marcellinus.
Miltiades .	*IV id. jan.* (Jan. 10th).	*VI non jul.* (July 2nd) (ordination).[3]
Julius . .	*prid. id. apr.* (April 12th).	*IV non. mart.* (March 4th). (Name should be Lucius.)
Liberius .	*VIII kal. oct.* (Sept. 24th).	*XVI kal. jun.* (May 17th) (ordination).
Damasus .	*IV id. dec.* (Dec. 10th).	*III id. dec.* (Dec. 9th). (Surely a mistake.)[4]
Innocent .	*IV id mart* (March 12th).	*XII kal. jan.* (Dec. 21st) (ordination), prid. id. Mart. (a mistake (?)).
Boniface .	*prid. non. sep.* (Sept. 4th).	*IIII kal. jan.* (Dec. 29th) (ordination).
Leo . . .	*prid. id. mart.* (March 14th)	*III. id. april* (Ap. 11th) (translation).

---

[1] We may quote a single example of such an error.   In three different codices of the Martyrology we read :

prid. id. Jan. (*Cod. Bern.*) .   .   .   Romae . . . Basilledis Tribuli Nagesi (?) Magdaletis.

(*Cod. Epter.*) .   .   .   .   .   . Tripoli Magdaletis Rom Basilis.

(*Cod. Wissenb.*) .   .   Romae Baseledis Tripoli Macidaletis.

June 12.—At Rome, Basillis ; in Tripoli, Magdales.

In the versions of the Middle Ages, however, we find the reading,

Romae, Baselidis Tripodis Magalis,

where the place-name *Tripoli* has become a saint Tripos.

[2] For further criticisms see Duchesne, *Lib. Pont.* under respective popes.

[3] So Duchesne : not here *translation*, as Dufourcq.   See *Études sur les* Gesta Martyrum *romains*, p. 95, and following pages for Martyrology of Jerome.

[4] Dufourcq, *op. cit.*, says this is the day of translation.   Cf. July 2nd, *supra*, p. 222.

These double papal entries require more minute investigation than we have been able to give them here, but are quoted as the kind of errors that appear in the Calendar.

Analysis of the Entries of the Roman Martyrs.—The Martyrology is obviously somewhat more detailed, even in the papal entries, than the Philocalian Calendar, and the notices of the saints are incomparably fuller. For while in the earlier Calendar we have but 47 Roman saints, or groups of saints, there appear in the Martyrology 213 saints, or groups of purely Roman saints, according to Dufourcq's [1] most useful and laborious reckoning. Of these, as he points out, 86 have no topographical indication except " Rome." Among these 86 are found some of the most famous names,—some of the popes, S. Agnes (Jan. 21st : *XII K feb.*), SS. John and Paul (June 26th : *VI K. Jul.*), S. Cecilia (Sep. 16th and Nov. 22nd : *XVI. K. Oct.* and *X K. dec.*), etc. For the remaining 127, different places of burial are given for 11. For 40 out of the entire 213 more than one day of deposition is noted. For about 20 of these 40, however, the fact of a translation or papal ordination can explain the discrepancy; but the facts of each case require most careful investigation on its own merits.

If we compare the names of martyrs inscribed in the Martyrology with our information from other sources,—*Gesta*, actual tombs, epigraphy,—we shall find some curious omissions.[2] Where are Clement the Consul and his wife Flavia Domitilla, both relations of the Emperor Domitian ; Acilius Glabrio, of a noble patrician family, who had served the state for generations, and whose first-century tomb forms the nucleus of the catacomb of S. Priscilla ; Justin Martyr,[3] and many another less well known?

Dufourcq has analysed the number of martyrs and the topographical indications found in the Calendar, and in the *Gesta* respectively, and notes that for each great cemetery-lined road of Rome, from two to fifteen martyrs are peculiar

---

[1] Dufourcq, *op. cit.* p. 18. The *total* number, of course, is much higher. For instance, " Parthenius and Calocerus," or " John and Paul," is each counted as " one group."

[2] See Dufourcq, *op. cit.* p. 95.   [3] *Supra*, p. 153.

to the *Gesta* and absent from the Calendar.   The general conclusion would seem to be that the two sets of documents are independent, and that the *Gesta* derive their information from oral tradition and other sources.[1]

Such is the history of the Martyrology, according to De Rossi, and to Duchesne, who has devoted twenty years to the study of it.   In practical agreement with them are Achelis, Harnack, Mommsen, Urbain, Dufourcq, and other scholars.[2]

This account of the Martyrology, however, has not passed quite unchallenged.

Views of Krusch : Martyrology compiled at Luxeuil in the Seventh Century.   Duchesne's Theory carries Conviction.—Krusch,[3] who has had the advantage of studying Duchesne's great work, while he agrees with Duchesne on the difficult question of the classification of the manuscripts, and the construction of the Martyrology, believes that the document was compiled, (1) not at Auxerre, but at Luxeuil, (2) nor yet in the sixth century, but about 627. Of the Italian version he will hear nothing; and further denies that Cassiodorus and Gregory the Great are referring to this work in the passages quoted above; and holds that the apocryphal introductory letters belong to the original compilation.   It would be too long to enter minutely into this controversy, and both parties to it are in agreement as to the composition of the document : as to its Gallican origin— both Luxeuil and Auxerre being in Burgundy—and even to its date within about forty years.   To most students the replies of Duchesne to Krusch will appear to vindicate amply the correctness of Duchesne's conclusions.[4]

Later Martyrologies : (1) Bede (Eighth Century).— We may complete this account of the Martyrology of Jerome

---

[1] *Supra*, p. 185.

[2] Harnack, *Theologische Literaturzeitung*, 1888, p. 351, Leipsic ; Mommsen, *Gestorum Pontificum Romanorum*, vol. i. p. xi, note, and p. xix, in series *Monumenta Germaniae Historica*, Berlin, 1898 ; Dufourcq, *Étude sur les* Gesta Martyrum *romains*, p. 77 ; Achelis, *Die Martyrologien . . . (op. cit.)*.

[3] See Bibliography—MARTYROLOGY OF JEROME.

[4] The whole controversy is found in the pages of the *Bulletin Critique*, *Analecta Bollandiana*, and the *Neues Archiv*, quoted in the Bibliography— MARTYROLOGY OF JEROME.

by a brief note of later Martyrologies depending mainly on it. They are all what we may call historical Martyrologies,[1] with biographies, more or less detailed, of the saints included in them.

First and foremost is the so-called *Martyrology of Bede*[2] of the early eighth century, based on the Martyrology of Jerome, on the *Liber Pontificalis*, and on other works. It was in use in the north of England, at Yarrow, Wearmouth, Iona, and Bangor.

(2) Little Roman Martyrology (Eighth Century).—Probably contemporary with this is the Little Roman Martyrology (*Martyrologium Romanum Parvum*), compiled at Rome in the eighth century.

(3) Of Rabanus Maurus, 850.—To the ninth century, about 859, belong the *Martyrology of Rabanus Maurus* and that of *Florus* of Lyons.

(4) Of Ado (Ninth Century).—The most important of all these Martyrologies is that of *Ado*,[3] composed at Lyons before he was Archbishop of Vienne, between 860 and 874. Ado makes use of all the earlier Martyrologies, except that of Maurus. It is much fuller in the biographical details than previous works. Notices are given of 178 Roman saints, or groups of saints, and to 129 of these are attached little biographies, varying in length from five lines to several pages, derived from various *Gesta* and *Passiones*. There is also an allusion in it to " A very ancient Martyrology " which Ado saw at Ravenna. This most interesting document has not been identified, but from the entries from it in Ado it can be shown to be quite distinct from the Martyrology of Jerome. Wherever the statements of Ado can be checked by other sources of information, he is found to be following ancient and authentic documents.

(5) Of Usuard (875): Roman Martyrology.—Another *Martyrology* was compiled by *Usuard*, a monk of S. Germain des Prés, in 875, who dedicated it to Charles the Bold. From it is directly derived the *Roman Martyrology* at present in use.

---

[1] *Supra*, p. 206. Cf. Quentin, *Martyrologes historiques du moyen age*, 1908.
[2] For texts of the Martyrologies following see Bibliography.
[3] See Bibliography and Dufourcq, *op. cit.* p. 31, and *infra*, p. 343.

CHAPTER XVIII

THE *SYLLOGAE*: THEIR SOURCES AND LITERARY STYLE

Inscriptions, secular and religious.—*Syllogae* of the sixth and seventh centuries.—*Syllogae* of the Carolingian epoch : influence of Alcuin.—The chief *Syllogae* and the geographical distribution of the manuscripts : (1) Northern French group—(2) S. Gall group.—Inscriptions in anthologies.—The subject-matter of the *Syllogae* and the original topographical arrangement.—The manuscripts and their deformation.—Date and literary style.—The authors.—Imitations from the classics.—Paganism of some Christian epitaphs.—Plagiarism in inscriptions.—Historical value of the inscriptions.

Inscriptions, Secular and Religious.—A considerable part of the history of Rome is written in the numerous inscriptions on the monuments, secular and religious. Of the originals scarcely one-fifth remain, but a certain number have been preserved in the collections known as *Syllogae*. We must confine ourselves here to the study of those *Syllogae* concerning Christian Rome which are earlier than the tenth century.[1]

Syllogae **of the Sixth and Seventh Centuries.**—*Syllogae* of Christian inscriptions were compiled as early as the sixth and seventh centuries, and were thus contemporary with some of the Itineraries, to which they are in some respects akin. The inscriptions contained in these *Syllogae* were taken down direct from the monuments, and arranged in topographical order with indications of locality affixed. Though none of these original *Syllogae* now exist, these facts can be deduced from the analysis of the later *Syllogae* depending on them.[2]

[1] There are many interesting local *Syllogae* (Milan, Nola, Tours, etc.), as well as mediaeval *Syllogae* of the twelfth century and later, such as those of Peter Mallius (twelfth century), Nicholas Laurentius (fourteenth century), and others.

[2] See Chaps. XIX., XX. For texts and full details see De Rossi, *Inscriptiones Christianae Urbis Romae*, t. ii. (" *I.C.*") (All the inscriptions quoted are found in this second volume of De Rossi.

The authors of the *Syllogae* are unknown. Perhaps they were members of the lower orders of clergy, perhaps scholars from the monasteries, perhaps those professional guides who are known to have existed in the great cities of the Roman Empire.

The interest in the Roman inscriptions spread far, and was especially keen in England, a real home of learning at that date. In the poetical works [1] of Aldhelm, Abbot of Malmesbury, and, later, Bishop of Sherbourne, are found inscriptions either derived from the *Syllogae*, or copied from the monuments themselves by Aldhelm when summoned to Rome by Pope Sergius. Aldhelm himself, when there, composed some verses in honour of SS. Peter and Paul,[2] which appear to have been used as inscriptions for S. Andrew's on the Vatican.[3]

Bede, too, quotes the epitaph of Cadwalla,[4] the Saxon king, and of Gregory the Great;[5] and the epitaph of Pope Boniface II. (530–532)[6] was borrowed for the English bishop, Boniface (d. 755), the apostle of the Germans. Turning far in the other direction, we find that Roman inscriptions are imitated in African basilicas,[7] and, nearer at home, in the cities of Italy.

Syllogae **of the Carolingian Epoch (Eighth and Ninth Centuries): Influence of Alcuin (735–800).**—At the close of the eighth century came the revival of learning, under the patronage of Charlemagne, due directly to the efforts of Alcuin and the band of scholars who were his pupils. One of the aspects of this many-sided movement was the interest taken in the inscriptions of Rome and in the ancient *Syllogae* and Itineraries, which resulted in new compilations based on the earlier documents.

The poems of Alcuin himself[8] consist largely of inscrip-

---

[1] *P.L.* 89, col. 291.   [2] *Ibid.* col. 297.

[3] Cf. De Rossi, *Inscriptiones Christianae Urbis Romae*, p. 257, Nos. 1, 2, with *P.L.* 89, col. 291 (ii.), 293 (iv.). Aldhelm also quotes *Virgo Maria tibi* (see *infra*, p. 282) in his *De re grammatica et metrica* (Mai, *Classicorum auctorum t. v.* p. 539).

[4] *Hist. Eccles.* v. c. 7 ; *I.C.* p. 70, No. 40.

[5] *Op. cit.* ii. c. 1 ; *I.C.* p. 112, No. 73.

[6] *I.C.* 126, No. 2.   [7] *Infra*, p. 310.

[8] *P.L.* 101, col. 738 ; Dümmler, *Poetae latini aevi Carolingi*, t. i. pp. 169–351, in *Mon. Germ. Hist.* ; *I.C.* p. 285.

tions—some original, some borrowed [1] either from the older *Syllogae* or from the monuments themselves. If we follow in the track of his labours,[2] extending to the length and breadth of Charlemagne's kingdom, we find that at every place with which he was connected he left some monument of learning; and among these are to be found some of the *Syllogae*. Alcuin was educated at York in the traditions of Bede; probably took the tonsure, and then migrated to the Court of Charlemagne, where he gathered round him a band of scholars, of whom a large proportion were English. He spent his days in spreading abroad learning and piety, and in the reorganization of the monasteries. He became himself Abbot of S. Martin's at Tours.

The Chief *Syllogae* **and the Geographical Distribution of the Manuscripts.**—Turning to the *Syllogae* [3] we find they originate mainly in two distinct districts—in N. France (and mainly in the N.E.) and in the monasteries more or less within the sphere of influence of S. Gall, near Lake Constance, namely, at Reichenau and Einsiedeln.

(1) Northern French Group of *Syllogae.*—Among the French *Syllogae*, the *Sylloge Turonensis* came from the actual monastery of which Alcuin was abbot. The *Sylloge Centulensis* (or *Corbeiensis*) was compiled by the Englishman Angilbert, a pupil of Alcuin and abbot of the Monastery of S. Richarius, Centula (modern S. Riquier, dep. Somme); later the manuscript was sold to the neighbouring Monastery of Corvie,[4] whose abbot, in earlier days, had been Adalard, also a pupil of Alcuin. These two *Syllogae*, then, depend directly on the influence of Alcuin. Further, the best manuscript of the Sylloge of Vatican Inscriptions (*Inscriptiones Vaticanae*) is found in Paris. To this group must be added the *Sylloge Virdunensis*, from Verdun (dep. Meuse), though this, as far as we know, has no connexion with Alcuin.

---

[1] e.g. *His solidata fides* . . . (Dümmler, *op. cit.* i. p. 345, No. III.) which Alcuin copied from the inscription in S. Peter *ad Vincula* in Rome (*I.C.* p. 110, No. 64), which is itself copied from Arator, *De actis apostolorum*, i. 1070. Many other examples might be given. Cf. *I.C.* p. liv.

[2] *De Vita Alcuini*, *P.L.* 101, especially cols. 52, 57, 59.

[3] For the history and analysis of each Sylloge see Chaps. XIX., XX.

[4] It is now in the library of S. Petersburg.

(2) **S. Gall Group.**—From the S. Gall[1] district, around Lake Constance where, tradition says, Alcuin himself taught, comes the *Sylloge Einsiedlensis* (or *Reichenavensis*), compiled at the monastery of Reichenau, and now preserved in the Benedictine monastery of Einsiedeln in Switzerland. The *Sylloge Laureshamensis* comes from Lorsch (Lauriacum), south-west Germany, not far from Einsiedeln. It was compiled in the ninth century by a monk of Lorsch, of which the Abbot was Samuel, another pupil of Alcuin. The little *Sylloge Wirceburgensis* from Würzburg (Germany), not far east of Lorsch, belongs geographically to this group. Our list of *Sylloge* will be complete if we add the *Sylloge of Cambridge*,[2] preserved in the University Library of that town.

The *Vetus Membrana Scaligeri*,[3] though it contains but a single Roman inscription, must be mentioned on account of its antiquity and fame. It is perhaps the oldest of the *Syllogae*, and consists of a mere fragment, probably of the sixth century. It was discovered in a French monastery by Pithou in the seventeenth century, and the single copy existing was made by Scaliger, and is now in the Vatican Library. It contains fourteen inscriptions in prose, secular and religious : of the cities of Rome (one only), Ravenna (four), Ariminum (Rimini) (one) and Treviri (Triers) in the Rhine district (eight), arranged in groups. The most ancient inscription is that at Ravenna (No. 2), relating how Theodoric (493–526) drained the marshes and wrought other improvements in that city.

Inscriptions in Anthologies.—Inscriptions, too, are sometimes found in the collected works of the poets who composed them.[4] They are also preserved by being quoted in histories, as in that of Bede.[5] They are found in collections of anthologies,[6] such as the *Anthologia Salmasiana*, derived from a sixth-century source, preserved in a Paris manuscript of the seventh century ; the *Anthologia Carmi-*

---

[1] This monastery was a centre of learning for many centuries ; it was peopled largely by English and Irish monks. Under Abbot Angilbert (924–933) the valuable library of manuscripts was taken to Reichenau on account of the threatened invasion by the Huns.

[2] Chap. XX. [3] *I.C.* p. 3. [4] *Supra*, pp. 231, 232.
[5] *Supra*, p. 231. [6] *I.C.* p. 238.

num in Codice Parisino 8071 of the eighth century, preserved in a manuscript of the tenth or eleventh; the
Anthologia Isidoriana of the seventh century, forming
part of the manuscript of the *Sylloge of Tours*; and many
others.

**The Subject-Matter of the *Sylloge* and Original
Topographical Arrangement.**—The contents of these
Syllogae consist mainly of Roman inscriptions covering the
period from the fourth to the ninth century. The subject-
matter of each Sylloge has been analysed by De Rossi
according to the original sources which compose it. The
Syllogae are then seen to contain much in common. They
all contain some at least of the inscriptions of S. Peter's,
derived from a sixth-century document of Vatican inscriptions (*Inscriptiones Vaticanae*). All alike, too, contain
inscriptions of suburban churches, and of the crypts of the
catacombs, derived from some Itinerary of the seventh
century. The third element common to all the *Syllogae* is
inscriptions of other basilicas and churches within the city,
derived, too, from early sources. Other inscriptions belong to
secular monuments (which often bear Christian inscriptions),
and to cities other than Rome (Spoleto, Ravenna, Ticino);
and sometimes to the monasteries which possessed the manuscripts (as Tours and S. Riquier (Centula)).[1]

From this analysis it is further evident that, in the prototypes from which the *Syllogae* were compiled, indications
of locality were appended to the inscriptions; and that they
were arranged, as were the Itineraries, in the topographical
order in which the pilgrims made their journey. It is probable, also, that these prototypes were complete in themselves.
For example, in the *Inscriptiones Vaticanae* if complete,
the list would proceed methodically from atrium, font, and
portico by way of side chapels, tombs, and shrines on to the
triumphal arch, the apse and the altar. A similar method
would be followed in the collection of inscriptions of the
urban stational[2] basilicas and other churches. It is certain,
too, that the inscriptions from the catacombs and suburban
shrines would be at least as complete as the Itineraries,

[1] *Infra*, pp. 248, 250. [2] *Supra*, pp. 13, 14.

and include *all* the great roads filled with sepulchres along which the pilgrim passed.

The Manuscripts of the *Syllogae*; their Deformation.— Such were the prototypes on which the *Syllogae* were based.

These prototypes passed through the hands of the eighth-century compilers, thence through the hands of various copyists, till they reached us, much changed from the originals, in manuscripts of the tenth, eleventh and twelfth centuries. The texts themselves of these manuscripts are faulty: not infrequently a few lines from one inscription are accidentally appended to another on a totally different subject. The indications of locality are often entirely lacking, and the inscriptions run on without any break. The original topographical order has been confused in many places. Moreover, any given portion of a Sylloge is usually incomplete. Many inscriptions of the urban basilicas are entirely omitted, a few only are given from S. Peter's, and the inscriptions of the suburban roads are frequently confined to two or three out of at least twenty— usually the Via Salaria and the Via Nomentana being chosen.

It is difficult to tell exactly how far the compilers and copyists are responsible for these errors. They are some-times obviously using incomplete originals, and the constant omission of the roads with which the pilgrims' way opened and closed, namely, the Via Flaminia and the Via Cornelia, suggests that these venerable guide-books had become worn in the pilgrims' hands, and had lost their first and last pages. Sometimes the scribe is using two incomplete versions which he has unskilfully pieced together, with repetitions and overlapping. On many of the manuscripts are corrections and notes; some by hands contemporary with the documents, or nearly so, and some as late as the seventeenth century.

Yet with all their defects the *Syllogae* have preserved a large number of inscriptions otherwise lost, and many traces of the original documents; for, in spite of omissions, there are still many topographical indications remaining, and even in the most confused *Syllogae* are found *groups* of inscriptions arranged in topographical order.

Further, the *Syllogae* mutually supply each other's defects—each gives some epitaph omitted in others, some place-name, or correct reading. From a variety of other sources, literary and monumental, light is thrown on these documents. There still remain, however, inscriptions not yet identified, which form the subject of many studies and of wide diversity of opinion among scholars.[1]

Date and Literary Style of the Inscriptions.—The inscriptions of the *Syllogae* are nearly all in verse—hexameters or elegiacs—and consist of two lines or more, the commonest length being of six or eight lines. They cover a period of six centuries, from the fourth to the ninth; and alike in contents and style reflect the vicissitudes of the ages in which they were composed. There is a note of exaltation in the early days of the triumph of the Church. Compare Constantine's conception of "*A world rising triumphant to the stars under the leadership of Christ*"[2] with the misery revealed in verses of the succeeding centuries, with their perpetual prayer for peace amid the successive invasions of Goth, Greek and Lombard.[3] And again we can trace in the inscriptions a short period of revived hopes under the rule of Theodoric and Justinian.

The Authors.—The style of the verses is as varied as the contents. The best of the inscriptions retain something of classic beauty, and are sometimes the work of well-known poets—of Paulinus, Bishop of Nola (353–431), of Ambrose of Milan (340–397), of Jerome, of Publius Optatianus Porphyrius of the court of Constantine, of Sidonius Apollinaris (431–489), Bishop of Clermont in Auvergne, of Prudentius the Spaniard (b. 438), of Anicius Bassus, consul in 408 and in 431, who wrote the epitaph of Monica (d. 387), mother of S. Augustine.[4]

To the majority of the inscriptions the name of some pope is attached, and often he was actually the maker of the verses, as well as of the buildings referred to in them.

---

[1] See Chap. XX.
[2] *Infra*, p. 278.
[3] *Infra*, p. 281.
[4] *Anthol. Isid.*, No. 2, in *I.C.* p. 252.

Damasus (366–384)[1] wrote nearly all the epitaphs of the catacombs, and many others as well; Boniface I. (418–423) those to S. Felicitas;[2] and various monuments once recorded the names of Celestinus (422–432), Sixtus (433–414), Symmachus (498–514) and Honorius (625–640).[3]

Imitation from the Classics.—As in art, ritual and philosophy, Christianity has ever embraced what seemed good, or at worst indifferent, in paganism, so in the inscriptions are found whole lines and phrases inspired directly by pagan sources, and especially by the poet Virgil. Sometimes the effect is happy; sometimes the verses read like a parody. Damasus' version[4]

> Tityre tu fido recubans sub tegmine Christi
> Divinos apices sacro modularis in ore

of the familiar lines of Virgil[5]

> Tityre tu patulae recubans sub tegmine fagi
> Silvestrem tenui Musam meditaris avena

is scarcely successful.

Paganism of Christian Inscriptions.—Some of the epitaphs indeed,—usually those of obscure or unknown persons,—bear no signs of Christianity, though some at least are known to belong to graves of Christians. Most of these are of quite remarkable beauty. As examples among many similar may be noted a group of five on the Via Salaria,[6] and another three on the Via Tiburtina,[7] all found in the *Sylloge Centulensis*; the last (No. 67) being the epitaph of an actor. In the *Sylloge Laureshamensis IV.* is the epitaph of Dionysius, a pious deacon and also a doctor, quite un-Christian in sentiment; followed by the exquisite inscription made by Dionysius himself to his wife Rhodine;[8] and in the same

---

[1] For collected poems see *Damasi epigrammata*, ed. Ihm, in series *Anthologia Latina*: Leipsic, 1895.

[2] *Infra*, p. 293.   [3] *Infra*, pp. 280–288.

[4] Epigram, No. 3.   [5] *Bucolica*, i. 1.

[6] *Sylloge Centulensis* ("*Cent.*"), Nos. 50–54 (in *I.C.* p. 90).

[7] Nos. 65–67 (in *I.C.* p. 93).

[8] *Sylloge Laureshamensis* ("*Laur.*") *IV.*, Nos. 49, 50 and 54 (forming one epitaph) (in *I.C.* p. 106); cf. in same Sylloge Nos. 76, 77, 78, 86, 90, 94, 101, 102.

collection are the inscriptions of a senator, and of an unknown person, both buried in S. Peter's, and equally devoid of all pious sentiments.

Plagiarism in Inscriptions.—Not only were inscriptions borrowed [1] from the poets, pagan or Christian, but certain phrases and lines seem common property of all writers of such verses, and occur again and again : they were, in fact, useful "tags" in an age when verse-writing did not come easy. Sometimes entire inscriptions were borrowed from one building to serve for another, and were slightly modified or enlarged to adapt them to the new situation. It was not unknown for a pope to add a line or two to an old inscription, claiming the honour of the work executed, or to substitute his own name for that of a predecessor— sometimes often with disastrous metrical effects. These borrowed inscriptions often travelled far. An inscription of the Vatican, *Justitiae sedes*,[2] and an inscription of S. Peter *ad Vincula*, composed by Sixtus III. (432–440), *Cede prius*,[3] are both found in a sixth-century inscription of a basilica at Tebessa (*Theveste*) in Numidia, North Africa ;[4] and the English Boniface, we have seen, lay at rest beneath the borrowed papal epitaph of his namesake.[5]

If some of the inscriptions are of rare beauty, the majority are somewhat commonplace, and frequently obscure in sense and defective in grammar and metre. Some of these, however, are inspired by a religious fervour which almost redeems their banality. The examples of inscriptions given in a subsequent chapter [6] will illustrate the diversity of style and subject-matter.

Historical Value of the Inscriptions.—Historically these inscriptions are of the highest importance. Often the entire history of the fabric of a church can be read in the verses of successive centuries affixed to its walls. The papal

---

[1] Many examples of plagiarism will be found in the next three chapters.
[2] *I.C.* p. 55, No. 8.
[3] *I.C.* p. 110, No. 67.
[4] *Bull. arch. crist.*, 1878, p. 7 ; 1879, p. 163 (see *infra*, p. 310).
[5] *Supra*, p. 231.
[6] Chap. XXI. The translations there attempted are as literal as possible, and, like their originals, sometimes fail in respect of sense and beauty.

inscriptions, extending over a period of four centuries,[1] frequently yield a complete biography : and a papal biography is a summary of the history of the Church—of her discipline, struggle with heretics, relation with the civil powers, internal strife, architecture and ritual. A history of dogma can be compiled from the dedicatory inscriptions for churches, baptisteries, altars and votive offerings. The history of many a martyr and of his cult can be traced from the inscription on the catacomb where he lay first, to that in the suburban church raised over him ; and thence to that in the urban basilica to which his body was transferred ; and finally the successive dedications of a single church reveal the ebb and flow of his popularity. Here, too, in the epitaphs can be read the story of many a stranger and pilgrim, great or obscure, who came to Rome and never returned : of Cadwalla the Saxon king who "purified by the grace of Christ in the water of regeneration straightway passed to heaven, still in his white baptismal robe," or of Elpis, the Sicilian woman "whom love for her husband drove far from her fatherland."

---

[1] Exclusive of the brief epitaphs of the earlier popes (see *infra*, p. 300 *et seq.*).

CHAPTER XIX

THE *SYLLOGAE*: ANALYSES

History, place of compilation, date, analysis of contents of the following :—
Sylloge Einsiedlensis (*Reichenavensis*), *Sylloge Laureshamensis*, *Sylloge Virdunensis*, *Sylloge Turonensis*, *Sylloge Centulensis* (*Corbeiensis*) *Inscriptiones Basilicae Vaticanae*, *Sylloge Wirceburgensis*.

IT remains to consider briefly the sources, date and birthplace of the more important *Syllogae*. The Analyses will show their contents and their topographical arrangement. From a comparison of these analyses, all inscriptions referring to any given church, shrine or locality which are found in two or more of the eight *Syllogae* in question could be grouped together for purposes of any special investigation.

Sylloge Einsiedlensis :—(*a*) **the Manuscript Eighth or Ninth Century.**—The *Sylloge Einsiedlensis*[1] (or *Sylloge Reichenavensis*) came originally from the monastery of Reichenau to the Benedictine monastery at Einsiedeln, and belongs to the Carolingian epoch—eighth or early ninth century. It exists, in a manuscript of the ninth or tenth century, as an appendix to the *Itinerarium Einsiedlense*.[2] It is followed by an exact liturgical description of the ceremonies of Holy Week, as the author saw them performed by the pope in Rome—a document of the highest value—and by a Latin anthology of no topographical interest. In De Rossi's opinion these sections of the manuscript are of the same age, by the same hand, and compiled at Reichenau. A very few leaves are missing.

---

[1] *I.C.* p. 9. The text is also printed with the Itinerary in Uhrlichs, *Codex urbis Romae Topographicus*, 1871. Cf. also Jordan, *Topographie der Stadt Rom im Alterthum*, vol. ii. pp. 156, 330 : Berlin, 1871.

[2] *Supra*, p. 119.

(*b*) **Character of the Sylloge.**—The Sylloge contains eighty-two entries, nearly all concerning Rome, each with definite topographical heading.   As the Itinerary of Ein-siedeln differed in some respects from the other Itineraries, —in arrangement, in the interest shown in secular as well as sacred monuments, and in the precision of topographical detail, — so the Sylloge possesses some of the peculiar characteristics of the Itinerary to which it is appended. In the first and second portions (Nos. 1–71) there is even a preponderance of secular over religious inscriptions.   In the brief third portion (No. 71–77) half the inscriptions (*i.e.* Nos. 73a, 73b, 74a) are taken straight from some Itinerary, and are a mere topographical list of names.   Jordan, indeed, believed that both Itinerary and Sylloge were derived from a common source.   De Rossi, however, pointing out marked differences in the topographical terms, and in other respects, between the documents, believes them to be derived from different originals.

Many of the inscriptions recorded in this Sylloge are peculiar to it.

(*c*) **Analysis of Component Parts.**—It can be divided into four parts, bearing traces of four distinct earlier sources, probably of the seventh century.

ANALYSIS OF THE *SYLLOGE EINSIEDLENSIS*

I. SECULAR AND RELIGIOUS (MAINLY URBAN)

1–60.—Secular inscriptions for bridges, aqueducts, columns, theatres, tombs, etc.   Among them certain Christian inscriptions for the churches of S. Peter (Nos. 6, 10, 11), S. Paul (Nos. 52, 53), SS. John and Paul (No. 51), S. Anastasia (No. 25), S. Sabina (No. 27), S. Pancras (No. 28), S. Sebastian (No. 34), The Library of Gregory the Great (No. 55).

II. SET OF INSCRIPTIONS FOR THE TOMB OF HADRIAN

61–71.—Of these, 61, 62, 63 are found in the preceding portion (Nos. 4, 5, 6).
  None of these seventy-one inscriptions are later than the sixth century.

16

III. CATACOMB INSCRIPTIONS (EXCEPT NO. 75)

72-77.—(*a*) VIA PINCIA (72, 73), with a passage (73a)
quoted from an Itinerary of the district; (*b*)
VIA APPIA (73b) being a portion of an Itinerary, (74); (*c*) ROAD from PORTA S. PETRI
to S. PAUL'S (74a), from an Itinerary; (*d*)
VIA OSTIENSIS (75 a pagan Greek epitaph)
(76); (*e*) VIA APPIA again (S. Sebastian, 77).

IV. INSCRIPTIONS OF PAPIAS IN NORTH ITALY

78-82.—Three inscriptions to Emperors, one to a flamen
and one, in Greek, for the base of a bronze
statue of S. Peter in the basilica of Ticinum
(Ticino), North Italy.

Corporis Laureshamensis Syllogæ: **Four Component Parts.**
—The composite document renamed by De Rossi *Corporis
Laureshamensis Syllogæ*[1] is found in a Codex of the Vatican
known as the Palatine, whence its old name *Codex Palatinus.*
It can be analysed into four component parts:

I. *Corp. Laur. Sylloge I.*, **Ninth Century: Thirty-Four
Inscriptions of Churches, many Urban.**—In the ninth century a certain monk from the monastery of Lauriacum (Lorsch)
in south-west Germany, made a collection of thirty-four inscriptions taken direct from Roman churches, *e.g.* S. Peter's (10 in
number), S. John Lateran (6), S. Anastasia (2), SS. John and
Paul (2), S. Maria in Trastevere (1), S. Cecilia (1), S. Laurence
in Damaso (3), S. Chrysogonus (1), SS. Cosmas and Damian
(1), S. Stephen (6), and S. Laurence on the Via Tiburtina (1).
The document is earlier than 846, in which year various
treasures, here described as existing, were destroyed by the
Saracens. The topographical indications at the head of the
inscriptions were probably added by a later hand.

This forms the first of the elements of the *Corporis Laureshamensis*, and is called by De Rossi *Corporis Laureshamensis
Sylloge I.*[2]

II. *Corp. Laur. Sylloge II.*, **Seventh Century: Pontifical
Epitaphs of S. Peter's.**—To complete his collection, the

[1] Nos. VIII., XI., XIII., XVI., in *I.C.*   [2] No. XIII., in *I.C.* p. 142.

monk of Lorsch incorporated with it three other older *Syllogae*. The second element, then, in our document is the *Corporis Laureshamensis Sylloge II.*,[1] a seventh-century document containing thirteen of the pontifical epitaphs in S. Peter's, from Anastasius (496–498) to John v. (684–686). Nine out of these thirteen inscriptions are of the seventh century. Most of them bear the heading $\overline{E_{PYT}}$ (*epitaphium*). They are not arranged in strict order of date. Arranged chronologically, the numbers of the inscriptions should run—IV., III., II., V., VI., I., IX., VII., X., VIII., XI., XII., XIII.

III. *Corp. Laur. Sylloge III.*: North Italian Epitaphs.—The third contribution, the *Corporis Laureshamensis Sylloge III.*,[2] is a local collection of thirty-six inscriptions of the Subalpine district and Po Valley (*Sylloge Circumpadana et Subalpina*). These inscriptions do not concern us here, but some of the epitaphs are of great poetic beauty.

IV. *Corp. Laur. Sylloge IV.*, Seventh Century: Urban and Suburban Epitaphs.—The most important element is the *Corporis Laureshamensis Sylloge IV.*,[3] a collection of the seventh century, containing one hundred and four inscriptions, secular, religious, and purely pagan, of basilicas, suburban tombs and other monuments. This list is extremely confused topographically, and there are very few indications of locality appended to the inscriptions. There are, however, traces of a certain order that once existed. The following analysis will give some idea of the contents, and the precise degree of disorder. It appears to be incomplete; whether we consider the inscriptions of the great churches,—of which three only are mentioned,—or of the catacomb shrines, of which few are given beyond those of the Via Salaria and Via Nomentana, or of the inscriptions, few in number and mostly unidentified, within the city.

[1] No. XI., in *I.C.* p. 124. [2] No. XVI., in *I.C.* p. 159.
[3] No. VIII., in *I.C.* p. 95.

ANALYSIS OF THE *CORPORIS LAURESHAMENSIS SYLLOGE IV.*

I. Basilicas

Nos.
1–3. S. Peter's, Vatican. 4, 5. S. Paul's. 6. S. Maria Maggiore.

II. Suburban Tombs

Nos.
7–12. Neighbourhood of S. Peter's.

13–19; [20. Via Ardeatina] . . .	Nos. 13–41.
21–28; [29. Via Labicana] . . .	Via Salaria and the adjacent road,
30; [31. Via Appia. 32. Via Ostiensis]	Via Nomentana
33–39; [40. Via Ostiensis] . . .	(except those in
41	brackets).

42–45. Via Ardeatina and adjoining Via Appia.
46–54. S. Laurence *in Agro Verano, i.e.* Via Tiburtina, and adjacent Via Labicana.
55–56; [57? 58. Via Salaria], 59–62; [63 ?], Via Appia and Via Ardeatina.

Ia. Basilicas and Churches

Nos.
64–68. S. Peter *ad Vincula*; [69? 70?]. 71 S. Sabina.
72–73. Tombs near S. Peter's, Vatican; [74–78?].
79–82. Inscriptions of S. Peter's, Spoleto.[1]

IIa. Suburban Tombs

Nos.

83–88; [89. S. Vitalis, Ravenna] . .	Via Salaria and Via Nomentana.
90–99	

100–103. Probably S. Laurence in Via Tiburtina.
104. Via Nomentana.

Sylloge Virdunensis, **Eighth Century :**—(*a*) **Date.**—The *Sylloge Virdunensis*[2] contains thirty-two inscriptions, of which many are peculiar to it. Internal evidence shows

---

[1] For the collocation of inscriptions from three different churches of S. Peter see *infra*, p. 252.
[2] No. XII., in *I.C.* p. 131.

that it was written at a period when the bodies of the martyrs were still in their catacomb tombs, *i.e.* before 817.[1] It was written, however, after Paul I. had removed the body of Pope Silvester from the catacomb church which bears his name, in S. Priscilla, to the urban monastery of *S. Silvestro in Capite*[2] in 761; for the heading in the Sylloge to the inscription of Silvester (No. 21) reads:

AD SCM SILVESTRUM UBI ANTE PAUSAVIT SUPER
ILLO ALTARE

i.e. (the inscriptions) above the altar of the church of S. Silvester where that pope formerly lay.

The latest of the inscriptions is that of Leo the Great (440–461), made by Sergius I. in 688.

(*b*) **The Manuscript.**—The Sylloge has been preserved in a manuscript of the tenth century in the Monastery of S. Vito, Verdun: it is now in the Library. It has been annotated by a later, though early, hand. In the original Sylloge there were full and accurate topographical indications, many of which are now lost. We can, however, discern very clear traces of a topographical arrangement in the document as we have it; though it is true, as Bonavenia[3] remarks, that many of the inscriptions are in wrong order, and that the headings (*i.e.* the name of the church or of the martyr) would often be misleading if we could not correct or supplement them from other sources. It is obviously incomplete as regards the list of cemeteries and the basilica inscriptions.

ANALYSIS OF THE *SYLLOGE VIRDUNENSIS*

I. Inscriptions of Urban Churches

Nos.

1, 2, 3. S. Peter *ad Vincula*.
     4. SS. Cosmas and Damian.
5, 6, 7. S. Laurence *in Damaso*.

---

[1] *Supra*, p. 17.
[2] The church for English-speaking Catholics in modern times.
[3] *La Sylloge di Verdun*: Rome, 1903.

II. Inscriptions of Suburban Cemeteries

Nos.

8–16. Via Salaria.
17, 18, [19?] Via Nomentana.
20–24. Via Salaria.
[25 and 26?] Via Salaria.

Ia. Urban Churches (probably a portion of Part I.)

Nos.

27. The Apostles (SS. James and Philip).
28. S. Maria Maggiore.
29. Lateran Basilica.

III.

After a heading, "We found these epitaphs in the church of S. Peter's," follows the beginning only of a list of papal epitaphs,—namely, three (Nos. 30, 31, 32) in S. Peter's,—followed by the words, "For the rest of this catalogue see the book of Hegesippus the historian." The heading suggests that the compiler of the Sylloge took down these inscriptions himself.

(c) **Value of Topographical Indications.**—The precise degree of topographical accuracy of this Sylloge can best be gauged by putting in their correct order, as the pilgrim would walk, the epitaphs of the Via Salaria and Via Nomentana :

Via Salaria

12, 13, 13a, 14, 15.—S. Felicitas group,[1] 1 mile N. of the city.
8, 9, 10, 16.—Chrysanthus and Darias group, 2 miles N. of the city.
11.—Saturninus' tomb,[2] quite near the last.
20.—Tomb of Alexander,[3] 2½ miles from the city.
21, 22, 23, 24.—Church of S. Silvester,[4] 3 miles from the city.
? 25, ? 26.

Via Nomentana

17, 18, 19.—S. Agnes in Via Nomentana, 1½ miles from city.

---

[1] In *Coemeterium Maximi* (see *Index Coemiteriorum, supra*, p. 98, and Appendix IV.).
[2] In *Coem. Thrasonis.*   [3] In *Coem. Jordanorum.*   [4] In *Coem. Priscillae.*

As the locality of the inscriptions Nos. 25 and 26 form the subject of a lively controversy, whose main outlines will be indicated later,[1] an analysis is appended here of that portion of the document. It is interesting in itself as an example of a connected portion of a Sylloge.

DETAILED ANALYSIS OF PART OF THE *SYLLOGE OF VERDUN.*[2]

21.—Ad Sanctum Silvestrum ubi ante pausavit super illo altare.
> [S. Silvester, in the Catacomb of S. Priscilla.]
> (10 lines, epitaph of Pope Siricius.)

22.—Epitaphium Marcelli papae.
> [S. Silvester, in the Catacomb of S. Priscilla.]
> (8 lines, epitaph of Pope Marcellus.)

23.—Epitaphium Sanctorum Felicis et Philippi Martyrum.
> [S. Silvester, in the Catacomb of S. Priscilla.]

QUI NATUM PASSUMQUE DEUM REPETISSE PATERNAS
SEDES ATQUE ITERUM VENTURUM EX AETHERE CREDIT
JUDICET ET VIVOS REDIENS PARITERQUE SEPULTOS
MARTYRIBUS SANCTIS PATEAT QUOD REGIA COELI
RESPICIT INTERIOR SEQUITUR SI PRAEMIA CHRISTI
> [S. Silvester, in the Catacomb of S. Priscilla.]

24.[3]—CULTORES DOMINI FELIX PARITERQUE PHILIPPUS
HINC VIRTUTE PARES CONTEMPTO PRINCIPE MUNDI
AETERNAM PETIERE DOMUM REGNUMQUE PIORUM
SANGUINE QUOD PROPRIO CHRISTI MERUERE CORONAS
HIC DAMASUS SUPPLEX VOLUIT SUA REDDERE VOTA

25.—Isti versiculi scripti sunt ad fontes:

SUMITE PERPETUAM SANCTO DE GURGITE VITAM
CURSUS HIC EST FIDEI MORS UBI SOLA PERIT
ROBORAT HIC ANIMOS DIVINO FONTE LAVACRUM
ET DUM MEMBRA MADENT MENS SOLIDATUR AQUIS

---

[1] *Infra*, p. 270 *et seq.*   [2] For translations see *infra*, pp. 270–272.
[3] De Rossi first saw that *23* and *24* were two distinct inscriptions.

AUXIT APOSTOLICAE GEMINATUM SEDIS HONOREM
CHRISTUS ET[1] AD CAELOS HANC DEDIT ESSE VIAM
NAM CUI SIDEREI COMMISIT LUMINA[2] REGNI
HIC HABET IN AMPLIS[3] ALTERA CLAUSTRA POLI

26.—Isti versiculi scripti sunt ubi pontifex consignat infantes:

ISTIC INSONTES CAELESTI FLUMINE LOTAS
PASTORIS SUMMI DEXTERA SIGNAT OVES
HUC UNDIS GENERATE VENI QUO SANCTUS AD UNUM
SPIRITUS UT CAPIAS TE SUA DONA VOCAT
TU CRUCE SUSCEPTA MUNDI VITARE PROCELLAS
DISCE MAGIS MONITUS HAC RATIONE LOCI

27.—Isti versiculi scripti sunt ad Apostolos insuper liminare:

(Distich of Pelagius.)

28.—Isti versiculi scripti sunt ad Sanctam Mariam Majorem.[4]

VIRGO MARIA TIBI . . . .

[Here follow inscriptions of the Lateran, S. Peter's, etc.]

Sylloge Turonensis :—(*a*) **Place and Date.**—Two local and dated inscriptions in the *Sylloge Turonensis*[5] give us the place and date of compilation of this Sylloge.[6] Both inscriptions belong to Tours: the second (No. 39) is an inscription on a votive tablet placed by Ionatus, otherwise unknown, "On a lofty mountain hanging over the greater monastery of S. Martin, patron of Tours" (*i.e.* in the famous monastery of Marmoutier), "while Bishop Chrodobertus ruled gloriously over it." As Chrodobertus was Bishop of Tours about

---

[1] MS. is *Xps . . . ad caelos.* (The *p* of *Xps* is a mistake from confusion with Greek Xρ.) De Rossi and Marucchi read *Christus et ad* . . . ; Bonavenia reads *Christus ut ad.* . . .

[2] De Rossi and Marucchi emend to *limina.*

[3] De Rossi and Marucchi emend to *templis.*

[4] See *infra*, p. 282.

[5] No. VI., in *I.C.* p. 58.

[6] *Supra*, p. 234.

670–676, the Sylloge was compiled at Tours in the seventh century.

(*b*) **Manuscripts.** — The Sylloge is preserved in two manuscripts of the eleventh or twelfth century, one at Klosterneuburg, near Vienna, and one in the Abbey of Gottwei in S. Austria.

(*c*) **Contents.**—It contains forty-two inscriptions. With the exception of those of Tours (Nos. 38, 39) and five from basilicas (Nos. 18, 19, 40, 41, 42), derived from a sixth-century source, these are all taken from the suburban cemeteries, and with few exceptions are of the fourth century, by Damasus. Very few of these are still in existence. The document depends on some seventh-century Itinerary. Though there are but three indications of locality (Nos. 15, 20, 29) in the whole of this portion, nearly all the epitaphs have been identified, and are found to be arranged in strict topographical order, proceeding, as in the case of the Itineraries,[1] in a clockwise direction, beginning with the Via Salaria Nova, thence by the Viae Nomentana, Tiburtina . . . round to S. Paul's on the Via Ostiensis. Certain roads are missing in the list—namely, the Viae Flaminia and Salaria Vetus at one end, which were the usual starting-points, and the Viae Portuensis, Aurelia, Cornelia, with S. Peter's, at the other end. The copyist was evidently using a version of which the first and last pages were missing. The following analysis will show the topographical arrangement.

ANALYSIS OF THE *SYLLOGE TURONENSIS*

I. Suburban Epitaphs

Nos.
1–4. Via Salaria Nova.
5, 6. Via Nomentana :—Basilica of S. Agnes.
7–10. Via Tiburtina :—S. Laurence *in Agro Verano*.
11–15. Via Labicana and near it.
16–17. Via Latina.
[18, 19. Misplaced : within the city, the basilica of SS. Philip and James.]

---

[1] *Supra*, Chaps. VII., VIII., pp. 93–126.

Nos.
20–27. Via Appia:—S. Sebastian (20, 21) and the
Catacomb of S. Callixtus (22–27).
28. Via Ardeatina.
29–37. Via Ostiensis and S. Paul's.

II. LOCAL INSCRIPTIONS OF TOURS
38, 39.

III. BASILICAS

40. Vatican (epitaph of Cadwalla, Saxon king)
added later.
[40a. Misplaced: "in praise of the island of Lerinum"
(Lérins).[1]]
41. SS. Cosmas and Damian.
42. S. Maria Maggiore.

Sylloge Centulensis : (*a*) **Place and Date of Compilation.**
—In the *Sylloge Centulensis*,[2] as in the *Sylloge Turonensis*,
an inscription in the Sylloge (No. 68) gives the place and
date of compilation, and, moreover, the probable author.
This inscription, a century later than any other in the
Sylloge, is the epitaph of a Scotch priest, Caidocus, buried
in the Monastery of S. Richarius in Centula (S. Riquier).
Tomb and inscription were made by Angilbert (740–814),
his fellow-countryman, the friend and pupil of Alcuin, and
Abbot of S. Richarius. At this period "Scotch" often
referred to an Irishman. The inscription is as follows:—

MOLE SUB HAC TEGITUR CAIDOCUS JURE SACERDOS
SCOTIA QUEM GENUIT GALLICA TERRA TEGIT
HIC DOMINI CHRISTI GAUDENS PRECEPTA SECUTUS
CONTEMPSIT PATRIS MENTE BEATUS OPES
HINC SIBI CONCREVIT CENTENA COPIA FRUCTUS
ET METIT AETHERII PRAEMIA LARGA SOLI
HUIC ANGILBERTUS FRETUS PIETATE MAGISTRA
ET TUMULO CARMEN CONDIDIT ET TUMULUM

[1] An island off Provence. The monastery, founded here by Honoratus,
Bishop of Arles, in the fifth century, was famous for its learning till the seventh.
The inscription was written by Dynamius (d. 601), a correspondent of Gregory
the Great. Cf. *supra*, p. 30.

[2] No. VII. in *I.C.* p. 72. Cf. De Rossi in *Bull. arch. crist.*, 1881, p. 5; also
1890, p. 123; and 1883, p. 7.

Beneath this monument is buried Caidocus, lawful priest,[1] whom the Scottish land bore, and the earth of Gaul covers.   He rejoiced to follow the precepts of Christ the Lord; and, blessed in spirit, despised the wealth of his father.   Hence there increased for him fruit a hundredfold, and he reaps a rich reward in the harvest fields of heaven. For him Angilbert made the epitaph on the tomb and also the tomb, trusting to be helped by his goodness.

The Sylloge, then, is of the eighth or early ninth century, and was probably compiled by Angilbert at Centula.

The library of this monastery was famous.   Angilbert was at least four times in Rome (once engaged in collecting relics for Alcuin), and from thence perhaps brought back some of the two hundred codices which he presented to the monastery, among them no doubt some of the sources of this Sylloge.

(*b*) **The Manuscript.**—The manuscript is in Lombard characters of the same period.   It was long preserved at the neighbouring monastery of S. Peter at Corvie, and is now in S. Petersburg, whence it was sent, on loan, to De Rossi by the Czar Alexander II. in 1881.   The document is annotated by a contemporary hand.

(*c*) **Contents.**—The Sylloge contains sixty-eight inscriptions, the latest being of the time of Pope Honorius (625–638), concerning whom there are no less than five, all made in his lifetime ; and it is certain that the sources of the eighth-century compilation belonged to the reign of this pope.   The inscriptions are incomplete, without local indications, and topographically confused.   It seems as if the copyist had before him two imperfect versions of the document and was endeavouring, somewhat unsuccessfully, to piece them together.   The Sylloge consists of two parts :

I. INSCRIPTIONS OF THE VATICAN BASILICA

(Nos. 1–9), depending on the *Inscriptiones Vaticanae* of the seventh century.   There follow three inscriptions (10–12)

---

[1] *Sacerdos* is frequently used for a *bishop*, which is the probable meaning here. Cf. *infra*, p. 289, note 1.   The difficult phrase, *Fretus pietate magistra=confidens auxilio pietatis.*   I am indebted to the kindness of Prof. Marucchi for this and other interpretations.

of S. Peter's at Spoleto, out of place, but inserted here on account of the connexion between the two churches.[1]

II. SUBURBAN INSCRIPTONS (SEVENTH CENTURY).

A series of suburban inscriptions (21–67), of which most belong to the Via Salaria. It is obviously incomplete and curiously confused. Though inferior in accuracy, it resembles portions of the *Sylloge Laureshamensis* and the *Sylloge Turonensis,*—all three depending on the same seventh-century suburban Itinerary.

ANALYSIS OF THE *SYLLOGE CENTULENSIS*

I. INSCRIPTIONS OF S. PETER'S

Nos.

1–9. S. Peter's. [10–12] S. Peter's, Spoleto.

II. SUBURBAN INSCRIPTIONS

13–20. Via Ostiensis and S. Paul's.
21–22. Via Tiburtina and S. Laurence.
21–43 [? 44]. Via Salaria and Via Nomentana.
45, 46. Via Appia.
47, 48. Via Labicana.
49. Via Latina.
50–54 [55 Ravenna]. Via Salaria.
56–67 (rather doubtful). S. Laurence, Via Tiburtina.

Inscriptiones Basilicae Vaticanae **(Seventh Century).**— Derived from some original document of the seventh century, and preserved in a mutilated manuscript of the Vatican of the fifteenth century, we have twelve inscriptions of the Vatican Basilica, named by De Rossi *Inscriptiones Basilicae Vaticanae*[2] (*e codice Pal. Vat.* 591). Unlike every other Sylloge, these are correctly arranged. They are all earlier than the seventh century, except four (Nos. 1–4), which belong to that century, of which the latest is the epitaph (No. 2) of Pope Agatho (678–682).

---

[1] *Supra*, p. 244. Cf. *Corp. Laur. IV.*, Nos. 79–82 of S. Peter's at Spoleto, appended to S. Peter's of the Vatican (72, 73) *and* to S. Peter *ad Vincula* (64–68).

[2] No. V. in *I.C.* p. 52.

A Paris manuscript of the ninth century has supplied another seven inscriptions of the Vatican Basilica, *Appendix Inscriptionum Basilicae Vaticanae (e codice Parisino,* 8071).[1]

Sylloge Wirceburgensis **of Ninth Century.**—Another series of ten inscriptions of basilicas is found in the small *Sylloge Wirceburgensis,*[2] of Würzburg. It is of the ninth century, and added by a later hand on a spare leaf of Cicero's *De Arte Rhetorica.* The inscriptions must be taken from some larger work. Nos. 1–5 bear indications of locality :

ANALYSIS OF THE *SYLLOGE WIRCEBURGENSIS*

No. 1. S. Paul's.   2. S. Sabina.   3 (and 9). S. Laurence *in Agro Verano* (?).   4 (and 7 and 8). S. Peter's. 5. S. Pancras.   6. S. Cecilia [7 and 8. S. Peter's]. [9. S. Laurence.]   10. S. Peter *ad Vincula.*

[1] No. V. in *I.C.* p. 56.   [2] No. XIV. in *I.C.* p. 155.

CHAPTER XX

THE NEW SYLLOGE OF CAMBRIDGE: THE *SUMITE* CONTROVERSY

The Sylloge of Cambridge, forming part of the *Liber Pontificalis*: the manuscript and the sources.—Analysis of the Sylloge, with quotations.— Peculiarities of the Sylloge: (*a*) Topographical errors, mainly in the Symmachus inscriptions: analysis of the subjects and localities of the inscriptions (*b*) Textual peculiarities, mainly in the same: ascriptions to Symmachus.—Conclusions from the analysis.—Explanation of false attributions.—The discussion concerning *Sumite* and *Istic* inscriptions: (*a*) Interpretations of the text of the Verdun Codex (*b*) The locality, according to the Sylloge of Verdun (1) Via Salaria or Via Nomentana? (2) S. Peter's or S. Priscilla?—(*c*) The locality, according to the Sylloge of Cambridge: (1) S. Michael's or (2) S. Priscilla, and then S. Michael, or (3) S. Peter's?

Sylloge of Cambridge, forming Part of the *Liber Pontificalis*. In 1910 Dr. Levison drew attention to the *Sylloge of Cambridge*, which forms part of a version of the *Liber Pontificalis* contained in a twelfth-century codex[1] of the University Library of Cambridge. The codex contains also other documents, some of the twelfth century and some earlier.

This new text of the *Liber Pontificalis* presents no particular features of interest. It records the deeds (*Gesta*) of the popes from Peter to Gelasius II. (1118–1119). A few pages are missing, among them those containing the *Gesta Sixti* (III.).

The special characteristics of this manuscript is the insertion, in the text of certain *Gesta*, of the inscriptions set up on the buildings, tombs, votive offerings, etc., connected with their heroes. These inscriptions are found in the Lives of several popes from Damasus (366–384) to John VII. (705–708), whose epitaph is the latest inscription in the

[1] KK. IV. 6. Most of the Sylloge has been transcribed by Levison, by Duchesne, and by Marucchi: See Bibliography—SYLLOGE OF CAMBRIDGE.

collection. The inscriptions are generally inserted immediately after the passage in the *Liber Pontificalis* describing the erection of the monument.

The Manuscript.—The manuscript is not very accurate, and some twelfth-century hand has constantly erased words and substituted others; the original words being often distinctly legible.

The Sources.—It is unknown from what source the twelfth-century scribe copied these inscriptions into his version of the *Liber Pontificalis*: what was its scope, what the method of arrangement, — topographical or biographical,—and in what fashion the copyist adapted the inscriptions to his work.[1] The date of the source is certainly of the eighth century, since the latest inscription is that of John VII. (705–708), whilst the fact that the history of the *Liber Pontificalis* is brought up to the year 1119, *i.e.* to Gelasius (1118–1119), proves the whole composite document to be of the twelfth century.

Analysis of the Sylloge.—The criticisms concerning these inscriptions will bear on the questions of (1) topographical attributions and (2) peculiarities of the text; and will be more easily appreciated after an analysis of the Sylloge and some quotations of the inscriptions.[2] The short quotation from the passage of the *Liber Pontificalis* which precedes each inscription, or set of inscriptions, will show the context of the latter. To the ordinary text of the *Liber Pontificalis* the author of the Sylloge of Cambridge frequently adds (1) words to introduce the inscriptions, and (2) headings to the inscriptions themselves. There are also (3) some extraordinary divergencies from the readings of the same inscriptions which we find in the other *Syllogae*.[3]

---

[1] *Infra*, p. 269.   [2] *Infra*, pp. 256–262.

[3] These *three* variations from the ordinary texts are all indicated by italics in the following quotations. Passages of the original omitted in the quotations are marked by dots. I have added in brackets the locality *ascribed* to each inscription in the Sylloge of Cambridge : these ascriptions are frequently incorrect. The inscriptions already familiar will be found in the *Inscriptiones Christianae II.* of De Rossi : some are quoted in this book, Chap. XXI. and elsewhere. I have numbered the inscriptions and lines for purposes of reference.

ANALYSIS OF THE NEW SYLLOGE OF CAMBRIDGE

. . . .

Gesta Damasi

. . . In quo loco platonam ipsam, ubi jacuerunt corpora sancta, versibus exornavit [1]
Versus Damasi papae.

[S. Sebastian on the Via Appia is implied.]

1. CINGEBANT LATICES [2] . . .

. . . .

. . . Qui etiam sepultus est Via Ardeatina in basilica sua . . . et cessavit episcopatum dies XXXI.[3]
Epitaphium Damasi

[Via Ardeatina, in his own basilica.]

2. QUI GRADIENS PELAGI [4] . . .
(There are no inscriptions for the next seven popes after Damasus.)

Gesta Leonis

. . . .

. . . Qui etiam sepultus est in basilica beati Petri, III. id April; et cessavit episcopatum dies VII. *Hujus corpus tempore Sergii papae de abdito inferioris secretarii translatum et in loco eminentiori est positum et super eum hoc epitaphium scriptum* : [5]
Epitaphium Leonis papae

[in S. Peter's].

3. HUJUS APOSTOLICI [6] . . .
(There are no inscriptions for the four popes after Leo.)

---

[1] *In that place* (S. Sebastian) *Damasus adorned with verses the platonia where the holy bodies* (of SS. Peter and Paul) *once lay.*

[2] CINGEBANT, see *infra*, p. 279.

[3] *He was buried on the Via Ardeatina in his own basilica . . . and the bishopric was vacant 31 days.*

[4] *Infra*, p. 290.

[5] *He was buried in the basilica of blessed Peter, April 11, and the bishopric was vacant 7 days. In the time of Sergius the pope his body was removed from the lower chamber and put in a higher place, and above him this epitaph is written.*

[6] *I.C.* p. 98, No. 1.

Gesta Anastasii

. . . Qui sepultus est apud beatum Petrum in Vaticanum XIII. kal. Dec. et cessavit episcopatum dies IV. *et hoc epitaphium in tumba ejus est scriptum.*

Epitaphium ejus.   [in S. Peter's].

4. LIMINA NUNC SERVO[1] . . .

Gesta Symmachi

.   .   .   .
Hic fecit basilicam Sancti Andreae apostoli apud beatum Petrum ubi fecit . . . arcus argenteos IV. singulos pensantes LX.[2]

5. INGREDERIS QUISQUAM RADIANTIS[3] . . .
                                    [S. Andrew on the Vatican].
(of which the concluding distich is):

(5) ORNAVIT PRAESUL VENERANDUS SYMMACHUS AEDES
(6) PRISCAQUE CESSERUNT MAGNO NOVITATIS HONORE

Oratorium Sancti Thomae apostolae . . . arcum argenteum qui pensat lib. XVI.

6. QUISQUIS AD AETERNAM[4] . . .
                              [Chapel of S. Thomas in S. Andrew's].

6a[5]. SYMMACHUS HAS ARCES CULTU MELIORE NOVAVIT
      MARMOREIS TITULIS NOBILITATE FIDE
      NIL FORMIDO VALET MORSUS CESSERE LUPORUM
      PASTORIS PROPRIUM CONTINET AULA GREGEM

Confessionem Sancti Cassiani et Sanctorum Proti et Hyacinthi . . .

---

[1] *I.C.* p. 126, No. 4.
[2] *Symmachus built the basilica of S. Andrew the apostle near S. Peter's, and made there . . . four silver arches each weighing 60 pounds.*
[3] *I.C.* p. 53, No. 5.   [4] *I.C.* p. 57, No. 19.
[5] *SYMMACHUS HAS ARCES* . . . is an inscription quite distinct in subject (and metre) from *QUISQUIS AD AETERNAM*, though the two are written as one in the codex. *Symmachus restored and adorned these arches with marble inscriptions, nobility, and faith: there is no more fear* (from schismatics); *the biting of the wolves* (sc. the followers of the antipope Laurence) *have ceased; this temple enfolds the true sheep of the Shepherd.* This inscription is new: the contents show the date to be about 507, the year of the restoration of peace.

Item basilicam SS. martyrum Proti et Jacinthi ubi fecit hos versus

[for the "basilica" (*i.e.* Confession) of SS. Protus and Jacinthus in S. Andrew's on the Vatican].

7. TEMPLA MICANT [1] . . .
        (closing with distich)
  (7) SYMMACHE QUAPROPTER VIVAX JAM FAMA PER AEVUM
  (8)   NARRABIT TITULIS AMPLIFICATA PIIS

7a. O LAETA JUCUNDA [2] . . .
        (ending with the distich)
  (5) SYMMACHUS ANTISTES TANTI SACRATOR HONORIS
  (6)   HAEC FECIT TITULIS COMMEMORANDA SUIS

Item ad fontem in basilica Sancti Petri apostoli . . . crucem ex auro cum gemmis, ubi includit lignum dominicum *ubi scripti sunt hi versus.*[3]

8. FORTIS AD INFIRMOS . . .
                        [Baptistery of S. Peter's].

Intra civitatem romanam, basilicam sanctorum Silvestri et Martini a fundamento construxit. . . . Ad beatum Johannen et Paulum fecit gradus post absidam *ubi super picturas veteris et novi testamenti hos versus fecit.*[4]
                        [SS. John and Paul].

9. TEMPLUM INGENS DOMINO . . .
    (lines 1–9 known, lines 10–17 are new)

Item ad archangelum Micaelem basilicam ampliavit et gradus fecit, et aquam introduxit *ad baptisterium cum his versibus.*[5]
                        [Baptistery of S. Michael].

---

[1] *I.C.* p. 246, No. 8.

[2] The last four lines of a familiar inscription, *I.C.* p. 246, No. 8a. This, again, is quite distinct from the *Templa micant* . . . which precedes.

[3] *Also in the baptistery of the basilica of S. Peter the apostle . . . he made a gold cross set with gems, and enclosed in it a relic of the Lord's cross, and wrote on it these verses.* See *infra*, p. 285. This inscription is new.

[4] *Within the city of Rome he built the basilica of SS. Silvester and Martin and raised it from the foundations. . . . At the church of blessed John and Paul he made steps behind the apse, where, above the pictures of the Old and New Testaments, he made these verses.* See *I.C.* p. 150, No. 21.

[5] *Also he enlarged the basilica of the archangel Michael, and made steps, and conveyed water to the baptistery with these verses.* See *infra*, pp. 270–277, for translations and discussion, and *supra*, pp. 247, 248.

10. SUMITE PERPETUAM . . .

          (lines 1–4 as usual)

(5) AUXIT APOSTOLICAE GEMINATUM SEDIS HONOREM [1]

(6)   CHRISTUS ET AD CAELOS HANC [2] DEDIT ESSE VIAM [3]

(7) NAM [4] CUI SIDEREI COMMISIT *LIMINA* [LUMINA] [5] REGNI

(8)   HIC HABET IN *TERRIS* ALTERA *REGNA* POLI [POLIS] [6]

(9) *SYMMACHUS HUNC STATUIT SACRI BAPTISMATIS USUM*

(10)   *SUB QUO QUIDQUID ERAT INCIPIT ESSE NOVUM*

11. ISTIC INSONTES CAELESTI FLUMINE LOTAS

(2)   PASTORIS SUMMI DEXTERA SIGNAT OVES

(3) HUC UNDIS *GENERANDE* VENI QUO SANCTUS AD UNUM

(4)   SPIRITUS [7] UT CAPIAS TE SUA DONA VOCAT

(5) TU CRUCE SUSCEPTA MUNDI VITARE PROCELLAS

(6)   DISCE MAGIS MONITUS HAC RATIONE LOCI

Item versus de eodem [8]   [Baptistery of S. Michael].

12. HAEC DOMUS EST FIDEI [9]. . .

Item ad S. Mariam [10]   [S. Maria].

13. JUSTICIAE SEDES . . .

      (As usual—with a new distich)

(5) *SYMMACHUS ISTA TIBI PERSOLVIT VOTA SACERDOS*

(6) *UT BENE QUOD MERUIT REDDERET IPSE DECUS* [11]

Item sub clipeo argenteo in arcu argenteo quem fecit in medio presbiterio [12]   [In choir of S. Maria (?)].

---

[1] Codex *amorem.*

[2] Codex *hinc.*

[3] Codex *vitam.*

[4] Codex *jam.*

[5] The original *lumina* of the Codex has been erased and *limina* substituted.

[6] The original *s* of *polis* has been erased, and *poli* is the reading.

[7] Codex *Christus.*

[8] sc. *baptisterio.*

[9] *I.C.* p. 68, No. 31.

[10] sc. *Majorem.* See *I.C.* p. 55, No. 8.

[11] *Symmachus the priest* (=*bishop*) *has made this offering to thee, and renders* (to this monument) *the glory which is due to it.*

[12] *Also on the silver shield on the silver arch which he made in the middle of the choir* (? of S. Maria Maggiore). These seven lines of verse are new and form *two* inscriptions: the first is for a votive offering of a silver shield; the second refers to the ceiling of S. Peter's.

14. VOTORUM COMPOS LAETUS TIBI MUNERA SOLVO
PARVA SALUTIFERAE REDDENS NUNC PRAEMIA LEGIS
SUSCIPE DONA PRECOR MENTIS PIA PIGNORA NOSTRAE

14a. SEDIS APOSTOLICAE PULCHRUM ET SUBLIME LACUNAR
ANTIQUAM SPECIEM VINCIT HONORE SUO
SYMMACHUS HOC PRAESTAT VENERANDUS IN URBE SACERDOS
NE POSSIT TEMPLO LONGA NOCERE DIES[1]

Item in Oratorio Salvatoris de Nominibus Ejus[2]
[Oratory of Our Saviour].

15. SPES, RATIO . . .

(the last line is new)

(8) *SYMMACHUS ISTA TIBI PIE JESU NOMINA LUSIT*

*Item supra portam urbis quae dicitur Porta Sancti Petri
quam ipse ornavit*   [The city gate called S. Peter's].

16. INNOVAT[3] ANTIQUUM . . .

(lines 1–4 in elegiacs, already known; 3 and 4 are new)

(3) *ANTISTES PORTAM RENOVAVIT SYMMACHUS ISTAM*

(4) *UT ROMA PER EUM NIHIL ESSET NON RENOVATUM*

*Item in lamina argentea regiae Sancti Petri quam ipse
fecit.*[4]   [The great silver doors of S. Peter's].

17. LUX ARCANA DEI . . .

(lines 1–17 as usual)

---

[1] (14) *Having won an answer to my prayers, joyful I offer gifts to Thee,
making now a little return for Thy law of salvation. I pray Thee receive these
gifts, the token of the gratitude of our heart.* (14a) *The fair and lofty ceiling of
the seat of the Apostle* (S. Peter's) *surpasses the ancient beauty by its splendour.
Symmachus the priest, honoured in the city, made this, that the passing of time
might not injure the temple.* (Should not the reading be *jure sacerdos* instead of
in urbe sacerdos? Cf. *supra*, p. 250, "*Caidocus jure sacerdos.*")

[2] *Also in the Oratory of Our Saviour* (? in S. Mary) *concerning the Holy
Name.* For the inscription see *infra*, p. 286.

[3] Codex *invocat*. For inscription see *I.C.* p. 99, No. 9.

[4] *Infra*, p. 282 ; *I.C.* p. 53, No. 3.

(18) SED BONUS ANTISTES DUX PLEBIS SYMMACHUS ARMIS (?)
(lines 19–24 as usual)

Item ad sanctam Mariam[1] Oratorium Sanctorum
Cosmae et Damiani a fundamento construxit (and so on,
the usual text of the *Liber Pontificalis*).

Gesta Hormisdadis

Eodem tempore fecit papa Hormisdas apud beatum
Petrum apostolum trabem . . . *in quo hi versus scripti sunt.*
[S. Peter's].

18. QUAMVIS PRAECIPUIS . . .
(inscription of 8 lines hitherto unknown)

(The remaining inscriptions are all correctly placed :
19. Inscription of FELIX IV. in SS. Cosmas and Damian.[2]
The next ten are all papal epitaphs, found at the end of the
reign of each pope.   The inscriptions are all known.
[S. Peter's].
Epitaphs of FELIX IV. (20): BONIFACE II. (21): JOHN II.[3]
(22): JOHN III. (23): JOHN I. (?) (24): BENEDICT I. (25):
GREGORY I. (26): BONIFACE III. (27): BONIFACE IV. (28):
DEUSDEDIT (29): BONIFACE V. (30).)

Gesta Honorii

. . . Fecit absida ejusdem basilicae (S. Agnes) ex
musibo (mosaic) ubi etiam et multa dona obtulit.
[S. Agnes, Via Nomentana].

31. VIRGINIS AULA MICAT VARIIS DECORATA METALLIS[4]
SED PLUS *EST MERITIS SPLENDIDA VIRGINEIS*

---

[1] These words of the *Liber Pontificalis* are repeated a second time, as the
passage was broken here to insert the inscriptions 13–17 (see above).

[2] *Infra*, p. 287.

[3] Four popes have no inscriptions recorded here—Agapetus, Silverius,
Vigilius, Pelagius I. : Pelagius II. is omitted after Benedict I., and Sabinian
after Gregory.

[4] *Infra*, p. 288.

31a. AUREA CONCISIS SURGIT PICTURA METALLIS[1]
ET COMPLEXA SIMUL CLAUDITUR IPSA DIES
FONTIBUS E NIVEIS AURORA *SUBIRE VIDETUR*
DISCUTIENS NUBES RORIBUS ARVA RIGANS
VEL QUALEM LUCEM *PER NEBULA PERVEHIT IRIS*
VEL QUI PURPUREO PAVO NITORE NITET
QUI POTUIT *NOCTI LUCEM PRAESTARE PROFUNDAE*
MARTIRIS E BUSTIS REPPULIT ILLE CHAOS
VIRGINIS AGNETIS MAGNO DEVOTUS HONORI
PRAESUL HONORIUS HAEC VOTA DICATA DEDIT
VESTIBUS ET FACTIS SIGNANTUR *PRAESULIS* ORA
LUCET ET ASPECTU LUCIDA CORDA GERENS

· · · · · · · ·

32. Epitaph of AGATHO : 33. of JOHN V. : 34. of JOHN VII.[2]

Peculiarities of the Sylloge : (*a*) Topographical Errors in the Following Inscriptions.—We have then, scattered about in the text of the *Liber Pontificalis*, a Sylloge of thirty-eight inscriptions.[3] Of these, six are hitherto unknown, namely, Nos. 6a, 8, 14, 14a, all of Symmachus ; No. 18 (of Hormisdas) ; and No. 34 (the epitaph of John VII.).

Of these thirty-eight inscriptions, nearly half, namely, sixteen, belong to Symmachus, and it is among these that nearly all the peculiarities of the Sylloge are seen.

Cingebant (No. 1).—The topographical errors are entirely confined to the Symmachus inscriptions (Nos. 5 to 17), with the exception of a single inscription of Damasus, *Cingebant* (No. 1). This familiar inscription is in reality a dedication for the Baptistery of the Vatican, made by Damasus. There

---

[1] *I.C.* p. 89, No. 42. See *infra*, p. 287, note 3. *Her picture arises all golden amid the cut mosaics, and seems to hold the very day itself. From the snowy sources the dawn seems to rise, and, scattering the clouds, to water the fields with its dew, like the rainbow lights that Iris draws across the heavens, or as a peacock shines in glowing splendour. He Who could spread light over the deep darkness of night, He has saved from ruin the shrine of the martyr. The Pope Honorius with deep devotion has consecrated these offerings to the glory of the Virgin, Agnes. In (pontifical) robes, bearing (a basilica in his hand) a sign of what he has wrought, his image gleams as bright as the joy in his heart.*

[2] There are no inscriptions inserted for the nine popes before Agatho, nor for the two after Agatho, nor for the three before John VII.

[3] Always counting as *two* inscriptions these which are in reality distinct, though written as one, *e.g.* 6 and 6a, 7 and 7a, 14 and 14a, 31 and 31a.

is no mention of this baptistery to introduce the quotation in the *Gesta Damasi* of the *Liber Pontificalis*; and so, in the Sylloge of Cambridge, the inscription has been inserted at random, and *happens* to follow the passage in the *Liber Pontificalis* describing the Catacomb of S. Sebastian on the Via Appia.

Symmachus Inscriptions: (Nos. 5–17).—Coming to the Symmachus inscriptions (5–17), there are at least seven attributions definitely wrong, and three more probably so, but so vaguely indicated in the Sylloge of Cambridge as to be unidentifiable.

Ingrederis (5), *Quisquis* (6).—The first two in reality belong to the atrium of S. Peter's, i.e. *Ingrederis* (5), a dedication, and *Quisquis* (6), the epitaph of John I. They should properly have been inserted *after* the portion of the text of the *Liber Pontificalis* describing the improvements executed in S. Peter's by Symmachus. Instead of that they follow the description of building executed in the Church of S. Andrew's on the Vatican.

Templa (7) and *O Laeta* (7a).—Of the next two, *Templa micant* (7) and *O Laeta* (7a) are correctly indicated as being in S. Andrew's on the Vatican. There is a mistake here, however. The verses (7) and (7a), given as one inscription, form *two*; one (7) belongs, as indicated, to the shrine of Protus and Jacinthus, the other (7a) to that of S. Sossius: the latter (7a) is therefore misplaced, and should come a few lines down after the reference to Sossius in the text of the *Liber Pontificalis*. We may note also that in the headline to the verses inserted by the scribe the shrine is described as "a basilica," instead of an "oratory" (*oratorium*, i.e. side chapel), or "confession" (*confessionem*)—the correct word used in the *Liber Pontificalis*.

Sumite (10) and *Istic* (11); *Haec Domus* (12).—The following three inscriptions, i.e. *Sumite* (10), *Istic* (11),—a distinct inscription from (10) though written all together,—and *Haec Domus* (12) all belong to baptisteries, and are ascribed here to a church of S. Michael; probably meaning S. Michael in the Via Urbana, near S. Pudentiana, since the other four churches of S. Michael in existence at the time of

Symmachus are excluded for various reasons.[1] The true position of *Sumite* and *Istic* is a matter of dispute;[2] *Haec Domus* belongs to the baptistery of S. Paul's.

Justiciae Sedes (13).—To insert the next inscription, *Justiciae sedes* (13), the text of the *Liber Pontificalis* is interrupted in the middle of a sentence, and the lines placed after the words *ad Sanctam Mariam* (apparently S. Maria Maggiore). Whatever may be the church intended, the true locality is S. Peter's.

Symmachus Has (6a), **Votorum** (14), **Sedes Apostolicae** (14a), **Spes Ratio** (15).—The new inscription *Symmachus has* (6a) probably belongs to the rest of that group in the Vatican. It is not clear what position the writer of the Sylloge of Cambridge intends to attribute to the following inscriptions—*Votorum* (14), for a votive offering, *Sedis apostolicae* (14a), which certainly belongs to S. Peter's, as the verses indicate, and *Spes Ratio*[3] (15): they might well all form a group with the last inscription, *Justiciae sedes* (13), falsely ascribed to S. Maria.

Analysis of the Subjects and Localities of the Inscriptions.—The local ascriptions for the rest of the Sylloge are correct. Having discovered, then, the correct ascriptions of locality we find that, out of a total of thirty-eight inscriptions, no less than twenty-one certainly belong to S. Peter's, or places on the Vatican immediately connected with it. The sixteen remaining include the epitaph of Damasus (2) on the Via Ardeatina, and inscriptions of SS. John and Paul (9), S. Paul (12), SS. Cosmas and Damian (19), S. Agnes (31 and 31a)—all most important churches which find a place in almost any collection. Of the rest it is almost certain that (6a) and (8) also belong to S. Peter, and extremely probable that some at least of certain others, *i.e.* Nos. 10 and 11, 14, 14a, 15, do so too.

[1] (a) A very ancient church on the *Via Salaria*, seven miles from the city; (b) S. Michael *in Fagana*, near Tivoli (*L.P.* ii. 40); (c) near the Vatican, with a baptistery since the time of Damasus; (d) S. Michael *ad Porticum Ottavium* (called *S. Paul* till 770).

[2] *Infra*, p. 270 *et seqq.*

[3] There was an Oratory of Our Saviour in S. Petronilla, one of the group of Vatican churches, but it did not exist earlier than 757.

Among these thirty-eight inscriptions there are no less than fourteen papal epitaphs, all of S. Peter's, except that of Damasus. It almost seems as if the source of the compilation were a Collection of Vatican Inscriptions,[1] or of Papal Epitaphs.

(*b*) **Textual Peculiarities : in the Following** :—As regards peculiarities of the text, the readings of the Sylloge of Cambridge often differ considerably from those of the older Syllogae. Since the familiar reading is often represented, without any important variations, in several of the older Syllogae, we may conclude that the readings of the latter represent more truly the original inscription, as it stood on the actual building, than does the text of the Sylloge of Cambridge.

In *Aurea Concisis* (31a).—Turning, for an example, to the familiar inscription *Aurea Concisis* (31a),[2] put up by Honorius (625–640) in the basilica of S. Agnes, Via Nomentana, we see from the lines in italics the considerable differences between the text of the Sylloge of Cambridge and that of the three older versions of the *Sylloge Centulensis*, *Sylloge Laureshamensis*, and *Sylloge Virdunensis*.

It is true that the Cambridge version is an improvement on the original—it makes sense, and it is poetical ; it is, in fact, like a set of boy's verses touched up by a master, and is probably the work of the twelfth-century copyist. But, by good fortune, the actual inscription can be read on the golden mosaic of the apse of S. Agnes—and it is in the older Syllogae that it is faithfully reproduced.

In Papal Epitaphs.—The papal epitaphs are, on the whole, more correct in reading, but there are considerable variations in some of them, as well as a false attribution to Benedict I. of the epitaph of Benedict II.

Several of the papal epitaphs have been curtailed, namely, those of Boniface III. (No. 27 in Sylloge of Cambridge), *Postquam mors Christi* ; of Deusdedit (29), *Cur titulata diu* ; of Boniface V. (30), *Da mecum gemitum*. That of Boniface IV. (28), *Vita hominum brevis*, has been almost rewritten.

[1] *Supra*, p. 252.   [2] *Supra*, p. 262.

In Ascriptions to *Symmachus* **: (1) in Verses already known** (5, 7, 7a) **or occurring in New Inscriptions** (6a, 14a). —Returning again to the Symmachus inscriptions, we find some peculiarities in the text. No less than ten of these inscriptions contain a line, or lines, naming Symmachus as the author of the work described. Of these, two inscriptions (6a, 14a) are entirely new; three (5, 7, 7a) are familiar inscriptions which already contained the Symmachus lines.

(2) In Verses newly added to Familiar Texts.— To the remaining five inscriptions already familiar (10, 13, 15, 16, 17) new lines have been added attributing the inscriptions to Symmachus. Are these attributions correct? Whether correct or not, how did they come to be inserted?

Sumite (10).—Of this group of five familiar inscriptions with Symmachus additions, the first is *Sumite* (10), known hitherto only in the Sylloge of Verdun. The whole question of the date and locality of this inscription will be discussed elsewhere.[1]

Justitiae (13).—In *Justitiae* (13), though the Symmachus couplet is an addition, yet the couplet itself (not the inscription) appears incorrectly, in the *Sylloge Centulensis*, as belonging to the basilica of S. Paul's, in the following form:[2]—

> Haec tibi *Honorius* persolvit vota sacerdos
> Ut bene quod meruit redderet ipse decus.

It may be noted that the inscription *Justitiae* really belongs to S. Peter's (though ascribed in the Sylloge of Cambridge to S. Maria). We may suppose either that the compiler, wishing to attribute this inscription to Symmachus (perhaps correctly), has borrowed, altered and added the Honorius *couplet* in S. Peter's. (It is true that *Honorius* does not scan, but verse was loosely written in those days.) Or, on the other hand, Honorius himself may, at some time, have borrowed the convenient Symmachus couplet. At all events, the *couplet* does not properly belong to the inscription *Justitiae*, though it may belong to Symmachus. That the compiler was in truth guilty of the offence suggested in the

---

[1] *Infra*, p. 270. [2] *I.C.* p. 81, No. 18.

former hypothesis, is amply proved in the case of the *Lux arcana* (17) inscription.

Lux Arcana (17).—This inscription was made by Honorius (626–638) for the great silver doors of S. Peter's : it celebrates the Incarnation, and gives a history of the successful suppression in 628 of the heresy in Istria which opposed that dogma. The name of Honorius occurs in line 18—*Sed bonus antistes dux plebis Honorius almus.* In the Sylloge of Cambridge we find the whole inscription under Symmachus (496–514), with the words *Symmachus armis* (?) substituted for *Honorius almus.* It may be noted that the inscription gives an account of the suppression of a heresy which arose more than a century later than the death of Symmachus.

In this case, then, it is perfectly clear that the compiler has inserted under Symmachus the inscription of a pope living more than a century later, and has falsified the inscription by changing the name *Honorius* to *Symmachus.*

Innovat (16).—*Innovat* (16) is correctly attributed to that gate of the city known as the *Porta S. Petri.* The Symmachus distich (which seems an echo of that in *Sumite* (10)) is in hexameters, the rest of the poem being in elegiacs. This in itself suggests a later addition. Moreover, it does not seem very likely that Symmachus performed the repairs mentioned, which in his time, under Theodoric the Goth, were the office of the State.[1] Under Justinian, the Church became responsible, and the inscription very probably belongs to a pope later than Symmachus, but has been adopted again for Symmachus by the compiler.

Spes Ratio (15).—The curious verses *Spes Ratio* (15) were already known and attributed to "Severus,"[2] and elsewhere to "Silvius."[3] In the Sylloge of Cambridge they are attributed (in an extra line) to Symmachus, and said to be in the "Oratory of Our Saviour" : from the context this oratory would appear to be in S. Maria.

Bonavenia is of opinion that the name of the author

---

[1] Duchesne, *Mélanges*, 1910, Nov.–Dec., p. 301.

[2] Fabricius, *Poetarum veterum ecclesiasticorum opera christiana*, p. 774, and p. 43*a* of Commentary : Bale, 1564.

[3] Reise, *Anthologia Latina*, ii. p. 162, No. 689 : Leipsic, 1906.

had been forgotten; that the true author was in fact Symmachus, and that in lapse of time his name, beginning with an S, was wrongly changed into Silverius and Severus. It seems a little difficult to accept this explanation : and the words *Silvius* and *Severus* appended to the original poem may look much alike in manuscript, and one may be a mistake for the other. Further, Bonavenia's explanation does not account for the additional line *Symmachus ista* in this poem. Here, again, it looks as if the twelfth-century scribe had adapted the inscription to Symmachus.

(3) **Two Inscriptions (6, 12) without Symmachus' Verses found under "Symmachus."**—All these inscriptions contain the Symmachus lines. There are two, however, without them found under Symmachus' reign, which must be excluded from the inscriptions which belong to this pope : *Quisquis ad aeternam* (6), which is the epitaph of John I. (523–526), who began to reign nine years after the death of Symmachus, and *Haec domus est* (12) of the Baptistery of S. Paul's.

Conclusions from the Analysis.—To sum up, then, the results of this investigation of the Symmachus inscriptions, we find that *topographically* only three inscriptions (7, 9, 16) out of sixteen are known to be correct, though there are seven more (6a, 8, 10 with 11, 14, 14a, 15) which may possibly be so ; the remaining six are certainly incorrect, namely, Nos. 5, 6, 7a, 12, 13, 17.

Concerning the *attributions* of the sixteen inscriptions attributed to Symmachus by the fact of inclusion under his reign, and also, generally, by the addition of the Symmachus verses, five attributions are certainly correct, namely, Nos. 5, 6a, 7, 7a, 9; seven are doubtful, namely, Nos. 8, 10 and 11, 12, 13, 14, 14a, 16; four are certainly wrong, Nos. 6, 13, 15, 17.

Most of the Symmachus inscriptions are inaccurate in *both* respects, and only about half the inscriptions are correct *either* topographically *or* in respect of the Symmachus attributions.

To explain these false attributions of place and persons two theories have been propounded :

Explanation of the False Attributions :—(*a*) **Transference of Inscriptions.**—The new attributions are to be explained by the fact that inscriptions were common property, and were freely borrowed for different buildings, and sometimes altered a little to adapt them to the new situation ; and that Symmachus did, in fact, *borrow* all these inscriptions. If this be so, Symmachus must have been a greater plagiarist than even most of his contemporaries ; whilst in the one case, *Lux arcana* (17), where the facts are really known, this explanation does not hold good.

(*b*) **The Work of the Twelfth-Century Scribe.**— The alternative explanation is that the twelfth-century scribe has inserted his inscriptions carelessly, probably taking them from some document which is arranged *topographically*. This would account for the fact that a whole group (Nos. 5, 6, and perhaps 6a, 7, 7a, 8) are approximately correct, *topographically* ; in that they all belong, in fact, to churches on the Vatican, and are attributed in the Sylloge to this region. If this be true, the blunder of inserting the epitaph of John I. (6) under Symmachus is quite natural, since that epitaph was in the Atrium of S. Peter's, as was inscription (5), and possibly (6a). Not content, however, with these random insertions, the scribe seems to have freely touched up the verses, and to have deliberately added the Symmachus verses to inscriptions which did not possess them. The case of *Lux arcana*[1] (17) supports this view. Yet these alterations and insertions in the twelfth century seem strangely purposeless. Had they been made at the beginning of the sixth century, an explanation might have been found in the strong partisan feeling for Symmachus in opposition to his rival, the anti-pope Laurence, a struggle indeed recorded in one of the inscriptions (6a). At this period there did exist a fragment of a *Liber Pontificalis* showing anti-papal feeling, and known as the *Laurentian fragment*.[2] It is possible to imagine the existence of a *Symmachan fragment* ; but there is absolutely no evidence of this, and the date of the inscriptions of the Sylloge, namely, of the fourth to the eighth century, about which there can be no doubt, precludes the supposition. The problem can-

---

[1] *Supra*, p. 267.   [2] *Supra*, p. 54.

not really be solved by a single explanation including all the inscriptions. Each case requires the most minute investigation on its own merits, and even then enough material is hardly forthcoming to provide an answer.

The Discussion concerning *Sumite* (18) **and** *Istic* (11). —Such a minute investigation has, however, been applied to the two inscriptions *Sumite* (10) and *Istic* (11). Perhaps it is worth while to indicate the main features [1] of the controversy concerning the interpretation, date and locality of these verses, as an example both of the method of using these documents, and of the application, to the solution of a single problem, of various branches of knowledge, not excluding some new information contributed by excavation.

The question had already been discussed long before the discovery of the Sylloge of Cambridge, the inscriptions being found in the Sylloge of Verdun.[2]

(*a*) **The Interpretation of the Text of the Verdun Codex.** —The first question that arises is that of the interpretation of the text of the Sylloge.

It is evident at once from the heading and contents that *Sumite* (25) is an inscription for a baptistery, *Istic* (26) for a *consignatorium*.[3]

The translation of *Sumite* as it stands in the Codex is :

> *For the Baptistery.* Put on everlasting life from this holy stream : this is the way of faith by which alone death perishes. The washing here in the divine spring strengthens our souls, and with the wetting of our limbs our spirits are made strong by the water. Christ increased the twofold honour of the apostolic seat when He granted this to be the way to the heavens. For he to whom Christ committed the lights of the starry realm, has other habitations in the wide spaces of heaven.

The sense of the last four lines is not very clear.

---

[1] For full details of the various points raised see Bibliography—SYLLOGAE *D*, and especially, for the new material, literary and monumental, Marucchi (*Nuovo Bullettino*) and Bonavenia (*Osservatore Romano*).

[2] *Supra*, p. 245 and pp. 247–248 for text. Except in cases of obvious copyist's blunders the text of the Codex has been given ; other readings and emendations are added in the footnotes.

[3] *Infra*, p. 284.

The somewhat violent emendations of De Rossi, accepted by most scholars, do not entirely elucidate matters, nor do the numerous alternative interpretations offered by them. A suggestion of Marucchi, accepted by Bonavenia (who on other matters is in disagreement with him), is helpful; he interprets *claustra* as meaning, *not*, as usual, "habitations," but as the *power of the keys* conferred on Peter.[1] The last four lines with De Rossi's reading, and Marucchi's interpretations appear to mean:

> Christ increased the twofold honour of the Apostolic seat and granted this (*i.e.* baptism) to be the way to heaven. For he (Peter) to whom He committed the care of the threshold (*limina*) of the starry realms, has here in this temple (*templis*) (built in his honour) other keys to the heavens (by way of baptism and confirmation).

There are still problems to elucidate. Does the *Honorem geminatum* mean the double gift to the convert of baptism and confirmation? or does it refer to *Peter*, and mean *either* the double honour he enjoys on earth in his church, and above, in the regions of heaven; *or* the double power of the keys to bind and loose; *or* the power to open the way to heaven by baptism and penance? And how is the twofold honour increased?

It seems very probable that between confusion of thought, and the inability to express so much dogma in so few lines the writer himself did not know exactly what he meant.

The meaning of *Istic* (26) is simpler:

> *These verses are written where the pope confirms the children.* Here the right hand of the chief shepherd signs the sheep, washed pure in the divine stream; Come hither, O thou born of water, to where the Holy Spirit calls each one, that thou mayst receive his gifts. Taking

---

[1] For a similar use of *claustra* compare the lines in the inscription made by Achilles, Bishop of Spoleto in 419, for the local church of S. Peter's—*Dixit enim tu es magno mihi nomine Petrus Et tibi caelorum fortia claustra dedi* (*Laur.* iv., No. 80, in *I.C.* viii. p. 114); and those in the inscription for the baptistery of the Lateran of almost the same date—*Petrus regia claustra tenens* (*Laur.* i. 15, in *I.C.* xiii. p. 148). For the Spoleto inscription see *Bull. arch. crist.*, 1871, 117.

272 ROME OF THE PILGRIMS AND MARTYRS

up thy cross learn to escape the storms of this world
admonished by the teaching of this place.

(*b*) **The Locality of** *Sumite—Istic* **according to the Sylloge
of Verdun.**—Whatever is the precise meaning of *Sumite*,
it is quite clear, as we have seen, that these inscriptions are
for a Baptistery and *Consignatorium* respectively. While
the cryptic references to the power of Peter would be quite
in place in any baptistery—where the adult convert had
to do penance for his sins, and make a profession of faith
previous to receiving the sacrament—they would yet be
peculiarly appropriate to a church dedicated to, or connected with, Peter. What further indications have we as
to locality?

Turning first to the Sylloge of Verdun [1] it will be seen
that *Sumite* (25) and *Istic* (26) come at the end of a series
of suburban inscriptions, all of the Via Salaria or Via
Nomentana. Of those closely preceding *Sumite*, Nos. 17–19
are of the Via Nomentana, No. 20 Via Salaria, also Nos.
21–24, of S. Silvester in the catacomb of S. Priscilla. [2]
Sumite and *Istic* are followed by inscriptions of the churches
of the Apostles (SS. James and Philip) (27), S. Maria
Maggiore (28) and others *within* the city.

(1) **On Via Salaria or Via Nomentana?**—We have
already noted [3] that no *absolute* reliance can be placed on
the topographical indications of this Sylloge. At the same
time, they are sometimes correct. Looking at the position
of *Sumite*, it seems probable that it belongs to the previous
group, that is, to the Via Nomentana-Salaria group, and
possibly even to S. Silvester itself. It might also belong
to the following group of churches within the city. Con-

---

[1] *Supra*, p. 245.

[2] There is practically no doubt that No. 23 does in truth belong here. It is
closely attached to No. 22, as also in the Sylloge of Tours (*I.C.* p. 62, No. 23).
It forms a portion of a creed due to that Pope Celestinus (423–432) who summoned
the Council of Ephesus to combat Nestorianism. Celestinus was buried in this
church of S. Silvester in S. Priscilla (for his epitaph see Sylloge of Tours, *I.C.*
vi. I, p. 63), and it would be very suitable to inscribe the creed near his grave.
The translation is : *And he believes that God was born and suffered and sought
again His Father's home : and that He will come again from heaven to judge
both the quick and the dead*, etc.

[3] *Supra*, p. 245.

sidering purely *literary* evidence, the heading AD FONTES would support the former supposition, since this phrase is constantly used to indicate the inscriptions of a baptistery of a church whose other inscriptions have just been quoted.[1] On the other hand, the eighth-century compiler may have been using a mutilated copy, or be copying carelessly, and the heading may have lost the name of the basilica.   To what actual baptistery within or without the city could these inscriptions refer?

Before approaching this question, the date of the inscriptions must be determined,—a somewhat difficult matter in the absence of the original stone.   They have usually been attributed to the fourth century.   Bonavenia, however (*before* the discovery of the Sylloge of Cambridge), judging from the inferior Latin, and the peculiar use of *claustra* (if it is so used here is a matter not finally decided), attributed them both to the fifth century and to the reign of Symmachus.

What baptisteries were there in the fourth and fifth centuries?   What identifications have scholars made?

(2) The Baptistery of S. Peter or the Catacombs of S. Priscilla.—Before the recent excavations in S. Priscilla, which he did not live to see, De Rossi attributed these inscriptions to S. Peter's on the Vatican; remarking that the position of the inscriptions in the Sylloge indicated a building on the Via Nomentana or Via Salaria, but that there was no baptistery there.   If the inscriptions belong to S. Peter's, the complete heading should read, *Ad fontes Basilicae Sancti Petri.*

Since then, Marucchi has discovered, in the Catacomb of Priscilla, on the Via Salaria, a portion of a building which is undoubtedly a baptistery; it is to this building that he would ascribe the two epitaphs, which do in fact close a series belonging mainly to the Via Salaria, and come immediately *after* a series of epitaphs (21–24) actually

---

[1] Cf. inscriptions for the baptisteries of the Vatican, *infra*, p. 279 (*I.C.*, p. 147, No. 10); S. Paul's (*I.C.*, p. 28, No. 53; cf. p. 68, No. 31); S. Laurence *in Damaso*, *infra*, p. 283 (*I.C.*, p. 135, No. 6); S. Anastasia (*I.C.*, p. 150, No. 19).

18

in the church of S. Silvester, in S. Priscilla. Moreover, the use of *Ad Fontes* supports this identification, as does the possibility of the close connexion of Peter with S. Priscilla through the family of Pudens, some of whom are buried there.[1]

Marucchi's hypothesis seems at first sight convincing. The question, however, arises, *did* the popes go out to the Catacomb of S. Priscilla two miles outside the city to baptize and confirm in the fourth or fifth centuries?

It would take too long to examine in detail this point, but the general results of research seem to indicate that they did not do so *habitually* at that date, and that therefore these inscriptions did not stand here. This does not, of course, disprove the use of the Baptistery of S. Priscilla in *primitive* times.

(*c*) **Locality of** *Sumite* **and** *Istic* **in the Sylloge of Cambridge : New Readings and Attributions.**—Bonavenia, always sceptical with regard to the topographical indications of the Sylloge, still adhered to De Rossi's theory that S. Peter's is the baptistery in question. The discussion had reached this point when Dr. Levison drew attention to the Sylloge of Cambridge.[2] In this document (1) *Sumite* (No. 10) and *Istic* (No. 11) are written as one inscription, instead of two ; (2) they are attributed to the baptistery of S. Michael ; and (3) *Sumite* ends with two additional lines ascribing the work to Symmachus. There are further, some differences in the readings. In this Codex, as in that of Verdun, the original word is *lumina* (in line 7 of *Sumite*). Modern scholars[3] changed this to *limina* in the Verdun, and the twelfth-century scribe also erased *lumina*, and substituted *limina* in the Sylloge of Cambridge.[4] In line 6 the new Sylloge reads *terris . . . regna* in place of the Verdun *amplis . . . claustra*.

---

[1] See *Nuovo Bullettino*, 1901, 1902, 1903, 1906, 1907, 1908, 1910 for a full description of excavations. It may be added that the *Istic* inscription is found in close connexion with what is supposed to be a portion of the epitaph to a certain Eucharis (which stood in S. Priscilla) in the *Anthologia e Codice Parisino*, 8071 (*I.C.* p. 247, No. 11). This proximity of text may possibly indicate the proximity of the originals, and so supports Marucchi's attribution.

[2] *Supra*, p. 254 *et seqq.*   [3] *Supra*, p. 248, notes.   [4] *Supra*, p. 259.

Do *Sumite—Istic* belong: (1) to S.Michael's, Via Urbana?
—As to the attribution of these inscriptions to the Baptistery
of S. Michael's, identified as S. Michael of the Via Urbana,[1]
nearly all authorities—Levison, Marucchi, Grisar and Bonavenia—are agreed that the inscriptions did, in fact, stand
here; they are also agreed as to the identification of the
church.   If this conclusion is correct, does not the text of
the Sylloge of Cambridge refer to S. Michael—"to whom
were committed the *lights* (*lumina*) of heaven, and who had
on earth (in his church) another heavenly dwelling (*regna
poli*)"—rather than to S. Peter?

Then arises the question—what of the different readings
and different local attributions? Here Marucchi and Bonavenia take different views.

Bonavenia already, as we have seen, before the discovery
of the Cambridge Sylloge, attributed *Sumite* and *Istic*
to the time of Symmachus, and never accepted the Priscilla
attribution.   The new Sylloge appears to confirm his
conjecture.   He holds that it was composed for the church
of S. Michael by Symmachus.   He accounts for the variations of reading by copyist's mistakes, and thinks that the
Sylloge of Verdun is mutilated—hence the absence of the
Symmachus distich—and that the heading there is also
incomplete, and should read, AD FONTES BASILICAE S.
MICHAELIS.

The difficulty in accepting the latter part of the explanation is that it contradicts the facts as we know them in the
case of the other Symmachus inscriptions.   It is *these* inscriptions whose text is deliberately changed, and to these
inscriptions that the Symmachus lines are always *added*.
Bonavenia appears to accept this explanation for all the
other inscriptions.[2]   As a further point against the authenticity of this attribution to S. Michael's, it may be noted that

---

[1] On the identification, see *supra*, p. 264, note 1.   It is perhaps just worth
noting, that both in the Sylloge of Verdun *and* of Cambridge, this inscription
is quite close to an inscription ascribed to S. Maria Maggiore, which stands
very near the church of S. Michael in question :—Verdun : *Sumite* No. 25, *Istic*
No. 26 (S. Maria Maggiore 283) ; and Cambridge : *Sumite* No. 10, *Istic* No. 11
(S. Maria 13).

[2] Except *Spes, ratio* (15), see *supra*, p. 267.

the information as to the building of a *Baptistery* of S. Michael is peculiar to the Cambridge manuscript. In the ordinary text of the *Liber Pontificalis* it is merely recorded that water was laid on to the basilica.

(2) **Or to S. Priscilla originally, and then S. Michael's ?** —Marucchi still believes that the inscriptions *Sumite* and *Istic* stood originally in the baptistery and *consignatorium* recently discovered in S. Priscilla; and that when Symmachus built his Baptistery of S. Michael, which had to serve too, as a *consignatorium*, he took the ancient inscriptions, combined them into one, and inserted the distich about himself. Various facts support this conclusion. There was a close connection between the church of S. Pudentiana, in whose parish S. Michael's stood, and the catacomb of S. Priscilla ; indeed, in the Middle Ages the crypts of S. Pudentiana were called *Coemeterium S. Priscillae*. Moreover, the difference of text in the Sylloge of Verdun and that of Cambridge could be accounted for by the fact that the two copyists were using *two different originals*. It was also quite in harmony with the practice of the time to borrow inscriptions. The thought, too, suggests itself that if Marucchi is correct in his hypothesis, perhaps the word *claustra* and *limina* stood in the Priscilla buildings with their association with Peter, and that *regna* and *lumina* stood in S. Michael's, as a happy adaptation in honour of the patron of the baptistery.

(3) **Or to S. Peter's ?**—Duchesne recognizes the number of false attributions in the Sylloge of Cambridge, and the fact of the addition of the Symmachus lines by the twelfth-century compiler. He includes among false ascriptions the local attribution to S. Michael of *Sumite* and *Istic*, and holds that the inscriptions should be ascribed to S. Peter's baptistery on the Vatican, which Symmachus did in fact repair.

In that case, apparently, the Symmachus lines would be genuine? If so, why do they not appear in the Verdun version? It may, of course, as Bonavenia holds, be mutilated.

There are difficulties whichever explanation we adopt,

and the material is not sufficient to form a final opinion;[1] but the investigation itself is valuable as an example of method, of the precise weaknesses of the Syllogae, and of the wide divergence of view among scholars on all such matters.

[1] Is it just possible that the inscriptions belong to S. Michael, 7 miles N. of Rome on the Via Salaria? If so, the heading of the Verdun Sylloge should be AD FONTES S. MICHAELIS, and the inscription would then stand in *correct position* in the Sylloge, namely, just after the inscriptions of S. Silvester, on the Via Salaria, 2 miles N. of Rome. The fact that *Sumite* occurs in the Sylloge of Cambridge among a set which are " within the city " (*Intra civitatem*) does not carry much weight in such a document.

CHAPTER XXI

THE *SYLLOGAE*: SOME EXAMPLES OF INSCRIPTIONS

Inscriptions mainly Urban: S. PETER (Nos. 1–6)—on papal authority, baptism, the Incarnation, etc. ; S. MARIA MAGGIORE (No. 7)—on the Incarnation ; S. LAURENCE IN DAMASO (8) and S. PRISCILLA (?) (No. 9) and AN AFRICAN CHURCH (10)—on baptism and confirmation ; the ORATORY OF THE CROSS in the Baptistery of S. PETER'S (?) (11)—on the Redemption and the Eucharist ; ORATORY OF THE SAVIOUR, S. PETER'S (?) (12)—on the Holy Name ; S. PAUL (13)—for a cantharus ; SS. COSMAS AND DAMIAN (14) ; S. AGNES (15). —*Inscriptions for secular buildings*: Archives of S. LAURENCE IN DAMASO (16) ; the LIBRARY of Gregory the Great (17).—*Inscriptions from suburban tombs, mainly by Damasus*: EPITAPH ON HIMSELF (18) ; in the PAPAL CRYPT OF S. CALLIXTUS (19, 20) ; of Gordianus, near VIA LABICANA (21) ; of Tiburtius on VIA TIBURTINA (22) ; Epitaphs by Boniface on S. Felicitas, VIA SALARIA (23, 24) ; Inscription of Vigilius on the VIA SALARIA (25).— Relics in S. STEPHEN on the Vatican, and in S. SILVESTER IN CAPITE (26).

Inscriptions mainly Urban: **S. Peter's.**—As might be expected, it is in the Basilica of S. Peter's that the inscriptions are most abundant and varied in character.

1. Of Constantine on the Triumphal Arch (Fourth Century).—The earliest of all is that of Constantine[1] over the triumphal arch of the basilica he had just erected on the site of the little memorial chapel of Pope Anacletus :

1. In Arcu Sancti Petri.

QUOD DUCE TE MUNDUS SURREXIT IN ASTRA TRIUMPHANS
HANC CONSTANTINUS VICTOR TIBI CONDIDIT AULAM

> Because under Thy leadership the world arose triumphant to the stars, Constantine the victor (*sc.* over his enemies at the Mulvian Bridge) has founded this temple to Thee.

[1] *Sylloge Einsiedlensis* (in *I.C.* p. 20, No. 6).

2 and 3. Damasus for the Baptistery (Fourth Century).

—In the crypt of S. Peter's is still to be seen the inscription of Damasus,[1] recording the discovery of the spring on the Vatican Hill destined to supply the new baptistery with water :

2. CINGEBANT LATICES MONTEM TENEROQUE MEATU
CORPORA MULTORUM CINERES ATQUE OSSA RIGABANT
NON TULIT HOC DAMASUS COMMUNI LEGE SEPVLTOS
POST REQUIEM TRISTES ITERUM PERSOLVERE POENAS
PROTINUS ADGRESSUS MAGNUM SUPERARE LABOREM
AGGERIS IMMENSI DEJECIT CULMINA MONTIS
INTIMA SOLLICITE SCRUTATUS VISCERA TERRAE
SICCAVIT TOTUM QUIDQUID MADEFECERAT HUMOR
INVENIT FONTEM PRAEBET QUI DONA SALUTIS
HOC CURAVIT MERCURIUS LEVITA FIDELIS

> Streams of water surrounded the (Vatican) hill, and, gently winding, drenched the bodies, bones and ashes of many.   Damasus could not endure that thus buried indiscriminately they should again suffer grievous pains when they had won peace.   So at once venturing on the great toil, he laid low the summit of the immense hill. Carefully scrutinising the inmost depths of the earth, he dried everything which the water had made sodden.   Then he discovered a spring which brings us the gift of salvation (*sc.* water for baptism).   Mercurius, the faithful deacon, executed this work.

For the baptistery itself Damasus wrote the following lines :[2]

3. Ad Fontes.

NON HAEC HUMANIS OPIBUS NON ARTE MAGISTRA
(line missing)
SED PRAESTANTE PETRO CUI TRADITA JANUA CAELI EST
ANTISTES CHRISTI COMPOSUIT DAMASUS

---

[1] *Inscriptiones Vaticanae* (in *I.C.* p. 56, No. 14) ; for a reproduction of the original, see P. Dionysius, *Vaticanae Basilicae Cryptae Monumenta*, p. 61, pl. xxvii., Rome, 1773.

[2] *Sylloge Laureshamensis* (in *I.C.* p. 147, No. 10).

UNA PETRI SEDES UNUM VERUMQUE LAVACRUM
VINCULA NULLA TENENT *quem lavat iste liquor.*

For the baptistery.

This is not the work of worldly wealth, nor of a
master's art (but the work of God, . . .); but
relying on Peter, to whom has been committed
the gate of heaven, Damasus the representative
of Christ, composed these lines. There is one
seat of Peter, one true baptism, and no chains
bind him whom this water has washed.

There are several more inscriptions for baptisteries with
which that of the Vatican may be compared—for S. Laurence
in Damaso,[1] written by Damasus; for S. Paul, the Lateran,
S. Anastasia and others.[2]

4. Simplicius on the Papal Power (Fifth Century).—
The idea of Damasus concerning the " one seat of Peter," and
himself as the representative of Christ, is developed in the
inscription[3] of Simplicius (468–483), which stood over the
entrance doors of S. Peter's, and shows the conception that a
fifth-century pope held of his office :

4. Super limina in introitu ecclesiae (S. Petri)

QUI REGNI CLAVES ET CURAM TRADIT OVILIS
QUI CAELI TERRAEQUE PETRO COMMISIT HABENAS
UT RESERET CLAUSIS UT SOLVAT VINCLA LIGATIS
SIMPLICIO NUNC IPSE DEDIT SACRA JURA TENERE
PRAESULI QUO CULTUS VENERANDAE CRESCERET AULAE

Above the threshold at the entry of the Church.

He Who handed over the keys of the kingdom
and the care of the sheepfold; He Who committed
to Peter the reins of heaven and earth, that he
should open to those imprisoned, and loose the
chains of those who are bound ; has now Himself
granted to Simplicius as ruler to wield the
sacred rights, that the worship in these holy
courts might increase.

[1] *Infra,* p. 283.
[2] For other churches, see *infra,* pp. 283, 284.
[3] *Laur.* i, (*I.C.* p. 144, No. 3).

5. Pelagius I. on the Incarnation (Sixth Century).—
The doctrine of the Incarnation is expounded, in opposition
to Nestorianism and kindred heresies, in an inscription of
Pelagius I. (555–559)[1] which stood, suitably enough, on some
part of the altar. The last verses throw light on the troubles
of the times:

5. In Altare Beati Petri.

VOX ARCANA PATRIS CAELI QUIBUS AEQUA POTESTAS
  DESCENDIT TERRAS LUCE REPLERE SUA .
HAEC DEUS HUMANAM SUMENS DE VIRGINE FORMAM
  DISCIPULOS MUNDO PRAECIPIENDA DOCET
QUAE MODO PELAGIUS PRAESUL CUM PLEBE FIDELIS
  EXERCENS OFFERT MUNERA SACRA DEO
UT ROMANA MANU CAELESTI SCEPTRA REGANTUR
  SIT QUORUM IMPERIO LIBERA VERA FIDES
PRO QUIBUS ANTISTES REDDENS HAEC VOTA PRECATUR
  SAECULA PRINCIPIBUS PACIFICATA DARI
HOSTIBUS UT DOMITIS PETRI VIRTUTE PER ORBEM
  GENTIBUS AC POPULIS PAX SIT ET ISTA FIDES

On the altar of blessed Peter.

The hidden Word of the Father, to Whom (*sc.* to
the Word and the Father) is equal power in
heaven, came down to fill earth with His light.
God, the Word, taking on Him human form from
a Virgin, taught His disciples what they were to
teach to the world. The faithful Pelagius, now
performing these instructions, as ruler, together
with the people, offers these holy gifts to God;
(and prays) that the Roman sceptre may be
wielded by a Divine hand, and that under that rule
the true faith may be free. For our princes, the
representative (of God) offering up these petitions,
prays that they may be granted a time of peace,
and that all enemies, being overcome throughout the world by the power of Peter, to all
the peoples there may be peace and this faith
(*sc.* in the Incarnation).

6. Honorius on the Incarnation (Seventh Century).—
These lines were evidently in the mind of Honorius (626–638)

[1] *Laur.* i. (*I.C.* p. 145, No. 7).

when he put up his inscription [1] directed against similar heresies on the great silver doors of S. Peter's :

6. Item in ostia majore Sancti Petri.

LUX ARCANA DEI VERBUM SAPIENTIA LUCIS
  ATQUE CORUSCANTIS SPLENDIDA IMAGO PATRIS
AD NOS DESCENDIT NEC QUO FUIT ESSE RECESSIT
  UT CAECAS MENTES ERUERET TENEBRIS
PLENUS HOMO IN NOSTRIS ET VERUS NASCITUR ISDEM
  VIRGINIS EX UTERO TOTUS UBIQUI DEUS

.   .   .   .

On the great door of S. Peter.

The hidden light of God, the Word, the Wisdom, and the resplendent Image of the dazzling light of the Father, came down to us, yet ceased not to be where [2] He was before : that He might deliver our blind spirits from darkness ; He is born perfect man among us, and likewise, from the womb of a Virgin, perfect all-present God.

There follows a passage concerning the power of Peter, an account of " The seven and tenfold pestilential schism " which arose in Istria, and was put down by Honorius, and the inscription concludes with a prayer to Peter, "the gentle guardian of the gates of heaven," to give quiet times to his flock.

7. S. Maria Maggiore : Sixtus III. on the Incarnation (Fifth Century).—The same idea is expressed in an inscription of Sixtus III. (432–440).[3] He beautified the basilica built by Liberius (352–356), and dedicated it to S. Mary, as a memorial of the victory over Nestorianism at the Council of Ephesus held under Celestinus (423–432).

7. In basilica Sanctae Mariae Majore.

VIRGO MARIA TIBI SIXTUS NOVA TEMPLA DICAVI
DIGNA SALUTIFERO MUNERA VENTRE TUO

---

[1] *Ins. Vat.* (*I.C.* p. 53, No. 3).

[2] Or, *quod*="He ceased not to be *what* He was before, *i.e.* God."

[3] *Sylloge Turonensis* (*I.C.* p. 71, No. 42). For another inscription on the same subject see *Laur.* iv. (*I.C.* p. 109, No. 63), probably set up in the palace of the widow of Boethius ; also an inscription of the fifth or sixth century in the palace of the Vandal king of Carthage, *Qualiter intacta* . . . (*I.C.* p. 241, No. 6).

TE GENETRIX IGNARA VIRI TE DENIQUE FETA
VISCERIBUS SALVIS EDITA NOSTRA SALUS
ECCE TUI TESTES UTERI TIBI PRAEMIA PORTANT
SUB PEDIBUSQUE JACET PASSIO CUIQUE SUA
FERRUM FLAMMA FERUS FLUVIUS SAEVUMQUE VENENUM
TOT TAMEN HAS MORTES UNA CORONA MANET

> O Virgin Mary, I, Sixtus, have dedicated a new
> temple to thee, an offering worthy of the womb
> that brought us salvation. Thou, a virgin, didst
> bear, a maiden didst thou bring forth our Salva-
> tion. Behold these martyrs, witnesses to Him
> Who was the fruit of thy womb, bear to thee
> their crowns of victory, and beneath their feet
> lie the instruments of their passion,—sword,
> flame, wild beast, river, and cruel poison: one
> crown alike awaits these divers deaths.

The latter part of the inscription refers evidently to a
representation of martyrs offering up their victorious crowns;
depicted, probably in mosaic, round the walls of the church.[1]

**8. S. Laurence *in Damaso*: Damasus for the Baptistery
(Fourth Century).**—Another inscription[2] for a baptistery,
also by Damasus, existed in S. Laurence *in Damaso*.

8. Item ad fontem (S. Laurentii in Damaso).

ISTE SALUTARES FONS CONTINET INCLITUS UNDAS
ET SOLET HUMANAM PURIFICARE LUEM
MUNIA SACRATI QUAE SINT VIS SCIRE LIQUORIS
DANT REGNATRICEM FLUMINA SANCTA FIDEM
ABLUE FONTE SACRO VETERIS CONTAGIA VITAE
O NIMIUM FELIX VIVE RENATUS AQUA
HUNC FONTEM QUICUMQUE PETIT TERRENA RELINQUIT
SUBJECIT ET PEDIBUS CAECA MINISTERIA

> This glorious spring contains the waters of salva-
> tion, and purifies human guilt; if you wish to
> know what are the gifts of the sacred stream,
> this holy river gives a triumphant faith. Wash
> away in the holy spring the stains of your old

---

[1] There are many examples of such representations still existing in churches
and on sarcophagi in Rome, Ravenna, and elsewhere.

[2] *Sylloge Virdunensis* (*I.C.* p. 135, No. 6). See *supra*, p. 247.

life; O thrice happy man, live, born again of water. Whoever seeks this spring forsakes earthly things, and tramples under foot the works of darkness.

9. S. Priscilla : Baptistery and *Consignatorium* (? Fifth Century). — We possess another inscription for a baptistery, followed immediately by one for a *consignato rium* (or place of confirmation) in the Sylloge of Verdun.[1] The locality of these inscriptions is, as we have seen, a subject of some discussion.

The rite of confirmation, or sealing (*consignatio*) with the sign of the cross with holy oil (*crisma*), was administered to the neophyte immediately after baptism; both rites being performed by the bishop—in Rome by the pope—sitting in the episcopal chair. Sometimes the neophyte passed from the font to the side of the baptistery; sometimes the rite was performed in a distinct building, the *consignatorium*.[2] There were *consignatoria* at the Vatican in the time of Symmachus (498–514), and in the Lateran in the time of Hilarius (461–468), both dedicated to the Holy Cross.

10. An African Church : for a *Consignatorium* (Fifth Century).—Of about the same date are two inscriptions, for baptistery and *consignatorium* respectively, for an African church unknown. This *consignatorium* also is dedicated to the Holy Cross, and the inscription[3] is as follows :

10. Versus Sanctae Crucis.

HINC CRUX SANCTA POTENS COELO SUCCESSIT ET ASTRIS
DUM RETINET CORPUS MISIT IN ASTRA DEUM
QUI FUGIS INSIDIAS MUNDI CRUCIS UTERE SIGNIS
HAC ARMATA FIDES PROTEGIT OMNE MALUM
CRUX DOMINI MECUM CRUX EST QUAM SEMPER ADORO
CRUX MIHI REFUGIUM CRUX MIHI CERTA SALUS
VIRTUTUM GENETRIX FONS VITAE JANUA CAELI
CRUX CHRISTI TOTUM DISTRUIT HOSTIS OPUS

---

[1] For text and general discussion see *supra*, pp. 247, 270 *et seqq.*

[2] The whole ceremony can be seen in Westminster Cathedral on Holy Saturday if there happens to be an adult baptism.

[3] *Anthologia Salmasiana* (in *I.C.* p. 241, No. 5).

The Holy Cross has risen mighty to the stars of heaven. While it retained the body (of our Lord) it set free God to return to the stars. Thou who dost flee the snares of this world, use the sign of the Cross. Armed with this, faith protects against all evil. The Cross of the Lord is with me, it is the Cross which I ever adore; the Cross is my refuge, the Cross is my assured salvation. Parent of virtues, fountain of life, gate of heaven, the Cross of Christ has utterly destroyed the work of the enemy.

11. *Oratory of the Holy Cross* **in the Baptistery of S. Peter's (?) : by Symmachus ; (498–514) on the Redemption and Eucharist.**—It was probably for the chapel of the Holy Cross in the baptistery of S. Peter's that Symmachus (498–514) put up the following inscription[1] concerning the Redemption and the Eucharist. The last two lines are familiar from the office of the Exaltation of the Cross.[2]

II. FORTIS AD INFIRMOS DESCENDENS PANIS ALENDOS
 HOC FRACTUS LIGNO EST UT POTUISSET EDI
 HIC AGNI MEMBRIS PROPRIO MORS DENTE LIGATA EST
 ET PRAEDAM PRAEDAE JAM GEMIT ESSE SUAE
 O MAGNUM PIETATIS OPUS MORS MORTUA TUNC EST
 QUANDO HOC IN LIGNO MORTUA VITA FUIT

The Strong One came down to the weak; and, Bread to those who need food, He was broken on the wood of the Cross, that we might feed on Him. On this Cross the limbs of the Lamb bound death with his own bonds,—death which now groans that it is preyed upon by its Prey. O great work of love! then death died when on this Cross our Life hung dead.

12. *Oratory of our Saviour,* **S. Peter's (?) : by Symmachus, in honour of the Holy Name.**—The new Sylloge[3] contains the inscription consisting of a series of invocations to the name of Jesus, a model, doubtless, for the "Litany

[1] MSS. KK. IV. 6, at Cambridge. See *supra*, p. 254.
[2] Roman Breviary, Sept. 14th. [3] MSS. KK. IV. 6, Cambridge.

of the Holy Name" and similar later compositions. It is here ascribed to Symmachus for "The Oratory of our Saviour." The poem was already known *without* the last line and attributed to a certain Silvius, or Severus.[1]

12. Item in Oratorio Salvatoris de nominibus Ejusdem.

SPES RATIO VIA VITA SALUS SAPIENTIA MENS MONS
JUDEX PORTA GIGAS REX GEMMA PROPHETA SACERDOS
MESSIAS SABBAOT RABBI SPONSUS MEDIATOR
VIRGA COLUMBA PETRA FILIUS EMMANUELQUE
VINEA PASTOR OVIS PAX RADIX VITIS OLIVA
FONS AGNUS PANIS ARIES VITULUS LEO JESUS
VERBUM HOMO RETE LAPIS TECTUM DOMUS OMNIA CHRISTUS
SIMMACHUS ISTA TIBI PIE JESU NOMINA LUSIT

> Hope. Reason. The Way. Life. Salvation.
> Wisdom. Mind. Mountain. Judge. Door.
> Giant. King. Jewel. Prophet. Priest. Messiah.
> Sabbaoth. Rabbi. Bridegroom. Mediator. Rod.
> Dove. Rock. Son and Emmanuel. Vineyard.
> Shepherd. Sheep. Peace. Root. Vine. Olive.
> Fountain. Lamb. Bread. Ram. Calf. Lion.
> Jesus. Word. Man. Net. Stone. Covering.
> House. All things Christ. Symmachus made
> this play on Thy Names, O gentle Jesus.

13. S. Paul : Leo I. for a *Cantharus* (Fifth Century).—In the Basilica of S. Paul is an example by Leo I. (440–461) of an inscription[2] for the basin of the fountain (*cantharus*) which stood in the centre of the atrium. It was here that the pilgrims would wash before actually entering the church.

13. Isti versiculi in atrio Sancti Pauli scripti sunt.

PERDIDERAT LATICUM LONGAEVA INCURIA CURSUS
QUOS TIBI NUNC PLENO CANTARUS ORE VOMIT
PROVIDA PASTORIS PRAE TOTUM CURA LEONIS
HAEC OVIBUS CHRISTI LARGA FLUENTA DEDIT
UNDE LAVAT CARNIS MACULAS SED CRIMINA PURGAT
PURIFICATQUE ANIMAS MUNDIOR AMNE FIDES

[1] *Supra*, p. 267.   [2] *Sylloge Centulensis* (*I.C.* p. 80, No. 13).

QUISQUIS SUIS MERITIS VENERANDA SACRARIA PAULI
INGREDERIS SUPPLEX ABLUE FONTE MANUS

> Through the neglect of ages the stream of waters
> had been lost which now the full-mouthed
> fountain pours forth for thee. The provident
> care in all things of your shepherd, Leo, gave
> these broad streams to the flock of Christ where-
> with to wash away the stains of the body. But
> faith, purer than this water, cleanses from guilt
> and purifies our souls. Whoever thou art who
> enterest as a suppliant to the shrine of Paul,
> made holy by his merits,—wash thy hands in
> this fountain.

14. SS. Cosmas and Damian: by Felix IV. (Sixth Century).—The Greek saints Cosmas and Damian were extremely popular in Rome. The inscription[1] on the apse of their basilica composed by Felix (526–530) is still in existence. The first two lines seem to have been suggested by the opening words of an inscription[2] of Symmachus (498–514) for an altar in S. Andrew on the Vatican containing relics of Protus and Jacinthus:

TEMPLA MICANT PLUS COMPTA FIDE QUAM LUCE METALLI

> Temples shine more glorious adorned with faith
> than with the light of precious metals.[3]

The verses of SS. Cosmas and Damian are as follows:

14. In Basilica Cosmae et Damiani.

AULA DEI CLARIS RADIAT SPECIOSA METALLIS
IN QUA PLUS FIDEI LUX PRETIOSA MICAT
MARTYRIBUS MEDICIS POPULO SPES CERTA SALUTIS
VENIT ET EX SACRO CREVIT HONORE LOCUS
OBTULIT HOC DOMINO FELIX ANTISTITE DIGNUM
MUNUS UT AETHERIA VIVAT IN ARCE POLI

> The temple of God shines glorious with bright

---

[1] *Tur.* (*I.C.* p. 71, No. 41).

[2] *Anthol. Cod. Paris* (*I.C.* p. 246 and note). Cf. *supra*, p. 258.

[3] The word *metallis* seems to be of somewhat general significance, including marbles, metal-work, and referring especially to mosaics. Cf. *supra*, pp. 261, 262.

metals; but the precious light of faith shines here more splendid. A certain hope of safety came to the people in their martyred physicians, and the church arose from the holy reverence paid them. Felix offered this gift worthy of its patron saint, that he himself might live in the heavenly city above.

15. S. Agnes: by Honorius (Seventh Century).—These verses again certainly inspired Honorius (625–640) in his distich [1] for the arch of S. Agnes in Via Nomentana.

15. Item in arcu.

VIRGINIS AULA MICAT VARIIS DECORATA METALLIS
SED PLUS NAMQUE [2] NITET MERITIS FULGENTIOR AMPLIS

The Court of the Virgin gleams adorned with divers precious metals: but she herself shines more glorious with her great merits.

Somewhat similar are the opening words of another inscription [3] in the apse of S. Agnes :

Sanctae Agnae (*sic*) Martyris.

AUREA CONCISIS SURGIT PICTURA METALLIS

Her image rises all in gold among the cut mosaics.

16. *Inscriptions for Secular Buildings*: Archives of S. Laurence *in Damaso*, by Damasus (Fourth Century).—The secular buildings, too, had their full share of inscriptions. As an example we may give the inscription Damasus set up in the portico adjoining the church of S. Laurence *in Damaso* where the ecclesiastical archives were kept.[4]

16. In Ecclesia beati Laurentii Martyris in qua requiescit Sanctus Damasus papa.

---

[1] *Tur.* (*I.C.* p. 63, No. 6). Cf. *supra*, p. 261.
[2] Is this word correct ?
[3] *Laur.* iv. (*I.C.* viii. p. 104, No. 36). Cf. *supra*, p. 262.
[4] *Laur.* i. (in *I.C.*, p. 151, No. 23). The body of Damasus was translated from the Via Ardeatina to S. Laurence *in Damaso* by Hadrian I. (772–795) ; see *Lib. Pont.*

HINC PATER [1] EXCEPTOR LECTOR LEVITA SACERDOS
CREVERAT HINC MERITIS QUONIAM MELIORIBUS ACTIS
HINC MIHI PROVECTO CHRISTUS CUI SUMMA POTESTAS
SEDIS APOSTOLICAE VOLUIT CONCEDERE HONOREM
ARCHIBIS FATEOR VOLUI NOVA CONDERE TECTA
ADDERE PRAETEREA DEXTRA LAEVAQUE COLUMNAS
QUAE DAMASI TENEANT PROPRIUM PER SAECULA NOMEN

> In the church of blessed Laurence the martyr,
> where rests S. Damasus, pope.

> Here my father grew up. He was clerk, reader,
> deacon, priest (probably *bishop*). Here he grew
> in grace through his good deeds. Here, as I
> grew old, Christ, in whom is the supreme power,
> willed to grant me glory of the apostolic seat (*i.e.*
> he became pope). I confess I wished to erect
> a new building for the archives, and to add
> columns on the left and right (*i.e.* make a
> portico), which should bear as their own the name
> of Damasus through the ages.

**17. Library of Gregory the Great, by Agapetus (Sixth
Century).**—Another inscription for a library is that over the
library of Gregory the Great on the Coelian Hill.[2] It had
been built by Pope Agapetus (535–536), and adorned with
representations of the Fathers of the Church, with Agapetus
among them.

17. In bibliotheca Sancti Gregorii qui est in Monasterio
    Clitauri ubi ipse dialogorum (sc. libros) scripsit.

SANCTORUM VENERANDA COHORS SEDET ORDINE *longo*
DIVINAE LEGIS MYSTICA DICTA DOCENS

---

[1] This reading, rather than the alternative *puer*, is accepted as correct by
most scholars,—so the verses would apply to the *father* of Damasus. If *puer* is
read, the whole inscription becomes autobiographical (see pp. 311 *et seqq.* for a
discussion on the life of Damasus). The word *sacerdos* (priest) is frequently
used by Damasus of a bishop; see his reference to himself (No. 42, ed. Ihm :
reddit sua vota sacerdos); and to the popes Miltiades (No. 12 : *pace sacerdos*),
Siricius (No. 93 : *magnus sacerdos*) and others. It is used by other popes in
their inscriptions of themselves :—*jure Sacerdos* = rightful bishop, or pope. Cf.
supra, pp. 250, 260; cf p. 290.

[2] *Eins.* (in *I.C.* p. 28, No. 55).

HOS INTER RESIDENS AGAPETUS JURE SACERDOS
CODICIBUS PULCHRUM CONDIDIT ARTE LOCUM
GRATIA PAR CUNCTIS SANCTUS [1] LABOR OMNIBUS UNUS
DISSONA VERBA QUIDEM SED TAMEN UNA FIDES

> For the library of Saint Gregory, which is in the
> Monastery on the slope of Clitaurus, where he
> wrote his Dialogues.
>
> A noble band of the saints is ranged around,
> teaching the mystic words of the divine
> law. Among these sits Agapetus, the lawful
> bishop; he fashioned with skill this fair place
> for the manuscripts. Equal is our gratitude
> to all these, even as the holy toil of each
> was the same. For divers were their voices, but
> one their faith.

Inscriptions for Suburban Tombs (Damasus, etc.).—By
far the largest number of inscriptions were written by
Damasus, and destined to adorn the martyrs' tombs. Some,
however, as we have seen, were for churches.[2] Later, we
will consider the group of his own family epitaphs from
which we gather some facts about his life.[3]

Among the surburban inscriptions, however, we note
the epitaph of Damasus[4] himself. It once stood, together
with that of his mother Laurentia, and his sister Irene,
in the basilica which he built for himself on the Via
Ardeatina, where the three lay side by side.

18. Epitaph on Damasus by Himself (Fourth Century), Via Ardeatina.

18. Epitaphium papae Damasi quod sibi edidit ipse.

QUI GRADIENS PELAGI FLUCTUS COMPRESSIT AMAROS
VIVERE QUI PRAESTAT MORIENTIA SEMINA TERRAE
SOLVERE QUI POTUIT LETALIA VINCULA MORTIS

---

[1] Or *Sanctis?*   [2] *Supra*, pp. 279, 283.

[3] On the epigrams of Damasus, see *Bull. Arch. Crist.*, 1884, p. 7. On
other inscriptions and details of his life, see *infra*, p. 311 *et seqq.*

[4] *Anthol. Isidor.* (in *I.C.* p. 252, No. 1). Many lines of this epitaph have
been borrowed for other inscriptions; see *I.C.* p. 170, No. 27; p. 323, No. 5.

POST TENEBRAS FRATREM POST TERTIA LUMINA SOLIS
AD SUPEROS ITERUM MARTAE DONARE SORORI
POST CINERES DAMASUM FACIET QUIA SURGERE CREDO

> He Who walking on the waves could calm the
> bitter waters, and Who grants life to the dying
> seeds of the earth; He Who could loose the mortal
> chains of Death; Who, after the darkness, could
> bring back to the upper world again, on the
> third day, the brother for his sister Martha: I
> believe He will make Damasus rise again from
> his ashes.

19. Papal Crypt, S. Callixtus: by Damasus.—Turning
to the martyrs' tombs, the epitaph which stood in the papal
crypt of S. Callixtus[1] strikes, as it were, the keynote of the
whole series:

19. HIC CONGESTA JACET QUAERIS SI TURBA PIORUM
CORPORA SANCTORUM RETINENT VENERANDA SEPULCRA
SUBLIMES ANIMAS RAPUIT SIBI REGIA CAELI
HIC COMITES SIXTI PORTANT QUI EX HOSTE TROPEA
HIC NUMERUS PROCERUM SERVAT QUI ALTARIA CHRISTI
HIC POSITUS LONGA VIXIT QUI IN PACE SACERDOS
HIC CONFESSORES CHRISTI QUOS GRAECIA MISIT
HIC JUVENES PUERIQUE SENES CASTIQUE NEPOTES
QUIS MAGE VIRGINEUM PLACUIT RETINERE PUDOREM
HIC FATEOR DAMASUS VOLUI MEA CONDERE MEMBRA
SED CINERES TIMUI SANCTOS VEXARE PIORUM

> If thou seekest them, here lies in little space
> a throng of holy ones. Their honoured
> sepulchres hold the bodies of the saints,
> but the realms of heaven have rapt away
> their lofty spirits. Here are the comrades
> (Laurence and his fellow deacons) of Sixtus
> (the martyred pope), who wrested victory
> from the enemy; here the band of our leaders
> who serve the altars of Christ (*i.e.* bishops
> of Rome). Here is laid the priest (Miltiades,
> 311–314) who lived long days in peace; here
> are the confessors of Christ whom Greece sent

[1] *Tur.* (*I.C.* p. 66, No. 23).

forth (the Greek martyrs Hippolytus, Adrias, Neo, etc.). Here are young men and boys, old men and children, whose will it was to preserve their virgin purity. I confess that I, Damasus, would fain have laid my limbs here, but I feared to trouble the holy ashes of the saints.

20. The Papal Crypt: List of Popes.—In this same crypt was a marble slab put up by Sixtus III. (432–440), inscribed[1] with the list of popes and others buried here:

20. SIXTUS (II.), DIONYSIUS, CORNELIUS, FELIX, PONTIANUS, FABIANUS, GAIUS, EUSEBIUS, MELCHIADES, STEPHANUS, URBANUS, LUCIUS, MANNUS (?), ANTEROS, NUMIDIANUS, LADICEUS, JULIANUS, POLYCARPUS, OPTATUS.

21. Gordianus, Martyr, near Via Labicana: by Damasus.—One of the most beautiful of the epitaphs[2] is that of the youthful martyr Gordianus, buried between the Via Labicana and Via Latina:

21. In Metropi (sic) Via.

HAEC QUICUMQUE VIDES NIMIO PERFECTA LABORE
DESINE MIRARI MINUS EST QUAM[3] MARTYR HABETUR
HIC AETATE PUER RUDIBUS JAM VICTOR IN ANNIS
TEMPORE SUB PAUCO MATURA LAUDE TRIUMPHANS
ASPERA INNOCUO MACULAVIT TELA CRUORE
ET SITIENS TENERO SUXIT SIBI SANGUINE PRAEDO
SIC VICTOR SUPERAS AURAS REGNUMQUE PETIVIT
ET NOS CAELESTI PLACIDOS DE SEDE REVISIT
NOMINE GORDIANUS CHRISTI QUEM PALMA CORONAT
MARMORE CONCLUDENS ARCHAM CINERESQUE BEATOS
PRESBYTER ORNAVIT RENOVANS VINCENTIUS ULTRO

You who look upon this grave, perfected with so great a labour, cease to wonder: it is less wondrous than the martyr it enshrines. He, a boy in age, a victor in his youthful years, in a little space triumphed, ripe for glory.

---

[1] *Tur.* (*I.C.* p. 66, No. 24). The names are in the genitive in the text.
[2] *Tur.* (*I.C.* p. 64, No. 15). [3] De Rossi emends to *quia.*

He stained the cruel weapons with his innocent blood : his murderer thirstily drank up the blood of the tender prey. Thus victorious he sought a supernal kingdom and from his heavenly dwelling visits us who enjoy peace. His name is Gordianus, whom the palm of Christ crowned. The priest Vincentius adorned and repaired the tomb at his own expense, enclosing the chest and the blessed ashes in marble.

22. Tiburtius, Via Tiburtina : by Damasus.—Another well known inscription[1] is that of Tiburtius on the Via Tiburtina :

22. TEMPORE QUO GLADIUS SECUIT PIA VISCERA MATRIS
EGREGIUS MARTYR CONTEMPTO PRINCIPE MUNDI
AETHERIS ALTA PETIT CHRISTO COMITANTE BEATUS
HIC TIBI SANCTUS HONOR SEMPER LAUDESQUE MANEBUNT
CARE DEO UT FOVEAS DAMASUM PRECOR ALME TIBURTI

At the time when the sword was piercing the heart of our holy mother (the Church), this glorious martyr, despising the prince of this world, sought, blessed one, with Christ as companion, the heights of heaven. Here (at the tomb) for ever shall be holy honour and praise to thee. O gentle Tiburtius, dear to God, I pray thee cherish Damasus.

23, 24. Epitaphs on S. Felicitas, Via Salaria ; by Boniface (Fifth Century).—Boniface I. (418–423) is the author of two epitaphs[2] to S. Felicitas for her church on the Via Salaria. The first represents her standing before the judge :

23. Epitaphium Sanctae Felicitatis.

DISCITE QUID MERITI PRAESTET PRO REGE FERIRI
FEMINA NON TIMUIT GLADIUM CUM NATIS OBIVIT
CONFESSA CHRISTUM MERUIT PER SAECULA NOMEN

---

[1] *Tur.* (*I.C.* p. 64, No. 12). The first line is repeated in two other epitaphs of Damasus, both on the Via Salaria (*I.C.* pp. 101 and 103, Nos. 21, 34a).
[2] *Vird.* (*I.C.* p. 136, Nos. 12, 13, 13a).

> Learn how great a merit it is, to be slain for
> Christ the King. A woman feared not the
> sword: she perished with her sons: having
> confessed Christ, she earned for ever her name
> (Felicitas).

In the second inscription, at the entrance to the church,
she is enjoying a somewhat Virgilian paradise :

24. Iste versiculi sunt scripti in introitu ecclesiae.

. . . .

CORPOREIS RESOLUTA MALIS DUCE PRAEDITA CHRISTO
AETHERIS ALMA PARENS ATRIA CELSA PETIT
INSONTES PUEROS SEQUITUR PER AMOENA VIRECTA
TEMPORA VICTRICIS FLOREA SERTA LIGANT
PURPUREAM RAPIUNT ANIMAM CAELESTIA REGNA
SANGUINE LOTA SUO MEMBRA TENET TUMULUS
SI TUMULUM QUAERIS MERITUM DE NOMINE SIGNAT
NE OPPRIMERE*r bello dux* FUIT ISTA MIHI

. . . .

> Freed from the pains of the body, with Christ as her
> leader, the gentle mother seeks the lofty dwell-
> ings of the heavens. Through green meadows
> she follows her innocent sons, and flowery
> wreaths bind her victorious temples. The
> realms of heaven have rapt away her shining
> spirit: the tomb contains her limbs washed
> in her own blood. If you seek her tomb, it is
> marked with the name (Felicitas) she earned.
> To me (who made the epitaph) she has been
> a (leader in conflict?) that I should not be
> overcome.

25. S. Vitalis, Via Salaria : by Vigilius (Sixth Century).
—An inscription [1] of Pope Vigilius (537–555) for the tombs
of SS. Vitalis, Martialis and Alexander on the Via Salaria
describes the restorations made after the Gothic devastation
of the northern suburbs :

25. Sancti Vitalis Martyris et Sancti Martialis et Sancti
Alexandri.

[1] *Laur.* iv. (*I.C.* p. 100, No. 18).

DUM PERITURA GETAE POSUISSENT CASTRA SUB URBE
MOVERUNT SANCTIS BELLA NEFANDA PRIUS
ISTAQUE SACRILEGO VERTERUNT CORDE SEPULCRA
MARTYRIBUS QUONDAM RITE SACRATA PIIS
QUOS MONSTRANTE DEO DAMASUS SIBI PAPA PROBATOS
AFFIXO MONUIT CARMINE JURE COLI
SED PERIIT TITULUS CONFRACTO MARMORE SANCTUS
NEC TAMEN HIS ITERUM POSSE LATERE FUIT
DIRUTA VIGILIUS NAM MOX HAEC PAPA GEMISCENS
HOSTIBUS EXPULSIS OMNE NOVAVIT OPUS

> When the Goths set their camps, destined to
> perish, against the city, they first waged a
> shameful war on the saints; and with sacrilegious
> hearts rifled those sepulchres once solemnly con-
> secrated to the holy martyrs. For pope Dama-
> sus, under the divine guidance, had proved them
> to be martyrs; and he put up inscriptions to
> them and commanded that they should be duly
> honoured. But the marble was broken, the
> sacred inscriptions perished; and a second time
> they could not escape the eyes of the foe.
> Vigilius the pope, lamenting over these ruins,
> after the enemy was expelled, restored all
> things.

**26. Relics in S. Stephen's and S. Silvester *in Capite* :
by Leo III., Paul I. (Eighth Century).**—Inscriptions, too,
are found in honour of the bodies of martyrs, or of their
relics, which have been translated to churches within the
city.

A prose inscription [1] by Leo (795–816) was set up over
an altar containing the relics of the martyred deacons
Stephen and Laurence in the monastic church of S. Stephen
on the Vatican.

26. SERVANTUR IN HAC ARA RELIQUIAE SANCTORUM
MARTYRUM ATQUE LEVITARUM STEPHANI ET
LAURENTII

> Preserved in this altar are the relics of the holy
> martyrs and deacons Stephen and Laurence.

Sometimes the inscription takes the form of a list of

---

[1] *Excerpta ex anthol. var.*, *I.C.* p. 275, No. 7.

names of such saints or relics. Such a one, of the eighth century, exists in the crypts of the Vatican Basilica.[1]

In the church of S. Silvestro *in Capite* there can still be seen a calendar of saints [1] whose bodies were brought here from the catacombs by Paul I. (757–768). Similar inscriptions are found in S. Praxed, S. Martin, and S. Cecilia [2] as well as in the provincial cities of Italy.

[1] Mai, *Script. Vet. Nov. V.*, pp. 44, 56 ; Dionysius, *Vat. Bas. Crypt. Mon.*, p. 101, pl. xxxix.

[2] Mai, *op. cit.* pp. 38, 46, 48.

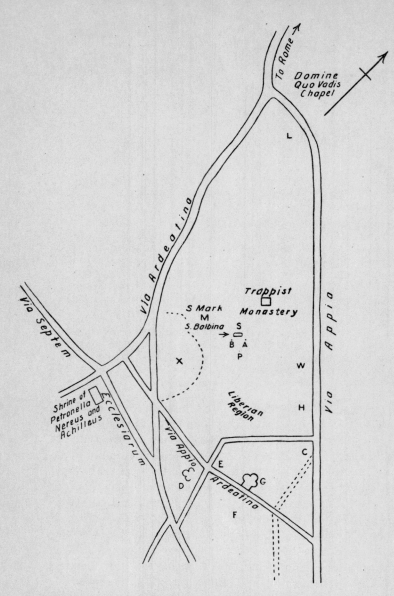

PLAN IV.—THE AREAS OF S. CALLIXTUS, VIA APPIA

Based on plans by Wilpert, Schneider, Scaglia, and Marucchi

From the *Journal of Roman Studies*, i., i. 1911 (London)

C, Crypts of Lucina with tomb of Cornelius. F, S. Callixtus proper with papal crypt and shrine of S. Cecilia. E, Shrine of Eusebius and area of Parthenius and Calocerus. H, Arenarium of Hippolytus. W, Area of S. Soteris (?). L, Ruins. M, Basilica of S. Mark and S. Balbina (?). A, Crypt of the Apostles (? Shrine of Damasus). B, Crypt of the Columns (? SS. Marcus and Marcellianus). P, Crypt of Laurentia's epitaph. S, Ancient stairs to A and B. G, Basilica called S. Sixtus and S. Cecilia (? S. Zephyrinus). D, Basilica called S. Soteris (? Basilica of SS. Marcus and Marcellianus). :::::::::: ancient road discovered by Schneider (*Nuovo Bullettino*, 1910).

CHAPTER XXII

DOCUMENT AND MONUMENT

Document and monument.—Itineraries as the key to the monuments : *Via Appia* and the identifications of the three cemeteries : (*a*) S. CALLIXTUS (Crypts of the popes, S. Cecilia, etc.) : (*b*) PRAETEXTATUS (S. Januarius) : (*c*) AD CATACUMBAS (SS. Peter and Paul, S. Sebastian).—Syllogae as key to the monuments : *Via Ardeatina*, DOMITILLA (SS. Nereus and Achilleus and S. Petronilla) : *North Africa*, an inscription.—Combination of documentary and monumental evidence applied to the life of Damasus (family epitaphs, etc.).—The tradition of S. Cecilia and the excavations.

Nobis quoque peccatoribus famulis tuis, de multitudine miserationum tuarum sperantibus, partem aliquam et societatem donare digneris cum tuis sanctis Apostolis et Martyribus : cum Joanne, Stephano, Matthia, Barnaba, Ignatio, Alexandro, Marcellino, Petro, Felicitate, Perpetua, Agatha, Lucia, Agnete, Caecilia, Anastasia et omnibus sanctis.[1]—*Canon Missae.*

Document and Monument.—In the attempt to establish certain facts in the history of Christian Rome of the first three centuries there are innumerable ways, and combinations of ways, in which the documents throw light on the monuments, and *vice versa*. The interpretations of the evidence, however, sometimes give rise to considerable variety of opinion, as we have seen in the minute discussion of the difficult questions raised in the attempts to determine the localities of the " Chair of Peter " by means of the Papyrus of Monza ;[2] and of the *Sumite* inscription by means of the two Syllogae, Verdun and Cambridge ;[3] and the true number of the Roman cemeteries in connexion with the *Index Coemiteriorum.*[4]

In the majority of cases, however, the relations between

[*Continued p.* 300.

[1] " *To us too, sinners, Thy servants, hoping in the multitude of Thy mercies, deign to give some part and share with Thy holy apostles and martyrs: with John, Stephen,*" etc.

[2] *Supra*, p. 110.   [3] *Supra*, p. 270.   [4] Appendix IV. p. 340.

INDEX Coemeteriorum[1] *from* Notitia Regionum XIV.	INDICES OLEORUM [of Monza].[2]		ITINERARIUM SALISBURGENSE.[3]
	PITTACIA.	INDEX OLEORUM.	
Coemeterium Praetextati ad s. Januarium via Appia.	[LABEL IV.] . . . Sca Sapientia, sca Spes, sca Fides, sca Caritas, sca Caecilia, scs Tarsicius, scs Cornelius et multa milia sanctorum.	Sce Sotheris Sce Sapientiae Sce Spei Sce Fides Sce Caritatis Sce Ceciliae Sci Tarsicii Sci Cornilii et multa milia sanctorum.	Postea pervenies via Appia ad s. Sebastianum martyrem, cujus corpus jacet in inferiore loco, et ibi sunt sepulchra apostolorum Petri et Pauli, in quibus XL annorum requiescebant. Et in occidentali parte ecclesiae per gradus descendis ubi s. Cyrinus papa et martyr pausat. Et eadem via ad aquilonem ad ss. martyres Tiburtium et Valerianum et Maximum. Ibi intrabis in speluncam magnam et ibi invenies s. Urbanum episcopum et confessorem, et in altero loco Felicissimum et Agapitum martyres et diaconos Syxti, et in tertio loco Cyrinum martyrem, et quarto Januarium martyrem. Et in tertia ecclesia rursum s. Synon [Zeno] martyr requiescit. Eadem via ad s. Caeciliam, ibi innumerabilis multitudo martyrum. Primus Syxtus papa et martyr, Dionisius papa et martyr, Julianus (?) papa et martyr, Flavianus [Fabianus] martyr, s. Caecilia virgo et martyr, LXXX martyres ibi requiescunt deorsum. Geferinus [Zephyrinus] papa et confessor sursum quiescit. Eusebius papa et martyr longe in antro quiescit. Cornelius papa et martyr longe in antro altero quiescit. Postea pervenies ad s. virginem Soterem et martyrem : eadem via venis ad ecclesiam parvam ubi decollatus est s. Xystus cum diaconibus suis, cujus corpus jacet ad Aquilonem.
Coemeterium Catacumbas ad s. Sebastianum via Appia.			
	[LABEL VIII.] Sci Sebastiani Scs Eutycius Scs Quirinus Scs Valerianus Scs Tiburtius Scs Maximus Scs Urbanus Scs Januarius	Here follow names from the two Viae Salaria. Sci Sebastiani Sci Eutycii Sci Quirini Sci Valeriani Sci Tiburti Sci Maximi Sci Urbani Sci Januari	
Coemeterium Calisti ad s. Xystum via Appia.			

[1] *Supra*, page 98.　　[2] *Supra*, page 105.　　[3] *Supra*, page 112.

298

EPITOME LIBRI DE LOCIS SANCTIS MARTYRUM.[4]	ITINERARIUM MALMESBURIENSE.[5] (Notitia Portarum . . .)	ITINERARIUM EINSIEDLENSE.[6]
Juxta viam Appiam in orientali parte civitatis ecclesia est s. Suteris [Soteris] martyris, ubi ipsa cum multis martyribus jacet, et juxta eandem viam ecclesia est s. Syxti papae ubi ipse dormit. Ibi quoque et Caecilia virgo pausat, et ibi s. Tarsicius et s. Geferinus [Zephyrinus] in uno tumulo jacent et ibi s. Eusebius et s. Calocerus et s. Parthenius per se singuli jacent et DCCC martyres ibidem requiescunt. Inde haud procul in coemeterio Calisti, Cornelius et Cyprianus in ecclesia dormiunt. Juxta eandem viam quoque ecclesia est multorum sanctorum, id est Januarii qui fuit de septem filiis Felicitatis major natu, Urbani, Agapiti, Felicissimi, Cyrini, Zenonis, fratris Valentini, Tiburtii, Valeriani et Maximi et multi martyres ibi requiescunt. Et juxta eandem viam ecclesia est s. Sebastiani martyris ubi ipse dormit ubi sunt sepulturae apostolorum in quibus XL annos quieverunt. Ibi quoque et Cyrinus martyr est sepultus.	Undecima porta et via dicitur Appia. Ibi requiescunt s. Sebastianus et Quirinus, et olim ibi requieverunt apostolorum corpora. Et paulo propius Roman sunt martyres Januarius, Urbanus, Xenon, Quirinus, Agapitus, Felicissimus. Et in altera ecclesia Tiburtius, Valerianus, Maximus, nec longe ecclesia s. Ceciliae martyris; et ibi reconditi sunt Stephanus, Sixtus, Zefferinus, Eusebius, Melchiades, Marcellus, Eutichianus, Dionysius, Antheros, Pontianus, Lucius papa, Optatus, Julianus(?), Calocerus, Parthenius, Tharsitius, Policamus, martyres. Ibidem ecclesia s. Cornelii et corpus. Et in altera ecclesia sancta Soteris, et non longe pausant martyres Hippolitus, Adrianus, Eusebius, Maria, Martha, Paulina, Valeria, Marcellus; et prope papa Marcus in sua ecclesia.	On Route 8 from De Septem Viis to Porta Metrovia :— In via Latina in dextera :[7] Sci Januarii, oratorium Sci Syxti. On Route 9 from S. Paul's via Ostiensis, down the via Ardeatina : Inde ad Scum. Soterum. Inde ad sanctum Sixtum. Ibi et scus. Favianus et Antheros et Miltiades. Inde ad scum. Cornelium ; inde ad scum. Sebastianum. Inde revertendo per viam Appiam ad ecclesiam ubi scs. Syxtus cum suis diaconibus decollatus est, inde ad portam Appiam. [Isolated names are found in other routes.]

---

[4] Supra, page 115.   [5] Supra, page 117.   [6] Supra, page 119.
[7] Porta Metrovia is S.E. of Rome.   The "In Via Latina in dextera" is the left-hand side of the Via Appia.

document and monument have been definitely determined; and a consideration of a few typical examples will be a sufficient indication of method.

Itineraries as the Key to the Monuments.—One of the most obvious methods of investigation, is to take the Itineraries, and excavate all along the routes indicated by them. Each martyr should then be looked up in the Philocalian Calendar and the Martyrology of Jerome: his *Acts* should be studied, his inscription sought in the *Syllogae,* and any possible reference in the *Liber Pontificalis* to himself or his shrine noted. The sum of this evidence should establish *some* facts concerning the martyrs.

This task of excavation was first attempted by De Rossi in the days when the greater part of the catacombs was unknown.[1]

Via Appia and the Identification of the *Three Cemeteries.*—As an illustration of this method of research we will select for examination an area familiar to all visitors to Rome, one which has been extensively excavated, and where new discoveries are being made yearly, namely, the Via Appia; and compare the written records with the actual monuments.

The Itineraries[2] record many shrines on this road: the *Index Coemiteriorum*[3] mentions three distinct cemeteries, as does the Philocalian Calendar[4] in the *Depositio Martyrum*: "XIII. kal. febr. Fabiani in Calisti, et Sebastiani in Catacumbas . . . VIII. id. augusti Xysti in Calisti, et in Praetextati, Agapiti et Felicissimi."

(a). **S. Callixtus : (1) Cornelius in the Crypt of Lucina.**

---

[1] For the catacombs, see Bibliography—ARCHAEOLOGY: Catacombs. An immense and somewhat controversial literature concerning the sites of the shrines of S. Callixtus has just grown up, stimulated by the discoveries there, chiefly in 1903, 1908, and 1910. For a summary of the whole question, and a complete bibliography, see E. Barker, "The Topography of the Catacombs of S. Callixtus," in *Journal of Roman Studies* (*J.R.S.*), vol. i. pt. i., London, 1911.

[2] *Supra*, pp. 93 *et seqq.* and 298, 299. It would take too long to collate here the Itineraries with the other documents.

[3] *Supra*, pp. 98, 99. [4] Appendix III. p. 337.

—The first step in the identification of these three areas was taken by De Rossi. In 1849 he discovered on the Via Appia, on a property known as the Vigna Ammendola, a fragment of an inscription which read—

. . . NELIUS MARTYR

This he recognized as a portion of the epitaph of Pope Cornelius who, as the documents tell us, was buried in the *Crypt of Lucina* [C on Plan IV.] on the Via Appia. Around this crypt grew the cemetery known later as S. Callixtus.

Excavating here in 1852, the remaining portion of the inscription was discovered:

COR . . .
EP

i.e. Cor(*nelius*) Bishop. It was found in a crypt adorned with a remarkable series of frescoes, some Pompeian in character, some Eucharistic in significance, all of the first or second century. Here assuredly was the Crypt of Lucina.

(2) **Crypt of S. Cecilia.**—In 1854, with the discovery of a large crypt [F] containing a series of papal epitaphs, and of the adjoining crypt, decorated with frescoes of S. Cecilia of the fifth to the seventh century, the identification of "*Calisti ad Xystum*"—situated on the right (west) side of the Via Appia, about one mile from the Porta Appia in the Aurelian Wall—was complete.[1]

(3) **Papal Crypt.**—Not only was the cemetery identified, but nearly every shrine mentioned in the Itineraries, the *Liber Pontificalis*, and the epigrams of Damasus (preserved in the *Syllogae* and in other documents), has been discovered. From these we learn that all the fifteen popes of the third century, with two exceptions,[2] and two of the fourth were buried here. Of these fifteen popes in S. Callixtus, ten lay

[1] *i.e.* as the name was applied in the time of the pilgrims. " S. Callixtus " now indicates an agglomeration of these, and various other centres, known in those days under different names.

[2] Callixtus (221–227) himself perished in a riot in the Trastevere, and was buried in the cemetery Calepodius: Marcellinus (296–304) (and several of the succeeding popes) lay in S. Priscilla. The name of Pope *Soter* (? 175–182) in the Itineraries is probably a mistake, owing to confusion with *Soteris*, a woman martyr who was buried in S. Callixtus [W ?]: *Soter* was buried in the Vatican. The name *Marcellus* is also a mistake ; he was buried in Priscilla.

actually in the papal crypt; we have the epitaphs of six of them inscribed on their tombs. These epitaphs, except that of Cornelius, are all in Greek, and of the form :

LUCIUS EP(iscopus).

The inscriptions of the two martyred popes read :

FABIANUS EPI(scopus) M(ar)T(y)R,

and

PONTIANUS EPISC(opus) M(ar)T(y)R.[1]

Though the epitaphs of some of the popes have been lost, the names are all given on the inscription put up in the papal chamber by Sixtus III.[2] (432-440); and for Sixtus II., though no epitaph is forthcoming, there are numerous pilgrims' *graffiti*[3] to prove his burial here. The five popes who lie in other parts of the catacomb are (1) Zephyrinus (199-217), who built and adorned the papal crypt, and at the time of the pilgrims lay quite near it in a chapel above ground,—probably that known as S. Sixtus and S. Cecilia [G], though the point is disputed ; (2) Cornelius (251-253), the discovery of whose tomb in the crypt of Lucina [C] has been described above ; (3) Eusebius (309-311), whose shrine [E] lies in the region to which he gave his name ; (4) Gaius (283-296), fragments of whose inscription have been found near the tomb of Eusebius ; (5) Miltiades (311-312), whose shrine has not been identified. The following table will elucidate monument and Itinerary :—

POPES OF THE THIRD CENTURY IN S. CALLIXTUS, ETC.

1.	.	.	(1) Zephyrinus (? 203-231)	.	Buried near the papal crypt in a chapel above ground: not certainly identified.	
[2	.	.	Callixtus .	.	.	in Calepodius.]
3	.	.	Urban	.	.	Inscribed tomb in papal crypt.
4	.	.	Pontianus	.	.	,, ,, ,,
5	.	.	Anteros .	.	.	,, ,, ,,
6	.	.	Fabianus	.	.	,, ,, ,,

---

[1] For the abbreviations of *Martyr* in both these inscriptions, and its possible later addition—also for an account of the discovery of the Pontianus inscription in 1910 by Mgr. Wilpert, and for a reproduction of it, see *J.R.S.*, *loc. cit.*

[2] *Supra*, p. 292.

[3] *Supra*, pp. 39, 40.

7	.	.	(2)	Cornelius	. . . Inscribed tomb in crypt of Lucina, S. Callixtus.
8	.	.	.	Lucius	Inscribed tomb in papal crypt.
9	.	.	.	Stephen	(name appears in Sixtus III.'s inscription in papal crypt.)
10	.	.	.	Sixtus II. . . .	,, ,, and pilgrims' *graffiti.*
11	.	.	.	Dionysius . . .	name in Sixtus III.'s inscription
12	.	.	.	Felix I.	,, ,, ,,
13	.	.	.	Eutychianus . . .	Inscribed tomb in papal crypt.
14	.	.	(3)	Gaius	fragmentary inscription in region of Eusebius, S. Callixtus.
[15	.	.	.	Marcellinus (296–308)	. in Priscilla.]
[16	.	.	.	Marcellus [1] (308–309)	. in Priscilla.]
17	.	.	(4)	Eusebius (309–311) .	. in S. Callixtus in the "Region of Eusebius."
18	.	.	(5)	Miltiades [2] (311–314)	. in S. Callixtus, not identified, but there is an inscription of Damasus.

[Cyprian and Optatus].—We find in the Itineraries the name of *Cyprian*, the martyred bishop of Carthage, connected with that of Cornelius; and that of another African bishop, *Optatus*, with the papal crypt. The reason of the mistake is that these bishops are depicted together with Cornelius and Sixtus II. in the Byzantine frescoes with which the crypt of Cornelius was adorned in the sixth century; perhaps as examples of bishops who worthily performed their office. All except Optatus were martyrs. According to the *Passion of Cornelius*,[3] Cyprian and Cornelius wrote to each other. None of the three were buried with Cornelius. But the festival day of S. Cyprian on September 14th was kept in this crypt in the fourth century, as we see from the Philocalian Calendar.

(4) Parthenius and Calocerus.—Other martyrs mentioned in the Itineraries are Parthenius and Calocerus, whose names the pilgrims have scrawled all over the wall in the region of Eusebius [E on Plan IV].

(5) Tarsicius.—The grave of the boy martyr Tarsicius has not been positively identified; but very possibly he was

---

[1] *Supra*, p. 71.

[2] The *possible* grave of Miltiades (or Melchiades) has been discovered in a great sarcophagus not far from the region of Eusebius.

[3] *Supra*, p. 69.

ultimately placed with Zephyrinus in the great grave of the basilica called S. Sixtus and S. Cecilia [G]. The existence of the grave is proved by the epitaph of Damasus.

(6) "An innumerable multitude of Martyrs."—"The innumerable multitude of martyrs," "The eight hundred martyrs," and such expressions in several Itineraries might well refer to the great collection of skeletons found in recent excavations under the Crypt of S. Cecilia, and other similar *ossuaria* found elsewhere in the catacomb. These are probably not the bones of martyrs.

(7) Pope Mark.—The foundation of the basilica of Pope Mark [M on Plan IV] has been identified beneath the garden of the present Trappist Monastery.

(8) Hippolytus, Paulina, etc.—The names of Maria, Neo, and the following Greek martyrs—Hippolytus, Adrias and Paulina—occur in two epitaphs said to be by Damasus.

(9) Fides, Spes, Caritas.—A fragment of inscription has been found near the crypt of S. Cecilia bearing the words PISTIS (Greek form of Fides) SPES . . .[1]

(*b*). Praetextatus; (1) Shrine of Januarius.—Leaving now the shrines of Callixtus, where is the *Coemeterium Praetextati ad S. Januarium?* Excavating near the road almost opposite S. Callixtus, De Rossi discovered in 1863 a great crypt, adorned with lovely frescoes of the earliest period, representing the seasons. The wall was covered with the *graffiti* of the pilgrims, a trifle misspelt: *Give us refreshment, Januarius, Agatopus* (Agapitus), *Felicissimum* (Felicissimus) *Martyrs.* The shrine is certainly that of Januarius, son of S. Felicitas, martyred with his mother in 162.

(2) *Spelunca Magna,* with Felicissimus and Agapitus.—The *Spelunca Magna* of the Itineraries has been discovered in the great main artery of the catacomb, which begins at the modern entrance; and the walls covered with the pilgrims' inscriptions (*graffiti*) bear witness to the presence of revered shrines. Among the *graffiti* here may be read again the names *Felicissimus* and *Agapitus,* the deacons of Pope Sixtus II. and colleagues of S. Laurence, all martyred with the pope on the Via Appia in 258. Frag-

[1] *Supra,* p. 109.

ments also of the epitaph of Damasus in their honour, already known from the *Syllogae*, have been found here.

(3) **Quirinus (Cyrinus).**—An inscription of the fourth or fifth century bears the names of the last-mentioned saints associated with that of Quirinus ; and another, of the third century, bears the name *Yacinthus* (Hyacinthus) *Martyr*, who is not mentioned in any of the Itineraries as being on the Via Appia.[1]

A ruined crypt near the *Spelunca Magna*, might be the shrine of Quirinus, martyred under Hadrian.

(4) **Urban, Bishop.**—The tomb of the Bishop Urban (not the pope), connected with S. Cecilia, may be revealed by further excavations but is at present unknown.

(5) **? S. Zeno : also the Family of Cecilia.**—Above the cemeteries are remains of little chapels in one of which perhaps S. Zeno, a martyr of the third century, lay ; and doubtless in one of them the husband and relatives of S. Cecilia—Tiburtius, Valerianus, and Maximus. An inscription bearing the name of the *Caecilii* shows that the family of S. Cecilia was connected with the cemetery.

(*c.*) **Ad Catacumbas: Shrines of (1) SS. Peter and Paul.**—The third of the cemeteries is found quite near, on the west side of the Via Appia ; namely, the cemetery *Ad Catacumbas*, of the first century, situated beneath the Church of S. Sebastian, originally built in the fourth century. These catacombs are now called S. Sebastian. Here has been discovered a sepulchral chamber known as the Platonia. It serves as a confessional to the church above. In the middle of the Platonia is a great double compartment divided in the centre by a slab of marble, and capable of holding two sarcophagi. This discovery, together with various literary evidence, including that of an epitaph of Damasus preserved in a manuscript, leaves little doubt that the bodies of Peter and of Paul did indeed rest here, for a period, in 258, after being removed from their own famous cemeteries in the Vatican and on the Via Ostiensis to an

[1] The names *Hyacinthus* and *Protus* are found in the Itineraries for the Via Salaria Vetus : inscriptions to both these martyrs have been found there.

20

obscure burial-place during the confiscation and possible desecration of the cemeteries under Valerian.[1]

(2) Quirinus (Cyrinus), Bishop of Siscia.—Here also has been found the long inscription of the beginning of the fifth century of Cyrinus, the martyred Bishop of Siscia in Pannonia.

(3) S. Sebastian.—Under the altar in the crypt of the church has been identified the place of burial of S. Sebastian, the soldier, martyred under Diocletian about 290.

(4) Eutychius.—An inscription of Damasus commemorates the martyr Eutychius, whose tomb further excavations may bring to light.

The Syllogæ, as a Key to the Monuments; Via Ardeatina: Domitilla.—Nearly all the documents, and especially the *Syllogae*, are used in identifying the position of the *Coemiterium Domitillae Nerei et Achillei ad S. Petronellam Via Ardeatina* mentioned in the *Index* and referred to in the Itineraries under the last three names only.[2] As to Flavia Domitilla, history relates that she was wife of Clement, the consul (95), who was nephew of Vespasian; and she herself was a near relation of three emperors. Clement was executed in 96, and Flavia banished to the Isle of Pandataria (in the Pontian group near Capua and Terracina), both on a charge of atheism.[3]

The name of Flavia Domitilla is omitted from the Martyrology of Jerome, but those of Nereus and Achilleus are found there—*May 12. At Rome: the anniversary of Nereus and Achilleus;*—and there is an inscription to them in the Sylloge of Einsiedeln.[4]

---

[1] Barnes, *S. Peter in Rome.* The period was probably just over a year, and not forty years, as the Itineraries state.

[2] It is worth noting that in this fourth-century *Index* the primitive name, of the *owner*, is given, while it is omitted in all the Itineraries. See *supra*, p. 102. For Nereus and Achilleus see pp. 307 *et seqq.*

[3] A charge of "atheism" certainly indicates that Clement and his wife were Christians. In spite of the division between scholars as to the identity of Flavia Domitilla, and the supposition of *two* martyrs of the name (arising out of various confusions and later legends), there is little doubt, I think, that there was but *one* Flavia Domitilla. On the whole question see Bibliography—CATACOMBS.

[4] *I.C.* p. 31, No. 74.

Finally, the *Gesta Nerei et Achillei* [May 12], of the sixth century, relate,—amidst a wealth of imaginative detail as to Flavia Domitilla, Petronilla, and others,—that Nereus and Achilleus, servants of Flavia Domitilla, were exiled with her to the Pontian islands, and executed under Trajan at Terracina ; and that Auspicius, servant of Flavia Domitilla, brought them home by ship and "buried them in the property of Domitilla in the sand pits (*crypta arenaria*) on the Via Ardeatina, one mile and a half from the city, near the sepulchre in which was buried Petronella, daughter of S. Peter. This information," the writer adds, "we obtained from Auspicius himself!"

What corroboration is there of these statements in the facts revealed by excavation?

Excavations in Domitilla.—A small portion of a cemetery on the Via Ardeatina was already known to Bosio, in the seventeenth century, and believed by him to be part of Callixtus.

(1) Inscriptions of Flavia Domitilla.—Inscriptions, however, found here in the beginning of the nineteenth century, bearing the name of Flavia Domitilla, niece of Vespasian, and referring to rights of burial granted by her, made it clear that in this catacomb was the *Coemiterium Domitillae*, distinct from Callixtus.

(2) Vestibule of the Flavii.—Excavations here in 1864-1865 revealed the noble, classic *Vestibule of the Flavii*, built, as might have been expected, in the style of the first century, adorned with Pompeian frescoes, and containing remains of sarcophagi. De Rossi then began to search for the shrine of Nereus and Achilleus.

(3) Basilica of Nereus and Achilleus.—In 1873, built over a catacomb of the end of the first century (the date given for the martyrdom of Nereus and Achilleus), was discovered a basilica of the fourth century. Was this the required basilica? Two fragments[1] of an inscription were discovered, and De Rossi instantly identified them as forming part of the epitaph preserved in the Sylloge of Einsiedeln[2]

[1] Indicated by capitals in the quotation following.
[2] *I.C.* p. 31, No. 74.

(and in other *Syllogae*) and attributed there to the graves of Nereus and Achilleus:

In Sepulchro Nerei et Achillei in Via Appia.

> militiae nomen dederant saeVumque gerebant
> officium pariter spectantes jussA TYranni
> praeceptis pulsante metu serviRE PARati
> mira fides rerum subito posueRE FURORem
> CONversi fugiunt ducis impia castrA RELINQUUNt
> PROIiciunt clypeos phaleras telAQ . CRUENTA
> CONFEssi gaudent Christi portarE TRIUMFOS
> CREDITE Per Damasum possit quid GLORIA CHRISTI

The verses relate how Nereus and Achilleus, soldiers and servants of the emperor, flung down their arms and confessed the faith of Christ.

The basilica was therefore identified beyond doubt as that of Nereus and Achilleus, built, as we learn in the *Liber Pontificalis*, by Pope Siricius between 390 and 395. But still further proof of identity was forthcoming. On a little broken column, probably belonging to the ciborium, was a sculptured relief of an execution bearing the name ACILLEUS. No doubt there was a similar column with the name NEREUS.

(4) Fresco of Petronilla.—Just behind the apse was a crypt painted with the figure of a woman leading another into Paradise. Over the former is inscribed the name of the saint mentioned in the Itineraries, PETRONELLA MART(YR), over the latter, VENERANDA DEP VII. IDUS JANUARIAS (Veneranda, buried January 7).

(5) Actual Graves of Nereus, Achilleus, and Petronilla.—Excavations undertaken here in May 1910[1] have revealed what appear to be traces of the original tombs of Nereus and Achilleus, and of Petronilla, in a cubicle cut out of the tufa. In the same cemetery have been found a group of first-century epitaphs of Narcissus—possibly the Narcissus mentioned in S. Paul's letter (Rom. xvi. 11)—and others. A " Nereus " is also mentioned in that epistle (ver. 15). Can this be the martyred Nereus?

[1] *Nuovo Bullettino*, 1911, p. 82; 1912, p. 111. For further details we await Marucchi's book, to be published some time in 1913.

It has been suggested,[1] however, that Nereus and Achilleus may, in reality, have had no connexion with Domitilla herself, and that they probably perished in Diocletian's persecution, which fell very heavily on soldiers. This would account for the fact that their names are remembered, while those of earlier martyrs are forgotten. The epitaphs seem quite in harmony with this supposition.

Authenticity of the Traditions of SS. Nereus and Achilleus.—The excavations then show that in the first century there was on the Via Ardeatina a cemetery of Flavia Domitilla, and that in the fourth century there was a cult of Nereus and Achilleus, reputed to be martyrs, of sufficient strength to cause the erection of a basilica over the supposed site of burial. There seems little reason to doubt the existence of these martyrs, or that their bodies lay in the catacomb. Gregory the Great once preached a festival sermon in their honour in this chapel, and it was just about that period, two centuries later than the erection of the basilica, that the *Gesta* were compiled. These may have depended on an earlier tradition, or they may have grown up under the inspiration of the monument of the fourth century; but if the sculpture and fresco of the basilica were inspired by a true tradition, as seems not unlikely, the *Gesta* may contain considerable elements of truth. There seems every probability, however, that Aurelia Petronilla, as a kinswoman of the Aurelii and Flavii, derived her second name from the Flavii, several of whom bore the cognomen *Petro*. There is no proof of the truth of the assertion in the *Gesta* that she was a daughter (either natural or spiritual) of Peter, and probably her name misled the writer.[2]

Thus, by document and monument, we have established the existence of many primitive martyrs, the position of their graves, and the fact of a very primitive cult.

We have once or twice used the *Syllogae* in the investigations of the monuments.

---

[1] *Studi e Testi*, 1909, fasc. 3, p. 43 (with bibliography).

[2] In the Vatican is the sarcophagus brought from here by Pascal I. (817–824) with the inscription *To Aurelia Petronilla dearest maiden*. See *Bull. arch. crist.*, 1879, p. 5.

Syllogae as a Key to a North African Inscription.—An example of the identification or elucidation of *inscriptions* by means of the *Syllogae* is afforded by excavations undertaken in 1877 by Bosredon in Tebessa, in North Africa. In a church there he found,[1] among other things, seven fragments of inscriptions of the sixth century, which we give below as first published. Some of the letters were scarcely decipherable, but the discovery of the key has made it possible to supply them correctly.

<table>
<tr><td align="center">1</td><td align="center">2</td></tr>
<tr>
<td>. . . EMUNUS+AECLESIA
ABET UNA FIDES+DON
ET CURA PROBANTI+TIST</td>
<td>VITATI CEDEVET
OTADICARECLI
E SEDES CRISTO</td>
</tr>
<tr><td align="center">3</td><td align="center">4</td></tr>
<tr>
<td>CEDE PRIUS NOMEN
REGIALI TANTI . . RV
HAEC PETRI PAULI QU</td>
<td>RESUNUM DUO
OR CELIBRE . . .
V . . ENMICO</td>
</tr>
<tr><td align="center">5</td><td align="center">6</td></tr>
<tr>
<td>UDIU . . . VES
. . . U . . . NUS M
. . C S P . . .</td>
<td>USTAS
ET
LIBENTE RESURGIT</td>
</tr>
</table>

7

EX OFFICINA DI
DONATI ET SIC
IVISV

Bosredon was quite unable to interpret these inscriptions. De Rossi, however, perceived that they formed part of an inscription [2] (preserved in the *Syllogae*) which once stood in S. Peter's *ad Vincula*, and was written in honour of the chains of S. Peter. The fragments, after the correction of errors, rearranged in the order 3, 2, 6, 5, 4, 1, are indicated below in capital letters and the omissions supplied. It will be seen that the text so formed varies somewhat from that of the *Syllogae*.

[1] *Bull. arch. crist.*, 1878, p. 7.   [2] *I.C.* 67, p. 110, No. 67.

3	2	6

CEDE PRIUS NOMEN *n*OVITATI CEDE VET USTAS
REGIA LAETANTER V OTA DICARE LI BET
HAEC PETRI PAULIQU E SEDES CRISTO LIBENTE RESURGIT [1]

5	4	1

UNU*m q*UESO *pa*RES UNUM DUO *sumit*E MUNUS
UNUS H*on* OR CELIBRE*t q*|*uos h*ABET UNA FIDES
*pr*ESB*yteri tam*EN HIC *opus est* ET CURA PROBANTI [2]

7 (and end of 1)

probably gives the names of the donor of the church, of the consecrating bishop (*antistes*) and of the stonemason's yard (*officina*).[3]

Combination of Documentary and Monumentary Evidence : Life of Damasus (1) in the *Liber Pontificalis*.—

Finally, as an illustration of the method of writing history from the combined evidence of document and monument, we will attempt to establish a few facts as to the life of Pope Damasus[4] in addition to those recorded in the brief biography of the *Liber Pontificalis*.

(2) In the *Epigrammata Damasi*.—

Of the numerous inscriptions made by Damasus,[5] one or two are of an autobiographical character.

(3) Inscription referring to Damasus' Father.—

Several facts about his father are recorded in an inscription[6] which Damasus composed for the portico adjoining the Church of S. Laurence *in Damaso* (near the Theatre

---

[1] This line has been expanded in the African version in a manner disastrous to the metre, and the following pentameter line of the Roman version, referring to Pope Sixtus III., entirely omitted for obvious reasons.

[2] The name of *Probantius*, author of the African work, is substituted for *Philippus* of the Roman inscription.

[3] In the same district were found some more fragmentary inscriptions, which, correctly pieced together, formed the well-known lines (preserved in the *Syllogae*, *I.C.* p. 145, No. 6), *Justitiae Sedes*, which stood in the apse of S. Peter's : *Bull. arch. crist.*, 1879, p. 163.

[4] The facts of Damasus' life are still obscure, and the evidence, literary and monumental, a subject of lively discussion. For a summary of the whole question see E. Barker, *S. Callixtus . . .* in *Journal of Roman Studies*, i. pt. i., 1911. See especially *Nuovo Bullettino*, 1903, p. 59 ; also *Bull. arch. crist.*, 1881 (p. 48), 1883 (62), 1884–5 ; Rade, *Damasus Bischof von Rom.*, 1882.

[5] *Supra*, pp. 279, 280, 283, 288–293, 301, 306.

[6] Quoted above, p. 289 (*I.C.* p. 151, No. 23).

of Pompey), which was built by him on the probable site of his father's house. In the time of Hadrian I. (772–795) the body of Damasus himself was removed to this church, as is recorded in the *Liber Pontificalis*.

Previous to this, as all the documents record, he was buried, together with his mother and sister, on the Via Ardeatina, in a basilica which he had himself built.

(4) Epitaph to Himself.—For himself he wrote the beautiful inscription recording his belief in the resurrection, which has been preserved in the *Syllogae*.[1]

(5) Epitaph to his Mother, Laurentia.—The name of his mother, and the inscription to her, were unknown till in 1902–3 Mgr. Wilpert discovered, exactly on the spot indicated by the Itineraries as the burial-place of Damasus [P, on Plan IV.], the *impression* on a great slab of what proved to be the lost epitaph.

HIC DAMASI MATER POSUIT LAURentia membra
QUAE FUIT IN TERRIS CENTUM MINUS octo per annos
SEXAGINTA DEO VIXIT POST FOEdera sancta
PROGENIE QUARTA VIDIT QUAE laeta nepotes

From this we gather that Laurentia, the mother of Damasus, lived to be ninety-two ; that she dedicated herself to God, *i.e.* lived as a widow or virgin for sixty years after taking holy vows (of virginity); that one of her children at least (exclusive of Damasus, and, as we shall see, of her daughter Irene) had grandchildren. At her great age, also, she must have lived to see her son pope, and probably survived her husband. It is clear that she died before Damasus (who, as we know, lived to be nearly eighty), since he wrote her epitaph.

Further, at a few yards from this spot, was discovered a fragmentary inscription of four letters :

A

NOS

Comparing this with the impressed inscription, Mgr. Wilpert saw that this fragment was a piece of the original

---

[1] *Supra*, p. 290. The reference there to *Martae* . . . *sorori* (sc. of Lazarus) has led to a mistake in the Itinerary *De Locis Sanctorum Martyrum*, where we read : *Prope (Viam Ardeatinam) Damasus papa depositus est et soror euis* Martha.

inscription, fitting in at the end of the first two lines (membrA, anNOS).

So much for the mother of Damasus. But we can learn something more about his family.

(6) And to his Sister, Irene.—Through the destruction of monuments, and the removal of material for building purposes, and for other reasons, many inscriptions have been discovered far from their original locality. It is in the Church of SS. Cosmas and Damian in the Roman Forum that Marucchi discovered, in 1880, a minute fragment of an inscription [1] (indicated in capitals in the following quotation), identified—thanks again to the *Syllogae*,[2] where it had been preserved—as forming part of the inscription of Irene, the sister of Damasus, which once stood on the Via Ardeatina:

> hoc tumulo sacrata DEO NUnc membra quiescunt
> hic soror est DAmasi noMEN SI QUAeris Irene
> voverat haec sese ChristO CUM VITA MAneret
> virginis ut meritum sanCTUS PUDOR IPSe probaret
> bis denas hiemes necdum complevERAT aetas . . .

. . . .

> In this tomb now lie her limbs, consecrated to God : here is the sister of Damasus : her name was Irene. As long as life lasted she vowed herself to Christ, that her holy purity should bring her the merit of virginity. Her days had not yet reached to twice ten winters (sc. she was not yet twenty) . . .

The rest is a eulogy of Irene.

Hence Actual Identification of Damasus' Father with Leo, the Bishop.—It is the double source (1) of the *Syllogae* which enable us to interpret the fragmentary inscriptions we are about to discuss, and (2) the sum of the knowledge concerning Damasus, derived from the inscriptions quoted above, which will enable us to identify the *subject* of another inscription, and so fill up some lacunae in the life of Damasus.

There existed, in the *Syllogae*, an inscription of Damasus,[3]

---

[1] *Nuovo Bullettino*, 1903, p. 82.   [2] *I.C.* p. 104, No. 42.

[3] *I.C.* p. 92, No. 62. The capitals in the following quotation indicate the actual inscription.

of which the *first* half of nearly every line was missing. In 1881 in the Agro Verano, near S. Laurence on the Via Tiburtina, was found an inscription in which the *last* half of the lines was missing: these two fragmentary inscriptions were fitted together, and the whole now reads:

OMNIA QUAEQue vides proprio quaesita labore
CUM MIHI GENTILis jamdudum vita maneret
INSTITUI CUPIENS CENSUM COgnoscere mundi
JUDICIO POST MULTA DEI MELIora secUTUS
CONTEMPTIS OPIBUS MALui cognoSCERE CHRIStum
HAEC MIHI CURA FUIT NUDOs vestIRE PETENTES
FUNDERE PAUPERIBUS QUIDQuid concESSERAT ANNUS

Immediately after these lines in the *Syllogae*, and forming part of the same inscription, were the lines following, of which also the original inscription had been found in 1857 in the same place as the inscription *Omnia quaeque*, to which it belongs:

PSALLERE ET IN POPULIS VOLUI Modulante PROPHETA
SIC MERUI PLEBEM CHRISTI RETIneRE SACERDOS
HUNC MIHI COMPOSUIT TUMULUM LAURENTIA CONJUX
MORIBUS APTA MEIS SEMPER VENERANDA FIDELIS
INVIDIA INFELIX TANDEM COMPRESSA QUIESCIT
OCTOGINTA LEO TRANSCENDIT EPISCOPUS ANNOS
DEP. DIE PRID. IDUS MARTIAS

Translated, the two inscriptions ran:

Everything which you see was acquired by my own toil while my life was that of a pagan (? *gentilis*). At first I desired to know the ways of the world: after much experience, by the judgment of God, I pursued worthier objects, and despising wealth chose rather to know Christ. My care was to clothe the naked who asked, to lavish on the poor whatever the year had yielded. I desired to perform the office of chanter and reader before the people. So as a priest I deserved to govern the people of Christ. My wife Laurentia made this tomb for me: her way of life was in harmony with mine: she was honourable and faithful. Cruel envy at length lies crushed and still. Leo the bishop lived over eighty years and was buried March 14.

If we compare this epitaph with that to Laurentia, mother

of Damasus; and with the inscription (*Hinc pater exceptor*) [1] referring to his unnamed father; the thought at once arises that Leo, the bishop of the *Omnia quaeque* epitaph, is none other than the father of Damasus. The biography of Leo the bishop, as here given, closely resembles that of Damasus' father. They both "chose the better way" (cf. *melioribus actis* with *meliora secutus*). It was evidently in fulfilment of his office as reader (*lector*) and deacon (*levita*) that Leo, as also the father of Damasus, chanted in church, cared for the poor, and looked after the accounts (*quidquid concesserat annus*). Both, too, are called *sacerdos*, a word often used of a *bishop*,[2] and Leo is actually called *bishop* as well. Each, too, had a wife Laurentia. These similarities seem sufficient proof of the identity of Damasus' father with Leo the bishop.[3]

If this identification is correct—and if then Leo died at over eighty and Laurentia at ninety-two, it is clear that the words of Laurentia's epitaph *deo vixit . . . sexaginta annos . . . post foedera sacra* refer, not to widowhood, but to a state of virginity. Does not the *moribus apta meis* of Leo's epitaph refer to this fact? And is not the *reason* for it supplied in the fact that "bishops, priests (*presbyteri*) and deacons (*diacones*) and all clerks" were compelled to separate from their wives by a canon of the Council of Elvira in 306?[4] Again, the *invidia infelix* appears to refer to the calumnies to which Damasus was subject even before his accession to the papacy.[5]

The Tradition of S. Cecilia and the Excavations.— In dealing with the *Gesta* and the traditions of the martyrs it has often been noted that even documents of little or no historical value—such as the *Acta Petri*,[6] the Passions of Procopius,[7] Pope Cornelius,[8] Nereus and Achilleus, Sebastian

---

[1] *Supra*, pp. 288-289. See Marucchi, *Nuovo Bullettino*, 1903, for this identification.

[2] *Supra*, p. 289, note 1.

[3] It is true that the name of Damasus' father is given as *Antonius* in the *Liber Pontificalis*. This, however, is the name of the *gens*, while Leo is either the cognomen, or the new name adopted by the convert on baptism.

[4] Labbé, *Concilia*, i. col. 1231, canon 33.   [5] *Lib. Pont.* (*sub* Damaso).

[6] *Supra*, pp. 194, 202.   [7] *Supra*, p. 195.   [8] *Supra*, pp. 69, 200.

—are usually correct as to the existence of a martyr and the place of his shrine ; as has been repeatedly shown by excavation and other sources of information. It is seldom, of course, that the actual body of the saint has been seen in comparatively modern times. There is, however, this proof of the truth of the tradition of S. Cecilia,[1] whose story, as told in her apocryphal Acts, has already been substantiated in some points by the monuments.

The Passion relates that Cecilia, after her martyrdom in her private house in the Trastevere, was buried in the crypt of the Caecilii in S. Callixtus. The house was excavated by Cardinal Rampolla in 1900. The crypt was long an object of pilgrimage in primitive times.

In the ninth century, during the removal of the bodies of the martyrs from the Catacombs to the urban churches, Pope Pascal sought in vain for that of S. Cecilia, which should have been near the papal crypt of S. Callixtus. We read in the "false diploma of Pascal I.," and also in the *Liber Pontificalis* (with slight variations of detail), how Pascal fell asleep in S. Peter's during Matins—sung usually soon after midnight—and dreamed that S. Cecilia appeared to him, and told him that he had already been so near her body that she might have spoken to him. Pascal, searching again, found the sarcophagus; which, as excavations have revealed, was blocked up by a wall raised to conceal it from the Lombards. He opened it, and found within the body of the martyr, "robed in gold tissue with linen clothes steeped in blood at her feet." The body was placed in S. Cecilia in the Trastevere, a church built over her house, dating from the fourth century, and rebuilt by this same Pascal I.

In 1599, on the occasion of again rebuilding S. Cecilia's Church, Sfondrati, its titular Cardinal opened the sarcophagus. In it was found the embalmed body of S. Cecilia, wrapt in cloth of gold with the blood-stained garments at her feet. "She was not lying upon her back like a body in a tomb, but upon the right side like a virgin in

---

[1] There is an excellent account of the entire subject in Cabrol, *Dict. Arch. Chrét.*

her bed, with her knees modestly drawn together, and seemingly asleep."

Pope Clement VIII. and all Rome flocked to see the body ; and before the tomb was closed again Maderno sculptured the marble portrait which now stands over her grave, and inscribed it with the words : " Behold the body of the most holy virgin Cecilia, whom I myself saw lying incorrupt in her tomb. In this marble I have made for you the image of that saint, in the very posture in which I saw her."

In Festo Omnium Sanctorum. 1912.

Gratia par cunctis, sanctus labor omnibus unus
dissona verba quidem sed tamen una fides.

FINIS.

PART II.—APPENDICES

ABBREVIATIONS

ACTA APOST. APOC. .	Lipsius, *Acta Apostolorum Apocrypha.*
ANAL. BOLL. . .	*Analecta Bollandiana.*
A.S.	Ruinart, *Acta Sincera.*
A.SS. . . .	*Acta Sanctorum* of the Bollandists.
BULL. ARCH. CRIST.	*Bullettino di archeologia cristiana.*
CABROL, DICT. . .	Cabrol, *Dictionnaire d'archéologie chrétienne et de liturgie.*
CORP. SCRIPT. LAT. .	*Corpus Scriptorum Ecclesiasticorum Latinorum.*
FUNK . . .	See *PP. Apost.*
H.E.	*Historia Ecclesiastica.*
I.C.	De Rossi, *Inscriptiones Christianae,* vol. ii.
L.P.	*Liber Pontificalis,* ed. Duchesne.
MIGNE . . .	See *P.G.* and *P.L.*
MOMBRITIUS . .	Mombritius, *Sanctuarium.*
MON. GERM. HIST. .	*Monumenta Germaniae Historica.*
N.B.	*Nuovo bullettino di archeologia cristiana.*
NEUES ARCHIV .	*Neues Archiv der Gesellschaft für ältere deutsche Geschichtskunde.*
P.G.	Migne, *Patrologia Graeca.*
P.L.	,, ,, *Latina.*
PP. APOST. . .	Funk, *Opera Patrum Apostolicorum.*
RÖM. QUART. . .	*Römische Quartalschrift.*
R.S.	De Rossi, *Roma Sotterranea.*
SURIUS . . .	Surius, *De probatis Sanctorum Historiis.*

I. BIBLIOGRAPHY [1]

A. GENERAL BIBLIOGRAPHY

1. (a) DICTIONARIES AND (b) HISTORY

(a) DICTIONARIES

*H. WACE and W. PIERCY [2]	A Dictionary of Christian Biography and Literature, to the End of the Sixth Century, 1 vol. London, 1911.
W. SMITH and H. WACE	A Dictionary of Christian Biography, 4 vols. London, 1877–1887. (Up to Charlemagne.)
*F. CABROL, O.S.B. .	Dictionnaire d'Archéologie chrétienne et de Liturgie. Paris, 1907. In progress. (The best dictionary for this subject.)
F. KRAUS . . .	Real-Encyklopädie der Christlichen Alter-thümer, 2 vols. Freiburg-im-Breisgau, 1880–1886.
W. SMITH and S. CHEETHAM	Dictionary of Christian Antiquities, 2 vols. London, 1875–1880.

Catholic Encyclopedia, 15 vols. New York, 1907. In progress.

DU CANGE and DUFRESNE	Glossarium mediae et infimae Latinitatis (ed. Favre), 10 vols. Niort, 1883–1887.
A. POTTHAST . .	Bibliotheca historica medii aevi, 2 vols. Berlin, 1896.

(b) HISTORY

BARDENHEWER, DUCHESNE, HARNACK, PFLEIDERER have all much to contribute on this period. A few books only are mentioned below. Compare Bibliography—ACTS OF MARTYRS.

[1] In Section A a few books only are mentioned, as likely to be most helpful to the student. But a reference to any one will give a full bibliography of the subject. It is hoped that Section B is practically complete, except for the bibliography of the Acts of the Martyrs, which is too vast, and of which a portion only bears on the history of the first three centuries. Reference is given to English translations (where they exist) of foreign works. Works of especial importance are indicated by a star.

[2] This is an abbreviated edition of that issued in 4 vols. in 1877.

A. HARNACK . . 1. *The Mission and Expansion of the Church in the first Three Centuries* (translation by J. MOFFATT, in Theological Translation Library), 2 vols. London, 1908.

„ . . 2. *The Constitution and Law of the Church in the first Two Centuries* (translation by F. POGSON, in Crown Theological Library), 1 vol. London, 1910.

A. HARNACK and 3. *Texte und Untersuchungen zur Geschichte*
GEBHARDT *der Altchristlichen Literatur*, 35 vols. Leipsic, 1883. In progress.

O. PFLEIDERER . *Primitive Christianity* (translation by W. MONTGOMERY, Theological Translation Library), 1 vol. London, 1911.

Cambridge Mediaeval History, planned by J. B. BURY. Vol. i. *The Christian Roman Empire and the Foundation of the Teutonic Kingdoms.* Cambridge, 1911. In progress. (There is much that is useful here. Bibliography.)

F. X. FUNK . . *Manual of Church History*, 2 vols. (English translation by L. CAPPADELTA. London, 1910.) (A useful brief general history with Bibliography. Vol i. goes up to the Middle Ages.)

*Mgr. L. DUCHESNE . *Histoire ancienne de l'Église*, 3 vols. Paris, 1908–1910. (Fourth edition.) (Transl., *The Early History of the Christian Church*, 1 vol. London, 1909–1912.)

* „ . *Origines du culte chrétien.* Paris, 1898.[1] (Transl., M'Clure, *Christian Worship: a Study of the Latin Liturgy up to the Time of Charlemagne.* London, S.P.C.K., 1912.) (These two books form the foundation of any study of the subject.)

E. LUCIUS . . *Die Anfänge des Heiligenkults in der christlichen Kirche.* Tübingen, 1904.

H. DELEHAYE, S.J. . *Les Origines du culte des martyrs.* Brussels, 1912.

CH. DE SMEDT . . 1. "L'organisation des églises chrétiennes jusqu'au milieu du IIIᵉ siècle," in *Revue des Questions historiques*, t. 44, p. 329. Paris, 1888.

„ . . 2. "L'organisation des églises chrétiennes au IIIᵉ siècle," in *Revue des Questions historiques*, t. 47. Paris, 1891. (Also printed separately.)

See also HARTMANN GRISAR in Bibliography—ITINERARIES. For Papal Correspondence and Councils, see Bibliography—PATRISTIC.

---

[1] Fourth edition in 1908.

21

2. PATRISTIC

(a) TEXTS

MIGNE . . . *Patrologiae Cursus Completus*, containing
Patrologia Latina and *Patrologia Graeca*,
387 vols. Paris, 1850–1884.
(Most useful for general reference. Contains a vast number of texts of Fathers from
the second century, councils, martyrologies,
liturgies, etc., with indices. For *critical*
study, some of the texts indicated below are
necessary.)

*Die Griechischen Christlichen Schriftstellern der ersten drei Jahrhun-
derte*, 19 vols. Leipsic, 1902. In progress.
(Excellent critical German edition, with
contributions by MOMMSEN, etc.)

*Corpus Scriptorum Ecclesiasticorum Latinorum. Vienna, 1866. In
progress.
(Tertullian, Augustine, Ambrose, etc.)

F. X. FUNK . 1. *Opera Patrum Apostolicorum*, 2 vols. Tübingen, 1881.

„ . 2. *Die Apostolischen Väter*, 1 vol. Tübingen and
Leipsic, 1901.
(These volumes contain texts of several
of the Apostolic Fathers, with some Latin
translations of Greek texts, and criticisms.
Also a few *Acta Martyrum*.)

GEBHARDT, HARNACK, *Patrum Apostolicorum Opera*, 4 vols. Leipsic,
and ZAHN 1876–1878.
(Texts in Latin and Greek.)

*LIGHTFOOT . . *Apostolic Fathers*, 6 vols. London, 1890.
(Text, translation and critical notes.)

Compare also ARMITAGE ROBINSON in *Texts and Studies*,
Cambridge, 1891 ; Mrs. GIBSON and Mrs. LEWIS on the *Didascalia* ;
HARNACK on the *Didaché*, etc.

P. F. KEHR . . *Regesta Pontificum Romanorum*, 2 vols. Berlin,
1906–1907.

PH. JAFFÉ . . *Regesta Pontificum Romanorum*, 2 vols. Leipsic, 1885–1888.

A. THIEL . . . *Epistolae Romanorum Pontificum*, 1 vol. 1868.

J. D. MANSI . . *Sacrorum Conciliorum Collectio*, 31 vols.
Florence, 1759–1798. Reprint, Paris, 1901.
In progress.

Cf. LABBÉ, HARDOUIN, HEFELE, and QUENTIN (*Jean-Dominique
Mansi et les grandes collections conciliaires.* Paris, 1900). For trans-
lations, see Bibliography: PATRISTIC—Translations, under WACE and
SCHAFF.

M. J. ROUET DE JOURNEL, S.J. . . *Enchiridion Patristicum*
H. DENZINGER (ed. C. BANNWART), S.J. .   „   *Symbolorum*
C. KIRCH, S.J. . . . . .   „   *Fontium*
                                        Historiae
            3 vols. London (Herder), 1910.

(*b*) TRANSLATIONS

A. ROBERTS and   *The Ante-Nicene Christian Library*, 25 vols.
   J. DONALDSON   Edinburgh, 1867–1872 and 1897.
                  (From Clement of Rome to Origen.)
E. B. PUSEY . . *Library of the Fathers of the Holy Catholic Church previous to the Division of East and West*, 49 vols. Oxford, 1837–1850.
*PH. SCHAFF . . *Select Library of the Nicene and Post-Nicene Fathers of the Christian Church.* First Series. 14 vols. New York, 1892.
*H. WACE and *Select Library of the Nicene and Post-Nicene
   PH. SCHAFF   Fathers of the Christian Church.* New Series. 14 vols. Oxford, 1890–1900. In progress. (Vol. xiv. is *The Seven Œcumenical Councils of the Undivided Church.*) (Cf. under " Texts," ARMITAGE ROBINSON, LIGHTFOOT.)
*O. BARDENHEWER . *Patrology: The Lives and Works of the Fathers of the Church.* 1 vol. Freiburg-im-Breisgau, 1908. (Eng. trans. by T. SHAHAN. An invaluable history with bibliography.)

3. ARCHAEOLOGY

(*a*) GENERAL

*G. B. DE ROSSI . *Inscriptiones Christianae urbis Romae vii° saeculo antiquiores*, 2 vols. Rome, 1857–1888.
*O. MARUCCHI . . *Epigrafia Cristiana.* Milan, 1910. (Eng. trans. by J. A. WILLIS. A most useful little volume.)
H. GRISAR   . . *Analecta Romana*, 2 vols. Rome, 1899. (A useful Collection of Dissertations on the Texts and Monuments of Rome.)

*H. LECLERCQ, O.S.B. *Manuel d'Archéologie Chrétienne*, 2 vols. Paris, 1907.
(Best general introduction to the subject.)

P. SYXTUS (SCAGLIA), O.C.R. *Notiones Archaeologiae Christianae*, vol. i. pars prior. Rome, 1908.
(Useful, up-to-date volume. Compare his other works, including a fine plan of the Catacomb of S. Callixtus.)

*O. MARUCCHI . . *Éléments d'Archéologie Chrétienne*. Paris, 1903. (Cf. his other works.)

(b) CATACOMBS

*G. B. DE ROSSI . *Roma Sotterranea Cristiana*, 2 vols. Rome, 1864–1867.
(The foundation of every other work on the subject.)

J. S. NORTHCOTE and W. BROWNLOW *Roma Sotterranea*, 2 vols. London, 1879.
(A condensed translation of De Rossi. Though of necessity in some respects out of date, this remains a most useful volume.)

O. MARUCCHI . . 1. *Roma Sotterranea Cristiana*. Nuova Serie. Vols. i. and ii. *Domitilla*. Rome, 1909–1913. (In progress.)

*   „   . . 2. *Le Catacombe Romane*, 1 vol. Rome, 1903.
(The best general account.)

Mgr. J. WILPERT . 1. *Die Papstgräben und die Cäciliengruft in der Katakombe des Hl. Kallistus*. Freiburg-im-Breisgau, 1909.
(Trans., *La Cripta dei Papi*. Rome 1910.)
(A most important work, including the most recent discoveries.)

*   „   . . 2. *Die Malereien der Katakomben Roms*, 2 vols. Freiburg-im-Breisgau, 1903.
(Trans., *Le Pitture delle Catacombe Romane*.)
(A magnificent volume of plates of frescoes already vanishing from the walls, with a volume of text of interpretations of frescoes. Compare WILPERT'S numerous other works.)

(Compare also DE ROSSI'S publication, *Bullettino di Archeologia Cristiana*, 1863–1894; and the continuation under MARUCCHI as *Nuovo Bullettino di Archeologia Cristiana*.[1] Rome, 1895. In

[1] Especially P. CROSTAROSA, "Noztiie storico-topografiche delle Catacombe Romane," in *Nuovo Bullettino di Archeologia Cristiana*, 1900, p. 321; being a useful description of the Catacombs, with a *plan showing their position relative to the roads.

progress. DE WAAL, *Römische Quartalschrift für christliche Alterthumskunde.* Rome, 1887. In progress. ACHELIS, "Die römischen Katakomben," in *Zeitschrift für die Neutestamentische Wissenschaft* (1911–1912), Giessen. In progress. All up-to-date information appears in the *Nuovo Bullettino* and *Römische Quartalschrift.* See also under Bibliography—ARCHAEOLOGY—General.

B. THE DOCUMENTS

1. LIBER PONTIFICALIS

(a) TEXT AND HISTORY

*Mgr. L. DUCHESNE . 1. *Liber Pontificalis,* 2 vols. Paris, 1886–1892. In "Bibliothèque des écoles françaises d'Athènes et de Rome." (Texts, critical notes, and complete historical introduction.)

" . 2. "Le *Liber Pontificalis* en Gaule," in *Mélanges d'archéologie et d'histoire,* 1882, p. 227.

T. MOMMSEN . . *Gestorum Pontificum Romanorum vol. i.: Libri Pontificalis pars prior.* Berlin, 1898, in *Monumenta Germaniae Historica.*

The BOLLANDISTS . *Acta Sanctorum, Propylaeum Maii.* Antwerp, 1685. (Text.)

ANASTASIUS BIBLIO-THECARIUS *De Vitis Romanorum Pontificum,* in Migne, *P.L.,* t. 127 and 128. (Text.)

H. GRISAR . . 1. *Analecta Romana,* t. i. Rome, 1899. (Excellent outline of the history of the *Liber Pontificalis,* following DUCHESNE'S theory.)

" . 2. "Der *Liber Pontificalis,*" in *Zeitschrift für Katholische Theologie,* vol. xi. p. 417. 1887.

F. G. ROSENFELD . *Ueber die Komposition des* Liber Pontificalis *bis zu Konstantin.* Marburg, 1896.

G. WAITZ . . . 1. "Ueber die verschiedenen Texte des *Liber Pontificalis,*" in *Neues Archiv der Gesellschaft für ältere deutsche Geschichtskunde,* 1879, p. 216. Hanover.

" . . 2. "Ueber den sogenannten *Catalogus Cononianus* der Päpste," *ibid.* 1884, p. 457.

" . . 3. "Ueber die Italienischen Handschriften des *Liber Pontificalis,*" *ibid.* 1885, p. 445.

G. WAITZ . . 4. "Ueber den sogenannten *Catalogus Felicianus* der Päpste," *ibid.* 1886, p. 217.

(*b*) THE PHILOCALIAN CALENDAR

*DUCHESNE . . *Op. cit., supra.*

*T. MOMMSEN . 1. *Chronographus anni cccliv* (i.e. Philocalian Calendar), in *Monumenta Germaniae Historica*, t. ix. (also called *Chronica Minora*, t. i.). Berlin, 1892.
(Text and notes.)

* „ . 2. "Ueber den Chronographen vom Jahre 354," in *Abhandlung der phil. hist. Classe der königlichen sächsischen Gesellschaft der Wissenschaften.*
(An illuminating study of the Philocalian Calendar, with a nearly complete text.)

„ . 3. *Corpus Inscriptionum Latinarum*, ed. MOMMSEN, i. p. 332.
(Text of Pagan Calendar in the Philocalian Calendar.)

MIGNE . . . *Patrologia Latina*, 13, col. 442 and 675.
(For Pagan Calendar.)

H. JORDAN and CH. HUELSEN
Topographie der Stadt Rom im Alterthum, Bd. ii. Berlin, 1871.
(Text of the geographical portion of the Calendar, i.e. the *Notitia Regionum xiv urbis Romae.*)

(*c*) PAPAL CHRONOLOGY

*A. BARNES . . *S. Peter in Rome.* London, 1906.
(The author discusses the whole Petrine question in the light of evidence, literary and monumental. He arrives at the same conclusion as Harnack, Lightfoot, and most modern scholars, that S. Peter was bishop of Rome, and was martyred there.)

*LIGHTFOOT . . *Apostolic Fathers*, pt. i. vol. i. p. 201. London, 1890.
(With bibliography and critical study of the Philocalian (Liberian) Calendar and Chronicle of Hippolytus.)

TH. MOMMSEN . "Ordo et spatia episcoporum Romanorum in Libro Pontificali," in *Neues Archiv*, vol. 21 p. 335. 1896.

R. A. LIPSIUS . 1. "Neue Studien zur Papstchronologie," in the *Jahrbuch für protestantische Theologie*, 1879, p. 385 ; 1880, p. 78 and p. 233.

LIPSIUS . . 2. *Chronologie der römischen Bischöfe, bis zur Mitte des vierten Jahrhunderts.* Kiel, 1869.
(Also contains a text of the papal biographies in the Philocalian Calendar.)

„ . . 3. *Die Papstverzeichnisse des Eusebios und der von ihm abhängigen Chronisten.* Kiel, 1868.

A. HARNACK . 1. "Die älteste christliche Datirung und die Anfänge einer bischöflichen Chronographie in Rom," in *Acta Minora.* (Academy of Berlin), 1892, pp. 617–658.

„ . 2. "Die Zeit des Ignatius," in *Jahrbuch für protesiantische Theologie.* Leipsic, 1880.

SEGNA . . . *De Successione Romanorum Pontificum.* Rome, 1897.

Cf. KEHR, JAFFÉ, THIEL in Bibliography—PATRISTIC.

2. THE ITINERARIES

(a) GENERAL TOPOGRAPHY AND PLANS

*HARTMANN GRISAR *Geschichte Roms und der Päpste im Mittelalter,* 3 vols. Freiburg, 1901.
(English translation, *History of Rome and the Popes in the Middle Ages,* by LUIGI CAPPADELTA. London, 1911.)
(Gives an admirable general idea of the topography of Rome, Christian and secular ; and of the history and the thought of the first five centuries : there is a plan (see *supra,* Plan I.), and full references to original authorities and to recent publications. The best introduction to more specialised studies.)

O. RICHTER . . *Topographie von Rom,* published in series *Handbuch der Klassischen Alterthums-Wissenschaft,* dritter Band, dritte Abtheilung. Munich, 1897.
(Good general topography and text of *Notitia Regionum xiv* with plans.)

H. JORDAN . . *Topographie der Stadt Rom im Alterthum,* zweiter Band. 2 Bde. Berlin, 1871–1907.

*R. LANCIANI . . *Forma Urbis Romae,* published by the " Regia Accademia Lyncaeorum " (ed. Hoepli, Milan).
(A magnificent series of forty-six large plans of Rome — pagan, Christian, and

modern, scale 1 : 1000; an indispensable companion to the Itineraries, etc., dealing with the interior of the city.)

*CH. HUELSEN and   *Forma Urbis Romae Antiquae.* Berlin, new
H. KIEPERT   edition, 1912.

(Plans, with Christian churches, the Fourteen Regions, etc., with alphabetical index and bibliography of monuments, both ancient and modern.)

CH. HUELSEN .   . *Romae Veteris Tabula.* Berlin, 1901.
AUGUST SCHNEIDER *Das alte Rom.* Leipsic, 1896.

(Five series of historical Maps of Rome, giving idea of general topography.)

C. A. J. SKEEL   . *Travel in the First Century after Christ.* Cambridge, 1901.

Compare also DE ROSSI, *Roma Sotterranea,* and CROSTAROSA, under Bibliography—CATACOMBS.

(b) GENERAL TEXTS

DE ROSSI.   .   . *Roma Sotterranea Cristiana,* i. pp. 128–183. Rome, 1864.

(Texts of Itineraries in parallel columns arranged according to the roads.[1] The easiest form in which to grasp them. *Good account of the documents.)

*C. L. URLICHS.   . *Codex Urbis Romae Topographicus.* Würzburg, 1871.

(Most useful volume of documents referring to topography of Rome ; contains nearly all the texts mentioned in chaps. vii. and viii. of this book.)

H. JORDAN   .   . *Topographie der Stadt Rom im Alterthum,* zweiter Band. 2 Bde. Berlin, 1871.

(Text of ITINERARIES on p. 537. In the *erster Band, dritte Abtheilung,* revised by HUELSEN, Berlin, 1907, are some useful plans, with the Regions, churches, roads.)

(c) MONOGRAPHS

I. *NOTITIA XIV REGIONUM*

O. RICHTER   .   . In *Topographie von Rom.* (See General Topography.)

---

[1] The same text is given in Scaglia, *Notiones Archeologiae Christianae,* i. p. 441, n a convenient little volume. See *supra,* p. 324.

II. *LATERCULUS POLEMII SILVII*

TH. MOMMSEN . *Monumenta Germaniae Historica auctorum antiquorum t. ix. (Chronicorum Minorum,* t. i.), p. 345. Berlin, 1892.

III. *INDEX COEMITERIORUM*

Cardinal RAMPOLLA. " Di un Catalogo cimiteriale Romano," in *Atti del II° ⋯⋯⋯⋯ Internazionale.* Rome, 1902.

DE ROSSI. . . In *Bullettino di archeologia cristiana,* 1878. Rome.

STEVENSON . . In *Nuovo Bullettino di archeologia cristiana,* 1897. Rome.

IV. *PAPYRI OF MONZA*

*A. SEPULCRI . . *I Papiri della Basilica di Monza e le reliquie inviate da Roma.* Milan, 1903, being a paper read before the " Congresso Storico Internazionale della Societa storica Lombarda."
(Text, photographs of the papyri, criticism, and full bibliography.)

G. BONAVENIA. . *La Silloge di Verdun e il papiro di Monza.* Rome, 1903.
(A good general account.)

V. *ITINERARIUM MALMESBURIENSE*

T. DUFF-HARDY . *Willelmi Malmesburiensis monachi Gesta regum Anglorum.* London, 1840.

VI. *ITINERARIUM EINSIEDLENSE*

*R. LANCIANI . . " L' Itinerario di Einsiedeln," in *Monumenti Antichi* of the Accademia dei Lincei, vol. i. p. 436. Milan, 1890.
(Plans, bibliography, etc. A most illuminating study of an Itinerary.)

CH. HUELSEN . . *La pianta di Roma dell' anonimo Einsiedlense.* Rome, 1907.
(Contains two good plans of Rome under the Empire,—one with the roads and cemeteries.)

VII. *ORDO ROMANUS* OF BENEDICT AND *MIRABILIA URBIS ROMAE*

R. LANCIANI . . *Op. cit., supra.*

3. ACTS OF THE MARTYRS[1]

(a) GENERAL HISTORY

P. ALLARD . 1. *Histoire des persécutions.* 4 vols. Paris, 1892–1898.

„ . 2. *Ten Lectures on the Martyrs.*
(English translation by L. CAPPADELTA. 1 vol. London, 1907. In the International Catholic Library.)

H. DOULCET . . *Essai sur les rapports de l'église chrétienne avec l'état romain.* Paris, 1883.
(With bibliography and chronological tables.)

B. AUBÉ . . 1. *Histoire des persécutions de l'église jusqu'à la fin des Antonins.* Paris, 1875.

„ . . 2. *Histoire des persécutions de l'église : la polemique païenne à la fin du second siècle.* Paris, 1878.

„ . . 3. *Les Chrétiens dans l'Empire romain de la fin des Antonins au milieu du IIIᵉ siècle* (A.D. 180–249). Paris, 1881.

„ . . 4. *L'Église et l'état dans la seconde moitié du troisième siècle* (A.D. 249–284). Paris, 1886.

LE NAIN DE TILLE-MONT *Mémoires pour servir à l'histoire ecclésiastique.* Second edition. 16 tomes. Paris, 1701.

O. BARDENHEWER . *Geschichte der altkirchlichen Literatur,* 2 vols. Freiburg-im-Breisgau, 1902.
*(Vol. ii. p. 611, *Die ältesten Märtyrerakten.* With bibliography.)

A. HARNACK . 1. *Geschichte der altchristlichen Literatur bis Eusebius,* erster Theil : *Die Ueberlieferung und der Bestand.* 2 Bde. Leipsic, 1893.
*(*Märtyrerakten* . . . In Bd. ii. p. 807.)

„ . 2. *Idem.,* zweiter Theil : *Die Chronologie der Literatur . . . bis Eusebius.* 2 Bde. Leipsic, 1897.
*(" *Martyrien* . . ." In Bd. ii. p. 463.)
(With complete bibliographies of individual *Acta.*)

C. J. NEUMANN . *Die römische Stadt und die allgemeine Kirche bis auf Diokletian.* Leipsic, 1890.

W. M. RAMSAY . *The Church in the Roman Empire before A.D. 170.* London, 1894.

[1] The Acts referred to in chapters ix.–xv. are nearly all in the *Acta Sanctorum* of the Bollandists, under the dates given ; or in the more convenient volume, the *Acta Sincera* of Ruinart ; and French translations of a large number are found in Leclercq, *Les Martyrs.* References, therefore, in those chapters are given only (1) to Acts *not* appearing in any of these volumes, or (2) to recent critical texts, when they exist.

E. G. HARDY . . *Christianity and the Roman Government.* London, 1894.
(An excellent little volume.)

P. E. VIGNEAUX . *Essai sur l'histoire de la Praefectura Urbis à Rome.* Paris, 1896.
(An admirable account of Roman criminal procedure.)

*H. LECLERQ, O.S.B. "Acta Martyrum," in CABROL, *Dictionnaire d'archéologie chrétienne et de liturgie.* Paris, 1907.

*H. DELEHAYE, S.J. . *Les légendes hagiographiques.* Brussels, 1906.
(Trans., *The Legends of the Saints,* by Mrs. V. M. CRAWFORD. 1907. An invaluable introduction to the study of hagiography.)

E. LE BLANT . . 1. *Les Actes des martyrs : supplément aux* Acta Sincera *de Dom Ruinart.* (See *supra,* chap. ix.)

" . . 2. *La Préparation au martyre.*
(Both published in *Mémoires de l'Académie des inscriptions et belles-lettres,* Paris, t. 30, 1881, and t. 28, 1879, respectively.)
This forms chapter ix. of the following :—

" . . 3. *Les Persécuteurs et les Martyrs.* Paris, 1893.

LE BOURGEOIS . *Les Martyrs de Rome d'après l'histoire et l'archéologie chrétienne.* Paris, 1897.

*A. DUFOURCQ . . *Étude sur les* Gesta Martyrum *romains.* Paris, 1900.
(A most important contribution to the study of the *Gesta.*)

CH. DE SMEDT, S.J. *Principes de la critique historique.* Paris, 1883.
(By the Editor of the *Analecta Bollandiana.* See *supra,* chap. ix.)

(*b*) TEXTS

J. BOLLANDUS, S.J. . *Acta Sanctorum quotquot toto orbe coluntur . . .,* 64 vols. Brussels, 1643. In progress.
(See *supra,* chap. ix. The edition of 1887 is the best.)

*T. RUINART, O.S.B. *Acta Sincera.* Paris, 1689.
(Contains nearly all the Acts referred to in chaps. ix to xv.)

MOMBRITIUS, O.S.B. *Sanctuarium sive Vitae Sanctorum.* Milan, 1475. Edited by the Monks of Solesmes, 2 vols. Paris, 1910.
(Arranged alphabetically ; contains a large number of texts.)

L. SURIUS . . *De probatis Sanctorum Historiis*, 6 vols. Lübeck, 1562.

O. VON GEBHARDT . *Acta Martyrum Selecta.* Berlin, 1902.
(A small volume with a few authentic texts.)

J. B. LIGHTFOOT . 1. *Apostolic Fathers*, pt. 2, vols. i.–iii. London, 1889.

„ . 2. *Miscellaneous Texts.* London, 1891.
(Texts, criticisms, and translations of the Passions of Ignatius and of Polycarp.)

O. VON GEBHARDT 1. *Texte und Untersuchungen* . . ., 14 Bde.
and A. HARNACK Leipsic, 1883–1896.

„ „ 2. *Texte und Untersuchungen.* Neue Folge, 15 Bde. Leipsic, 1897–1906.
(See especially 1888, 1893-5-6-7.)

*ANALECTA BOLLANDIANA, 30 vols. Brussels, 1882. In progress.
Bibliographia Hagiographica Graeca, 2 vols. Brussels, 1895.
Bibliographia Hagiographica Latina. Paris, 1893.
(All these volumes are the work of the Bollandists, see *supra*, chap. ix.)
Bibliotheca Cassinensis seu codicum manuscriptorum qui in tabulario Cassinensi asservantur series, 5 vols. Monte Cassino, 1873–1880, 1894.

A few new texts or new versions appear from time to time in the following publications.

TEXTS AND STUDIES, ed. J. ARMITAGE ROBINSON. Cambridge, 1901 . . . (For S. Perpetua and for the Scillitan martyrs ; texts and translations) ; STUDI E TESTI, Rome, 1900 . . . ; STUDIA BIBLICA, ed. S. DRIVER, Oxford, 1895. . . Compare also BARDENHEWER and HARNACK under Bibliography—ACTS OF MARTYRS : General History ; and LUCIUS and DELEHAYE, under General Bibliography—HISTORY.

(c) TRANSLATIONS

J. CARNANDET et *Les Actes des Saints* . . *d'après les Bollandistes.*
J. FÈVRE Vols. i.–iv. January. Lyons, 1866.

„ „ Vols. i.–iv. Lyons, 1865–1867.
(History, criticism, martyrologies : incomplete.)

P. GUÉRANGER, O.S.B. *Les Actes des martyrs.* 4 vols. 1853–1863.
(A useful collection of Passions, translated from the *Acta Sanctorum*, Ruinart, etc. Arranged in centuries.)

DROURY DE MAU- *Les Actes des martyrs.* Paris, 1708.
PERTUIS
(Translation of Ruinart's *Acta Sincera.* A most useful volume.)

*H. LECLERQ, O.S.B. *Les Martyrs: Recueil des pièces authentiques*, 7 vols. Paris, 1902.

(An invaluable book, containing nearly all the Acts referred to in this book. Only the first three volumes deal with records of the early martyrs ; and with those only which have some claim to authenticity. Good bibliography and criticisms.)

F. C. CONYBEARE . *Monuments of Early Christianity.* London, 1894.

(Translations of a few of the *Acta*, with good notes.)

A few other texts and translations may be found among the books in Bibliography—PATRISTIC.

S. BARING-GOULD . *The Lives of the Saints*, 16 vols. London, 1897.

(A modern version of the lives of a selected number of Saints derived from the *Acta Sanctorum*, etc. Extremely useful for reference, and to gain a knowledge of the tradition. Somewhat similar is ALBAN BUTLER, *Lives of the Fathers, Martyrs . . .* 2 vols. London, 1833.)

4. THE MARTYROLOGY OF JEROME AND OTHERS

H. ACHELIS . . *Die Martyrologien, ihre Geschichte und ihr Wert*, in *Abhandlungen der Königlichen Gesellschaft der Wissenschaften*, phil.-hist. Klasse, Neue Folge, Bd. iii., Nr. 3. Berlin, 1900.

A. URBAIN . . *Ein Martyrologium der christlichen Gemeinde zu Rom am Anfang des V^{ten} Jahrhunderts.* Leipsic, 1901. Published in *Texte und Untersuchungen*, Neue Folge, Bd. vi. (or xxi. in entire edition), Heft 3.

H. LIETZMANN . *Die drei ältesten Martyrologien.* Bonn, 1903.

*DE ROSSI and DUCHESNE "Martyrologium Hieronymianum" in *Acta Sanctorum*, November, t. ii., 1894.

(Introduction, four parallel columns of texts of the manuscripts, bibliography.)

SOCII BOLLANDIANI 1. *Martyrologium, ex Codice Bernensi*, 289, 1 vol. Brussels, 1881.

(The most convenient volume of the text for general reference.)

SOCII BOLLANDIANI 2. *Martyrologium Hieronymianum ex Codice Trevirensi*, 1 vol.   Brussels, 1883.

        (This Codex is not given in Duchesne's edition.)

*DUCHESNE   1. (With a brief note by DE ROSSI), " Les Sources du Martyrologe Hieronymien " in *Mélanges d'archéologie et d'histoire*, 1885, p. 120.

        (The best and easiest general introduction.)

„   ·   2. "A propos du Martyrologe Hieronymien " in *Analecta Bollandiana*, xvii. (1898) p. 421 ; and " Un dernier mot sur le Martyrologe Hieronymien," *ibid.*, xx. (1901) p. 241 ; cf. also criticism (on " Passiones Vitaeque Sanctorum " of Krusch) in *Bulletin Critique*, 1897, pp. 301, 325.

DE ROSSI .   ·   *Roma Sotterranea*, ii. p. xvi.

H. GRISAR   ·   *Analecta Romana*, vol. i. p. 231.   Rome, 1899.

B. KRUSCH   ·   1. "Zur Afra—legende und zum Martyrologium Hieronymianum " in *Neues Archiv der Gesellschaft für ältere deutsche Geschichtskunde*, xxiv. (1899) p. 289 ; 2. " Zum Martyrologium Hieronymianum, *ibid.* t. xx. (1895) p. 437 ; 3. "Nochmals das Martyrologium Hieronymianum, *ibid.* t. xxvi. (1901) p. 349 ; 4. "Nochmals die Afra—legende und das Martyrologium Hieronymianum," in *Mittheilungen des Instituts für Oesterreichische Geschichtsforschung*, t. 21, p. 1.   Innsbruck, 1900.

A. DUFOURCQ .   ·   *Étude sur les* Gesta Martyrum *romains.* Paris, 1900.

        (Throughout this study there is constant reference to the Martyrologies, especially to that of Jerome.   It affords a most instructive example of the method of using the documents.)

BEDAE VENERABILIS *Martyrologia*, in *P.L.*, 94, col. 799.

Martyrologium Romanum Parvum, in *P.L.*, col. 143 (cf. DE ROSSI, *R.S.*, ii. p. xxvii).

BEATI RABANI MAURI *Martyrologium*, in *P.L.*, 110, col. 1121.

FLORI DIACONI .   ·   *Martyrologium*, in *P.L.*, 119, col. 95.

ADONIS ARCHIEPISCOPI VIENNENSIS *Martyrologium*, in *P.L.*, 123, col. 146.

USUARDI MONACHI .   *Martyrologium*, in *P.L.*, 123, col. 602.

Martyrologium Romanum . . . *Martyrologium vetus Romanum* . . .
Martyrologium Adonis, edited by H. ROSWEYDE, 1 vol. Antwerp,
1613.
(A beautiful edition with index.)
Martyrologium Romanum. Rome, 1873.
(Now in use.)
Martyrologe romain, par deux prêtres du clergé de Paris. Paris, 1848.
(Translation of *Mart. Rom.* A useful volume with index of saints.)
H. QUENTIN . . *Les Martyrologes historiques du moyen age.*
Paris, 1908.

5. THE SYLLOGAE

(*a*) GENERAL HISTORY

De Rossi . . . Inscriptiones Christianae urbis Romae septimo
saeculo antiquiores, 2 vols. Rome, 1861–
1888.
(Vol. ii. contains the texts of the Syllogae,
with historical introduction and notes.)
H. Grisar . 1. Analecta Romana, vol. i. p. 76. Rome, 1899.
" . . 2. "Die altchristlichen Inschriften Roms im
früheren Mittelalter" in *Zeitschrift für Kathol-*
ische Theologie, 1889, p. 90. Innsbruck.

(*b*) SYLLOGE OF VERDUN

G. BONAVENIA . . La Sylloge di Verdun, 1 vol. Rome, 1903.

(*c*) SYLLOGE OF CAMBRIDGE

Manuscript, KK. iv., 6, folio 238 in the University Library at Cambridge.
W. LEVISON . . In *Neues Archiv der Gesellschaft für ältere*
deutsche Geschichtskunde, vol. 35, fasc. 2,
p. 333, 1910.
DUCHESNE . . *Le recueil épigraphique de Cambridge,* in
Mélanges d'archéologie et d'histoire, Nov.-
Dec. 1910, Paris and Rome.

(*d*) SOME CRITICAL DISCUSSIONS ON (*b*) AND (*c*)

MARUCCHI . . In *Nuovo Bullettino di archeologia cristiana,*
1901, 1902, 1903, 1906, 1907, 1908, 1910.
DE ROSSI . . . In *Bullettino di archeologia cristiana,* 1867,
p. 33.

BONAVENIA and   In *Osservatore Romano*, 1910, May 18 and 31 ;
MARUCCHI   June 6, 7 and 8; July 6 (cf. also May 8 and 21).
ZETTINGER . . *Römische Quartalschrift*, 1902, p. 345.
DE WAAL . . *Ibid.*, 1908, p. 42.

II. LIST OF THE POPES

WITH DATES, PLACES OF BURIAL, ETC.

P . . =recognized as a martyr in the Philocalian Calendar.
L.P. . =   ,,   ,,   ,,   *Liber Pontificalis*.
L.P.(2) =   ,,   ,,   ,,   ,,   (second edition only).
V . . =buried in the Vatican.
C . . =   ,,   Catacomb of S. Callixtus.
Pr . . =   ,,   ,,   S. Priscilla.

V. . . (42).[1] Peter, L.P., P.
V. . . (67). Linus, L.P.
V. . . (78). Anacletus, L.P.
(90). Clement, L.P. (buried in Greece).
V. . . (112). Evaristus, L.P.
(?) . . (121). Alexander, L.P. (Via Nomentana (?)).
V. . . (132). Sixtus I., L.P.
V. . . (142). Telesphorus, L.P.
V. . . (154). Hyginus, L.P.
V. . . (158). Pius I., L.P.
V. . . (167). Anicetus, L.P. (2).
V. . . (175). Soter, L.P.
V. . . (182). Eleutherius, L.P.
V. . . (189). Victor, I., L.P.
C. . . (199). Zephyrinus, L.P.
(217). Callixtus, L.P., P. (Calepodius).
C. . . (222). Urban, L.P.
C. . . (230). Pontianus, L.P.
C. . . (235). Anteros, L.P.
C. . . (236). Fabianus, L.P., P.
C. . . (251). Cornelius, L.P.
C. . . (253). Lucius, L.P.
C. . . (254). Stephen, L.P.
C. . . (257). Sixtus II., L.P., P.
C. . . (259). Dionysius, L.P.
C. . . (269). Felix I., L.P.

C. . . (275). Eutychianus, L.P.(2).
C. . . (283). Gaius, L.P. (2).
Pr. . . (296). Marcellinus, L.P.
Pr. . . (308). Marcellus, L.P. (2).
C. . . (309). Eusebius.
C. . . (311). Miltiades.

PEACE OF THE CHURCH.

Pr. . . (314). Silvester.
Near C. (336). Mark.
(337). Julius I. (Calepodius).
Pr. . . (352). Liberius.
(355). Felix II. (Via Aurelia).
(366). Damasus (Via Ardeatina and S. Laurence).
Pr. . . (384). Siricius.
{(399). Anastasius I. (ad Ursum Pileatum).
{(401). Innocent I.
V. . . (417). Zosimus.
(418). Boniface I. (Via Salaria, near S. Felicitas).
Pr. . . (422). Celestinus.
(432). Sixtus III. (in S. Laurence).

---

[1] The dates are extremely uncertain during the first and second centuries. The dates are not given in Duchesne (*Liber Pontificalis*) till Pontianus, A.D. 230,

V. . . (440).	Leo the Great.	V. . . (530).	Boniface II.
(461).	Hilary (S. Laurence).	V. . . (533).	John II.
		V. . . (535).	Agapetus.
V. . . (468).	Simplicius.	(536).	Silverius (Pontian Islands).
V. . . (483)	Felix III.		
V. . . (492).	Gelasius I.	(537).	Vigilius (Via Salaria).
V. . . (496).	Anastasius II.		
V. . . (498).	Symmachus.	V. . . (555).	Pelagius I.
V. . . (514).	Hormisdas.	V. . . (560).	John III.
V. . . (523).	John I.	V. . . (574).	Benedict I.
V. . . (526).	Felix IV.	V. . . (574).	Gregory the Great.

III. (A) DEPOSITIO EPISCOPORUM and (B) DEPOSITIO MARTYRUM of the PHILOCALIAN CALENDAR (FOURTH CENTURY), with (C) A LIST OF THE MARTYRS in it arranged alphabetically

A. DEPOSITIO EPISCOPORUM

[Dec. 27]	. . VI. Kal. Januarias . . .	Dionisi, in Calisti.
[Dec. 30]	. . III. Kal. Januar. . . .	Felicis, in Calisti.
[Dec. 31]	. . Prid. Kal. Januar. . . .	Silvestri, in Priscillae.
[Jan. 10]	. . . IIII. Idus Januarias . .	Miltiadis, in Calisti.
[Jan. 15]	. . XVIII. Kal. Feb. . . .	Marcellini, in Priscillae.
[March 5]	. . III. Non. Mar.	Luci, in Calisti.
[April 22]	. . X. Kal. Mai	Gai, in Calisti.
[Aug. 2]	. . . IIII. Non Augustas . .	Steffani, in Calisti.
[Sep. 26]	. . VI. Kal. Octob. . . .	Eusebii, in Calisti.
[Dec. 8]	. . . VI. Id. Decemb. . . .	Eutichiani, in Calisti.
[Oct. 7]	. . . Non. Octob.	Marci, in Balbinae.
[Apr. 12]	. . . Prid. Idus Apr.	Juli, in Via Aurelia, miliario III., in Calisti.

B. DEPOSITIO MARTYRUM

[Dec. 25]	. . VIII. Kal. Janu. . . .	Natus Christus, in Betleem Judeae.

Mense Januario.

[Jan. 20]	. . . XIII. Kal. Feb.. . . .	Fabiani, in Calisti, et Sebastiani, in Catacumbas.
[Jan. 21]	. . . XII. Kal. Feb.	Agnetis, in Nomentana.

Mense Februario.

[Feb. 22]	. . . VIII. Kal. Mart. . . .	Natale Petri de Catedra.

22

Mense Martio.

[March 7] . . Non. Mart. . . . . . Perpetuae et Felicitatis, Africae.

Mense Maio.

[May 19] . . XIIII. Kal. Jun. . . . Partheni et Caloceri, in Calisti, Diocletiano VIIII. et Maximiano VIII. Cons. [304].

Mense Junio.

[June 29] . . III. Kal. Jul. . . . . Petri, in Catacumbas ; et Pauli Ostense, Tusco et Basso Cons. [258].

Mense Julio.

[July 10] . . . VI. Id. Jul. . . . . . Felicis et Filippi, in Priscillae ; et in Jordanorum, Martialis, Vitalis, Alexandri ; et in Maximi, Silani ; hunc Silanum martirem Novati furati sunt ; et in Praetextati, Januari.

[July 30] . . . III. Kal. Aug. . . . . Abdos et Sennes, in Pontiani, quod est ad Ursum piliatum.

Mense Augusto.

[Aug. 6] . . . VIII. Id. Aug. . . . . Xysti, in Calisti ; et in Praetextati, Agapiti et Felicissimi.

[Aug. 8] . . . VI. Id. Aug. . . . . . Secundi, Carpophori, Victorini et Severiani Albano ; et Ostense VII. ballistaria, Cyriaci, Largi, Crescentiani, Memmiae, Julianae et Smaragdi.

[Aug. 11] . . III. Id. Aug. . . . . . Laurenti, in Tiburtina.

[Aug. 13] . . Id. Aug. . . . . . . Ypoliti, in Tiburtina ; et Pontiani, in Calisti.

[Aug. 22] . . XI. Kal. Sep. . . . . Timotei, Ostense.

[Aug. 28] . . V. Kal. Sep. . . . . . Hermetis, in Basillae, Salaria Vetere.

Mense Septembre.

[Sep. 5] . . . Non. Sept. . . . . . Aconti, in Porto, et Nonni et Herculani et Taurini.

[Sep. 9] . . . V. Id. Sept. . . . . . Gorgoni, in Labicana.

[Sep. 11] . . . III. Id. Sept. . . . . Proti et Jacinthi in Bassillae.

[Sep. 14] . . . XVIII. Kal. Oct. . . . Cypriani Africae. Romae celebratur in Calisti.

[Sep. 22] . . . X. Kal. Oct. . . . . . Basillae, Salaria Vetere, Diocletiano VIIII. et Maximiano VIII. Cons. [304].

Mense Octobre.

[Oct. 14] . . . Prid. Id. Oct. . . . . Calisti, in Via Aurelia,
miliario III.

Mense Novembre.

[Nov. 9] . . . V. Id. Nov. . . . . . Clementis, Semproniani
Claudi, Nicostrati, in comitatum.
[Nov. 29] . . III. Kal. Dec. . . . . Saturnini, in Trasonis.

Mense Decembre.

[Dec. 13] . . Id. Dec. . . . . . . Ariston, in Portum.

C. LIST OF MARTYRS IN THE PHILOCALIAN CALENDAR

G. . =found also in the Passionary of Gregory (sixth century).
A. . =   ,,   ,,   Martyrology of Ado (ninth century).

ROME.

Abdon (and Sennen) (A.). Acontius. Agapitus (G., A.) (and Felicis-
simus). Agnes (A.). Alexander (and Felix). Ariston. Basilla.
Callixtus (G., A.). Calocerus (and Parthenius) (A.). Carpophorus
(Victorinus and Severianus). Claudius and Clement (and Semproni-
anus). Crescentianus. Cyriacus (G., A.). Fabianus. Felicissimus (A.)
(and Agapitus). Felix (and the other six sons of Felicitas). Gorgonius.
Hippolytus. Hermes (A.). Herculanus. Jacinthus (A.) (and Protus).
Januarius (and Felix). Juliana. Largus (and Smaragdus) (G.). Laurence
(A.). Martialis (and Felix). Memmia. Nicostratus. Nonnius. Parthe-
nius (and Calocerus) (A.). Peter and Paul App. (A.). Philip (and Felix).
Pontianus. Protus (and Jacinthus). Saturninus. Sebastian (A.).
Secundus. Sempronianus. Sennen (and Abdon) (A.). Severianus (and
Carpophorus). Silanus (and Felix). Sixtus II. (A.). Smaragdus. Taur-
inus. Timotheus. Victorinus (and Carpophorus). Vitalis (and Felix).

AFRICA.

Cyprian, Perpetua and Felicitas.

IV. INDEX COEMITERIORUM XVI
AND THE TRUE NUMBER OF THE CEMETERIES

THE answer to the question whether the *Index* is complete or other-wise depends partly on the variations in the codices.[1]

Besides the (**1.**) Vatican Codex there are three other versions of the Index.

2. *Index Chigiana.* The second of these is known as the *Index Chigiana,* having been discovered in that library by Giorgi. It was pub-lished by De Rossi.[2] It is preserved in a manuscript of the eleventh century appended to the Dialogues of Pope Gregory the Great. This list gives an additional cemetery, the *Cimiterium Aproniani ad Sanctam Eugeniam*[3] *Via Latina,*—making seventeen in all. It is in almost the same somewhat faulty topographical order as the Vatican Codex.

3. *Index Laurenziana.* The third version of the Index is preserved in a twelfth-century manuscript formerly in Lord Ashburnham's library, and now in the *Biblioteca Laurenziana* in Florence, and has been pub-lished by Stevenson.[4] There is a list of seventeen cemeteries, arranged this time in good topographical order.

4. Cardinal Rampolla's Catalogue. A fourth version of the *Index* was discovered by Cardinal Rampolla[5] in a fifteenth-century Codex of the Vatican, also based on a document of the fourth century. This Codex was transcribed in Rome, as an appendix to the famous work of Frontinus, "On the Aqueducts of the City" (*De Aquaductibus Urbis*).[6] It is beautifully written ; various readings from other manu-scripts are given in the margin, and signed by Johann Vynck, one of the learned German clerks who worked in the papal library for that fine scholar Pope Nicholas V. (1447–1455). A study of the manuscripts on which this document is based throws light on the number of the cemeteries. On what manuscript, then, does this Catalogue depend?

There are three ancient manuscripts of Frontinus : (1) The oldest, of the thirteenth or fourteenth century, at Monte Cassino. (2) A manuscript

---

[1] For texts of the three codices, see *supra,* p. 98.

[2] See *Bullettino di archeologia cristiana,* 1878, p. 44.   [3] *Supra,* p. 193.

[4] Stevenson in *Nuovo Bullettino di archeologia cristiana,* 1897, p. 255. This article gives a good summary of the whole question with further bibliography. Both Giorgi and Stevenson believe the *Index* to be incomplete ; the latter inserts sixteen cemeteries which he believes omitted from the original list.

[5] Rampolla, *op. cit.,* Bibliography—ITINERARIES–INDEX, to whose work I am in-debted for this paragraph.

[6] Frontinus was Commissioner of Waterworks in A.D. 97. His work, *De Aqua-ductibus,* was discovered in 1429, and frequently reproduced since. C. Herschel, in *The Two Books on the Water Supply of the City of Rome,* Boston, 1899, has published a fine edition of his works.

of 1345 in the Vatican, called *Urbinate*, and closely resembling the manuscript of Monte Cassino. (3) A somewhat imperfect manuscript of the fifteenth century in the Vatican, called the Vatican manuscript.

Now, the manuscript of Vynck contains several important facts absent from all three manuscripts mentioned above. He was therefore copying from some other document, which is at present undiscovered. It is possible, however, to determine the date of this prototype. We note first that Vynck's version contains information concerning the Aurelian Wall not found in the *Notitia* and *Curiosum*.[1] Moreover, it describes fully the wall as it was originally built by Aurelian (270-275) and Probus (276-282), but ignores the modifications made in it by Honorius in 403 in his attempt to protect Rome against the Goths. It is therefore obvious that Vynck's original manuscript was written not later than 403. The number of cemeteries given in it as existing at this period is sixteen; the fact is mentioned twice in different parts of the text, and also the words occur "*Cymiteria XVI.*"

Having now examined all the manuscripts, we can discuss the question whether the *Index* is mutilated or not.

The number of the cemeteries as given in the *Index*. De Rossi, followed by Scaglia, Giorgi and Stevenson, is of opinion that the *Index* of the Vatican is mutilated. It must be remembered that these scholars all wrote before the discovery of Rampolla's catalogue. In support of his view De Rossi quotes the scholar Fiorenti, who, in his notes to the *Martyrologium Hieronymianum*, asserts that he saw at Lucca a manuscript which contains a list of twenty-one cemeteries. De Rossi thinks that in this Lucca manuscript we have the original *complete* prototype of the various Indexes, giving the correct number of twenty-one cemeteries. This manuscript, however, has not been found; and the evidence of the three other manuscripts quoted by Rampolla seems to indicate that the original documents on which they are based contained the names of sixteen or seventeen cemeteries only.

V. LIST OF PASSIONS IN THE PASSIONARY OF GREGORY (Sixth Century)[2]

A = occurs in the Martyrology of Ado
P =   ,,   Philocalian Calendar

Jan. 14 . . . Felix [Romanus], priest (A.).
Aug. 8 . . . Sisinnius, Cyriacus (P.), (A.), Smaragdus and Larcius (Largus) (P.).

[1] *Supra*, p. 95; the collation of fifteen manuscripts of the *Notitia* shows that the prototype was mutilated in the last page,—hence the omission of information on this wall.
[2] The text is given in Dufourcq, *Les Gesta Martyrum romains*, p. 81.

Feb. 7	.	.	Juliana, Virgin [of Cumae or Nicomedia]
„ 14	.	.	Valentine
May 3	.	.	Alexander, hermit and pope (A.)
„ 10	.	.	Januarius, priest
			Domitilla Virgin, niece of Domitian
May 12	.	.	Marcellus, Nereus and Archilleus (A.)
			Petronilla
			Sulpicius and Servilianus
May 19	.	.	Praxed and Pudentiana (A.)
June 2	.	.	Marcellinus and Peter (A.)
„ 9	.	.	Primus and Felicianus (A.)
„ 18	.	.	Processus and Martinianus (A.)
July 29	.	.	Pope Felix (II.) (A.)
„ 10	.	.	Rufina and Secunda (A.)
Aug. 11	.	.	Susanna (A.)
„ 14	.	.	Eusebius (A)
„ 23?	.	.	Agapitus (P.) (A.)
„ 25	.	.	Genesius the mime (A.)
„ 29	.	.	Serapia (A.)
Sept. 14	.	.	Pope Cornelius (A.)
„ 22	.	.	Mauritius
Oct. 14	.	.	Pope Callixtus (P.) (A.)
Nov. 23	.	.	Clement, pope and martyr [from Gregory of Tours]
Nov. 1	.	.	Caesarius (A.)
„ 9	.	.	Theodore [Greek]
„ 24	.	.	Chrysogonus

Donatus, bishop ⎫
Sept. 21 . . . Alexander, bishop and martyr ⎬ Tuscan

April 17 . . . Savinus, bishop with deacons ⎫
 Marcellus and Superantius ⎪
Jan. 1 . . . Concordius ⎬ All Umbrian
Feb. 4 . . . Laurence of Spoleto ⎪
March . . . John *Penarensis* ⎪
Dec. 22 . . . Gregory of Spoleto ⎭

(Note these are all Roman martyrs except Juliana of Cumae [Feb. 7], Theodore the Greek [Nov. 9], Donatus and Alexander the Tuscans, and the last five, who are Umbrians.)

VI. LIST OF SEVENTY-SEVEN MARTYRS OF THE FIRST THREE CENTURIES

WHOSE PASSIONS ARE REFERRED TO

IN ADO'S MARTYROLOGY (NINTH CENTURY)[1]

P=found in Philocalian Calendar.
G=found in Passionary of Gregory.

	Period of Martyrdom.	Names of Martyrs.	Reference in *A.SS.* or elsewhere.
P	Decius	Abdon and Sennen (P.)	See Laurence
	Diocletian	Abundius	Sept. 16
G	Domitian	Achilleus	See Nereus
	Diocletian	Adauctus	See Felix
P G	Decius	Agapitus (P., G.)	See Laurence
P	Diocletian	Agnes (P.)	Jan. 21
G	Trajan	Alexander pope (G.)	May 3
	Diocletian	Alexander Romanus	May 13
	,,	Anastasia	Mombritius, i. 200 (ed. 1910)
	Decius	Anatolia and Victoria	July 9
	Diocletian	Anthimius	May 11
	Julian	Apollonia	Feb. 9
	Diocletian	Apuleius	See Marcellus
	,,	Auceia	See Luceia
	Aurelian	Aurea	Aug. 24
	Decius	Aurelianus	May 22
	Trajan	Balbina	See Hermes
	Aurelian	Basilis	June 12
	Diocletian	Beatrix (Viatrix)	See Simplicius
	Julian	Bib(b)iana	*Bibl. Casin.*, iii., fl. 191
	Diocletian	Boniface	May 14
	Sep. Severus	Bonosa	July 15
G	Domitian	Caesarius (G.)	Nov. 1
	Al. Severus	Calepodius	May 10
P G	Sep. ,,	Callixtus (P., G.)	Oct. 14
P	Decius	Calocerus and Parthenius (P.)	May 19
	Al. Severus (?)	Cecilia	Nov. 23, Mombritius, i. 332
	Aurelian	Chrysanthus and Darias	Aug. 25

[1] For this list with nearly all the details I am indebted to Dufourcq, *Les* Gesta
Martyrum *romains*. I have arranged it alphabetically for purposes of reference.
The text of Ado is in *P.L.* 123, and in Rosweyde, *Martyrologium Romanum* . . .
Antwerp, 1613. For references see Bibliography—ACTS OF MARTYRS, and AB-
BREVIATIONS (p. 319). The story of most of these martyrs, according to the tradi-
tion of the sixth century, is found in English in Baring-Gould, *Lives of the Saints*.

List of Seventy-three Martyrs—*continued.*

	Period of Martyrdom.	Names of Martyrs.	Reference in *A. SS.* or elsewhere.
G	Trajan	Clement, pope (G.)	Mombritius, i. p. 341
G	Decius	Cornelius, pope (G.)	Schelestratus, *Antiq. Eccles.*, i. 188
	Diocletian	(Quattuor) Coronatorum	*Sitzungsberichte,* Berlin, xlvii., 1292
P	,,	Crescenti(an)us (P.)	Sept. 14
G P	Decius	Cyriaca	Aug. 21, *Anal. Boll.*, ii. 247
	Diocletian	Cyriacus (P., G.)	*Anal. Boll.*, ii. 247
	Aurelian	Darias	See Chrysanthus
	Decius	Digna and Merita	Sept. 22
	Trajan	Eleutherius	*Studi e Testi*, 1901, 6
	Marcus Aurelius	Eugenia	*P.L.*, 21, 1105
G	Julian	Eusebius (G.)	Aug. 14
	Marcus Aurelius	Eusebius and Pontianus	Aug. 25
	,,	Eustathius	*Anal. Boll.*, iii. 65, 172
P	Decius	Felicissimus (P.)	See Laurence
P	Marcus Aurelius	Felicitas	Künstle, *Hagiographische Studien*, Paderborn, 1894
	Diocletian	Felix and Adauctus	Aug. 30
G	,,	Felix Romanus (G.)	Jan. 14
G	Julian	Felix II., pope (G.)	*Anal. Boll.*, ii. 322
G	Diocletian	Felicianus	See Primus
	,,	Flora	See Lucilla
	,,	Geminianus	See Lucia
G	,,	Genesius (G.)	Aug. 25
	Trajan	Getulius	June 10
	Julian	Gordianus	May 10
	Decius	(Sanctorum) Graecorum	*R.S.*, iii. 201
	Trajan	Hermes (P.) and Balbina	March 31 [May 3]
P	Domitian	Hyacinthus (Jacinthus) (P.)	July 26 (Sept. 11 ?)
	Julian	John and Paul	June 25 and 26
	Decius	Justinus	Sept. 17 (April 13 ?)
P	,,	Laurence, with Abdon, Sennen, Sixtus II., Agapitus, Felicissimus (P.)	Surius, iv. 607

List of Seventy-three Martyrs—*continued.*

	Period of Martyrdom.	Names of Martyrs.	Reference in *A.SS.* or elsewhere.
	Diocletian	Leopardus	Sept. 30
	„	Lucia and Gemini-anus	*Bibl. Cass.*, iii., fl. 270
	„	Luceia and Auceia	June 25
	Marcus Aurelius	Lucilla and Flora	July 29
G	Diocletian	Marcellinus and Peter (G.)	June 2
G	„	Marcellus, pope	Jan. 16
G	„	Marcellus and Apuleius	Oct. 7
	Julian	Marinus	*Cat. Brux.*, ii. 184
	Aurelian	Marius and Martha	Jan. 19
	Severus	Martina or Tatiana	Jan. 1
	Decius	Merita	See Digna
	Trajan	Montanus	July 17
G	Domitian	Nereus and Achilleus (G.)	May 12
	„	Nicomedes	Mombritius, ii.
	Diocletian	Pancras	*Anal. Boll.*, x. 52
	Decius	Parthenius (P.)	See Calocerus
P	Trajan	Pastor	July 26
	Julian	Paul	See John
	Diocletian	Peter (G.)	See Marcellinus
G	Nero	Peter and Paul (P.)	*Acta Apost. Apoc.*
P	Marcus Aurelius	Pontianus	See Eusebius
P	Decius	Pontius	Baluze, *Miscellanea*, i. 29, 75
G	Trajan	Potentiana and Praxed (G.)	May 19
G	Diocletian	Primus and Felicianus (G.)	June 9
	Nero	Prisca	Jan. 18
G	„	Processus and Martinanus (G.)	July 2
	Aurelian	Restituta	*Bibl. Cass.*, iii., fl. 12
	Diocletian	Restitutus	May 29
G	Decius	Rufina and Secunda (G.)	July 10
	Diocletian	Rufus	*Anal. Boll.*, viii. 168
P	„	Sebastian (P.)	Jan. 20
	Decius	Secunda	See Rufina
P	„	Sennen (P.)	See Laurence
G	Trajan	Serapia (G.) and Sabina	Aug. 29

List of Seventy-three Martyrs—*continued.*

	Period of Martyrdom.	Names of Martyrs.	Reference in *A.SS.* or elsewhere.
	Diocletian	Simplicius and Beatrix (Viatrix)	July 29
P	Decius	Sixtus II., pope (P.)	See Laurence
	Trajan	Sophia	*Bibl. Casin.,* iii. 276
	Decius	Stephen, pope	Aug. 2
G	Diocletian	Susanna (G.)	Aug. 11
	Trajan	Symphorosa	July 18
	Severus	Urban	May 25
	Decius	Victoria	See Anatolia

VII. LIST OF MARTYRS WHOSE PASSIONS ARE REFERRED TO IN THE CHAPTERS ON THE ACTS OF THE MARTYRS [1]

A.SS.—*Acta Sanctorum* of the Bollandists
A.S.—*Acta Sincera* of Ruinart

Name.	Day.	Reference.
Caesarius	Nov. 4 [Nov. 1]	*A.SS.*
Euphemia	Sept. 16	*A.S.*
Maximus	May 14	*A.S.*
Neon in *Acta S. Speusippi*	Jan. 17	*A.SS.*
Eustratius	Dec. 12	Surius
Genesius of Arles	Aug. 25	*A.S.*
Cassian in *Passio Marcelli*	Oct. 30 [Dec. 3]	*A.S.*
Cyprian	Sept. 14	*Cypriani Epistolae* ed. Hartel, III.
Felix Romanus	Jan. 14	*A.S.*
Victor Maurus	May 8	*A.SS.*
Vincent of Saragossa	Jan. 22	*A.S.*
Saturninus	Feb. 11	*A.S.*

[1] These are arranged approximately in the order in which they are mentioned : for the page, see Index ; for the full titles of the references, see Bibliography— ACTS OF MARTYRS, and ABBREVIATIONS (p. 319). It is sometimes impossible to be sure of the correct day of the anniversary.

List of Martyrs—*continued.*

Name.	Day.	Reference.
Euplus	Aug. 12	*A.S.*
Pionius	Mar. 12	*A.S.*
Symphorianus	Aug. 22	*A.S.*
Martyrs of Lyons		Eusebius, *Hist. Eccles.*
Flavia Domitilla	May 12	*A.SS.*
Clement the Consul		
Acilius Glabrio		
Epictetus and Astion	.	Rosweyde, *Vitae Patrum* and *P.L.* 73, 593
Lucianus	Jan. 7	*A.S.*
Irenaeus of Sirmium	Mar. 25	*A.S.*
Phileas of Alexandria	Feb. 4	*A.SS.*
Scillitan Martyrs	July 17	*Anal. Boll.*, 1889, 1897
Maxima, Donatella and Secunda	July 30	*Anal. Boll.*, 1889
Typasius	Jan. 11	*Anal . Boll.*, 1890
Maximilian	Mar. 12	*A.S.*
Justin Martyr (Sep. 17)	Apr. 13	*Studi e Testi*, 1902
Fructuosus	Jan. 21	*A.S.*
Ignatius	Feb. 1	Lightfoot, *op. cit.*, BIBLIOGRAPHY
Polycarp	Apr. 25	„ „
Martyrs of Vienne and Lyons (Blandina, Pothinus, &c.)	June 2	Eusebius, *Hist. Eccles.*
Martyrs of Alexandria		„ „
Procopius	Nov. 22 [July 8]	*A.SS. Propylaeum,* and *Anal. Boll.*, 1897
Perpetua and Felicitas	Mar. 6	Texts and Studies, 1891
Jacobus and Marianus	Apr. 12	*Studi e Testi*, 1900
Carpus Papylus & Agathonice	Apr. 13	*Revue Archéologique*, 1881
Apollonius	Apr. 8	*Anal. Boll*, 1895
Crispina	Dec. 5	*Studi e Testi*, 1902
Montanus and Lucius (and Flavian)	Feb. 24	*Anal Boll.*, 1899
Acacius	Mar. 31	*A.S.*
Agape, Irene and Chione	Apr. 3	*St di e Testi*, 1902
Felix, Bp. of Tibiuca	Aug. 30	*Anal. Boll.*, 1897 and 1903
Phileas and Philoromus	Feb. 4	*Anal. Boll.*, 1897
Thecla		*A.S.*

List of Martyrs—*continued.*

Name.	Day.	Reference.
Symphorosa and Seven Sons	July 17	*A.SS.*
Hippolytus	Aug. 13	*A.S.*
Sixtus II.	Aug. 6	*A.SS.*
Laurence	Aug. 10	*A.S.* and Surius, IV. 607
Agnes	Jan. 21	*A.S.*
Sebastian	Jan. 20	*A.SS.*
Agatha	July 25 [Feb. 5]	„
Ciricus and Julitta	June 16	*Anal. Boll.*, 1882
George	Apr. 23	*A.SS.*
Eleutherius	Apr. 13	*Studi e Testi*, 1901
Felix and Adauctus	Aug. 30	*A.SS.*
Digna and Merita	Sep. 22	„
Leo and Paregorius	June 30	*A.S.*
Marciana	Jan. 9	*A.SS.*
Nereus and Achilleus	May 12	„
Cornelius, pope	Sep. 14	Schelstratus, *Antiq. Eccles.*, i. 188
Eugenia	Dec. 25	Conybeare, *Monuments of Early Christianity;* and in *P.L.* 21
Peter and Paul	June 29	*Acta Apost. Apoc.* (Lipsius)
Andrew	Nov. 30	„ „
Thomas	Dec. 21	„ „
Cyriacus	[Aug. 8; see *A.SS.*, Jan. 16]	*Anal. Boll.*, 1883, 247
Anastasia	Dec. 25	*A.SS.*
Julian and Basilla	Jan. 9	„
Cosmas and Damian	Sep. 27	„
Clement, pope	Nov. 23	*P.G.*,ii. 617; Mombritius, i. 341; Funk, *P. P. Apost.*, 180
Chrysanthus and Darias	Oct. 25	*A.SS.*
S. Pancras	May 4	*Anal. Boll.*, 1891, 52
S. Cecilia	Nov. 23	Mombritius, i. 332
Urban in *Passio S. Ceciliae*	Nov. 23	Surius, Nov. 22
Callixtus, pope	Oct. 14	*A.SS.*
Stephen, pope	Aug. 2	„
Alexander, pope	May 3	„
Gaius [July 1], pope, in *Passio Susannae*	Aug. 11	„
Susanna	Aug. 11	Surius, iv. 597

List of Martyrs—*continued*.

Name.	Day.	Reference.
Marcellus, pope	Jan. 16	*A.SS.*
Eusebius, pope	Sep. 26	
Greek Martyrs		,,
		R.S., iii. 202
Sebastian	Jan. 20	*A.SS.*
John and Paul	June 25 and 26	,,
Pontianus, pope	Aug. 13	,,
Processus and Martinianus	July 2	,,
Nereus and Achilleus	May 12	,,
Sixtus II., pope	Aug. 6	*A.SS.* and Surius, iv. 607

INDEX

REFERENCES to subjects treated fully and indexed in the chapter headings are made as follows, *e.g.* Acta Martyrum, 127 (ch. hd.) seqq., 134 (ch. hd.) seqq.

Brackets indicate a sub-heading, *e.g.* Popes, burial-places of . . . (mentioned in *L.P.*) 69 ; (in *M.H.*) 200.

The names of documents are in italics.

The names of martyrs from the Martyrologies cannot always be identified.

The words *Acta, Passiones, Gesta, Vitae* are practically equivalent in the Index. The word *basilica* may indicate anything, from S. Peter's on the Vatican to a tiny memorial chapel in the Catacombs. The word *Cemetery (Coemiterium)* is used consistently, and is equivalent to *Catacomb*.

ABBREVIATIONS

Ap.	apostle.
A.SS. . . .	*Acta Sanctorum.*
B.	bishop.
Bas. . . .	basilica.
Cem. . . .	cemetery.
Coem. . . .	coemiterium.
Ch.	church, oratory, basilica.
E.	emperor.
K.	king.
L.P. . . .	*Liber Pontificalis.*
M.	counted as martyr in the documents.
M.H. . . .	*Martyrology of Jerome.*
P.	pope.
Phil. Cal. . .	*Philocalian Calendar.*
S.	shrine of, a general term for cemetery or church of martyrs.
V.	virgin.

A

Abbreviations of names of books, 319

Abdon and Sennen MM. of Persia, 343, 345 ; S. 99, 116, 338, 339, 345

Abundius M., 343

Acacius B.M. of Antioch, *Acts of,* 147, 173

,, patriarch of Constantinople, excommunicated, 65

Academy, French, 131

Acca B., England, 38

Achaia, 214

Achelis, H., on *Martyrology of Jerome,* 228

Achilles B. of Spoleto, 43, 44, 271 n. 1

Achilleus MM., Nereus and ; see Nereus

Acontius M., 338, 339

Acta (=transactions), made at domiciliary visits, 138, 139

,, *Martyrum,* 65, 68, 73, 127 (ch. hd.) seqq., 134 (ch. hd.) seqq., 146 (ch. hd.) seqq., 161 (ch. hd.) seqq., 178 (ch. hd.) seqq., 300 ; see *Gesta Martyrum*

,, *Proconsularia,* 134 (ch. hd.) seqq., 146 (ch. hd.) seqq., 197

,, *Publica,* 136

Acta Sanctorum of the Bollandists, 35, 128 seqq., 187, 196, 197; passages discussed, 343 seqq.

Acts, see *Acta*; of popes, see *Liber Pontificalis, Gesta*

Adalard, Abbot of S. Peter's, Corvie, 232

Adam, 51

Adamnan, Abbot, Ireland, 119

Adauctus MM., Felix and, see Felix and Adauctus MM.

Ado, Archbishop of Vienne, *Martyrology of*, 183; comparison with *Passional of Gregory*, 341; with *Phil. Cal.*, 339; with *Calendar of Ravenna*, 132, 229; Roman *Gesta* in, 201–202, 206, 229, 343 seqq.

Adrias (or Adrianus) M. (Greek), S. and inscription of, 291–292, 299, 304

Adriatic, 26

Aemilianae, titulus (? or ch. of Four Crowned Saints), 12

Aemilianus, judge of Fructuosus M., 157 seqq.

Aemilius, Consul (of 259), 157

Africa, *Acta Martyrum* read liturgically in, 181; Calendars of, 211 n. 3, 219; *Calendar* of fourth cent. (basis of *M.H.*), 205, 207, 216, 218–220; *Martyrology of Carthage* of sixth cent., 219; Council at Hippo (of 393), 179; inscriptions in churches of, 231, 238, 284–285, 310–311; invaders from, 7; martyrs of, 52, 135, 138, 147 seqq., 156, 215, 338, 339; see Alexandria, Carthage, Cirta, Scilli; pilgrims from, 18, 36; popes and bishops from, 54, 66; revenues to Roman churches from, 88, 90

Agape (love feast), 80

Agape, Irene and Chione MM. of Thessalonica, 138; *Acts of*, 173

Agapetus P., 56; epitaph and inscriptions, 261 n. 3, 289

Agapitus and Felicissimus MM., 72, 261, 342, 343, 344; cf. 291; S. and ch. of, 15, 53, 72, 298, 299, 338, 339; (excavations at), 304

Agatha M., 181; Coem. Lucinae ad S. Agatham ad Girulum, Via Aurelia, 99, 105, 125; (ch. of), 15; ch. of S. Agatha *dei Goti*, in Suburra, 13, 122; monastery of, 121

Agatho P., epitaph of, 252, 262

Agathonice M., see Carpus, Papylus and

Agellius M., 215

Ager Veranus, on Via Tiburtina, 72, 244, 249, 253, 314

Agiulphus, deacon of Gregory of Tours, 31, 33

Agnes M., 181, 227, 343; cem. of (also called Emerentiae, Ostrianum, Majus, ad Nymphas, or Fontis S. Petri), 98, 100, 105, 111, 124; (basilica of, in cem.), 15, 85, 101, 113, 115; (inscriptions in), 246, 249, 261, 264, 265, 288

Alaric the Goth, 6, 18, 42, 86, 88

Alban M. of England, 217

Alcala, Justus M. of, 41

Alcuin and the *Syllogae*, 112, 231 seqq., 250

Aldhelm B. of Sherbourne, 231

Alessio, S. on the Aventine (old S. Boniface), 14

Alexander, P.M. [May 3], 49, 53; decrees of, 79, 80; martyrdom of, 68; *Passion of*, 200

,,   M. [July 10], son of Felicitas, of Via Salaria, 338, 339; Coem. Jordanorum ad S. Alexandrum, 98, 106, 107, 110, 118, 246

,,   M. of Via Nomentana, 68, 200 n. 5

,,   Romanus M. [May 13], 343

,,   B.M. of Tuscany, 342

,,   (Severus) E., 72, 203, 204

,,   II., Czar, 251

Alexandria, 179, 201; *Calendar of*, 219; Clement of, 193; Cyril of, 44; Dionysius B. of, 162; see Eulogius B. of; martyrs of, 145, 162, 173; church revenues for S. Peter's from, 90

Alfred K. of England, educated in Rome, 24

Alfrid K. of Northumbria, 119

Allard, P. on *A.SS.*, 130

Alps, 33

Alta Semita, region called, 12

Altar, martyrs' tombs form, 28, 47

Altinum, Heliodorus B. of, 212, 217

Alypius, B. of Thagaste, Augustine's letter to, 27

Amalasuenta, Queen, 57

Amantius B. of Como, 29

Amasia in Pontus, shrine of Euphemia M. at, 134

Amator B. of Auxerre, 210

Ambrose B. of Milan, friend of Emp. Theodosius, 3 ; and anniversaries of martyrs, 28 ; references to martyrs, 181 ; in *M.H.*, 217 ; friend of Chromatius, 212 ; inscriptions by, 236

Ammendola, Vigna, 301

Amphitheatrum Castrense, 121, 123

Anachronisms in the *Gesta*, 186, 188 ; in the *L.P.*, 59, 75 seqq.

Anacletus (or Cletus) P.M., name and order of succession, 49, 53, 54 ; decrees of, 10 ; builds memorial chapel (memoria) to Peter, 8, 9, 84, 89, 278

Analecta Bollandiana, 129 ; cf. 344 seqq.

Anastasia M., of Persia, 195, 215, 343 ; titulus of, 11, 12, 13 ; (inscriptions for), 241 ; translation of relics, 113, 115

Anastasius I. P., 37

    ,,   II. P., life of in *L.P.*, 54, 56, 58, 60, 61, 64 ; decrees of, 75 ; epitaph of, 243, 257

    ,,   M., ch. of, 124

    ,,   patriarch of Antioch, 32

    ,,   Bibliothecarius, reputed author of *L.P.*, 62

Anatolia and Victoria MM., 343

Andrew Ap. M., in *M.H.*, 214 ; *Passion of*, 194 ; ch. of on Vatican, 263 ; (inscriptions for), 231, 257, 258, 287 ; ch. of S. Andrew Catabarbara on the Esquiline, 5, 14

Angels, worship of, 45

Angilbert, English abbot of S. Richarius, Centula, author of *Sylloge Centulensis*, 232 ; and of inscription

to Caidocus, 250 ; removes library to Reichenau, 233 n. 1

Anglo-Saxon, see English ;—*Chronicle*, 37 ;—Kings, 22 n. 1

Anicetus P.M., order of succession, 49, 53 ; a Syrian, 66 ; martyrdom of, 67 n. 4

Anicius, 23

Anii, 23

Anniversaries (natales), of apostles, see Peter, Peter and Paul ; of bishops and popes, see *Depositio Episcoporum* ; of martyrs, see *Depositio Martyrum* ; see Martyrs, *Acta Martyrum* ; of Mithras, 51 ; of ordinations of popes, 74, 224, 226 ; see *Calendars, Martyrologies*

Ansa, Lombard queen, hospice of on Mt. Garganus, 26

Anteros P.M., martyrdom of, 68 ; decrees of, 76, 182 ; in *M.H.*, 220 ; tomb and epitaph, 292, 299, 302

Anthemas, patriarch, deposed for heresy, 58

Anthimius M., 343

Anthologia Carminum, 234

    ,,   *Isidoriana*, 234

    ,,   *Latina*, 240

    ,,   *Salmasiana*, 233

Anthologies, inscriptions in, 233

Antioch, Anastasius, patriarch of, 32 ; *Calendar of*, 219 ; church revenues from for S. Peter's, 90 ; Fabius B. of, 162 ; Ignatius B.M. of, q.v. —in Pisidia, see Acacius B.M.

Antoninus, E., 64

Antonius M., companion of Marcellus P.M., 73

Antwerp, Rosweyde of and *A.SS.*, 129

Anulinus, judge, 109, 137

Apocalypse, known to writers of *Acta Martyrum*, 166

Apocryphal *Gesta* of fifth century, 73, 138, 178–204 ; rejection by Church, 67, 76, 181 seqq., 192 seqq. ; sources of *L.P.*, 74, 81, seqq. ; see *Acta Martyrum, Gesta Martyrum*

Apollinaris, Sidonius, B. of Clermont-Ferrand, 36, 236

Apollo, 95 ; temple of, 70, 89

23

Apollonia M., 343

Apollonius M., *Acts of*, 147, 169

Apostasy, 140, 142, 177 ; cf. 73

Apostles (sc. Twelve), 49 ; in *M.H.*, 211, 212, 214 ; founders of churches, 49 ; *Canons of*, 55, 74, 75

,, (sc. SS. James and Philip), ch. of, see James and Philip, ch. of

,, (sc. SS. Peter and Paul), see Peter, Paul, Peter and Paul ; Catacumbas, basilica of, Ad ; ch. of (titulus Apostolorum, or t. Eudoxiae, called Ad Vincula Petri), see Peter, ch. of, Ad Vincula ; Tropaea Apostolorum, 9 ; see Peter, Memoria of

Appia, Via, 2, 15, 67, 69, 70, 72, 73, 99, 104, 105, 106, 115, 116, 125, 215, 220, 221, 222, 263, 304, 305 ; excavations on, and collation of monument and document, 297 (ch. hd.)—306 ; inscriptions of, 240, 250, 252, 256 ; collated lists of shrines on, from the *Itineraries*, 298, 299

Apronianus, Coem. Aproniani ad S. Eugeniam, 99, 102, 215, 340

Apuleius M., 343

Aqua Salvia, 124

Aqueducts, 2 ; Aqua Claudia (or Julia, Marcia, Tepula), 121, 123 ; Forma Virginis, 120 ; Lateranensis, 121, 123 ; *De Aquaeductibus* of Frontinus, 340

Aquileia, Chromatius B. of, 212 ; martyrs of in *M.H.*, 215, 217 ; Riparius of, 45

Aquilinus M. of Scilli, 153

Aquitaine, Desiderius B. of, 45

Aravatius (or Servatius) B. of Tongres, 36

Archangels, worship of, 45

Archives, judicial (*archivium proconsulis*), 134, 136 ; of Church, 74, 75, 91, 213, 216 ; see Laurence *in Damaso*, ch. of

Arculf, B. (of France), 119

Ardeatina, Via, 2, 15, 99, 107, 116,

125, 264, 306 ; excavations on, and collation of document and monument, 307–309 ; inscriptions of, 244, 250, 256

Argiletum, 121

Arians, 13 n. 8, 82, 194

Ariminum (Rimini), inscriptions of, 233

Ariston M., 339

Aritus M. of Aquileia, 215

Arles, Council of, 140 ; Hilary B. of, 36 ; Honoratus B. of, 215 ; Sapaudius B. of, 30 ; Genesius M. of, *Acts of*, 135

Armenia, revenues from for S. Peter's, 90 ; Armenian version of *Acts of Eugenia*, 193

Armitage Robinson on *Acts of Perpetua*, 165

Arverni (Auvergne), district of, 209

Asceticism, praise of in *Gesta*, 194, 195 ; (fasting), 26, 64, 74, 75, 77, seqq., 162 ; (virginity), 18, 118, 292, 313, 315

Ashburnham, Lord, library of, 340

Asia, 162 ;—Minor, 219 ; see *Greek Menology* of

Associations, illegal, 138, 142

Asterius B. of Amasia, 134, 187

,, priest of Rome, 203

Astion M., 144

Athanagines M. of Nicomedia, *Acts of*, 194

Atheism, charge of, 306

Auceia M., 343

Audeinus M., 215

Augurius M., companion of Fructuosus, 157, 158, 216

Augustalis, reader, 158

Augustine, Archbishop of Canterbury, 207

,, B. of Hippo, correspondence with Paulinus of Nola, 36 ; inscriptions by, 236 ; martyrs, references to, 20, 22, 41 (*De Cura pro mortuis gerenda*), 42, 80, 151, 157, 165, 181 ; on paganism of Christians, 4, 26 n. 2, 27 seq. ; on papa succession, 54; on traditores, 138 seqq.; *De origine animae*, 167; *De Trinitate*, 202; see Monica

Augustus E., 2

Aunarius (or Aunacharius) B. of Auxerre, 209, 212

Aurelia, Via, 2, 15, 52, 53, 99, 105, 113, 115, 116, 117, 125, 203, 221, 222, 337

Aurelian E., 341; Wall of, 2, 94, 117, 118, 121, 301, 341

Aurelianus M., 343

Aurelii, 309

Aurelius Repentinus, poet, 40

Auspicius, servant of Domitilla, 307

Autun (Augustodunum), 60, 208-209; see Gallic

Auvergne (Arverni), 209, 236

Auxerre (Autussiodorum), see Germanus B. of; place of origin of *M.H.*; 204 (ch. hd.), 208-211, 228; see Gallic

Aventine, 5, 14, 96

Aventinus, region called, 13

Avitus B. of Vienne, 30

,,   B. of Arverni (Auvergne), 209, 210

B

Babylon, martyrs of, 219

Baiae, martyrs of in *M.H.*, 217

Balbina M., 343; Coem. Balbinae ad Marcum et Marcellianum, 52, 99, 125, 337; (titulus Balbinae), 13; ch. of on Aventine, 5

Bangor, *Martyrology of Bede* used at, 229

Baptism, of Cadwalla, 239; of Constantine, 81; of converts, 10, 76; of Dinocrates, 167; dogma concerning, see Baptisteries, inscriptions for; of martyrs, 136, 145, 169; Mithraic, 3; by Thecla, 194; in Westminster Cathedral, 284 n. 2

Baptisteries, circular, built on pagan models, 9; of S. Germanus, Auxerre, 210; of Lateran, 225; inscriptions for: of African church unknown, 284; of S. Anastasia, 273 n. 1, 280;

of Lateran, 271 n. 1, 280; of S. Laurence *in Damaso*, 280, 283; of S. Michael Archangel, 258, 259, 263, 264, 274-277; see infra *Sumite-Istic* inscriptions; of S. Paul, 264, 268, 273 n. 1, 280; of S. Peter, Vatican, 258, 262, 273, 279, 280, 285; of S. Priscilla, 247-248, 273-274, 284; *Sumite-Istic* inscriptions, 244 (ch. hd.), 247, 248, 270-277

Barbarian invasions of Rome, 6, 7, 17, 18, 36, 64, 86, 97, 187, 220, 225

Bardenhewer on *Gesta Martyrum*, 196

Baronius on *Gesta Martyrum*, 128, 131, 173

Basileus, Coem. Basilei ad S. Marcum, 99

Basilica(s), Christian, 8, 9; ad Corpus, see Laurence, basilica of; for stations, (at Auxerre), 212; (in Rome), 13 seq.; pagan, 5, 8, 97

Basilis M., 343

Basilla M. [Sep. 22] of Via Salaria, Coem. Basillae ad S. Hermen, 98, 106, 118, 215, 338, 339

Bassus, consul (of 258), 52, 72, 157

,,   Anicius, consul (of 408), 236

,,   Junius, consul (of 317), 5

Baths, 3, 6, 9; list of, 124; of Constantine, 121, 122; of Diocletian, 120; of Timothy (or Novatus), 5, 154; of Trajan, 81

Bauso M., 106, 108

Beatrix (or Viatrix) M., 116, 117, 346

Bede, and Alcuin, 232; *Martyrology of*, 55, 183, 206, 207, 229; and relations of English to Rome, 28, 37 seqq., 83; quotes *Liber Pontificalis*, 55, 58, 61; and Roman inscriptions, 231, 233; on an *Itinerary*, 118

Belgium, home of *A.SS.* 129

Belisarius invades Italy, 25, 57, 58, 64

Benedict I. P., epitaph of, 261, 265

,,   II. P., epitaph of, 265

,,   the Canon, *Ordo Romanus* of, 123 seqq.

Benedictine, Leclercq a, 130, 131; monastery at Einsiedeln, 233; of Monte Cassino, 195, 340, 341; Ruinart a, 130

Beneventum, martyrs of in *M.H.*, 217
Berne, Codex of, see *Codex*
Bethlehem, 43, 45, 52, 214
Bib(b)iana M., ch. of on Esquiline, 14, 117, 121, 122, 343
Biblias M. of Lyons, 177
Biscop Benedict of England, 38
Bishops of Rome. See Popes
Blastro M., 106, 108
Blessing of fruits of earth, 80; of houses, 80; of pilgrim's staff and scrip, 37 n. 4, 93
Boethius, widow of, 282 n. 3
Bollandists, 129–130, 131, 207; see *Acta Sanctorum, Analecta Bollandiana*
Bollandus, 129
Bonavenia on *Syllogae*, 245, 267, 268, 271; on *Sumite-Istic* inscriptions, 273–277
Boniface I. P., edicts of, 81; in *M.H.*, 222–226; inscriptions by 227, 293; builds ch. of S. Felicitas, 15
    ,,   II. P., in *L.P.*, 60; epitaph of, 231, 261, cf. 238
    ,,   III., and IV., and V., PP., epitaphs of, 261, 265
    ,,   M. of Via Salaria, S. of, 106, 108, 115, 118
    ,,   M. [May 14], 343
    ,,   , ch. of (S. Alessio on Aventine), 14
    ,,   B., England, 231, 238
Bonosa M., 343
Bordeaux, Delphinius B. of, 37; Paulinus of, 36
Bosio, excavations in catacombs by, 17 n. 3, 307
Bosredon, excavations in Africa by, 310
Brandea (cloths) laid on apostles' tombs, 29, 31, 32, 33
Brest, Julianus M. of, 210
Breviaria, of *Martyrologies*, 206; of the *Notitia*, 95
Britain, 43, 119; relations to Rome, 18, 30; (Lucius), 83; see English
British Isles, manuscripts of *Martyrologies* in, 206; see England

Brutii, 23
Burgundy, place of origin of *M.H.*, 226; *Cononian Abridgment of L.P.* in monastery of, 60
Burial, 97; ad Sanctos, 41; confraternity, 10; of martyrs, see *Depositio Martyrum*; of popes, see Popes; revels at burials, 26 seqq.
Busaeus, first prints *L.P.*, 62
Byzanti (or Pammachii) titulus (ch. of SS. John and Paul), 12, 13
Byzantine restoration in Italy, 57–59; frescoes, 122, 303

C

Cadwalla K., in Rome, 23, 239; epitaph of, 231, 250
Caeciliae, titulus (S. Cecilia in Trastevere), 13; see Cecilia
Caecilii, tombs of, in S. Callixtus, 305, 306
Caelimontium, region of, 12
Caesar, slaves of household of, 154, 186; cf. Narcissus
Caesarea in Cappadocia, Procopius M. of, 162, 163, 196
    ,,   in Palestine, Procopius M. of, 195, 196; Eusebius B. of, 179, 213; see Eusebius
Caesarius M., deacon, 128, 342, 343
Caidocus, Scotch priest, epitaph of, 250, 251
Calabria, 75
Calendar(s), 133; of Africa, 205, 211 n. 3, 216, 218–220; (of *Alexandria*), 219; (of *Carthage*), 218–220, cf. 205; of East, 196, 216, 219; (of *Antioch*), 219; (of *Asia Minor* or *Greek Menology*), 179, 205, 218, 219; (*Ferial of Eusebius*), 213; *Calendar of Miltiades*; see infra *Roman*; Oriental, see of East; Pagan, 51, 133; *Roman Calendar* (or of *Miltiades*, of 312), 52, 114, 180, 183, 216, 218, 220 seqq., 224 seqq.; see *Philocalian Calendar*; of *Ravenna*, 132; of saints in S. Silvester, 296
Calepodius M. priest, 203, 343; Coem.

Calepodii ad S. Callixtum (or ad S. Pancratium), 203, 221, 222, 223, 302, 339

Callixtus P.M., public works of, 84; martyrdom of, 51, 67; in *Calendars*, 201, 339, 342, 343; *Passion* of, 200, 203, 204; shrine of in Calepodius, see Calepodius; ch. of in Trastevere, 203; Coem. Callixti ad S. Sixtum, 40, 51, 52, 53, 70, 72, 73, 99, 125, 215, 221, 222, 298, 299, 337, 338, 339, cf. 105; (inscriptions and graffiti of), 40, 291, 292, 302; see Cecilia, Damasus (inscriptions), Excavations, Frescoes, Popes (tombs in)

Calocerus, MM., Parthenius and, see Parthenius

Calopus M., 116

Cambridge text of *L.P.*, and *Sylloge of*, see *Sylloge of*

Canon(s), of *Apostles*, 55, 74, 75; *Book of Canons of Apostles*, 75; *Collection of Canons of Apostles*, 81; *of Councils*, 74; of Scripture, 47, 182, cf. 153; *of Mass*, see *Mass*

Canterbury, Cathedral of, 39; Nothelm, Arbp. of, 37; saints of in *Calendars*, 207

Cantharus, inscription for, 286; see Fountain

Capito, consul, 64

Capitoline Hill, 2, 121, 122, 203; museum on, 94

Cappadocia, martyrs of, 155, 156

Capua, 217, 306

Cardinals, titles of, 11

Caritas M., 105, 109, 298, 304

Carlo Borromeo, St., 130

Carmelite order, 129

Carolingian epoch, 231, 240; see Charlemagne

Carpophorus MM., Secundus and, see Secundus

Carpus, Papylus and Agathonice MM. of Pergamos, *Passion of*, 147, 169; (Carpus), 145, 176

Carthage, 282 n. 3; *Calendars* of, 219–220; martyrs of, 52, 138, 141, 151, 152, 165, 171, 173

Carthusian, Surius a, 128

Cassian(-us) M. of Africa, 135
    ,,   and Hyacinthus MM., epitaph of, 257

Cassino, Monte, *manuscripts* and *Passionary* of Benedictine Monastery of, 195, 340, 341

Cassiodorus of Vivarium, 7, 61, 75; and *Martyrology of Jerome*, 215–217, 228

Catabarbara, St. Andrew, 5

Catabulum, in (transport service), 71

Catacombs, identical with cemeteries, q.v.

Catacumbas ad S. Sebastianum, Coem. Ad (shrine of SS. Peter and Paul), 52, 69, 85, 99, 106, 125, 188, 263, 298, 299, 305, 337; basilica of, 15, 307 seq.; (inscriptions of), 241, 256; monastery of, 85

Catalogue of Popes, Roman (fifth cent.), 54, 56; see Popes

Catana, martyrs of, 138, 217

Cecilia M., 227, 305, 343; titular ch. of in Trastevere, 8, 13, 120, 121, 316; (inscriptions of), 242, 253, 296; crypt of, in S. Callixtus, 40, 105, 109, 298, 315–317; oratory of SS. Sixtus and, in S. Callixtus, 302, 304; statue of, by Maderno, 317; tradition of, illustrated by excavation, 315–317; *Passion of*, 69, 194, 200, 202, 316

Celestinus P., 114, 282; gifts to church, 86; epitaph, 237, 247, 272 n. 2
    ,,   M., 118

Cemeteries (or Catacombs), 2, 11, 94 n. 1, 101 n. 1, 102, 195, 227, 297, 306; *Index Coemiteriorum XVI.*, 96 seqq., 124 n. 2, 298, 300, 306, 340; *Index Coem.* in *Mirabilia urbis Romae*, 124 seqq.; monuments of, see Churches, suburban; organization of, 10, 76, 77; see Damasus, Excavations, Frescoes, Pilgrimages, Translation of bodies

Centula (S. Riquier), 232; monastery of, 234; see *Sylloge of*

Centumcellae (Civita Vecchia), 69, 70

Ceres, temple of, 95

Chains of Peter and Paul, 28, 29; see Peter, ch. of *ad Vincula*

Chair of Peter (sedes ubi prius sedit Petrus or Cathedra Petri), see Peter, Chair of

Chalcedon, Council of, 59

Charita M., 154

Charitas, see Caritas

Chariton M., 154

Charlemagne, 23, 25, 120, 183, 231, 232; see Carolingian epoch

Charles the Bold, 229

Charta Cornutiana, 92

Charters of foundations of churches, 38, 39, 91

Chartres, library of, 129

Chigiana, Biblioteca and *Index*, 98 n. 1, 340

Childebert K., 30, 32

Chione M. See Agape, Irene and Chione

Christ, 3, 43, 44, 45, 46, 47, 52, 65, 145, 153, 154, 164, 173, 175, 181, 190, 211, 213, 239, 281, 282, 285; confession of faith in, 154, 190, 239, 247, 272 n. 2; names of, 23, 28, 46, 145, 166, 177, 214, 281, 282, 285; Passion and Redemption of, 28, 190, 211, 212; (inscription), 284; see Cross; Resurrection of, 211, 290; see Christmas, Easter, Eucharist, Incarnation

Christmas, 52 (and n. 4), 53, 64, 79, 211, 337

Chrodobertus B. of Tours, 248

Chromatius and Heliodorus BB., *letters of* in *M.H.*, 212 seqq.

Chronica Francica, 61

Chronicle, *Anglo-Saxon*, 37; *of Eadmer*, 39; *of Hippolytus*, 50 seqq.

Chrysanthus and Darias MM., 33, 343; S. and inscription of, 105, 107, 110, 118, 242, 246; *Passion of*, 194, 200

Chrysogonus M., 342; titulus Chrysogoni, in Trastevere, 13, 120

Church, 4, 71 n. 2, 159, 175, 239, 267; archives of, 74, 75, 152, 153, 213, 216; books of, 92, 162, 163; (authenticity of *Gesta*), 192 seqq., 181

seqq.; (Canon of Scripture), 47' 182; (destruction of), 138 seqq., 142, 145, 151, 153, 179; doctrin of, 167, 194, see Christ, confession of faith in; in East, 25, 64, 188 n. 3; see Antioch, Constantinople, Palestine; organization of, 9, 10, 43, 77, 181, see Popes; revenues of, 84–92; (from East), 88, 90; see *Calendars*, Councils, Heretics, Liturgy, Pagans, Peace of Church, Persecutions

Churches, dedications of in *Calendars*, 206; foundations by Apostles, 49; parish churches (tituli), 10; list of, 12, 13; stational churches, list of, 13, 14; in Rome in sixth century, 87, 97; suburban churches, 87; (list of), 15; for inscriptions see *Syllogae* and under names of churches, and martyrs, and popes

Cicero, manuscript of, 253

Cillo, 5

Circus Flaminius, region of, 12;— Maximus, region of, 12

Circumpadana et Subalpina, Sylloge, see *Sylloge Laureshamensis*

Ciricus (Cyriacus) and Julitta (June 16) MM., *Passion of*, 182

Cirta, 138; martyrs of, 168

Cittinus M. of Scilli, 152, 153

Claudian, consul, 152

Claudius, Clement and Sempronianus MM., 339

Clement P.M., 49, 53, 54, 74, 342, 344; decrees and writings of, 75, 76, 136 n. 5, 182, 193; martyrdom of, 67; *Passion of*, 68, 200

,, VII. P., 317

,, M., consul, 142, 227, 306

,, M. of Chersonnesus, 200 n. 3

,, of Alexandria, 193

Clermont (-Ferrand), (Arvernum) in Auvergne, 209; Sidonius B. of, 36, 236

Cletus, P., 53, 54

Clivum Cucumeris, Coem. ad Sanctam Columbam ad Caput S. Joannis in, 98, 102, 106, 124

Cloths as relics, see Brandea

Clovis K. of Franks, 86

Codex of Berne (*C. Bernensis*), *of Corvie* (*C. Corbeiensis*), *of Epternach* (*C. Epternacensis*), *of M.H.*, 206, 207 ; *of Palatine* (*C. Palatinus*) in the Vatican, 242, see *Sylloge Laureshamensis* ; *of Vienna* (*C. Vindobonensis*) *of Passionary of Gregory*, 201

Coelian Hill, 25, 96, 113, 114, 117, 289

Coinred K., 24

Collection of Ancient Martyrdoms of Eusebius, 179, 183, 216

Colosseum, 2, 122

Columbam S., Ad, see Clivum Cucumeris

Commodillae, ad SS. Felicem et Adauctum, coem., 99, 101, 102 ; epitaph of Felix and Adauctus, 119, 187 ; basilica of, 15

Communion, 28, see Eucharist

Como, Amantius B. of, 29

Concordius M., of Umbria, 342

Confirmation, of King Alfred, 24; inscriptions concerning, 248, 254 (ch. hd.), 259, 270–277, 278 (ch. hd.), 284

Conon P., 58

Cononian Abridgment of L.P., 60, 61

Constance, Lake, monasteries round, 232, 233

Constantina Empress, and the head of S. Paul, 32 seqq.

Constantine E., 5, 9, 14, 15, 21, 95, 193, 211, 212, 236 ; baptism of, 81 ; gifts to church, 84, 85, 88 seqq., 101, 180, 278 ; basilica of, see Lateran ; Baths of, 121, 122 ; horse of, 121

Constantinople, 5, 65, 96 ; Council of, 59

Cordova, martyrs of, 216

Corinthians, Clement's letter to, 49

Cornelia, Via, 2, 15, 99, 101, 105, 116, 117, 120, 215, 235, 249

Cornelius P.M., in *Calendars*, 222, 223, 342, 343 ; martyrdom of and *Passion*, 67, 69, 200, 303 ; Crypt of

(or Crypt of Lucina), 70, 105, 298, 299 ; (excavations, frescoes, and epitaph), 292, 300 seqq. ; (chapel of), 15

Coronatorum Quattuor, MM. (Four Crowned Saints), 344 ; titular church of (or t. Aemilianae), 12

Corvie, see *Codex of* ; monastery of, 232 ; see *Sylloge of Corvie*

Council(s), annual papal, 74 ; of Arles, 140 ; Canons of, 74 ; of Chalcedon, 59 ; of Constantinople, 59 ; *Collection of Councils* of Dionysius, 74, 75 ; of Elvira, 315 ; of Ephesus, 59, 272 n. 2, 282 ; of Gregory I., 11 ; of Hippo, 179 ; of Milan, 213, 217 ; of Nicaea, 59, 81 ; œcumenical, 59, 74 ; Roman (of 499), 11, 87 ; (of 595), 77 ; of Silvester, 183

Crescentiae, titulus (? San Sisto), 12

Crescenti(an)us M., 40, 72, 73, 118, 338, 339, 344

Cross of Christ, 284 ; ch. of Holy Cross (Sessorian Basilica, S. Croce in Gerusalemme), 5, 14, 85, 121, 123 ; Invention of, 83, 211, 212 ; (*Acts of Invention* of, *De Inventione Crucis*), 182 ; relics of, 14, 29, 31 ; sign of, 174, 284, 285 ; inscriptions for the Chapel of the Holy Cross (for a consignatorium in Africa), 284 ; in Baptistery of S. Peter's, 185 ; see Confirmation, inscriptions for

Crusade, 117

Cumae, Juliana M. of, 342

Curia Senatus, 5, 122

Curiosum Urbis Romae regionum XIV., 95, 97, 341

Curubis in Africa, 148, 149

Cuthbert B., in *Martyrology*, 207

Cybele, 3, 125

Cyprian B.M., 80, 140, 168, 172, 174, 176, 179, 218, 299 ; in *Calendar*, 52, 338, 339 ; correspondence of, 70, 137, 143, 193 ; *Acts of* (*Acta Cypriani*), 141, 143, 147 seqq., 153, 163, 181 ; *Passion of*, 163 seqq. ; Commemoration in Crypt of Cornelius, 303

Cyprus, 88, 91

Cyrenus M., companion of Marcellinus P.M., 73

Cyriaca M. [Aug. 21], 344 ; cem. of on Via Tiburtina, 72

Cyriaci, titulus (? ch. of in Suburra), 11, 12

Cyriacus, Largus and Smaragdus MM. [Aug. 8], in *Calendars*, 338, 339, 341, 344 ; *Passion of Cyriacus*, 194 ; Coem. Cyriaci Via Ostiense, 100, 125; ch. of in Suburra (? titulus Cyriaci), 121, 122

Cyricus, see Ciricus

Cyril of Alexandria, 44

Cyrinus (or Quirinus) M., companion of Agapitus M., in Praetextatus, 298, 299, 305

,,   B.M., of Siscia in Pannonia, in Ad Catacumbas, 106, 217, 298, 299, 306

Cyrrhus, Theodoret B. of, 25

D

Dadas M. (? of Ephesus), companion of Maximus, 135

Dalmatia, martyrs of, in *M.H.*

Damasus P., Life of, 211–315, see *infra* Inscriptions of; (apocryphal letters of Jerome and, in *L.P.*), 55, 56; (and in *M.H.*), 223, 224, 226. Public works of, 101, 180, 295; (in Basilica Damasi of Via Ardeatina), 15, 85, 100, 256, 290, 312–313, 314, 315; (in S. Laurence *in Damaso* or titulus Damasi), 12, 85 ; (in S. Peter, Vatican), 262, 279–280, 283–284, 288–289. Inscriptions of, 237, 254, 265 ; (autobiographical and family), 311–315; (epitaph of himself), 256, 264, 290–291 ; (of father, Leo), 289, 311, 313–315; (of mother, Laurentia), 290, 312–313, 314, 315 ; (of sister, Irene), 312–313; (of martyrs in general), 50, 55, 101, 180–181, 237, 249, 295; (of SS. Peter and Paul, Ad Catacumbas), 85, 188 n. 2, 305 ; (of popes in Papal Crypt of S. Callixtus), 41, 291–292, 301, 303 ; (of other martyrs in the Catacombs), 187–188, 290–293, 304–305, 308

Darias MM., Chrysanthus and, see Chrysanthus

Dativus M., 215

Decius E., 70, 72, 141, 147

Delehaye on *Gesta Martyrum*, 130, 131, 169, 185–196

Delphinius B. of Bordeaux, 37

Depositio Episcoporum and *Depositio Martyrum* of *Calendar of Autun* (Augustodunum), 208 seqq. ; *of Auxerre* (Autussiodorum), 208 seqq. ; of the *Philocalian Calendar*, 51–52, 73, 98 n. 1, 100, 114, 303, 337 seqq., cf. 341 seqq.

De Rossi, excavations of in catacombs, 18 ; (in Viae Appia and Ardeatina), 300–309; on *Index Coemiteriorum*, 340 ; on *Itineraries*, 94, 97, 100, 116 n. 1 ; on *M.H.*, 206, 207, 209, 228 ; on *Syllogae*, 234, 240, 251, 271, 273–277, 310–311

Desiderius B. of Aquitaine, 45

,,   K. of Lombards, 26

Deusdedit P., epitaph of, 261, 265

Diana, temple of, 125

Digna and Merita MM., 344, 345; *Passion of*, 188

Dinocrates, brother of S. Perpetua, vision concerning, 167

Diocletian E., Baths of, 120, 124 ; destruction of documents under, 138 seqq., 179 ; persecution of, 10, 69, 70, 73, 77, 109, 134, 141, 144, 156, 179, 180, 186, 188, 195

Diogenes M., 115

Dionysius P.M., decrees of, 76 ; in *Calendars*, 51, 337 ; (in *M.H.*), 222, 223, 226 ; S. of, 298, 299 ; (and epitaph), 292, 293

,,   deacon, epitaph of, and inscription by, 237

,,   B. of Alexandria, 162

,,   monk of Scythia, compiler of *Canons of Councils*, etc., 74, 75

Dominanda V., 118

"Domine, quo Vadis," ch. of, 124

Domitian E., 227 ; persecution of, 10, 141

Domitilla, Flavia, 142, 227, 306, 307, 309, 342 ; coem. Domitillae, Nerei et Achillei ad S. Petronillam, 99, 102 ; (excavations in and inscriptions), 307 seq.

Donata V., of Via Salaria, 118
,, M., of Scilli, 152, 153
Donatella MM., Maxima and, see Maxima
Donatists, 54 n. 1, 220 n. 2
Donatus B., of Tuscany, 342
Doxology, 153, 156, 160, 163, 171
Duas Lauros ad SS. Petrum et Marcellinum, coem. Ad, 98, 124
Duchesne, an Academician, 131 ; on inscriptions, 276 ; on *L.P.*, 48–92 ; on *M.H.*, 205–229 ; on notarii, 183
Dufourcq on *Itineraries*, 114, 116 n. 1 ; on *M.H.*, 226, 228 ; on *Roman Calendar*, 114 n. 1 ; on Roman *Gesta*, 199–205 ; on *Passionary of Gregory*, 201
Dynamius, 250 n. 1

E

Eadburga, Abbess of Thanet, 88
Eadmer, Chronicle of, 39
East, see Asceticism, *Calendars, Martyrologies*, Church, *Gesta*, Heretics, Monasteries
Easter, 23, 64, 77, 212 ; see Christ, Resurrection of
Ecclesiastical Annals, see Baronius
,, *History*, see Bede, Eusebius
Egypt, revenues to S. Peter's from, 90 ; see Alexandria
Egyptian giant, Perpetua's vision of, 168
Einsiedeln, Itinerary of (Itinerarium Einsiedlense), 109, 119–123, 241 ; monastery of, 119 ; see *Sylloge of Einsiedeln*
Eleutherius, P.M., 49 ; and conversion of Lucius, K. of Britain, 83 ; decrees of, 78
,, M., 344 ; *Passion of*, 187
Elfleda, queen of England, 38
Elijah, prophet, in *A.SS.*, 129
Elpis of Sicily, epitaph of, 239

Elvira, Council of, 315
Ely, ch. of S. Peter, 39
Emerentianae, coem., see Agnes, cem. of
Emeritus M., 215
Emperors, Arian, 82 ; edicts of, 4 n. 3, 6, 7, 142 ; see Persecutions ; gifts to church, 84–92 ; as pilgrims to Rome, 21 seqq. ; prayers for, 152, 281 ; worship of, 142, 158 ; see under names of emperors
England, 118, 217, 229 ; relations to Rome, 23 seqq., 37 seqq., 231, 232 ; monks of, 233 n. 1, 250 seq. ; see Alcuin, Angilbert, Bede, Caidocus, William of Malmesbury ; and under the names of kings
Ephesus, Council of, 59, 272 n. 2, 282 ; see Maximus, M. of
Epictetus, priest, 144
Epiphanius, *Adversus Haereses* of, 54
Epternach, see *Codex of Epternach*
Equitii or Silvestri, titulus (SS. Silvester and Martin), 12 ; see Silvester
Esdras, Book of, 47
Esquiliae, region of, 12
Esquiline, 2, 5, 14, 87, 92, 96
Ethelswitha, sister of King Alfred, 24
Ethelwulf, K., 24
Ethiopia, 18
Eucharis, epitaph of in S. Priscilla, 274 n. 1
Eucharist, see Martyrs, anniversaries of ; celebrated by martyrs, 138, 143, 158, 172, cf. 186 ; frescoes of in Catacombs, 166, 301 ; Perpetua's vision of, 166 ; milk as symbol of, 166 ; see Mass
Eudoxia, empress, 22, 122 ; titulus Eudoxiae (or Apostolorum), 12 ; see Peter, ch. of *ad Vincula*
Euelpistus M., companion of Justin M., 154, 156
Eugenia M., 344 ; *Acts of*, 193 ; coem. Aproniani ad S. Eugeniam, 99, 215, 340
Eulogius B. of Alexandria, correspondence of Gregory the Great and, 183, 201, 216 ; cf. 132
,, M., of Tarragona, companion of Fructuosus, 157, 158, 216

Euphemia, St., ch. of, 121, 122
,, M., of Pontus, 134, 135
Euphrates, 91
Euplus M., of Catana, 138
Eusebius P.M. [Sep. 26], *Passion of*, 200, 202 ; in *Calendars*, 222, 342, 344 ; region of in S. Callixtus, 303 ; (tomb and epitaph), 52, 292, 298, 299, 302, 303, 337
,, M. [Aug. 14], Rome, in S. Callixtus, 299, 342, 344
,, and Pontianus MM. [Aug. 25], Rome, 344
,, historian, 9, 49, 50, 54, 140, 161, 162, 170, 179, 183, 195, 216, 219
Eustathius M., 344
Eustochium, daughter of Paula, friend of Jerome, 26, 43
Eustratius, 135
Euticetus M., 215
Eutychianus P.M., in *Calendars*, 67 n. 4, 222, 223, 337 ; decrees of, 80 ; tomb of, 299 ; (and epitaph) 303
Eutychius M., S. of, 106, 298 ; (and epitaph), 306
Evaristus P.M., order of succession, 49 ; decrees of, 10, 81
Excavations in Catacombs, in Calepodius, 203 ; in S. Callixtus, 67, 297 (ch. hd.), 300–304 ; (inscriptions in), 250, 291, 292 ; (in Crypt of Cecilia), 40, 105, 109, 298, 301, 304, 315–317 ; (in Papal Crypt), 69, 85, 99, 125, 316 ; (inscriptions in), 291, 292 ; cf. 51, 52, 72, 73 ; in Ad Catacumbas, 305–306 ; in Via Latina, 193 n. 3 ; in Domitilla, 307 seqq. ; in Praetextatus, 304 ; see Frescoes
Exeter, 39
Expansion of original documents in *Gesta*, 179, 186, 189–191, 195

F

Fabianus P.M., buildings of, 84 ; decrees of, 10, 76, 182 ; martyrdom of, 51, 52, 67, 68 ; tomb of, 221, 223, 298, 300, 337, 339 ; (and epitaph), 292, 302
Fabius B. of Antioch, 162

Fasciolae, titulus (ch. of SS. Nereus and Achilleus), 13, 187 ; see Nereus
Fasting, see Asceticism
Fathers of Church, fresco representing, 289 ; see Augustine, Jerome, etc.
Fausta, princess, 9
Faustinus M., of Via Portuensis, translation of, 117
,, of Africa, 215
Feasts, funeral (parentalia), 28 ; (agape), 80 ; see Anniversaries, *Calendars* (pagan)
Felician Abridgment of L.P., 59–61
Felicianus MM., Primus and, see Primus
Felicissimus MM., Agapitus and, see Agapitus
Felicitas M., of Via Salaria, and her seven sons, in *Calendars*, 52, 344 ; coem. Felicitatis, 106, 108, 115, 118, 124, 198, 299, 304 ; (and epitaph), 293 ; (basilica of), 15
,, M., of Carthage, companion of Perpetua, 165, 168, 176, 338, 339
,, M., of Milan, 215
Felix I. P.M. [Dec. 30], in *Calendars*, 223, 337, 342 ; tomb of, 51, 292 ; (epitaph), 303
,, II. P.M. [July 29], in *Calendars*, 224, 334 ; life of in *L.P.*, 82
,, III. P., in *L.P.*, 56, 66 ; builds S. Agapitus, 15
,, IV. P., buildings by, 15, 86, 122 ; inscriptions by, 261, 287 ; in *L.P.*, 60
,, M., son of Felicitas, of Via Salaria, S. of, 106, 107, 118, 338, 339 ; epitaph in S. Silvester, 247
,, M., of Via Aurelia, 116
,, and Adauctus MM., of Rome [Aug. 30], on Via Ostiensis, 344 ; for cemetery see Commodillae
,, (and Saturninus) MM. of Carthage, 142
,, M. of Nola, 26

INDEX

363

Felix M. of Scilli, 153

" B.M. of Tibiuca, *Acts of*, 173

" of Tarragona, friend of Fructuosus B.M., 159

" Cirta, flamen, 139, 140

" Romanus M., priest [Jan. 14], in *Calendars*, 341, 344 ; *Acts of*, 137 ; *Vita S. Felicis presbyteri*, 187 ; Coem. ad insalatos (sic) ad S. Felicem Via Portuensi, 99, 125 ; (Basilica Julii in), 15

Ferial of Eusebius, 213 ; see *Calendars, Martyrologies*

Fides M., 105, 298, 304

Filocalus, see Philocalus

Fiorentini on *Index Coemiteriorum*, 341

Flaminia, Via, 14, 15, 98, 100, 101, 105, 113, 114, 115, 235, 249

Flavia Domitilla, see Domitilla

Flavian M. ("Fravianus"), 215

" M. of Carthage, companion of Montanus and Lucius, 172, 176

" (-us) judge (in *Passion of Procopius*), 163, 196

" Nichomachus, 3

Flavii, 309 ; Vestibule of, in cem. of Domitilla, 307

Flora M., 344

Florence, Biblioteca Laurenziana of, 340

Florus of Lyons, Martyrology of, 183, 229

Forbidden Books, Index of, 130

Forgeries, 81 seqq., 183 ; of *Gesta*, 192 seqq.

Fortunatus B.M., 215

Forums, 2, 6 ; of Carthage, 138 ; Forum Romanum, 5, 6, 86, 120, 121, 122 ; (Region of), 12 ; of Smyrna, 170

Four Crowned Saints, ch. of (Aemilianae titulus), 12

Fountain, of St. Peter's Church Vatican, 25 ; of S. Peter (Fons S. Petri), 120, 121 ; see Agnes, cem. of ; of S. Paul's, 286

Fourteen regions of Rome, see *Notitia regionum XIV*

France, mainly manuscripts and libraries of, 30, 60, 206, 207, 232 ; see Gaul, and under names of cities

Franks, 25, 86 ; see Gaul

Fredegaire, 61

Frescoes and paintings, in the Roman Catacombs in general, 133, 159 n. 1, 177, 301 ; in S. Callixtus, 166 ; (in Crypt of Cornelius or Lucina), 301, 303 ; (of Cecilia), 301 ; in Domitilla (Vestibule of Flavii), 307 ; (of Petronella), 308 ; in Praetextatus (S. Januarius), of seasons, 304 ; on Via Tiburtina (S. Hippolytus), 186. Other frescoes, (of Euphemia) 134, (of Eleutherius) 187, (in Library of Gregory I.) 187, (in S. Maria Maggiore) 283

Friesland, 38

Frisians, 25, 207

Fructuosus B.M. of Tarragona, 168, 174, 216 ; *Passion of*, 147, 157 seqq., 181

Fulgentuis B. of Ruspe, Africa, 36

G

Gabinius, proconsul, 135

Gaius P.M., edicts of, 77, 82 ; martyrdom of in *Passion of S. Susanna*, 70, 200 ; tomb, excavations and epitaph, 52, 292, 302

" ("Gagus") M., 215

" priest, on apostles' tombs, 9

Galerius Maximus, proconsul, 149, 150, 151

Gall, S., monastery of, 232, 233

Galla Placidia, empress, 22

Gallic origin of *M.H.*, 207-212, 228 ; see Gaul

Gallienus E., 141, 148, 150, 157 ; Arch of, 123

Gallus, a Christian, 40

Games, gladiatorial, 4

Garganus, Mount, hospice of, 26

Gaul, 45, 83 ; bishops of, 209, 210 ; martyrs and saints of, 146, 208-210 ; pilgrims from, 34, 36, 37 n. 2 ; see France, Gallic, and under names of towns

Gelasius I. P., 56, 57 ; buildings of, 86 ; decrees of (*De recipiendis*), 182, 192, 193, 194 ; *Sacramentary* of, 79

,, II. P., 254, 255

Generosa M., of Scilli, 153

,, cem. of, 117

Genesius M., of Arles, *Acts of*, 135, 342, 344

Genseric, 4, 6

George (Georgius) M., *Passion of*, 182 ; ch. of (San Giorgio in Velabro), 13, 121, 122

Germain, S. des Prés, Usuard of, 229

Germanus, B. of Auxerre, 30, 37, 210 ; in *M.H.*, 208–210 ; ch. of (Baptistery), 210

Germany, Germans, 18, 183, 206, 231, 233, 242

Gerusalemme, S. Croce in, see Cross, ch. of

Gesta, Martyrum, 56, 67, 73, 127, 178–204, 220, 227, 228, 229, 315 ; in East, 146, 207 ; and iconography and current literature, 166 ; hagiographers and *Gesta*, 185–198 ; heretics and, 182 ; in liturgy, 178, 179, 180, 181, 183 ; monastic use of, 180 ; oriental influence on, 195 ; Roman *Gesta*, 199 (ch. hd.)—208 ; tradition and *Gesta*, 185–198 ; *Liber Pontificalis* and, 67 seqq., 200 ; see *Acta Martyrum*

,, *Regum Anglorum*, 117

Getulius M., 344

Giorgi on *Index Coemiteriorum*, 341

Girulum, see Agatha

Glabrio, consul, 72

,, Acilius, M., consul, 227

Gloria in excelsis, 64, 79

Gloucester, S. Peter's, 39

Golden Legend (*Legenda Aurea*), 127

Golgotha, 211, 212

Gordianus M., 344 ; epitaph of, 292 ; Coem. Gordiani foris Portam Latinam, on Via Latina, 124

Gorgonius M., 338, 339

Goths, 13 n. 8, 18, 64, 80, 97, 267 ; in-

vasions of, 236, 294, 295, 341 ; kings, 57, 59 ; see Theodoric, Theodatus

Gottwei, Abbey of, 249

Graffiti, 20, 39, 40, 302, 303, 304

Gratian E., 100

Greek, hero Hippolytus, 187 ; invasions of Italy, 236 ; language for liturgy, 78, 79 ; for papal inscriptions, 302, 303 ; liturgy, 163 ; martyrs, 195, 287 ; the "Greek Martyrs" (Sancti Graeci), 342, 344 ; (*Gesta* of), 202 ; (inscription of), 291 ; popes, 66, cf. 64 ; see *Calendars*

Gregory I., the Great, P., 11, 14, 30, 31, 32, 37, 61, 78, 79, 88, 132, 250 n.1, 309, 340 ; Council of, 77 ; epitaph of, 231, 261 ; inscription for his library, 241, 289 ; *letter to Eulogius*, 132, 183, 201, 215 ; *Passionary of*, 132, 183, 201, 216 ; and Theodelinda, 102, 103, 107, 108

,, of Tours, 29, 36, 68, 210 ; (*De Gloria Martyrum*), 31, 33, 200 ; and *L.P.*, 60, 61

,, of Spoleto, 342

Grisar on Roman topography, 2 n. 1 ; on *Sumite-Istic* inscriptions, 275

H

Hadrian, P., 312 ; *letter to Charlemagne*, 183 ; epitaphs, 241

,, St., ch. of, 5, 13, 121, 122

Harnack on *Acta Martyrum*, 130, 169, 196 ; on *L.P.*, 66 n. 4 ; on *M.H.*, 228

Hegesippus, historian, 49, 246

Helena, Empress, 14, 123, 211, 212 ; ch. of, see Cross, ch. of ; coem. inter duas lauros ad S. Helenam, 98, 124

Heliodorus B., see Chromatius

Herculanus M., 106, 108, 118, 338, 339

Hercules, 96

Herennienus, subdeacon, 172

Heretics, 54, 58, 65, 74, 75, 78, 81, 128, 239, 257 n. 5, 267, 281, 282 ; and *Gesta*, 182, 192–195 ; see Arians, Donatists, Istria, Manichaeans, Marcionites, Nestorians

Hermes M. [May 3 and Aug. 28] of Via Salaria, 338, 339 ; coem. Basillae ad S. Hermetem or coem. Hermetis, 98, 106, 108, 118, 124 ;—and Balbina, 344

Hierarchy, discipline of, 74-77, 82, 315 ; grades of, 139, 219, 289 ; persecution of, 141, 143, 147 ; cf. 139

Hierax M., 155

Hilaria M., 118

Hilarina V., 118

Hilarion, 194

Hilary P., 59, 75, 284 ; gifts to church, 86

  ,, B. of Arles, 36

Hippo, Council of, 179 ; see Augustine B. of

Hippolytus B.M. of Via Tiburtina, Chronicle of, 50, 51, 53 ; legend of, 186 ; shrine of, 21, 98, 165, 338, 339 ; (ch. of), 225

  ,, M., Greek, of S. Callixtus, S. and epitaph of, 291, 299, 304

  ,, Greek hero, 187

Holy City, temple of (t. Sacrae Urbis), 5, 122

Holy week, 240

Homer, 163

Homobonus, 30

Honoratus, B. of Arles, 250 n. 1, 215

Honorius P., 92, 119, 251, 267 ; buildings of, 113, 115, 122 ; inscriptions by, 237, 261, 265, 266, 281, 288 ; monastery of, 121, 123

  ,, E., 2, 4, 5, 6, 8, 22 n. 1, 95, 341

Hormisdas P., 32, 54, 64, 77, 86, 262 ; inscription by, 261

Hospices for pilgrims, 25, 26

Huns, 4, 36, 233 n. 1

Hyacinthus (Jacinthus, Yacinthus) M., 305, 344 ; see Protus

Hyginus P., 49

I

Iconium, martyrs of, 155, 173 ; see Thecla

Idols, 6, 27, 35

Ignatius M. [Dec. 25], Rome, 215

  ,, B.M. [Feb. 1], of Antioch, 175 ; Acts of, 147, 161, 190; Acts (of fourth cent.), 190–191 ; Letter to Romans, 161

Ina, K. of Wessex, 23

Incarnation, inscriptions on, 267, 281, 283

Index Coemiteriorum, see Cemeteries

  ,, of Forbidden Books, 130

  ,, Oleorum (of Monza), 103 seqq.

India, revenues for Roman Church from, 88

Innocent I. P., 75 ; cem. of, 125 ; in M.H., 221–226

Inquisition, office of, 130

Insalatos, see Felix Romanus

Inscriptiones Vaticanae, see Syllogae

Inscriptions, 278 (ch. hd.)–296 ; see Baptisteries, Damasus, Syllogae ; and under names of Churches, Martyrs, Popes

Interpolation, theory of, 130, 197

Inventories of ecclesiastical properties, 87 seqq., 139, 140

Iona, 229

Ionatus, 248

Irenaeus, B. of Lyons, papal records of, 49, 53, 66 ; on Ignatius, 162

  ,, M., of Sirmium, 114

Irene MM., Agape and, see Agape, Irene and Chione

  ,, V., see Damasus

Isidore of Spain, 6

Isis, 3 ; and Serapis, region of, 12

Istra, heresy of, 267, 282

Italy, Martyrology of N. Italy, 216

Itineraries, 15, 65, 87, 93 (ch. hd.)–111, 112 (ch. hd.)–126, 133, 203, 220, 225, 230, 231, 249 ; list of shrines from, on Via Appia collated, 298–299 ; and collated with monuments on Via Appia, 297 (ch. hd.)–306 ; It. De locis sanctis martyrum, 13, 97, 112, 113, 115 seqq., 299 ; It. Einsiedlense, 109, 119 seqq., 240, 241, 299 ; see Curiosum urbis, Index Coemiteriorum, Notitia Regionum, Notula oleorum

J

Jacinthus, see Hyacinthus
Jacobus de Voragine and *Golden Legend*, 128
,,   and Marianus MM., *Passion of*, 147, 168 seqq.
James, brother of our Lord, 211, 212, 244
,,   (sc. SS. James and Philip), ch. of (Ad Apostolos, SS. Jacobi et Philippi, Basilica Julia, Santi Apostoli), 13, 14, 272; inscriptions for, 246, 248, 249
Janiculum, 2, 96, 121
Januaria M., Rome, 215
,,   M., Scilli, 153
Januarius M., son of Felicitas, Via Salaria, 72; coem. Praetextati ad S. Januarium, 99, 106, 298, 299, 338, 339; (frescoes in), 304
,,   priest, 342
,,   catechumen of Carthage, 172
Jason M., 105, 107, 118
Jerome, 36, 193, 236; on Catacombs, 20; on cult of martyrs and pilgrimages, 26, 42 seqq.; and on *L.P.*, 54 seqq.; *Martyrology of Jerome*, 211–217; see *Martyrologies*
Jerusalem, 18, 40, 43, 162, 196, 211, 212; see Cross, ch. of; *Itinerary of*, 119
Jesuits and *A.SS.*, 129 seqq.
Jesus, invocation of Names of, 285; see Christ
Jews, enmity to Christians, 141, 170; kings of, 51
John M., of Via Salaria, coem. ad caput Joannis in Clivum Cucumeris, 98, 102, 106, 124
,,   and Paul MM., 33, 37, 105, 114, 115, 120, 121, 227, 344; *Gesta* of, 202; epitaphs of, 241, 242, 258, 264; ch. of, see Byzanti, titulus
,,   Penarensis M., of Umbria, 342

John, Abbot, the pilgrim, 103 seqq.; see Monza
,,   Ap., Assumption of, 211, 212, 214
,,   Baptist, 211, 212; *Invention of Head of*, *Acts of*, 182
Jordan, H., historian, 241
Jordanorum ad S. Alexandrum Via Salaria, coem., 98, 102, 110, 111, 125
Judas, Ap., 214
Julia, Basilica, see SS. James and Philip, ch. of
Julian(us), E., 44
,,   deacon, of France, 30
,,   priest of Carthage, 150
,,   subdeacon of Carthage, 150
,,   M., of Via Appia, 292, 298, 299
,,   M., of Carthage, companion of Montanus and Lucius, 172
,,   M., of Brest, 210
,,   and Basilissa MM. [Jan. 9], *Acts of*, 194
Juliana, vestal, 203
,,   M. of Cumae or Nicomedia, 342
Julii, Basilica (S. Felix [Jan. 14], Via Portuensis), 15
,,   et Callixti, titulus (S. Maria in Trastevere, q.v.), 13; cf. Julia (Basilica)
Julitta M., see Ciricus
Julius P., edicts of, 76, 82, 92; buildings of, 15, 101; in *Calendars*, 221, 224, 226, 337; coem. Julii, Via Aurelia, 52, 125
Junius Bassus, consul, 5
Jupiter, 23
Justin M., 180, 227, 344; on liturgy, 78; *Acts of*, 153 seqq.
,,   E., gifts to church, 86
,,   priest, 106
Justinian E., 7, 25, 57 seqq., 64, 122, 236, 267; gifts to church, 86
Justus M., of Alcala, 41

K

Keys of SS. Peter's and Paul's, as relics, 29, 31, 38
Klosterneuberg, 249
Krusch on *M.H.*, 228

L

Labicana, Via, 2, 15, 98, 116, 123, 124, 238 ; inscriptions of, 244, 249, 252, 292

Ladder, Perpetua's vision of brazen, 165

Ladiceus (?), in inscription, 292

Laetantius M., of Scilli, 153

Land, revenues of church from, 80, 90, 92

Largus ("Larcius") and Smaragdus MM., 338, 339, 341

Lateran, basilica of (Constantinian Basilica, S. John, S. Giovanni in Laterano), 9, 13, 85, 86, 123 ; inscriptions of, 242, 246, 248 ; baptistery of, 225, 271 n. 1 ; consignatorium of, 284 ; hospital of, 123 ; museum of, 50

Laterculus Polemii Silvii, 96

Latina, Via, 2, 15, 45, 99, 105, 116, 124, 292, 299, 340 ; inscriptions of, 249, 252

Laurence, anti-pope, 54, 65, 257 n. 5, 269

,, M., 181, 195, 304, 344 ; *Gesta*, 72, 202 ; coem. in Agro Verano ad S. Laurentium and basilica of Via Tiburtina, 15, 41, 53, 85, 88, 98, 100, 101, 105, 106, 115, 124, 338, 339 ; (inscriptions of), 242, 244, 249, 252, 253, 291, 295, 314 ; titulus Damasi (S. Laurence *in Damaso*), 12 ; (archives of), 288, 311 ; (inscriptions for), 242, 245, 280, 283 ; ch. of S. Laurence *in Formonso* (or Panisperna), 121, 122 ; titulus Lucinae (S. Laurence *in Lucina*), 12 ; hospice of, 25 ; relics of, 29, 30, 33, 37, 42

,, M., of Spoleto, 342

,, scribe of *M.H.*, 205, 207

Laurentia, see Damasus

Laurentian fragment of L.P., 54, 269

Laurenziana, Biblioteca and *Index*, 98 n. 1, 340

Laureshamensis, Sylloge, see *Sylloge Laureshamensis*

Lauros ad SS. Petrum et Marcellinum, coem. Ad duas, 98, 124

Le Blant on *A.SS.*, 130, 145, 197

Leclercq on *A.SS.*, 130, 131, 169, 196

Leo I. (the Great), P., 3, 4, 20, 22, 24, 25 ; decrees of, 79 ; inscriptions by, 286 ; epitaph of, 256 ; gifts and buildings, 15, 86 ; in *M.H.*, 221, 224, 225, 226 ; *Sacramentary of*, 3, 79

,, II. P., translations of bodies, 117

,, III. P., inscription by, 295

,, IV. P., buildings of, 120

,, B., father of Damasus (?), 313–315 ; see Damasus

Leo and Paregorius MM., *Passion of*, 188

Leontius, consul, 31

Leopardus M., 345

Lérins (Lerinum), monastery of, 30, 250

Lesbos, 97

Leuparic, priest, 30

Levison, Dr., on *Sylloge of Cambriage*, 254, 274

Leyden, manuscript of, 60

Liber Generationis, 50, 51 ;—*Martyrum*, 201 ;—*Pontificalis*, 9, 10, 15, 101, 182, 202, 206, 220, 229 ; 48 (ch. hd.) seqq., 63 (ch. hd.) seqq., 84 (ch. hd.) seqq. ; (collated with monuments), 300 seqq. ; (relation to *Gesta Martyrum*), 68 seqq., 200 ; (relation to *Syllogae* in *manuscript of Cambridge*), see *Sylloge of Cambridge*

Liberalis, M., 106, 108

Liberia, Basilica (S. Maria Maggiore, q.v.), 13, 14, 85

Liberian Calendar, see *Philocalian Calendar*

Liberianus M., 155

Liberius P., 56, 58 ; buildings of, 14, 85, 282 ; *Gesta of*, 82 ; in *M.H.*, 221–226

Linus P.M., 49, 53, 62, 64

Lion, legend of Marciana M. and, 188

Little Roman Martyrology (*Martyrologium Romanum Parvum*), 229

Liturgy, 14 n. 1, 74, 240; papal decrees concerning, 78 seqq.; in Greek, 78, 79; Greek liturgy, 163; litanies, 211, 212; office in S. Peter's, 183; relation of *Martyrologies* and *Gesta* to, 62, 73, 133, 166, 178, 179, 181, 183, 206, 207; vessels for, 18, 69, 87, 89, 97; see Eucharist, Mass, Stations

Local, inscriptions in *Syllogae*, 248, 250; entries in *Martyrologies*, 206, cf. 208 seqq.

Locis Sanctis Martyrum, De, 299; see *Itineraries*

,, *Sanctorum Martyrum, De*, 112

Lombard, invasions, 17, 236, 316; kings and pilgrims, 26, 32, 102, 103 109; handwriting, 103, 251; see Monza, Theodelinda

London, Mellitus B. of, 9, 37

Lorsch (Lauriacum), monastery of, 242, 243; see *Sylloge of*

Lucca, *Index coemiteriorum* at, 341

Luceia and Auceia MM., 345

Lucia and Geminianus MM., 345

Lucia in Orpheo (Orthea?), ch. of, 121, 122

Lucian(us) M., of Antioch, 144

,, priest, 172

Lucina, matron, buries Paul on Via Ostiensis, 124

,, buries Peter and Paul in Ad Catacumbas (in 258), 69; and Marcellus P.M. in Priscilla (in 309), 71; and Cornelius P.M. (in 258) in Crypt of Lucina, 70; see Cornelius, Crypt of

coem. Lucinae ad S. Agatham ad Girulum, Via Aurelia, 99, 105, 125; (basilica of S. Agatha), 15

M. (?) of Via Salaria, 106

Lucius P.M., decrees of, 77; martyrdom of, 68, 72; in *M.H.*, 223; shrine, excavations and epitaph, 52, 292, 299, 302, 303, 337

Lucius MM., Montanus and, see Montanus

,, K. of Britain, 83

Lullus B. of Mayence, 88

Luxeuil and *M.H.*, 228

Lydus, historian, 136

Lyons, bishops of in *M.H.*, 209; see Florus of; martyrs of, 142, 143, 162, 175, 176, 208, 209

M

Maccabees, mother of, 169

Macedonia M., a Montanist, 170

Macedonian kings, 51

Macellum Magnum, 5

Macrinus E., 203

Macrobius Candidianus, procurator, 151

Maderno, sculptor, 317

,, agic, 44

Magnilianus, clerk, 135

Magnus M., companion of Laurence, 72

Majorian, E., 7, 8

Malmesbury, William of, 117

,, *Itinerary of* (*Itinerarium Malmesburiense*), 117 seqq.; monastery of, 118, 231

Manes and Manichaeans, 78, 194

Mannus (?), inscription, 292

Mappala, Africa, 151

Marcellianus MM., Marcus and, see Marcum

Marcellinus P.M., *Passion of*, 72 seqq.; in *Calendars*, 221 n. 2, 223 n. 7, 337

,, and Peter MM., 345; see Duas Lauros

Marcellus P.M., 73; decrees of, 10, 76; martyrdom and *Passion of*, 71, 200; in *Calendar*, 345; (in *M.H.*), 215, 222, 226; S. of, 106, 107, 110, 111, 124, (epitaph) 247; titulus Marcelli, in Via Lata, 12, 71 (and n. 4)

,, M., of Via Appia, 299

,, M. (Nereus and Achilleus), 342

,, M., centurion of Tangiers, 135, 157

,, and Apuleius MM., 345

,, and Superantius MM., of Umbria, 342

Marciana M., Passion of, 189
Marcianus M., 116
Marcion, Poem against, 54
Marcionites, 170
Marcum et Marcellianum MM., coem.
    Balbinae ad. SS., 99, 167
Marcus (Mark) P., in *M.H.*, 222 ; coem.
    Basilei ad S. Marcum, 52,
    99, 107, 299, 377, (bas.) 15 ;
    ch. of (titulus Marci), 12, 13
  ,,   husband of Lucina, 7
Marcus Aurelius E., 64
Maria (Mary), Virgin, in *M.H.*, 211 ;
    inscriptions to, 281 seqq. ; churches
    of : S. Maria Antiqua, 5, 13, 121,
    122 ;—Major (Maggiore), 13, 121,
    122, 125, 225, 264, 275 n. 1, 299 ;
    (inscriptions of), 244, 246, 248, 250,
    259, 260, 267, 272, 282 seqq. ;—
    Rotunda, 13 ;—in Trastevere, 13,
    120, 121 ; (inscription of), 242
Marinus M., 345
Marius and Martha MM. [Jan. 19],
    345
Marmoutiers (S. Martin, Tours), monas-
    tery of, 248
Marriage, see Hierarchy, Asceticism
Mars, temple of, 70
Martha M. [Jan. 16], 215, 299
  ,,   sister of Lazarus, in inscription,
    290, 312 n.
Martialis M., son of Felicitas, 106,
    107, 110, 118, 338, 339 ; epitaph of,
    294
Martin, S., monastery of, at Tours,
    232, 248
  ,,   ch. of, in Suburra (Titulus
    Equitii or Silvestri), 12, 121,
    123, 296
Martina (Tatiana) M., 345
Martinianus MM., Processus and, see
    Processus
Martyrology(ies), 65, 67, 133, 300 ;
    see Ado, Bede, Gregory ; *of Jerome*
    (*Martyrologium Hieronymianum*),
    205(ch. hd.) seqq., 218(ch. hd.) seqq. ;
    cf. 62, 73, 179, 183, 186, 203, 300,
    306 ; later Martyrologies, list of, 183,
    228,229; *Martyrologium Universale*,
    see *Calendars*
    24

Martyrs, word in inscriptions, 302 n. 1 ;
    anniversaries of, 16, 27, 28, 79, 80,
    137, 143, 179, 186, 213, 216; auto-
    biographies of, 116, 161, 162, 171,
    192 ; burial *ad Martyres*, 41, 42 ;
    cult of, 16 (ch. hd.) seqq., 35 (ch. hd.)
    seqq., 84 seqq., 180, 279 ; in liturgy,
    17, 20, 47, 79, 80, 179, 186, 213,
    214, 216 ; representations of in
    frescoes, etc., 283, 303, 308, 317 ;
    translation of bodies of, 17, 113, 117,
    295, 305, 316 ; voluntary nature of
    martyrdom, 194 ; see *Calendars*,
    Damasus, Inscriptions, Mass
Marucchi, 271, 273, 274, 313
Mass, Canon of, 53 n. 1, 67, 78 seqq. ;
    for Christmas, 64 ; of stations, 14 n. 1,
    158 ; see Eucharist, Martyrs
Materialism, 41 seqq., 186
Matthias Ap., in *M.H.*, 214
Mauritius (Maurice) M., 342
Maurus M., 105, 107, 118
Maurus, Rabanus, Martyrology of, 183,
    229
Mausolea, 9
Maxentius E., 71, 122
Maxilitani SS., of Africa, 219
Maxima, Donatella and Secunda MM.,
    of Africa, *Passion of*, 156
Maximillian(us) M., of Via Salaria, 106,
    108, 118
  ,,   M., of Numidia, *Acts
    of*, 157
Maximus M., of Via Salaria, coem.
    Maximi ad S. Felicitatem,
    98
  ,,   M., in Praetextatus, kins-
    man of Cecilia, 298, 299,
    305
  ,,   M. [May 14], of Ephesus (?)
    Passion of, 135, 157
  ,,   consul, 72
Mayence, *L.P.* first printed in, 62
Medals as relics, 29
Melchiades P., see Miltiades
Mellitus, B. of London, 37
Memmia M., 338, 339
Memoria of Peter, 9, 84, 278 ; see
    Peter, ch. of, on Vatican
Menology, Greek, 179, 205, 218, 219

Metalla, meaning of word, 287 n. 3
Metrodorus M., a Marcionite, 170
Mercia, 24, 39
Mercury, temple of, 95
Merita MM., Digna and, see Digna
Metrovia Via, 292, 299
Mica Aurea, 120, 121
Michael archangel, 14, 275; baptistery of, 258, see *Syllogae* (*Sumite-Istic* inscriptions); ch. of *in Fagana*, Tivoli, 264; *ad Porticum Ottavium* ("S. Paul" till 770) of Via Salaria, 264, 277 n. 1; on Via Urbana, 263, 264 n. 1; on Vatican, 264, see *supra* baptistery
Milan, *Edict of*, 3, 28, 43, 102, 128, 215, 217, 236; see Peace of Church; Council of, 213, 217; *Sylloge of*, 230 n. 1
Milevis, Optatus B. of, 9
Miltiades (Melchiades) P., decrees of, 78; in *M.H.*, 221–226; tomb and epitaph of, 52, 291, 299, 302, 303, 337
Mirabilia urbis Romae, 123
Mistranslations in *Gesta*, 186 seqq.
Mithra, 3, 51
Molinae, 120, 121
Moluccas, 88
Mombritius, *Sanctuarium* of, 128
Mommsen, on *L.P.*, 61; on *M.H.*, 228
Monasteries, libraries of, 132; life of, 24; *Martyrologies* and *Gesta* adapted for, 130, 180, 206, 207; in East, 180; of Centula (S. Richarius), 232, 234, 250, 251; of Corvie (S. Peter), 232, 251; of Einsiedeln, 232, 233, 240; of S. Gall, 232, 233; of Gottwei (Abbey), 249; of Lérins (Lerinum), 250; of Lorsch (Lauriacum), 242, 243; of Malmesbury, 118, 231; of Monte Cassino, 195; of Reichenau, 232, 233, 240; of Rome (S. Agatha), 121, (Mt. Clitaurus, of Gregory I.) 290, (S. Callixtus, Trappist) 304, (Honorius) 121 and 123, (S. Silvester *in Capite*) 245, (S. Stephen, Vatican) 295; of Verdun (S. Vitus), 245; of Vivarium, 75, 215

Monica, mother of Augustine, 28; epitaph of, 236
Montanists, 170
Montanus and Lucius MM., 147, 171, 174, 176; *Passion of*, 171 seqq.
Monte Cassino, manuscripts of, 195
Montorio, temple of Apollo *in*, 70; S. Peter's *in*, 121
Monuments, collation of, with documents, 125, 126, 297 (ch. hd.) seqq.; destruction of, 187, 313; see Excavations, Frescoes, Pagan, *Syllogae*
Monza, Cathedral of, 31, 102, 109, 110; *Papyrus of*, 94, 102 seqq.; treasure of, 34, 102 seqq.
Moon and sun, worship of, 45
Mosaics, 123, 261, 262, 283, 287, 288
Mother of Gods, temple of, 95
Mulvian Bridge, battle of, 278

N

Nabor and Felix MM., 215
Name, Holy, invocations of, 285; litany of, 285
Naples, 57, 58, 217
Narcissus, of S. Paul's epistle, inscription of, 308
Nartzalus M., of Scilli, 152, 153, 190
Natales, see Anniversaries
Neo, Greek martyr in S. Callixtus, S. and epitaph of, 291, 292, 304
Neon M., *Acts of*, 135
Nereus and Achilleus MM., *Passion of*, 193, 194, 202, 307, 309, 315; in *Calendars*, 342, 345; Coem. Domitillae Nerei et Achillei, 99; (titular church of, t. Fasciolae), 13, 15, 187, 198; (inscriptions and frescoes), 119, 307, 308
Nero E., 70, 141
Nestorians, 272 n. 2, 282
Nicaea, Council of, 59, 81
Nicholas v. P., 340
Nichomachus, Flavianus, 3
Nicomedes M., 345
Nicomedia, 81 n. 3, 219, 342
Nicostratus, Claudius and Sempronianus MM., 339
Noah, 51

Nola, Felix M. of, 26 ; see Paulinus B. of; *Sylloge of*, 230 n. 1

Nomentana, Via, 2, 15, 52, 68, 85, 88, 98, 100, 101, 105, 110, 111, 113, 115, 116, 117, 124, 215, 221, 235, 243, 288, 337 ; inscriptions of, 244, 245, 246, 249, 252, 261, 272, 273 ; see Agnes

Nonnius M., 339

Northumbria, 119, 207

Notaries, 76, 92, 134 seqq., 182

Nothelm, Archbishop of Canterbury, 37

Notitia Dignitatum, 95, 97, 99

    ,,   *Ecclesiarum* (*Itin. Salisburgense*), 112 seqq.

    ,,   *Portarum* . . . (*Itin. Malmesburiense*), 117 seqq.

    ,,   *Regionum XIV.*, 51, 95, 97, 99, 341

Notula oleorum, 03 seqq., see Monza

Novatus, Baths of, 5 ; see Timothy, Baths of

Numidia, 9, 88 ; (inscription), 238 ; confessors and martyrs of, 143, 151, 157

Numidianus, in inscription, 292

Nundinarius, deacon of Cirta, 138

O

Œcumenical councils, 59, 74

Offa K., 24

Oftfor B. of Worcester, 38

Oil as a relic, 30, 31, 102, 111 ; for chrism, 284

Oleorum, Index, see Monza

Olybrii, 23

Optatus B. of Milevis, 9, 54 ; name in S. Callixtus, 292, 299, 303

Ordinations, feasts of papal, 74, 224, 226

Ordo Romanus of Benedict the Canon, 123

Orpheus, fresco of, 187 ; ch. of Lucia *in Orpheo* (*Orthea*?), 121, 122

Ossuaria, in catacombs, 304

Ostiensis, Via, 2, 9, 15, 52, 99, 100, 101, 105, 115, 116, 119, 120, 125, 299, 305, 338 ; inscriptions of, 244, 249, 250, 252

Oswald K., 207

Oswy K., 37

Otho II. E., 22 n. 1

P

Paeonius M., companion of Justin M., 155

Pagans, paganism, 78, 191 ; *Calendar*, 51 ; in Church, 3, 4, 10, 26, 27 seq. ; (in inscriptions), 237 ; converts from, 77, 196 ; monuments of, 4 seqq., 95 seqq. ; transition from, to Christianity, 1, 3 seqq., 19 ; writers of, 132, 133, 135

Palatine, 25, 96, 121, 122 ; *Codex Palatinus* (or *Vaticanus*), see *Sylloge of Lorsch*

Palatium, region, 12

Palestine, 213 ; martyrs of, 162 ; see Caesarea, Eusebius, Jerusalem

Palladius B. of Saintes (Santones), 30

Pallas, temple of, 70

Palmatius, consul, 203

Palumbas (Columbas), see Clivum Cucumeris

Pammachius, see Byzanti

Pamphilius M., 115, 118

Pancras M., 345 ; relics of, 30, 33, 37 ; *Gesta of*, 200, 202 ; cem. and bas. (see Calepodius), 15, 99, 105, 113, 116, 203 ; (inscriptions), 241, 253

Pandataria, island of, 306

Pannonia, martyrs of, 217, 306 ; see Cyrinus

Pantheon, 13

Papebroch and *A.SS.*, 129

Papias, N. Italy, inscription of, 242

Papylus MM., Carpus and, see Carpus

Papyri of Monza, see Monza

Paradise, 168, 177, 294, 308

Paregorius MM., Leo and, see Leo

Parentalia, 28

Paris, 129, 195, 252

Parishes, 76 ; see Tituli

Parthenius and Calocerus MM., 303, 338, 339, 345

Pascal P., *False diploma of*, 316 ; translation of bodies, 17, 316

Passionary, of Gregory, see Gregory ; *Latin*, 162, 195

Pastor M., 215, 345

Paternus, proconsul, 141, 148, 149
Patras, 214
Paul Ap. M., 153, 158, 182, 194, 306,
    308, 345; martyrdom of, 124;
    Acts of, 194 ; shrine and basilica
    on Via Ostiensis, 14, 15, 18,
    32, 35, 52, 70, 85, 86, 97
    ("Churches of Blessed Apos-
    tles"), 99, 100, 101, 116, 124,
    299, 305, 338; (hospice of),
    25 ; (inscriptions for), 241, 244,
    249, 250, 252, 253, 264, 266,
    268; (inventory of), 88, 91 ;
    see Catacumbas, Ad ; ch. of
    (later S. Michael *ad Porticum
    Ottavium*), 264.   See Peter and
    Paul App.
    ,,   I. P., translation of bodies, 17,
        117, 245, 295
    ,,   M., Via Salaria, 118
    ,,   M., see John and Paul MM.
    ,,   B. of Cirta, 138
    ,,   deacon, inscription by, 26
Paula, friend of Jerome, 26, 43
Paulina, Greek martyr in Callixtus, 105,
        118, 299 ; epitaph of, 304
    ,,   V., on Via Salaria, 118
Paulinus B. of Nola, 26, 36, 41 seqq.,
        217, 236
    ,,   B. of London, 207
    ,,   M., 116
Pavia, 24
Peace of Church, 8, 15, 16, 52, 64,
    84, 141, 179, 205, 225, 236, 291 ;
    see Milan, *Edict of*
Pelagius I. P., inscriptions and epi-
    taph, 248, 261 n. 3, 281
    ,,   II. P., 30, 119 ; buildings of,
        115 ; epitaph, 261 n. 3
    ,,   British monk, 83
Penance, 74, 76, 112
Penda K., 39
Pergamos, martyrs of, 169, 215
Perpetua M., 52, 145, 174, 176, 218,
    338, 339 ; *Passion of*, 165 seqq., 171
    181
Persecutions, 82, 114, 141 seqq., 147,
    213, 225 ; cf. 291 seqq. ; caused by
    Jews, 141, 170 ; by pagan enmity,
    141, 203 ; of Vandals, 202   see

Diocletian, Domitian, Valerian, Acts
    of Martyrs
Persia, martyrs of, 113, 219   monarchs
    of, 51
Peter Ap. M., in Rome, 8, 10, 24, 36,
    42, 49, 53, 124, 154 n. 1, 187,
    307, 309; martyrdom of, 70,
    121; *Acts of*, 194, 202, 315;
    Feast of, 26, see Peter and Paul ;
    Feast of Chair of (or Cathedra,
    or Sedes Petri), 22, 25, 52, 104,
    106, 107, 110, 111, 211, 297,
    337 ; Fountain of, 120, 121 ;
    Fontis S. Petri, coem., see
    Agnes, cem. of ; prison of,
    120, 121 ; power of (inscrip-
    tions), 271–277, 279–281 ; see
    Popes, inscriptions of ; Porta
    S. Petri (inscription), 260, 267 ;
    Shrine of on Via Appia, see
    Catacumbas, Ad ; on Vatican,
    99, 100, 305. See *infra* ch. of
    on.   Churches dedicated to, in
    ROME :—on Vatican, the Mem-
    oria of Anacletus, 9, 84, 278 ;
    (enlarged to basilica of Con-
    stantine), 3, 6, 14, 15 ; (pilgrims
    to), 18, 21 seqq.; (papal tombs
    in), 55, 64, 70, 116 ; see under
    names of popes ; 97 ("Chur-
    ches of Apostles") ; (crypts of),
    296 ; (landed property and in-
    ventory of), 88 seqq. ; (inscrip-
    tions of), 235, 238, 241, 242,
    244, 248 seqq., 256, 260, 261,
    263 seqq., 269, 273 seqq., 278
    seqq. ; (liturgy of), 183 ; *in
    Montorio*, 121 ; *ad Vincula*,
    12, 13, 87, 121, 122, 125, 225;
    (inscriptions of), 232 n. 1, 238,
    244, 245, 253, 310 ;   see
    Apostles, (titular) church of.
    At SPOLETO, 44 ; (inscrip-
    tions), 244, 251, 271 n. 1.   At
    CORVIE, 232.   In England,
    list of churches, 38, 39.   See
    Peter and Paul
    ,,   and Paul App. MM., 24 ; Feast
        (anniversary, natalis), in *Cal-
        endars*, 4, 36, 42, 218, 333,

339, 345; inscriptions, 231, 241, 256, 311; portraits of, 29; see Catacumbas (Ad), Paul Ap. M.

Peter and Marcellinus MM., see Marcellinus

Peterborough, Cathedral, 39

Petersburg, St., 251

Petro, cognomen, 309

Petronilla, 99, 107, 342; excavations and frescoes, 307 seqq.; ch. of, on Vatican, 264

Phileas and Philoromus MM. of Alexandria, *Acts of*, 145, 173, 175

Philip and James App., see James and Philip

,, and Felix MM., sons of Felicitas, Via Salaria, 106, 107, 118, 338, 339; epitaph, 247

,, Neri, St., 128

Philocalian (*Liberian*) *Calendar*, 22, 50 seqq., 56, 63, 66, 67, 73, 95, 98 n. 1, 100, 114, 180, 186, 201, 203, 223 seqq., 227, 300, 303; see *Liber Pontificalis*

Philocalus, 50; see *Philocalian Calendar*

Philomelium, church of, 162

Philoromus MM., Phileas and, see Phileas

Philosophumena, 68

Pilate, 190; Palace of, 121, 122, 123

Pilgrims, 16 (ch. hd.) seqq., 35 (ch. hd.) seqq., 180, 186, 188, 234, 249, 304

Pionius M., *Passion of*, 147, 157, 169 seqq.

Pistis M., 109, 304

Pithou, 233

Pittacia ampullarum, see Monza

Pius I. P.M., 5; order of succession, 49, 53, 54

,, II., 56

Placentia, martyrs of, 217

Plagiarism in *Gesta*, 191, 198; in inscriptions, 237, 238, 266 seqq., 276

Platonia, see Catacumbas (Ad)

Po, valley of, inscriptions, 243

Polemii Silvii Laterculus, 96

Policamus M., 299

Polycarp B.M., 162, 175; *Acts of*, 147

,, in inscription, 292

Pompey, theatre of, 311

Pomponia Graecina, 142

Pontian islands, 58, 306, 307

Pontiani ad Ursum Pileatum, coem., Via Portuensis, 99, 102, 105, 125, 338

Portianus P.M., martyrdom and *Passion of*, 67, 68, 72, 200; in *Calendars*, 51, 222, 223, 226, 229; shrine, excavations at and epitaph, 302

,, and Eusebius MM., 345

Pontius M., 345

,, author of *Passion of Cyprian* 163

Popes, decrees of, 73 seqq., 192. Burial places (mentioned in *Phil. Cal.*), 51 seqq., 377 seqq.; (and in *L.P.*), 69 seqq.; (and in *M.H.*), 200 seqq.; in S. Callixtus, 302 seq.; (in papal crypt of), 55, 67, 70, 72 73, 85, 291, 301 seqq.; in Priscilla, see Celestinus P., epitaph of, Liberius P., in *M.H.*, Marcellinus P., Marcellus P., Silvester P., Siricus P., epitaph of; in Vatican, 55, 64, 70, 116. Inscriptions of and by, 231, 236, 238, 242, 243, 246, 261, 265, 291, 292. List of, 336. Ordinations, anniversaries of, 74, 224, 226. Power of, in inscriptions, 279 seqq., 289; see Peter, power of. *Gesta* of, 200 seqq., 346 seqq.; see *Liber Pontificalis*, and under names of popes

Porta Appia, 124, 125; Aurelia, 118, 121; Capena, 12; Cornelia, 118; Flaminia, 115, 118, 120; Latina, 124; Nomentana, 118, 120; S. Petri, 118, 120, 260; Porticiana, 118; Praenestina, 121, 123; Tiburtina, 118; Trigemina, 95

Portuensis, Via, 2, 15, 99, 104, 116, 125, 249

Potentiana, see Pudentiana

Pothinus B.M. of Lyons, 176

Praenestina, Via, 121

Praesens, consul, 151

Praetextati ad S. Januarium, coem., 53, 69, 72, 99, 102, 125, 298; excavations in, 304

Praxed M., S. of on Via Salaria, 118, 342; titulus Praxedis, 12, 123, 296 (inscription)

Primus and Felicianus MM., 113, 117, 342, 345

Prisca M., 118, 345; titulus Priscae, 13

Priscilla, 122, 274; coem. Priscillae ad S. Silvestrum, and basilica, 15, 29, 40, 52, 56, 71, 73, 98, 102, 106, 107, 110, 111, 115, 118, 124, 221, 227, 337, 338; (inscriptions), see *Syllogae, Sumite-Istic* inscription; (of Eucharis), 274; (in basilica), 246, 247 seq., 272 seqq.; (baptistery of), 284; (excavations in), 273; see Popes, burial-places in Priscilla; coem. Priscillae (or Crypts of S. Pudentiana), 276

Probus E., 341

Processus and Martinianus MM., 105, 116, 342, 345; *Gesta* of, 202

Procopius, historian, 7, 57
,, M., *Acts of*, 147, 162, 163, 195, 315

Profuturus, *letter of Pope Vigilius* to, 79

Protus and Jacinthus (Hyacinthus) MM., S. and bas., 106, 108, 118, 338, 339; (inscriptions for), 119; inscriptions for in S. Andrew, Vatican, 257, 258, 263, 287; see Hyacinthus

Prudentius, poet, 6, 21, 23, 157, 181, 186, 236

Pudens, host of Peter, 8, 122, 154 n. 1, 274; titulus Romanus or Pudentis or Pudentianae, 5, 11 n. 6, 12, 87, 121, 122, 276

Pudentiana, 118, 154 n. 1, 342; see Pudentis, titulus

Puteoli, martyrs of, 217

Q

Quattuor Coronatorum (? titulus Aemilianae), 12

Quintilian M., 135

Quirinal, 2

Quirinus M., of Via Salaria, 118
,, of Praetextatus, see Cyrinus
,, of Ad Catacumbas, see Cyrinus

R

Rampolla, Cardinal, on *Index Coemiteriorum*, 100, 340; and excavations in house of S. Cecilia, 316

Ravenna, Theodoric at, 65; quarter called, 203; martyrs of, 217; *Calendar of*, 132, 229; inscriptions of, 233, 252, (of Vitalis M.) 244

Regions, Fourteen, 2; list of, 12, 13; seven ecclesiastical, 75, 76, 182

Reinach, S., on *Analecta Bollandiana*, 129

Relics, 28 seqq., 151, 160, 186, 191, 206, 251; inscriptions for, 295

Repentinus, Aurelius, 40

Restituta M., 345

Restitutus M., 215, 345

Rhaetia, 217

Rhine, pilgrims from, 18

Rhodine, epitaph of, 237

Richarius, see Centula

Ricimer, 13 n. 8

Rimini (Ariminum), inscription of, 233

Riparius B. of Aquileia, 45

Ripon, 38, 39

Rogantina V., 118

Rogatianus, catechumen, 157

Romanus M., companion of Sixtus II., 72

Romulus, Rotunda of, 5, 86, 95, 122

Rosweyde, H., on *A.SS.*, 129, 131

Rufina and Secunda MM., 116, 342, 345

Rufinus, 67, 193 (on *Gesta*)

Rufus, consul, 64
,, M., 345

Ruinart, *Acta Sincera* of, 130, 131, 197

Rusticius, judge of Justin M., 154 seqq.

S

Sabina M., 345; titulus Sabinae, 13, 14, (inscriptions of) 241, 244, 253

Sabinian P., epitaph, 261 n. 3

Sabinus, deacon, 41

Sacerdos, meaning of, 251 n. 1, 289 n. 1
Sacra, Via, 86
Sacrae Urbis Templum, 5
Sacramentary of Gelasius, 79 ; *of Leo*, 3, 79
Saintes (Santones), Palladius, B. of, 30
Saints, 307 ; see Martyrs
Salaria, Via, 2, 15, 73, 88, 98, 105 seqq., 110, 111, 115, 116, 118, 119, 124, 215, 221, 222, 235, 237, 243, 293, 338 ; inscriptions of, 244, 246, 249, 252, 272, 273, 294, 298
Salzburg, Codex of, 112 seqq.
Samuel, Abbot of Lorsch, 233
Sanctuarium of Mombritius, 128
Sanctus, title of, 11
Sapaudius, B. of Arles, 30
Sapientia M., 105, 109, 298
Saracen invasions, 242
Saragossa, Vincent M. of, 138
Sardinia, 72
Sarum Missal, 93
Saturn, Temple of, 6 ; quarter of at Sextii, 149
Saturnina V., 118
Saturninus, consul, 64
,,   proconsul, Africa, 152, 153, 190
,,   M.[Nov. 29], of Via Salaria, Coem. Thrasonis ad S. Saturninum, 98, 105, 107, 118, 124, 339, (inscription) 246
,,   M. [Dec. 25], of Pergamos, 215
,,   M. [Feb. 11], of Carthage, *Acts of*, 138, 142, 173
,,   M. [Jan. 16], of Africa, 215
Saturus M., companion of Perpetua, 165, 166
Savinus B., of Tuscany, 342
Saviour, Our, oratory of, in S. Petronilla and in S. Maria Maggiore, inscriptions for, 260, 264 (and n. 3), 267, 285
Saxons, 25, 231, 239 ; see English
Scala Santa, 122, 123
Scaliger on *Index Coemiteriorum*, 341 ; *Vetus Membrana Scaligeri*, 233
Schneider on *Itineraries*, 20 n. 1, 94 n. 1, 108 n. 2

Schola Francorum, 25
Scilli, martyrs of, in *M.H.* (SS. Scillitani), 219 ; *Acts of*, 147, 151 seqq., 189
Scipio, consul, 64
Scotland, Caidocus of, 250
Scythian, Dionysius the, 75
Scythopolis, Procopius M. of, 162
Sebastian M., 106, 181, 337, 339, 345 ; *Gesta* of, 202, 315 ; see Catacumbas (Ad)
Secunda M. [July 17], of Scilli, 152, 153
,,   and Maxima MM. [July 30], see Maxima
,,   and Rufina MM., near Via Cornelia, 116, 345
Secundus and Carpophorus (Carpoferus) MM., 338, 339
Sedes Petri, see Peter, Chair of
Semetrius M., 118
Sempronianus M., 339
Sennen MM., Abdon and, see Abdon
Septisolium, 187
Sepulcri on *Papyrus of Monza*, 104, 108, 109
Serantina V., 118
Serapia M., 342, 345
Sergius I. P., 231 ; inscription by, 245, 256
,,   ch. of St., 121
Servian Wall, 2
Servilianus M., 342
Sessorian Basilica, see Cross, ch. of Holy
Settaliano, library, 110
Severianus (and Carpophorus) MM., 338, 339
Severinus P., 92
Severus, Marcus Successus, in inscription, 40
,,   author of *Spes Ratio*, 267, 268, 286
,,   Alexander, E., 72, 203, 204
,,   Septimius, E., arch of, 120, 121 ; plan of, 5, 94, 141
,,   friend of Paulinus of Nola, 36
,,   M., companion of Laurence, 72

Sexti in Africa, 149, 150
Shepherd of Hermas, 166
Sherbourne, 38, 231
Sicily, 88, 239
Sighere K., 24
Silanus M., son of Felicitas, 118, 338, 339
Silvanus B. of Cirta, 138 seqq.
Silverius P., in *L.P.*, 56 seqq., 60, 65 ; epitaph of, 261 n. 3
Silvester P., 64, 67, 114 ; *Constitutum Silvestri*, 81, 82, 183 ; public works, 15, 84, 85 ; in *Calendars*, 52, 223, 337 ; translation of body, 245 ; *Acts of*, 83, 182 ; *Book of*, 116 ; shrine of, see Priscillae ad S. Silvestrum, coem. ; ch. of in Suburra (titulus Silvestri or Equitii, i.e. SS. Silvester and Martin),'121, 123, 258 ; ch. of, *in Capite*, and monastery, 245, 296 ; Gate of, 118
Silvius, author of *Spes Ratio*, 267, 286
Simphroniana M., 215
Simplicius P., monuments and inscriptions, 5, 14, 15, 280
,,   (Simplex), Faustinus and Beatrix, MM., 117, 346
Siricius P., edicts of, 75, 81 ; public works of, 86, 87, 308 ; epitaph of, 247 ; in *M.H.*, 224
Sirmium, Irenaeus M. of, 144
Sirmius M., 215
Siscia, see Cyrinus B. of
Sisinnius M., 341
Sixtus I. P.M., 49, 68
,,   II. P.M., martyrdom of, 67, 68, 71, 124, 147, 168, 181, 304 ; *Passion*, 68, 200 ; in *Calendars*, 51, 53, 218, 222, 338, 339, 346 ; see Callixti ad S. Sixtum, coem. ; oratory of (? titulus Crescentiae), 12, 15, 225 ; oratory called SS. Sixtus and Cecilia, 302, 304
,,   III. P., buildings by, 15, 86, 87, 225 ; inscriptions by, 85, 237, 238, 282, 292, 302, 303 ; *Gesta de Purgatione Sixti*, 82, 83, 254
,,   M., Via Salaria, 115

Smaragdus MM., Largus and, see Largus
Smyrna, martyrs of, 162, 169
Sophia M., 105, 346
Sosimus P., see Zosimus
Sossius M., inscription to, 263
Soter P.M., 49, 53
Soteris M., S. and bas., 15, 105, 126, 298, 299
Spain, martyrs of, 147, 181 ; see Cordova, Tarragona, Valentia ; pilgrims from, 18 ; pope from, 236 ; Vigilantius of, 44
Spelunca Magna, in Praetextatus, 304
Speratus M., of Scilli, 152, 153, 189, 190
Spes, M., 105, 109, 298, 304
Spoleto, see Achilles B. of ; martyrs of, 217 ; inscriptions, 234, 244, 251
Stations, churches for, 234 ; in Rome, list of, 13 ; in Auxerre, 212 ; of martyrs in prison, 158
Stephen P.M., decrees of, 80 ; *Passion of*, 200 ; in *Calendars*, 52, 222, 337, 346 ; tomb and epitaph, 299, 303
,,   M., companion of Laurence, 72
,,   M., of Jerusalem, 181 ; ch. (and monastery) on Vatican, inscription for, 295 ; on Coelian (S. Stefano Rotundo), 5, 113, 117, (inscription) 242 ; on Via Latina, and Via Tiburtina, 15
Suburra, 121, 122
Sulpicius and Servilianus MM., 342
Sumite-Istic inscriptions, see Baptisteries
Sun worship, 3, 45, 95
Surius, *De probatis sanctorum historiis*, 128
Susanna M., 342, 346 ; *Passion of*, 70, 200
Syagrius B. of Autun, 216
Sylloge(ae), 65, 230 (ch. hd.) seqq., 240 (ch. hd.) seqq., 300 ; collated with monuments of Via Appia and Via Ardeatina, 301, 306 seqq. ; and with other inscriptions, 310 seqq. ; *Sylloge of Cambridge*, 233, 254 (ch. hd.) seqq., 285, 297 ; of *Centula* (or of *Corvie*) (*Centulensis* or *Corbeiensis*) 232,

237, 250 seqq., 265 ; *Circumpadana et Subalpina*, part of *S. Lauresha-mensis*, q.v. ; of *Einsiedeln* (or of *Reichenau*) (*Einsiedlensis* or *Reich-enavensis*), 119, 233, 240 seqq., 306, 307, 308 ; of Lorsch (Lauriacum) (*Laureshamensis* or *Palatinus* or *Vaticanus*), 233, 237, 242 seqq., 252, 265 ; of *Milan*, 230 n.1 ; of *Nola*, 230 n.1 ; of *Tours* (*Turonensis*), 232, 234, 248 seqq., 272 n. 2 ; of *Vatican inscriptions* (*Inscriptiones Vaticanae*), 232, 234 ; the *Vetus Membrana Scaligeri*, 233 ; S. of *Verdun* (*Virdu-nensis*), 232, 244 seqq., 266, 297 ; see *Sumite-Istic* inscriptions ; of *Würzburg* (*Wirceburgensis*), 233, 253

Symmachus P., 30, 54, 65, 77, 78, 81, 82, 83, 284 ; inscriptions by, 257–277, 285 seqq. ; cf. *Sumite-Istic* inscriptions, 272 seqq. ; public works of, 15, 25, 86, 126, 263 ; Symmachan fragment of *L.P.*, 269

Symphorosa M., 174, 176

Synod, of Bishops, 81 ; Roman (of 494), 182 ; (of 605), 37 ; see Councils

Syria, 25, 49, 66

Syriac Abridgment, see *Calendars, Greek Menology*

Syracuse, martyrs of, 217

T

Tangiers, martyrs of, 157

Tarpeian Hill, 96

Tarragona, martyrs of, 157, 168, 216

Tarsicius M., 105, 298, 299, 303

Taurinus M., 339

Taurobolium, 3

Tebessa (Theveste), martyrs of, 169 ; basilica (inscriptions), 238, 310

Telesphorus P.M., 49, 64, 180 ; decrees of, 77, 79 ; martyrdom of, 67, 68

Temple, of Ceres, 95 ; of Cybele, 125 ; of Diana, 125 ; of Isis, 3 ; of Jupiter, 23 ; of Mars, 70 ; of Mother of Gods, 95 ; Templum Pacis, region of, 12 ; of Pantheon, 13 ; of Romulus, 4 ; Templum Sacrae Urbis, 5 ; of Saturn, 5 ; of Venus, 125

Terracina, 306, 307

Tertullian, 49, 145, 165, 193, 202

Thagaste, Alypius B. of, 27

Thanet, 88

Thecla M., 194 ; *Passion of*, 173 ; cem. of, 99

Theoctista, 32

Theodatus, K. of Goths, 57, 59, 65

Theodelinda, Queen of Lombards, 31, 102, 103, 107, 108

Theodora, Empress, 58

Theodorae, Basilica, 14

Theodore P., 113, 117

,, M., Greek, 342 ; ch. of, 121, 122

Theodoret B. of Cyrrhus, 25

Theodoric, K. of Goths, 7, 57, 59, 61, 64, 65, 83, 215, 233, 236, 267 ; gifts to church, 86

Theodorius, Fl. Valila, 92

Theodosius, E., 3, 4, 6, 7, 22, 213

Theophorus, 190

Thessalonica, martyrs of, 138, 173

Theveste, see Tebessa

Thomas, Ap. M., *Passion of*, 194 ; oratory, in S. Andrew, Vatican, in-scription for, 257

Thrasonis ad S. Saturninum, coem., 98, 102, 110, 111, 124

Three children in fiery furnace, 159

Tiber, 2, 203

Tibiuca, Felix B.M. of, 173

Tiburtina, Via, 2, 15, 50, 53, 85, 88, 98, 100, 101, 105, 115, 116, 124, 237, 249, 293 ; inscriptions of, 252

Tiburtius M., brother of S. Cecilia, 69 ; S. and inscription, 106, 293, 305

Ticabis, Typasius M. of, 156

Ticino (Ticinum), 234, 242

Tigridae, titulus (? t. Priscae), 13

Tillemont on *A.SS.*, 128, 132

Timedus M., 215

Timothy (Timotheus), *Epistle to*, 49, 63

,, B.M., of Via Ostiensis, 99, 100, 116, 338, 339

,, (or Novatus), Baths of, 5, 154

Tithes, 24

Titulus Romanus, see Pudens

Tituli, 2, 10 n. 1, 87, 187 ; list of, 12

Tivoli (Tibur), 92, 264 n. 1
Toledo, Inquisition at, 130
Tongres, Servatius B. of, 36
Torquatus, tribune, 203
Totila, K., 59
Tours, ch. of, 31 ; inscription at, 250 ; martyrs and saints of, 208, 248 seqq. ; monastery of, 234 ; see Gregory of, *Sylloge of*
Trajan E., 121, 122, 190, 307
Tranquillianus M., 35
Translation of bodies of martyrs, etc., 11, 17, 69, 115, 119, 226, 227, 245, 256, 295
Transtiberim, see Trastevere ; region, 13
Trappist monastery of S. Callixtus, 304
Trastevere, 2, 121 ; see Callixtus, ch. of, Cecilia, house and ch. of, Chrysogonus, ch. of, Maria, ch. of
Treasurer of Holy See (Vestiarius Sanctae Sedis), 92
Treviri (Triers), inscription of, 233
Tropaea apostolorum, 9
Tuscan saints, 342
Tuscus, consul, 72
Turburbitani SS., 219
Typasius M., *Passion of*, 156

U

Umbilicum, 121, 122
Umbria, martyrs of, 201, 342
Urban 1. P.M., in Callixtus, Passion of (in *Passion of Cecilia*), 68 seq., 200, 346 ; S. and epitaph, 292, 302, 305
,,   11. P., 117
,,   B.M., friend of Cecilia, in Praetextatus, 69, 102, 298, 299
Urbinate, manuscript called, 341
Ursum pileatum, see Pontiani ad
Usuard, Martyrology of, 183, 229

V

Valentia, martyrs of, 216
Valentin (Valentinus) M., S. and bas., 14, 15, 98, 100, 101, 113, 115, 342
,,   patron of Philocalus, 50

Valentinian E., 7, 22, 83, 86
Valeria M., 299
Valerian (Valerianus) M., betrothed to Cecilia, 69, 106, 298, 299, 305
,,   E., 72, 77, 141, 150, 151, 157
,,   B. of Auxerre, 210
Valerius, Cardinal, 130
Vandals, 36, 202, 220, 282 n. 3
Vatican, 2, 99 ; churches on : see Andrew, Michael, Peter, Petronilla, Stephen ; inscriptions for churches of, see *Sylloge of Vatican inscriptions* ; library of, 233 ; *Codices of*, 340, 341 ; see *Sylloge of Lorsch* ; see Popes, tombs of in
Velabrum, 98 ; see George M.
Veneranda, fresco of, 308
Venus, street of, 149 ; temple of, 125
Veranus, Ager, on Via Tiburtina, 72, 244, 249, 253, 314
Verdun, monastery of, 245 ; see *Sylloge of Verdun*
Verona, 54, 217
Vespasian E., 306, 307
Vestia M. of Scilli, 152, 153
Vestiarius Sanctae Sedis, 92
Vestinae titulus (S. Vitalis), 12
Vetri (gilt glasses), 29
Veturinus M. of Scilli, 153
Via Lata, hospice of, 25 ; region of, 12 ; see Marcellus P.
Vici, 3, 96
Vicomagistri, 2, 96
Victor P.M., 49, 78 ; edicts of, 81 ; martyrdom, 68
,,   B. of Vita, 202
,,   secretary of Felix the flamen, 139
,,   M., of Aquileia, 215
,,   the Moor M., *Acts of*, 137
Victoria MM., Anatolia and, see Anatolia
Victoriana M., 215
Victorianus M. of Aquileia, 215
Victorinus M., 338, 339
Vienna Salzburg-, Codices, 112 seqq.
Codex Vindobonensis, 201

Vienne, Avitus B. of, 30 ; see Ado, Arbp. of ; martyrs (and *Acts of*), 143, 147, 162, 208

Vigilantius on cult of martyrs, 44 seqq.

Vigilius P., 58, 59, 79 ; inscriptions, 261 n. 3, 294

Vigna Ammendola, 301

Viminal, 2, 122

Vincent(ius) M., deacon of Sixtus II., 72

,, M. of Saragossa, *Acts of*, 138

,, priest, 292, 293

Vincula, Ad, see Peter, ch. of *ad Vincula*

Virgil, 237, cf. 294

Virgin, virginity, see Asceticism, Mary

Visions of martyrs, 177 ; of Cyprian, 149 ; at Fructuosus' martyrdom, 159, 160 ; of Jacobus and Marianus, 168 ; of Montanus, 172 ; of Perpetua, 165 seqq. ; of Quartellosa, 171 ; of Servatius, 36

Vita, Victor B. of, 202

Vitalian P., 37

Vitalis M., son of Felicitas, 106, 107, 110, 118, 338, 339, (inscription for) 294 ; titular church of (t. Vestinae), 12, 121, 122

,, M. of Ravenna, ch. of, 294

Vitus M., ch. of (S. Vito), 121, 122

Vivarium, monastery of, see Cassiodorus

Vynck on *Index Coemiteriorum*, 340 seqq.

W

Wearmouth, Biscop Benedict of, 38

Westminster, S. Peter's Abbey, 39 ; Cathedral of, 284 n. 2

Wigbert B. of Sherbourne, 38

Wighard, 37

Wilfred, Arbp. of York, 38

William of Malmesbury, 117

Willibrord, of Ripon, 38, 205 n. 1, 207

Wilpert, excavations in catacombs, 302, 312 seq.

Wirceburgensis, see *Sylloge of Würzburg*

Witigis the Goth, 17, 57, 59, 64

Worcester, Oftfor B. of, 38

Wulferus K., 39

Würzburg, Codex of, 112 seq. ; see *Sylloge of*

X

Xystus, see Sixtus

Y

Yarrow, 183, 229

York, Wilfred of, 38 ; Alcuin at, 232

Z

Zaccarias of Mitylene, 97

Zeno M., 126

Zephyrinus P.M., 49 ; edicts of, 77, 81 ; buildings of, 84 ; tomb of, 298, 302, 304

Zmaragdus M., see Smaragdus

Zoe M., 35

Zosimus P., 67, 224

Printed by
MORRISON & GIBB LIMITED
Edinburgh

A SELECTION OF BOOKS PUBLISHED BY METHUEN AND CO. LTD., LONDON 36 ESSEX STREET W.C.

CONTENTS

	PAGE
General Literature	2
Ancient Cities	13
Antiquary's Books	13
Arden Shakespeare	14
Classics of Art	14
'Complete' Series	15
Connoisseur's Library	15
Handbooks of English Church History	16
Handbooks of Theology	16
'Home Life' Series	16
Illustrated Pocket Library of Plain and Coloured Books	16
Leaders of Religion	17
Library of Devotion	17
Little Books on Art	18
Little Galleries	18
Little Guides	18
Little Library	19

	PAGE
Little Quarto Shakespeare	20
Miniature Library	20
New Library of Medicine	21
New Library of Music	21
Oxford Biographies	21
Four Plays	21
States of Italy	21
Westminster Commentaries	22
'Young' Series	22
Shilling Library	22
Books for Travellers	23
Some Books on Art	23
Some Books on Italy	24
Fiction	25
Books for Boys and Girls	30
Shilling Novels	30
Sevenpenny Novels	31

A SELECTION OF
MESSRS. METHUEN'S
PUBLICATIONS

IN this Catalogue the order is according to authors. An asterisk denotes that the book is in the press.

Colonial Editions are published of all Messrs. METHUEN's Novels issued at a price above 2s. 6d., and similar editions are published of some works of General Literature. Colonial Editions are only for circulation in the British Colonies and India.

All books marked net are not subject to discount, and cannot be bought at less than the published price. Books not marked net are subject to the discount which the bookseller allows.

Messrs. METHUEN's books are kept in stock by all good booksellers. If there is any difficulty in seeing copies, Messrs. Methuen will be very glad to have early information, and specimen copies of any books will be sent on receipt of the published price *plus* postage for net books, and of the published price for ordinary books.

This Catalogue contains only a selection of the more important books published by Messrs. Methuen. A complete and illustrated catalogue of their publications may be obtained on application.

Abraham (G. D.). MOTOR WAYS IN LAKELAND. Illustrated. *Demy 8vo.* 7s. 6d. net.

Adcock (A. St. John). THE BOOK-LOVER'S LONDON. Illustrated. *Cr. 8vo.* 6s. net.

*Ady (Cecilia M.). PIUS II.: THE HUMANIST POPE. Illustrated. *Demy 8vo.* 10s. 6d. net.

Andrewes (Lancelot). PRECES PRIVATAE. Translated and edited, with Notes, by F. E. BRIGHTMAN. *Cr. 8vo.* 6s.

Aristotle. THE ETHICS. Edited, with an Introduction and Notes, by JOHN BURNET. *Demy 8vo.* 10s. 6d. net.

Atkinson (C. T.). A HISTORY OF GERMANY, 1715-1815. *Demy 8vo.* 12s. 6d. net.

Atkinson (T. D.). ENGLISH ARCHITECTURE. Illustrated. *Third Edition. Fcap. 8vo.* 3s. 6d. net.
A GLOSSARY OF TERMS USED IN ENGLISH ARCHITECTURE. Illustrated. *Second Edition. Fcap. 8vo.* 3s. 6d. net.
ENGLISH AND WELSH CATHEDRALS. Illustrated. *Demy 8vo.* 10s. 6d. net.

Bain (F. W.). A DIGIT OF THE MOON: A HINDOO LOVE STORY. *Tenth Edition. Fcap. 8vo.* 3s. 6d. net.

THE DESCENT OF THE SUN : A CYCLE OF BIRTH. *Fifth Edition. Fcap. 8vo.* 3s. 6d. net.
A HEIFER OF THE DAWN. *Seventh Edition. Fcap. 8vo.* 2s. 6d. net.
IN THE GREAT GOD'S HAIR. *Fifth Edition. Fcap. 8vo.* 2s. 6d. net.
A DRAUGHT OF THE BLUE. *Fifth Edition Fcap. 8vo.* 2s. 6d. net.
AN ESSENCE OF THE DUSK. *Third Edition. Fcap. 8vo.* 2s. 6d. net.
AN INCARNATION OF THE SNOW. *Third Edition. Fcap. 8vo.* 3s. 6d. net.
A MINE OF FAULTS. *Third Edition. Fcap. 8vo.* 3s. 6d. net.
THE ASHES OF A GOD. *Second Edition. Fcap. 8vo.* 3s. 6d. net.
BUBBLES OF THE FOAM. *Fcap. 4to.* 5s. net. Also *Fcap. 8vo.* 3s. 6d. net.

Balfour (Graham). THE LIFE OF ROBERT LOUIS STEVENSON. Illustrated. *Eleventh Edition. In one Volume. Cr. 8vo.* Buckram, 6s. Also *Fcap. 8vo.* 1s. net.

Baring (Hon. Maurice). LANDMARKS IN RUSSIAN LITERATURE. *Second Edition. Cr. 8vo.* 6s. net.
RUSSIAN ESSAYS AND STORIES. *Second Edition. Cr. 8vo.* 5s. net.
THE RUSSIAN PEOPLE. *Demy 8vo.* 15s. net.

Baring-Gould (S.). THE LIFE OF NAPOLEON BONAPARTE. Illustrated. *Second Edition. Royal 8vo.* 10s. 6d. *net.*
THE TRAGEDY OF THE CÆSARS: A STUDY OF THE CHARACTERS OF THE CÆSARS OF THE JULIAN AND CLAUDIAN HOUSES. Illustrated. *Seventh Edition. Royal 8vo.* 10s. 6d. *net.*
THE VICAR OF MORWENSTOW. With a Portrait. *Third Edition. Cr. 8vo.* 3s. 6d. *Also Fcap. 8vo.* 1s. *net.*
OLD COUNTRY LIFE. Illustrated. *Fifth Edition. Large Cr. 8vo.* 6s. *Also Fcap. 8vo.* 1s. *net.*
A BOOK OF CORNWALL. Illustrated. *Third Edition. Cr. 8vo.* 6s.
A BOOK OF DARTMOOR. Illustrated. *Second Edition. Cr. 8vo.* 6s.
A BOOK OF DEVON. Illustrated. *Third Edition. Cr. 8vo.* 6s.

Baring-Gould (S.) and Sheppard (H. Fleet-wood). A GARLAND OF COUNTRY SONG. English Folk Songs with their Traditional Melodies. *Demy 4to.* 6s.
SONGS OF THE WEST. Folk Songs of Devon and Cornwall. Collected from the Mouths of the People. New and Revised Edition, under the musical editorship of CECIL J. SHARP. *Large Imperial 8vo.* 5s. *net.*

Barker (E.). THE POLITICAL THOUGHT OF PLATO AND ARISTOTLE. *Demy 8vo.* 10s. 6d. *net.*

Bastable (C. F.). THE COMMERCE OF NATIONS. *Sixth Edition. Cr. 8vo.* 2s. 6d.

Beckford (Peter). THOUGHTS ON HUNTING. Edited by J. OTHO PAGET. Illustrated. *Third Edition. Demy 8vo.* 6s.

Belloc (H.). PARIS. Illustrated *Third Edition. Cr. 8vo.* 6s.
HILLS AND THE SEA. *Fourth Edition. Fcap. 8vo.* 5s. *Also Fcap. 8vo.* 1s. *net.*
ON NOTHING AND KINDRED SUBJECTS. *Third Edition. Fcap. 8vo.* 5s.
ON EVERYTHING. *Third Edition. Fcap. 8vo.* 5s.
ON SOMETHING. *Second Edition. Fcap. 8vo.* 5s.
FIRST AND LAST. *Second Edition. Fcap. 8vo.* 5s
THIS AND THAT AND THE OTHER. *Second Edition. Fcap. 8vo.* 5s.
MARIE ANTOINETTE. Illustrated. *Third Edition. Demy 8vo.* 15s. *net.*
THE PYRENEES. Illustrated. *Second Edition. Demy 8vo.* 7s. 6d. *net.*

Bennett (Arnold). THE TRUTH ABOUT AN AUTHOR. *Crown 8vo.* 6s.

Bennett (W. H.). A PRIMER OF THE BIBLE. *Fifth Edition Cr. 8vo.* 2s. 6d.

Bennett (W. H.) and Adeney (W. F.). A BIBLICAL INTRODUCTION. With a concise Bibliography. *Sixth Edition. Cr. 8vo.* 7s. 6d. *Also in Two Volumes. Cr. 8vo. Each* 3s. 6d. *net.*

Benson (Archbishop). GOD'S BOARD. Communion Addresses. *Second Edition. Fcap. 8vo.* 3s. 6d. *net.*

***Berriman (Algernon E.).** AVIATION. Illustrated. *Cr. 8vo.* 10s. 6d. *net.*

Bicknell (Ethel E.). PARIS AND HER TREASURES. Illustrated. *Fcap. 8vo. Round corners.* 5s. *net.*

Blake (William). ILLUSTRATIONS OF THE BOOK OF JOB. With a General Introduction by LAURENCE BINYON. Illustrated. *Quarto.* 21s. *net.*

Bloemfontein (Bishop of). ARA CŒLI: AN ESSAY IN MYSTICAL THEOLOGY. *Fifth Edition. Cr. 8vo.* 3s. 6d. *net.*
FAITH AND EXPERIENCE. *Second Edition. Cr. 8vo.* 3s. 6d. *net.*

***Boulenger (G. A.).** THE SNAKES OF EUROPE. Illustrated. *Cr. 8vo.* 6s.

Bowden (E. M.). THE IMITATION OF BUDDHA. Quotations from Buddhist Literature for each Day in the Year. *Sixth Edition. Cr. 16mo.* 2s. 6d.

Brabant (F. G.). RAMBLES IN SUSSEX. Illustrated. *Cr. 8vo.* 6s.

Bradley (A. G.). THE ROMANCE OF NORTHUMBERLAND. Illustrated. *Third Edition. Demy 8vo.* 7s. 6d. *net.*

Braid (James). ADVANCED GOLF. Illustrated. *Seventh Edition. Demy 8vo.* 10s. 6d. *net.*

Bridger (A. E.). MINDS IN DISTRESS. A Psychological Study of the Masculine and Feminine Minds in Health and in Disorder. *Cr. 8vo.* 2s. 6d. *net.*

Brodrick (Mary) and Morton (A. Anderson). A CONCISE DICTIONARY OF EGYPTIAN ARCHÆOLOGY. A Handbook for Students and Travellers. Illustrated. *Cr. 8vo.* 3s. 6d.

Browning (Robert). PARACELSUS. Edited with an Introduction, Notes, and Bibliography by MARGARET L. LEE and KATHARINE B. LOCOCK. *Fcap. 8vo.* 3s. 6d. *net.*

Buckton (A. M.). EAGER HEART: A CHRISTMAS MYSTERY-PLAY. *Eleventh Edition. Cr. 8vo.* 1s. *net.*

Bull (Paul). GOD AND OUR SOLDIERS. *Second Edition. Cr. 8vo.* 6s.

Burns (Robert). THE POEMS AND SONGS. Edited by ANDREW LANG and W. A. CRAIGIE. With Portrait. *Third Edition. Wide Demy 8vo.* 6s.

Calman (W. T.). THE LIFE OF CRUSTACEA. Illustrated. *Cr. 8vo.* 6s.

Carlyle (Thomas). THE FRENCH REVOLUTION. Edited by C. R. L. FLETCHER. *Three Volumes. Cr. 8vo.* 18s.
THE LETTERS AND SPEECHES OF OLIVER CROMWELL. With an Introduction by C. H. FIRTH, and Notes and Appendices by S. C. LOMAS. *Three Volumes. Demy 8vo.* 18s. *net.*

Chambers (Mrs. Lambert). LAWN TENNIS FOR LADIES. Illustrated. *Second Edition. Cr. 8vo.* 2s. 6d. *net.*

Chesser (Elizabeth Sloan). PERFECT HEALTH FOR WOMEN AND CHILDREN. *Cr. 8vo.* 3s. 6d. *net.*

Chesterfield (Lord). THE LETTERS OF THE EARL OF CHESTERFIELD TO HIS SON. Edited, with an Introduction by C. STRACHEY, and Notes by A. CALTHROP. *Two Volumes. Cr. 8vo.* 12s.

Chesterton (G. K.). CHARLES DICKENS. With two Portraits in Photogravure. *Eighth Edition. Cr. 8vo.* 6s.
Also Fcap. 8vo. 1s. *net.*
THE BALLAD OF THE WHITE HORSE. *Fourth Edition. Fcap. 8vo.* 5s.
ALL THINGS CONSIDERED. *Seventh Edition. Fcap. 8vo.* 5s.
TREMENDOUS TRIFLES. *Fifth Edition. Fcap. 8vo.* 5s.
ALARMS AND DISCURSIONS. *Second Edition. Fcap. 8vo.* 5s.
A MISCELLANY OF MEN. *Second Edition. Fcap. 8vo.* 5s.

*Clausen (George). ROYAL ACADEMY LECTURES ON PAINTING. Illustrated. *Cr. 8vo.* 5s. *net.*

Conrad (Joseph). THE MIRROR OF THE SEA: Memories and Impressions. *Fourth Edition. Fcap. 8vo.* 5s.

Coolidge (W. A. B.). THE ALPS: IN NATURE AND HISTORY. Illustrated. *Demy 8vo.* 7s. 6d. *net.*

Correvon (H.). ALPINE FLORA. Translated and enlarged by E. W. CLAYFORTH. Illustrated. *Square Demy 8vo.* 16s. *net.*

Coulton (G. G.). CHAUCER AND HIS ENGLAND. Illustrated. *Second Edition. Demy 8vo.* 10s. 6d. *net.*

Cowper (William). POEMS. Edited, with an Introduction and Notes, by J. C. BAILEY. Illustrated. *Demy 8vo.* 10s. 6d. *net.*

Cox (J. C.). RAMBLES IN SURREY. Illustrated. *Second Edition. Cr. 8vo.* 6s.
RAMBLES IN KENT. Illustrated. *Cr. 8vo.* 6s.

Crawley (A. E.). THE BOOK OF THE BALL: AN ACCOUNT OF WHAT IT DOES AND WHY. Illustrated. *Cr. 8vo.* 3s. 6d. *net.*

Crowley (H. Ralph). THE HYGIENE OF SCHOOL LIFE. Illustrated. *Cr. 8vo.* 3s. 6d. *net.*

Davis (H. W. C.). ENGLAND UNDER THE NORMANS AND ANGEVINS: 1066–1272. *Third Edition. Demy 8vo.* 10s. 6d. *net.*

Dawbarn (Charles). FRANCE AND THE FRENCH. Illustrated. *Demy 8vo.* 10s. 6d. *net.*

Dearmer (Mabel). A CHILD'S LIFE OF CHRIST. Illustrated. *Large Cr. 8vo.* 6s.

Deffand (Madame du). LETTRES DE LA MARQUISE DU DEFFAND A HORACE WALPOLE. Edited, with Introduction, Notes, and Index, by Mrs. PAGET TOYNBEE. *Three Volumes. Demy 8vo.* £3 3s. *net.*

Dickinson (G. L.). THE GREEK VIEW OF LIFE. *Eighth Edition. Cr. 8vo.* 2s. 6d. *net.*

Ditchfield (P. H.). THE OLD-TIME PARSON. Illustrated. *Second Edition. Demy 8vo.* 7s. 6d. *net.*
THE OLD ENGLISH COUNTRY SQUIRE. Illustrated. *Demy 8vo.* 10s. 6d. *net.*

Dowden (J.). FURTHER STUDIES IN THE PRAYER BOOK. *Cr. 8vo.* 6s.

Driver (S. R.). SERMONS ON SUBJECTS CONNECTED WITH THE OLD TESTAMENT. *Cr. 8vo.* 6s.

Dumas (Alexandre). THE CRIMES OF THE BORGIAS AND OTHERS. With an Introduction by R. S. GARNETT. Illustrated. *Second Edition. Cr. 8vo.* 6s.
THE CRIMES OF URBAIN GRANDIER AND OTHERS. Illustrated. *Cr. 8vo.* 6s.
THE CRIMES OF THE MARQUISE DE BRINVILLIERS AND OTHERS. Illustrated. *Cr. 8vo.* 6s.
THE CRIMES OF ALI PACHA AND OTHERS. Illustrated. *Cr. 8vo.* 6s.
MY PETS. Newly translated by A. R. ALLINSON. Illustrated. *Cr. 8vo.* 6s.

Dunn-Pattison (R. P.). NAPOLEON'S MARSHALS. Illustrated. *Second Edition. Demy 8vo.* 12s. 6d. *net.*

THE BLACK PRINCE. Illustrated. *Second Edition. Demy 8vo. 7s. 6d. net.*

Durham (The Earl of). THE REPORT ON CANADA. With an Introductory Note. *Demy 8vo. 4s. 6d. net.*

Egerton (H. E.). A SHORT HISTORY OF BRITISH COLONIAL POLICY. *Third Edition. Demy 8vo. 7s. 6d. net.*

Evans (Herbert A.). CASTLES OF ENGLAND AND WALES. Illustrated. *Demy 8vo. 12s. 6d. net.*

Exeter (Bishop of). REGNUM DEI. (The Bampton Lectures of 1901.) *A Cheaper Edition. Demy 8vo. 7s. 6d. net.*

Ewald (Carl). MY LITTLE BOY. Translated by ALEXANDER TEIXEIRA DE MATTOS. Illustrated. *Fcap. 8vo. 5s.*

Fairbrother (W. H.). THE PHILO-SOPHY OF T. H. GREEN. *Second Edition. Cr. 8vo. 3s. 6d.*

ffoulkes (Charles). THE ARMOURER AND HIS CRAFT. Illustrated. *Royal 4to. £2 2s. net.*

*DECORATIVE IRONWORK. From the xIIth to the xvIIIth Century. Illustrated. *Royal 4to. £2 2s. net.*

Firth (C. H.). CROMWELL'S ARMY. A History of the English Soldier during the Civil Wars, the Commonwealth, and the Protectorate. Illustrated. *Second Edition. Cr. 8vo. 6s.*

Fisher (H. A. L.). THE REPUBLICAN TRADITION IN EUROPE. *Cr. 8vo. 6s. net.*

FitzGerald (Edward). THE RUBA'IYÁT OF OMAR KHAYYÁM. Printed from the Fifth and last Edition. With a Commentary by H. M. BATSON, and a Biographical Introduction by E. D. ROSS. *Cr. 8vo. 6s.*

*Also Illustrated by E. J. SULLIVAN. *Cr. 4to. 15s. net.*

Flux (A. W.). ECONOMIC PRINCIPLES. *Demy 8vo. 7s. 6d. net.*

Fraser (E.). THE SOLDIERS WHOM WELLINGTON LED. Deeds of Daring, Chivalry, and Renown. Illustrated. *Cr. 8vo. 5s. net.*

*THE SAILORS WHOM NELSON LED. Their Doings Described by Themselves. Illustrated. *Cr. 8vo. 5s. net.*

Fraser (J. F.). ROUND THE WORLD ON A WHEEL. Illustrated. *Fifth Edition. Cr. 8vo. 6s.*

Galton (Sir Francis). MEMORIES OF MY LIFE. Illustrated. *Third Edition. Demy 8vo. 10s. 6d. net.*

Gibbins (H. de B.). INDUSTRY IN ENGLAND: HISTORICAL OUT-LINES. With Maps and Plans. *Seventh Edition, Revised. Demy 8vo. 10s. 6d.*

THE INDUSTRIAL HISTORY OF ENGLAND. With 5 Maps and a Plan. *Nineteenth Edition. Cr. 8vo. 3s.*

ENGLISH SOCIAL REFORMERS. *Third Edition. Cr. 8vo. 2s. 6d.*

Gibbon (Edward). THE MEMOIRS OF THE LIFE OF EDWARD GIBBON. Edited by G. BIRKBECK HILL. *Cr. 8vo. 6s.*

THE DECLINE AND FALL OF THE ROMAN EMPIRE. Edited, with Notes, Appendices, and Maps, by J. B. BURY. Illustrated. *Seven Volumes. Demy 8vo.* Illustrated. *Each 10s. 6d. net. Also in Seven Volumes. Cr. 8vo. 6s. each.*

Glover (T. R.). THE CONFLICT OF RELIGIONS IN THE EARLY ROMAN EMPIRE. *Fourth Edition. Demy 8vo. 7s. 6d. net.*

VIRGIL. *Second Edition. Demy 8vo. 7s. 6d. net.*

THE CHRISTIAN TRADITION AND ITS VERIFICATION. (The Angus Lecture for 1912.) *Cr. 8vo. 3s. 6d. net.*

Godley (A. D.). LYRA FRIVOLA. *Fourth Edition. Fcap. 8vo. 2s. 6d.*

VERSES TO ORDER. *Second Edition. Fcap. 8vo. 2s. 6d.*

SECOND STRINGS. *Fcap. 8vo. 2s. 6d.*

Gostling (Frances M.). AUVERGNE AND ITS PEOPLE. Illustrated. *Demy 8vo. 10s. 6d. net.*

Gray (Arthur). CAMBRIDGE. Illustrated. *Demy 8vo. 10s. 6d. net.*

Grahame (Kenneth). THE WIND IN THE WILLOWS. *Seventh Edition. Cr. 8vo. 6s.*

*Also Illustrated. *Cr. 4to. 7s. 6d. net.*

Granger (Frank). HISTORICAL SOCI-OLOGY: A TEXT-BOOK OF POLITICS. *Cr. 8vo. 3s. 6d. net.*

*Gretton (M. Sturge).** A CORNER OF THE COTSWOLDS. Illustrated. *Demy 8vo. 7s. 6d. net.*

Grew (Edwin Sharpe). THE GROWTH OF A PLANET. Illustrated. *Cr. 8vo. 6s.*

Griffin (W. Hall) and **Minchin (H. C.).** THE LIFE OF ROBERT BROWNING. Illustrated. *Second Edition. Demy 8vo. 12s. 6d. net.*

Haig (K. G.). HEALTH THROUGH DIET. *Second Edition. Cr. 8vo. 3s. 6d. net.*

Hale (J. R.). FAMOUS SEA FIGHTS: FROM SALAMIS TO TSU-SHIMA. Illustrated. *Second Edition. Cr. 8vo. 6s. net.*

Hall (H. R.). THE ANCIENT HISTORY OF THE NEAR EAST FROM THE EARLIEST TIMES TO THE BATTLE OF SALAMIS Illustrated. *Second Edition. Demy 8vo. 15s. net.*

Hannay (D.). A SHORT HISTORY OF THE ROYAL NAVY. Vol. I., 1217-1688. Vol. II., 1689-1815. *Demy 8vo. Each 7s. 6d.*

Hare (B.). THE GOLFING SWING SIMPLIFIED AND ITS MECHANISM CORRECTLY EXPLAINED. *Third Edition. Fcap. 8vo. 1s. net.*

Harper (Charles G.). THE AUTOCAR ROAD-BOOK. With Maps. *Four Volumes. Cr. 8vo. Each 7s. 6d. net.*

    Vol. I.—SOUTH OF THE THAMES.

    Vol. II.—NORTH AND SOUTH WALES AND WEST MIDLANDS.

    Vol. III.—EAST ANGLIA AND EAST MIDLANDS.

    *Vol. IV.—THE NORTH OF ENGLAND AND SOUTH OF SCOTLAND.

Harris (Frank). THE WOMEN OF SHAKESPEARE. *Demy 8vo. 7s. 6d. net.*

Hassall (Arthur). THE LIFE OF NAPOLEON. Illustrated. *Demy 8vo. 7s. 6d. net.*

Headley (F. W.). DARWINISM AND MODERN SOCIALISM. *Second Edition. Cr. 8vo. 5s. net.*

Henderson (M. Sturge). GEORGE MEREDITH: NOVELIST, POET, REFORMER. With a Portrait. *Second Edition. Cr. 8vo. 6s.*

Henley (W. E.). ENGLISH LYRICS: CHAUCER TO POE. *Second Edition. Cr. 8vo. 2s. 6d. net.*

Hill (George Francis). ONE HUNDRED MASTERPIECES OF SCULPTURE. Illustrated. *Demy 8vo. 10s. 6d. net.*

Hind (C. Lewis). DAYS IN CORNWALL. Illustrated. *Third Edition. Cr. 8vo. 6s.*

Hobhouse (L. T.). THE THEORY OF KNOWLEDGE. *Demy 8vo. 10s. 6d. net.*

Hobson (J. A.). INTERNATIONAL TRADE: AN APPLICATION OF ECONOMIC THEORY. *Cr. 8vo. 2s. 6d. net.*

PROBLEMS OF POVERTY: AN INQUIRY INTO THE INDUSTRIAL CONDITION OF THE POOR. *Eighth Edition. Cr. 8vo. 2s. 6d.*

THE PROBLEM OF THE UN-EMPLOYED: AN INQUIRY AND AN ECONOMIC POLICY. *Fifth Edition. Cr. 8vo. 2s. 6d.*

GOLD, PRICES AND WAGES: WITH AN EXAMINATION OF THE QUANTITY THEORY. *Second Edition. Cr. 8vo. 3s. 6d. net.*

Hodgson (Mrs. W.). HOW TO IDENTIFY OLD CHINESE PORCELAIN. Illustrated. *Third Edition. Post 8vo. 6s.*

Holdich (Sir T. H.). THE INDIAN BORDERLAND, 1880-1900. Illustrated. *Second Edition. Demy 8vo. 10s. 6d. net.*

Holdsworth (W. S.). A HISTORY OF ENGLISH LAW. *Four Volumes. Vols. I., II., III. Demy 8vo. Each 10s. 6d. net*

Holland (Clive). TYROL AND ITS PEOPLE. Illustrated. *Demy 8vo. 10s. 6d. net.*

Horsburgh (E. L. S.). WATERLOO: A NARRATIVE AND A CRITICISM. With Plans. *Second Edition. Cr. 8vo. 5s.*

THE LIFE OF SAVONAROLA. Illustrated. *Cr. 8vo. 5s. net.*

Hosie (Alexander). MANCHURIA. Illustrated. *Second Edition. Demy 8vo. 7s. 6d. net.*

*Howell (A. G. Ferrers).** ST. BERNARDINO OF SIENA. Illustrated. *Demy 8vo. 10s. 6d. net.*

Hudson (W. H.). A SHEPHERD'S LIFE: IMPRESSIONS OF THE SOUTH WILTSHIRE DOWNS. Illustrated. *Third Edition. Demy 8vo. 7s. 6d. net.*

Humphreys (John H.). PROPORTIONAL REPRESENTATION. *Cr. 8vo. 5s. net.*

Hutton (Edward). THE CITIES OF SPAIN. Illustrated. *Fourth Edition Cr. 8vo. 6s.*

THE CITIES OF UMBRIA. Illustrated. *Fifth Edition. Cr. 8vo. 6s.*

THE CITIES OF LOMBARDY. Illustrated. *Cr. 8vo. 6s.*

*THE CITIES OF ROMAGNA AND THE MARCHES. Illustrated. *Cr. 8vo. 6s.*

FLORENCE AND NORTHERN TUSCANY WITH GENOA. Illustrated. *Second Edition. Cr. 8vo. 6s.*

SIENA AND SOUTHERN TUSCANY. Illustrated. *Second Edition. Cr. 8vo. 6s.*

VENICE AND VENETIA. Illustrated. *Cr. 8vo. 6s.*

ROME. Illustrated. *Third Edition. Cr. 8vo. 6s.*

COUNTRY WALKS ABOUT FLORENCE. Illustrated. *Second Edition. Fcap. 8vo. 5s. net.*

A BOOK OF THE WYE. Illustrated. *Demy 8vo. 7s. 6d. net.*

Ibsen (Henrik). BRAND. A Dramatic Poem, translated by WILLIAM WILSON. *Fourth Edition. Cr. 8vo. 3s. 6d.*

Inge (W. R.). CHRISTIAN MYSTICISM. (The Bampton Lectures of 1899.) *Third Edition. Cr. 8vo. 5s. net.*

Innes (A. D.). A HISTORY OF THE BRITISH IN INDIA. With Maps and Plans. *Cr. 8vo. 6s.*
ENGLAND UNDER THE TUDORS. With Maps. *Fourth Edition. Demy 8vo. 10s. 6d. net.*

Innes (Mary). SCHOOLS OF PAINTING. Illustrated. *Second Edition. Cr. 8vo. 5s. net.*

Jenks (E.). AN OUTLINE OF ENGLISH LOCAL GOVERNMENT. *Second Edition.* Revised by R. C. K. ENSOR *Cr. 8vo. 2s. 6d. net.*
A SHORT HISTORY OF ENGLISH LAW: FROM THE EARLIEST TIMES TO THE END OF THE YEAR 1911. *Demy 8vo. 10s. 6d. net.*

Jerningham (Charles Edward). THE MAXIMS OF MARMADUKE. *Second Edition. Fcap. 8vo. 5s.*

Jevons (F. B.). PERSONALITY. *Cr. 8vo. 2s. 6d. net.*

Johnston (Sir H. H.). BRITISH CENTRAL AFRICA. Illustrated. *Third Edition. Cr. 4to. 18s. net.*
THE NEGRO IN THE NEW WORLD. Illustrated. *Demy 8vo. 21s. net.*

Julian (Lady) of Norwich. REVELATIONS OF DIVINE LOVE. Edited by GRACE WARRACK. *Fourth Edition. Cr. 8vo. 3s. 6d.*

Keats (John). POEMS. Edited, with Introduction and Notes, by E. de SÉLINCOURT. With a Frontispiece in Photogravure. *Third Edition. Demy 8vo. 7s. 6d. net.*

Keble (John). THE CHRISTIAN YEAR. With an Introduction and Notes by W. LOCK. Illustrated. *Third Edition. Fcap. 8vo. 3s. 6d.*

Kempis (Thomas à). THE IMITATION OF CHRIST. From the Latin, with an Introduction by DEAN FARRAR. Illustrated. *Fourth Edition. Fcap. 8vo. 3s. 6d.*

*THOMAE HEMERKEN A KEMPIS DE IMITATIONE CHRISTI. Edited by ADRIAN FORTESCUE. *Cr. 4to. £1 1s. net.*

Kipling (Rudyard). BARRACK-ROOM BALLADS. *117th Thousand. Thirty-fourth Edition. Cr. 8vo. Buckram. Also Fcap. 8vo. Cloth, 4s. 6d. net; leather, 5s. net.*

THE SEVEN SEAS. *97th Thousand. Twenty-first Edition. Cr. 8vo. Buckram, 6s. Also Fcap. 8vo. Cloth, 4s. 6d. net; leather, 5s. net.*

THE FIVE NATIONS. *81st Thousand. Eleventh Edition. Cr. 8vo. Buckram, 6s. Also Fcap. 8vo. Cloth, 4s. 6d. net; leather, 5s. net.*

DEPARTMENTAL DITTIES. *Twenty-Third Edition. Cr. 8vo. Buckram, 6s. Also Fcap. 8vo. Cloth, 4s. 6d. net; leather 5s. net.*

Lamb (Charles and Mary). THE COMPLETE WORKS. Edited, with an Introduction and Notes, by E. V. LUCAS. *A New and Revised Edition in Six Volumes. With Frontispiece. Fcap. 8vo. 5s. each.* The volumes are :—
I. MISCELLANEOUS PROSE. II. ELIA AND THE LAST ESSAYS OF ELIA. III. BOOKS FOR CHILDREN. IV. PLAYS AND POEMS. V. and VI. LETTERS.

Lane-Poole (Stanley). A HISTORY OF EGYPT IN THE MIDDLE AGES. Illustrated. *Cr. 8vo. 6s.*

Lankester (Sir Ray). SCIENCE FROM AN EASY CHAIR. Illustrated. *Seventh Edition. Cr. 8vo. 6s.*

Lee (Gerald Stanley). INSPIRED MILLIONAIRES. *Cr. 8vo. 3s. 6d. net.*
CROWDS : A STUDY OF THE GENIUS OF DEMOCRACY, AND OF THE FEARS, DESIRES, AND EXPECTATIONS OF THE PEOPLE. *Cr. 8vo. 6s.*

Lock (Walter). ST. PAUL, THE MASTER BUILDER. *Third Edition. Cr. 8vo. 3s. 6d.*
THE BIBLE AND CHRISTIAN LIFE. *Cr. 8vo. 6s.*

Lodge (Sir Oliver). THE SUBSTANCE OF FAITH, ALLIED WITH SCIENCE : A CATECHISM FOR PARENTS AND TEACHERS. *Eleventh Edition. Cr. 8vo. 2s. net.*
MAN AND THE UNIVERSE : A STUDY OF THE INFLUENCE OF THE ADVANCE IN SCIENTIFIC KNOWLEDGE UPON OUR UNDERSTANDING OF CHRISTIANITY. *Ninth Edition. Demy 8vo. 5s. net. Also Fcap. 8vo. 1s. net.*

THE SURVIVAL OF MAN: A STUDY IN UNRECOGNISED HUMAN FACULTY. *Fifth Edition. Wide Cr. 8vo.* 5s. *net.*

REASON AND BELIEF. *Fifth Edition. Cr. 8vo.* 3s. 6d. *net.*

MODERN PROBLEMS. *Cr. 8vo.* 5s. *net.*

Loreburn (Earl). CAPTURE AT SEA. *Cr. 8vo.* 2s. 6d. *net.*

Lorimer (George Horace). LETTERS FROM A SELF-MADE MERCHANT TO HIS SON. Illustrated. *Twenty-fourth Edition. Cr. 8vo.* 3s. 6d. *Also Fcap. 8vo.* 1s. *net.*

OLD GORGON GRAHAM. Illustrated. *Second Edition. Cr. 8vo.* 6s. *Also Cr. 8vo.* 2s. *net.*

Lucas (E. V.). THE LIFE OF CHARLES LAMB. Illustrated. *Fifth Edition. Demy 8vo.* 7s. 6d. *net.*

A WANDERER IN HOLLAND. Illustrated. *Fourteenth Edition. Cr. 8vo.* 6s.

A WANDERER IN LONDON. Illustrated. *Fifteenth Edition, Revised. Cr. 8vo.* 6s.

A WANDERER IN PARIS. Illustrated. *Tenth Edition. Cr. 8vo.* 6s. *Also Fcap. 8vo.* 5s.

A WANDERER IN FLORENCE. Illustrated. *Fourth Edition. Cr. 8vo.* 6s.

THE OPEN ROAD: A LITTLE BOOK FOR WAYFARERS. *Twenty-first Edition. Fcap. 8vo.* 5s. *India Paper,* 7s. 6d. *Also Illustrated. Cr. 4to.* 15s. *net.*

THE FRIENDLY TOWN: A LITTLE BOOK FOR THE URBANE. *Seventh Edition. Fcap. 8vo.* 5s.

FIRESIDE AND SUNSHINE. *Seventh Edition. Fcap 8vo.* 5s.

CHARACTER AND COMEDY. *Sixth Edition. Fcap. 8vo.* 5s.

THE GENTLEST ART: A CHOICE OF LETTERS BY ENTERTAINING HANDS. *Seventh Edition. Fcap. 8vo.* 5s.

THE SECOND POST. *Third Edition. Fcap. 8vo.* 5s.

HER INFINITE VARIETY: A FEMININE PORTRAIT GALLERY. *Sixth Edition. Fcap. 8vo.* 5s.

GOOD COMPANY: A RALLY OF MEN. *Second Edition. Fcap. 8vo.* 5s.

ONE DAY AND ANOTHER. *Fifth Edition. Fcap. 8vo.* 5s.

OLD LAMPS FOR NEW. *Fourth Edition. Fcap. 8vo.* 5s.

*LOITERER'S HARVEST. *Fcap. 8vo.* 5s.

LISTENER'S LURE: AN OBLIQUE NARRATION. *Ninth Edition. Fcap. 8vo.* 5s.

OVER BEMERTON'S: AN EASY-GOING CHRONICLE. *Tenth Edition. Fcap. 8vo.* 5s.

MR. INGLESIDE. *Tenth Edition. Fcap. 8vo.* 5s.

*LONDON LAVENDER. *Fcap. 8vo.* 5s.

THE BRITISH SCHOOL: AN ANECDOTAL GUIDE TO THE BRITISH PAINTERS AND PAINTINGS IN THE NATIONAL GALLERY. *Fcap. 8vo.* 2s. 6d. *net.*

HARVEST HOME. *Fcap. 8vo.* 1s. *net.*

A LITTLE OF EVERYTHING. *Third Edition. Fcap. 8vo.* 1s. *net.*

See also Lamb (Charles).

Lydekker (R.). THE OX AND ITS KINDRED. Illustrated. *Cr. 8vo.* 6s.

Lydekker (R.) and Others. REPTILES, AMPHIBIA, FISHES, AND LOWER CHORDATA. Edited by J. C. CUNNINGHAM. Illustrated. *Demy 8vo.* 10s. 6d. *net.*

Macaulay (Lord). CRITICAL AND HISTORICAL ESSAYS. Edited by F. C. MONTAGUE. *Three Volumes. Cr. 8vo.* 18s.

McCabe (Joseph). THE EMPRESSES OF ROME. Illustrated. *Demy 8vo.* 12s. 6d. *net.*

THE EMPRESSES OF CONSTANTINOPLE. Illustrated. *Demy 8vo.* 10s. 6d. *net.*

MacCarthy (Desmond) and Russell (Agatha). LADY JOHN RUSSELL: A MEMOIR. Illustrated. *Fourth Edition. Demy 8vo.* 10s. 6d. *net.*

McDougall (William). AN INTRODUCTION TO SOCIAL PSYCHOLOGY *Seventh Edition. Cr. 8vo.* 5s. *net.*

BODY AND MIND: A HISTORY AND A DEFENCE OF ANIMISM. *Second Edition. Demy 8vo.* 10s. 6d. *net.*

Maeterlinck (Maurice). THE BLUE BIRD: A FAIRY PLAY IN SIX ACTS. Translated by ALEXANDER TEIXEIRA DE MATTOS. *Fcap. 8vo. Deckle Edges.* 3s. 6d. *net. Also Fcap. 8vo.* 1s. *net.* An Edition, illustrated in colour by F. CAYLEY ROBINSON, is also published. *Cr. 4to.* 21s. *net.* Of the above book Thirty-three Editions in all have been issued.

MARY MAGDALENE: A PLAY IN THREE ACTS. Translated by ALEXANDER TEIXEIRA DE MATTOS. *Third Edition. Fcap. 8vo. Deckle Edges.* 3s. 6d. *net. Also Fcap. 8vo.* 1s. *net.*

*OUR ETERNITY. Translated by ALEXANDER TEIXEIRA DE MATTOS. *Fcap. 8vo.* 5s. *net.*

*Maeterlinck (Mme. M.) (Georgette Leblanc).** THE CHILDREN'S BLUEBIRD. Translated by ALEXANDER TEIXEIRA DE MATTOS. Illustrated. *Fcap. 8vo.* 5s. *net.*

Mahaffy (J. P.). A HISTORY OF EGYPT UNDER THE PTOLEMAIC DYNASTY. Illustrated. *Cr. 8vo.* 6s.

Maitland (F. W.). ROMAN CANON LAW IN THE CHURCH OF ENGLAND. *Royal 8vo.* 7s. 6d.

Marett (R. R.). THE THRESHOLD OF RELIGION. *New and Revised Edition. Cr. 8vo.* 5s. *net.*

Marriott (Charles). A SPANISH HOLIDAY. Illustrated. *Demy 8vo.* 7s. 6d. *net.*
THE ROMANCE OF THE RHINE. Illustrated. *Demy 8vo.* 10s. 6d. *net.*

Marriott (J. A. R.). ENGLAND SINCE WATERLOO. With Maps. *Demy 8vo.* 10s. 6d. *net.*

Masefield (John). SEA LIFE IN NELSON'S TIME. Illustrated. *Cr. 8vo.* 3s. 6d. *net.*
A SAILOR'S GARLAND. Selected and Edited. *Second Edition. Cr. 8vo.* 3s. 6d. *net.*

Masterman (C. F. G.). TENNYSON AS A RELIGIOUS TEACHER. *Second Edition. Cr. 8vo.* 6s.
THE CONDITION OF ENGLAND. *Fourth Edition. Cr. 8vo.* 6s. *Also Fcap. 8vo.* 1s *net. Also Fcap. 8vo.* 1s. *net.*

Mayne (Ethel Colburn). BYRON. Illustrated. *Two Volumes. Demy 8vo.* 21s. *net.*

Medley (D. J.). ORIGINAL ILLUSTRATIONS OF ENGLISH CONSTITUTIONAL HISTORY. *Cr. 8vo.* 7s. 6d. *net.*

Methuen (A. M. S.). ENGLAND'S RUIN : DISCUSSED IN FOURTEEN LETTERS TO A PROTECTIONIST. *Ninth Edition. Cr. 8vo.* 3d. *net.*

Miles (Eustace). LIFE AFTER LIFE; OR, THE THEORY OF REINCARNATION. *Cr. 8vo.* 2s. 6d. *net.*
THE POWER OF CONCENTRATION : How TO ACQUIRE IT. *Fourth Edition. Cr. 8vo.* 3s. 6d. *net.*

Millais (J. G.). THE LIFE AND LETTERS OF SIR JOHN EVERETT MILLAIS. Illustrated. *New Edition. Demy 8vo.* 7s. 6d. *net.*

Milne (J. G.). A HISTORY OF EGYPT UNDER ROMAN RULE. Illustrated. *Cr. 8vo.* 6s.

Mitchell (P. Chalmers). THOMAS HENRY HUXLEY. *Fcap. 8vo.* 1s. *net.*

Moffat (Mary M.). QUEEN LOUISA OF PRUSSIA. Illustrated. *Fourth Edition. Cr. 8vo.* 6s.
MARIA THERESA. Illustrated. *Demy 8vo.* 10s. 6d. *net.*

Money (L. G. Chiozza). RICHES AND POVERTY. *New and Revised Issue. Cr. 8vo.* 1s. *net.*
MONEY'S FISCAL DICTIONARY, 1910. *Second Edition. Demy 8vo.* 5s. *net.*
THINGS THAT MATTER : PAPERS ON SUBJECTS WHICH ARE, OR OUGHT TO BE, UNDER DISCUSSION. *Demy 8vo.* 5s. *net.*

Montague (C. E.). DRAMATIC VALUES. *Second Edition. Fcap. 8vo.* 5s.

Moorhouse (E. Hallam). NELSON'S LADY HAMILTON. Illustrated. *Third Edition. Demy 8vo.* 7s. 6d. *net.*

Morgan (C. Lloyd). INSTINCT AND EXPERIENCE. *Second Edition. Cr. 8vo.* 5s. *net.*

Nevill (Lady Dorothy). MY OWN TIMES. Edited by her Son. *Second Edition. Demy 8vo.* 15s. *net.*

O'Donnell (Elliot). WERWOLVES. *Cr. 8vo.* 5s. *net.*

Oman (C. W. C.). A HISTORY OF THE ART OF WAR IN THE MIDDLE AGES. Illustrated. *Demy 8vo.* 10s. 6d. *net.*
ENGLAND BEFORE THE NORMAN CONQUEST. With Maps. *Third Edition, Revised. Demy 8vo.* 10s. 6d. *net.*

Oxford (M. N.). A HANDBOOK OF NURSING. *Sixth Edition, Revised. Cr. 8vo.* 3s. 6d. *net.*

Pakes (W. C. C.). THE SCIENCE OF HYGIENE. Illustrated. *Second and Cheaper Edition.* Revised by A. T. NANKIVELL. *Cr. 8vo.* 5s. *net.*

Parker (Eric). A BOOK OF THE ZOO. Illustrated. *Second Edition. Cr. 8vo.* 6s.

Pears (Sir Edwin). TURKEY AND ITS PEOPLE. *Second Edition. Demy 8vo.* 12s. 6d. *net.*

Petrie (W. M. Flinders.) A HISTORY OF EGYPT. Illustrated. *Six Volumes. Cr. 8vo.* 6s. each.

VOL. I. FROM THE IST TO THE XVITH DYNASTY. *Seventh Edition.*
VOL. II. THE XVIITH AND XVIIITH DYNASTIES. *Fifth Edition.*
VOL. III. XIXTH TO XXXTH DYNASTIES.
VOL. IV. EGYPT UNDER THE PTOLEMAIC DYNASTY. J. P. MAHAFFY.
VOL V. EGYPT UNDER ROMAN RULE. J. G. MILNE.
VOL. VI. EGYPT IN THE MIDDLE AGES. STANLEY LANE-POOLE.

2

RELIGION AND CONSCIENCE IN ANCIENT EGYPT. Illustrated. *Cr. 8vo.* 2s. 6d.

SYRIA AND EGYPT, FROM THE TELL EL AMARNA LETTERS. *Cr. 8vo.* 2s. 6d.

EGYPTIAN TALES. Translated from the Papyri. First Series, ivth to xiith Dynasty. Illustrated. *Second Edition. Cr. 8vo.* 3s. 6d.

EGYPTIAN TALES. Translated from the Papyri. Second Series, xviiith to xixth Dynasty. Illustrated. *Second Edition. Cr. 8vo.* 3s. 6d.

EGYPTIAN DECORATIVE ART. Illustrated. *Cr. 8vo* 3s. 6d.

Pollard (Alfred W.). SHAKESPEARE FOLIOS AND QUARTOS. A Study in the Bibliography of Shakespeare's Plays, 1594–1685. Illustrated. *Folio. £1 1s. net.*

Porter (G. R.). THE PROGRESS OF THE NATION. A New Edition. Edited by F. W. Hirst. *Demy 8vo. £1 1s. net.*

Power (J. O'Connor). THE MAKING OF AN ORATOR. *Cr. 8vo. 6s.*

Price (L. L.). A SHORT HISTORY OF POLITICAL ECONOMY IN ENGLAND FROM ADAM SMITH TO ARNOLD TOYNBEE. *Seventh Edition. Cr. 8vo.* 2s. 6d.

Pycraft (W. P.). A HISTORY OF BIRDS. Illustrated. *Demy 8vo. 10s. 6d. net.*

Rawlings (Gertrude B.). COINS AND HOW TO KNOW THEM. Illustrated. *Third Edition. Cr. 8vo. 6s.*

Regan (C. Tait). THE FRESHWATER FISHES OF THE BRITISH ISLES. Illustrated. *Cr. 8vo. 6s.*

Reid (Archdall). THE LAWS OF HEREDITY. *Second Edition. Demy 8vo. £1 1s. net.*

Robertson (C. Grant). SELECT STATUTES, CASES, AND DOCUMENTS, 1660–1832. *Second, Revised and Enlarged Edition. Demy 8vo. 10s. 6d. net.*

ENGLAND UNDER THE HANOVERIANS. Illustrated. *Second Edition. Demy 8vo. 10s. 6d. net.*

Roe (Fred). OLD OAK FURNITURE. Illustrated. *Second Edition. Demy 8vo.* 10s. 6d net.

*Rolle (Richard).** THE FIRE OF LOVE and THE MENDING OF LIFE. Edited by Frances M. Comper. *Cr. 8vo.* 3s. 6d. net.

Ryan (P. F. W.). STUART LIFE AND MANNERS: A Social History. Illustrated. *Demy 8vo.* 10s. 6d. net.

* **Ryley (A. Beresford).** OLD PASTE. Illustrated. *Royal 8vo. £2 2s. net.*

St. Francis of Assisi. THE LITTLE FLOWERS OF THE GLORIOUS MESSER, AND OF HIS FRIARS. Done into English, with Notes by William Heywood. Illustrated. *Demy 8vo.* 5s. net.

'Saki' (H. H. Munro). REGINALD. *Third Edition. Fcap. 8vo.* 2s. 6d. net.

REGINALD IN RUSSIA. *Fcap. 8vo.* 2s. 6d. net.

Sandeman (G. A. C.). METTERNICH. Illustrated. *Demy 8vo.* 10s. 6d. net.

Schidrowitz (Philip). RUBBER. Illustrated. *Demy 8vo.* 10s. 6d. net.

Schloesser (H. H.). TRADE UNIONISM. *Cr. 8vo.* 2s. 6d.

Selous (Edmund). TOMMY SMITH'S ANIMALS. Illustrated. *Twelfth Edition. Fcap. 8vo.* 2s. 6d.

TOMMY SMITH'S OTHER ANIMALS. Illustrated. *Sixth Edition. Fcap. 8vo.* 2s. 6d.

JACK'S INSECTS. Illustrated. *Cr. 8vo. 6s.*

Shakespeare (William).

THE FOUR FOLIOS, 1623; 1632; 1664; 1685. Each £4 4s. net, or a complete set, £12 12s. net.

THE POEMS OF WILLIAM SHAKESPEARE. With an Introduction and Notes by George Wyndham. *Demy 8vo. Buckram, 10s. 6d.*

Shaw (Stanley). WILLIAM OF GERMANY. *Demy 8vo.* 7s. 6d. net.

Shelley (Percy Bysshe). POEMS. With an Introduction by A. Clutton-Brock and notes by C. D. Locock. *Two Volumes. Demy 8vo. £1 1s. net.*

Smith (Adam). THE WEALTH OF NATIONS. Edited by Edwin Cannan. *Two Volumes. Demy 8vo. £1 1s. net.*

Smith (G. F. Herbert). GEM-STONES AND THEIR DISTINCTIVE CHARACTERS. Illustrated. *Second Edition. Cr. 8vo.* 6s. net.

Snell (F. J.). A BOOK OF EXMOOR. Illustrated. *Cr. 8vo. 6s.*
THE CUSTOMS OF OLD ENGLAND. Illustrated. *Cr. 8vo. 6s.*

'Stancliffe.' GOLF DO'S AND DONT'S. *Fifth Edition. Fcap. 8vo. 1s. net.*

Stevenson (R. L.). THE LETTERS OF ROBERT LOUIS STEVENSON. Edited by Sir SIDNEY COLVIN. *A New and Enlarged Edition in four volumes. Fourth Edition. Fcap. 8vo. Each 5s. Leather, each 5s. net.*

Storr (Vernon F.). DEVELOPMENT AND DIVINE PURPOSE. *Cr. 8vo. 5s. net.*

Streatfeild (R. A.). MODERN MUSIC AND MUSICIANS. Illustrated. *Second Edition. Demy 8vo. 7s. 6d. net.*

Surtees (R. S.). HANDLEY CROSS. Illustrated. *Fcap. 8vo. Gilt top. 3s. 6d. net.*
MR. SPONGE'S SPORTING TOUR. Illustrated. *Fcap. 8vo. Gilt top. 3s. 6d. net.*
ASK MAMMA; OR, THE RICHEST COMMONER IN ENGLAND. Illustrated. *Fcap. 8vo. Gilt top. 3s. 6d. net.*
JORROCKS'S JAUNTS AND JOLLITIES. Illustrated. *Fourth Edition. Fcap. 8vo. Gilt top. 3s. 6d. net.*
MR. FACEY ROMFORD'S HOUNDS. Illustrated. *Fcap. 8vo. Gilt top. 3s. 6d. net.*
HAWBUCK GRANGE; OR, THE SPORTING ADVENTURES OF THOMAS SCOTT, ESQ. Illustrated. *Fcap. 8vo. Gilt top. 3s. 6d. net.*

*Suso (Henry). THE LIFE OF THE BLESSED HENRY SUSO. By HIMSELF. Translated by T. F. Knox. With an Introduction by DEAN INGE. *Cr. 8vo. 3s. 6d. net.*

Swanton (E. W.). FUNGI AND HOW TO KNOW THEM. Illustrated. *Cr. 8vo. 6s. net.*
BRITISH PLANT - GALLS. *Cr. 8vo. 7s. 6d. net.*

Symes (J. E.). THE FRENCH REVOLUTION. *Second Edition. Cr. 8vo. 2s. 6d.*

Tabor (Margaret E.). THE SAINTS IN ART. With their Attributes and Symbols Alphabetically Arranged. Illustrated. *Third Edition. Fcap. 8vo. 3s. 6d. net.*

Taylor (A. E.). ELEMENTS OF METAPHYSICS. *Second Edition. Demy 8vo. 10s. 6d. net.*

Taylor (Mrs. Basil) (Harriet Osgood). JAPANESE GARDENS. Illustrated. *Cr. 4to. £1 1s. net.*

Thibaudeau (A. C.). BONAPARTE AND THE CONSULATE. Translated and Edited by G. K. FORTESCUE. Illustrated. *Demy 8vo. 10s. 6d. net.*

Thomas (Edward). MAURICE MAETERLINCK. Illustrated. *Second Edition. Cr. 8vo. 5s. net.*

Thompson (Francis). SELECTED POEMS OF FRANCIS THOMPSON. With a Biographical Note by WILFRID MEYNELL. With a Portrait in Photogravure *Twentieth Thousand. Fcap. 8vo. 5s. net.*

Tileston (Mary W.). DAILY STRENGTH FOR DAILY NEEDS. *Twentieth Edition. Medium 16mo. 2s. 6d. net.* Also an edition in superior binding, *6s.*
THE STRONGHOLD OF HOPE. *Medium 16mo. 2s. 6d. net.*

Toynbee (Paget). DANTE ALIGHIERI. HIS LIFE AND WORKS. With 16 Illustrations. *Fourth and Enlarged Edition. Cr. 8vo. 5s. net.*

Trevelyan (G. M.). ENGLAND UNDER THE STUARTS. With Maps and Plans. *Fifth Edition. Demy 8vo. 10s. 6d. net.*

Triggs (H. Inigo). TOWN PLANNING: PAST, PRESENT, AND POSSIBLE. Illustrated. *Second Edition. Wide Royal 8vo. 15s. net.*

Turner (Sir Alfred E.). SIXTY YEARS OF A SOLDIER'S LIFE. *Demy 8vo. 12s. 6d. net.*

Underhill (Evelyn). MYSTICISM. A Study in the Nature and Development of Man's Spiritual Consciousness. *Fourth Edition. Demy 8vo. 15s. net.*

Urwick (E. J.). A PHILOSOPHY OF SOCIAL PROGRESS. *Cr. 8vo. 6s.*

Vardon (Harry). HOW TO PLAY GOLF. Illustrated. *Fifth Edition. Cr. 8vo. 2s. 6d. net.*

Vernon (Hon. W. Warren). READINGS ON THE INFERNO OF DANTE. With an Introduction by the Rev. Dr. MOORE. *Two Volumes. Second Edition. Cr. 8vo. 15s. net.*
READINGS ON THE PURGATORIO OF DANTE. With an Introduction by the late DEAN CHURCH. *Two Volumes. Third Edition. Cr. 8vo. 15s. net.*

READINGS ON THE PARADISO OF DANTE. With an Introduction by the BISHOP OF RIPON. *Two Volumes. Second Edition. Cr. 8vo.* 15s. net.

Vickers (Kenneth H.). ENGLAND IN THE LATER MIDDLE AGES. With Maps. *Demy 8vo.* 10s. 6d. net.

Wade (G. W. and J. H.). RAMBLES IN SOMERSET. Illustrated. *Cr. 8vo.* 6s.

Waddell (L. A.). LHASA AND ITS MYSTERIES. With a Record of the Expedition of 1903-1904. Illustrated. *Third and Cheaper Edition. Medium 8vo.* 7s. 6d. net.

Wagner (Richard). RICHARD WAGNER'S MUSIC DRAMAS. Interpretations, embodying Wagner's own explanations. By ALICE LEIGHTON CLEATHER and BASIL CRUMP. *Fcap. 8vo.* 2s. 6d. each.
THE RING OF THE NIBELUNG.
   Fifth Edition.
LOHENGRIN AND PARSIFAL.
   Second Edition, rewritten and enlarged.
TRISTAN AND ISOLDE.
TANNHÄUSER AND THE MASTERSINGERS OF NUREMBURG.

Waterhouse (Elizabeth). WITH THE SIMPLE-HEARTED. Little Homilies to Women in Country Places. *Third Edition. Small Pott 8vo.* 2s. net.
THE HOUSE BY THE CHERRY TREE. A Second Series of Little Homilies to Women in Country Places. *Small Pott 8vo.* 2s. net.
COMPANIONS OF THE WAY. Being Selections for Morning and Evening Reading. Chosen and arranged by ELIZABETH WATERHOUSE. *Large Cr. 8vo.* 5s. net.
THOUGHTS OF A TERTIARY. *Small Pott 8vo.* 1s. net.
VERSES. A New Edition. *Fcap. 8vo.* 2s. net.

Waters (W. G.). ITALIAN SCULPTORS. Illustrated. *Cr. 8vo.* 7s. 6d. net.

Watt (Francis). EDINBURGH AND THE LOTHIANS. Illustrated. *Second Edition. Cr. 8vo.* 10s. 6d. net.

***R. L. S.** Cr. 8vo.* 6s.

Wedmore (Sir Frederick). MEMORIES. *Second Edition. Demy 8vo.* 7s. 6d. net.

Weigall (Arthur E. P.). A GUIDE TO THE ANTIQUITIES OF UPPER EGYPT: FROM ABYDOS TO THE SUDAN FRONTIER. Illustrated. *Second Edition. Cr. 8vo.* 7s. 6d. net.

Wells (J.). OXFORD AND OXFORD LIFE. *Third Edition. Cr. 8vo.* 3s. 6d.
A SHORT HISTORY OF ROME. *Twelfth Edition.* With 3 Maps. *Cr. 8vo.* 3s. 6d.

Whitten (Wilfred). A LONDONER'S LONDON. Illustrated. *Second Edition. Cr. 8vo.* 6s.

Wilde (Oscar). THE WORKS OF OSCAR WILDE. *Twelve Volumes. Fcap. 8vo.* 5s. net each volume.
I. LORD ARTHUR SAVILE'S CRIME AND THE PORTRAIT OF MR. W. H. II. THE DUCHESS OF PADUA. III. POEMS. IV. LADY WINDERMERE'S FAN. V. A WOMAN OF NO IMPORTANCE. VI. AN IDEAL HUSBAND. VII. THE IMPORTANCE OF BEING EARNEST. VIII. A HOUSE OF POMEGRANATES. IX. INTENTIONS. X. DE PROFUNDIS AND PRISON LETTERS. XI. ESSAYS. XII. SALOMÉ, A FLORENTINE TRAGEDY, and LA SAINTE COURTISANE.

Williams (H. Noel). A ROSE OF SAVOY: MARIE ADÉLAIDE OF SAVOY, DUCHESSE DE BOURGOGNE, MOTHER OF LOUIS XV. Illustrated. *Second Edition. Demy 8vo.* 15s. net.
THE FASCINATING DUC DE RICHELIEU: LOUIS FRANÇOIS ARMAND DU PLESSIS (1696-1788). Illustrated. *Demy 8vo.* 15s. net.
A PRINCESS OF ADVENTURE: MARIE CAROLINE, DUCHESSE DE BERRY (1798-1870). Illustrated. *Demy 8vo.* 15s. net.
THE LOVE AFFAIRS OF THE CONDÉS (1530-1740). Illustrated. *Demy 8vo.* 15s. net.

***Wilson (Ernest H.).** A NATURALIST IN WESTERN CHINA. Illustrated. *Demy 8vo.* £1 10s. net.

Wood (Sir Evelyn). FROM MIDSHIPMAN TO FIELD-MARSHAL. Illustrated. *Fifth Edition. Demy 8vo.* 7s. 6d. net.
   Also Fcap. 8vo. 1s. net.
THE REVOLT IN HINDUSTAN (1857-59). Illustrated. *Second Edition. Cr. 8vo.* 6s.

Wood (W. Birkbeck) and **Edmonds (Col. J. E.).** A HISTORY OF THE CIVIL WAR IN THE UNITED STATES (1861-65). With an Introduction by SPENSER WILKINSON. With 24 Maps and Plans. *Third Edition. Demy 8vo.* 12s. 6d. net.

Wordsworth (W.). POEMS. With an Introduction and Notes by NOWELL C. SMITH. *Three Volumes. Demy 8vo.* 15s. net.

Yeats (W. B.). A BOOK OF IRISH VERSE. *Third Edition. Cr. 8vo.* 3s. 6d.

PART II.—A SELECTION OF SERIES

Ancient Cities

General Editor, SIR B. C. A. WINDLE

Cr. 8vo. 4s. 6d. net each volume

With Illustrations by E. H. NEW, and other Artists

BRISTOL. Alfred Harvey.

CANTERBURY. J. C. Cox.

CHESTER. Sir B. C. A. Windle.

DUBLIN. S. A. O. Fitzpatrick.

EDINBURGH. M. G. Williamson.

LINCOLN. E. Mansel Sympson.

SHREWSBURY. T. Auden.

WELLS and GLASTONBURY. T. S. Holmes.

The Antiquary's Books

General Editor, J. CHARLES COX

Demy 8vo. 7s. 6d. net each volume

With Numerous Illustrations

*ANCIENT PAINTED GLASS IN ENGLAND. Philip Nelson.

ARCHÆOLOGY AND FALSE ANTIQUITIES. R. Munro.

BELLS OF ENGLAND, THE. Canon J. J. Raven. *Second Edition.*

BRASSES OF ENGLAND, THE. Herbert W. Macklin. *Third Edition.*

CELTIC ART IN PAGAN AND CHRISTIAN TIMES. J. Romilly Allen. *Second Edition.*

CASTLES AND WALLED TOWNS OF ENGLAND, THE. A. Harvey.

CHURCHWARDEN'S ACCOUNTS FROM THE FOURTEENTH CENTURY TO THE CLOSE OF THE SEVENTEENTH CENTURY.

DOMESDAY INQUEST, THE. Adolphus Ballard.

ENGLISH CHURCH FURNITURE. J. C. Cox and A. Harvey. *Second Edition.*

ENGLISH COSTUME. From Prehistoric Times to the End of the Eighteenth Century. George Clinch.

ENGLISH MONASTIC LIFE. Abbot Gasquet. *Fourth Edition.*

ENGLISH SEALS. J. Harvey Bloom.

FOLK-LORE AS AN HISTORICAL SCIENCE. Sir G. L. Gomme.

GILDS AND COMPANIES OF LONDON, THE. George Unwin.

*HERMITS AND ANCHORITES OF ENGLAND, THE. Rotha Mary Clay.

MANOR AND MANORIAL RECORDS, THE. Nathaniel J. Hone. *Second Edition.*

MEDIÆVAL HOSPITALS OF ENGLAND, THE. Rotha Mary Clay.

OLD ENGLISH INSTRUMENTS OF MUSIC. F. W. Galpin. *Second Edition.*

14   METHUEN AND COMPANY LIMITED

The Antiquary's Books—continued

OLD ENGLISH LIBRARIES. James Hutt.

OLD SERVICE BOOKS OF THE ENGLISH CHURCH. Christopher Wordsworth, and Henry Littlehales. *Second Edition.*

PARISH LIFE IN MEDIÆVAL ENGLAND. Abbot Gasquet. *Third Edition.*

PARISH REGISTERS OF ENGLAND, THE. J. C. Cox.

REMAINS OF THE PREHISTORIC AGE IN ENGLAND. Sir B. C. A. Windle. *Second Edition.*

ROMAN ERA IN BRITAIN, THE. J. Ward.

ROMANO-BRITISH BUILDINGS AND EARTH-WORKS. J. Ward.

ROYAL FORESTS OF ENGLAND, THE. J. C. Cox.

SHRINES OF BRITISH SAINTS. J. C. Wall.

The Arden Shakespeare.

Demy 8vo.   2s. 6d. net each volume

An edition of Shakespeare in Single Plays ; each edited with a full Introduction Textual Notes, and a Commentary at the foot of the page

ALL'S WELL THAT ENDS WELL.

ANTONY AND CLEOPATRA. *Second Edition.*

AS YOU LIKE IT.

CYMBELINE.

COMEDY OF ERRORS, THE

HAMLET. *Third Edition.*

JULIUS CAESAR.

*KING HENRY IV. PT. I.

KING HENRY V.

KING HENRY VI. PT. I.

KING HENRY VI. PT. II.

KING HENRY VI. PT. III.

KING LEAR.

KING RICHARD II.

KING RICHARD III.

LIFE AND DEATH OF KING JOHN, THE.

LOVE'S LABOUR'S LOST. *Second Edition.*

MACBETH.

MEASURE FOR MEASURE.

MERCHANT OF VENICE, THE. *Second Edition*

MERRY WIVES OF WINDSOR, THE.

MIDSUMMER NIGHT'S DREAM, A.

OTHELLO.

PERICLES.

ROMEO AND JULIET.

TAMING OF THE SHREW, THE.

TEMPEST, THE.

TIMON OF ATHENS.

TITUS ANDRONICUS.

TROILUS AND CRESSIDA.

TWO GENTLEMEN OF VERONA, THE.

TWELFTH NIGHT.

VENUS AND ADONIS.

WINTER'S TALE, THE.

Classics of Art

Edited by DR. J. H. W. LAING

With numerous Illustrations.   Wide Royal 8vo

ART OF THE GREEKS, THE. H. B. Walters. 12s. 6d. net.

ART OF THE ROMANS, THE. H. B. Walters. 15s. net.

CHARDIN. H. E. A. Furst. 12s. 6d. net.

DONATELLO. Maud Cruttwell. 15s. net.

FLORENTINE SCULPTORS OF THE RENAIS-SANCE. Wilhelm Bode. Translated by Jessie Haynes. 12s. 6d. net.

GEORGE ROMNEY. Arthur B. Chamberlain. 12s. 6d. net.

Classics of Art—continued

GHIRLANDAIO. Gerald S. Davies. *Second Edition.* 10s. 6d. net.

LAWRENCE. Sir Walter Armstrong. £1 1s. net.

MICHELANGELO. Gerald S. Davies. 12s. 6d. net.

RAPHAEL. A. P. Oppé. 12s. 6d. net.

REMBRANDT'S ETCHINGS. A. M. Hind. Two Volumes. 21s. net.

RUBENS. Edward Dillon. 25s. net.

TINTORETTO. Evelyn March Phillipps. 15s. net.

TITIAN. Charles Ricketts. 15s. net.

TURNER'S SKETCHES AND DRAWINGS. A. J. Finberg. *Second Edition.* 12s. 6d. net.

VELAZQUEZ. A. de Beruete. 10s. 6d. net.

The 'Complete' Series.

Fully Illustrated. Demy 8vo

THE COMPLETE ASSOCIATION FOOTBALLER. B. S. Evers and C. E. Hughes-Davies. 5s. net.

THE COMPLETE ATHLETIC TRAINER. S. A. Mussabini. 5s. net.

THE COMPLETE BILLIARD PLAYER. Charles Roberts. 10s. 6d. net.

THE COMPLETE BOXER. J. G. Bohun Lynch. 5s. net.

THE COMPLETE COOK. Lilian Whitling. 7s. 6d. net.

THE COMPLETE CRICKETER. Albert E. KNIGHT. 7s. 6d. net. *Second Edition.*

THE COMPLETE FOXHUNTER. Charles Richardson. 12s. 6d. net. *Second Edition.*

THE COMPLETE GOLFER. Harry Vardon. 10s. 6d. net. *Thirteenth Edition.*

THE COMPLETE HOCKEY-PLAYER. Eustace E. White. 5s. net. *Second Edition.*

THE COMPLETE HORSEMAN. W. Scarth Dixon. *Second Edition.* 10s. 6d. net.

THE COMPLETE LAWN TENNIS PLAYER. A. Wallis Myers. 10s. 6d. net. *Third Edition, Revised.*

THE COMPLETE MOTORIST. Filson Young. 12s. 6d. net. *New Edition (Seventh).*

THE COMPLETE MOUNTAINEER. G. D. Abraham. 15s. net. *Second Edition.*

THE COMPLETE OARSMAN. R. C. Lehmann. 10s. 6d. net.

THE COMPLETE PHOTOGRAPHER. R. Child Bayley. 10s. 6d. net. *Fourth Edition.*

THE COMPLETE RUGBY FOOTBALLER, ON THE NEW ZEALAND SYSTEM. D. Gallaher and W. J. Stead. 10s. 6d. net. *Second Edition.*

THE COMPLETE SHOT. G. T. Teasdale-Buckell. 12s. 6d. net. *Third Edition.*

THE COMPLETE SWIMMER. F. Sachs. 7s. 6d. net.

THE COMPLETE YACHTSMAN. B. Heckstall-Smith and E. du Boulay. *Second Edition, Revised.* 15s. net.

The Connoisseur's Library

With numerous Illustrations. Wide Royal 8vo. 25s. net each volume

ENGLISH FURNITURE. F. S. Robinson.

ENGLISH COLOURED BOOKS. Martin Hardie.

ETCHINGS. Sir F. Wedmore *Second Edition.*

EUROPEAN ENAMELS. Henry H. Cunynghame.

GLASS. Edward Dillon.

GOLDSMITHS' AND SILVERSMITHS' WORK. Nelson Dawson. *Second Edition.*

ILLUMINATED MANUSCRIPTS. J. A. Herbert. *Second Edition.*

IVORIES. Alfred Maskell.

JEWELLERY. H. Clifford Smith. *Second Edition.*

MEZZOTINTS. Cyril Davenport.

MINIATURES. Dudley Heath.

PORCELAIN. Edward Dillon.

FINE BOOKS. A. W. Pollard.

SEALS. Walter de Gray Birch.

WOOD SCULPTURE. Alfred Maskell. *Second Edition.*

Handbooks of English Church History

Edited by J. H. BURN. *Crown 8vo. 2s. 6d. net each volume*

THE FOUNDATIONS OF THE ENGLISH CHURCH. J. H. Maude.

THE SAXON CHURCH AND THE NORMAN CONQUEST. C. T. Cruttwell.

THE MEDIÆVAL CHURCH AND THE PAPACY. A. C. Jennings.

THE REFORMATION PERIOD. Henry Gee.

THE STRUGGLE WITH PURITANISM. Bruce Blaxland.

THE CHURCH OF ENGLAND IN THE EIGHTEENTH CENTURY. Alfred Plummer.

Handbooks of Theology

THE DOCTRINE OF THE INCARNATION. R. L. Ottley. *Fifth Edition, Revised. Demy 8vo. 12s. 6d.*

A HISTORY OF EARLY CHRISTIAN DOCTRINE. J. F. Bethune-Baker. *Demy 8vo. 10s. 6d.*

AN INTRODUCTION TO THE HISTORY OF RELIGION. F. B. Jevons. *Fifth Edition. Demy 8vo. 10s. 6d.*

AN INTRODUCTION TO THE HISTORY OF THE CREEDS. A. E. Burn. *Demy 8vo. 10s. 6d.*

THE PHILOSOPHY OF RELIGION IN ENGLAND AND AMERICA. Alfred Caldecott. *Demy 8vo. 10s. 6d.*

THE XXXIX ARTICLES OF THE CHURCH OF ENGLAND. Edited by E. C. S. Gibson. *Seventh Edition. Demy 8vo. 12s. 6d.*

The 'Home Life' Series

Illustrated. Demy 8vo. 6s. to 10s. 6d. net

HOME LIFE IN AMERICA. Katherine G. Busbey. *Second Edition.*

HOME LIFE IN FRANCE. Miss Betham-Edwards. *Sixth Edition.*

HOME LIFE IN GERMANY. Mrs. A. Sidgwick. *Second Edition.*

HOME LIFE IN HOLLAND. D. S. Meldrum. *Second Edition.*

HOME LIFE IN ITALY. Lina Duff Gordon. *Second Edition.*

HOME LIFE IN NORWAY. H. K. Daniels *Second Edition.*

HOME LIFE IN RUSSIA. A. S. Rappoport.

HOME LIFE IN SPAIN. S. L. Bensusan *Second Edition.*

The Illustrated Pocket Library of Plain and Coloured Books

Fcap. 8vo. 3s. 6d. net each volume

WITH COLOURED ILLUSTRATIONS

THE LIFE AND DEATH OF JOHN MYTTON, ESQ. Nimrod. *Fifth Edition.*

THE LIFE OF A SPORTSMAN. Nimrod.

HANDLEY CROSS. R. S. Surtees. *Fourth Edition.*

MR. SPONGE'S SPORTING TOUR. R. S. Surtees. *Second Edition.*

JORROCKS'S JAUNTS AND JOLLITIES. R. S. Surtees. *Third Edition.*

ASK MAMMA. R. S. Surtees.

THE ANALYSIS OF THE HUNTING FIELD. R. S. Surtees.

THE TOUR OF DR. SYNTAX IN SEARCH OF THE PICTURESQUE. William Combe.

THE TOUR OF DR. SYNTAX IN SEARCH OF CONSOLATION. William Combe.

THE THIRD TOUR OF DR. SYNTAX IN SEARCH OF A WIFE. William Combe.

LIFE IN LONDON. Pierce Egan.

WITH PLAIN ILLUSTRATIONS

THE GRAVE: A Poem. Robert Blair.

ILLUSTRATIONS OF THE BOOK OF JOB. Invented and Engraved by William Blake.

Leaders of Religion

Edited by H. C. BEECHING. *With Portraits*

Crown 8vo. 2s. net each volume

CARDINAL NEWMAN. R. H. Hutton.

JOHN WESLEY. J. H. Overton.

BISHOP WILBERFORCE. G. W. Daniell.

CARDINAL MANNING. A. W. Hutton.

CHARLES SIMEON. H. C. G. Moule.

JOHN KNOX. F. MacCunn. *Second Edition.*

JOHN HOWE. R. F. Horton.

THOMAS KEN. F. A. Clarke.

GEORGE FOX, THE QUAKER. T. Hodgkin.
Third Edition.

JOHN KEBLE. Walter Lock.

THOMAS CHALMERS. Mrs. Oliphant. *Second Edition.*

LANCELOT ANDREWES. R. L. Ottley. *Second Edition.*

AUGUSTINE OF CANTERBURY. E. L. Cutts.

WILLIAM LAUD. W. H. Hutton. *Fourth Edition.*

JOHN DONNE. Augustus Jessop.

THOMAS CRANMER. A. J. Mason.

LATIMER. R. M. and A. J. Carlyle.

BISHOP BUTLER. W. A. Spooner.

The Library of Devotion

With Introductions and (where necessary) Notes

Small Pott 8vo, cloth, 2s.; leather, 2s. 6d. net each volume

THE CONFESSIONS OF ST. AUGUSTINE. *Eighth Edition.*

THE IMITATION OF CHRIST. *Sixth Edition.*

THE CHRISTIAN YEAR. *Fifth Edition.*

LYRA INNOCENTIUM. *Third Edition.*

THE TEMPLE. *Second Edition.*

A BOOK OF DEVOTIONS. *Second Edition.*

A SERIOUS CALL TO A DEVOUT AND HOLY LIFE. *Fifth Edition.*

A GUIDE TO ETERNITY.

THE INNER WAY. *Second Edition.*

ON THE LOVE OF GOD.

THE PSALMS OF DAVID.

LYRA APOSTOLICA.

THE SONG OF SONGS.

THE THOUGHTS OF PASCAL. *Second Edition.*

A MANUAL OF CONSOLATION FROM THE SAINTS AND FATHERS.

DEVOTIONS FROM THE APOCRYPHA.

THE SPIRITUAL COMBAT.

THE DEVOTIONS OF ST. ANSELM.

BISHOP WILSON'S SACRA PRIVATA.

GRACE ABOUNDING TO THE CHIEF OF SINNERS.

LYRA SACRA. A Book of Sacred Verse *Second Edition.*

A DAY BOOK FROM THE SAINTS AND FATHERS.

A LITTLE BOOK OF HEAVENLY WISDOM. A Selection from the English Mystics.

LIGHT, LIFE, and LOVE. A Selection from the German Mystics.

AN INTRODUCTION TO THE DEVOUT LIFE.

THE LITTLE FLOWERS OF THE GLORIOUS MESSER ST. FRANCIS AND OF HIS FRIARS.

DEATH AND IMMORTALITY.

THE SPIRITUAL GUIDE. *Second Edition.*

DEVOTIONS FOR EVERY DAY IN THE WEEK AND THE GREAT FESTIVALS.

PRECES PRIVATAE.

HORAE MYSTICAE. A Day Book from the Writings of Mystics of Many Nations.

Little Books on Art

With many Illustrations. Demy 16mo. 2s. 6d. net each volume

Each volume consists of about 200 pages, and contains from 30 to 40 Illustrations, including a Frontispiece in Photogravure

ALBRECHT DÜRER. L. J. Allen.

ARTS OF JAPAN, THE. E. Dillon. *Third Edition.*

BOOKPLATES. E. Almack.

BOTTICELLI. Mary L. Bonnor.

BURNE-JONES. F. de Lisle.

CELLINI. R. H. H. Cust.

CHRISTIAN SYMBOLISM. Mrs. H. Jenner.

CHRIST IN ART. Mrs. H. Jenner.

CLAUDE. E. Dillon.

CONSTABLE. H. W. Tompkins. *Second Edition.*

COROT. A. Pollard and E. Birnstingl.

EARLY ENGLISH WATER-COLOUR. C. E. Hughes.

ENAMELS. Mrs. N. Dawson. *Second Edition.*

FREDERIC LEIGHTON. A. Corkran.

GEORGE ROMNEY. G. Paston.

GREEK ART. H. B. Walters. *Fourth Edition.*

GREUZE AND BOUCHER. E. F. Pollard.

HOLBEIN. Mrs. G. Fortescue.

ILLUMINATED MANUSCRIPTS. J. W. Bradley.

JEWELLERY. C. Davenport. *Second Edition.*

JOHN HOPPNER. H. P. K. Skipton.

SIR JOSHUA REYNOLDS. J. Sime. *Second Edition.*

MILLET. N. Peacock. *Second Edition.*

MINIATURES. C. Davenport. *Second Edition.*

OUR LADY IN ART. Mrs. H. Jenner.

RAPHAEL. A. R. Dryhurst.

RODIN. Muriel Ciolkowska.

TURNER. F. Tyrrell-Gill.

VANDYCK. M. G. Smallwood.

VELAZQUEZ. W. Wilberforce and A. R. Gilbert.

WATTS. R. E. D. Sketchley. *Second Edition.*

The Little Galleries

Demy 16mo. 2s. 6d. net each volume

Each volume contains 20 plates in Photogravure, together with a short outline of the life and work of the master to whom the book is devoted

A LITTLE GALLERY OF REYNOLDS.

A LITTLE GALLERY OF ROMNEY.

A LITTLE GALLERY OF HOPPNER.

A LITTLE GALLERY OF MILLAIS.

The Little Guides

With many Illustrations by E. H. NEW and other artists, and from photographs

Small Pott 8vo. Cloth, 2s. 6d. net; leather, 3s. 6d. net each volume

The main features of these Guides are (1) a handy and charming form; (2) illustrations from photographs and by well-known artists; (3) good plans and maps; (4) an adequate but compact presentation of everything that is interesting in the natural features, history, archæology, and architecture of the town or district treated

CAMBRIDGE AND ITS COLLEGES. A. H. Thompson. *Third Edition, Revised.*

CHANNEL ISLANDS, THE. E. E. Bicknell.

ENGLISH LAKES, THE. F. G. Brabant.

ISLE OF WIGHT, THE. G. Clinch.

LONDON. G. Clinch.

MALVERN COUNTRY, THE. Sir B.C.A. Windle.

NORTH WALES. A. T. Story.

The Little Guides—*continued*

OXFORD AND ITS COLLEGES. J. Wells. *Ninth Edition.*

ST. PAUL'S CATHEDRAL. G. Clinch.

SHAKESPEARE'S COUNTRY. Sir B. C. A. Windle. *Fifth Edition.*

SOUTH WALES. G. W. and J. H. Wade.

WESTMINSTER ABBEY. G. E. Troutbeck. *Second Edition.*

BERKSHIRE. F. G. Brabant.

BUCKINGHAMSHIRE. E. S. Roscoe.

CHESHIRE. W. M. Gallichan.

CORNWALL. A. L. Salmon. *Second Edition.*

DERBYSHIRE. J. C. Cox.

DEVON. S. Baring-Gould. *Third Edition.*

DORSET. F. R. Heath. *Second Edition.*

DURHAM. J. E. Hodgkin.

ESSEX. J. C. Cox.

HAMPSHIRE. J. C. Cox. *Second Edition.*

HERTFORDSHIRE. H. W. Tompkins.

KENT. G. Clinch.

KERRY. C. P. Crane. *Second Edition.*

LEICESTERSHIRE AND RUTLAND. A. Harvey and V. B. Crowther-Beynon.

MIDDLESEX. J. B. Firth.

MONMOUTHSHIRE. G. W. and J. H. Wade.

NORFOLK. W. A. Dutt. *Third Edition, Revised.*

NORTHAMPTONSHIRE. W. Dry. *Second Edition, Revised.*

NORTHUMBERLAND. J. E. Morris.

NOTTINGHAMSHIRE. L. Guilford.

OXFORDSHIRE. F. G. Brabant.

SHROPSHIRE. J. E. Auden.

SOMERSET. G. W. and J. H. Wade. *Second Edition.*

STAFFORDSHIRE. C. Masefield.

SUFFOLK. W. A. Dutt.

SURREY. J. C. Cox.

SUSSEX. F. G. Brabant. *Third Edition.*

WILTSHIRE. F. R. Heath.

YORKSHIRE, THE EAST RIDING. J. E. Morris.

YORKSHIRE, THE NORTH RIDING. J. E. Morris.

YORKSHIRE, THE WEST RIDING. J. E. Morris. *Cloth, 3s. 6d. net; leather, 4s. 6d. net.*

BRITTANY. S. Baring-Gould.

NORMANDY. C. Scudamore.

ROME. C. G. Ellaby.

SICILY. F. H. Jackson.

The Little Library

With Introduction, Notes, and Photogravure Frontispieces

Small Pott 8vo.   Each Volume, cloth, 1s. 6d. net

Anon. A LITTLE BOOK OF ENGLISH LYRICS. *Second Edition.*

Austen (Jane). PRIDE AND PREJUDICE. *Two Volumes.*
NORTHANGER ABBEY.

Bacon (Francis). THE ESSAYS OF LORD BACON.

Barham (R. H.). THE INGOLDSBY LEGENDS. *Two Volumes.*

Barnett (Annie). A LITTLE BOOK OF ENGLISH PROSE.

Beckford (William). THE HISTORY OF THE CALIPH VATHEK.

Blake (William). SELECTIONS FROM THE WORKS OF WILLIAM BLAKE.

Borrow (George). LAVENGRO. *Two Volumes.*
THE ROMANY RYE.

Browning (Robert). SELECTIONS FROM THE EARLY POEMS OF ROBERT BROWNING.

Canning (George). SELECTIONS FROM THE ANTI-JACOBIN : With some later Poems by GEORGE CANNING.

Cowley (Abraham). THE ESSAYS OF ABRAHAM COWLEY.

The Little Library—*continued*

Crabbe (George). SELECTIONS FROM THE POEMS OF GEORGE CRABBE.

Craik (Mrs.). JOHN HALIFAX, GENTLEMAN. *Two Volumes.*

Crashaw (Richard). THE ENGLISH POEMS OF RICHARD CRASHAW.

Dante Alighieri. THE INFERNO OF DANTE. Translated by H. F. CARY.
THE PURGATORIO OF DANTE. Translated by H. F. CARY.
THE PARADISO OF DANTE. Translated by H. F. CARY.

Darley (George). SELECTIONS FROM THE POEMS OF GEORGE DARLEY.

Dickens (Charles). CHRISTMAS BOOKS. *Two Volumes.*

Ferrier (Susan). MARRIAGE. *Two Volumes.*
THE INHERITANCE. *Two Volumes.*

Gaskell (Mrs.). CRANFORD. *Second Edition.*

Hawthorne (Nathaniel). THE SCARLET LETTER.

Henderson (T. F.). A LITTLE BOOK OF SCOTTISH VERSE.

Kinglake (A. W.). EOTHEN. *Second Edition.*

Lamb (Charles). ELIA, AND THE LAST ESSAYS OF ELIA.

Locker (F.). LONDON LYRICS.

Marvell (Andrew). THE POEMS OF ANDREW MARVELL.

Milton (John). THE MINOR POEMS OF JOHN MILTON.

Moir (D. M.). MANSIE WAUCH.

Nichols (Bowyer). A LITTLE BOOK OF ENGLISH SONNETS.

Smith (Horace and James). REJECTED ADDRESSES.

Sterne (Laurence). A SENTIMENTAL JOURNEY.

Tennyson (Alfred, Lord). THE EARLY POEMS OF ALFRED, LORD TENNYSON.
IN MEMORIAM.
THE PRINCESS.
MAUD.

Thackeray (W. M.). VANITY FAIR. *Three Volumes.*
PENDENNIS. *Three Volumes.*
HENRY ESMOND.
CHRISTMAS BOOKS.

Vaughan (Henry). THE POEMS OF HENRY VAUGHAN.

Waterhouse (Elizabeth). A LITTLE BOOK OF LIFE AND DEATH. *Fourteenth Edition.*

Wordsworth (W.). SELECTIONS FROM THE POEMS OF WILLIAM WORDSWORTH.

Wordsworth (W.) and Coleridge (S. T.). LYRICAL BALLADS. *Second Edition.*

The Little Quarto Shakespeare

Edited by W. J. CRAIG. With Introductions and Notes

Pott 16mo. 40 Volumes. Leather, price 1s. net each volume

Mahogany Revolving Book Case. 10s. net

Miniature Library

Demy 32mo. Leather, 1s. net each volume

EUPHRANOR: A Dialogue on Youth. Edward FitzGerald.

THE LIFE OF EDWARD, LORD HERBERT OF CHERBURY. Written by himself.

POLONIUS; or, Wise Saws and Modern Instances. Edward FitzGerald.

THE RUBÁIYÁT OF OMAR KHAYYÁM. Edward FitzGerald. *Fourth Edition.*

The New Library of Medicine

Edited by C. W. SALEEBY. *Demy 8vo*

CARE OF THE BODY, THE. F. Cavanagh. *Second Edition.* 7s. 6d. net.

CHILDREN OF THE NATION, THE. The Right Hon. Sir John Gorst. *Second Edition.* 7s. 6d. net.

DISEASES OF OCCUPATION. Sir Thos. Oliver. 10s. 6d. net. *Second Edition.*

DRINK PROBLEM, in its Medico-Sociological Aspects, The. Edited by T. N. Kelynack. 7s. 6d. net.

DRUGS AND THE DRUG HABIT. H. Sainsbury.

FUNCTIONAL NERVE DISEASES. A. T. Schofield. 7s. 6d. net.

HYGIENE OF MIND, THE. T. S. Clouston. *Sixth Edition.* 7s. 6d. net.

INFANT MORTALITY. Sir George Newman. 7s. 6d. net.

PREVENTION OF TUBERCULOSIS (CONSUMPTION), THE. Arthur Newsholme. 10s. 6d. net. *Second Edition.*

AIR AND HEALTH. Ronald C. Macfie. 7s. 6d. net. *Second Edition.*

The New Library of Music

Edited by ERNEST NEWMAN. *Illustrated. Demy 8vo.* 7s. 6d. net

BRAHMS. J. A. Fuller-Maitland. *Second Edition.*

HANDEL. R. A. Streatfeild. *Second Edition.*

HUGO WOLF. Ernest Newman.

Oxford Biographies

Illustrated. Fcap. 8vo. Each volume, cloth, 2s. 6d. net *; leather,* 3s. 6d. net

DANTE ALIGHIERI. Paget Toynbee. *Third Edition.*

GIROLAMO SAVONAROLA. E. L. S. Horsburgh. *Sixth Edition.*

JOHN HOWARD. E. C. S. Gibson.

ALFRED TENNYSON. A. C. Benson. *Second Edition.*

SIR WALTER RALEIGH. I. A. Taylor.

ERASMUS. E. F. H. Capey.

ROBERT BURNS. T. F. Henderson.

CHATHAM. A. S. McDowall.

CANNING. W. Alison Phillips.

BEACONSFIELD. Walter Sichel.

JOHANN WOLFGANG GOETHE. H. G. Atkins.

FRANÇOIS DE FÉNELON. Viscount St. Cyres.

Four Plays

Fcap. 8vo. 2s. net

THE HONEYMOON. A Comedy in Three Acts. Arnold Bennett. *Second Edition.*

THE GREAT ADVENTURE. A Play of Fancy in Four Acts. Arnold Bennett. *Second Edition.*

MILESTONES. Arnold Bennett and Edward Knoblauch. *Sixth Edition.*

KISMET. Edward Knoblauch. *Second Edition.*

TYPHOON. A Play in Four Acts. Melchior Lengyel. English Version by Laurence Irving. *Second Edition.*

The States of Italy

Edited by E. ARMSTRONG and R. LANGTON DOUGLAS

Illustrated. Demy 8vo

A HISTORY OF MILAN UNDER THE SFORZA. Cecilia M. Ady. 10s. 6d. net.

A HISTORY OF PERUGIA. W. Heywood. 12s. 6d. net.

A HISTORY OF VERONA. A. M. Allen. 12s. 6d. net.

22 METHUEN AND COMPANY LIMITED

The Westminster Commentaries

General Editor, WALTER LOCK

Demy 8vo

THE ACTS OF THE APOSTLES. Edited by R. B. Rackham. *Sixth Edition.* 10s. 6d.

THE FIRST EPISTLE OF PAUL THE APOSTLE TO THE CORINTHIANS. Edited by H. L. Goudge. *Third Edition.* 6s.

THE BOOK OF EXODUS. Edited by A. H. M'Neile. With a Map and 3 Plans. 10s. 6d.

THE BOOK OF EZEKIEL. Edited by H. A. Redpath. 10s. 6d.

THE BOOK OF GENESIS. Edited, with Introduction and Notes, by S. R. Driver. *Ninth Edition.* 10s. 6d.

ADDITIONS AND CORRECTIONS IN THE SEVENTH AND EIGHTH EDITIONS OF THE BOOK OF GENESIS. S. R. Driver. 1s.

THE BOOK OF THE PROPHET ISAIAH. Edited by G. W. Wade. 10s. 6d.

THE BOOK OF JOB. Edited by E. C. S. Gibson. *Second Edition.* 6s.

THE EPISTLE OF ST. JAMES. Edited, with Introduction and Notes, by R. J. Knowling. *Second Edition.* 6s.

The 'Young' Series

Illustrated. *Crown 8vo*

THE YOUNG BOTANIST. W. P. Westell and C. S. Cooper. 3s. 6d. net.

THE YOUNG CARPENTER. Cyril Hall. 5s.

THE YOUNG ELECTRICIAN. Hammond Hall. 5s.

THE YOUNG ENGINEER. Hammond Hall. *Third Edition.* 5s.

THE YOUNG NATURALIST. W. P. Westell. *Second Edition.* 6s.

THE YOUNG ORNITHOLOGIST. W. P. Westell. 5s.

Methuen's Shilling Library

Fcap. 8vo. 1s. net

BLUE BIRD, THE. Maurice Maeterlinck.

*CHARLES DICKENS. G. K. Chesterton.

*CHARMIDES, AND OTHER POEMS. Oscar Wilde.

CHITRÀL: The Story of a Minor Siege. Sir G. S. Robertson.

CONDITION OF ENGLAND, THE. G. F. G. Masterman.

DE PROFUNDIS. Oscar Wilde.

FROM MIDSHIPMAN TO FIELD-MARSHAL. Sir Evelyn Wood, F.M., V.C.

HARVEST HOME. E. V. Lucas.

HILLS AND THE SEA. Hilaire Belloc.

HUXLEY, THOMAS HENRY. P. Chalmers-Mitchell.

IDEAL HUSBAND, AN. Oscar Wilde.

INTENTIONS. Oscar Wilde.

JIMMY GLOVER, HIS BOOK. James M. Glover.

JOHN BOYES, KING OF THE WA-KIKUYU. John Boyes.

LADY WINDERMERE'S FAN. Oscar Wilde.

LETTERS FROM A SELF-MADE MERCHANT TO HIS SON. George Horace Lorimer.

LIFE OF JOHN RUSKIN, THE. W. G. Collingwood.

LIFE OF ROBERT LOUIS STEVENSON, THE. Graham Balfour.

LIFE OF TENNYSON, THE. A. C. Benson.

LITTLE OF EVERYTHING, A. E. V. Lucas.

LORD ARTHUR SAVILE'S CRIME. Oscar Wilde.

LORE OF THE HONEY-BEE, THE. Tickner Edwardes.

MAN AND THE UNIVERSE. Sir Oliver Lodge.

MARY MAGDALENE. Maurice Maeterlinck.

OLD COUNTRY LIFE. S. Baring-Gould.

OSCAR WILDE: A Critical Study. Arthur Ransome.

PARISH CLERK, THE. P. H. Ditchfield.

SELECTED POEMS. Oscar Wilde.

SEVASTOPOL, AND OTHER STORIES. Leo Tolstoy.

TWO ADMIRALS. Admiral John Moresby.

UNDER FIVE REIGNS. Lady Dorothy Nevill.

VAILIMA LETTERS. Robert Louis Stevenson.

VICAR OF MORWENSTOW, THE. S. Baring-Gould.

Books for Travellers

Crown 8vo. 6s. each

Each volume contains a number of Illustrations in Colour

AVON AND SHAKESPEARE'S COUNTRY, THE. A. G. Bradley.

BLACK FOREST, A BOOK OF THE. C. E. Hughes.

BRETONS AT HOME, THE. F. M. Gostling.

CITIES OF LOMBARDY, THE. Edward Hutton.

CITIES OF ROMAGNA AND THE MARCHES, THE. Edward Hutton.

CITIES OF SPAIN, THE. Edward Hutton.

CITIES OF UMBRIA, THE. Edward Hutton.

DAYS IN CORNWALL. C. Lewis Hind.

FLORENCE AND NORTHERN TUSCANY, WITH GENOA. Edward Hutton.

LAND OF PARDONS, THE (Brittany). Anatole Le Braz.

NAPLES. Arthur H. Norway.

NAPLES RIVIERA, THE. H. M. Vaughan.

NEW FOREST, THE. Horace G. Hutchinson.

NORFOLK BROADS, THE. W. A. Dutt.

NORWAY AND ITS FJORDS. M. A. Wyllie.

RHINE, A BOOK OF THE. S. Baring-Gould.

ROME. Edward Hutton.

ROUND ABOUT WILTSHIRE. A. G. Bradley.

SCOTLAND OF TO-DAY. T. F. Henderson and Francis Watt.

SIENA AND SOUTHERN TUSCANY. Edward Hutton.

SKIRTS OF THE GREAT CITY, THE. Mrs. A. G. Bell.

THROUGH EAST ANGLIA IN A MOTOR CAR. J. E. Vincent.

VENICE AND VENETIA. Edward Hutton.

WANDERER IN FLORENCE, A. E. V. Lucas.

WANDERER IN PARIS, A. E. V. Lucas.

WANDERER IN HOLLAND, A. E. V. Lucas.

WANDERER IN LONDON, A. E. V. Lucas.

Some Books on Art

ARMOURER AND HIS CRAFT, THE. Charles ffoulkes. Illustrated. *Royal 4to. £2 2s. net.*

ART AND LIFE. T. Sturge Moore. Illustrated. *Cr. 8vo. 5s. net.*

BRITISH SCHOOL, THE. An Anecdotal Guide to the British Painters and Paintings in the National Gallery. E. V. Lucas. Illustrated. *Fcap. 8vo. 2s. 6d. net.*

*DECORATIVE IRON WORK. From the xith to the xviiith Century. Charles ffoulkes. *Royal 4to. £2 2s. net.*

FRANCESCO GUARDI, 1712-1793. G. A. Simonson. Illustrated. *Imperial 4to. £2 2s. net.*

ILLUSTRATIONS OF THE BOOK OF JOB. William Blake. *Quarto. £1 1s. net.*

JOHN LUCAS, PORTRAIT PAINTER, 1828-1874. Arthur Lucas. Illustrated. *Imperial 4to. £3 3s net.*

OLD PASTE. A. Beresford Ryley. Illustrated. *Royal 4to. £2 2s. net.*

ONE HUNDRED MASTERPIECES OF PAINTING. With an Introduction by R. C. Witt. Illustrated. *Second Edition. Demy 8vo. 10s. 6d. net.*

ONE HUNDRED MASTERPIECES OF SCULPTURE. With an Introduction by G. F. Hill. Illustrated. *Demy 8vo. 10s. 6d. net.*

ROMNEY FOLIO, A. With an Essay by A. B. Chamberlain. *Imperial Folio. £15 15s. net.*

*ROYAL ACADEMY LECTURES ON PAINTING. George Clausen. Illustrated. *Crown 8vo. 5s. net.*

SAINTS IN ART, THE. Margaret E. Tabor. Illustrated. *Second Edition, Revised. Fcap. 8vo. 3s. 6d. net.*

SCHOOLS OF PAINTING. Mary Innes. Illustrated. *Cr. 8vo. 5s. net.*

CELTIC ART IN PAGAN AND CHRISTIAN TIMES. J. R. Allen. Illustrated. *Second Edition. Demy 8vo. 7s. 6d. net.*

'CLASSICS OF ART.' See page 14.

'THE CONNOISSEUR'S LIBRARY.' See page 15.

'LITTLE BOOKS ON ART.' See page 18.

'THE LITTLE GALLERIES.' See page 18.

Some Books on Italy

ETRURIA AND MODERN TUSCANY, OLD. Mary L. Cameron. Illustrated. *Second Edition. Cr. 8vo. 6s. net.*

FLORENCE : Her History and Art to the Fall of the Republic. F. A. Hyett. *Demy 8vo. 7s. 6d. net.*

FLORENCE, A WANDERER IN. E. V. Lucas. Illustrated. *Fourth Edition. Cr. 8vo. 6s.*

FLORENCE AND HER TREASURES. H. M. Vaughan. Illustrated. *Fcap. 8vo. 5s. net.*

FLORENCE, COUNTRY WALKS ABOUT. Edward Hutton. Illustrated. *Second Edition. Fcap. 8vo. 5s. net.*

FLORENCE AND THE CITIES OF NORTHERN TUSCANY, WITH GENOA. Edward Hutton. Illustrated. *Second Edition. Cr. 8vo. 6s.*

LOMBARDY, THE CITIES OF. Edward Hutton. Illustrated. *Cr. 8vo. 6s.*

MILAN UNDER THE SFORZA, A HISTORY OF. Cecilia M. Ady. Illustrated. *Demy 8vo. 10s. 6d. net.*

NAPLES : Past and Present. A. H. Norway. Illustrated. *Third Edition. Cr. 8vo. 6s.*

NAPLES RIVIERA, THE. H. M. Vaughan. Illustrated. *Second Edition. Cr. 8vo. 6s.*

PERUGIA, A HISTORY OF. William Heywood. Illustrated. *Demy 8vo. 12s. 6d. net.*

ROME. Edward Hutton. Illustrated. *Third Edition. Cr. 8vo. 6s.*

ROMAGNA AND THE MARCHES, THE CITIES OF. Edward Hutton. *Cr. 8vo. 6s.*

ROMAN PILGRIMAGE, A. R. E. Roberts. Illustrated. *Demy 8vo. 10s. 6d. net.*

ROME OF THE PILGRIMS AND MARTYRS. Ethel Ross Barker. *Demy 8vo. 12s. 6d. net.*

ROME. C. G. Ellaby. Illustrated. *Small Pott 8vo. Cloth, 2s. 6d. net ; leather, 3s. 6d. net.*

SICILY. F. H. Jackson. Illustrated. *Small Pott 8vo. Cloth, 2s. 6d. net ; leather, 3s. 6d. net.*

SICILY : The New Winter Resort. Douglas Sladen. Illustrated. *Second Edition. Cr. 8vo. 5s. net.*

SIENA AND SOUTHERN TUSCANY. Edward Hutton. Illustrated. *Second Edition. Cr. 8vo. 6s.*

UMBRIA, THE CITIES OF. Edward Hutton. Illustrated. *Fifth Edition. Cr. 8vo. 6s.*

VENICE AND VENETIA. Edward Hutton. Illustrated. *Cr. 8vo. 6s.*

VENICE ON FOOT. H. A. Douglas. Illustrated. *Second Edition. Fcap. 8vo. 5s. net.*

VENICE AND HER TREASURES. H. A. Douglas. Illustrated. *Fcap. 8vo. 5s. net.*

VERONA, A HISTORY OF. A. M. Allen. Illustrated. *Demy 8vo. 12s. 6d. net.*

DANTE AND HIS ITALY. Lonsdale Ragg. Illustrated. *Demy 8vo. 12s. 6d. net.*

DANTE ALIGHIERI : His Life and Works. Paget Toynbee. Illustrated. *Cr. 8vo. 5s. net.*

HOME LIFE IN ITALY. Lina Duff Gordon. Illustrated. *Third Edition. Demy 8vo. 10s. 6d. net.*

LAKES OF NORTHERN ITALY, THE. Richard Bagot. Illustrated. *Fcap. 8vo. 5s. net.*

LORENZO THE MAGNIFICENT. E. L. S. Horsburgh. Illustrated. *Second Edition. Demy 8vo. 15s. net.*

MEDICI POPES, THE. H. M. Vaughan. Illustrated. *Demy 8vo. 15s. net.*

ST. CATHERINE OF SIENA AND HER TIMES. By the Author of 'Mdlle. Mori.' Illustrated. *Second Edition. Demy 8vo. 7s. 6d. net.*

S. FRANCIS OF ASSISI, THE LIVES OF. Brother Thomas of Celano. *Cr. 8vo. 5s. net.*

SAVONAROLA, GIROLAMO. E. L. S. Horsburgh. Illustrated. *Cr. 8vo. 5s. net.*

SHELLEY AND HIS FRIENDS IN ITALY. Helen R. Angeli. Illustrated. *Demy 8vo. 10s. 6d. net.*

SKIES ITALIAN : A Little Breviary for Travellers in Italy. Ruth S. Phelps. *Fcap. 8vo. 5s. net.*

UNITED ITALY. F. M. Underwood. *Demy 8vo. 10s. 6d. net.*

WOMAN IN ITALY. W. Boulting. Illustrated. *Demy 8vo. 10s. 6d. net.*

PART III.—A SELECTION OF WORKS OF FICTION

Albanesi (E. Maria). SUSANNAH AND ONE OTHER. *Fourth Edition.* Cr. 8vo. 6s.
THE BROWN EYES OF MARY. *Third Edition.* Cr. 8vo. 6s.
I KNOW A MAIDEN. *Third Edition.* Cr. 8vo. 6s.
THE INVINCIBLE AMELIA; OR, THE POLITE ADVENTURESS. *Third Edition.* Cr. 8vo. 3s. 6d.
THE GLAD HEART. *Fifth Edition.* Cr. 8vo. 6s.
OLIVIA MARY. *Fourth Edition.* Cr. 8vo. 6s.
THE BELOVED ENEMY. *Second Edition.* Cr. 8vo. 6s.

Bagot (Richard). A ROMAN MYSTERY. *Third Edition* Cr. 8vo. 6s.
THE PASSPORT. *Fourth Edition.* Cr. 8vo. 6s.
ANTHONY CUTHBERT. *Fourth Edition.* Cr. 8vo. 6s.
LOVE'S PROXY. Cr. 8vo. 6s.
DONNA DIANA. *Second Edition.* Cr. 8vo. 6s.
CASTING OF NETS. *Twelfth Edition.* Cr. 8vo. 6s.
THE HOUSE OF SERRAVALLE. *Third Edition.* Cr. 8vo. 6s.
DARNELEY PLACE. *Second Edition.* Cr. 8vo. 6s.

Bailey (H. C.). STORM AND TREASURE. *Third Edition.* Cr. 8vo. 6s.
THE LONELY QUEEN. *Third Edition.* Cr. 8vo. 6s.
THE SEA CAPTAIN. Cr. 8vo. 6s.

Baring-Gould (S.). IN THE ROAR OF THE SEA. *Eighth Edition.* Cr. 8vo. 6s.
MARGERY OF QUETHER. *Second Edition.* Cr. 8vo. 6s.
THE QUEEN OF LOVE. *Fifth Edition.* Cr. 8vo. 6s.
JACQUETTA. *Third Edition.* Cr. 8vo. 6s.
KITTY ALONE. *Fifth Edition.* Cr. 8vo. 6s.
NOÉMI. Illustrated. *Fourth Edition.* Cr. 8vo. 6s.
THE BROOM-SQUIRE. Illustrated. *Fifth Edition.* Cr. 8vo. 6s.

Bladys of the Stewponey. Illustrated. *Second Edition.* Cr. 8vo. 6s.
PABO THE PRIEST. Cr. 8vo. 6s.
WINEFRED. Illustrated. *Second Edition.* Cr. 8vo. 6s.
ROYAL GEORGIE. Illustrated. Cr. 8vo. 6s.
IN DEWISLAND. *Second Edition.* Cr. 8vo. 6s.
MRS. CURGENVEN OF CURGENVEN. *Fifth Edition.* Cr. 8vo. 6s.

Barr (Robert). IN THE MIDST OF ALARMS. *Third Edition.* Cr. 8vo. 6s.
THE COUNTESS TEKLA. *Fifth Edition.* Cr. 8vo. 6s.
THE MUTABLE MANY. *Third Edition.* Cr. 8vo. 6s.

Begbie (Harold). THE CURIOUS AND DIVERTING ADVENTURES OF SIR JOHN SPARROW, BART.; OR, THE PROGRESS OF AN OPEN MIND. *Second Edition.* Cr. 8vo. 6s.

Belloc (H.). EMMANUEL BURDEN, MERCHANT. Illustrated. *Second Edition.* Cr. 8vo. 6s.
A CHANGE IN THE CABINET. *Third Edition.* Cr. 8vo. 6s.

Bennett (Arnold). CLAYHANGER. *Eleventh Edition.* Cr. 8vo. 6s.
THE CARD. *Sixth Edition.* Cr. 8vo. [6s.
HILDA LESSWAYS. *Seventh Edition.* Cr. 8vo. 6s.
BURIED ALIVE. *Third Edition.* Cr. 8vo. 6s.
A MAN FROM THE NORTH. *Third Edition.* Cr. 8vo. 6s.
THE MATADOR OF THE FIVE TOWNS. *Second Edition.* Cr. 8vo. 6s.
THE REGENT: A FIVE TOWNS STORY OF ADVENTURE IN LONDON. *Third Edition.* Cr. 8vo. 6s.
ANNA OF THE FIVE TOWNS. Fcap. 8vo. 1s. net.
TERESA OF WATLING STREET. Fcap. 8vo. 1s. net.

Benson (E. F.). DODO: A DETAIL OF THE DAY. *Sixteenth Edition.* Cr. 8vo. 6s.

Birmingham (George A.). SPANISH GOLD. *Sixth Edition. Cr. 8vo. 6s.*
Also Fcap. 8vo. 1s. net.
THE SEARCH PARTY. *Sixth Edition. Cr. 8vo. 6s.*
Also Fcap. 8vo. 1s. net.
LALAGE'S LOVERS. *Third Edition. Cr. 8vo. 6s.*
THE ADVENTURES OF DR. WHITTY. *Fourth Edition. Cr. 8vo. 6s.*

Bowen (Marjorie). I WILL MAINTAIN *Eighth Edition. Cr. 8vo. 6s.*
DEFENDER OF THE FAITH. *Seventh Edition. Cr. 8vo. 6s.*
A KNIGHT OF SPAIN. *Third Edition. Cr. 8vo. 6s.*
THE QUEST OF GLORY. *Third Edition. Cr. 8vo. 6s.*
GOD AND THE KING. *Fifth Edition. Cr. 8vo. 6s.*
THE GOVERNOR OF ENGLAND. *Second Edition. Cr. 8vo. 6s.*

Castle (Agnes and Egerton). THE GOLDEN BARRIER. *Cr. 8vo. 6s.*

*Chesterton (G. K.). THE FLYING INN. *Cr. 8vo. 6s.*

Clifford (Mrs. W. K.). THE GETTING WELL OF DOROTHY. Illustrated. *Third Edition. Cr. 8vo. 3s. 6d.*

Conrad (Joseph). THE SECRET AGENT: A SIMPLE TALE. *Fourth Edition. Cr. 8vo. 6s.*
A SET OF SIX. *Fourth Edition. Cr. 8vo. 6s.*
UNDER WESTERN EYES. *Second Edition. Cr. 8vo. 6s.*
CHANCE. *Cr. 8vo. 6s.*

Conyers (Dorothea). SALLY. *Fourth Edition. Cr. 8vo. 6s.*
SANDY MARRIED. *Third Edition. Cr. 8vo. 6s.*

Corelli (Marie). A ROMANCE OF TWO WORLDS. *Thirty-Second Edition. Cr. 8vo. 6s.*
VENDETTA; OR, THE STORY OF ONE FOR-GOTTEN. *Thirtieth Edition. Cr. 8vo. 6s.*
THELMA: A NORWEGIAN PRINCESS. *Forty-third Edition. Cr. 8vo. 6s.*
ARDATH: THE STORY OF A DEAD SELF. *Twenty-first Edition. Cr. 8vo. 6s.*
THE SOUL OF LILITH. *Seventeenth Edition. Cr. 8vo. 6s.*
WORMWOOD: A DRAMA OF PARIS. *Nineteenth Edition. Cr. 8vo. 6s.*
BARABBAS: A DREAM OF THE WORLD'S TRAGEDY. *Forty-sixth Edition. Cr. 8vo. 6s.*
THE SORROWS OF SATAN. *Fifty-eighth Edition. Cr. 8vo. 6s.*
THE MASTER-CHRISTIAN. *Fourteenth Edition. 179th Thousand. Cr. 8vo. 6s.*
TEMPORAL POWER: A STUDY IN SUPREMACY. *Second Edition. 150th Thousand. Cr. 8vo. 6s.*

GOD'S GOOD MAN: A SIMPLE LOVE STORY. *Sixteenth Edition. 154th Thousand. Cr. 8vo. 6s.*
HOLY ORDERS: THE TRAGEDY OF A QUIET LIFE. *Second Edition. 120th Thousand. Cr. 8vo. 6s.*
THE MIGHTY ATOM. *Twenty-ninth Edition. Cr. 8vo. 6s.*
Also Fcap. 8vo. 1s. net.
BOY: A SKETCH. *Thirteenth Edition. Cr. 8vo. 6s.*
Also Fcap. 8vo. 1s. net.
CAMEOS. *Fourteenth Edition. Cr. 8vo. 6s.*
THE LIFE EVERLASTING. *Sixth Edition. Cr. 8vo. 6s.*
JANE: A SOCIAL INCIDENT. *Fcap. 8vo. 1s. net.*

Crockett (S. R.). LOCHINVAR. Illustrated. *Third Edition. Cr. 8vo. 6s.*
THE STANDARD BEARER. *Second Edition. Cr. 8vo. 6s.*

Croker (B. M.). THE OLD CANTON-MENT. *Second Edition. Cr. 8vo. 6s.*
JOHANNA. *Second Edition. Cr. 8vo. 6s.*
THE HAPPY VALLEY. *Fourth Edition. Cr. 8vo. 6s.*
A NINE DAYS' WONDER. *Fourth Edition. Cr. 8vo. 6s.*
PEGGY OF THE BARTONS. *Seventh Edition. Cr. 8vo. 6s.*
ANGEL. *Fifth Edition. Cr. 8vo. 6s.*
KATHERINE THE ARROGANT. *Seventh Edition. Cr. 8vo. 6s.*
BABES IN THE WOOD. *Fourth Edition. Cr. 8vo. 6s.*

*Danby (Frank). JOSEPH IN JEOPARDY. *Fcap. 8vo. 1s. net.*

Doyle (Sir A. Conan). ROUND THE RED LAMP. *Twelfth Edition. Cr. 8vo. 6s.*
Also Fcap. 8vo. 1s. net.

Drake (Maurice). WO₂. *Fifth Edition. Cr. 8vo. 6s.*

Findlater (J. H.). THE GREEN GRAVES OF BALGOWRIE. *Fifth Edition. Cr. 8vo. 6s.*
THE LADDER TO THE STARS. *Second Edition. Cr. 8vo. 6s.*

Findlater (Mary). A NARROW WAY. *Fourth Edition. Cr. 8vo. 6s.*
THE ROSE OF JOY. *Third Edition. Cr. 8vo. 6s.*
A BLIND BIRD'S NEST. Illustrated. *Second Edition. Cr. 8vo. 6s.*

Fry (B. and C. B.). A MOTHER'S SON. *Fifth Edition. Cr. 8vo. 6s.*

Harraden (Beatrice). IN VARYING MOODS. *Fourteenth Edition. Cr. 8vo. 6s.*
HILDA STRAFFORD and THE REMIT-TANCE MAN. *Twelfth Edition. Cr. 8vo. 6s.*
INTERPLAY. *Fifth Edition. Cr. 8vo. 6s.*

Hauptmann (Gerhart). THE FOOL IN CHRIST : EMMANUEL QUINT. Translated by THOMAS SELTZER. *Cr. 8vo. 6s.*

Hichens (Robert). THE PROPHET OF BERKELEY SQUARE. *Second Edition. Cr. 8vo. 6s.*

TONGUES OF CONSCIENCE. *Third Edition. Cr. 8vo. 6s.*

FELIX : THREE YEARS IN A LIFE. *Tenth Edition. Cr. 8vo. 6s.*

THE WOMAN WITH THE FAN. *Eighth Edition. Cr. 8vo. 6s. Also Fcap. 8vo. 1s. net.*

BYEWAYS. *Cr. 8vo. 6s.*

THE GARDEN OF ALLAH. *Twenty-second Edition. Cr. 8vo. 6s.*

THE BLACK SPANIEL. *Cr. 8vo. 6s.*

THE CALL OF THE BLOOD. *Eighth Edition. Cr. 8vo. 6s.*

BARBARY SHEEP. *Second Edition. Cr. 8vo. 3s. 6d. Also Fcap. 8vo. 1s. net.*

THE DWELLER ON THE THRESHOLD. *Cr. 8vo. 6s.*

THE WAY OF AMBITION. *Fourth Edition. Cr. 8vo. 6s.*

Hope (Anthony). THE GOD IN THE CAR. *Eleventh Edition. Cr. 8vo. 6s.*

A CHANGE OF AIR. *Sixth Edition. Cr. 8vo. 6s.*

A MAN OF MARK. *Seventh Edition. Cr. 8vo. 6s.*

THE CHRONICLES OF COUNT ANTONIO. *Sixth Edition. Cr. 8vo. 6s.*

PHROSO. Illustrated. *Ninth Edition. Cr. 8vo. 6s.*

SIMON DALE. Illustrated. *Ninth Edition. Cr. 8vo. 6s.*

THE KING'S MIRROR. *Fifth Edition. Cr. 8vo. 6s.*

QUISANTÉ. *Fourth Edition. Cr. 8vo. 6s.*

THE DOLLY DIALOGUES. *Cr. 8vo. 6s.*

TALES OF TWO PEOPLE. *Third Edition. Cr. 8vo. 6s.*

A SERVANT OF THE PUBLIC. Illustrated. *Sixth Edition. Cr. 8vo. 6s.*

THE GREAT MISS DRIVER. *Fourth Edition. Cr. 8vo. 6s.*

MRS. MAXON PROTESTS. *Third Edition. Cr. 8vo. 6s.*

Hutten (Baroness von). THE HALO. *Fifth Edition. Cr. 8vo. 6s. Also Fcap. 8vo. 1s. net.*

'The Inner Shrine' (Author of). THE WILD OLIVE. *Third Edition. Cr. 8vo. 6s.*

THE STREET CALLED STRAIGHT. *Fourth Edition. Cr. 8vo. 6s.*

THE WAY HOME. *Second Edition. Cr. 8vo. 6s.*

Jacobs (W. W.). MANY CARGOES. *Thirty-third Edition. Cr. 8vo. 3s. 6d.* Also Illustrated in colour. *Demy 8vo. 7s. 6d. net.*

SEA URCHINS. *Seventeenth Edition. Cr. 8vo. 3s. 6d.*

A MASTER OF CRAFT. Illustrated. *Tenth Edition. Cr. 8vo. 3s. 6d.*

LIGHT FREIGHTS. Illustrated. *Eleventh Edition. Cr. 8vo. 3s. 6d. Also Fcap. 8vo. 1s. net.*

THE SKIPPER'S WOOING. *Eleventh Edition. Cr. 8vo. 3s. 6d.*

AT SUNWICH PORT. Illustrated. *Tenth Edition. Cr. 8vo. 3s. 6d.*

DIALSTONE LANE. Illustrated. *Eighth Edition. Cr. 8vo. 3s. 6d.*

ODD CRAFT. Illustrated. *Fifth Edition. Cr. 8vo. 3s. 6d.*

THE LADY OF THE BARGE. Illustrated *Ninth Edition. Cr. 8vo. 3s. 6d.*

SALTHAVEN. Illustrated. *Third Edition. Cr. 8vo. 3s. 6d.*

SAILORS' KNOTS. Illustrated. *Fifth Edition. Cr. 8vo. 3s. 6d.*

SHORT CRUISES. *Third Edition. Cr. 8vo. 3s. 6d.*

James (Henry). THE GOLDEN BOWL. *Third Edition. Cr. 8vo. 6s.*

Le Queux (William). THE HUNCHBACK OF WESTMINSTER. *Third Edition. Cr. 8vo. 6s.*

THE CLOSED BOOK. *Third Edition. Cr. 8vo. 6s.*

THE VALLEY OF THE SHADOW. Illustrated. *Third Edition. Cr. 8vo. 6s.*

BEHIND THE THRONE. *Third Edition. Cr. 8vo. 6s.*

London (Jack). WHITE FANG. *Ninth Edition. Cr. 8vo. 6s.*

Lowndes (Mrs. Belloc). THE CHINK IN THE ARMOUR. *Fourth Edition. Cr. 8vo. 6s. net.*

MARY PECHELL. *Second Edition. Cr. 8vo. 6s.*

STUDIES IN LOVE AND IN TERROR. *Second Edition. Cr. 8vo. 6s.*

THE LODGER. *Crown 8vo. 6s.*

Lucas (E. V.). LISTENER'S LURE : AN OBLIQUE NARRATION. *Ninth Edition Fcap. 8vo. 5s.*

OVER BEMERTON'S : AN EASY-GOING CHRONICLE. *Tenth Edition. Fcap. 8vo. 5s.*

MR. INGLESIDE. *Ninth Edition. Fcap. 8vo. 5s.*

LONDON LAVENDER. *Sixth Edition. Fcap. 8vo. 5s.*

Lyall (Edna). DERRICK VAUGHAN, NOVELIST. *44th Thousand. Cr. 8vo. 3s. 6d.*

Macnaughtan (S.). THE FORTUNE OF CHRISTINA M'NAB. *Sixth Edition. Cr. 8vo. 2s. net.*
PETER AND JANE. *Fourth Edition. Cr. 8vo. 6s.*

Malet (Lucas). A COUNSEL OF PERFECTION. *Second Edition. Cr. 8vo. 6s.*
COLONEL ENDERBY'S WIFE. *Sixth Edition. Cr. 8vo. 6s.*
THE HISTORY OF SIR RICHARD CALMADY: A ROMANCE. *Ninth Edition. Cr. 8vo. 6s.*
THE WAGES OF SIN. *Sixteenth Edition. Cr. 8vo. 6s.*
THE CARISSIMA. *Fifth Edition. Cr. 8vo. 6s.*
THE GATELESS BARRIER. *Fifth Edition. Cr. 8vo. 6s.*

Mason (A. E. W.). CLEMENTINA. Illustrated. *Eighth Edition. Cr. 8vo. 6s.*

Maxwell (W. B.). THE RAGGED MESSENGER. *Third Edition. Cr. 8vo. 6s.*
VIVIEN. *Twelfth Edition. Cr. 8vo. 6s.*
THE GUARDED FLAME. *Seventh Edition. Cr. 8vo. 6s.*
Also Fcap. 8vo. 1s. net.
ODD LENGTHS. *Second Edition. Cr. 8vo. 6s.*
HILL RISE. *Fourth Edition. Cr. 8vo. 6s.*
Also Fcap. 8vo. 1s. net.
THE COUNTESS OF MAYBURY: BETWEEN YOU AND I. *Fourth Edition. Cr. 8vo. 6s.*
THE REST CURE. *Fourth Edition. Cr. 8vo. 6s.*

Milne (A. A.). THE DAY'S PLAY. *Fourth Edition. Cr. 8vo. 6s.*
THE HOLIDAY ROUND. *Second Edition. Cr. 8vo. 6s.*

Montague (C. E.). A HIND LET LOOSE. *Third Edition. Cr. 8vo. 6s.*
THE MORNING'S WAR. *Cr. 8vo. 6s.*

Morrison (Arthur). TALES OF MEAN STREETS. *Seventh Edition. Cr. 8vo. 6s.*
Also Fcap. 8vo. 1s. net.
A CHILD OF THE JAGO. *Sixth Edition. Cr. 8vo. 6s.*
THE HOLE IN THE WALL. *Fourth Edition. Cr. 8vo. 6s.*
DIVERS VANITIES. *Cr. 8vo. 6s.*

Ollivant (Alfred). OWD BOB, THE GREY DOG OF KENMUIR. With a Frontispiece. *Twelfth Edition. Cr. 8vo. 6s.*

THE TAMING OF JOHN BLUNT. *Second Edition. Cr. 8vo. 6s.*
THE ROYAL ROAD. *Second Edition. Cr. 8vo. 6s.*

Onions (Oliver). GOOD BOY SELDOM: A ROMANCE OF ADVERTISEMENT. *Second Edition. Cr. 8vo. 6s.*
THE TWO KISSES. *Cr. 8vo. 6s.*

Oppenheim (E. Phillips). MASTER OF MEN. *Fifth Edition. Cr. 8vo. 6s.*
THE MISSING DELORA. Illustrated. *Fourth Edition. Cr. 8vo. 6s.*
Also Fcap. 8vo. 1s. net.

Orczy (Baroness). FIRE IN STUBBLE. *Fifth Edition. Cr. 8vo. 6s.*
Also Fcap. 8vo. 1s. net.

Oxenham (John). A WEAVER OF WEBS. Illustrated. *Fifth Edition. Cr. 8vo. 6s.*
THE GATE OF THE DESERT. *Eighth Edition. Cr. 8vo. 6s.*
* Also Fcap. 8vo. 1s. net.
PROFIT AND LOSS. *Fourth Edition. Cr. 8vo. 6s.*
THE LONG ROAD. *Fourth Edition. Cr. 8vo. 6s.*
Also Fcap. 8vo. 1s. net.
THE SONG OF HYACINTH, AND OTHER STORIES. *Second Edition. Cr. 8vo. 6s.*
MY LADY OF SHADOWS. *Fourth Edition. Cr. 8vo. 6s.*
LAURISTONS. *Fourth Edition. Cr. 8vo. 6s.*
THE COIL OF CARNE. *Sixth Edition. Cr. 8vo. 6s.*
THE QUEST OF THE GOLDEN ROSE. *Fourth Edition. Cr. 8vo. 6s.*
MARY ALL-ALONE. *Third Edition. Cr. 8vo. 6s.*

Parker (Gilbert). PIERRE AND HIS PEOPLE. *Seventh Edition. Cr. 8vo. 6s.*
MRS. FALCHION. *Fifth Edition. Cr. 8vo. 6s.*
THE TRANSLATION OF A SAVAGE. *Fourth Edition. Cr. 8vo. 6s.*
THE TRAIL OF THE SWORD. Illustrated. *Tenth Edition. Cr. 8vo. 6s.*
WHEN VALMOND CAME TO PONTIAC: THE STORY OF A LOST NAPOLEON. *Seventh Edition. Cr. 8vo. 6s.*
AN ADVENTURER OF THE NORTH: THE LAST ADVENTURES OF 'PRETTY PIERRE.' *Fifth Edition. Cr. 8vo. 6s.*
THE SEATS OF THE MIGHTY. Illustrated. *Nineteenth Edition. Cr. 8vo. 6s.*
THE BATTLE OF THE STRONG: A ROMANCE OF TWO KINGDOMS. Illustrated. *Seventh Edition. Cr. 8vo. 6s.*

THE POMP OF THE LAVILETTES. *Third Edition. Cr. 8vo. 3s. 6d.*

NORTHERN LIGHTS. *Fourth Edition. Cr. 8vo. 6s.*

THE JUDGMENT HOUSE. *Cr. 8vo. 6s.*

Pasture (Mrs. Henry de la). THE TYRANT. *Fourth Edition. Cr. 8vo. 6s. Also Fcap. 8vo. 1s. net.*

Pemberton (Max). THE FOOTSTEPS OF A THRONE. Illustrated. *Fourth Edition. Cr. 8vo. 6s.*

I CROWN THEE KING. Illustrated. *Cr. 8vo. 6s.*

LOVE THE HARVESTER: A STORY OF THE SHIRES. Illustrated. *Third Edition. Cr. 8vo. 3s. 6d.*

THE MYSTERY OF THE GREEN HEART. *Fifth Edition. Cr. 8vo. 2s. net*

Perrin (Alice). THE CHARM. *Fifth Edition. Cr. 8vo. 6s. Also Fcap. 8vo. 1s. net.*

THE ANGLO-INDIANS. *Sixth Edition. Cr. 8vo. 6s.*

Phillpotts (Eden). LYING PROPHETS. *Third Edition. Cr. 8vo. 6s.*

CHILDREN OF THE MIST. *Sixth Edition. Cr. 8vo. 6s.*

THE HUMAN BOY. With a Frontispiece. *Seventh Edition. Cr. 8vo. 6s.*

SONS OF THE MORNING. *Second Edition. Cr. 8vo. 6s.*

THE RIVER. *Fourth Edition. Cr. 8vo. 6s.*

THE AMERICAN PRISONER. *Fourth Edition. Cr. 8vo. 6s.*

KNOCK AT A VENTURE. *Third Edition. Cr. 8vo. 6s.*

THE PORTREEVE. *Fourth Edition. Cr. 8vo. 6s.*

THE POACHER'S WIFE. *Second Edition. Cr. 8vo. 6s.*

THE STRIKING HOURS. *Second Edition. Cr. 8vo. 6s.*

DEMETER'S DAUGHTER. *Third Edition. Cr. 8vo. 6s.*

THE SECRET WOMAN. *Fcap. 8vo. 1s. net.*

Pickthall (Marmaduke). SAÏD, THE FISHERMAN. *Eighth Edition. Cr. 8vo. 6s. Also Fcap. 8vo. 1s. net.*

'Q' (A. T. Quiller-Couch). THE MAYOR OF TROY. *Fourth Edition. Cr. 8vo. 6s.*

MERRY-GARDEN AND OTHER STORIES. *Cr. 8vo. 6s.*

MAJOR VIGOUREUX. *Third Edition. Cr. 8vo. 6s.*

Ridge (W. Pett). ERB. *Second Edition. Cr. 8vo. 6s.*

A SON OF THE STATE. *Third Edition. Cr. 8vo. 3s. 6d.*

A BREAKER OF LAWS. *A New Edition. Cr. 8vo. 3s. 6d.*

MRS. GALER'S BUSINESS. Illustrated. *Second Edition. Cr. 8vo. 6s.*

THE WICKHAMSES. *Fourth Edition. Cr. 8vo. 6s.*

SPLENDID BROTHER. *Fourth Edition. Cr. 8vo. 6s. Also Fcap. 8vo. 1s. net.*

NINE TO SIX-THIRTY. *Third Edition. Cr. 8vo. 6s.*

THANKS TO SANDERSON. *Second Edition. Cr. 8vo. 6s.*

DEVOTED SPARKES. *Second Edition. Cr. 8vo. 6s.*

THE REMINGTON SENTENCE. *Cr. 8vo. 6s.*

Russell (W. Clark). MASTER ROCKA-FELLAR'S VOYAGE. Illustrated. *Fourth Edition. Cr. 8vo. 3s. 6d.*

Sidgwick (Mrs. Alfred). THE KINS-MAN. Illustrated. *Third Edition. Cr. 8vo. 6s.*

THE LANTERN-BEARERS. *Third Edition. Cr. 8vo. 6s.*

THE SEVERINS. *Sixth Edition. Cr. 8vo. 6s. Also Fcap. 8vo. 1s. net.*

ANTHEA'S GUEST. *Fourth Edition. Cr. 8vo. 6s.*

LAMORNA. *Third Edition. Cr. 8vo. 6s.*

BELOW STAIRS. *Second Edition. Cr. 8vo. 6s.*

Snaith (J. C.). THE PRINCIPAL GIRL. *Second Edition. Cr. 8vo. 6s.*

AN AFFAIR OF STATE. *Second Edition. Cr. 8vo. 6s.*

Somerville (E. Œ.) and Ross (Martin). DAN RUSSEL THE FOX. Illustrated. *Seventh Edition. Cr. 8vo. 6s. Also Fcap. 8vo. 1s. net.*

Thurston (E. Temple). MIRAGE. *Fourth Edition. Cr. 8vo. 6s. Also Fcap. 8vo. 1s. net.*

Watson (H. B. Marriott). ALISE OF ASTRA. *Third Edition. Cr. 8vo. 6s.*

THE BIG FISH. *Third Edition. Cr. 8vo. 6s.*

Webling (Peggy). THE STORY OF VIRGINIA PERFECT. *Third Edition. Cr. 8vo. 6s. Also Fcap. 8vo. 1s. net.*

THE SPIRIT OF MIRTH. *Sixth Edition.* *Cr. 8vo. 6s.*

FELIX CHRISTIE. *Third Edition. Cr. 8vo. 6s.*

THE PEARL STRINGER. *Third Edition. Cr. 8vo.* 6s.

Westrup (Margaret) (Mrs. W. Sydney Stacey). TIDE MARKS. *Second Edition. Cr. 8vo.* 6s.

Weyman (Stanley). UNDER THE RED ROBE. Illustrated. *Twenty-third Edition. Cr. 8vo.* 6s.
Also Fcap. 8vo. 1s. net.

Whitby (Beatrice). ROSAMUND. *Second Edition. Cr. 8vo.* 6s.

Williamson (C. N. and A. M.). THE LIGHTNING CONDUCTOR: The Strange Adventures of a Motor Car. Illustrated. *Twenty-first Edition. Cr. 8vo.* 6s. *Also Cr. 8vo. 1s. net.*
THE PRINCESS PASSES: A ROMANCE OF A MOTOR. Illustrated. *Ninth Edition. Cr. 8vo.* 6s.
LADY BETTY ACROSS THE WATER. *Eleventh Edition. Cr. 8vo.* 6s.
Also Fcap. 8vo. 1s. net.

THE BOTOR CHAPERON. Illustrated. *Eighth Edition. Cr. 8vo. 6s.*
*Also Fcap. 8vo. 1s. net.

THE CAR OF DESTINY. Illustrated. *Seventh Edition. Cr. 8vo. 6s.*

MY FRIEND THE CHAUFFEUR. Illustrated. *Twelfth Edition. Cr. 8vo.* 6s.

SCARLET RUNNER. Illustrated. *Third Edition. Cr. 8vo.* 6s.

SET IN SILVER. Illustrated. *Fourth Edition. Cr. 8vo.* 6s.

LORD LOVELAND DISCOVERS AMERICA. *Second Edition. Cr. 8vo.* 6s.

THE GOLDEN SILENCE. *Sixth Edition. Cr. 8vo.* 6s.

THE GUESTS OF HERCULES. *Third Edition. Cr. 8vo.* 6s.

THE HEATHER MOON. *Fifth Edition. Cr. 8vo.* 6s.

THE LOVE PIRATE. Illustrated. *Second Edition. Cr. 8vo.* 6s.

THE DEMON. *Fcap. 8vo. 1s. net.*

Wyllarde (Dolf). THE PATHWAY OF THE PIONEER (Nous Autres). *Sixth Edition. Cr. 8vo.* 6s.

Books for Boys and Girls

Illustrated. Crown 8vo. 3s. 6d.

GETTING WELL OF DOROTHY, THE. Mrs. W. K. Clifford.

GIRL OF THE PEOPLE, A. L. T. Meade.

HEPSY GIPSY. L. T. Meade. *2s. 6d.*

HONOURABLE MISS, THE. L. T. Meade.

MASTER ROCKAFELLAR'S VOYAGE. W. Clark Russell.

ONLY A GUARD-ROOM DOG. Edith E. Cuthell.

RED GRANGE, THE. Mrs. Molesworth.

SYD BELTON: The Boy who would not go to Sea. G. Manville Fenn.

THERE WAS ONCE A PRINCE. Mrs. M. E. Mann.

Methuen's Shilling Novels

Fcap. 8vo. 1s. net

ANNA OF THE FIVE TOWNS. Arnold Bennett.

BARBARY SHEEP. Robert Hichens.

**BOTOR CHAPERON, THE. C. N. & A. M. Williamson.

BOY. Marie Corelli.

CHARM, THE. Alice Perrin.

DAN RUSSEL THE FOX. E. Œ. Somerville and Martin Ross.

DEMON, THE. C. N. and A. M. Williamson.

FIRE IN STUBBLE. Baroness Orczy.

**GATE OF DESERT, THE. John Oxenham.

GUARDED FLAME, THE. W. B. Maxwell.

HALO, THE. Baroness von Hutten.

HILL RISE. W. B. Maxwell.

JANE. Marie Corelli.

Methuen's Shilling Novels—*continued.*

*JOSEPH IN JEOPARDY. Frank Danby.

LADY BETTY ACROSS THE WATER. C. N. and A. M. Williamson.

LIGHT FREIGHTS. W. W. Jacobs.

LONG ROAD, THE. John Oxenham.

MIGHTY ATOM, THE. Marie Corelli.

MIRAGE. E. Temple Thurston.

MISSING DELORA, THE. E. Phillips Oppenheim.

ROUND THE RED LAMP. Sir A. Conan Doyle.

SAÏD, THE FISHERMAN. Marmaduke Pickthall.

SEARCH PARTY, THE. G. A. Birmingham.

SECRET WOMAN, THE. Eden Phillpotts.

SEVERINS, THE. Mrs. Alfred Sidgwick.

SPANISH GOLD. G. A. Birmingham.

SPLENDID BROTHER. W. Pett Ridge.

TALES OF MEAN STREETS. Arthur Morrison.

TERESA OF WATLING STREET. Arnold Bennett.

TYRANT, THE. Mrs. Henry de la Pasture.

UNDER THE RED ROBE. Stanley J. Weyman.

VIRGINIA PERFECT. Peggy Webling.

WOMAN WITH THE FAN, THE. Robert Hichens.

Methuen's Sevenpenny Novels

Fcap. 8vo.   *7d. net*

ANGEL. B. M. Croker.

BROOM SQUIRE, THE. S. Baring-Gould.

BY STROKE OF SWORD. Andrew Balfour.

*HOUSE OF WHISPERS, THE. William Le Queux.

HUMAN BOY, THE. Eden Phillpotts.

I CROWN THEE KING. Max Pemberton.

*LATE IN LIFE. Alice Perrin.

LONE PINE. R. B. Townshend.

MASTER OF MEN. E. Phillips Oppenheim.

MIXED MARRIAGE, A. Mrs. F. E. Penny.

PETER, A PARASITE. E. Maria Albanesi.

POMP OF THE LAVILETTES, THE. Sir Gilbert Parker.

PRINCE RUPERT THE BUCCANEER. C. J. Cutcliffe Hyne.

*PRINCESS VIRGINIA, THE. C. N. & A. M. Williamson.

PROFIT AND LOSS. John Oxenham.

RED HOUSE, THE. E. Nesbit.

SIGN OF THE SPIDER, THE. Bertram Mitford.

SON OF THE STATE, A. W. Pett Ridge.

Printed by MORRISON & GIBB LIMITED, *Edinburgh*